The Intimate Environment
Exploring Marriage and the Family

Second Edition

Arlene Skolnick
University of California, Berkeley

Little, Brown and Company   Boston   Toronto

Library of Congress Catalog Number: 77-84526

ISBN-0-316-797006

10 9 8 7 6 5 4 3

MV

Published simultaneously in Canada by Little, Brown & Company (Canada) Limited

Printed in the United States of America

Produced by Ken Burke & Associates

Text designer: Christy Butterfield
Copyeditor: Judith Fillmore
Photo researcher: Audrey Ross
Illustrator: Boardworks
Compositor: Typothetae

Text Credits

85   From *Self and Others*, 2nd edition revised, by R. D. Laing. Copyright © 1961, 1969 by R. D. Laing. Reprinted by permission of Pantheon Books, a division of Random House, Inc., and Tavistock Publications.

239   From *Lines on Reading D. H. Lawrence, Sherwood Anderson, et al.* by John Haynes Holmes. Reprinted by permission of Roger Holmes.

288   From Dr. Haim Ginott's column, "Being a Parent," King Features Syndicate, which appeared in the *San Francisco Sunday Examiner and Chronicle*, February 11, 1973. Reprinted by permission of Dr. Alice Ginott.

Photo Credits

Preface

In the few years since the first edition of this book appeared, there has been a remarkable growth of public interest in the family. "Family" has become a "buzz" word, a sexy topic. Much of this interest reflects the widespread fear that the family is falling apart. Although previous generations also thought they were observing the demise of the family, never before have so many people felt they could see its collapse before their very eyes.

Every day seems to bring forth a new book or article explaining why the family is becoming an endangered species, or disputing the popular assumption that it is doing so. A new nostalgia about the family is in vogue. For some people, stimulated by the television series *Roots,* it has meant a search into their own family history. For others, it has meant a longing for some past golden age when the family was supposedly strong and stable.

In response to the current changes and public concern about them, politicians and policy makers have become newly aware of the family. Both major parties in the presidential campaign of 1976 pledged themselves to "strengthening" the family. There is a growing interest in the idea that public and private policies should be based on assessments of their impact on families. A White House Conference on the Family is being planned, and numerous study groups, conferences, and commissions ponder the current state of the family and its future.

The past decade has also seen an outpouring of important new scholarship on the family. Some of the most exciting work has come from historians, but an increasing number of other disciplines and professions have joined the sociologists and anthropologists to whom the family field used to belong. Not only has this work changed many of our old ideas about the family and provided new insights, but also it has revealed how much more we need to know—about families in the past as well as in our own times.

In this edition, I have tried to incorporate the new scholarship on the family, as well as to speak to many of the issues that concern students and the general public. For example, there is a new first chapter that attempts to put the current perceptions of a "crisis" in the family in perspective.

There are also new chapters on class and racial differences in American family life, and on love and the development of intimate relationships. On the other hand, many of the issues discussed in the first edition are relevant both to the new scholarship and to the emerging public debates on the family, and these have been retained: What is a family? What is family normality? Are current family changes pathological, or simply changes? What is the impact of the larger society on the family?

The general outlook of the book remains the same. Several paragraphs from the Preface to the first edition sum up my approach to the study of the family, and I would like to quote them:

> One particular casualty of recent history is the assumption that human activity functions to maintain the stability and harmony of the social order. Starting out from this assumption, which dominated the social sciences during the 1950s and '60s, one is inevitably driven to conclude that the family plays a key role in assuring social stability, continuity, and consensus. If, however, one assumes that change and conflict are natural conditions of social life, that social institutions are maintained by sanctions, rewards, and social pressures rather than by consensus, and that values and ideals are a poor guide to how people actually behave, then one is free to construct an alternative vision of family life. This book is an attempt to begin to construct such a vision.
>
> In contrast to the prevailing assumptions about the necessity and naturalness of the family, this book begins with the assumption that the family is problematic in every sense of the term. We do not really know, for example, whether, and in what ways, it is useful to think of the family as a constant in all human societies. The very concept of the family is also problematic because it exists at several levels of reality. At one level the family is the stream of behavior that flows in families; but the family is also a mental construction in the heads of family members and observers of family life. The relations among the different levels of reality are neither direct nor constant in their indirection. For example, it would be wrong to assume that family ideologies are always maps of behavior, but it would also be wrong to conclude that they are always smokescreens. Besides, what people think is happening is an important part of what really is happening.
>
> Finally, the family is problematic in an emotional sense. Family life is the place where, as one writer put it, "you're dealing with life-and-death voltages." Dramatists and novelists, from the Greek tragedians to Eugene O'Neill to the writers of soap operas, have always portrayed the intimacies of family life in terms of love *and* hate, devotion *and* cruelty, sacrifice *and* spite. Until very recently, however, students of marriage and the family have tended to overlook the inconsistencies and ironies of family life in favor of such orderly conceptions as family harmony on one side and breakdown on the other.

Paradoxically, by emphasizing the problematic nature of the family, this book is able to be unpessimistic about the future of the family. If there is no definition of the family that will hold across all cultures and periods, and if the family is a concept rather than a biological reality, then novel forms of the intimate environment may be equally valid. If conflict between the generations and the sexes is part of human history, then today's situation is not such a radical departure from the past. If the normal family is a myth, then perhaps the craziness we observe in family life is also part of the human condition. What we are witnessing may not be so much the breakdown of the family as an institution, as the destruction of myths and assumptions about family living that were never true in the first place.

Arlene Skolnick

Berkeley, California
April 1978

Acknowledgments

I would still like to thank first of all the institution that indirectly led me to enter the field of family studies by failing to come through with jobs promised during the time my husband was being courted. As I have since come to learn, my experience was not unusual for dual-career academic couples. I am now grateful for what seemed at the time a personal crisis, for if I had not been pushed by unemployment, I would never have left the narrower paths of social and developmental psychology for the wider interdisciplinary wilds of family studies.

I am also, and unironically, grateful to my husband, Jerome H. Skolnick, for the countless number of ways he has supported and encouraged me through the inception, writing, and revision of this book. It was his suggestion that we embark together on a study of the family, which solved the unemployment problem for me. The result of our joint efforts that year was *Family in Transition,* which raised some of the issues that this book attempts to explore more deeply. Throughout the writing of this book, Jerry has been, as always, my severest critic and best friend, a difficult feat in view of the complications my writing introduced into our domestic life. I would also like to thank my children, Michael and Alexander, who had to share me and our household with a demanding sibling, this book.

I owe a special debt of gratitude to the people who read the manuscript or parts of it and provided valuable comments: William J. Goode, Deborah Kaufman, Barbara Laslett, Barbara Richardson, and Zick Rubin, as well as other, anonymous, reviewers. Also, I would like to thank Ken Burke, the production supervisor, who transformed the manuscript into a book and made it possible for me to enjoy the process of bookmaking, as well as Milton Johnson of Little, Brown, who provided so much support and encouragement.

My thanks also to the various people who helped with the research and typing, especially Evy Bogen, Rod Watanabe, Wendy Rakocy, and Tina Miller.

Since the first edition of this book appeared, I have had so many conversations about its general themes with so many people that it is difficult to name them all. I would particularly like to acknowledge conversations with William J. Goode, Arlie Hochschild, John Irwin, Barbara Laslett, Marcia Rosenbaum, Lilian Rubin, Ann Swidler, and Lenore Weitzman, as well as my colleagues at the Childhood and Government Project, the Center for the Study of Law and Society, and the Institute of Human Development, all at the University of California, Berkeley.

Arlene Skolnick

Contents

The Intimate Environment

Chapter One
The Family in Our Time: Perspectives on the Current "Crisis" in the American Family

☐ *To study the history of the American family is to conduct a rescue mission into the dreamland of our national self-concept. No subject is more closely bound up with our sense of a difficult present—and our nostalgia for a happier past.*

John Demos, *"The American Family in Past Time"*

4

This is a time of change for the family—many would call it a time of trouble. The public image of American family life has been remarkably transformed in recent years. Before the mid-1960s, the American family seemed to represent the most developed version of a timeless family unit. No one denied that there were family problems such as illegitimacy, marital unhappiness, divorce, and conflicts between parents and children, but these were seen as exceptions to the usual state of family life and were blamed on individual shortcomings. Social scientists assumed that mother, father, and child formed the fundamental human group, held together by interlocking needs built into human nature. Any attempt to tamper with the nuclear family, its division of labor between the sexes, or its patterns of child rearing could result in the downfall of "civilization."

Now, as the United States enters its third century, many people feel that the American family is falling apart, losing its functions, and abandoning its responsibilities. Recent statistics seem to offer evidence of a crisis in American family life. The divorce rate has risen and the birth rate has decreased. Fewer people of marriageable age get married. The supposedly typical family with the husband the sole breadwinner and the wife a full-time homemaker has become a statistical minority. Increasing numbers of women are in the labor force, married or not. The extended-family household has practically disappeared, and large numbers of people live alone.

Besides all these measurable changes, numerous people are involved in relationships and living arrangements that may not be recorded in official statistics—unmarried couples living together, married couples living apart or practicing "open" marriage, or in any number of ways trying to alter the traditional terms of married life. Another change, hard to document statistically but evident to everyone, is an atmosphere of increased frankness about sexuality.

Formerly taboo subjects are openly discussed, and formerly taboo sexual practices, such as homosexuality, have emerged as defensible ways of life. Many people see this permissive climate as a threat to the stability of the family.

Such changes in adult life, however, are less worrisome to many people than the possibility that the family is failing in its responsibilities to children. One prominent social scientist argues that today's families have become little more than dormitories, quick-service restaurants and consumption units, in which "the flickering blue parent" of television has replaced the real parent.[1] Another argues that in terms of current divorce rates, single-parent households, child abuse, and other statistics, the middle-class family now is approaching the level of disorganization typical of poor families in the 1960s.[2]

Public attitudes seem to be shifting away from the child-centeredness of the fifties and sixties toward a view of children and child rearing as costly and burdensome.[3] Cross-national studies suggest that Americans are spending less time on child care than they did in the past and less time than parents in other countries.[4] The large family of the 1950s, with its three, four, and five children, no longer seems desirable to many people in a time of overpopulation, inflation, and a great emphasis on self-realization. Nor does the idea of living for or through one's children seem as attractive as it once did. A recent poll found that 43 percent of those surveyed seemed to represent a new breed of American parents—more self-oriented and less willing to make sacrifices for their children than traditional parents. Further, a Gallup poll recently found that 10 percent of a representative sample of American parents reported that they were sorry they had children—a percentage that translates into approximately 5.5 million parents of children under eighteen who regret having had those children.[5]

To many, the chief threat to the traditional

family seems to arise from recent changes in women's behavior and attitudes. Not only are women entering the work force in increasing numbers, but movement toward equality between the sexes has spread surprisingly wide and far. Those who see the family as based on a dominant, breadwinning male and a submissive, economically dependent female—a view held by many conservatives and some radical feminists—feel that family life and sexual equality are incompatible.

For other observers, the chief threat to the American family is coming from another source—changing American values. A traditional ethic, based on hard work, thrift, responsibility, and self-denial, seems to have been replaced by a new "fun morality"[6] stressing enjoyment and self-fulfillment. Daniel Bell[7] argues that the Protestant ethic has given way to "a psychedelic bazaar," a "pop hedonism" based on play, fun, display, and spending. Tom Wolfe[8] writes of the growing popularity of new "awareness" and "personal growth" therapies and new religious cults as evidence of an increasing preoccupation with the self. He labels the 1970s "The Me Decade." In the past, he argues, people lived for their ancestors and their children, as part of the stream of generations. Now they live for their own self-fulfillment.

Some writers attribute the new hedonism to the hippie counterculture of the 1960s and the spread of its style in music, clothing, group therapy, and the ideology of "doing your own thing" to the masses. Others trace the change to a shift in the economic system from an earlier form of capitalism based on thrift and hard work to a later form requiring the mass consumption of goods to keep the system working. Whatever the cause, the new hedonism seems incompatible with family stability: we may come to treat relationships the way we treat cars and clothing, to be used for a short time and then replaced by later models. "One of the gravest indictments of our society," writes

Christopher Lasch,[9] "is . . . that it has made deep and lasting friendships, love affairs, and marriages so difficult to achieve." He finds that the new therapies aimed at getting rid of inhibitions and increasing "awareness" end up intensifying the problems they were intended to cure. "Arising out of a pervasive dissatisfaction with the quality of personal relations," writes Lasch, the consciousness movement "encourages people not to make too large an investment in love and friendship, to avoid excessive dependence on others, and to live for the moment—the very conditions that created the crisis of personal relations in the first place."

This analysis of the plight of the family seems to represent the prevailing view today, just as the notion of the happy, stable, nuclear family dominated the "togetherness" era of the 1950s. And just as some scholars dissented from the prevailing views at that time, so do some dissent now from the notion that the family is doomed. Without denying that family life is changing, these scholars argue that such changes need not be viewed as signs of decay or disintegration. To see the family as declining, it is necessary to point to some previous era when the family was "stronger" or conformed more to ideal norms. It is difficult, however, to identify that era. As one historian concludes, "there is no Golden Age of the Family gleaming at us from far back in the historical past."[10]

Although those who argue that the family is "here to stay"[11] are undoubtedly more nearly right than those who see signs of family disintegration and decay everywhere, the family is different than it was in the past, the society it inhabits is different, and Americans as individuals are different.

The only way to begin to understand these changes is to take a long look in the rearview mirror of recent and past history. Unless we examine, however briefly, what family life was like in the past—and more importantly, how people perceived it—we are likely to assume that somewhere in history there really was long-lost era of family stability and serenity.

There are other uses of looking at the family in past times. As we live our personal lives from day to day, it is sometimes hard to see the influence of larger social forces on ourselves and others. It is easier to see the interplay of public issues and private life in another era—just as an old photograph bears the unmistakable imprint of a distinct time and place while we cannot see the mark of history in pictures we take of ourselves today.

Only Yesterday: The Fifties Revisited

If any period in American history can claim to be a golden age of the family, it would be the two decades after World War II, especially the 1950s. Many people, confronted with the difficulties of the present, look back with longing for the era of togetherness and the affluent society, of the baby boom and the suburban way of life. The nostalgia began when the sixties turned into the seventies. In 1972, *Newsweek* carried a feature story entitled: "Yearning for the Fifties: The Good Old Days."

Movies like *American Graffiti, The Last Picture Show,* and *Let the Good Times Roll,* and television shows such as "Happy Days" recreate a simpler and more stable time. Nor is this nostalgia confined to pop culture. Writing in the intellectual journal *Commentary,* John Mander proclaimed the 1950s to be "the happiest, most stable, most rational period the Western world has known since 1914."[12]

Given the discouraging kinds of problems that face us as we approach the 1980s, it is tempting to look back at the fifties as a golden age of normality, stability, and prosperity. As Morris Dickstein puts it: "The lure of the fifties hints that history moves like a pendulum; it speaks to our wish to have done with these problems; it tells us we can return unscathed to an idealized time before life grew complicated. . . ."[13]

The lure must be resisted, for the image of the fifties as an untroubled time distorts what life was really like back then. The upheavals of the sixties unmasked tensions that simmered beneath the surface of conformity, domesticity, and respectability. The smug tranquility of the fifties was fragile as well as duplicitous.

Yet we cannot really understand the current situation of the family without looking back at the 1950s. For one thing, as we've already noted, the period represents the stable norm from which the current changes in family life are seen as deviations. It is not merely that statistical indicators, such as the marriage rate, the divorce rate, and the birth rate, are often compared with those of the fifties. Rather, the social-science and popular models of the family we use today were largely constructed during the fifties. They incorporated the assumptions and apparent realities of family life at the time.

Indeed, despite the upheavals of the past fifteen years, many of the ideas and attitudes of the fifties persist today. The social and sexual tensions that burst forth in the sixties remain unresolved. The solutions that once promised to solve them—communes, open marriage, the sexual revolution, sex-role equality—have either been frustrated or tried with mixed results.

The Family in Postwar Perspective

During the postwar era the middle-class American family seemed to be the most highly

This picture contains many symbols of American society and family life in the 1950s: the newly opened supermarket, the overflowing shopping basket, the children with their balloons, going along on the ride to the family car, the smiling faces.

developed expression of basic human nature. Family textbooks could state unapologetically that they were based on the American middle class because that was the ideal norm toward which everyone was striving. The underlying conception of America among most social scientists, not just those in the family field, was that of a "middle-class society in which some people were simply more middle class than others."[14]

Deviation from the standard family pattern was attributed to psychopathology, poverty, or just misfortune. Little or no consideration was given to the possibility that different life styles might be workable alternatives to the nuclear-family life style. Each field—sociology, anthropology, psychology—supported in its own way the idea of the nuclear family as a necessary and therefore universal institution. Some scholars did object to the general consensus. Like the little child who pointed out that the emperor wore no clothes, one sociologist complained that the social scientists, "despite all their elaborate theories and technical research devices, are doing little more than projecting certain middle-class hopes and ideals onto a refractory reality."[15] But the climate of opinion and the prevailing social life did not support such critical views.

The Way We Were

The social scientists' model of the nuclear family, with its two-by-two division into age and sex roles, reflected the prevailing realities of the United States of the 1950s. The ambitious middle-class husband of the fifties fulfilled the "instrumental" male role. The suburban housewife and mother fulfilled her assigned "expressive" role as socializer of children and domestic mainstay. The baby boom and the popular preoccupation with child-rearing experts confirmed the family's role as a social institution whose primary function was to "integrate" individuals into society.

Only Yesterday: The Fifties Revisited

An earlier generation of sociologists had predicted that the coming of a large-scale, urban-industrial society would cause the disintegration of the family. Their predictions seemed to be refuted by statistics showing that more people than ever were marrying, that they were marrying younger and producing record numbers of babies. Fewer women were choosing childless careers. Even the rising divorce rates were interpreted as showing the importance of the family: people were not rejecting marriage but were trying to perfect it, as indicated by the prevalence of remarriages.

At-homeness or togetherness was more than an ideology, it was a statistical reality as well.[16] The "natural habitat" of the midcentury city dweller alternated between work and home. Studies of the mushrooming metropolitan areas in the United States and other advanced societies revealed a social order centered around "the single-family dwelling unit, the conjugal family, selected kinfolk, the job, and the mass media—the latter consumed in the home."[17] The earlier theorists of the city had seen the city dweller as a sophisticated cosmopolitan, participating in the rich cultural and public life that cities made possible, or else as a rootless person drifting through a fragmented and anonymous life, devoid of intimate human relationships. Yet few urban areas and relatively few individuals lived up to either the cosmopolitan or the fragmented version of the urban stereotype. Summarizing the findings of a number of studies, Greer wrote: "The picture that emerges is of a society in which the conjugal family is extremely powerful among all types of population."[18]

But earlier theorists were confirmed in their assertions concerning the weakening of the community life that had existed in earlier times and still exists within the small town and some neighborhoods. In the metropolitan areas where most Americans came to live in the postwar years, the community "as a solid pha-

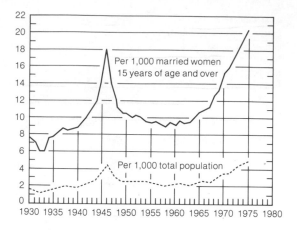

Divorce rates for the United States, 1930–1975. During 1975, for the first time, more than one million divorces were granted in the United States. The total was 1,036,000, which represented an increase of 6 percent over the total of 977,000 divorces granted in 1974.

The more specific rate, divorces per 1,000 married women, reached a record high for the third consecutive year. This rate was 20.3 for 1975, indicating that more than 2 percent of all married women in the United States divorced during this year. Before 1973, the highest level for this rate was 17.9, recorded in 1946. The divorce rate per 1,000 married women has increased each year since 1963. (Source: National Center for Health Statistics.)

lanx of friends and acquaintances does not exist; if individuals are to have a community in the older sense of communion, they must make it for themselves."[19] Thus family and friends fill the sociability gap created by the decline of the community and old kind of neighborhood. Even in the most "neighborly" neighborhoods, Greer notes, the family tends to be weakly identified with the local community.

The inward-turning, intensified family life of the fifties and early sixties contributed to a general mood of complacency and celebration in the social sciences as well as the mass media. But there was more to the national mood than celebration. There was a pervasive hostility—a kind of McCarthyism of marriage and the family—toward anyone who dared deviate from prescribed sex roles: the single adult, the working woman, the childless wife or husband, the "weak" male. Homosexuality was so far beyond the pale that nobody argued against it. At best it was seen as an extreme form of mental illness; more often the homosexual served in both literature and real life as a symbol of evil, decadence, and corruption.

In their book on the fifties, Douglas Miller and Marian Nowak[20] give many examples of the hostility toward deviation from standardized sex roles. Singleness was regarded almost as a contagious disease. One of the influential books of the time, *Modern Woman, The Lost Sex,*[21] argued that bachelors over thirty should receive psychotherapy, and that all spinsters should be forbidden by law to teach children, on grounds of emotional incompetence.

The Paradox of Female Roles   While bachelors and women teachers were condemned for being single, married women were condemned for working. An article on the American woman in a 1956 issue of *Life* denounced the "disease" of working women.[22] The culture of the 1950s abounded in contradictions, and the whole area of women and work contained several.

Paradoxically, despite the image of the normal woman as the happy housewife with no commitment outside the home, and the corresponding image of the working woman as a deviant, more women than ever joined the work force during the 1950s. The rise in women working is now recognized as one of the most obvious and widespread changes in the American family since World War II.

Actually, women's participation in the labor force has been climbing since the nineteenth century. But the most rapid increase occurred during the postwar era. Thus the percentage of women working doubled from 1900 to 1940, but then it tripled from 1940 to 1970. The most striking increase was in the number of working mothers. Between 1940 and 1975 the labor-force participation of women with children under eighteen increased from 29 percent to 47 percent—in other words, nearly half of all mothers were employed. These figures are all the more striking when we realize that much of the increase has occurred in mothers with children under six.[23]

Before World War II, most working wives had come from the lower class; by the late fifties women of all classes were working or looking for jobs. As historian Peter Filene[24] observes, the large influx of women into the labor market effectively closed the question that had been debated for a hundred years: should a woman, particularly a mother, work outside the home? The issue had become as obsolete as the debate over whether or not women should attend college. Nevertheless, although the statistical reality of women's entry into the labor force became apparent by the middle fifties, the social and psychological implications of this change in family life would not be recognized until a decade and a half later.

Typically, the women's jobs were secondary to family. Women worked before they got married and they went back to work at convenient points in the family life cycle—after the youngest child started school and in the empty-nest period after the children left home. Sometimes they went to work at other times—when there were young children at home—if the family finances seemed to demand it. Most women have worked in "the pink-collar ghetto"[25]—in jobs at the bottom of the work hierarchy such as clerical or sales work. At every level of work, however, from the most unskilled to the most technically demanding job, women have been paid less than men.

Despite the image of "the affluent society," few families felt that they had enough money to cover all their needs and wants. Working-class women took jobs to make ends meet, to cover the gap left when the husband's paycheck went to pay last month's bills; middle-class women went to work to pay for the remodeling of the garage or for the children's braces and music lessons.

Two decades later, in the aftermath of the women's movement, we have learned that even jobs with low pay and low prestige can provide some degree of satisfaction.[26] Contributing to the family budget by bringing home a paycheck, and showing that one's hours have a cash value, can give women a feeling of usefulness and self-esteem. Many find the companionship of coworkers a relief from the isolation of the household. And working can give a woman a sense of independence and the ability to hold her own during a marital struggle.

Women have felt free to say these things to researchers during the 1970s, but two decades ago most working women denied they were working for any other reason than to serve family needs. To have hinted at finding fulfillment in one's work would be to open oneself to the charge of being an unnatural woman. Some women did manage to follow careers, or to find and admit satisfaction in work, but the majority of women, whatever they have thought inwardly, conformed outwardly to the "feminine mystique."

The general hostility toward the idea of women working was focused on two particular kinds of women: working mothers and career women. Working mothers received the most criticism. There were more of them, and, more importantly, their working raised questions

Labor-force participation rates of married women by presence and age of children, 1950–1974. Married women with or without children under age eighteen have entered the labor force in increasing proportions over the past quarter century; the pace of the increase for women with preschool children has accelerated in the past few years. (Source: U.S. Bureau of Labor Statistics.)

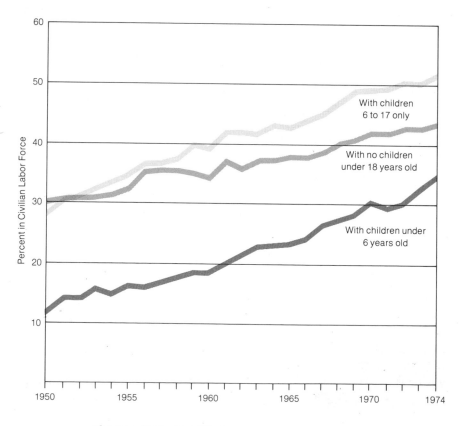

about their children's well-being. Not only the mass media but also the combined voices of psychiatry and social science, citing case histories and statistics, warned about the harm that could come to children if mothers worked outside the home. Dr. Spock, in his book that was the bible of child care in the postwar era, repeated the warnings. Worried mothers wrote the Children's Bureau asking, "Am I making my child into a juvenile delinquent because I have to work?" Despite the agonies of guilt this literature undoubtedly produced, there is now, according to one recent review of the research literature, a remarkable consensus among investigators that the mother's outside employment is not a crucial variable in the child's well-being and development.[27]

But the poorly designed research studies that "documented" the harmful effects of the working mother were not the basis of the popular prejudice; more likely the studies themselves reflected the prejudice. The notion that woman's place was in the home was so ingrained in the culture of the fifties, so woven into the fabric of psychological and sociological thinking, that it would have been unreasonable to think that such a deviation from natural femininity could fail to harm children.

Some writers of the time allowed that women could work without violating their natures if they took jobs that had little prestige, made few demands on their time, and conceded authority to men. A woman who pursued a career, or took her work seriously, was denying her femininity and trying to be a man—she was an obvious case of penis envy. Hostility against the "unnatural" career woman could be expressed in viciously direct terms. Writing in *Esquire* in 1954, Merle Miller, later to emerge from the closet as a homosexual, denounced "that increasing and strident minority of women who are doing their damnedest to wreck marriage and home life in America, those who insist on having both husband and career.

They are a menace and they have to be stopped."[28]

Thus women were caught in a double bind: if they took their work seriously, they were condemned as unwomanly deviants; if they failed to take work seriously, they were open to the charge of being frivolous. Their lack of commitment could be used to excuse low pay and exclusion from responsible jobs.

But that was only one of the tightropes women had to walk in the fifties. There was also the sexual tightrope: women were supposed to make themselves attractive to men but were not supposed to "tease"; they were not supposed to be "frigid" but they were not to go "too far" or "all the way" lest they lose their status as "nice girls." Alex Schulman has written of "the war in the back seat"[29] that went on between young men and women in the forties and fifties. Boys demanded sex while making it clear they would never marry a girl with a "reputation." "Petting" was a major form of sexual activity among the unmarried in the fifties, and it embodied the contradictory demands of the time. The Kinsey reports devoted considerable attention to it. By the 1970s, as Paul Robinson notes, the word has practically disappeared from our sexual vocabulary. "Indeed, one cannot read Kinsey's discussion of petting without being immediately transported into the distinctive sexual ambience of the 1940s and 1950s, with its uniquely frustrating synthesis of permissivism and restraint. . . ."[30]

Contradictory Male Roles Male roles were also caught in a tangle of contradictions. On the one hand, the Victorian patriarch was held up as a model for husbands and fathers, although few living examples were ever observed. Mostly, it was his disappearance that was lamented. Psychiatrists warned about the dire effects of the "passive" or "ineffectual" male. The "weak" father and his partner in psychiatric crime, the dominant mother, were blamed, as one critic put it, for "everything from homosexuality to ingrown toenails."[31] Comic strips and television made millions laugh by poking fun at the emasculated male in the form of Dagwood Bumstead, Ozzie Nelson, George Gobel, and Robert Young.

On the other hand, the ideology of male domination was contradicted by the ideology of the democratic family. The marriage and family literature, as well as the popular media, reported that the happiest marriages were equal partnerships. The doctrine of "togetherness" prescribed that the wife share in the husband's job by discussing his problems and entertaining his associates. Leisure time and sexual satisfaction were also to be shared. In fact, the bedroom was the scene of the most complete equality; the marriage manual of the time most decidedly did not call for the return of the Victorian patriarch, who inflicted his animal need on his sexless and saintly wife. Rather, the good husband must see to it that his wife got satisfaction, preferably at the same moment he did. This was a difficult

demand for both partners because of the widely held view that a vaginal orgasm, produced by the husband in attaining his satisfaction, was the only legitimate kind.

The ideology of togetherness also applied to housework. Family-life author Paul Landis found in the increased sharing of housework by both spouses evidence for the "twentieth century democratizing of the American home"; studies of household decision making and task responsibilities reported high levels of male participation.[32]

The ideal of household democracy conflicted with the patriarchal ideal *and* reality. Studies purporting to show such household democracy reveal actually little time put in by males, as well as great selectivity in what tasks they performed. Men's share of the household chores tended to consist largely of "male tasks" such as fixing things and yard work; even here, males participated only about half the time.[33] Women did more of the time-consuming, daily chores that must be done repeatedly and are

The automobile revolutionized American courtship. The unchaperoned date, or just going for a drive, replaced the visit in the family parlor.

The Family in Our Time

never finished because they are always being undone by the family—making beds, doing the laundry, washing dishes, and so on. Sometimes male participation consisted of little more than "helping" the wife at tasks defined as her responsibility. At any rate, various studies found that male participation was less than equal. Men did seem to participate more in child care, but mostly they gave bottles to babies or played with older children; they tended to avoid diaper changing and the messier and more tedious aspects of caring for children. Nevertheless, fathers were providing more affection and companionship to their children than men in their father's generation.

Even though men were not living up to the ideal of the democratic divison of labor in the home, their participation in any but the most "masculine" of household tasks was outside the traditional male role. Washing the dishes even occasionally, or helping one's wife do them, did not fit the image of the Victorian patriarch retreating from the dinner table to relax with pipe and slippers. Even the advocates of togetherness and equality seemed to be uncomfortable with the idea, and the solution they proposed could have come from Orwell's *Animal Farm:* husband and wife were equal, but one was more equal than the other. Thus *McCall's* magazine, in a 1954 issue proclaiming the new era of togetherness, warned: "For the sake of every member of the family, the family needs a head. This means Father, not Mother. . . ."[34] In 1958, the singer Pat Boone wrote a best-selling book in which he described his family as "The happy home corporation." "I do believe marriage is a fifty-fifty deal," he noted, "but every corporation has to have a president who, when the chips are down, can say, 'it's going to be this way.' "[35]

In sum then, the family ideology of the fifties created difficulties for both men and women; each was faced with contradictory demands on the self and contradictory expecta-

tions of the other. It was in fact the classic double-bind situation: men and women were given incompatible scripts to enact; if they carried out one, they failed at the other, and no one pointed out the contradiction, thus breaking its spell. What people were saying was often not what people were doing, but again, no one pointed out the discrepancy. Everyone was under the additional obligation to have a happy and perfect family life. The illusions of the "happy home corporation" persisted unchallenged until the 1960s, when many of the children who had been the supposed beneficiaries of togetherness turned against it.

The Big Boom

If the tensions and contradictions within family life in the fifties escaped notice at the time, it may have been because of the seemingly miraculous abundance of the postwar economy. At the start of the 1940s, one-third of the country remained ill-housed, ill-fed, and ill-clothed. Millions faced seemingly endless unemployment, and relatively few had any hope of owning a new house or car, or sending a child through college. World War II ended the depression and started a boom that lasted well into the 1960s.

The war put an end to hard times for many families. During the war years, the proportion of families living on less than $2,000 a year dropped from three-quarters to one-quarter of the population. Family income more than doubled between 1939 and 1969. For the first time a majority of Americans no longer had to worry about being able to obtain the basic necessities of food, clothing, and shelter. Instead, they could take these for granted, and indulge in expenditures on a spectacular scale for items that had once been luxuries: new homes, television sets, wall-to-wall carpeting, cars, boats, hi-fi sets, travel, and so on.[36]

Coming after four years of war and twelve years of depression, the boom set off a mood of celebration and hope; it was as if, as one writer put it, "milk and honey appeared suddenly to a people who had been trudging across an eco-

A scene from the Great Depression of the 1930s. Government job programs helped to reduce unemployment, but it was World War II that put an end to the Depression.

nomic Sinai for a decade and a half."[37] Suddenly people could find jobs, get married, buy new homes, and, most significantly of all, have babies again. The birth rate shot up from its all-time historic low in the 1930s to an all-time historic high in the 1950s.[38]

Long-held ideals about the family and its style of life were first able to be put into practice on a mass scale at this time. People valued family privacy during the colonial era, but crowded households and the scrutiny of family relationships by neighbors empowered by religion to mind other people's business interfered with the realization of the ideal.[39] At the begin-

The Family in Our Time

ning of the nineteenth century, the single-family detached house came to be viewed as the ideal setting for domestic life and had great influence on architects and designers. But it was not until the postwar suburban area, supported by the massive government financing of VA and FHA programs, as well as private financing through banks and insurance companies, that the dream of the single-family home came to be realized on a large scale.

The general prosperity overshadowed in both popular awareness and the social sciences the poverty of a considerable minority of the population. The eye of the social scientist was firmly focused on the middle-class majority and its remarkable affluence. It was easy for a social scientist to slip from description to celebration. Here is Greer, for example, commenting on the freedom and affluence of the modern urban individual:

> . . . [he] has a freedom in the symbol spheres that has never been widespread before in any society. There are some one thousand television hours available each week to the Los Angeles resident. His relative wealth, literacy, and privacy allow an exploration of meaning never before possible to the rank and file of any society.[40]

Admittedly, all social problems had not been solved. There were still slums, bigotry, and sudden eruptions of violence. But in the perspective of the fifties, these seemed to be peripheral matters. Compared to the problems of the past—scarcity, mass unemployment, ethnic and class conflict, political instability, epidemics—these difficulties seemed trivial. Even when poverty was "discovered" in the early sixties, the answer to it seemed obvious and easy. The solution seemed mainly to be a technical one: to incorporate the disadvantaged and culturally deprived into the general affluence and well-being. The middle-class family pattern was held up as the model for the disadvantaged to follow.

Indeed, the "inadequate" family life of the poor, particularly the black poor, was held to be the major reason why those groups had not yet "made it" into the great middle class.

Most intellectuals and social scientists had joined in the celebration of the American way of life. Those who did not were not troubled by the problems that surfaced in the 1960s—racism, poverty, and the abuse of American power in the world. Rather, they were concerned about the cultural consequences of the affluence they could see around them—materialism, conformity, and the vulgarity of mass culture. William Whyte criticized the docile conformity of "the organization man" in the book of that title, David Riesman criticized the conforming "other-directed" personality of *The Lonely Crowd*. The writer Edmund Wilson is reported to have said after reading *Life* magazine that he did not belong to the country depicted there.[41]

Only a handful of social critics rejected the social and economic foundations of the affluent society. In 1958, Richard Chase asked: "Of what value is the new competence in family life, if while we have achieved it, we have surrendered control of the material resources of the country?" He went on:

> It is time to ask ourselves if a fruitful and human life will be possible at all in an America full of the flashy and insolent wealth of a permanent war economy, brutalized slums, rampant and dehumanizing Levittowns, race hatred, cynical exploitation and waste of natural resources, government by pressure group, by executive abdication, and by Congressional expediency, vulgarization and perhaps the destruction of the schools, not to mention the sporadic flash and fallout of "nuclear devices."[42]

Chase's book was ignored at the time. The dominant mood of the day was optimistic.

Looking to the future, social scientists saw more of the same—an extension of affluence and middle-class life styles to those "left out" or

This couple told the photographer: "We enjoy having these things."

"left behind" in their pockets of poverty, more technology, more economic growth, all leading to a more stable and balanced social order. The "age of ideology" was over and would not return.

The key to it all was continued abundance. Until the late sixties, it looked as if economic growth could go on forever. Even the counterculture rebels of the 1960s, who rejected most of the assumptions of postwar America, took continued abundance for granted. Indeed, as we shall see in more detail a little later, they criticized the society for not fully realizing that the end of economic scarcity was at hand. For mainstream opinion leaders during the fifties and early sixties, prosperity was in the process of solving all social problems. Social harmony would be guaranteed, as Hodgson put it, "by distributing the consumption of goods so lavishly that it would not seem urgent to distribute them equally."[43]

And Then the Deluge

The postwar mood of complacency and consensus was first shattered by the outbreak of social unrest in the mid-1960s—the growth of black militancy, the emergence of student dissent, the antiwar movement, the rise of the counterculture, and riots and fighting in the streets. In the tranquility of the fifties no one had foreseen anything like these developments. Even more unlikely in those days than the "politics of protest" was the emergence of a politics of the family. At the beginning of the sixties it was only the universality of the middle-class family life style that was called into question with the discovery of poverty. By 1970 virtually every assumption of the family and sex-role ideology of the fifties was under attack. Their validity was challenged by rebellious students, the commune movement, women's liberation, gay liberation, and the spread of nonmarital cohabitation. In a relatively short time such notions as the "obsolescence" and "crisis" of the nuclear family passed from being heresies of the counterculture to mass-media clichés.

In retrospect, the whole postwar way of life, not just its assumptions about women, the family, and home, was founded on illusion and contradiction. First, the image of America as an affluent society was seriously flawed: some parts of the population were excluded altogether from the American dream of affluent suburbia, and others had only a precarious hold on it. Second, the affluent society produced new sources of discontent in many of those who had been its most favored beneficiaries. Finally, there was a fundamental flaw at the very heart of the postwar life style, in the economic engine that drove it through a decade and a half of prosperity. Each of these themes will be discussed in greater detail.

The Limits of Affluence

As is true with most myths, there was some basis in reality for the myth of the affluent worker. During the postwar era, American workers enjoyed a level of material well-being that contrasted dramatically with the standard of living of workers in other countries and with American workers in previous decades. In the ideology of the times, however, this rise in living standards was elevated to the mythical notion that class differences and inequality had been abolished.

Furthermore, although living conditions did improve in the postwar era for a majority of middle- and upper-income families, they deteriorated for millions of poor and low-income families. The growth of the suburbs that benefited the nonpoor majority imposed heavy costs on the less advantaged. In fact, the process tended to worsen existing social, economic, and family inequalities.

Most people tend to think of the mass migration to the suburbs in the past thirty years as being due to some unplanned social force or simply to individual families making decisions to move. In fact, however, government policies played a large role in both the growth of the suburbs and the erosion of the cities.

One set of policies helped millions of Americans move out of large cities to the spacious environments of the suburbs: the provision of FHA insurance and mortgages for suburban development (but not inner-city housing), federal support for highways connecting suburbs to the central cities, and the tax advantages given to homeowners but not renters.

Meanwhile, the inner-city environment was being worsened by another set of policies. The flight of the middle class in itself led to the deterioration of the cities, since it resulted in a greater concentration of the poor and the traditional correlates of poverty—crime, drug use, and other forms of delinquency and despair. Adding to the problem was the large influx of blacks and other poor who were being driven off the land by the mechanization of southern agriculture.[44]

Very-low-income families were concentrated still further by the big public-housing projects that were being built in most major cities. These now are widely recognized as the most dangerous and unhealthy environments for children and families, yet millions had no alternative but to live in them. Further, urban-renewal and highway-construction policies led to even more concentration and isolation of the poor. Meanwhile, these same policies were breaking up poor and working-class neighborhoods that had contained cohesive communities and strong social ties. Finally, welfare policies were encouraging the breakup of families by providing support only to women and children.

By the 1960s American society had become more sharply segregated than it had been in the past; it had become two societies: a black inner

An urban ghetto. The postwar exodus to the suburbs contributed to the deterioration of America's cities.

city surrounded by a collar of white suburbs. Further, in addition to the more obvious racial segregation, there was increasing separation of people by income level, age, and life style. Retirement communities for the elderly were a postwar innovation; and, by the end of the 1960s, real-estate developers all over the country were offering housing exclusively for "swinging singles."

In short, during the postwar era the environments for poor and low-income urban families, especially minorities, had worsened "precisely *because* middle- and upper-income

households—especially whites—had deliberately excluded the former from sharing in the improved quality of the neighborhood environment."[45] Few of those who joined the great postwar exodus to the suburbs realized that they were the beneficiaries of government policies. Still less did they realize that they had contributed to deterioration of family environments in the inner city. Yet they eventually suffered the consequences of the urban crisis all the same. In the mid-sixties, American families could gather around the TV sets at dinner to watch American cities go up in smoke.

While poor black families trapped in the inner cities bore the brunt of the urban crisis, white ethnic and working-class families bore a disproportionate share of the costs of the changing urban landscape. Working-class and lower-middle-income neighborhoods were more likely than upper-middle-class ones to lie in the path of the expanding black population, an urban-renewal project, or a new highway. For most lower- and middle-income families, their home is the biggest investment. Further, as Andrew Levison points out, workers' homes are not simply a piece of property, "but something which has absorbed so much of their income, so many hours of work, and closed out so many alternatives, that losing it is like making all the sacrifices futile."[46] Thus the "changing" of a working-class white neighborhood

Segregation by age has increased in recent years.

Some studies show that older people prefer living in their own communities.

Only Yesterday: The Fifties Revisited

TABLE 1   *INCREASE SINCE 1970 IN THE NUMBER OF PRIMARY INDIVIDUALS LIVING ALONE BY AGE AND SEX*

Year and Sex	All Ages	Under 35 Years	35 to 64 Years	65 Years and over
1975				
Both sexes	13,939	2,947	4,984	6,008
Male	4,918	1,710	1,918	1,290
Female	9,021	1,237	3,066	4,718
1970				
Both sexes	10,851	1,449	4,333	5,071
Male	3,532	809	1,550	1,174
Female	7,319	640	2,783	3,897
Increase 1970 To 1975				
Both sexes	3,088	1,498	651	937
Male	1,386	901	368	116
Female	1,702	597	283	821
Percent Increase 1970 To 1975				
Both sexes	28.5	103.4	15.0	18.5
Male	39.2	111.4	23.7	9.9
Female	23.3	93.3	10.2	21.1

Source: U.S. Bureau of the Census. (Numbers in thousands)

could provoke fury and even violence. Often housing did lose its value as neighbors rushed to sell after a black family moved in. In short, the transformation of the American landscape in the postwar era resulted in a white backlash as well as the black uprisings of the sixties.

The Contradictions of Affluence

However shocking were the black riots of the sixties, or the attempts of white backlashers to stop the integration of a school or neighborhood, these acts were easily comprehensible. People were responding to their own obvious self-interests. The other revolts and social movements of the sixties were less understand-

able at first glance. Why would children of the most advantaged part of the population—the children of affluence and togetherness—rise up in protest? And why would that seemingly most privileged person on earth—the upper-middle-class educated housewife—denounce her very privileges as a form of oppression? And why would large numbers of successful, affluent men and women become fascinated with Indian gurus, Eastern religions, encounter groups, sexual experimentation, meditation, alternative family forms, and faddish therapies?

Paradoxically, the postwar prosperity gave rise to new, undreamed-of discontents and longings. And just as the "affluent society" produced dissatisfaction among the have-nots and the have-lessers—the blacks and the white working class—it produced a new rebellious class within its own privileged midst—its children. Some of the reasons for these discontents had been anticipated by the same social scientists who had stressed how well the family was functioning in modern society. Parsons had noted that when the family lost its economic functions and the home was no longer a workshop or a business, the women, children, and old people were left in an ambiguous position outside the occupational world. Goode, looking at family change in countries now undergoing modernization, noted a number of contradictions between the ideology of the conjugal family and the realities of life in an urban-industrial society. He too saw the woman's role as a particular point of strain in the system: "modernization" offers woman equality and liberation from the restrictions of the kin group, yet it leaves her in an isolated household with increased burdens of child rearing.[47]

The male role in modern society also generates strain. Under constant pressure to produce, achieve, and support, most men spend their lives at work they do not like. At the higher levels of the occupational scale, work is often intrinsically rewarding, but life at the top has its own discontents: the scientist, the artist, the company manager, the professor may judge themselves in relation to heroes of achievement farther up the scale than themselves, rather than by their distance from those below. Thus the home and family are assigned the role of refuge and retreat from the harshness of the occupational world, a difficult if not impossible assignment.

The contradictions of family life first became apparent among the well-educated, technically and professionally skilled part of the population. It is largely this group that has given rise to student dissenters, the counterculture, and the women's-liberation movement.

The middle-class woman of the postwar period was more likely than her working-class sister to experience the contradiction between the ideology that men and women are equal and the realities of life, particularly of marriage. After receiving the same education, middle-class young men and women went in very different directions: he participated in the larger

In the 1970s, increasing numbers of Americans have involved themselves in Eastern religions, and meditation, and various new therapies.

Only Yesterday: The Fifties Revisited

world and, despite complaints about the rat race, found some degree of daily social interaction and stimulation in his work; she retreated into the home. The contrast was greatest when the husband was a professional who enjoyed his work or a businessman who traveled to interesting places and indulged in expense-account living. The wife of a factory worker, however, had less cause for envy. In the same way the middle-class child who has been raised "democratically" is sensitized to discrepancies between the ideal of treating young people as "persons," human beings whose views are to be taken seriously, and the actual powerlessness of the dependent young in families, schools, and the larger society.

The most ironic source of discontent has been affluence itself. People brought up in relative economic security, political freedom, and affluence simply take these for granted as facts of life rather than as goals or values to organize their lives around. Kurt Back[48] has suggested that the emergence of the encounter-group movement in America is one expression of the discontents of affluence. In the past, he observes, most people's lives were devoted to simply surviving—to meeting basic needs for food, clothing, and shelter. People believed that in a society where such needs would be fulfilled everyone would be happy. During the sixties we learned the fallacy in that assumption. As George Bernard Shaw once quipped: "There are two tragedies in life: one is not getting what you want; the other is getting it." Many affluent Americans of the 1960s were to demonstrate the truth of the second half of that statement.

I Buy, Therefore I Am A number of observers have pointed out that the United States today is in an uncomfortable transition between the work ethic—stressing hard work, savings, and the repression of impulse—which remains the official ideology, and a hedonistic ethic appropriate for a mass-consumption society. Since World War II the American economy has required high levels of spending and consumption to maintain prosperity. There has been a growing emphasis on immediate rather than deferred gratification. The credit-card economy stresses leisure-time activities—boating, fishing, skiing, camping—as providing the central meaning of life and definitions of self.

Daniel Bell,[49] points out that in a modern capitalist economy, the motives for the acquisition of goods are *wants*, not *needs*. The distinction is derived from the writings of Aristotle. Human needs, he believed, have natural limits built into them—food to satisfy hunger, clothes and shelter for warmth, sexual intercourse, care during sickness, and so on. To acquire anything beyond the satisfaction of these basic needs would be unnatural. In a mass-production, capitalist society, however, *needs* are replaced by *wants*—which are unlimited and insatiable.

Advertising, of course, is the basic means used to produce these wants. It puts us on a hedonistic treadmill. Ironically, while promising to satisfy needs and wants, it is a powerful stimulant to discontent on a mass scale. Advertising constantly bombards us to be dissatisfied with what we already own, and tries to stimulate appetites for more, bigger, and better, and newer things.

Modern advertising focuses less on the product itself and more on the mind of the consumer—particularly on his or her self-image. Beginning in the 1920s, advertisers explicitly aimed at developing a critical self-consciousness in the buyer. In 1929 Helen and Robert Lynd noted that the new type of ad tried "to make the reader emotionally uneasy, to bludgeon him with the fact that decent people don't live the way he does."[50]

But the discontents that advertising stimulates are not always directed at the self; the other side of consumerism is a deep skepticism concerning all advertising claims, and a "scrutinizing, evaluating, and questioning [of] all areas of life from the environment, to education, to automobiles, and . . . even to politics."[51]

Fun Morality Another reason affluence fails to satisfy is that it is based on a "fun morality," as Martha Wolfenstein[52] describes it, that contains a paradoxical injunction: one is obligated to have a good time. Although the Protestant ethic could give rise to feelings of guilt and worthlessness, it offered the possibility of trying to satisfy one's conscience through hard work. Fun morality is more elusive. Play becomes permeated by the work ethic; one asks: am I having enough fun, a good-enough orgasm, a happy-enough marriage? Not only does happiness tend to elude such introspection, but being permitted to satisfy impulses may weaken the pleasure of anticipation:

In the past when work and play were more sharply isolated, virtue was associated with one and the danger of sin with the other. Impulse gratification presented possibilities of intense

excitement as well as of wickedness. Today we have attained a high degree of tolerance of impulses, which at the same time no longer seem capable of producing such intense excitement as formerly.[53]

Knowledge and Dissent Still another source of contradiction and discontent has been the spread of higher education to large masses of people after World War II.

The very dependency of the key institutions on an intelligentsia of educated professionals makes for a less-stable society. Along with providing the trained manpower, this same intelligentsia is just as likely to provide the major critics and rebels of the social order. Thus student protesters, insurgent intellectuals who protest government policies, as well as "phone phreaks"—electronics experts who use their expertise in opposition to the owners and managers who depend on them—symbolize the contradictions of advanced modern society. Dissent in the society arises not from the

Between 1950 and 1975, the percent of adults completing four or more years of high school almost doubled. (Source: U.S. Bureau of the Census.)

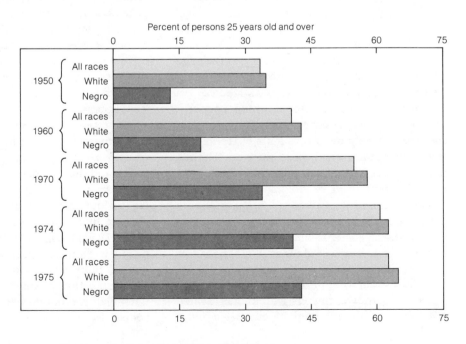

Only Yesterday: The Fifties Revisited

failures of socialization but from its successes. The critical faculties required by highly educated professionals lead them to question the very legitimacy of the order they serve.

Lipset and Dobson present some dramatic statistics documenting how the occupational structures of such advanced countries as the United States and the Soviet Union have changed in recent years. Between 1930 and 1965, for example, while the general work force in the United States increased by half, the number of engineers almost quadrupled and the number of scientists increased almost ten times over.[54] In addition, there has been expansion in the numbers and influence of other kinds of knowledge and cultural workers — teachers, artists, writers, journalists, people in the media.

Why are there such strong tendencies for intellectuals to constitute a dissenting force, to bite the hand that feeds them? The answer seems to be that creative work of any kind — scientific or artistic — seems to call for a certain skepticism, a critical detachment from prevailing ideas. Once a person develops critical or independent thinking in work, he or she will likely be critical also in matters outside that special field of work.

Moreover, when existing knowledge changes rapidly, it is not possible to train young persons with skills that will last a lifetime. An engineering student, a computer programmer, a student of business administration — none of these can simply be taught a set of techniques that will remain valid from then on. Rather, they must be taught to be flexible — there have been different ways of looking at the problem in the past, and the future will bring still more innovation. The more broadly a person has been educated, the easier it will be for him or her to change occupations or skills several times over.

The Transformation of the Self   The spread of higher education in the postwar era has created not only a different kind of citizen — a more critical and skeptical one — but also a different kind of personality. Although the lack of money, education, and success can produce unhappiness, having these things doesn't guarantee happiness. Education, in particular, seems to change people's needs, values, and self-perceptions. A number of studies dealing with the impact of income and education on people's sense of well-being have discovered what one writer calls a "Richard Cory complex."[55] Richard Cory was the subject of a poem by Arlington Robinson; he had looks, social status, and money, but one day he went home and put a bullet through his head.

When researchers such as Angus Campbell and his associates[56] asked people questions about how satisfied they felt, whether they regarded their lives as interesting or boring, enjoyable or miserable, and so forth, they discovered a surprising interaction effect between education and income. They found that the people who gave themselves the highest happiness ratings were those who did not finish high school but were earning more than $12,000 a year. College graduates, however, were not very happy regardless of how much they earned. College graduates with low incomes were happier than other people in that income category. But in the group of people making the most money, the college graduates were the least happy.

The reason for this discontent seems to be that education doesn't merely impart skills but transforms the way people feel about themselves and the world. Education seems to make people more introspective — more able and willing to look inside themselves and thus more likely to find weaknesses. One study conducted in the 1950s found that people with more education were more likely to have negative self-images than those with less education.[57] Further, education changes values: college graduates value economic security less than other people do; they also feel that having an important or exciting life is more important than having money. And they care more about the psychological aspects of their jobs than the economic ones. Since these values are more intangible than the size of one's paycheck, it is harder to measure one's success or failure.

Bringing Up Father: Adulthood as a Stage of Development   The increased emphasis on the psychological needs of adults has resulted in a new view of adulthood. The idea of development, once applicable only to growing children, is applied to adults as new stages of adult life are "discovered."

Keniston has argued that the dramatic increase in higher education has created a new stage of the lifespan—"youth"—on a mass scale:

> Like childhood and adolescence it was initially granted only to a small minority but is now being rapidly extended to an ever-larger group. I will call this stage "youth" and by that I mean both a further phase of disengagement from society and the period of psychological development that intervenes between adolescence and adulthood. This stage, which continues into the twenties and sometimes into the thirties, provided opportunities for intellectual, emotional, and moral development that were never afforded to any other large group in history.[58]

Although Keniston speaks of youth as a "psychological stage," he warns that not all college students are in this stage—that some are "adolescents" psychologically and some are adults. Nor are affluence and education necessary for the experience of youth: "There are poor and uneducated young men and women, from Abraham Lincoln to Malcolm X, who have had a youth, and rich educated ones who have moved straightaway from adolescence to adulthood."[59]

It might be more useful to think of "youth" not as a developmental stage but as a particular kind of cultural outlook or world view or psychological perspective. The psychological themes of youth may be less a postponement of adulthood than a redefinition of it. What Keniston describes as youth may well be an experience that for many people will extend over most of the lifespan.

Keniston's stage of youth resembles what Robert J. Lifton has called the "protean" life style. It used to be that growing up resulted in a finished product, a person whose character was set by the end of adolescence, and who would change only under the most extreme conditions, such as a religious conversion. Now, Lifton argues, we live in an age of identity crises that may last a lifetime. Settled identities may change to other settled identities, and more than once. Thus the conditions of life in the twentieth century have produced a new kind of individual, whom Lifton calls "protean man," after the mythological figure who could take the form of any living thing.[60]

There have been various other ways of viewing the cultural shift to a more fluid kind of adulthood personality. Christopher Lasch has written gloomily of the "new narcissism"—a type of personality that is chronically bored, unable to form deep and lasting friendships or marriages, and constantly seeking instant intimacy and "emotional titillation without involvement and dependence."[61]

By contrast, Lifton argues that the "protean" self is by no means pathological, and "in fact may be one of the central adaptive patterns of our day." The "new narcissism" may represent only the darker potential of the new personality style; tolerance, flexibility, and generosity may be its more prevalent virtues. Also in a more optimistic vein, Gail Sheehy, in her best-selling book *Passages,* has popularized a developmental view of adulthood—that is, adults are described as passing through stages, each with its own characteristic crisis and resolution.[62]

However one views these changes in adult personality, they have profound implications for both the society and the family. As Ralph Turner[63] has pointed out, in recent years we have witnessed a significant change in how people define their "true selves," a shift from institutional to impulsive definitions. In the past, most people identified themselves with their social roles—husband, wife, worker, student, parent. Impulses that seemed to threaten these roles—extramarital adventure, leaving the job, or being free of family responsibilities—would be regarded as alien urges that should be suppressed. Today, for many people, it is these impulses that are defined as the true self to which one owes primary allegiance.

The End of the Boom

The third flaw in postwar America was the bursting of the economic bubble.

If, during the 1950s, a seer had made predictions about the events that were to take place in America during the sixties and seventies—the assassinations of a president and national leaders, riots in the cities, the waging of a war in a small country across the Pacific that would arouse massive protests, Watergate—the coming of a prolonged economic crisis might not top the list of surprising events. But the end of the era of ever-increasing abundance may make the most drastic alterations of all on the lives of individuals and families.

It wasn't until the 1970s that this flaw became apparent. The disastrous combination of inflation, the energy crisis, recession, and unemployment that hit the country in 1973 put a final end to the postwar era. It became dramatically clear that the expectation of growing abundance, taken for granted in both the fifties and the sixties, was fundamentally wrong—an illusion.

The postwar era and its life styles had been based on three basic assumptions about the economy: that unlimited economic growth was good, that it was possible, and that economists possessed the technical know-how to control both inflation and unemployment.

By the late sixties, there was increasing awareness that growth brought costs as well as benefits. The automobile was a prime example. It polluted the air and damaged the physical and social environment of both the city and the country. A luxury in the twenties, it had become a necessity in the fifties. The early dream of driving freely through the countryside gave way to the reality of the daily morning and afternoon traffic jam. Each year more people were killed in traffic accidents than during the entire Vietnam war. Moreover, the car fragmented society, isolating people, including family members, from one another, separating home and work, increasing social stratification. Other forms of technology had similar built-in problems. Perhaps the ultimate insult of technology was the announcement by scientists in the spring of 1977 that human mothers' milk had become so polluted by chemicals in the environment that if it were sold in stores it would have to be banned as carcinogenic.[64]

By the 1970s it became clear that untrammeled growth not only was causing problems, but could not go on even if we wanted it to: the image of boundless abundance was replaced by the image of scarcity. Wants and technological ingenuity might be infinite, but natural resources were limited; people began to talk of "the spaceship earth," of "small is beautiful," of "survival," of "lifeboat ethics."

Finally, during the 1970s, economists lost confidence in their ability to control and even predict the national economy. They fell into warring camps disputing what went wrong and how to solve it, and the latest editions of the leading textbooks on economics talked of doubt, change, disaffection, and uncertainty.

In retrospect, it is striking how little the dissenters of the sixties disagreed with the basic assumption of unlimited economic growth. They assumed that scarcity was no more. The only problem that remained was distribution — and this was really not a problem. For example, Philip Slater argued that the key to understanding the difference between the counterculture of dissenters and the mainstream, "old" culture is the concept of scarcity; in the old culture both economic and sexual gratification are in short supply:

> The core of the old culture is scarcity. Everything in it rests on the assumption that the world does not contain the wherewithal to satisfy the needs of its human inhabitants. From this it follows that people must compete with each other for these scarce resources — lie, swindle, steal, if necessary.[65]

By contrast the "new culture" believes that human wants are easy to satisfy, and the means for doing so plentiful.

Another of the most influential figures on the left agreed. Herbert Marcuse criticized the American society of the fifties, but accepted its belief in limitless growth. He foresaw a time when automation would be so complete that the necessity to work would become obsolete — limitless abundance would lead to limitless leisure.[66] Michael Harrington, whose book *The Other America* had helped in the rediscovery of poverty, worried about how people would adjust to the end of scarcity and the necessity to work hard. No one foresaw that the end of prosperity was just around the corner.[67]

Thus for many people the decade of the seventies has been, as Morris Dickstein puts it, a time of "pinched possibilities, failed Utopian visions, exhausted psychological resources."[68]

There is some evidence that people are turning again toward home, family, and private life as a source of meaning. Many of those who questioned the fifties life style are forming committed relationships, getting married, even having children. A survey of college graduates of 1972 revealed that, to a greater extent than students a decade earlier, they expected family life and individual needs to take priority over careers as a way of retaining a feeling of self-worth, self-determination, and self-fulfillment in society.[69]

Yet this is not to suggest that the values of the fifties are returning. Ironically, the political movements of the sixties have had their major impact on private life and experience. Pollster Daniel Yankelovich has identified "a new breed of American parent" born out of the student rebellion, the counterculture, and women's liberation. Forty-three percent of the people in his study fit the model of the new-style parent, concerned with self-fulfillment, questioning of all authority, including their own, and skeptical of traditional values such as success, religion, patriotism, and marriage.[70]

Even people who did not identify with the protest movements of the 1960s have been subtly changed by them. Although a majority of Americans rejected militant protest or extreme life styles, the ideas of the women's-liberation movement have spread far and wide into the mainstream of the American population. A poll of the readers of a women's magazine of the early seventies revealed that a majority believed women to be second-class citizens, a view that had been held by a small minority only a few years earlier.[71] More recently, a *New York Times*-CBS poll found a majority of Americans believing that marriages in which both partners work and share the housework and child care are "a more satisfying way of life" than traditional marriages.[71a]

The results of numerous other surveys show that, despite a conservative backlash such as "the total woman" movement or the antihomosexual vote in Miami in June of 1977, Americans have been becoming more experimental in their private lives, more tolerant of racial, sexual, and political minorities, and more restless in their search for meaning in life.[72] As one writer sums it up, what remains from the 1960s is not so much changes in political or economic institutions, but "in the way people think and act toward each other."[73]

Yet there are obstacles in the way of seeking refuge in the family from the troubles of the times. A stagnating economy can undermine the family at the same time that it creates work-related discontents that drive people deeper into personal life. All families are pinched by inflation, but young people starting out their family lives are particularly vulnerable to the difficulties of finding jobs in a time of high unemployment or buying a house when prices are soaring out of sight. Many women must work, whether they want to or not, to maintain the family's standard of living. Childless couples put off having children, and those who already have them are facing the fact that many communities, even in the suburbs, are becoming less supportive environments for raising children than they used to be. In short, it is difficult to escape the profound impact of economic realities on family life. As one economist puts it:

If unemployment and underemployment continue in the future, the blessings of familism are likely to be compromised from all sides: from the pressures of inadequate income, from the blows to ego and family status of unemployment, by the drain on psychological and emotional resources of jobs which provide less challenge than educational careers have prepared individuals for, by the strain on marital relations of changing relations between men and women.[74]

Looking Backward: A Heritage of Family "Crisis"

Given the difficult world of the 1970s, and the seeming intractability of the economic and ecological problems that confront us, it is little wonder that many people have given up hope of finding utopia in the future and instead are looking for it in the past. We have already examined the current nostalgia for the fifties and have pointed out the reasons why the idealized image of that decade is distorted. Other historical eras also seem to provide us with images of a more stable and harmonious family life, if not of a perfect society. For many people, the 1930s, as depicted in the television show "The Waltons," calls up an image of solid families struggling together against economic adversity.

For the Victorian era, we can conjure up an image out of *Life with Father*—the stern pater-familias seated at the head of the table, surrounded by his properly behaved wife and offspring, only a mischievous glint in their eyes suggesting lively spirits beneath the decorum. Or we can go back even farther to images of the sturdy pioneer family, working together to build a new home on the frontier. Or we can go back to the early Puritan family in the colonies, bound together by a common core of religious belief and a community of fellow believers. And, along with all these specific images, there is the generalized one that William Goode called "the classical family of Western nostalgia"[75]—the image of a large, happy household bursting with kin, down on grandpa's farm.

The realities of family life in the past, however, to the extent that we can learn about them, seem to bear little resemblance to our idealized images. Looking backward past the 1950s, past World War II and the Depression, into the early decades of the twentieth century, and backward still farther into the nineteenth century, one gets a very different picture of the current family "crisis." Rather than a fall from grace, the past fifteen years represent a return to issues of family life and sex roles that had been simmering for almost a century before they were erased from memory by "the long amnesia" that set in with the Depression of the 1930s and was to last for more than thirty years. The fifties were an unusual period in American history not only because of affluence, but also because people did not worry about the conditions and future of the family.

Reading contemporary material from almost any previous era of America's past, one finds a pervasive sense of uncertainty about the family, a longing for a more stable, harmonious past, and frequent calls for reform to bring the reality more in line with the image. Several related themes recur again and again, their specific form set by the particular era. These are:

1. What happens to parental—or more precisely, paternal—authority in a society where change is a constant and where sons need not inherit their fathers' skills and occupations to find places for themselves?

2. What holds a family together when they are no longer a self-sufficient economic unit dependent on each other's labors?

3. What is "woman's place" in a society based, at least in principle, on human equality?

4. What is to be the role and place of women and children when production moves from home to factory and fathers become the family breadwinner?

America the Changeable

In 1888 James Bryce observed in *American Commonwealth:* "America is change."[76] Change has been the major constant in American life, and there have always been a great many Americans who found it disturbing. Social change often transforms family life. It disrupts traditional family roles and breaks up the continuity of generations. No matter what the form of the change—whether immigration, revolution, or the introduction of a factory or other new technology—it calls for alterations in the family's way of doing things; parents can no longer use their experience as a guide for the young. Although we inherited much of our culture from Europe, the ecology and conditions of life in the New World worked drastic alterations on that culture. In a country based on both immigration and a constantly expanding frontier, there has never been a time when an older generation could pass on to its children a society and landscape exactly like those it had known in its youth.

Concern about loss of parental control over children began early in our history. Although the seventeenth-century settlers tried to "strengthen" and "preserve" the home, as Oscar and Mary Handlin observed, "it was not an effective instrument of social control in the New World. The laws with monotonous regularity tried to shore up the institution; the preambles which described the need were a desperate commentary on the failure."[77]

What many viewed with alarm as a loss of social control was a shift in authority relations within the family. The position of the young was strengthened in the American environment. Young people approaching adulthood, unlike their counterparts in Europe, did not have to wait to inherit their parents' land, but could settle on the frontier. "It was a basic part of the New World experience," observes John Demos, "that families should be continually divided, and that at least some elderly people should be left to fend for themselves"[78] The ability to leave the family strengthened the hand of the young within the family as well; they could use the threat of leaving as a weapon in struggles with parents.

Indeed, a surprising degree of looseness in the bonds between parents and children could be found well into the nineteenth century. Many young people in their early teens left their families to make their own way in the world. The courts often legitimized these realities by terminating the mutual rights and obligations between parents and the children who had left home.[79] By the end of the nineteenth century, however, children could no longer be absorbed in an increasingly industrialized economy—they would be "runaways," not young persons in search of work.

If the departure of the young for the frontier created one kind of family drama, another kind of drama was repeated through the whole course of American history in the lives of immigrant families: the young were often more competent in the new environment than their foreign-born parents. In making their way in the New World they would almost inevitably reject their parents' traditions if not the parents themselves. As the Handlins put it:

. . . injunctions to preserve fidelity to the home rang hollow, unpersuasive when voiced by elders who had themselves deserted the places of their birth. Then too, the fathers, fumbling through the forests for paths they did not recognize, lost the ability to assure their sons of the way and thus lost the authority to lead. The old wisdom did not hold in a land strange in soil and climate. . . .[80]

Besides the changes brought about by social and geographic mobility, the growth of industry and of cities changed the American way of life, as have accompanying changes in knowledge, education, communication, and government policy. Change in all areas of life is a characteristic of modernized societies, and as historians have recently been putting it, America was "born modern."

To take but one example of the continuity of change in America, consider a man interviewed by the Lynds as part of their study of "Middletown."[81] When seen by the Lynds, he was one of the oldest citizens of "Middletown"—their pseudonym for Muncie, Indiana. He had been a leading local physician in the 1890s, and his memory reached back to the 1840s. Within his lifetime, local transportation had changed from the horse to the railroad and the car, "grain . . . ceased to be cut . . . by thrusting the sickle into the ripened grain as in the days of Ruth, . . . getting a living and making a home . . . ceased to be conducted under one roof, education . . . ceased to be a luxury accessible only to the few."[82]

His own field of medicine had been revolutionized by the development of the X-ray, anesthetics, and the germ theory of disease. He had experienced the discovery of electricity and the invention of the telephone, the telegraph, and radio, not to mention countless other innovations.

This enormous change within a single lifetime was not unique to this man, to his part of the country, or even to his generation. Indeed, much of *Middletown* is a study of changes in progress at the time, and their impact on people's lives; the Lynds witnessed the automobile and the movies revolutionizing small-town society, changing leisure-time activities, and creating new tensions between parents and children. The automobile "blasted its way" through previously unquestioned rules such as: "rain or shine, I never miss a Sunday morning at church," "a high-school boy does not need much spending money," and "parents ought always to know where their children are." Many people perceived the home to be "endangered" when riding in cars replaced the

The Family in Our Time

traditional visit in the family parlor as the way unmarried young people got together.

Indeed, the worries of many parents were justified. The movies revealed a sophisticated world of sexuality, which the parents of Middletown had tried to keep "out of sight and out of mind," and the automobile gave young people a place to act out their learning. "Dating" and "petting" were invented during the period.

The Lynds also witnessed the coming of assembly-line production and its transformation of the industrial worker from master craftsman to just another part of the machine, replaceable and unskilled. It became possible for a boy of nineteen to turn out a greater amount of work than his forty-five-year-old father; indeed, it was not unusual for fathers to be laid off during slack times while sons continued to hold jobs. "Whether one is temperamentally well disposed toward social change or resistant to it," the Lynds concluded, "the fact remains that Middletown's life exhibits at almost every point either some change or some stress arising from failure to change."[83]

The same might be said about almost any other place and time in American history. Despite the pervasiveness of change, Americans have been ambivalent about it. On the one hand, they have had faith in progress, in new technology, and in new ideas. On the other hand, they have often been unwilling to accept the social consequences of change.

For example, at the turn of the century, many people, including many scholars, worried about the fate of the family in industrial society. They feared that when the family "surrendered" its functions to other institutions—manufacturing to the factory, education to the state, health care to the hospital, and so on—it could only wither away.

These anxieties seemed to be confirmed by divorce rates. The divorce rate has been rising relentlessly since the middle of the nineteenth century. Between 1860 and 1914, the divorce rate per thousand marriages had quadrupeled while the marriage rate remained constant. There had been 7,000 divorces in 1860, 56,000 in 1900, and 100,000 in 1914. As historian Peter Filene observed, in an era when "many people believed that a kiss signified engagement and a marriage was forever, divorce was considered an ominous symptom not only of family disintegration, but of moral decay."[84]

The other sign of crisis in the family was the decline in the birth rate. Not only had the overall birth rate declined, but the drop was greatest among native, white, middle-class families; the birth rate among immigrant women was nearly twice as high. Theodore Roosevelt called it "race suicide." "A race is worthless and contemptible," he wrote in 1903, "if its men cease to be willing and able to work hard and to fight hard, and if its women cease to breed freely."[85]

During the early decades of the twentieth century, other political figures and social scientists, in numerous speeches, writings, and conferences, denounced the breakdown of family life. As late as 1929, a presidential commission reporting to President Hoover one month before the stock-market crash, was still sounding the alarm about the crisis in American family life and morality:

> Birth control, race riots, stoppage of immigration, . . . governmental corruption, crime and racketeering, the sprawl of great cities, . . . international relations, urbanism, . . . shifting moral standards, . . . the status of womankind, labor, child training, mental hygiene, the future of democracy and capitalism, . . . all of these grave questions demand attention if we are not to drift into zones of danger.[86]

The Woman Question

Throughout the nineteenth century, concern with the fate of the family in urban-industrial society was mixed up with the issue of women's proper role. The women's-rights movement, although it never won over a majority of women, had been an important part of nineteenth-century America and had provoked widespread and often bitter debates. Indeed, many of the ideas and proposals of the women's movement today were first put forth over a century ago. And much of the feminine-mystique ideology that prevailed in the 1950s had derived from arguments that had been made against nineteenth-century feminism. Freud, for example, although he was not quite the misogynist he is often assumed to have been, argued against the case for female equality that was being made by such writers as John Stuart Mill, Henrik Ibsen, and George Bernard Shaw. Ironically, during "the long amnesia" from the 1930s to the 1960s, the feminist half of the debate was forgotten. By the 1950s, young women would have no experience of organized feminism or the arguments it had made.

Along with getting the vote, the feminist movement from its earliest days was concerned with the suffocating restrictions that had been placed on women in the nineteenth century. The removal of production from home to factory resulted in a new ideology glorifying and sentimentalizing the home and the woman who maintained it. An enormous outpouring of writings on family life prescribed proper behavior for women and children. The new ideology saw the world as sharply divided between a chaotic, threatening public world and the home as a private retreat. The woman's role was to provide perfect peace, emotional comfort, and moral uplift to husband and children. The early feminists, observed John Demos, "despised all this adoring rhetoric on woman-in-the-home; they sought to expose this myth of domesticity for what it really was."[87]

Other important issues that concerned the women's movement of the time were the right

The working woman is not a new phenomenon.

The Family in Our Time

to work, the right to a college education, and—trivial as it sounds—the reform of women's dress. In the 1850s, feminists provoked a furor by rebelling against the restrictive clothing styles that symbolized women's status. Instead of the conventional way of dressing with its tight corsets and hoop skirts, they proposed a "bloomer" outfit consisting of pantaloons and tunic.

The passage in 1920 of the Nineteenth Amendment, granting women the right to vote, marked both the highest achievement and the beginning of the end of the feminist movement that had begun a century earlier. A number of reasons have been advanced for the decline of feminism: having achieved its major goal, the movement lost its purpose; the conservative political climate of the 1920s did not support social-protest movements. But perhaps a more fundamental reason was that feminism was undone by the sexual revolution that began in the twenties. Most feminist women had been Victorians in their sexual attitudes, despite the presence of a few well-publicized advocates of free love in their midst. The majority had assumed that sex was unpleasant, that celibacy did not imply deprivation, and that being a spinster was an honorable role.

By the 1920s, these attitudes had changed. A new kind of rebellious woman appeared in the figure of the flapper—girls with "bobbed hair and powdered noses, with fringed skirts just above the knees and hose folled below, with a cigarette in one hand and a man in the other."[88] "Flaming youth"—and its smoking, drinking, jazz, and petting—became a major topic of public and private debate; the new generation outranged both feminists and traditional Victorian conservatives. Although the majority of women did not model themselves on the flapper, the new sensuality she represented spread from the far-out fringe to the middle-class center.

As the Kinsey reports were later to document, the incidence of premarital intercourse among middle-class women did rise sharply during the twenties. Thus the twenties destroyed one of the basic hopes of nineteenth-century feminism and Victorianism in general—that there could be a single standard of morals compelling men to be as chaste as women. This proved unworkable. The twenties showed, as William O'Neill observed, that: "if men and women could not be equally chaste, they could at least be equally promiscuous."[89]

The feminist movement that had been an important part of American public life died in the crash of 1929. Despite the movement's loss of momentum in the twenties, the issues were still being debated. Magazines carried articles about equal marriage, cooperative nurseries, and combining work and career. The crash and the Great Depression that followed ended the debates about sexual equality and made the other "new woman," the flapper, irrelevant.

In the struggle for economic survival, the needs of the male breadwinner came first. One out of four men were unemployed, and millions more feared losing their jobs. Public opinion turned with a vengeance against women who seemed to be taking jobs away from men and their families. In fact, most women in the labor force, as today, were in female occupations, and the majority of male occupations hired few or no women. Also, just as today, most women worked out of necessity to support their families with or without a husband in the home. Despite the economic realities of women's work, her place was still in the home.

World War II brought an even greater discrepancy between women's work and the ideology of women's roles. Women moved in record numbers into every level of factory work and business. "Rosie the riveter" became a popular image of women's contribution to the war effort, and almost 200,000 women put on uniforms and joined the WACs and the WAVEs. The federal government provided day-care centers for the children of working mothers, although there were never enough places to meet the need. But all this changed behavior did not result in changed attitudes—once again, women's work was defined as a temporary expedient.

But it was not always defined that way by women themselves. Surveys taken at the time showed that a majority of women wanted to continue with the work they had done during the war.[90] But neither the government, nor labor, nor the men returning to their old jobs

Poster used to recruit women to war jobs during World War II. After the war, women were pressured to return to the home.

Longing won't bring him back sooner...
GET A WAR JOB!
SEE YOUR U. S. EMPLOYMENT SERVICE
WAR MANPOWER COMMISSION

were eager to see women remain on the job. The government, fearful of another depression and worried about employment problems of returning veterans, ended its child-care programs, and in other ways encouraged women to withdraw from the labor market. Social scientists, the mass media, and groups such as the Child Welfare League and the Family Service Association joined in the task of mobilizing women to return to the home.

Women did leave the niches they occupied in the male world, but many continued to keep a hand in the world of work, in the women's jobs they had traditionally occupied. Working or not, however, most women of childbearing age contributed to the baby boom. The traditional role as housekeeper and childbearer was joined to the newer ideas about sex. The long amnesia had finally snuffed out the memory of both feminist protests and the fear of family disintegration that had haunted earlier generations.

The Return of the Repressed

We have come full circle. After the smug illusions of the fifties and the turmoil and utopian hopes of the sixties, we are left with unresolved problems that had been put aside for fifty years.

It seems as if all the chickens have come home to roost at once. The belief in "progress" that sustained over a century of technological growth has, both literally and figuratively, run out of steam. The faith that unlimited economic growth could do away with poverty and inequality without challenging the basic distribution of wealth and power in the country has proved to be an illusion. And the issues of family life raised by a century of feminist agitation have also come to demand an answer now—how can we combine sexuality, sex-role equality, work, and domesticity into a rewarding life for both men and women?

Summary

In times of change and uncertainty, people often look nostalgically back to "the good old days" of some earlier period. Many feel that the post-World War II era, especially the 1950s, was an era of contentment, prosperity, and family stability. It is important to examine the realities of family life and attitudes during that era because it often serves as a baseline against which we measure current changes.

Despite the idealized image of the era, the postwar life style was both fragile and contradictory. The revolts that broke out in the 1960s—of blacks, young people, and women— were a product of tensions that were either created or repressed during the fifties. Three flaws undermined the postwar American way of life. First, a majority of American families did not enjoy the level of affluence that was portrayed in the mass media as typical. Blue-collar or working-class families struggled to maintain a modest level of material comfort, while the poor and minorities were excluded altogether. In fact, the growth of the suburbs during the postwar era imposed heavy costs on the disadvantaged. America became a society divided between angry, despairing inner-city ghettos surrounded by white suburbs. Working-class, white, ethnic families also suffered from the changing urban landscape. The result was an increase in racial, ethnic, and class tensions by the end of the 1960s.

A second flaw appeared in another set of tensions that arose paradoxically from affluence itself. The chief beneficiaries of the postwar life style, the educated upper-middle class, discovered that once basic survival needs could be taken for granted, new sources of striving and discontent arose. Many of the young people who had experienced the greatest advantages as children came to be the most dissatisfied with American society. They created a counterculture based on both political opposition and alternative life styles. Eventually, these attitudes spread from the fringes to influence the mainstream of the American population.

Women also rebelled against the "feminine mystique" of domesticity that had prevailed during the postwar era. The influence of the women's movement also spread well beyond its original middle-class origins. It raised far-reaching questions about family life, child rearing, work, and sexuality that have challenged almost every aspect of American society.

The final flaw in the postwar way of life lay in the economic forces that drove it. Economists, policy makers, and social theorists during the fifties assumed that economic growth could go on forever, and that abundance and technology could solve all problems. By the 1970s it had become clear that there were limits to growth, that technology produces disastrous side effects, and that many serious problems— inflation, unemployment, the energy crisis, and so on—seem to have no quick and easy solutions.

Earlier periods of American history do not reveal any other golden ages of the family either. America has always been a land based on change, and change has always had disturbing effects on the family. From colonial times, Americans have worried about the younger generation and the stability of the home.

Many of the family issues that confront us today were first raised during the nineteenth century, when industrialization and other social changes swept the society and created a new set of pressures on the family. Rather than witnessing a decline in the family over the past decade and a half, we are recovering from a long amnesia during which important family issues were ignored. We are finally taking up the unfinished business of working out the relations of men and women, parents and children, home and work, family and society in a modernized, industrial, bureaucratic society.

Source Notes

1. Keniston, 1975.
2. Bronfenbrenner, 1974.
3. Boocock, 1975.
4. Robinson and Converse, 1972; Szalai, 1972.
5. *McCall's,* November 1975.
6. Wolfenstein, 1954.
7. Bell, 1976, p. 54 ff.
8. Wolfe, 1976, p. 27 ff.
9. Lasch, 1976, p. 10
10. Demos, 1976, p. 29.
11. Bane, 1976.
12. Mander, 1969.
13. Dickstein, 1977, p. 27.
14. Bottomore, 1966, p. 105.
15. Moore, 1958, p. 408.
16. Grazia, 1962.
17. Greer, 1962, p. 94.
18. Ibid., p. 93.
19. Ibid., p. 94.
20. Miller and Nowak, 1977.
21. Farnham and Lundberg, 1947.
22. Coughlan, 1956.
23. *Handbook on Women Workers,* 1976, Chap. 1, Sect. 8.
24. Filene, 1975, p. 175.
25. Howe, 1977.
26. Rubin, 1976.
27. Herzog and Sudia, 1973, p. 212.
28. Miller, 1954, quoted in Miller and Nowak, 1977, p. 164.
29. Schulman, 1977.
30. Robinson, 1976, p. 63.
31. Levenson, 1972, p. 73.
32. Landis, 1955.
33. Boone, 1958.
34. *McCall's,* 1954, quoted in Friedan, 1963, p. 43.
35. Boone, 1958, pp. 83–84.
36. Grazia, 1962; Hodgson, 1977; Miller, 1965.
37. Hodgson, 1977, p. 52.
38. Glick, 1975.
39. Flaherty, 1972; B. Laslett, 1973.
40. Greer, 1962, pp. 104–105.
41. Wilson, quoted in Miller and Nowak, 1977.
42. Chase, quoted in Dickstein, 1977, p. 64.
43. Hodgson, 1977, p. 51.
44. Gutman, 1976.
45. Downs, 1977, p. 176.
46. Levison, 1974, p. 106.
47. Goode, 1963.
48. Back, 1972.
49. Bell, 1976.
50. Lynd and Lynd, 1929, p. 82.
51. Gartner and Reissman, 1974, p. 9.
52. Wolfenstein, 1954.
53. Ibid., p. 75.
54. Lipset and Dobson, 1972.
55. Tavris, 1975.
56. Campbell et al., 1976.
57. Gurin and Feld, 1960.
58. Keniston, 1971a, p. 309.
59. Ibid., p. 17.
60. Lifton, 1969.
61. Lasch, 1976, p. 11.
62. Sheehy, 1976.
63. Turner, 1976.
64. *San Francisco Chronicle,* 1977.
65. Slater, 1970, p. 103.
66. Marcuse, 1964.
67. Harrington, 1966.
68. Dickstein, 1977, p. 272.
69. Gottlieb, 1974.
70. Yankelovich, 1977.
71. Tavris and Jayaratne, 1973, p. 68.
71a. *New York Times,* 1977.

72. Wuthnow, 1976.
73. Starr, 1977, p. 54.
74. Grubb, 1977, p. 44.
75. Goode, 1963.
76. Bryce, 1888, quoted in Hodgson, 1977, p. 14.
77. Handlin and Handlin, 1971, pp. 15-16.
78. Demos, 1976, p. 16.
79. Marks, 1975.
80. Handlin and Handlin, 1971.
81. Lynd and Lynd, 1929.
82. Ibid., p. 10.
83. Ibid., p. 498.
84. Filene, 1975, p. 37.
85. Roosevelt, 1903, quoted in Kennedy, 1970, p. 42.
86. Hoover Commission, 1929, quoted in Hodgson, 1977, p. 14.
87. Demos, 1976, p. 21.
88. Filene, 1975, p. 134.
89. O'Neill, 1969, p. 94.
90. Childhood and Government Project, 1977.

Chapter Two
In Search of the Family

☐ *One difficulty in the psychological sciences lies in the familiarity of the phenomena with which they deal. A certain intellectual effort is required to see how such phenomena can pose serious problems or call for intricate explanatory theories. One is inclined to take them for granted as necessary or somehow "natural."*

Noam Chomsky, *Language and Mind*

☐ *Nobody knows what really goes on in a family.*

"Betty Neumeyer," in Paul Wilkes, *Trying Out the Dream:*
A Year in the Life of an American Family

In Search of the Family

There is, as William Goode observes, a striking paradox about the family. For several generations, the family has seemed to have been in a state of constant decline, yet it shows no signs of disappearing. Perhaps, he concludes, "disorganization is *endemic* to family life," and "the normal course of daily life is made up of dissolving pressures, together with the repeated and often stumbling reassertions of stable patterns."[1]

Current and past debates about the decline of the family conceal more fundamental disagreements about what the "family" really is. Even those who argue against the idea that the contemporary family is declining or decaying do not agree with one another about the meaning of current trends. Some see the family functioning as well as ever; some see it functioning as badly as ever. Some see continuity between past and present families; some see today's family life as shifting to new and diverse patterns. There is also disagreement about the facts of family change over time. Does the history of the family trace the decline of the large, extended patriarchal family and the rise of the nuclear family? Or has the extended family survived and even been strengthened in modern times?

At a more basic level, there is disagreement about how to measure the current and changing state of family life. Shall we look at household structure, who lives with whom? Shall we consider the relationships of family members with outsiders? Or are emotional relations among nuclear-family members the chief index to the nature of family and changes affecting it?

The disagreements and uncertainties concerning the present state of the family and its past history illustrate another paradox concerning the family: despite its familiarity to us all, it is actually a problematic and elusive subject of study. To understand the current state of the family, we must analyze in greater detail the obstacles that stand in the way of knowing about family life.

The Unknown Family

We approach the study of the family with a great handicap: we know both too much and too little. In no other field of study is there such a great temptation to use one's own experience as a basis for wide-ranging generalizations. Yet, rather than being the easiest of subjects to study, the family may be one of the hardest. Like anthropologists who often find their own culture harder to study than an exotic one, perhaps only a person who has never lived in a family is really qualified to study them. As R. D. Laing puts it:

> The first family to interest me was my own. I still know less about it than I know about many other families. This is typical . . . .[2]

And, even more surprisingly, he admits:

> The most common situation I encounter in families is when what *I* think is going on bears almost no resemblance to what anyone in the family . . . thinks is happening. . . . Maybe no one knows what is happening.[3]

The anthropologist Ray Birdwhistell argues that the family is an extremely difficult form for social scientists to study, not only in their own culture but in other cultures also. He concludes that everywhere family processes are both idealized and camouflaged.[4] Social scientists look out through the blinders and filters imposed on them as members of a particular culture. They deal with people who may hold unrealistic assumptions about their own family systems. As an anthropological field worker,

Birdwhistell was struck by the discrepancy between the actual behavior of people in their family life and the accounts people gave of their family systems:

> What even the most sophisticated interviewer gets when he asks about the family is a set of personalized stereotypes—the stereotype obscured by anecdotes which purportedly report personal experiences, but which are no less banal by virtue of this pseudo-individuality.[5]

Families, like governments or organizations or even individuals, do not find candor a necessary ingredient for their day-to-day functioning. Quite the opposite. One of the discoveries of recent family research is that families have myths, secrets, and information-processing rules that determine the kind of communication that goes on—what can be said and, more important, what can't be said. Families filter information not only about the wider culture, but also about their own functioning. Or, as Laing puts it, families practice mystification: they have complicated stratagems for keeping people in the dark about what is going on, and in the dark that they are in the dark.

Sanctity and Secrecy

Besides familiarity and mystification, other obstacles handicap the study of the family: it is morally sacred, and it is secret. The family in America includes two moral dimensions, a religious one based on Judeo-Christian family ideals, and a legal one relating to the laws of marriage, economic obligations between husband and wife, parents and children, and so on.[6] Thus the happenings of family life are the concern of others besides the family members themselves; they have a public dimension. Yet,

paradoxically, because privacy is also a cherished value, the family is perhaps the most secret institution in American society. To a greater extent than in other societies and in our own historical past,[7] American family life goes on behind closed doors. The home is a "backstage area"[8] where people can be relaxed, informal, and off guard precisely because they cannot be observed by outsiders.

As a result of this privacy, family life in America is marked by what sociologists call "pluralistic ignorance," a term usually applied to sexual experience. We know what goes on in our own household or bedroom, but we have little or no direct knowledge of what really goes on in other peoples'. Thus we know where our own family life falls short of the *ideal* norms—the way family life is supposed to be—but we do not know where it fits in *statistical* norms—the extent to which other families also may be departing from prescribed behavior. As Goffman puts it, people are aware of how their own "backstage" behavior differs from how they act "in public," but they are not in a position to come to the same conclusion about others.[9]

Until very recently family scholarship has paid relatively little attention to the "backstage" aspects of family life. Despite the vast literature on family life spreading across several disciplines, practically everything social scientists know about the family has been derived from questionnaires and interviews obtained from family members seen alone.[10] Often only one member of a family, usually the wife,[11] serves as an informant about the rest of the family.

There are, of course, some very good ethical reasons for respecting family privacy. Keyhole peeping and eavesdropping, electronic and otherwise, would be hard to justify as research methods. In recent years, however, researchers have found a compromise between privacy and research. They have begun to observe family interaction live with the consent of those being observed. Although these glimpses of family life do not give a view that is truly "backstage" or unobserved, they nevertheless have led to new conceptions of what families are, and how they are to be understood. Viewing live family interaction has reclaimed for social science some of the insights into family life that previously had been found only in the writings of novelists and playwrights."[12] We shall explore these insights later.

The Definition Problem

In much of this chapter we are going to explore what people mean when they speak of families and "the family." The family has proved to be an elusive concept, in spite of our conviction that we know what families are all about. Trying to pin down the meaning of the term is not just an intellectual game. There is, as we shall see, genuine doubt among those who have thought about the matter just what it is

that distinguishes families from nonfamilies, and whether there is a single definition of family that applies to all times and places.

Definitions of the family have important consequences in peoples' lives. The assumption that one form of "the family" is not only the most desirable but also the most real and observable form avoids interesting intellectual issues, dictates social policies that stigmatize certain family and sexual behaviors as pathological deviance, and at the same time fails to direct attention to the potentials for psychological and physical harm in ordinary family life.

The definition problem is important for another reason. There is a widespread belief, encouraged by family textbooks and popular writings on the family as well as by some distinguished scholars, that the nuclear family is universal, found in every known human society. Many people interpret this belief to mean that the family as we know it or would like it to be in our society occurs everywhere. Yet the very

Even with four fewer children, this would still be a family according to the American definition of the term. Would it still be a family without any of the children?

In Search of the Family

term "family" is ambiguous. Murdock observes that "the layman and even the social scientist often apply it to several social groups which, despite . . . similarities, exhibit important points of difference."[13]

Does "the family" mean the nuclear family—the married couple and their offspring? Is the husband-wife relationship the core of the family, or is it the mother-child pair? Does "family" include the family tree—the aunts, uncles, cousins, grandparents? Does it include the dead, whose influence some researchers have detected two generations beyond the grave? If "the family" means the nuclear family,

is the whole family as a unit "the unity of interacting personalities," as Burgess[14] put it? Or is the family a separate reality for each member —the child's view of the family may not be the parental view; the wife's view may not be that of the husband.

What is the irreducible basis of the concept of family: blood ties, marriage, living together, a sense of identification, a sense of obligation? Some combination of these? How does the quality of experience in groups called families differ from that in nonfamily groups? Will any definition apply across all cultures and historical periods?

Conceptions of the Nuclear Family

Discussions about the nuclear family are often confused because the term is used in a variety of ways. In American society the nuclear family refers to an observable group of people who live together and are set off from the rest of society in a number of tangible ways; the universal nuclear family of the anthropologists is more abstract. It is "abstract" because it does not imply that the nuclear family lives together, or acts as a unit, or is behaviorally similar from one society to another.

The classic statement as to the universality of the nuclear family was made by Murdock in 1949:

> The nuclear family is a universal social grouping. Whether as the sole prevailing form of the family or as the basic unit from which more complex familial forms are compounded, it exists as a distinct and strongly functional group in known society.[15]

In addition, Murdock postulated the following characteristics of the family: common residence, economic cooperation, socially approved

sexual relationships, reproduction, and child rearing.

Since Murdock's assertion that the nuclear family is a cultural universal, an imperative found in all societies, anthropologists have been debating the validity of the statement. In general, even those who argued for the idea of a universal nuclear family were well aware that family life as a day-to-day reality was not the same everywhere. In many societies, for example, husbands and wives are not expected to be emotionally close to one another and may not even eat or sleep together.

Murdock himself argued that the nuclear family is one of three distinct family organizations found in human society. The other two were the *polygamous family,* formed by the marriage of one man to two or more women, or one woman to two or more men, and the *extended family.* The extended family forms when a married couple joins the parents of one of the spouses, and three generations live under one roof or close to each other. Murdock argued, however, that the nuclear families were still separate units in these complex forms of the family. Other scholars disagreed that these larger family organizations could be viewed as being made up of nuclear families; rather, it seemed, the nuclear families were submerged in them.[16]

Other arguments about the universality of the nuclear family involve changing or stretching definitions. For example, the collective living and child-rearing arrangements of the Israeli kibbutz can be seen as an exception to the nuclear-family principle, or as a confirmation of it, depending on how the family and its functions are defined.[17] Another series of debates concerns the Nayar, a warrior caste in India.[18] Among these people, households consisted of brothers and sisters, and the children of the sisters and their daughters. One of the remarkable features of the Nayar was the complete separation between the roles of husband, biological father, and legally designated father. That is, marriages in this society were formal rituals, after which the spouses need never have anything more to do with each other. In fact, if a husband did develop a fondness for his wife, this would cause fear and concern among the relatives of each spouse. Men and women were free to take lovers. Neither the woman's husband nor the biological father had any rights over the child; the legitimate father of a child was one of the mother's lovers who agreed to pay for the birth expenses.

In viewing the customs of the Nayar, it is possible for one group of anthropologists to argue that these people do not have the institutions of marriage, fatherhood, and legitimacy, and for another group to argue with equal fervor that they do, however differently these institutions may be defined. Both sides would agree that there is little resemblance between the contemporary nuclear family as a group of people who live together and the family life of the Nayar.

David Schneider and Raymond Smith[19] have recently tried to clarify the confusion surrounding the concept of the nuclear family by pointing to three different ways of talking about it. It is necessary to distinguish the nuclear family as a *cultural symbol,* as a *set of norms or roles,* and as a *residential or domestic unit.*

The Nuclear Family as a Cultural Symbol

The nuclear family as a cultural symbol is deeply rooted in Western culture. The nuclear family is what people in these cultures mean by the term "family." It is represented in images of the Holy Family, in family photographs, and in mass-media depictions of family life. Thus, for family textbook writers, many social scientists, and the American public, "the family" is a married couple and their children. Society seems to be divided into nuclear-family groups, each living in a home of its own. Any deviation from the parent-child unit living together is not quite a family and needs explanation. It may be a "broken home" or some other variation from the expected pattern.

> A married couple without children does not quite make a family. Neither do a married woman and her children without a husband nor a married man and his children without a wife. For the married couple without children, one may say, "They have no family," or "Their family has not arrived yet," if they are very young. "Family" here means that the addition of children will complete the unit. . . . And of course one may say of an older couple, "Their family has all grown up and is married, each has a family of his own now."
>
> This last example makes clear another condition which is part of the definition of the family in American kinship. The family, to be a family, must live together.[20]

This description of American kinship usages may strike the reader as obvious to the point of being funny. But that is exactly the purpose of Schneider's study. The essence of any system of cultural symbols and definitions is what people in that culture take for granted.

As Schneider points out,[21] the anthropologist must act like a child. He has to learn the names for things, how to use the names correctly, and the values and dangers that lurk around them. Thus Schneider is spelling out the basic cultural premises of the American system that a native or anthropologist from another culture would have to know in order to understand the kinship system.

One of the striking features of the way Americans think about the family, Schneider notes, is the emphasis on the family as natural. The underlying image of the family is of a man and a woman united in physical love, whose children are seen as the "flesh and blood" of both parents.

Other cultures define the family differently. The traditional Chinese family, for example, is defined as a long line of fathers and sons, including remote ancestors and unborn descendants. A man remains a member of his family throughout his life. "He is identified with the family from birth, and every action concerning him, up to and including his death, is in the context of that group."[22] Women provide the links in the male chain of descent, but they are not included in anyone's genealogy. A woman is not a member of her husband's family, and although she is a temporary member of her father's household, she is not a member of his family either.

The Nuclear Family as a Normative System

Although all Americans share the cultural symbolism of the nuclear family described above, there is great variation in how different segments of the population define their obligations to various family members. Schneider and Smith[23] distinguish between two broad codes of family conduct: a middle-class one in which the husband and wife are the "solid core around which the whole system revolves," and a working-class, ethnic, or black pattern with an emphasis on help, cooperation, and solidarity with a network of kin, centering around a parent and his or her grown children.

The book and the movie *The Godfather* portray one version of the kin network and rich, extended-familial culture of Italian-Americans. Although the film perpetuates the myth that Italians have a special propensity toward crime, it presents a fairly accurate picture of this family culture.[24]

More often, however, kin networks in American families are focused on the mother. Although much has been written about the "matriarchal" black family, working-class white families often have an equally strong emphasis on ties between mothers and grown children, even where there are few female-headed households. The same is true of English working-class families. Thus one English mother of five reported to an interviewer: "I couldn't get on without me mother. I could get on without me husband—I don't notice him."[25]

These descriptions, it should be noted, are greatly oversimplified. Not all working-class or ethnic families follow the pattern ascribed to them, nor do all middle-class families follow the middle-class style. The obligations and attitudes of a son toward his mother, for example, may vary with the kind of work he does, how old he is, the region of the country they live in, the particular ethnic group they belong to, as well as personal and familial idiosyncrasies. Further, at the high end of the socioeconomic scale, upper-class families often emphasize the continuity of generation and have less emphasis on the independent nuclear family. Finally, people's beliefs about their kin obligations do not necessarily predict their behavior, a problem we shall examine in more detail in the next chapter.

A rural black family.

The difficulties of describing American family life in terms of one or even two typical patterns is illustrated by the work of John Spiegel. Spiegel and his associates decided to learn as much as they could about the structure and function of family life in the United States, in order to define "the normal American family." Spiegel[26] describes a remarkable search for "the family" amid the welter of real families in their varied day-to-day existence. Instead he found "the most astonishing variance in their structure and function."[27] It was difficult, for example, to know where to draw the boundaries around the family. Some families seemed to extend laterally—that is, to include relatives such as aunts, uncles, and cousins—whereas others extended vertically to include grandparents and great-grandparents.

The complexities reached into the very heart of the nuclear unit itself—the relations between husbands and wives, and parents and children. Spiegel writes:

> Not only were various and differing functions assigned to the family in different social milieus, but even those functions which were apparently universal, such as the socialization of children, the satisfaction of sexual needs, or the biological and material maintenance of the members of the family, were carried out in such various ways with such differing implications that it proved impossible to obtain meaningful patterns without reference to the surrounding social system.[28]

But the complications did not end there. Beyond the occupational structure, Spiegel writes, was another level of human behavior: the level of cultural and subcultural values. For example, middle-class families in the United States emphasize planning for the future, hard work, and individual initiative. But the United States has a mixed cultural heritage that complicates the picture. Each ethnic group seems to relate to the dominant value system in its own way.

Misunderstandings can arise between people who grow up in different kinship patterns. Some of Birdwhistell's[29] Kentucky subjects, for example, who lived in extended families, had very different conceptions and definitions of "family" from their friends, neighbors, and even spouses who had grown up in more nuclear or, as Birdwhistell calls them, segmented families. The interdependent or extended-family members seemed to define family in terms of blood kinship. They expected to continue all their lives the intense involvement with kinfolk they had known as children. They would not expect this involvement to be affected by reaching maturity, marrying, or work. In fact, the main purpose of Birdwhistell's research was to learn why some rural Kentuckians would migrate to other areas of the country and try to be "successful," while others who seemed much like them would remain behind in their hometowns. He believes he found the explanation in the different family patterns of the movers and nonmovers.

The family in the extended-family pattern is a very different entity from the series of separate units in space and time that make up the nuclear family. The traditional family is continuous in space and time, unbounded by household walls, and immortal. Marriage, birth, maturity, even death do not reduce the central unit. The genetic family tree defines not only genetic connections, but ongoing obligations and involvements. Rather than the marriage of grown children leaving behind an empty nest, the in-law line may add additional family members:

If the marriage is, in family terms, a good one, the affinal relatives/in-laws of the family member become one's own "almost like family." And as these affinal relatives meet at funeral, church, and family gatherings, they gain kinship status and are called by kinship terms.[30]

Yet Birdwhistell's interviewees did not perceive the unique quality of their family life. When asked directly about their family relationships, the "interdependent" family people talked in the stereotyped terms and imagery of the nuclear-family model. It was as if the nuclear-family imagery had blotted out the experiences of those who had a very different life style from the standard husband-wife, parent-child unit. And if there was any awareness of being different, it was stated with a sense of shame.

People who hold to one of the foregoing family patterns are likely to see people in the other family model as not quite healthy or normal psychologically. For example, Birdwhistell[31] notes that his nuclear-family subjects tended to define people with extended-family ties as immature, dependent, and lacking in ambition. The traditional people, on the other hand, were likely to feel that people with the nuclear-family emphasis were cold, selfish, and too driven by ambition.

The Nuclear Family as a Domestic Group

So far, we have discussed two ways of talking about the nuclear family. The first deals with the nuclear family as a cultural symbol—a set of images and definitions of what the family is. Second, we discussed the nuclear family as a normative system, a code of conduct concerning how particular family members should act toward one another, what obligations they have to each other, and so on. We contrasted two

An "extended" family.

different patterns of family norms: one was a "middle-class" pattern centered on the husband-wife-children unit, with grown children emotionally and economically independent of their parents; the other pattern—generally found among working- or lower-class, ethnic, or black families—emphasizes ties between extended-family members, especially between grown children and their own parents, particularly the mother, and places less emphasis on the husband-wife bond. The issue that concerns us here is the third way of talking about the nuclear family—the nuclear family as a household unit.

House, Home, and Family   One of the main assumptions in the middle-class definition of family is that a family lives together in a home. The terms "home" and "family" are used almost interchangeably. We know of course that in reality some families do not live together, and some people live together who are not families. But we tend to define these situations as abnormal and unfortunate or immoral.

Until recently most social scientists also tended to assume that home and family were equivalent. Common residence was one of the defining attributes of the family. For example, Murdock defined the family as a social group characterized by common residence, as well as economic cooperation and reproduction.[32] Households were thought of as containers or shells for family members, not as something to be considered separately.

Yet including the notion of household as part of the definition of the family has created many problems. For one thing, home and family are logically different, as Bohannan[33] has pointed out. Family has to do with kinship relations, whereas home is a place, a spatial concept. Bohannan argues that households or homes perform the functions usually ascribed to the family—they provide food and shelter and raise children. The distinction between household and family must be made because in many societies around the world families do not usually form households, and households may not be composed of families. Nuclear-family members often do live together, but it is also very common for husbands and wives and even for children not to live together under the same roof. Thus situations regarded as unfortunate, if not unusual, in our society turn out to be regarded as the usual and normal way of living in many other societies.[34]

The confusion between households and families has sometimes made it difficult to understand how the family in the past differed from today's families. Recent studies have shown that for the past four hundred years in England, most households have consisted of nuclear families, not large groups of kin.[35] Yet the meaning of this finding is unclear. Household composition may not reflect obligations, emotional ties, or the exchange of money, goods, and services. For example, parents may *expect* to live with their married children, but if the children marry late and the parents die relatively young, the extended-family household may exist for only a short time in the life cycle.[36]

Schneider and Smith[37] observe that even though the lower-class or ethnic family pattern does not emphasize the nuclear family, most households consist of the nuclear-family unit. But in these families, household boundaries do not define who is considered "close family." Often it is hard to tell which household a given individual belongs to at any particular time.

. . . [T]he composition of lower-class households can be more diverse without being considered unusual, there can be more coming and going on the part of those who live together, and ties maintained across household boundaries may be as intense as those between persons who live together.[38]

Although Schneider and Smith, among others, argue that there is nothing inherently abnormal or disorganized in the family patterns of the poor and working classes, and that the differences between them and middle-class families should not be interpreted as deviations

A household in New York's Spanish Harlem. Among the poor and near-poor household composition is often more diverse and fluid than in middle-class families.

Conceptions of the Nuclear Family

from a "normal" standard, much family research has been conducted using American middle-class patterns as the norm.

Variations in Residence Patterns When nuclear-family members live apart, most often it is the father-husband who lives apart from the rest of the family. Among some peoples—the Iroquois, for example—households consisted of mothers and daughters and daughters' children, while the men engaged in hunting or warfare. In some societies adult men may live in men's houses, apart from their wives and children; and sometimes all-male households consist of brothers.

In most of these male living situations, the father lives nearby his wife or wives and their children, and visits fairly often. Such an arrangement would be considered "common residence" by many anthropologists. But Stephens raises this question: how close must the father be in order to be counted as living with a wife and children? Fifty feet? A mile? Perhaps the extreme of distance is that found among a people in Kenya, where the mother-child households are located on widely separated farms.[39] Among the Navaho also, a man may marry unrelated women who live at considerable distances from one another.[40]

Another question can be raised: how often must a father visit, and how long must he stay, in order to be considered part of the household? Or, to put it another way, how long must he be gone in order not to be counted as a member of the household? Sometimes work or warfare take the father-husband away for years at a time. Is he then to be considered as "living with" his wife and children? It is also unclear whether the father should be counted in the household if his job requires him to live away from the rest of the family and maintain a separate residence.

Besides those instances when father lives apart from the rest of the family, there are many cases of children normally living separate from their parents. The Israeli communes (kibbutzim) are probably the best-known example. But in societies where the mother-child household prevails, boys usually move away from home at or before the onset of sexual maturation. The boys may merely sleep out and eat at home or move to the village of another relative.[41]

Even younger children sometimes live away from home. Among the Ibo, boys of five or six leave their mothers' houses and live with boys their age from the same compound.[42] Samoan children wander around from one relative's household to another, choosing where they will stay and for how long.[43] Closer to home, in Europe and America in past centuries it was a common practice for children past the age of seven or so to leave home to become apprentices or servants in other households.[44] And, of course, seven-year-old boys in upper-class British families are to this day sent off to boarding schools.

Finally, there are instances where infants do not live at home. During most of European history, when of course there were no feeding bottles, many babies were sent off to wet nurses or to baby farms to be nursed; they returned home, if they survived, after weaning, during the second or third year. Stephens notes two societies where infants leave home after weaning; among these two African peoples, the Hehe and the Thonga, the grandmother typically takes the child to her home after it has been weaned, and returns it to its parents several years later.[45]

Nonkinsmen in the Home Another reason for analyzing family and household separately—besides the *absence* of nuclear-family members—is that the household can also *include* people who are not members of the immediate family.

The idea of outsiders living in the family is alien to most contemporary Americans. Even relatives such as in-laws tend to be defined as

In the past, many households contained servants. Rich people have always had nurse-maids to help care for their children. Some still do.

The belief that every family should have a home of its own seems like a truism to which almost every American would assent without further thought. . . . Furthermore, each family should consist only of a husband, wife, and their minor children. All other forms of living are seen as having great disadvantages.[47]

The feeling that the nuclear family should occupy its own home without outsiders appears to be relatively recent, historically speaking. According to John Laslett,[48] one of the major features of the Western European family over the past several centuries has been the presence of servants in the household. Until the early 1900s, for example, servants were the largest single occupational group in England. Four-fifths of all young people would have the experience of either growing up with or being servants—the vast majority, of course, were the latter.

Households of European peasant and craftsmen families in the distant and recent past commonly contained servants, apprentices, and lodgers. Servants, usually young people employed by the family with whom they lived, shared the family's food and shelter as part of their wages. They were not a distinct social class; being a servant for several years during one's youth could be part of the experience of the most respectable and well-off families.[49] John Laslett labels these as "life-cycle servants," to distinguish them from people who would be servants all their lives.[50]

Lodgers typically worked outside the family with whom they lived. In peasant households these servants and lodgers tended to be part of the family rather than simply "employees" or "tenants."

The legal definition of the household was very precise in Austria; it meant all the people living in the same house under the authority of the head of the household, whether or not they were members of the family. Moreover, as Otto

outsiders. It is taken for granted that households should consist only of husband, wife, and their minor children. Recent census data reveal an increasing tendency for unmarried adults of all ages to live alone, and almost 20 percent of American households consist of one person.[46] As Margaret Mead described some time ago:

Conceptions of the Nuclear Family

Brunner has pointed out in his marvelous essay on the concept of the household in European history, *the word "family" was not commonly used in German until the eighteenth century— before that people spoke of belonging to a house or a household.* The *Universal Lexicon,* for example, defined the family as "a number of persons subject to the power and authority of the head of the household either by nature or by law"—"nature" referred to children, "law" to wife and servants. The idea that the entire household and not only the nuclear-family group was the real basis of the peasant-family organization was championed in the nineteenth century by the German sociologist Wilhelm Riehl. . . .[51]

In preindustrial England the households of craftsmen also included more than the immediate or nuclear family. In the year 1619 the bakers of London described a typical bakery and its expenses.[52] The bakery was a household as well as a workshop; it contained thirteen or fourteen people, including the baker and his wife and children, plus paid employees, apprentices, and servants. This group too was called a family:

> . . . All these people at in the house. . . . Except for the journeymen [paid employees], they were all obliged to sleep in the house at night and live together as a family.
>
> The only word used at that time to describe such a group of people was "family." The man at the head of the group, the entrepreneur, the employer, or the manager, was then known as the master or the head of the family. He was father to some of its members and in place of father to the rest. There was no sharp distinction between his domestic and his economic functions. His wife was both his partner and his subordinate. . . .[53]

The key to the size of the household in preindustrial times was economic need. Homes were workplaces. When the farm or the craft needed and could support more hands, the household group expanded. In hard times, it contracted. The baker's household described above was atypically large.

In America, also—well into the twentieth century, in fact—servants, boarders, and lodgers were found in a sizable proportion of families at some point in their lives. Although taking in boarders was more common among poorer families, the practice could be found among the more affluent also.[54]

The decline of boarding seems to have been associated with the rise, during the twentieth century, of a belief that the household should contain only the nuclear-family group, and the practical condition that enabled this value to be acted upon—the availability of private homes and apartments, and the widespread ability to pay for them. Sociologist Barbara Laslett[55] has argued that family privacy, in principle and practice, distinguishes the modern nuclear family from its counterpart in the past. With the variety of other new life styles in recent years, households have once again become more complex and open: adolescents may leave home, other peoples' children may move in, and single people—of either sex, and with or without children—form households. The evidence from anthropology and history suggests that such "deviations" are not rare and, further, that the private, self-contained, nuclear-family household is a modern life style that has occurred only within the twentieth century, and mainly in America.

A House Is Not a Home   Recently some of the same problems that plagued the concept of the family have been raised with regard to the household. Consider, for example, the situation of a group of college students who share an apartment or a house, but have all their meals out and send all their dirty clothes to the laundry. Should this group be called a household? Or consider this situation: among the

The caption of this picture is "Five cents a night"—the price of lodging in this turn-of-the-century home. The practice of taking in boarders and lodgers was not confined to the poor.

Ashanti, an African people,[56] husbands and wives do not live together. Each partner lives with his or her relatives on the mother's side. Yet the wife prepares meals for the husband and children, and he provides his wife and children with clothes. The nuclear family doesn't form a household, yet they seem to be involved in household activities in a way that the college roommates are not. Then there is the situation in which households carry on domestic functions but are not composed of families. The arrangement of the two divorced men on the "Odd Couple" television show illustrates this kind of household.

In order to deal with distinctions like these, Bender[57] has suggested that we ought to distinguish between "coresidence"—the roommate or dormitory situation—and "domestic" functions or activities, which have to do with the basic day-to-day necessities and trivia of living—the provision and preparation of food, the cleaning and mending of clothing, and the care of children:

Conceptions of the Nuclear Family

One is dealing, then, not with two distinct social phenomena—families and households—but with three distinct social phenomena: families, coresidential groups, and domestic functions. All three frequently correspond, both ideally and in fact (this is reflected in at least one meaning of our folk term "home," which implies a family residing together functioning as a domestic unit). The three also can and sometimes do vary independently. . . .[58]

In sum, then, Bender proposes that the term "family" be reserved for kinship relations. Family members may or may not live together and may or may not engage in domestic relations. People can live together and carry on domestic functions without being families. Or people can simply live together without sharing in domestic activities.

In modern societies, of course, domestic functions need not be performed by the family. Indeed, this is one of the most important features that set off modern societies from traditional or preindustrial ones. Laslett, for example, describes how institutional life in pre-industrial England was almost unknown; most people spent all of their days in small familial groups: "There were no hotels, hostels, or blocks of flats for single persons, and very few hospitals and none of the kind we are familiar with, almost no young men and women living own their own."[59]

Yet the concept of domesticity seems to capture an important part of the essence of what we mean by family, and it is useful to distinguish it from kinship on one side and living under one roof on the other. Domesticity involves both intimacy and trivia. Sharing meals, for example, appears to represent a higher degree of intimacy—of communion—than merely living together under the same roof. Berkner[60] notes that servants in peasant households usually ate with the family, out of the same pot. Later, when the relation between master and servant became less patriarchal and more like that of boss and worker, the practice of eating together stopped.

The Meaning of Kinship

Perhaps at this point the reader is bothered by all this scholarly nit-picking about the definition of the family and household. Surely the family and kinship are based on the solid bedrock of biology: parenthood and sexual intercourse! But the social facts of family life often violate the biological facts in various ways. In some societies, for example, it is necessary to distinguish between the *genitor*—the biological father—and the *pater*—the man who plays the father role. Thus, among the Tallensi, an African society, any child a woman bears belongs to her husband's descent group. Even though he knows he is not the biological father of the child, the husband is said to experience all the emotions of true fatherhood, while the genitor is said to feel no fatherly emotions at all.[61]

Kin relations also violate biology through fictional relationships such as adoption and godparenting. Such relationships are common in many societies, although only recently have they been studied to any great extent. Two kinds of fictional relationships occur. In one kind the fictionalization is so complete that everybody involved "forgets" the relationship isn't real. For example, an orphan might join the household of a relative, treat its members as parents and siblings, and be treated as a "real" child.[62] The other kind of fictional kinship maintains the distinction between fictional and real, as in the godparent relation, which was widespread in Mediterranean Europe and Latin America. Such fictional relations may tell us more about the true nature of kinship than those instances where the biological facts and the social facts coincide.

David Schneider, for example, has argued that kinship has as much to do with real biological facts as supernatural beliefs have to do with the real nature of ghosts and spirits.[63] Both kinship and religion, he argues, are systems of cultural beliefs that originate in people's heads, rather than in some reality out there.

To be sure, there are biological facts, but kinship systems make use of these facts in various symbolic ways. The biological relationships involved in kinship and marriage

represent something other than what they are . . . they represent diffuse, enduring solidarity. They symbolize those kinds of interpersonal relations which human beings as biological beings must have if they are to be born and grow up. They symbolize trust . . . they stand for the fact that birth survives death, and that solidarity is enduring. . . .[64]

Schneider does not suggest that actual family life is characterized by perfect love, trust, and solidarity, only that the family *symbolizes* these ideal qualities. For example, the symbolic meaning of kinship is shown when people in social movements call themselves brothers and sisters, and people in communes call themselves "families."

The Politics of Family Definitions

Much research in the social sciences, especially that about the family, is guided by concern with social problems of one kind or another. What one defines as a problem, however, depends greatly on what one defines as normal and what as problematic.[65] The definition of the normal family as a married couple with their children residing together leads to conceiving of any variation as a social problem—for example, common-law unions, husband and wife living apart, illegitimacy, homosexual unions, bachelorhood, spinsterhood, and even childlessness.[66] In the same way, definitions of age and sex roles dictate what is to be defined as normal and what as problematic. The family literature is full of concern about such "problems" as broken homes, working mothers, illegitimacy, dominant wives, weak fathers and husbands, and children being given too much or too little love, independence, or discipline. Many of these problems derive what are essentially political assumptions about how people should live.

There may indeed be much that is problematic about atypical family situations, but the assumption that the heart of the difficulty lies in deviations from the usual family forms and norms obscures what the real problem might be. Rodman discusses the prevailing assumptions concerning family problems as follows:

Are interfaith marriages the problem or is it organized religion and its demands that is the problem? Are "illegitimacy," "desertion" and "common law" unions *problems* of the lower class, or are they *solutions* of the lower class to more basic problems?[67]

The issue of illegitimacy provides a particularly useful instance of the way value judgments enter into social-science concepts and methodology. At first glance illegitimacy would seem to be an easy concept to define and measure. A child is either legitimate or not at birth, and the fact enters into the birth records. Most people define a child as illegitimate at birth if its mother is unmarried, as do the public agencies who calculate illegitimacy rates. Actually, however, illegitimacy can come about in other ways. For example, the mother may be married to one man, but have a child fathered by another. Or the mother may be separated or divorced at the time of birth. A child is also illegitimate if the parents live together as a stable couple but are not married. Some researchers have argued that illegitimacy statistics are not as "hard" and accurate as they are generally supposed to be. Teele and Schmidt,[68] for example, argue that

official statistics tend to underreport illegitimate births to white women and to married women, and thus to overestimate the degree to which illegitimate births occur among blacks and the unmarried. They also question the practice of labeling children as illegitimate. Philip Hauser, himself a demographer, argues that demographers and statisticians use "inherited and probably inaccurate conceptual frameworks." He states:

> I think it is important to remember that the standards we employ are based on our own categories of legitimate and illegitimate births. According to our standards, half the population in Latin America is illegitimate, and all of the population with whom I lived for two years in Burma is illegitimate and I'm not sure what that means.[69]

What *does* "illegitimacy" mean? Is it a social problem, and if so, why? Is illegitimacy itself the problem, striking at the very basis of the social order and jeopardizing the "continuity of society"?[70] Or is illegitimacy only a symptom

During the 1960s, the commune movement challenged the traditional definition of what "family" means. Although the movement declined, many communes still exist.

In Search of the Family

of other social problems such as poverty and discrimination? Or is the problem of illegitimacy located in those who label children as illegitimate in order to "punish" and "brutalize" unwed mothers and their children?[71] A few years ago, a San Francisco minister introduced his new grandchild to his congregation. His daughter and the father of the child had decided—responsibly, he thought—that they didn't want to marry. His only regret about the baby, he said, was that the child was valued less by the society than other infants, as indicated among other things by the word "bastard" as a term of abuse.

In recent years, as an increasing number of white middle-class women choose to keep their out-of-wedlock children, there has been some lessening of the tendency to stigmatize a child because of the conditions of its birth. Thus the white middle class may be moving closer to the attitudes of the black community. As Robert Staples observed, while it is not true that blacks are untroubled by illegitimacy, "children have a value independent of the legitimacy of their conception. In essence there is no such thing as an illegitimate child in the black community. All children are legitimate and have a value to their families and their community."[72]

There is no way to decide "scientifically" on the correct answers to the preceding questions about illegitimacy. How one answers them depends on basic assumptions about society and human nature.

Malinowski, the distinguished anthropologist, has written of the principle of legitimacy as a universal social law:

> . . . The most important moral and legal rule concerning the physiological side of kinship is that no child should be brought into the world without a man—and one man at that—assuming the role of sociological father, that is, guardian and protector, and male link between the child and the rest of the community.

I think this generalization amounts to a universal sociological law and as such I have called it in some of my previous writings *The Principle of Legitimacy.*[73]

Sociologists and anthropologists have built an extensive literature trying to show that the numerous exceptions to Malinowski's law were only apparent and not real. For example, there has been a debate concerning woman-headed households, particularly in the countries of the Caribbean.[74] In these areas illegitimate births are as high as 70 to 80 percent of total births. On one side of the argument, the proponents of the universal nuclear family and the principle of legitimacy argue that these woman-headed or matriarchal households are abnormal, incomplete, or disorganized forms of the family. Further, the argument goes, the people who live in such arrangements think so too, because they value the nuclear family as an ideal in spite of their inability to live up to it.

The other side of the argument states that to assume a variant family form must be abnormal is scientifically untenable: "The first job of science is, after all, to study what *is*, not what might be or could be."[75] Rather than assume at the outset that a given family form is pathological, we should assume that any variations we find are equally viable alternatives, at least until the contrary is demonstrated.

The Family, Science, and Values

It is questionable whether it is possible to study the family in the same way that natural scientists can study chemical reactions, the movement of the earth's crust, or the actions of DNA. In recent years the idea that the physical sciences can serve as models for sociology and psychology has come under increasing criticism. In this view the notion of a "value-free" social science is a myth that allows values to operate covertly, to sneak in the back door. That social scientists differ among themselves on basic assumptions points to important differences between the study of human social life and the natural sciences. Gordon Allport observes: "The theories of social psychology are rarely, if ever, chaste scientific productions. They usually gear into the prevailing political and social atmosphere."[76]

Even the most scientific-minded and determinedly neutral social scientist must choose what to study and analyze, and in so choosing inevitably becomes involved in value judgments concerning human nature and society. Gouldner[77] writes that social and social-psychological theories contain at least two parts or elements. One is the set of statements that makes up the theory itself—for example, Freud's theory of psychosexual development, Parsons' theory of the nuclear family, the various theories of personality and learning in psychology. The other part of any social theory is a set of tacit beliefs about the world, society, and human nature. These beliefs or "domain assumptions," as Gouldner calls them, rarely if ever enter into discussions of the theory, but they help determine why the sociologist or psychologist finds certain theories convincing and others not.

It is impossible to write about the family or do research in the field without choosing among contrasting assumptions about society and human nature. For example, is society a necessary curb on people's impulse—the only force that keeps people from murdering, raping, and plundering each other—or is "the whole of our present civilization . . . a captivity that man has somehow imposed on himself?"[78] Is the individual realized most fully by forming ties with other people, or are all social bonds a form of bondage? Are people inexorably shaped by their life events and circumstances, or do they retain some freedom of choice in their actions? Are human beings creatures of purpose, choice,

and reason, or is their behavior determined by the contingencies of reinforcement to which they have been exposed? Does "science" demand that human behavior be explained without making any statements about people's thoughts, feelings, and intentions? Or is it impossible to understand behavior without such statements? These sorts of questions can't be answered by going out and doing research; they have to be answered before any research can be done. How researchers answer them determines what they will choose to study and the kind of interpretations they will make.

Thus value judgments and assumptions enter into methodology in fairly direct ways. They dictate what questions shall be asked and how they shall be answered. For example, the concept of the universal nuclear family as the basic social atom or unit dictates that researchers hunt for the similarities among family systems, both in our own culture and others. Differences in family forms and functions must be handled mainly as apparent challenges to the universal nuclear-family doctrine.

Scientific arguments often concern not so much facts but how facts are to be interpreted. For example, we noted the debates about how to interpret the statistical facts concerning the prevalence of woman-headed households in the Caribbean. Does such prevalence indicate social disorganization? An adaptive response to poverty? A subculture with different values? Or does it merely indicate an alternative way of living? Should the researcher focus attention on how people actually behave, how they think they behave, how they think they ought to behave, or all three of these? Sometimes arguments center around what is or is not a fact: Has there been a sexual revolution in the United States in recent years? Is the nuclear family found in all societies?

Social scientists who disagree about these matters often find it hard to carry on a discussion with each other. It is very much like a political disagreement—they find themselves talking past each other, and using the same terms with very different meanings. They just don't speak the same language. They differ ideologically. They have different paradigms or models of reality.

Summary

The most familiar subjects are often the most difficult to study because we take them for granted. This is especially true of the family. In America the nuclear family—two parents and their minor children—in a home of their own is defined as *the family*. Variations from this pattern are seen as unfortunate and abnormal. It also has been widely believed that the middle-class American family pattern is universal.

When we look at family life in other societies, however, at our own historical past, or at different ethnic groups and social classes in America, we find that variations in family form and living arrangements are rather common. Nuclear-family members are often found living apart. The household may contain nonkin living together as a family. Households themselves may only be places where people sleep, while eating, child care, and other domestic functions occur elsewhere.

In trying to understand family life, family scholars have used a variety of different approaches or frameworks of interpretation. As in the rest of social science, family scholars disagree on basic assumptions concerning the nature of the individual, the family, and society.

Source Notes

1. Goode, 1976, p. 513.
2. Laing, 1971, p. 67.
3. Ibid., p. 77.
4. Birdwhistell, 1966.
5. Ibid., p. 211.
6. Ball, 1972.
7. B. Laslett, 1973.
8. Goffman, 1959, pp. 106–140.
9. Ibid., p. 132.
10. Framo, 1965, p. 410.
11. Safilios-Rothschild, 1969.
12. Henry, 1971, p. 456.
13. Murdock, 1949, p. 1.
14. Burgess, 1926.
15. Murdock, 1949, p. 2.
16. Levy, 1955.
17. Spiro, 1954.
18. Gough, 1959.
19. Schneider, 1968; Schneider and Smith, 1973.
20. Schneider, 1968, p. 33.
21. Ibid., p. 9.
22. Wolf, 1972, p. 32.
23. Schneider and Smith, 1973.
24. Gambino, 1975.
25. Kerr, 1958, p. 40.
26. Spiegel, 1971.
27. Ibid., p. 144.
28. Ibid.
29. Birdwhistell, 1966.
30. Ibid., p. 209.
31. Ibid.
32. Murdock, 1949, p. 1.

33. Bohannan, 1963.
34. Bender, 1967, p. 493.
35. P. Laslett, 1972.
36. Berkner, 1972.
37. Schneider and Smith, 1973.
38. Ibid., p. 53.
39. Stephens, 1963, p. 16.
40. Bender, 1967, p. 494.
41. Stephens, 1963.
42. Bender, 1967.
43. Mead, 1928, p. 36.
44. Aries, 1962; Demos, 1970; Morgan, 1944.
45. Stephens, 1963, p. 17.
46. Kobrin, 1976.
47. Mead, 1949, p. 309.
48. J. Laslett, 1977.
49. Berkner, 1972; Morgan, 1944.
50. J. Laslett, 1977.
51. Berkner, 1972, p. 411 (italics added).
52. P. Laslett, 1965.
53. Ibid., p. 2.
54. Modell, 1972.
55. B. Laslett, 1973.

56. Fortes et al., 1947, p. 168.
57. Bender, 1967.
58. Ibid., p. 495.
59. P. Laslett, 1965, p. 11.
60. Berkner, 1972, p. 412.
61. Zelditch, 1964, p. 465.
62. Fallers, 1965, p. 77.
63. Schneider, 1965.
64. Schneider, 1968, p. 116.
65. Skolnick and Currie, 1973.
66. Ball, 1972.
67. Rodman, 1965, p. 450.
68. Teele and Schmidt, 1970.
69. Hauser, 1970, p. 148.
70. Goode, 1964, p. 21.
71. Teele and Schmidt, 1970, p. 144.
72. Staples, 1971, p. 135.
73. Malinowski, in Coser, 1964, p. 13.
74. Adams, 1968; Goode, 1964, p. 28; Smith, 1956.
75. Adams, 1968, p. 47.
76. Allport, in Lindzey and Aronson, 1968.
77. Gouldner, 1970, p. 29.
78. Laing, in Boyers and Orill, 1969, p. 245.

Chapter Three
Ideal and Reality in Family and Society

□ *Social thought, unlike natural science, tends to be cyclical, returning to its roots periodically for sustenance, reassessment, reformulation. The study of man is passing through such a period now. . . . The comfortable assumption of the social sciences that human activity functions to assure the continuity and stability of the structures of society has fallen victim to the evidence of the recent past.*

Robert Murphy, *The Dialectics of Social Life*

Ideal and Reality in Family and Society

Human Nature, Society, and the Family

Every theory of the family implies a set of assumptions about human nature and society. As a matter of fact, all of us employ such assumptions whether we are aware of them or not. For example, many people would agree with such statements as the following: the family is the basic unit of society; a civilization cannot "survive" if its family system does not work well; it is "natural" or "instinctive" for people to form families. Thus the family seems to represent both social necessity and individual biological inclination.

This duality has led one writer to describe the family as "a slippery concept":

> The study of human life—or of behavior in general—has focused on three classes of elements (or systems): the individual, the family or small intimate group, and the society or culture. In this kind of classification, the family is inevitably in the middle. Perhaps because it is in the middle, it tends to be a slippery concept. It is slippery not only in definition, but also in focus. It is rare to complete an article or book whose title indicates it is about the family without finding the discussion sliding away from the family either to the individual or to the society, or even both.[1]

In short, the study of the family often seems to be an extension of the study of the individual on the one hand, or of the society on the other. Psychologists and psychiatric writings emphasize the individual, stressing how the family serves individual needs and shapes the personality of children. Sociologists view the family as part of the larger society. Both approaches to the family may impede understanding family life as a distinct reality in itself.

Is it possible . . . to study the family without reference to either the individual or the society? Sometimes, faced with the difficulties of sticking to a framework for viewing the family, one is led to wonder whether . . . the concept of the family is a reification. Is it perhaps less "real," particularly in the context of modern social conditions, than the concept of society itself?[2]

Functionalism and the Family

Like Monsieur Jourdan, who was surprised to learn that he had been speaking prose all his life, most people are probably unaware that the ideas they take for granted about the family and the relations within the family represent a particular brand of sociological thought. When we speak of the "survival" of a society, or the "need" of a society for a stable family life or for the orderly replacement of one generation by another, we are speaking in terms of a *functional* model of society whether we realize it or not.

It is impossible, of course, to summarize a complex body of thought like functionalism in a few paragraphs. Functionalism itself is not a unified body of thought, but has several opposing schools within its general outlook. Nevertheless, all brands of functionalism assume that human activities are organized to assure the continuity and stability of society. Society is viewed as a structure—an organization of interrelated parts—rather than as a collection of discrete elements. The "parts" of society may be thought of as institutions such as the family or the schools, social roles such as mother, father, worker, manager, or social practices and customs. The way these parts fit together in functional thought is not, however, like a clock or some other complex mechanical structure, but rather like a living organism.

If we were to examine the body of an animal, we could assume that any organ we found would play some vital role in keeping the animal alive. In the same way a functional analyst assumes that social customs or institutions persist because they serve a necessary social function, some ongoing usefulness to the society as a whole. Further, a living organism tends to be in a state of dynamic equilibrium or homeostasis: for example, a warm-blooded animal maintains a constant body temperature in spite of changes in the surrounding temperature. The functionalist sees society as also maintaining such a dynamic equilibrium; the society is not static, but changes are adjusted to smoothly.

Functionalism has come under increasing criticism in recent years. For example, the habit of thinking of society as an organism has been attacked as arbitrary and misleading. The assumption that certain practices and institutions are like vital organs predetermines that they are both necessary and sound.

If a social institution is as necessary to society as the liver is to the body, it would be dangerous to change it or remove it. By ignoring alternatives to contemporary social structures, functionalism tends to assume that things *must* be as they are, especially in the area of familial and sexual statuses and roles. Moreover, by implying—without arguing the point—that the fundamental goal of society is the same as that of an individual organism—that is, surviving and maintaining a steady state—the organismic metaphor turns out to support conservative positions.

This is obviously not a public-image, formal family portrait. But we do not know if it is an accurate picture of this family's "backstage" relationships.

Human Nature, Society, and the Family

Perhaps the most pointed criticism of functionalism has been offered by sociologist Ralf Dahrendorf,[3] who argues that functional sociology employs a utopian vision, in the tradition of a long line of writers beginning with Plato. Dahrendorf's point-by-point comparison of utopia with the social system as posited by functional sociology is important in two respects: first, it enlarges our understanding of the relation between the institution of the family and society; and, second, it suggests what is basically wrong with the traditional understandings of family life.

Utopia and Its Discontents

Most utopias, whether "good" ones like Plato's Republic or "bad" ones like Orwell's 1984, tend to have a number of common features. First, nothing ever changes. Utopias are suspended in time, beyond or outside history. They have no past, or only a vague one, and no future. Not only are utopias isolated in time, but also in space. Often they are located on islands or remote planets. Outside influences are simply irrelevant—in no way is it possible to disrupt their essential tranquility.

Second, there is nothing to argue about in utopia. Everybody agrees on goals and values, and on the ways and means for reaching these goals. Most utopian writers, says Dahrendorf, make it clear that in their society, conflict about values and institutional arrangements simply cannot arise or is just unnecessary. Thus there are no strikes or revolutions, or even parliaments in which opposing groups compete for power. Equality is not a feature of most utopias; in fact, they are often caste societies—for example, some people in Brave New World were genetically engineered to be the working drones of the society. But again, everyone accepts the power arrangements as they are. The op-

pressed in utopias do not see themselves as oppressed, and do not revolt.

In some of the literary utopias, such as Brave New World or 1984, the plot centers around a nonconformist who does not go along with the system. This nonconformist is often an outsider of some kind, such as a survivor from a previous society. It is something of a problem for the utopian writer to explain how a dissident can arise in a "perfect" social structure: ". . .'outsiders' are not (and cannot be) products of the social structure of utopia, but deviants, pathological cases infected with some unique disease."[4]

Since utopias consist of mortal beings, they face the problem of producing and training new generations of utopians. This creates a major risk to the stability of utopia, and utopian writers have given a good deal of attention to such matters. They have to figure out how sexual intercourse and reproduction will be managed, how children will be cared for and educated, and how these children will be assigned to their work positions.

Dahrendorf points out that the inventors of utopias could solve all these problems in one stroke by making people immortal, but they usually avoid this solution. Nevertheless, the utopian world operates as if people were immortal—that is, new generations replace their parents just as body cells replace each other, preserving the intactness of the body. Everything that happens in utopia serves to uphold the existing state of affairs.

Dahrendorf embarked on his travels in utopia to advance a major critique of functionalism, particularly the work of Talcott Parsons in The Social System. Dahrendorf argues that the vision of society in this brand of sociology corresponds point by point with all the elements of utopia. Any social system—for example, American society—is seen by the functional theorists as a community with a self-correcting equilibrium, based on consensus and isolated in time and space. In the social-system model of society, change is not absent but is seen as abnormal or unusual, something that has to be explained. Dahrendorf and other critics take functional sociology to task for generating a conservative complacency about society and its problems, and also for being boringly unconcerned with "riddles of experience." He feels that theory and research "have both largely dispensed with that prime impulse of all science and scholarship, the puzzlement over specific, concrete, and . . . empirical problems. Many sociologists have lost the simple impulse of curiosity. . . ."[5]

There is no need to go into details of Dahrendorf's indictment of sociological theory as essentially utopian. It should be noted, however, that the comparison does an injustice to utopian writers. They constructed their ideal societies to make moral criticisms or even indictments of existing societies. Functional sociologists, by contrast, implicitly justify the status quo in their models of society.

What alternative is there to the utopian social system of functional sociology? Along with a number of others, Dahrendorf has suggested a conflict model of society. Utopian definitions of the normal and expectable, as opposed to the unusual and in need of explanation, should be turned on their heads. Thus change and conflict are to be seen as constants in society. Instead of assuming that social organizations remain the same until something happens to change them, Dahrendorf suggests we assume that change is constant unless something intervenes to stop it. The task of the sociologist should be to try to determine what is interfering with the normal process of change.

In the same vein, Dahrendorf argues that conflict is always present in social life. We should become suspicious or curious to find a social organization or society that exhibits no conflict, although the conflict need not be violent or uncontrolled.

Finally, the conflict model of society is based on the notion of constraint. Rather than being held together by consensus, societies and social organizations are based on the coercion of some by others. This is the source of conflict and change. Constraints lead to conflict, and conflict leads to change. Dahrendorf acknowledges that the idea that conflict is always present in social life is not a pleasant one, but it is indispensable for an understanding of social problems.

The essential elements of the conflict model of society that Dahrendorf suggests[6] can be summarized as follows:

1. Every society is subjected at every moment to change.

2. Every society experiences social conflicts.

3. Every element in society can contribute to change.

4. Every society rests on the constraint of some members by others.

Certain other distinctions between the two kinds of models should be noted. Functionalists tend to think of societies as total systems with needs of their own, apart from the individuals and groups that make up the society. Conflict models, on the other hand, view societies as settings within which struggles between classes, factions, interest groups, and individuals are acted out. These conflicts and the conflicting factions, not the social system, are the focus of interest.[7]

There is also an important difference in how the two models handle conflict and change. Functionalists do not deny that conflict and change exist, but they assume that social systems adapt smoothly to such disturbances, or else that conflict and change actually make the society more stable and integrated. Conflict theorists generally recognize that both conflict and cooperation are pervasive and normal features of human life. Unlike the functionalists, however, they do not see conflict as an unusual or pathological condition.[8]

Finally, there is some confusion about whether functionalism is a particular theory or whether all social theories are functional theories. For example, it has been argued that functional analysis is nothing more than the basic operating procedure of all social scientists—they look at aspects of social life and try to determine how they are related, their causes and effects, and so on. This is true, but it is also misleading. Lumping all social scientists together as analysts of social functions obscures the differences between them. There is no name of consequence in the history of the social sciences who is not in some measure concerned with relationships between parts of culture.

> The contrast between different kinds of sociocultural theories is not built around the question of whether sociocultural systems have parts which are integrated with or affected by other parts, but rather, which parts, and how often, and with what kind of effect, and for how long?[9]

For the structural-functional model of society, social institutions like the family and religion function to maintain social stability and consensus. For Marx, social institutions serve the interests of the dominant class. For Freud, social institutions control human instincts and anxieties. Thus religion, for example, can be interpreted as an institution binding people in society together, as the opiate of the masses, or as an "illusion," as Freud put it, created by the childish dread of being alone in the world. The family may be seen as performing the functions necessary for the survival of society, as perpet-uating the power structure, or as satisfying basic instincts.

The Family as a Little Utopia　We have devoted so much space to this issue because of its direct relevance to the study of the family. The traditional social scientist's views of the family fit the utopian model in two distinct ways: as part of the utopian social system as a whole, and as a miniature utopia in itself. As part of the social system, the family carries out vital functions: it helps maintain the equilibrium of the system by replacing and training new generations. As we saw earlier, utopian writers from Plato on have been preoccupied with the family and education. The introduction of children into the social system brings with it an element of risk. There is always the possibility of a generation gap to threaten the stability of the system. Social theorists have also been strikingly preoccupied with the family and with the "problem" of socialization, including both education and assignment of people to occupational slots. Like the utopian writers, functional sociologists speak in terms of the survival of the society:

> It is readily apparent that what will terminate a society will not disintegrate an individual, at least not when he is viewed mainly as a biological organism. It should be evident, however, that the ways in which society meets its imperatives for survival have implications for the individual's socialization and that in actuality the requisites of continuing social life come down to what is largely a set of requirements for individual socialization.[10]

In short, the functional view of the family fits the utopian model of regulated, orderly change: "Children are born and socialized and allocated until they die; new children are born, and the same thing happens all over again."[11]

As a little world unto itself, the family in both popular and professional thought is also a

Conflict may be a normal part of family life, but we don't often see it in photographs.

utopia. The family is suspended in time and isolated in space; it is outside of history and not deeply affected by social surroundings. Major historical changes, such as the industrial revolution, do have their effect on the family, but these are only a matter of changing the relative importance of one of the basic functions. The family, like society, is assumed to adapt to change. In advanced industrial societies, for example, the state takes over the education of older children, but the nuclear family emphasizes infant care and emotional support for its members.

The family as a little social system also fits the model of utopian harmony and consensus. Like most utopias the family is a system of unequal statuses, a hierarchy in which the order of priority is men/women, adults/children. Yet in the conventional assumptions this class or caste system does not give rise to conflict, nor is it even recognized as such by the family members. For in living up to their prescribed roles, they are presumed to be carrying out their natural functions. Thus, in acting out the roles of male, female, and child, each person acts out his or her own biological and psychological predestination. Further, mother and father are also acting out the cultural rules learned in their own families: they are replacing their own parents.

The infant's need for care matches the mother's need to mother. The needs of mother and children for economic support match the need of the husband-father to fulfill his masculine nature by providing for his family. In short, the family is envisioned as a system of perfectly interlocking needs.

Perhaps an example will illustrate the way these ideas are usually presented. The following description of the nuclear family comes from a book by a well-known professor of psychiatry, one of the leading theorists of the family in that field. This description of the normal nuclear family serves to introduce the author's theory of the family origins of schizophrenia, which he assumes results from a failure to live up to the following norms:

1. The nuclear family is composed of two generations, each with different needs, prerogatives, and tasks. . . . The parents . . . seek to merge themselves and their backgrounds into a new unit that satisfies the needs of both and completes their personalities in a relationship that is permanent for them. . . . The parents serve as guides, educators, and models for the offspring. They provide nurturance and give of themselves so that the children can develop. . . .

2. The family is also divided into two genders with differing but complementary functions and role allocations as well as anatomical differences. The feminine role derives from the woman's biological structure and is related to nurturance of children and the maintenance of a home, leading to emphasis upon interest in interpersonal relations and emotional harmony—an expressive-affectional role. The male role is related to the support and protection of the family and leads to an emphasis upon instrumental-adaptive leadership characteristics. . . .

3. The bonds between family members are held firm by erotic and affectional ties. . . .

4. The family forms a shelter for its members within the society and from the remainder of society. . . . However, the family must reflect and transmit the societal ways. . . .[12]

The family system outlined above can in no way give rise to serious strain or conflict. It contemplates no conflict over age, sex roles, or power relations. There is no room for any distance between the person and the role. Dissent from these role norms places the dissident outside the system as it normally functions. And, in fact, that precisely is Lidz's theory of schizophrenia: it arises from parental failures to observe their proper age and sex positions. For Lidz and many other psychiatrists, it is all perfectly clear: there are sick families over here and well families over there. Thus, surprisingly, clinical work with troubled families seems to reinforce, rather than challenge, the utopian image of family life. We will return to this paradox later.

Psychoanalysis and Utopia We noted earlier that utopian stories often center around a nonconformist who rebels against the system. But how can a perfect social system give rise to a nonconformist in the first place? The writers of utopian fiction solve the problem by making the rebel an outsider—a visitor from another society or a survivor from a previous era. Thus the outsider is not a product of the social structure of utopia, but a deviant "infected with some unique disease."[13]

How does the functional model of society deal with the problem of deviance and nonconformity? One way is by pointing to the hidden functions performed by seemingly dysfunctional behavior such as conflict and criminality—some sociologists have argued that society needs deviants to remind the rest of us what moral rules are. But a more basic way functional models deal with deviance is to attribute it to the dark depths of human nature. Following the eighteenth-century philosopher Thomas Hobbes, these models assume that human beings are at heart so murderous and anarchic that strong societies are needed to prevent a war of all against all. The most recent and influential version of the Hobbesian view is found in some of Freud's work, particularly his later writings.

Psychoanalysis has contributed to utopian views of family life from two directions; its conception of society or "civilization" and its conception of human nature. Freud's notion of "civilization" corresponds to the utopian social system of sociology, with one exception: Freud's civilization has as its fatal flaw innate sexual and aggressive drives. These drives, which Freud referred to as libido, or the id, play the role of original sin in the fall from paradise. "Every individual is virtually an enemy of culture," wrote Freud in *The Future of an Illusion*.[14]

Thus psychoanalysis abets the conservative thrust of the functional view of society in two ways. It accounts for social conflict and pathology in a way that does not challenge the legitimacy or perfection of the social system. And, second, it suggests that, since the troubles that beset us arise from dark, unruly forces in human nature, there is little use in trying to change social conditions.

Freudian ideas have been used in another way to support the idea of a balanced social system. Parsons finds in Freud's concept of *internalization* an explanation of how the social system perpetuates itself smoothly from one generation to the next. In Freudian theory, a major step in the development of the child is its identification with the parent of the same sex. The moral dictates taught by the parents, according to Freud, are taken into the child's own personality, where they become the superego or conscience. Parsons expanded the concept of internalization. Instead of just moral dictates, the child incorporates all of the culture, including values, roles, and knowledge. The child's personality becomes a mirror image of the social world around him or her. Thus the requirements of the society are translated into individual motivation; people come to want to do what they have to do, and the society functions smoothly.[15]

This view of internalization has been criticized as a distortion of Freud's own thinking. As Dennis Wrong puts it, "The concept of internalization as it is used by many social scientists presents an oversocialized view of human nature, one that is infinitely malleable and capable of accepting the demands of any social system."[16]

Preaching Versus Practicing

The relationship between people's values and attitudes on the one hand and their actual behavior on the other is one of those perennial problems that plague the social sciences. Are people's ideals reliable guides to their behavior? Or are norms and behavior two separate realms that have nothing to do with each other? Or are norms a kind of smoke screen that obscures what is really going on?

Social scientists have disagreed in their answers to these questions. Some, in particular those functionalists who assume society tends toward a state of balance, assume that there must be a close fit between values and behavior.

The defects of such assumptions about the relation between ideal and reality are pointed out by Marvin Harris.[17] Warning anthropologists to avoid the temptation to write descriptions of exotic cultures in terms of their ideals, he offers the following ethnography of American life, written in ideal terms:

> If permitted to develop unchecked, the tendency to write ethnographies in accord with the . . . rules of behavior will result in an unintentional parody of the human condition. Applied to our own culture, it would conjure up a way of life in which men tip their hats

to ladies . . . unwed mothers are a rarity . . . chewing gum is never stuck under tables and never dropped on the sidewalk; television repairmen fix television sets; children respect their aged parents; rich and poor get the same medical treatment; taxes are paid in full; all men are created equal; and our defense budget is used only for maintaining peace.[18]

People may give lip service to a value such as honesty, faithfulness in marriage, or not losing one's temper with one's children, but circumstances may override commitment to such behavior in practice. There may even be counternorms that may turn out to be stronger in practice than the ideal. What is a counternorm? Jules Henry illustrates one with his observations on cheating in American high schools. In spite of the lip service paid to the idea that cheating is wrong, there is a great deal of pressure to engage in it. This pressure comes from the grading system, from the children as a group, and even from the teachers who seem to be indifferent to the cheating going on under their noses. Henry notes that a child who refuses to share test answers with a classmate would be the real deviant in the social system of the high school he observed. Further, he notes, "An honest adolescent life could be a crippling preliminary for many phases of contemporary culture."[19]

Likewise, Goode has written that the family *preaches* nonviolence but *teaches* violence:

. . . parents and other moral authorities constantly exhort young children against violence, but their own behavior belies that advice. We are all trained for violence. The child does learn that force is very effective at stopping others, and that force or its threat can change other people's calculations of profit and loss. The child experiences this directly, and watches it in others—the fright of his mother when his father is furious, arguments and threats among the neighbors, battles with his own siblings, and so on.[20]

Similarly, the norms of marital faithfulness have a highly problematic relation to actual behavior. Again, the rules and pressures against observing the norms often seem to

Family mealtime illustrates the contrast between the way family life is supposed to be and the way it often is. Eating together is a ritual that symbolizes the family's unity. Often, however, mealtimes become the occasion for scolding children, airing grievances, or complaining about the food. Or, as this picture shows, family members may find they have little to say to one another.

Ideal and Reality in Family and Society

dominate those in favor of the norms. Extramarital sex seems to be an institutionalized part of American life that coexists, however uncomfortably, with the monogamy principle. Morton Hunt's book, *The Affair,*[21] describes the social system of extramarital affairs and the discomforts caused by the discrepancy between people's beliefs and behavior.

Hunt's book and such works as the study of upper-middle-class marriages by Cuber and Harroff[22] reveal considerable social and environmental pressure on people to have extramarital affairs. Advertising and the mass media eroticize everyday life in America. Flirtation games are played in work settings as well as at parties. Travel and business provides the opportunity for liaisons with minimal risks of embarrassment and entanglements. In some social and business circles, an insistence on strict monogamy would render one as deviant as the high-school student who refused to offer examination answers to a classmate.

The reader should not leap to the conclusion, based on these examples, that American society is necessarily marked by a greater discrepancy between norms and behavior than that found in other societies. There is little evidence anywhere of a culture whose ideal norms are reliable guides to what people actually do. Harris[23] points out that even the kinship rules of "primitive" peoples, sometimes described as the most binding of social norms, often fail to be carried out in practice. For example, a rule may dictate that a young man has to marry his mother's brother's daughter. Some anthropologists, however, when actually tabulating who was married to whom, have found more exceptions to the rule than cases where it seemed to have been followed. And in one culture where the divorce rate approaches 100 percent, people still express the wish at every wedding that the marriage be a permanent one. Because of social science and the mass media, however, we may be more *aware* of discrepancies between our ideals and our behavior than are other cultures.

As a research strategy and a general approach to the family, asking "What is actually going on?" will generally lead to a different set of findings and a different view of the phenomena than asking "What are family norms and roles?" Questions about norms and roles are important, but they should not be taken as descriptions of observable behavior.

The sociological concept of role —as, for example, "the mother role," "the father role"— may be similarly misleading as a guide to understanding actual behavior. The term "role" was utilized to emphasize that people often seem to follow cultural scripts, rather than merely expressing their particular personalities. Thus one can analyze the roles of mother, salesperson, college president, police officer, and so on as something apart from the individual personalities of the particular people who occupy those roles. Accordingly, societies and cultures may be described as being made up of "role relationships."

Like many other valuable constructs in the social sciences, however, the idea of role is sometimes overextended. People may play several and conflicting roles. Does the role of "mother" accurately describe actual mother-child interaction in a culture? Often the "mother role" is assumed to dominate the existence of the woman occupying it. Presumably it overrides other roles:

> Granted that mothers have idiosyncratic differences—the personality peeping through —nevertheless it is held that the role of mother can be separated from individual mothers. . . . But the mother is also a wife . . . and mother-wife may be president of the women's club. . . . What are the criteria for telling when she is wife, when mother, when president, in the contexts of situations making up her daily life?

Preaching Versus Practicing

. . . The "role of mother" requires symbols at such high levels of abstraction . . . that one is forced to minimize the realities of observation in order to create one stereotype for an entire society.[24]

In the studies that have observed and measured what goes on between parents and children in households—that is, in the natural habitat of family life—a very different picture emerges of the "mother role." A child may receive its mother's undivided attention no more than a half-hour or an hour a day. The rest of the time the mother is busy with other things. What goes on between mother and child seems to be a by-product of the horde of small and seemingly trivial events and pressures that make the parent's day a good or a bad one, a harried or a calm one, a tired or an energetic one. To those investigators who have been observing the complex realities of family life—from events such as the preparing and eating of meals, putting children to bed, greetings and leavetakings, to patterns such as the organization of household time and space—norms and roles are, as concepts, simply too broad and abstract to be useful.

Although ideals and images and role definitions cannot be taken at face value as guides to behavior, they cannot be ignored either. Looking at behavior only, without some idea of what the behavior means to the participants, is misleading also. Consider the behavioral fact of a parent spanking a child. To understand the meaning of this event, one would have to know its context—why it occurred. If the parent were a modern, permissive parent who did not believe in spanking, the situation would signify a different meaning for both parent and child than if, say, the parent belonged to a culture teaching that physical discipline was good for children, that a parent who did not spank children was neglecting his or her duty. The modern family differs from its historical counterparts in its ideals and images of family life. The beliefs in close emotional bonds between husbands and wives and parents and children, and in personal happiness as the chief justification for marriage, enter into people's perceptions and experience of the daily events of family life. So these beliefs and norms cannot be ignored. They influence relationships even if they do not accurately describe them.

Psychiatry and the Idealization of Family Life

It is easy to see how defining family life in terms of cultural norms can lead to a utopian view of the family. And it is easy to see how sociologists and anthropologists, interviewing people about their family values and practices, can arrive at often idealized conceptions of family life. Interviewees tend to present themselves in a favorable light. Besides, they may sincerely hold to certain values, but have trouble carrying these out in real life. Finally, of course, people are not completely aware of how they are acting, of how their family behavior would look to an observer.

At first glance it would seem that psychiatrists, social workers, marriage counselors, and other clinicians who help troubled families would be in a much better position to make unidealized assessments of family life. In fact, one might expect that coming into daily contact with family miseries kept private from the rest of the world would lead clinicians to exaggerate the dark side of family life. Paradoxically, however, clinicians have contributed to the utopian or sentimentalized model of the family: the clinicians' experiences with troubled families seem to reinforce idealized conceptions of "the family," rather than challenge them. Thus the idealized model of the family remains the standard by which the "sick" families are judged:

> Studies of the family have, with a few memorable exceptions, accepted the sentimental model—statistics are made of units derived from this model; anecdotes are collected; and formalistic abstractions are derived from it. . . . Focusing upon the family's pathologies serve(s) to *reinforce the sentimental model by the assumption that the pathology-less family has the shape of the sentimental model.* . . . The pathologies are defined as variations from the sentimental model, and the sentimental model is reinforced in its supposed shape by the shape of its supposed pathologies.[25]

The Medical Model

The medical model of pathology stands behind the psychiatric assumption that normal families differ considerably from the families whose children become psychiatric patients. In recent years there has been a great deal of debate about the value of applying concepts of physical health and illness to matters of thoughts, feelings, and personalities. The issue has many ramifications, but the aspect that concerns us here has to do with the kind of thinking the medical model leads to—the kinds of inferences the psychiatrist draws about normality by observing patients. Suppose, for example, a patient (child) were to describe a parent as acting in some way that parents are not "supposed" to act—for example, cruel, irrational, neglectful, bizarre, impervious to what the patient says. What conclusion can the psychiatrist make about the normality of these parents? Assuming that the psychiatrist believes the child, can he or she infer that the parents are very different from most parents, only a little different, or typical?

Actually, the psychiatrist cannot legitimately draw any conclusion about prevailing child-rearing practices and parental behavior from patients. There is no way of knowing whether and how much and in what ways patients differ from the general population. The question is a matter for scientific investigation. To answer it, a study would have to be carried out comparing families having children in psychiatric treatment with families having children who had never been psychiatric patients. As a matter of fact, several such epidemiological studies have been carried out. They generally conclude that people who become psychiatric clients or patients represent only the tip of an iceberg:

> Studies from many countries confirm the picture of a high and persistent burden of neurosis in the population, the differences in rates between different studies probably reflecting differing criteria, rather than real differences in prevalence.[26]

Even if one did find differences between the families of schizophrenics and other families, there would be no way of knowing whether the differences came after the schizophrenia or before, unless the family had been studied before the patient got "sick."

When using a model of thinking borrowed from physical medicine, the psychiatrist may fail to perceive any problem in comprehending the normal family world. Thus the medical model leads to utopian conceptions of family life without any help from social theories! Medicine is based on the popular opposition of health and disease: if a patient comes to a doctor complaining of a symptom such as an itchy rash, the doctor easily understands "normality"—it is the absence of the symptom. In the realm of behavior, such thinking can lead to the erroneous conclusion that normal behavior and family life must be the exact opposite of what the psychiatrist confronts:

In order to understand the psychiatrist's thinking, one must bear in mind that his daily activities revolve around mental abnormalities and that concern with the psychological norm falls into the periphery of his endeavors. . . . The diagnosis of normality is made by exclusion, and if a psychiatrist can label a feature it is by implication pathological and undesirable. Therefore *anything that is called by a name is implicitly abnormal. . . .* Since the psychiatrist's attention is focused upon deviation, and since he has little or no training in normal psychology, *he tends to construct a hypothetical norm by averaging the exact opposite of those features he sees in his patients.*[27]

Freud and Family Psychology

Freud and his followers have made an enormous contribution to the understanding of the family. Freud's discoveries of the impact and lasting significance of early experiences must be included in any serious understanding of the family. Freud's discoveries derived from his invention of a new social situation—a new form of human interaction and communication.

In psychoanalysis the patient talks at length about whatever comes to mind to a fully attentive and sympathetic listener who will not interrupt or censure, no matter how outrageous the thoughts expressed might be. Using this method, Freud "opened new vistas on our inner world, just as Columbus opened up new vistas on our outer world."[28] He explored large areas of inner life that had seemed too disturbing or too unimportant to study: dreams, fantasies, slips of the tongue, seemingly irrelevant—and irreverent—thoughts.

In these explorations, Freud discovered that the impact of the family on the child was much greater than anyone had suspected. Most important perhaps was his discovery of the child as a person, capable of sensuous feelings, fantasy, and suffering. The prevailing view during the nineteenth century was that the child was essentially a nonperson, someone whose view of things should not be taken seriously. As women were placed on a pedestal, the child was sentimentalized as an adorable innocent. Such sentimentalization coexisted with economic exploitation of children in mines and factories, and savage disciplinary measures in homes and schools.[29]

Freud destroyed Victorian illusions about childhood innocence and family serenity. His discovery of infantile sexuality was perhaps the most shocking of all his findings; it aroused the most indignation. Yet Freud also discovered— or rediscovered—passions in adults that had been denied by idealized conceptions of family life. Freud was fond of stating that the essential themes of his theories were based on the intuitions of poets and playwrights.[30] The conflicts and strivings Freud found lurking beneath the surface of ordinary family life were the same passions dramatized by Shakespeare and the Greek tragedians. The lustful, murderous impulses between husbands and wives and parents and children that one could see acted out in *Hamlet, King Lear, Oedipus Rex, Medea,* and other classic works are ever-present but secret undercurrents in ordinary family life.

The Freudian theory of the family is thus a conflict theory, with conflict not only between family members but also within them. Freud's most important concepts are those of *repression* and *ambivalence.* Repression is the mechanism by which a person keeps wishes and fantasies outside his or her awareness; it explains why we may not be aware even in ourselves of the passions we see acted out overtly on the stage. The concept of *ambivalence* points to the duality of many of our wishes and fantasies. We not only love *or* hate, we can love *and* hate at the same time. We want intimate relationships, but we want our freedom and individuality; we want deep sexual intimacy with one person, but at the same time we want to sample sexual experiences with as many people as possible.

Despite Freud's antiutopian vision of family relations, psychoanalysis on the whole has reinforced the sentimental model of the nuclear family because Freud and his followers tended to ignore the everyday realities of family life in favor of inherited instincts—this despite Freud's stress on child rearing in the formation of personality. Nathan Ackerman, himself a psychoanalyst, has pointed to such incongruities in Freud's approach to the family:

> The Freudian theory focuses attention on the role of the family in the shaping of personality, but it gives priority to inborn instincts. It dramatizes the biological core of man, while diminishing the role of society. . . .
>
> Child-parent relations are the core of the psychoanalytic view of human development . . . . Yet in psychoanalysis direct observations of family interaction have not been carried out until recently, and only now is their importance beginning to be recognized.[31]

One reason for Freud's lack of concern for the everyday realities of family life stemmed from his emphasis on the child as a biological organism. He defined development as a progression through a series of innate maturational stages. These stages Freud conceived to be universal, hence only partly influenced by differences in individual experiences or social conditions. Parents, in Freud's theory, also have a relatively fixed part to play; they are the tamers of the child's instincts:

> Freud conceived the family as the instrument for disciplining the child's biologically fixed instinctual urges and enforcing repression of their spontaneous release. He described the child as a polymorphous, perverse little animal. The child epitomizes animal pleasure. The parent personifies reality and the restraints of society. . . . In this aspect of family relations, parent and child are . . . virtual enemies to one another.[32]

The emphasis on parent-child relations as the taming of impulse has several implications. For one thing it implies that a certain amount of suffering on the part of children is inevitably part of growing up. Psychoanalytic writers often argue against the notion that childhood can ever be a happy, conflict-free time of life. Even the most loving and beloved parents can be transformed in the child's imagination into witches and monsters:

> If we look closely into the life of a small child, we find that such transformations take place . . . when we are compelled to interfere with the child's pleasure. . . . The child begins life as a pleasure-seeking animal; his infantile personality is organized around his own body. In the course of rearing, the goal of exclusive pleasure seeking must be modified drastically. . . .
>
> So there are no ways in which a child can avoid anxiety. If we banished all the witches and ogres from his bedtime stories and policed his life for every conceivable source of danger, he would still succeed in constructing his own imaginary monsters out of the conflicts of his own life.[33]

The problem with this point of view is that it assumes that all the witches and monsters in a child's life are imaginary. It implies that in family government the virtues are with the rulers, and the vices with the ruled. The assumption of parental virtue, however, was wryly challenged by Herbert Spencer, the nineteenth-century philosopher whose career overlapped Freud's:

The current assumption respecting family government, as respecting national government, is that the virtues are with the rulers and the vices with the ruled. Judging by educational theories, men and women are entirely transfigured in their relations to offspring. The citizens we do business with, the people we meet in the world, we know to be very imperfect creatures. In the daily scandals, in the quarrels of friends, in bankruptcy disclosures, in lawsuits, in police reports, we have constantly thrust before us the pervading selfishness, dishonesty, brutality. Yet when we criticize nursery management and canvass the misbehavior of juveniles, we habitually take for granted that these culpable persons are free from moral delinquency in the treatment of boys and girls.[34]

The psychiatric idealization of the family in fact contradicts the analyst's clinical knowledge of parental behavior. It also contradicts the psychoanalytic view of persistent human nature. Thus the witches and monsters of the child's imagination may reflect accurate perceptions of veiled or not-so-veiled parental hostility.[35]

Freud seems to have been curiously disinterested in the daily realities of family life. Far from blaming his patients' families for their children's disorders, Freud overlooked or rejected much negative information, even in his own published case histories. He blamed his patients' troubles on their own wayward impulses, rather than on parental treatment.

During the early part of his career, Freud thought that his adult patients had become neurotic because they had been seduced by their parents. Later he realized that his patients' reports of seduction were fantasies rather than real events. Impressed with the power of unconscious, conflicting wishes, he came to view neuroses as a "pathology of desire"[36] rather than as a product of family life.

Freud and his followers came to focus most of their theoretical and clinical attention on the inner psychological world of their patients, and regarded their actual family life as having only limited significance. Some of Freud's most famous case histories reveal a striking disinterest in family relations.

The case of Little Hans[37], for example, is considered the classic statement on the Oedipus complex. It describes Freud's analysis of a phobia in a five-year-old boy. Erich Fromm[38] uses the published case to show Freud's bias in favor of parental figures. Freud, he argues, attributes qualities to Hans's parents as models of enlightened parenthood which contradict the facts he presents. Both parents were among Freud's closest adherents. Little Hans was treated by Freud, with his father as an intermediary, because he developed a strong fear of horses. According to Freud the boy's parents were determined to raise him without coercion, bullying, or ridicule. They were, in short, rebelling against the prevailing child-rearing practices of their time and place — turn-of-the-century Vienna.

As often happens when people set out to raise their children by new principles, the old ones have a way of persisting. For example, Little Hans's mother, according to Freud, told Hans the following at various times: that she would have his penis cut off, that she would abandon him, and that she had a penis. She also threatened to beat him with a carpet beater. At the same time Hans's mother was described as being seductive in various ways. Yet none of what the mother did entered into Freud's diagnosis of what troubled Hans. Freud attributed the phobia only to Oedipal wishes that arose from Hans's inner depths. His amorous feelings toward his mother and his fear of castration were not related by Freud to his mother's seductiveness or actual threats! The case is a remarkable demonstration of how concrete incidents in day-to-day family life can be at odds with the professed beliefs and values of the parents, as well as with professional estimates of the parents as people.

Similar observations have been made of the case of Dora, an eighteen-year-old girl who was brought to Freud for treatment of hysteria.[39] Once again Freud overlooked the family situation as a source of Dora's troubles and attributed her problems solely to her unrecognized sexual wishes toward her father and toward her father's friend and his wife. This family situation was more extreme than Little Hans's. Dora's father was having an affair with the friend's wife and was trying to offer Dora to this man so his own affair could continue. Freud was aware of this situation but considered it irrelevant to Dora's problems and to her treatment. He was concerned only with tracing her hysterical symptoms to their presumed origins in sexual wishes.

New Directions in Family Studies

New trends in the study of the family suggest some profound changes in our assumptions about ordinary family life. Each of the new trends in its own way is undermining traditional concepts of family normality. As we noted earlier, both the average person and the family expert tend to think of family problems as a kind of pathology attacking an otherwise healthy system, like a germ invading the body. This way of looking at the family forces us to think of problems as separate from normal family life, and of normal families as separate from pathological families. Tolstoy once wrote, "Happy families are all alike, but each unhappy family is unhappy in its own way." Like Tolstoy many observers put normal families in one pile and schizophrenic or child-battering families in another. Then they develop a theory of what goes on in normal families and a different theory to explain what goes on in pathological families. They keep the two or three kinds of families in airtight, logical compartments, paying little or no attention to the similarities, as opposed to the differences, between the types of families or to the process by which one type changes into another.

Newer studies in family history, family interaction, and family violence are undermining this polarized way of looking at families. In different ways they suggest that definitions of family normality and pathology are much harder to draw than had been thought. Further, these new approaches emphasize variations among families rather than similarities.

Perhaps the major contribution of the new historical studies is to show that although the nuclear family has existed for many centuries, the set of ideas and practices that make up the nuclear-family ideology is a relatively recent invention in Western society. French historian Aries[40] has traced the rise of the private nuclear family out of the "torrent" of general sociability in the Middle Ages. Aries draws an important distinction between the family as a biological unit and the ideas about that unit in a particular society or historical period. Thus there are mothers and fathers and children in every society, but the importance of the nuclear unit in social life can vary.

Aries' most striking contribution, however, is the notion of childhood as a social invention. The idea that the psychological bonds between husbands and wives have changed over time is a familiar one. Most people know, for example, that in the past in our culture, and in many other places today, marriages are not based on love but are arranged by families. We are not surprised to learn that the emotional aspects of marriage are conditioned by the historical and cultural setting. It is more surprising to learn that parental feelings toward children may be equally variable.

When infant- and child-mortality rates are extremely high, as they were in the early years of the modern era, infants do not count for much in their parents' feelings. That children were born to die was taken to be a fact no one could do much about. "All mine die,' said Montaigne casually, as a gardener might speak of cabbages.' "[41] Although infants were not quite human in these times, children over the age of seven were considered miniature adults. People did not think of childhood as a separate stage of life, with its own distinct psychological nature.

The historical evidence also undermines certain ideas about parenthood, childhood, and society that have been almost axiomatic among many anthropologists, sociologists, and psychoanalytic writers. Some examples of these ideas include the notions that parents have an innate desire to care for their young children; that there is an intuitive wisdom about the child-rearing methods of any culture; and, finally, that every society has a vested interest in children and in the child-rearing process, and therefore provides rewards and support for parents' efforts. On all these points, as we shall explain in more detail later, the historical evidence suggests that, unfortunately for children, none of these supposedly built-in benevolent forces can be counted on.

Other historical studies indicate that even deeply concerned and well-off families used child-rearing methods that were not only harmful but downright lethal. Writing of seventeenth-century France, David Hunt finds that, without bottles or good baby foods, there was great difficulty in nourishing infants during the first months of life. In a world where life was short and uncertain, and resources of all kinds were scarce, the infant was regarded as less

than human, a gluttonous little animal who sucked away his mother's blood as he nursed.[42]

Hunt had started his research with the expectation of finding that parents intuitively followed their own instincts and the wisdom of their culture in raising their children. He found instead a society-wide "breakdown" of parental care: parents were unprepared to deal with their children, the conditions of daily life seriously hindered their efforts, and children suffered. Hunt notes that when we are dealing with a distant society like seventeenth-century France, it is easy to see the plight of children and to accept the notion that this plight related to the political and social order in which they live. "We lack the corresponding understanding of parenthood and society today."[43]

Such an understanding can be found, however, in two areas of family research whose findings have not received as much general attention as they deserve. These studies involve family violence and interaction in families of schizophrenics. These two kinds of studies have been carried out independently by different researchers, using different methods and a different vocabulary. Both sets of studies began with groups of people who were thought to represent extreme forms of pathology. Yet each set of studies ended with findings that made it harder than ever to draw the line between normal and pathological. In particular they revealed a dark side of "normal" family life that in the past had been explored only in literary works.

The Violent Family

Nothing could be more opposed to the image of the loving and happy family than the idea of physical violence between husbands and wives and parents and children. If such cases are brought to our attention, we tend to assume that the violent individual must be deranged and disreputable. Yet, according to a number of recent studies, force and violence may be a fundamental part of family life. As the introduction to an anthology on family violence puts it, "it would be hard to find a group or institution in which violence is more of an everyday occurrence than it is within the family."[44]

Some of the findings of the studies on family violence are not new, but they had not previously been included in a general analysis of ordinary family life. For example, studies of murderers and their victims reveal that the single most frequent category of murderer-victim relationship is that of family members. More policemen are killed or injured dealing with family fights than with any other kind of crime.

Rather than considering the more sensational cases as abnormal exceptions to the usual state of family life, these researchers argue that they represent just the tip of the iceberg:

> Underneath the surface is a vast amount of conflict and violence—including bitter feelings, anger, hatred, much physical punishment of children, pokes and slaps of husbands and wives, and not altogether rare pitched battles between family members.[45]

Although the family traditionally is viewed as place of love and solidarity, the family in fact is one of the few groups in society empowered by law and tradition to use physical force and restraint on its members. In every state, for example, it is legal for parents to strike their children; many Americans see physical punishment as the most desirable form of punishment, and even more believe that parents are morally obliged to use it if their children cannot be controlled in any other way.[46] There is also widespread support for the idea that husbands are "entitled" to use physical force to keep their wives in line, and that the wife who is beaten by her husband must have provoked him.[47] As Straus observes, "the actual or implicit threat of physical coercion is one of many factors underlying male dominance in the family.[48]

Although it can be argued that there is a big difference between a spanking and the kind of beating that comes to the attention of police, in practice it has proved difficult to define the dividing line between legitimate and illegitimate acts of family violence. Gelles concluded from a study of both violence-prone and ordinary families that violence is more widespread and more severe than the image of the happy family suggests:

> Neither the 57% violent figure for the entire sample nor the 37% violent sample for the neighbor [control group] families can serve as definitive estimates of the extent of the family violence in society. But taking into account the figures on the extent of conjugal violence, it is indeed common in American families. Furthermore, these incidents . . . are not isolated attacks nor are they just pushes and shoves. In many families violence in patterned and regular and often results in broken bones and sutured cuts.[49]

Similarly, the research on child battering points to a continuity rather than a sharp break with normal child-rearing methods. Some battering parents seem only to have exaggerated notions of obedience and of the capacities of very young children to respond to commands. Such parents are likely to be righteous about their acts, arguing that they were only trying to teach their child not to be spoiled or disrespectful. For other parents the injuries that bring in the authorities are more like momentary outbursts of anger in the course of "normal" discipline.

In looking for the causes of child abuse, research points beyond the motives and weaknesses of the particular parent and toward the physical and social environment surrounding parents and children. What happens to the child in the course of a day often seems to be a by-product of what happens to the parent in his or her adult life outside the realm of parent-hood—a fight with the spouse, troubles with the boss, money worries, the household workload, illness. If stresses mount too high, the parent may be overwhelmed and explode at the child. In short, a host of actors apart from the child determine the parent's mood and the time and energy the parent has for child care. All this seems obvious—we see it even in television commercials: "I'm not going to let a headache MAKE ME SCREAM AT MY KIDS!" Yet this knowledge tends to be ignored in most family research and in the sentimental mythology of family life as a refuge from the stresses of the outside world.

Rather than being a refuge from the stresses, strains, and irrationality of the outside society, the family often seems to transmit or even magnify these strains. The isolated nuclear family seems to be a particularly efficient magnifier of strain because so few people are involved. Husband and wife look to each other to make up for whatever deprivation they have suffered in their social and work lives, and the adults have absolute power over the children. A good deal of truth appears in the comic strip

showing the boss yelling at the husband, the husband coming home and yelling at the wife, the wife yelling at the child, and finally the child kicking the dog. Periods of unemployment are usually accompanied by increases in child abuse and wife beating.[50]

Anthropologists have pointed out how American culture is extreme in letting parents and children be alone together, shut off in their own houses and away from the watchful eyes and sharp tongues that regulate parent-child relations in other cultures. This isolation sets the stage not only for physical abuse but for the more usual and common psychological abuse.

Madness and the Family

Like the studies of family violence, the studies of families of schizophrenics began with a group of people in a category clearly labeled "pathological" and "not like other families," and they have concluded with a set of concepts that make the line between the normal and the pathological—"them" and "us"—harder than ever to draw. The studies of the families of schizophrenics form one part of an important

Couples in a family therapy session.

Ideal and Reality in Family and Society

shift in psychiatric thinking that has taken place in the past fifteen to twenty years. The issues surrounding schizophrenia, its nature and causes, remain unclear. But the concepts that have come out of these studies have produced profound and revolutionary implications for understanding family life, as well as human behavior in general.

These studies developed a new therapy, a new methodology, and ultimately a new set of concepts that have been hailed as major scientific discoveries.[51] The new therapy was family therapy. Rather than seeing the individual patient alone, psychiatrists started to observe and to treat whole families. The new methods of research grew out of the new therapy. With whole families coming together in hospitals and clinics, it became possible to observe the intimate conversations and interactions of family members in ways that had never before been available to researchers. Furthermore, a whole new technology was now available to record and preserve the record of what people said and did. Movies, tape recorders, videotape, and so forth caught the words, looks, and gestures of family members, so it was no longer necessary to depend on anyone's memory. "Instant replay" became possible in the study of family interaction. Researchers could study a family scene again and again, picking up the more subtle aspects that had been missed the first time, or changing their definitions of what had gone on.

The new techniques transformed the family psychiatrist into a kind of anthropologist. Each family was like a newly discovered tribe, with its own language, rules, roles, and rituals. In looking at families this way, the researchers discovered that they lacked a vocabulary to describe what they saw. Psychiatry and psychoanalysis had many terms to describe the behavior and inner states of the single person, but very few terms to describe the interaction between two or more people.

To fill this information gap, concepts were borrowed from many fields, some seemingly far removed from psychiatry—information theory, logic, ecology, general-systems theory, sociology, existentialism, and Marxism. Oddly enough, no name has yet emerged for this new science. Several have been suggested, but none has stuck. "Communication theory" is perhaps used most often, but it refers mainly to one particular version of the new approach, that of Gregory Bateson and his associates. Other suggested names are "clinical sociology,"[52] "social psychiatry,"[53] and "interpersonal psychiatry."[54]

"Communicational psychiatry" failed to prove its initial assumptions: it did not discover a set of behavior patterns unique to schizophrenic families. Rather, it seems to have discovered patterns common to many families. The following features are some of those first found in families with a schizophrenic member:

The "politics of experience": struggles over definitions of what is really going on, over whose experience is to be defined as real, and whose experience is to be invalidated

Imperviousness: ignoring what the other person says

Mystification: doing something that is really in your own interests, but insisting you are doing it for the other person's good—for example, a parent tells a child "You're sleepy, dear—go to bed" when in fact the child is not tired, and the parent merely wants the child out of the way

A parent caring for a child only as an extension of himself or herself, not as a separate person

Mother and father as enemy camps; a cold war in the household

Mother and father united in a "holy alliance" against the rest of the world

Double-bind or paradoxical communications, such as glaring at a child and ordering him or her to kiss you at the same time; saying such things as "Don't take me seriously" or "Be spontaneous"

Too great a boundary between the family and the rest of the world—everyone outside the family is a suspicious character

Too little boundary between the family and the rest of the world: outsiders or other relatives constantly intruding on intimate family matters

Family secrets that everyone is aware of but doesn't dare discuss

A parent being preoccupied with the child's inner state: his or her moods, feelings, and general happiness

A parent mislabeling the child's inner states—stating that the child is hungry or sleepy when he or she is neither

A parent reacting to a child's statements or acts by belittling the child with sarcasm: "You can always depend on John—to do the wrong thing"

These findings were not so much discoveries as a rediscovery of what intuitive observers of the human scene had known all along: most families have small and large skeletons in their closets; the most mature-seeming people have foibles and weaknesses that emerge only in the presence of members of their family; family members conspire together to create a favorable impression for the outside world; family members may say one thing but imply another—"Don't worry about leaving me with all the dinner dishes—go and enjoy yourselves"; every family has its own unique set of rules, myths, communication networks, secret alliances, loves, and hates.[55]

Accordingly, the concept of a psychiatrically "normal" family is coming to seem as abstract and empty as the concept of a "universal" nuclear family that is the same everywhere. The more family interaction was studied, the harder it became to think that there was a normal "type" of family that could be contrasted with an abnormal "type."

The enthusiasm engendered by the new research gave way to disillusionment among those who had been hoping for an answer to the riddle of schizophrenia. But the less the new findings tell us about what is unique to schizophrenic families, the more they tell us about family life in general.

Jules Henry, an anthropologist who studied families of schizophrenics by living in their homes, raises the question as to how far these newly discovered patterns reach among families never labeled as "sick." Are they the inevitable result of people living together? Are they peculiar to Americans? To the isolated, urbanized nuclear family? He writes:

I worry that we have here, perhaps, a sudden discovery of the contemporary *family* rather than the pathologic family, unless of course we urge that in our culture, most families are pathogenic, in some sense—a position I take in this book.[56]

A somewhat different way of looking at family interaction is suggested by Lennard and Bernstein.[57] Rather than defining most families as "pathogenic," these researchers suggest that though ordinary family life can often be a difficult interactional environment, most people can cope with these difficulties most of the time. Just as our bodies have immune systems enabling us to live in a germ-filled environment without being sick constantly, so most of us are psychologically robust enough to deal with the emotional ups and downs of family interaction. Pathology such as schizophrenic reactions may occur when the level of interactional difficulty in a family exceeds the ability of a family member to cope with it. Some persons may be especially vulnerable to conflict, hostility, or emotional demands, and some families are more difficult interactional environments than others. When a vulnerable person finds himself or herself in a particularly difficult family, chances are that he or she will either try to withdraw from the family or develop symptoms that will lead to becoming a psychiatric patient.

Lennard and Bernstein were led to their conclusion concerning the difficulties of the family context by research comparing small-group interaction in families and other groups. They looked at "schizophrenic families," "normal families," and a variety of groups of unrelated people—for example, small groups that had participated in psychological experiments or therapy or discussion. One of their major measures was the ratio between positive interactions—agreeing, supporting, affirming—and negative interactions—disagreeing, contradicting, criticizing. As anticipated, they found that the "schizophrenic" families had lower ratios of positive to negative interactions. But to their surprise, the differences between the "normal" families and those with a schizophrenic member were not as wide as previous clinical descriptions had led them to believe. Furthermore, family groups, whether with a schizophrenic member or not, contrasted with the groups of unrelated people:

. . . Family contexts as a whole, whether or not they involve families with a mentally ill member, exhibit lower concordance ratios than any other form of social context on which we had data available. Moreover, family interaction process does not meet the criteria set forth by Bales for a viable, task-oriented system. . . . The family interactional environment then must be considered as a difficult context for interaction—an observation that is, needless to say, not inconsistent with common experience.[58]

In a more poetic way, Laing has described "the happy family" as a collusive game, an agreement, usually unspoken, among family members to put on a good front and to deny conflicts, even among themselves, but especially in front of the neighbors:

So we are a happy family and we have no
    secrets from one another.
If we are unhappy/we have to keep it a secret.
And we are unhappy that we have to keep it a
    secret.
And unhappy that we have to keep secret/the
    fact/that we
Have to keep it a secret
And that we are keeping all that secret.
But since we are a happy family you can see
This difficulty does not arise.[59]

Summary

The family often has been studied from the point of view of either the society as a whole or the individual. Both of these approaches can lead to idealized conceptions of family life. The view of society as a balanced social system leads to a utopian vision of family and society as conflict-free and harmonious. Clinical work with individuals and families often leads the clinician to assume that the patients are troubled only by personal failings rather than by social strains besetting families in general. Recent work in history, family interaction, and family conflict is undermining such idealized models of family life.

Source Notes

1. Troll, 1969, p. 222.
2. Ibid., p. 223.
3. Dahrendorf, 1958.
4. Ibid., p. 117.
5. Ibid., p. 123.
6. Ibid.
7. Lenski, 1966.
8. For a more detailed treatment of the differences between functional and conflict models, see Chamblis, 1973.
9. Harris, 1968, p. 521.
10. Inkeles, 1968, pp. 81−82.
11. Dahrendorf, 1958, p. 121.
12. Lidz, 1963, pp. 51-53.
13. Dahrendorf, 1958, p. 117.
14. Freud, 1898, p. 4.
15. Parsons and Bales, 1955.
16. Wrong, 1961, p. 192.
17. Harris, 1968.
18. Ibid., p. 59.
19. Henry, 1963, pp. 205-206.
20. Goode, 1971, p. 630.
21. M. Hunt, 1969.
22. Cuber and Harroff, 1965.
23. Harris, 1968.
24. Chapple, 1970, p. 272.
25. Birdwhistell, 1966, p. 211 (italics in original).
26. Ryle, 1967, p. 135.
27. Ruesch and Bateson, 1968, p. 71 (italics added).
28. Stierlin, 1976, p. 278.
29. Coveney, 1967.
30. Ellenberger, 1970, p. 460.
31. Ackerman, 1958, pp. 27-30.
32. Ibid., p. 28.
33. Fraiberg, 1959, pp. 14-15.
34. Spencer, 1946, p. 87 (originally 1858).
35. Bakan, 1971a, pp. 64ff.
36. Ricoeur, 1973, p. 982.
37. Little Hans, 1909.
38. Fromm, 1970, pp. 90-100.
39. Chesler, 1971.
40. Aries, 1962.
41. Plumb, 1972, p. 156.
42. D. Hunt, 1970, p. 121.
43. Ibid., p. 196.
44. Steinmetz and Straus, 1974, p. 3.
45. Ibid., p. 6.
46. Stark and McEvoy, 1970.
47. Ibid.; Gelles, 1972.
48. Straus, quoted in Gelles, 1972, p. 14.
49. Gelles, 1972, p. 192.
50. Steinmetz and Straus, 1974.
51. Henry, 1971, p. 455; see also Rabkin, 1970.
52. Lennard and Bernstein, 1969.
53. Rabkin, 1970.
54. Sullivan, 1953.
55. Framo, 1965, 1972.
56. Henry, 1971, p. 455.
57. Lennard and Bernstein, 1969.
58. Ibid., p. 185.
59. Laing, 1969, p. 100.

Chapter Four
Social Change and the Intimate Environment

☐ *The sociological imagination enables its possessor to understand the larger historical scene in terms of its meaning for the inner life and the external career of a variety of individuals. . . . The first fruit of this imagination—and the first lesson of the social science that embodies it—is the idea that the individual can understand his own experience and gauge his own fate only by locating himself within his period. . . . We have come to know that every individual lives, from one generation to the next, in some society, and that he lives it out within some historical sequence. By the fact of his living he contributes, however minutely, to the shaping of this society and to the course of its history, even as he is made by society and by its historical push and shove.*

The sociological imagination enables us to grasp history and biography and the relations between the two within society.

C. Wright Mills, *The Sociological Imagination*

How does our own family life compare with family life in other times and places? Leaving aside for the moment that we actually know little about family life as it is lived in contemporary families, what can we say about the experience of motherhood and fatherhood in the Middle Ages or of being a child in a band of hunters? Is family life essentially "the same" everywhere or does it vary significantly from time to time and place to place? What is the connection between family change and changes in the rest of society?

In the course of this chapter, we shall see that there are no simple answers to these questions, and, as was noted in the first chapter, no agreement among scholars as to the best way to describe current and past changes in family life. In spite of the confusions and uncertainties in the historical study of the family, however, recent research has produced some extremely important findings and laid to rest some long-held assumptions about the family.

Also in spite of the various debates among family scholars today, they agree on some fundamental issues. One of these points of agreement is that there have been some major turning points in history. As Immanuel Wallerstein observes, "One such generally recognized watershed . . . is the so-called neolithic or agricultural revolution. The other great watershed is the creation of the modern world."[1] Another point on which most scholars would agree is that these changes have produced profound changes in personal and family life.

Although some family scholars have been concerned with prehistoric changes in family life, more of them have been concerned with the second process—modernization. Currently, the term "modernization" is the subject of intense debate. There is great disagreement about what it is that defines the modern era, about what causes modernization to happen, and whether it is really useful to think of all "traditional" societies as similar to one another. Above all, scholars disagree about the meaning of modernization. Does it represent progress and enlightenment? Or was the "world we have lost" a more human place than the world we have now? Or is "modernization" just another form of exploitation and class struggle?

History of the Family

The study of family life in other places, of course, is very different from the study of family life in other times. No matter how remote or exotic an existing group, it is possible to study their family behavior firsthand. The historian, by contrast, faces the task or reconstructing history. Before the past decade there was a great deal of skepticism about trying to reconstruct family life and family change in past eras. William Goode asserted that "not a single history of the U.S. family would meet modern standards of historical research."[2]

Until recently most historians avoided studying the family, leaving the topic to anthropologists and sociologists. This avoidance can be attributed in part to the practical problems mentioned by Goode: the scarcity of documentary materials and the hesitancy of historians to venture into the alien territory of the social sciences. More important perhaps was the general tendency of historians to focus on public events rather than private experience, and on elites rather than on ordinary people.

In the past decade, however, a renewed interest in the history of the family has resulted from new methodologies as well as new definitions of the task of history. It has been stimulated in part by a commitment to understanding what life was like in all segments of society in past ages, not just the top social strata. The current interest in the family has also been stimulated by the generation gap, the women's movement, and anxieties about the future of the family.

For the new scholars of the family in history, reconstructing past family life does not appear to be an impossible task. As Tamara Hareven[3] points out, historians neglected the family not only because materials were lacking but also because they failed to ask the right questions.

Now new ways of using existing materials have been discovered. A number of important techniques have been borrowed from the field of demography, enabling historians to trace population changes, mobility, fertility, birth control, infant mortality, illegitimacy, and even marriages with pregnant brides. One highly significant development is a technique known as family reconstruction; using records of births, deaths, marriages, land transfers, and wills, the historian can reconstruct the family and household patterns of large numbers of ordinary people who had previously been considered lost forever in the depths of time.

Using the family-reconstruction technique, for example, Philip Greven[4] was able to trace the structures of individual families in Andover, Massachusetts, beginning with the first settlers and continuing through four generations. Greven emphasizes the role of the land in the family lives of farmers—the subtle ways in which inheritance patterns and the availability of land influenced relations between fathers and sons:

> By studying the families of four successive generations of residents of Andover, I have sought to answer one of the most crucially important questions that can be asked about the nature and history of the family: Did the structure and the character of families change through time and place to place? The answer, as this study demonstrates, is affirmative; families did change, and patterns of family structure, patterns of relationships between fathers and sons, patterns in the transmission of land, and patterns in demographic experience all gradually altered in the course of the seventeenth and eighteenth centuries. Because of these complex and almost continuous changes . . . one can describe the family as having a history. The nature of the family was as mutable as the circumstances shaping the lives of the men, women, and children who were born, matured, and died in this community and others.[5]

John Demos's study[6] of the Plymouth colony presents another attempt to reconstruct the intimacies of everyday family life in the colonial era. Demos tries to depict the concrete realities of the family by a detailed study of colonial houses, who lived in them, their furnishings, clothing, child-rearing methods, the tasks carried out in the households, and the relations between households and the larger community. More recently, the new methods have been used to document the nature of black family life during slavery and the post-Civil War era.[7]

Not surprisingly, the further such studies get from such facts as births, deaths, and household arrangements in making interpretations about the experiences of family life, the more debate their conclusions elicit. For example, Demos and Greven disagree about the quality of emotional life in colonial households: Greven sees life in the first generation of Andover settlers as harmonious, in part because of the abundance of land; Demos suggests that the crowded households built frustrations and resentments that were expressed in disputes with other families.

In a relatively short span of time, however, the recent work of historians has revised many notions about the family that had been held by family scholars as well as the public. We have learned that the typical household in centuries past was not necessarily filled with large

*Black family in early
twentieth century.*

numbers of kin; sexual behavior was not frozen at a constant level until the sexual revolution of the 1920s; and people did not have the same ideas and emotions about children that they have now. As noted in the last chapter, the new historical studies have also blurred the line between normality and pathology. Historians have analyzed nonmarital sexuality, illegitimacy, and generational conflict as part of family life itself, rather than as a separate category of deviance.

In spite of its achievements, however, the new history of the family has probably raised more questions that it has answered. Much of this research has been concerned with the impact of modernization on the family. It has chosen to look for this impact in changes over time in the size and composition of the average household. At first, historians were attracted to the study of household structure for several reasons: first, it is easy to obtain quantifiable data about it, since the household is the basic unit used by census takers in many countries; second, the prevailing social-science generalizations seemed to suggest that the history of the family should be viewed as the decline of the great extended patriarchal household and the rise of the isolated nuclear family. Further, to many historians, household structure seemed to be the key to the emotional environments of family life—an extended-family household seemed to create a "radically different set of emotional arrangements"[8] than those found in the nuclear family.

The principal finding of the new family history is, as already noted, that the nuclear family prevailed in many areas of Western Europe well before the industrial revolution. How then can we explain how the modern family differs from its historical counterpart? Before trying to answer this question, let's first examine the earlier development of family life.

Evolutionary Theories of the Family

To understand the development of the study of family change in the social sciences, we should recognize the importance of two overlapping controversies: the debate with Marxism and the use of evolutionary theories in the social sciences. The emphasis on the biological constancy and functional necessity of the family came about in part as reaction against nineteenth-century theories about how the family evolved through the stages of human evolution. One of the leading theorists of cultural evolution was an American, Lewis Henry Morgan, a Republican lawyer who practiced anthropology as a hobby.

The prevailing verdict on Morgan in works on the family is negative; he is generally assumed to have been thoroughly discredited, along with other fanciful nineteenth-century thinkers on the family. Perhaps the most important reason for Morgan's rejection was that his theory of family evolution became the basis for the Marxian theory of the family. Marx and Engels saw in Morgan's scheme a confirmation of the Marxian theory of history, which originally had been applied only to Western societies. Engels's *The Origin of Private Property, the Family and the State* is based largely on Morgan's work. Morgan's ideas, as interpreted by Engels, became the official anthropological dogma of the Communist Party of the Soviet Union.

The fate of Morgan's reputation on the two sides of the Cold War is an interesting example of how far political considerations can intrude into scholarly matters. In the Soviet Union Morgan was revered, whereas in the West he was considered wildly and totally wrong. Harris[9] argues that the attack on Morgan had profound consequences for anthropology for the first forty years of the twentieth century; for this period of time anthropologists no longer used the comparative method, and did not try to generalize about the processes of historical and cultural change.

Morgan and Engels were neither as historically correct as their supporters claimed, nor as wrong as Western social science insisted. Marxist ideas on the family certainly deserve discussion not only for general intellectual reasons, but also for more contemporary ones— they have been rediscovered in the new feminist movement.

Morgan's Scheme

As an anthropological hobbyist, Morgan became fascinated with the kinship terminology of American Indian tribes and decided to investigate the number of different types of kinship systems. He was intrigued to learn, for example, that the Iroquois used the same term for one's mother and one's mother's sister. Some of a person's cousins—the children of the father's sister and the mother's brother—were called cousins, but the children of the mother's sister and the father's brother were called brothers and sisters rather than cousins. On the basis of questionnaires sent to government officials and missionaries, Morgan learned that the kinship systems of groups all around the world fell into a rather small number of types.

Morgan eventually came to believe that kinship terms reflected marriage rules and family patterns, which in turn reflected stages of economic development. He constructed an elaborate scheme correlating technological development, social and political structure, and the family.[10] Morgan divided human history into three broad stages: savagery, barbarism, and civilization. Further subdivisions were as follows:

Savagery

Lower:	fruit and nut subsistence
Middle:	fish subsistence and fire
Upper:	bow and arrow

Barbarism

Lower:	invention of pottery
Middle:	domestication of animals in the Old World; irrigation and cultivation of maize in the New World
Upper:	iron tools

Civilization — invention of phonetic alphabet and writing

Morgan believed that each of these periods had its own style of life and culture. Thus he assumed that knowing one aspect of a society's culture would make it possible to predict all the rest. Further, he held that the sequence represented a series of necessary evolutionary stages; any existing society could be placed in one of the categories.

In the same way, Morgan believed that family institutions have also gone through successive stages of development. He postulated five such forms, each with its own type of marriage:

1. *Consanguine:* group marriage between actual brothers and sisters

2. *Punaluan:* a form of group marriage in which a group of brothers marries a group of sisters; brother-sister incest is taboo

3. *Pairing family:* a transitional form between group marriage and monogamy: single pairs of men and women would marry but either could end the marriage at any time, as well as cohabit with others at any time

4. *Patriarchal family:* marriage of one man with several wives

5. *Monogamian:* based on monogamy and an increase in female equality

Morgan's Errors

The errors in Morgan's scheme are many and serious. For example, he wrongly assumed that kinship terminology reflects actual marriage patterns. Thus, because the Hawaiians call all their aunts and uncles "mother" and "father," and all their cousins "brother" and "sister," Morgan believed that a group of sisters and brothers must have intermarried. But group marriage probably never existed as an institutionalized form. Pairing arrangements with incest prohibitions within the nuclear family, however, appear to be universal in every known society.[11]

Morgan made other mistakes.[12] First, he failed to relate the kinship or other aspects of social structure to the stages of technology in any sort of systematic way—that is, he did not explain why a particular form of subsistence should lead to a particular form of the family. Second, his technological sequences contain drastic errors; the earliest stage of human society, Morgan's period of "savagery," was based on hunting as well as gathering. The invention of agriculture—*not* the invention of pottery—was the revolutionary development that ushered in the next great stage of human history. Third, use of iron and writing systems are not the correct criteria for defining civilizations. Finally, Morgan erred in insisting that, historically, matrilineal descent preceded patrilineal descent. Morgan and others had argued that, because of group marriage as well as ignorance of the father's role in reproduction, the earliest stages of human culture recognized only descent from the mother, since a child's mother was always certain.

Engels and others extended this notion into the theory of matriarchy and mother-right. According to this theory there was an historical stage of matriarchy when women ruled human society and female deities were worshiped. This was followed by a universal defeat of the female sex by patriarchy, accompanied by the rise of private property.

Since the matriarchy notion has recently been revived as part of the women's movement, it will be useful to quote Marvin Harris's review of the controversy (Harris, it should be noted, is a defender of Morgan's work). About the controversy between the matriarchy theory and its opponents, he has this to say:

> . . . Here Morgan was a participant in one of the most heated and useless discussions in the history of the social sciences. He and his supporters were opposed by an equally numerous group, who argued for the reverse priority. Both groups were wrong, constituting one of those rare cases of diametrically opposed positions about which it is impossible to say that either contained a grain of truth.[13]

Descent rules — the question of whether a child belongs to the mother's or the father's line — seem to reflect residence patterns, whether a married couple lives with the wife's or the husband's people. Residence patterns in turn reflect local economic, technological, and environmental conditions. Groups at the same general level of economic development, however, can have varying descent rules. Besides, how descent is reckoned has little to do with either the status of women or knowledge of paternity:

> The occurrence of matrilineal descent has no bearing on the status of women, since mother's brother rather than mother is gener-

ally head of the descent group. Furthermore, the idea that matrilineality is a result of confusion concerning paternity is wholly confounded by the numerous cases of primitive peoples who deny that the male is necessary for conception, but who regard themselves as descended from a line of males, and by the universal recognition of some degree of kinship with both maternal and paternal relatives, regardless of the nature of the unilineal rule.[14]

Modern Evolutionism, Technology, and Family Life

In spite of Morgan's errors, he was right in believing that family and other aspects of social organization are tied to economic pursuits and technological development. Contemporary anthropologists are also concerned about the relation between social organization and technology, economic activities, and such environmental features as population density, disease, and food supply.[15]

Broadly speaking, Morgan's threefold division of societal development is still used by today's comparative anthropologists, although their terms differ somewhat: the divisions are "hunting-and-gathering societies," "agricultural societies," and "industrial societies." Again, these types represent a set of historical changes and also a set of categories into which any society can be placed.

As in Morgan's scheme, societal development or complexity influences family life. Modern theorists, however, do not leave the connections between society and family as vague and unspecified as Morgan did. Nor, incidentally, do they assume a mechanical sort of economic determinism; instead, they realize that how a society provides for basic needs, and the abundance it can produce, sets off a chain of influential consequences. For example, the sheer amount of food a society is able to produce determines how many and how densely people can live together. Further, more surplus frees people from agriculture and permits specialization in crafts and other occupations.

Modern scholars also agree with Morgan and Engels on the significance of the agricultural revolution as a major turning point in human history. The transition from hunting and gathering to the invention of agriculture made possible a settled way of life, the birth of individual and family property in land, herds, houses, and other objects, and the rise of unequal social classes and the state. Although the nuclear family tends to be the major family unit in hunting societies, the extended kin group characterizes agricultural societies.

A second major transition is the shift from agrarian to industrial society. In industrial societies the nuclear family once again emerges as the dominant household form. Blumberg and Winch[16] have documented this pattern for more than nine hundred societies. Not only does the structure of the family vary, but also the psychological quality of life. In general there are marked contrasts in the relations between men and women and parents and children over the range of societal development. Let us consider the family more closely under these major shifts in technology.

Hunting-and-Gathering Societies

For 99 percent of human history, hunting and gathering constituted the major means of subsistence.

> To date, the hunting way of life has been the most successful and persistent adaptation man has ever achieved. . . . It is still an open question whether man will be able to survive the exceedingly complex and unstable ecological conditions he has created for himself. If he fails in this task, interplanetary archeologists of the future will classify our planet as one in which a very long and stable period of small-scale hunting and gathering was followed by an apparently instantaneous efflorescence of technology and society rapidly leading to extinction. . . . The origin of agriculture and thermonuclear destruction will appear as essentially simultaneous.[17]

About 175 contemporary hunting-and-gathering cultures have been studied in detail, including Eskimos, Bushmen of the Kalahari Desert in southern Africa, forest Pygmies, and many Canadian and South American Indian groups.[18] These living groups of hunters cannot be regarded as fossils—precise replicas of human society as it existed ten to fifteen thousand years ago—but they do offer clues to earlier family and social organization.

Although the technology of hunters is rudimentary, and they lack "social complexity," they are not primitive in mentality. Nor do hunting societies live up to the image of "bloodthirsty savages." Nineteenth-century anthropologists, including Morgan, erroneously concluded that people in simpler societies were less intelligent than people in 'civilized' societies. Eighteenth-century philosophers erroneously thought hunters epitomized a simple "state of nature." But in religion, morality, art, and etiquette their culture is at least as elaborate as ours, and in one respect it is more eleborate. Some hunting groups possess enormously complex kinship systems. Moreover, there is no primitive language; the languages associated with primitive technologies may be more elaborate than the languages of some advanced societies. Still, the underlying structure of all human languages is identical, and any human infant placed in any group at birth will grow up a native speaker of whatever language prevails.

Although hunters live in many different environments with varying cultures, anthropologists consider it useful to analyze hunting societies as a major societal type:

> In spite of their varied environments, hunters share certain features of social life. They live in bands of about 20 to 200 people, the majority of bands having fewer than 50. Bands are divided into families, which may forage alone in some seasons. Hunters have simple but ingenious technologies. Bows and arrows, spears, skin clothing, and temporary leaf or wood shelters are common. Most hunters do some fishing. The band forages and hunts in a large territory and usually moves camp often.
>
> Social life is egalitarian. There is of course no state, no organized government. Apart from religious shamans or magicians, the division of labor is based only on sex and age. Resources are owned communally; tools and personal possessions are freely exchanged. Everyone works who can. Band leadership goes to whichever man has the intelligence, courage, and foresight to command the respect of his fellows. Intelligent older women are also looked up to.[19]

Marriage and sex practices in hunting societies in some ways resemble those in modern societies more than those in the agrarian states at the middle range of societal complexity. Hunting societies tend to be relaxed sexually; there is premarital sexual freedom, special times of sexual license for people not married to each other, and a "pragmatic" approach to adultery. The best-known example of the relaxed sexual customs that tend to prevail among hunters is the Eskimo custom of the wife sleeping with male guests as part of normal hospitality.

Kathleen Gough[20] notes that although group marriage does not exist among hunters, mating has more of a group character than in

Eskimo family. Hunting societies, like industrial societies, tend to have independent nuclear families.

Hunting-and-Gathering Societies

agrarian or industrial societies. There is less differentiation between the band and the nuclear family than in our society—the band is as much part of everyone's daily environment as the family.

Although elders arrange marriages, couples usually know each other and have some choice.

> Both sexual and companionate love between individual men and women are known and deeply experienced. With comparative freedom of mating, love is less often separated from or opposed to marriage than in archaic states or even than in some modern nations.[21]

Relations between parents and children also appear to be more relaxed in hunting societies than in more complex ones. Stephens[22] suggests that this may result from the greater authoritarianism of stratified states with central political leadership. When society is organized as a pyramid, with a king or chief at the top and social groups arranged in layers beneath him, children and women are likely to be at the bottom. Furthermore, children may be better treated in hunting societies because hunters seem to enjoy their work and life more than farmers or workers in industrial societies. Although the productivity of hunters is low, they do not work at hunting endlessly. They are not harried; indeed, many hunting peoples are extremely leisured. One anthropologist calls hunting society "the original affluent society."[23] Children in hunting societies, as part of their socialization, do the kinds of things that are intrinsically enjoyable for small children in any culture. Turnbull describes the way children's play in one hunting society imperceptibly changes into adult work:

> . . . At an early age, boys and girls are "playing house."
>
> They will also play at hunting, the boys stretching out their little bits of net while the girls beat the ground with bunches of leaves and drive some poor tired old frog in toward the boys. . . . One day they find that the games they have been playing are not games any longer, but the real things, for they have become adults. Their hunting is now real hunting; their tree climbing is in earnest search of inaccessible honey, in the pursuit of elusive game, or in avoiding malicious forest buffalo. It happens so gradually that they hardly notice the change at first, for even when they are proud and famous hunters their life is still full of fun and laughter.[24]

Finally, obedience is not a major value among hunters and gatherers. A study by Barry, Child, and Bacon[25] compared child-training practices and child behavior in societies having different types of subsistence economy. They found that hunting-and-fishing societies emphasized achievement, independence, and self-reliance, whereas agricultural societies stressed compliance and obedience. If crops and animals must be tended regularly, disobedience or even innovation can endanger the food supply for months. Thus farmers and herders must be cautious and responsible. Since hunters cannot store food, cautiousness and responsibility are not so crucial.

In recent years hunting-and-gathering societies are coming to be viewed in a new light. In the nineteenth century peoples with low levels of technological development were considered savages, living fossils with mental capacities between civilized people and apes. Civilization was regarded as progress up the ladder of human perfection. If, as nineteenth-century "false Darwinism" had it, evolution was the survival of the fittest, then simple societies obviously were unfit. Now, however, assessing the alienation of modern society and the environmental crises, anthropologists and others are coming to reevaluate the "advantages" of civilization.

Societies of the Middle Range

The agricultural revolution represented a major step in the advance of "civilization" or, to use a less value-loaded term, societal complexity. Hunting-and-gathering societies depend wholly on what nature provides for food, clothing, and shelter. Since they are always on the move, possessions are a burden, and even infants, the very old, and the very sick may have to be abandoned in times of short supply.

Agriculture made it possible for people to settle in one place, and enormous consequences followed. The ownership of property and its hereditary transmission appeared on the scene. Surplus wealth led to the growth of population, increased population density, and a greater division of labor: people could specialize in crafts and trade. With the increase in population, larger social units began to appear, resulting in the rise of cities and the emergence of the centralized state ruled by kings or other hereditary monarchs, about 4000 B.C.[26] Military conquests of one people by another became possible, and they contributed to the increasing stratification of society into different social classes.

The characteristic form of the family in agrarian societies is the large kin group, whether the unilineal descent groups of preliterate peoples or the extended families of European peasants.[27] These kin groups are also hierarchically organized along patriarchal principles.

The agricultural revolution ushered in a way of life with its own social and psychological characteristics. The first farmers had more in common with modern peasants than with the prehistoric hunters who preceded them.

It might be said that for the individual, the revolutionary psychological change was the substitution of routine and hard work for excitement and uncertainty, while the social counterpart was a new stability demanding greater discipline and more government.[28]

The other important contrast between agrarian societies and those at either end of the scale of societal complexity is the importance in them of the extended patriarchal family.

The Patriarchal Family Observed

"Traditional" family systems, although differing among themselves, contrast sharply with the Western industrial family. In each, the role of the individual is defined by heredity and long tradition: the extended-family group, whether or not it lives in the same household, is an economic unit tied to durable property of some kind; and deviation from community norms is severely sanctioned.

Societies at the middle of the scale of societal complexity tend to exhibit the most extreme patterns of age and sex subordination within the family. Indeed, William Stephens calls them "deference societies,"[29] characterized by ritualized expressions of respect, submissiveness, and obedience. Deference customs between sons and fathers involve such behavior as the following:

1. Not addressing father by his first name

2. Using verbal restraint when speaking to father; speaking in a low voice; not arguing

3. Kneeling or bowing when greeting father

4. Not touching father

5. Not being permitted to eat with father

6. Father has a seat of honor

7. Father and son not supposed to laugh and joke together

8. Strict obedience rules for children

Deference behavior demanded of wives is similar to that demanded for sons. Wives may also be excluded from gatherings attended by husbands.

In studying deference customs cross-culturally, Stephens discovered an all-or-none effect: if there is one deference relationship, there tend to be others. The hub of it all is the child-to-father relationship. If the children must defer to father, there are usually deference rules for elder male relatives, as well as wife-to-husband deferences.

Patterns of subordination are illustrated in a classic study of the Irish peasant family system, first published in 1940 by Arensberg and Kimball.[30] Children in these families begin their work lives very early and attain sociological adulthood very late. A man remains a "boy" verbally and socially until his father dies or retires and he inherits the family farm or his share of it. Thus some men of forty-five and even fifty are still "boys." Even though the sons do the major work of the farm, they have no control over the spending of farm income.

. . . Thus, the . . . farmer and his sons are often seen at fairs and markets together, but it is the farmer father who does the bargaining. Once when one of the authors asked a countryman about this at a potato market, he explained that he could not leave his post for long because his full-grown son "isn't well-known yet and isn't a good hand at selling."

. . . Even at forty-five and fifty, if the old couple have not made over their farm, the countryman remains a boy in respect to farm work and in the rural vocabulary. . . . The

Peasant family in Portugal.

Social Change and the Intimate Environment

division of labor in the masculine sphere between father and sons, then, is more than an economic arrangement. It is very directly part of the systems of controls, duties, and sentiments which make up the whole family life. . . . [31]

Along with a subordination of the young, there is a sharp differentiation between sex roles and derogation of women. Farm duties are divided into men's and women's work. Some tasks are divided according to heaviness of the labor, but many divisions are arbitrary, although those involved do not consider them so. They assume that the distribution of tasks corresponds to the natural propensities of the sexes. Thus selling eggs and milking cows are "natural" for women, and plowing is "naturally" a male activity. "There is . . . an entire body of popular belief and superstition surrounding the dichotomy in farm labor."[32]

Cernea provides a similar description of the Rumanian peasant family. About the position of the woman in the family he writes:

The inequality between husband and wife in the traditional Rumanian peasant family was enormous. Both societal and family values and rules reinforced that inequality. As several sociological investigations found, unwritten but very powerful village norms required that the woman should bow to the man and greet him first. A wife should not walk beside her husband but follow behind him; when he stopped to chat with another villager, she should stop at a definite distance behind him, not interfere with the conversation, wait, and start again only after her husband starts walking. At home she was "the humble servant of her husband, for all his needs, under the penalty of being beaten."[33] Out in the agricultural field, she had to perform a considerable share of the hardest activities, side by side with her husband. Advanced pregnancy was not a reason to discontinue work, and giving birth to a child in the field was reported as a common occurrence.[34]

In cultures where deference roles apply in the family, they appear to generate an emotional climate of reserve, lacking in spontaneity. Not only is the behavior of the deferent person inhibited, but so is the behavior of the person in the superior position. Extreme power inequality seems to generate stiff, formal behavior from everyone in the family, and may even result in family members avoiding each other; indeed, some societies prescribe patterns of apartness and estrangement.[35] In the most patriarchal societies, where the father is most all-powerful over his children, he is often quite inhibited in his dealings with them. He may order them around, but he doesn't play or laugh with them or let them sit on his lap. Here is an example of such a family climate from a study of Tepoztlan, Mexico:

The husband avoids intimacy with members of his family [in order] to be respected by them. He expects them to demonstrate their respect by maintaining a proper social distance. His contacts with the children are brief and reserved. The Tepoztlan husband expects his wife to see that the children are quiet when he is at home, and it is her obligation to teach them to fear him. Men are generally not talkative at home and contribute little to family conversation, nor do they seek or expect their children to confide in them. When the husband is at home during the day, he sits apart from the rest of the family; at night, he eats alone or with his grown sons and goes out, or retires soon after. . . . [36]

What accounts for such family patterns? Scholars have offered political explanations based on the structure of authority in the larger society, as well as economic explanations based on the control over resources within the family. Stephens attributes the authoritarianism of traditional family life to the autocratic state. He examined family customs in fifty-one societies: those with extremely high deference patterns

*Father and son at a
sheep market in Ireland.*

were parts of kingdoms; tribal groups tended to be low in deference. Stephens describes the difference between tribes and kingdoms as follows:

>These are the defining attributes of the kingdom: a state, nobles and commoners, an agrarian economic base, exploitation of commoners by nobles, and a state religion.
>
>The other type of society—the tribe—is a society without a state. It is not subject to ''a centralized organ of political control, with coercive power over the populace,'' with an army and tax collectors. Although the tribe may evince some rudimentary form of social stratification, it does not have ''nobles'' who have the power to economically exploit ''commoners.'' . . . The tribe's subsistence may come from one or several of three sources: agriculture, animal husbandry, hunting (and/or fishing), and gathering.
>
>A tribe never embraces cities. A kingdom may . . . . Some kingdoms are also characterized by a group of culture traits that are commonly termed ''civilization''—large public works and esoteric arts and sciences (written languages, mathematics, astronomy, and so forth). Tribes never have ''civilization,'' thus defined.
>
>The tribe was the first political form to appear. During the earliest periods of human history, people managed to get along without any sort of state government whatsoever. . . .[37]

Social Change and the Intimate Environment

Between the time the first centralized states developed—about 4000 B.C.—and about two hundred years ago, the history of the world was made by kingdoms. (Tribes may have histories, too, but these are unrecorded.) Traditional European societies that preceded the modern democratic state belong to this same general cross-cultural type—that is, kingdoms.

Others explain the family patterns of traditional societies differently. Cernea[38] suggests that the economic infrastructure of the peasant family accounts for the extreme subordination of women and children. The father not only exercises power as head of the household, but also owns and manages the family's labor and property. Further, agriculture, unlike industrialism, encourages caution and conservation rather than innovation. When slow social change is valued and traditional ways are rewarded, the elders are thought to possess superior wisdom, heightening still further their position vis-à-vis the young.

The patriarchal family was not restricted to peasants cultivating the land; it appeared in other preindustrial settings where the whole family group was an economic unit. For example:

> The household of a property-owning family in seventeenth-century England was a complicated economic enterprise that included not only children and relatives but servants, apprentices, and journeymen from different social classes. At its head was the *paterfamilias* who worked alongside his wife, children, employees, and wards. He was solely responsible for the economic and spiritual welfare of his family and represented in his person the supposed unity and independence of the family.[39]

Even during the early stages of industrialism, during the domestic or putting-out system, whole families working in their homes could be part of the manufacturing process:

> Weaving had offered an employment to the whole family, even when spinning was withdrawn from the home. The young children winding bobbins, older children watching for faults, picking over the cloth, or helping to throw the shuttle in the broadloom; adolescents working a second or third loom; the wife taking a turn at weaving in and among her domestic employments.[40]

The Patriarchal Family Idealized

In this book so far we have dealt at length with the familiar idealizations of the nuclear family in our contemporary culture. We have seen in the previous chapter how the nuclear family, in the writings of some students of the family, is presumed to be a harmoniously balanced social system providing for the satisfaction of human needs and societal stability. But the other family systems have also been justified in exactly the same terms. Since the nineteenth century, critiques of the nuclear family have been made from the right and from the left, contrasting the nuclear family with an idealized version of a different family system.

The conservative defense of the patriarchal family was developed by scholars who mourned the passing of the old monarchial regimes based on hereditary status, religion, tradition, and blood ties. They combined a utopian vision of feudal society with an acute insight into the strains of modern industrial ones. In traditional society people knew their duty and their place, and life was stable and cohesive. To these scholars the traditional family seemed to symbolize the principle of "authority without resentment."

For the scholars in this tradition the modern family is a disastrous social form. In fact, the popular cliché that the decline of family life leads to the downfall of civilization orginated with this group of scholars. People who state the cliché today believe they are talking about the nuclear family, but it was the decline of the traditional family that was lamented in the original formulation of the idea. Thus Zimmerman[41] wrote that the decline of patriarchal authority in the Roman family led to the demoralization of society and ultimately the downfall of Rome. Zimmerman argued that familistic values, which dictated that people subordinate their own needs to those of the family, gave way to individualism, leading to the breakdown of morality, authority, and social cohesiveness. Zimmerman thought the same process might be happening in the United States during the twentieth century.

Zimmerman's work was influenced by that of Frederic Le Play, a nineteenth-century French scholar. Like a number of other French scholars of the family and the old regime in France—that is, of France before the French Revolution—Le Play contrasted two extreme forms of the family, the patriarchal and the "unstable" or conjugal family, with an intermediate form, the stem family, which Le Play thought of as ideal. In the patriarchal family, sons and sometimes daughters remain in their parent's home after marriage. When the household grows too large, some members leave to create a new patriarchal unit. Le Play saw the patriarchal family as a more primitive form, and emphasized that most of these families would be found in agriculture.

In the stem family only one heir inherits and lives in the ancestral home and lands. The others are given "dowries" and can become independent, although the ancestral home remains a permanent center for all the members of the family. The direct heir usually inherits the same profession as the father. Le Play thought the stem family "answered all the legitimate instincts of humanity. This is why public order prevails everywhere it exists in strength."[42] The patriarchal system was too limiting, since all

the sons were confined to the father's household and occupation, but Le Play saw it as a sound system nevertheless. But for the "unstable" family he had not a single good word to say.

Le Play saw the "unstable" family prevailing among factory workers as well as among the wealthy classes of France. He noted that the individual under the new family regime could rapidly reach a high social position, because he could dispose freely of his inheritance and his income. He need no longer provide for the needs of relatives. For Le Play, however, mobility and achievement were not particularly attractive values. The detachment from the larger family that made mobility possible also made the "unstable" family vulnerable to disorganization as a result of illness, death, and financial need. People not only could rise but also could rapidly fall into misery and pauperism. Le Play believed that happiness in private life was guaranteed in the stem family, because it balances tradition and novelty, liberty and restraint, individualism and association. As for the individualism of the new family system, Le Play had this to say:

> The advantages which certain people derive from the unlimited extension of individual desires appear greater than they are in reality. Where individualism becomes dominant in social relations, men rapidly move towards barbarism.[43]

Because his values are so contrary to contemporary American ones, it is easier to see how they influence Le Play's analysis than a piece of work whose assumptions come closer to our own. His work serves as a useful model of how ideological biases intertwine with valid description and astute analysis.

Le Play disregarded the strains within the traditional society and family, but his analysis of the weaknesses of the modern family is still valid: its vulnerability to crisis, and its replacement of duty and obligation by individual freedom. Le Play has traditionally been regarded by sociologists as a mere propagandist for reactionary political positions. Yet actually Le Play engaged in field work and made careful observations of families in a large number of European societies. Many of his insights were stated in the form of testable hypotheses about the social conditions associated with each form of the family.[44]

Another idealization of traditional or feudal society may be found in Philippe Aries's *Centuries of Childhood*.[45] Aries describes medieval society as a big, happy, sociable mixture of young and old, rich and poor, from which the middle classes came to withdraw over the centuries of their rise to social power. His glossing over of the social inequalities of the medieval society places Aries in the conservative tradition; class distinctions were sharply marked by dress and manner, but people of different ranks were physically and emotionally close to each other:

> The valet never left his master, whose friend and accomplice he was, in accordance with an emotional code to which we have lost the key today. . . . The haughtiness of the master matched the insolence of the servant and restored, for better or worse, a hierarchy which excessive familiarity was perpetually calling into question.[46]

Although Aries's praise of medieval times and his rejection of modern society and the whole modernizing process—mass education, industrialism, achievement motivation—places him in a conservative camp, the value he places in individualism puts him on the opposite side from such writers as Le Play.

The conservative historians denounced individualism because it opposed the hereditary duties and customs of the traditional family. Aries argues that individualism has triumphed over the family. In his view the increasing power of the intense, tightly knit nuclear family has flourished at the expense of the individual and also has destroyed the richly textured communal society of medieval times.

Strains in the Patriarchal Family

Considerable evidence indicates that the traditional-family system was never as harmonious as its defenders would have us believe. It is interesting to contrast the idealized versions of traditional-family life in Le Play and others with actual studies of peasant families showing the household and inheritance patterns of the patriarchal and stem family. Wherever studies of peasant families have been carried out, one finds the same picture of individual subordination to the demands of the land and to a patriarchal authority structure.[47] As Berkner points out:

> The peasant's entire household may have looked like a big happy family, but it was held together by legal restrictions imposed in the peasant community and by the limited opportunities offered by the rural economy.[48]

Among peasants the father's parental authority is enhanced by his economic roles as manager, owner, and decision maker. The demands of the peasant father for obedience and discipline are strengthened to the extent that the children have no choice as to what they will be or where they will live: they will be farmers or farmers' wives. In short, the traditional peasant family imposes a life of toil and obedience and raises "virtually insurmountable barriers to possible attempts at escape."[49]

The chief source of strain appears to have been in the father-son relationship. For the son the hardest time was when he was full grown, waiting to inherit the farm in order to marry and achieve a man's status. For the father the hardest time was the retirement period, when the farm was transferred to the son during the father's lifetime. Such strains could be deduced from the prevalence of separate living quarters for the retired couple, and of detailed legal contracts setting forth the specific right the father retained after relinquishing the farm to the heir:

> When, for example, Joseph and Anna Maria Pichler decided to retire in October 1784, they drew up a contract with their son Johann and his bride Gertraud, selling them their house and fields for 100 florings. Joseph deducted 20 florings from the price as a wedding gift . . . and asked that the rest be paid in installments of 20 florings every . . . September 29. . . . They reserved the right to live in *Stubl* [retirement room] rent-free for the rest of their lives, the use of a small piece of meadow and a section of garden to grow cabbage and potatoes, and a yearly supply of seven bushels of wheat, thirty-two batches of hay, and two piles of wood.[50]

The prolongation of the lifespan in relatively modern times obviously increased this source of strain:

> The dutiful son mourned the day when his parents passed promptly to their reward . . . . That was as it should be and he inherited their place. But there were no attitudes proper for the situation in which the old people lived on and on while their successor waited impatiently.[51]

Marriage in this system was part of the family business rather than an individual affair of the heart. Stone[52] describes the bitter family struggles in the English nobility that led to the acceptance of the woman's right to a veto over marriages arranged by parents. During the early part of the period, marriages among the nobility were arranged as important business

transactions, without regard to the wishes of the marrying couple. It was common, for example, for small children to be bartered in advance by their families. Stone argues that these practices were supported by an ideology of strict parental control over children. These beliefs in the natural subjugation of children paralleled the political doctrine of the divine right of kings. In addition, noble sons as well as daughters were totally dependent economically on their parents—another instance of similarity between the extreme ends of the social scale. In trying to account for the modification of parent-child relations that resulted in the right of a child to say "no" to the parent's choice of a spouse, Stone refers to the several ideological currents at the time that favored individualism in religion, economics, and politics: the rise of the Protestant ethic, the growth of capitalism, and the growing challenge to the institution of absolute monarchy.

Besides the influence of new ideas, however, transportation affected the social lives of young people. The opening of roads and of a coach service between London and countryside led to the development of a "social season" in London. The nobility from all over England would come together every year for the balls and other events of the season. The increased social contacts resulting from the festivities may have made the old obligation to marry someone picked out by one's parents more objectionable. It was one thing to marry a stranger chosen by father when you didn't know any other young men and women; it was something else to have to do so after having met the entire field of eligible young people during the season.

Today, wherever the process of breaking away from traditional kinship patterns occurs, it tends to go along with the same sense of personal liberation. When a shift toward modernization takes place in underdeveloped countries, the resentments generated by traditional-family systems play an important role in enhancing change. Both modernization and the nuclear family, Goode notes, appeal to intellectuals, to the young, to women, and to the disadvantaged in general:

> . . . The ideology of the conjugal family is a radical one, destructive of the older traditions in almost every society. . . . Its appeal is almost as universal as that of "redistribution of the land." It asserts the equality of individuals, as against class, caste, or sex barriers.[53]

This does not mean, however, that in patriarchal families people constantly chafe under their restrictions. In spite of their built-in strains, these family structures can remain stable for centuries, sustained by duty, law, and lack of other opportunities. Like most revolutions, the revolution in family patterns requires that some alternative vision, some other way of doing things, becomes available or necessary to large numbers of people. Such change can be facilitated by a number of factors—literacy, improved transportation, access to market towns and outside jobs, or a poor harvest or too many sons for the land to support. All these factors promote migration of sons and brothers from the family farm, while illiteracy and isolation perpetuate traditional-family structures.[54]

"Modern" Society, "Modern" Family

We realize that the world we live in and the lives we lead differ from those of the past. Modern Western societies of Europe and America seem to contrast both with their own past and with non-Western societies. Social scientists, including economists and historians as well as sociologists and anthropologists, have been much concerned with describing and analyzing such changes. Societies are often divided into two contrasting types: industrial/preindustrial, modern/traditional, advanced/underdeveloped, complex/simple, urban/folk, literate/preliterate. Each term accents a different aspect of the contrast between two types of society. None of the terms is completely satisfactory to the scholars involved.

We noted earlier that there is widespread agreement among social scientists that great changes occurred in the European world over the past several centuries—changes that affected the rest of the globe as well. It is also agreed that these changes involved all realms of life—political, economic, social, and psychological. Yet there is intense debate about the meaning and usefulness of the term "modernization" to refer to these events.

The term seems least objectionable as a simple description of an historical process. The problem, however, is that the term "modernization" has acquired a host of additional meanings. For example, it has been associated with the idea of "progress," implying that modern societies are necessarily superior to traditional societies. The term "development" has been used as a synonym for modernization, adding evolutionary notions of natural progress to the idea of superiority. In the work of many scholars, "development" is abstracted from European origins and viewed as "an inexorable force" affecting all people in the same way.[55]

Stripped of these additional meanings, however, modernization can be studied as an historical phenomenon like any other.[56] Despite the controversies, the concept of traditional versus modern societies seems a useful one. Traditional societies may not resemble one another, and modernization may or may not have increased the sum total of human well-being, but the concept does point to significant differences between societies. In short, it seems useful to regard a society as traditional if ways of behavior in it continue with little change from one generation to the next. If behavior continues unchanged, certain other characteristics usually occur. Custom, rather than law, tends to regulate behavior. Social relations tend to be hierarchical rather than "democratic," and occupations and social positions are inherited. As Hagen observes, a society could not continue to be traditional unless these conditions prevailed. Finally, it should be noted that although modernized societies are also marked by custom, hierarchy, and the inheritance of social position, "the differences in degree and scope are such that without undue distortion of reality they may be thought of as differences in type."[57]

The preceding cautions should be kept in mind when using the accompanying table (Table 4-1), which summarizes some of the major contrasts that scholars have drawn between the modern and the traditional family. It should be noted that different scholars have emphasized different contrasts. Further, on several of the items, they disagree as to whether traditional and modern families do differ from each other.

The categories in the table represent ideal types—broad patterns rather than firm and certain distinctions. In any particular country, historical period, or social class, however, everything does not change all at once. In general the "modern" family pattern is found more completely and is more widespread in the middle class. Even today some aspects of the traditional pattern occur in families at the extreme ends of the socioeconomic-class scale. Kinship, for example, is more important among American families in the social register and among the poor than it is in middle-class groups. And Japanese society has combined an advanced economy with a traditional patriarchal-family system.

Industrialism and the Family

Despite the possibility of citing major contrasts between the modern and traditional families, scholars still disagree on the essential difference between "modern" and "traditional" social organization as well as the family. Is it the presence of large factories, the growth of cities, widespread literacy, the spread of democratic ideas, the separation of kinship from other aspects of life? Or is it all of these taken together? It is similarly difficult to offer definitive answers to questions about the relation between social change and family life: does family life really change drastically in the transition to modern society? In what aspects is there an underlying stability and continuity? Finally, what aspects of family life do change—household living arrangements, who lives with whom, the quality of emotional relationships, the economic functions of the family, the ideas people have about marriage and family?

One source of confusion in discussions about the family and industrialization is the assumption that in modern societies all families are nuclear, whereas in the past all families were large, extended kin groups. Goode describes as a myth the "classical family of Western nostalgia": the stereotype of a happy life down on the farm, where lots of kinfolk and their children live in a big rambling house.[58] Recent work by historians has shown that the nuclear-family form predominated in Western Europe and America long before the coming of industrialism.

Another misleading assumption, found not only among laymen but also among family scholars, is the belief that the coming of factories destroyed the large kin group down on the farm. The correlation between industrial society and the nuclear family is often interpreted, in an overly literal and simplistic way, to mean that the nuclear family comes about *only* in an industrial society, and that the presence of

TABLE 4-1   "TRADITIONALISM" VS. "MODERNISM" IN FAMILY FORM, FUNCTION, AND IDEOLOGY

"Traditionalism"	"Modernism"
1 Kinship is organized principle of society; almost everything a person does is done as a member of a kinship group..	Kinship is differentiated from economic, political, and social life; recruitment to jobs is independent of one's relatives.
2 Sons inherit father's status and occupation.	Individual mobility based on "merit."
3 Low geographic and social mobility.	High geographic and social mobility.
4 The extended or complex family may be basic unit of residence and domestic functions—e.g., meals and child care.	Conjugal or nuclear family is basic unit of residence and domestic functions.
5 Most adults work at home; the home is workshop as well as school, hospital, old-age home.	Separation of home and work; household consumes rather than produces.
6 Dominance of parents over children, men over women.	Relatively egalitarian relations within nuclear family in ideals and practice.
7 Kinship bonds override economic efficiency and maximization of individual gain.	Advancement and economic gain of individuals prevails over kin obligations.
8 Ideology of duty, tradition, individual submission to authority and to fate.	Ideology of individual rights, equality, freedom, self-realization.
9 Little emphasis on emotional involvement within nuclear family; marriage not based on love; predominant loyalty of individual is to blood kin, rather than spouse; children are economic rather than emotional assets, but subordination and dependency of children on parents may continue as long as parent lives—in Europe parent-child bonds may be reduced further by practice of apprenticing children to other families at an early age.	Intense involvement of spouses, parents, and children with each other; ideologies of marital happiness and adjustment; great concern with child's development, current adjustment, and future potential, but sharp break with parental authority upon attaining adulthood.
10 Little or no psychological separation between home and community; broad communal sociability; no large-scale institutions.	Sharp line of demarcation between home and outside world; home is a private retreat and outside world is impersonal, competitive, threatening.
11 High fertility and high death rates, especially in infancy; rapid population turnover—death a constant presence in families.	Low, controlled fertility and low death rates, especially low in infancy; death a phenomenon of old age.

factories leads in some inexorable way to the breakup of large kin groups. Often studies use literal models of industrialism to attack the idea that technological change leads to family change: thus, for example, a study might be done in country X to show that large industry moved in and did not at once destroy all existing kin ties. Or a study might attempt to show that working in factories did not destroy the kin ties of a group of nineteenth-century immigrants to America who came with extended-family structures. Or a study might argue that the nuclear

"Modern" Society, "Modern" Family

family existed in Europe and America before industrialization, therefore technology does not cause family change.

The problem with such studies is that they attack straw men: simplistic and mechanical versions of the relation between economic and family change. The presence of large factories is only one of a number of factors that set off a modern or advanced society from a more traditional one. "Industrialism" is a convenient metaphor, a shorthand reference to a host of social changes that occur when a society modernizes: cities grow in size and importance; population size and density increase; demands arise for literacy and other trained skills; communication and transportation systems improve; and the rate of social change increases. Each of these changes by itself could have profound effects on family life. Yet the term may be misleading in its emphasis on factories as the essential ingredient of modern life and the most important factor in family change.

Indeed, some scholars have argued that industrialization is not even an essential part of modernization. The historian E. A. Wrigley,[59] for example, argues that a society might become modernized before becoming industrialized, and that this in fact occurred in Europe beginning in the sixteenth century. The essence of modernization in this view is the existence of commerce and trade, a money economy, and the values of economic self-interest and rationality—rationality being defined in a narrow sense as "that which maximizes economic returns either to the individual, the nuclear family, or the state," as opposed to the larger kin group.[60] Such rationality also implies that people are recruited to jobs on the basis of ability rather than hereditary status. Once kinship is no longer the basis of economic life, social, occupational, and geographic mobility tend to increase. All these changes together weaken kinship bonds by making them less necessary and less enforceable.

Individualism and the Family

The economic and psychological separation of individuals and the nuclear family from the larger kin group can occur in preindustrial or primitive societies as well as modern and industrial ones. Thus, in a survey of 250 societies, Murdock notes that the development of the nuclear (neolocal) family is favored by any influence that emphasizes the individual:

> Individualism in its various manifestations, e.g., private property, individual enterprise in the economic sphere, or personal freedom in the choice of marital partners, facilitates the establishment of independent households by married couples. A similar effect may be produced by individual migration, or by pioneer life in the occupation of new territory, or by the expansion of trade and industry, or by developing urbanization. . . . Even a change in architecture might exert an influence, e.g., the supplanting of a large communal house by a form of dwelling suited to the occupancy of a single family.[61]

Another seemingly paradoxical finding about the nuclear family is that it appears in the most advanced, modern countries as well as in the most technologically simple. That is, the nuclear family appears as the dominant form in hunting societies such as the Eskimo, the extended family predominates in agricultural societies, then the nuclear family reappears in modern conditions. In other words, if all known societies were listed in the order of their complexity along the horizontal part of a graph and family type plotted on the vertical part of the scale, the relationship between societal development or complexity and family form would be curvilinear, as indicated in the accompanying graph. Why should this be so?

To answer this question, Nimkoff and Middleton examined more than five hundred societies for which detailed ethnographic infor-

This chart indicates that the percent of societies with extended-family households reaches highest in agricultural societies.[62]

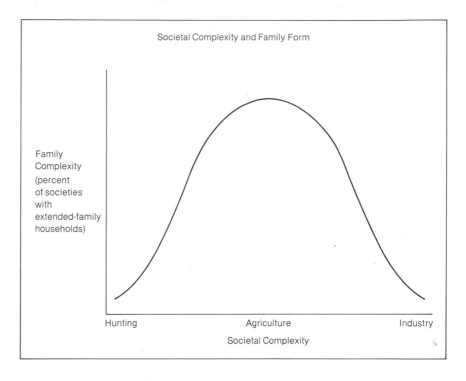

Societal Complexity and Family Form

Family Complexity (percent of societies with extended-family households)

Hunting   Agriculture   Industry

Societal Complexity

mation existed. They concluded that modern industrial societies in some important ways resemble simpler hunting-and-gathering societies. Both hunting and modern societies tend to individualize the worker.

The modern industrial society, with its small independent family, is then like the simpler hunting and gathering society . . . for some of the same reasons, namely limited need for family labor and physical mobility. The hunter is mobile because he pursues the game, the industrial worker, the job.[63]

The variables associated with the appearance of the extended family were the reverse of the foregoing ones: an ample and stable food supply, the use of the family as the unit of labor, geographic immobility, and family-owned property, especially in the form of land. Payment in money also has individualizing effects. In peas-

ant societies labor tends to be unpaid family labor. Property in the form of money rather than family-owned land or durable goods also favors the nuclear family over the extended family.

Winch and Blumberg[64] found some striking parallels between Nimkoff and Middleton's variables and the correlates of extended families in American society today. That is, geographic mobility, family property, and the family as a unit of labor also account for variations in the extent to which American families are involved with extended kin. Winch and Blumberg also found that certain ethnic groups in American society, particularly Jews and Italians, tended to have stronger extended-family ties than others; they account for these differences in terms of length of time since immigration, social class, and occupational traditions. Thus the closer a group is to its immigrant roots, the stronger the

---

"Modern" Society, "Modern" Family

extended-family ties. Also certain occupations such as storekeeping tend to encourage the maintenance of extended-family ties. In short, family patterns vary within industrial societies, and this variation can be explained in much the same terms as variation in family form among different kinds of societies.

The work of Winch and Blumberg also sheds light on the relationship between industrialism and the nuclear family. When they arranged 933 industrial societies in order of their complexity, they found that the nuclear family began to emerge *before* industrialism. In other words, the curve of extended familism took a downward turn in societies that were still mainly agricultural but complex, as indicated by their having irrigation, towns with more than five thousand people, and three or more levels of political hierarchy. These are indicators of societal complexity because they are complicated kinds of social organization, requiring specialized skills. They also show that the society is producing enough food to release some people from agriculture. These cross-cultural findings parallel the historical findings that the nuclear family emerged in Europe before the industrial revolution.

Economic Change, Ideology, and Private Life

In discussions of family change, the issue is sometimes posed in an either/or fashion, either technological change "causes" family change independent of people's wishes and feelings, or family values and ideologies are completely independent of economic factors. Such discussions also overlook the fact that modernization changes individuals as well as families. It is more useful to think of individual, family, and social change as a complex interplay of several sets of factors.

Scholars have pointed above all to individualism and a certain kind of individualistic rationality when trying to define the essential difference between modern and traditional societies. As Wrigley[65] puts it, it is not that traditional societies are irrational, but they define rationality differently. Traditional rationality may mean working only enough to supply one's minimal wants, or it may mean staying together in large kin groups even though the family lands can scarcely support everyone. In modern Western terms, however, rationality has come to mean maximizing economic gain. Wrigley argues that, once begun, modernization sets off a chain reaction of psychological effects that further increase the momentum of change; rationality and individualism "eat like acid" into the fabric of traditional society, destroying the web of rights and obligations as well as the structure of traditional authority.

But individualism has other meanings in addition to the economic one. It involves a heightened awareness of the self as a separate, unique individual. A person living in an unchanging, traditional social world, where there are no alternatives to the influence of family and community, can take that world for granted and live with a minimum of self-awareness. The individual is embedded in the family, just as the family is embedded in the community. From the very beginning, however, the rise of capitalism in the West was associated with a heightened self-awarness:

> Christianity has always encouraged a certain degree of self-consciousness in the form of the conscience .. . . But Puritans and other Protestants viewed social behavior as a sign of inward grace and argued that no church ritual or other outward act could determine for certain whether an individual was "saved." One indication of the expansion of self-consciousness was the proliferation of diaries in the

seventeenth century. More broadly, the same period saw the invention of silvered mirrors, the spread of autobiography, the building of chairs instead of benches, the spread of private lodgings, and the rise of self-portraits. In this period sincerity became a dominant social ideal.[66]

The coming of large-scale industry, bureaucratic organizations, and, above all, the separation of work from family life caused by these developments resulted in further increases in the sense of the separateness of the self. The awareness of discrepancy between our inner selves and the roles we are playing in work and public life creates the need for intimate relationships—a private world where we can express our real and whole selves. Thus the family comes to have a whole new set of demands placed on it in advanced industrial societies. Whether the family can in fact meet these demands is a theme we shall be pursuing throughout this book.

Literacy

Another major individualizing force in modern life is the widespread ability to read. Some scholars have suggested that the spread of literacy is the most meaningful feature of modernization, antedating industrial development.[67] For example, Parsons considers the invention of writing the dividing line between primitive and intermediate societies, and the extension of literacy from elite groups to the whole population a major distinguishing feature of modern societies. The growth of commerce and industry would be almost unthinkable without the existence of written records, bookkeeping, and accounting systems.

Though literacy spreads because of economic need, it has profound psychological consequences. Literacy fosters the same tendencies

toward rationality and individualism that are encouraged by the economic aspects of modernization. Preliterate people are not unsophisticated, simple, or at a lower stage of intellect; rather, they are skilled in a different medium of communication—the oral tradition. Using human memory capacities that remain undeveloped where literacy prevails, people who live entirely in the oral tradition can store enormous amounts of information, experience, and entertainment, and they can reproduce this information with astonishing accuracy.

Literacy is a decisive dividing line in individual development also. There is by now an impressive body of research evidence showing that many psychological changes once thought to represent the unfolding of the innate capacities of the human mind may actually be the result of literacy.[68] Such skills as the capacity for abstract thought and the ability to make logical inferences, for example, now appear to develop from the outside in rather than the inside out. Or, as Jerome Bruner[69] puts it, cognitive development may be to a large degree the internalization of technology. David Riesman[70] has summarized some of the consequences of the transition from the oral tradition to literacy. Writing tends to foster hierarchies of skill rather than age. In the oral tradition the status of the old is enhanced by their role as storehouses of experience and lore.

Another effect of literacy is to individualize the person, separating him or her from the primary group of family and kinspeople and the world of immediate experience. Books permit detachment and a critical attitude. Just as the ability to write improves the conversation one carries on with oneself, so the ability to read makes it possible to "converse" with people in distant times and places. Reading a book in the presence of others is an isolating act. We noted earlier the finding that geographic and social mobility is associated with the breakdown of extended-kinship relations. Riesman has emphasized that reading is the mental equivalent of mobility—you can leave home in your imagination:

> Thus the book helps liberate the reader from his group and its emotions, and allows the contemplation of alternative responses and the trying on of new emotions. . . .
>
> At the same time, while the book helped people break away from family and parish, it

linked them into noncontiguous associations of true believers. The Polish peasant who learned to read and write became identified with the urban world of progress and enlightenment, of ideology and Utopia, even while still in the peasant world. [71]

If literacy is used as an indicator of modernity, Western Europe began to change centuries before the first factories appeared on the scene. The growth of cities, trade, and, perhaps

Modern families don't usually work together, but they often play together.

Social Change and the Intimate Environment

above all, the growth of empire during the age of exploration accelerated demand for people who could read and write. A recent study by the economic historian Carlo M. Cipolla[72] traces the beginnings of the literacy revolution in Western Europe to the eleventh century.

The spread of literacy was accompanied by three different interpretations of its significance. Some saw it merely as a skill necessary to run the economy. Others saw it as a means of opening many minds to the benefits of civilization. Still others saw the spread of literacy as a subversive threat to the stability of the social order. Two arguments were used against the extension of literacy to the poor: first, that it would make people despise the place in life that they had been born to; and second, that they would read seditious books and pamphlets that would "render them insolent to their superiors; and in a few years the result would be that the legislature would find it necessary to direct the strong arm of power towards them."[73] All these predictions came true. Education did encourage peasants to leave the fields, seditious books and pamphlets were written and read, and they did play a role in the French and American revolutions. In general, literacy fostered the same tendencies toward rationality and individualism that are also promoted by the economic and political aspects of modernization.

Psychological Quality of the Intimate Environment

We are now in a position to answer the question posed at the beginning of this chapter. What is it that sets the modern family off from its historical counterparts? We have seen that the classical family of Western nostalgia—the large household bursting with kin—is largely a myth. In America and Western Europe the nuclear family was the prevailing unit, although peasant families were extended during part of the life cycle, and the household often contained nonkinsmen in the form of peasants and servants. How then was family life different in the past?

The answer, now emerging in the work of a number of scholars, lies in the psychological and emotional aspects of family life, not household structure. What seems to have changed is the psychological quality of the intimate environments of family life, and the relation between the family and the larger community. Within the home the family has become more intense emotionally, while the ties between home and the outside community have become more tenuous.

In the past the line of demarcation between the family and the outside world was not as marked as in our time. Edward Shorter, in his book, *The Making of the Modern Family,*[74] compares the family in traditional society to a ship moored in a harbor:

. . . the family . . . was held firmly in the matrix of a larger social order. One set of ties bound it to the surrounding kin . . . who dotted the regime's social landscape. Another set fastened it to the wider community, and gaping holes in the shield of privacy permitted others to enter the household freely and, if necessary, preserve order. A final set of ties bound this elementary family to generations past and future. Awareness of ancestral traditions and ways of doing business would be present in people's minds as they went about their day. Because they knew that the purpose of life was preparing coming generations to do as past ones had done, they would have clear rules for shaping behavior within the family. . . .[75]

The modern family has broken these ties to the surrounding community and the chain of generations. The home has become a private retreat, and ties to family members within the home have intensified as ties to outsiders have weakened. Above all, it is domesticity—"the family's awareness of itself as a precious emotional unit that must be protected with privacy and isolation from outside intrusion"[76]—that distinguishes the modern family.

Other writers emphasize changes in the social landscape as a cause of the family's withdrawal. Industrialization did not create the nuclear-family structure in Europe, but it did change the quality of family life. It destroyed, as Laslett[77] puts it, the "familial texture" of society; the removal of economic functions from the patriarchal family created the mass society. The transformation of the world outside the home from a small community into a place of impersonal, large-scale institutions transformed the home itself and the family. There began to be a sense of a gulf between the home and the society at large; each came to be perceived as a separate sphere of life. The home came to be idealized as an "Edenic retreat" from the harsh realities of nineteenth-century industrial soci-

ety, a place of perfect love, companionship, and moral regeneration.[78] Demos describes the kind of gulf that separates the modern American family from society, in contrast to continuity between family and community in colonial times:

> . . . The family becomes a kind of shrine for upholding and exemplifying all of the softer virtues—love, generosity, tenderness, altruism, harmony, repose. The world at large presents a much more sinister aspect. Impersonal, chaotic, unpredictable, often characterized by strife and sometimes by outright malignity, it requires of a man that he be constantly "on his guard."[79]

In the next chapter we explore some of the issues scholars have raised concerning the paradoxical place of the family in modern society: as it has lost its economic functions, it has come to loom larger psychologically.

Summary

In recent years scholars have become increasingly interested in family change. Rather than considering the family as essentially "the same" everywhere, they have been looking at how broader aspects of society affect family life. The relationship between the family, technological change in general, and industrialism in particular has been the subject of much confusion and debate. Rather than being a product solely of modern society, however, the nuclear family emerges whenever the individual is set off from the large family group. Thus hunting societies also have the nuclear family. Furthermore, in Western societies the nuclear-family structure appeared before the industrial revolution of the nineteenth century. It emerged in early modern times when towns grew in size and number, trade and handicrafts increased in importance, a monetary economy replaced barter, and literacy spread, along with other indicators of societal complexity. In short, the nuclear-family structure in Europe seems to have emerged in the context of mercantile, rather than industrial, capitalism. Industrial capitalism, however, altered the quality of family life by separating the workshop from the hearth and the family from society, leading to the enhancement of the psychological over the social and economic functions of the family.

Source Notes

1. Wallerstein, 1974, p. 3.
2. Goode, 1964, p. 105.
3. Hareven, 1971.
4. Greven, 1970.
5. Ibid., pp. 16-17.
6. Demos, 1970
7. Fogel and Engerman, 1976; Gutman, 1976.
8. Demos, 1972, p. 562.
9. Harris, 1968.
10. Morgan, 1870, 1877.
11. Harris, 1968, p. 186.
12. Ibid.
13. Ibid., p. 187.
14. Ibid.
15. Alland, 1967.
16. Blumberg and Winch, 1972.
17. Lee and DeVore, 1968, p. 3.
18. Gough, 1971.
19. Ibid., p. 765.
20. Ibid.
21. Ibid.
22. Stephens, 1963.
23. Sahlins, 1968.
24. Turnbull, 1971, pp. 128-129.
25. Barry, Child, and Bacon, 1959.
26. Gough, 1971.
27. Blumberg and Winch, 1972; Winch and Blumberg, 1968.
28. Hawkes, 1963, p. 354.
29. Stephens, 1963, p. 324.
30. Arensberg and Kimball, 1968.
31. Ibid., pp. 53-55.
32. Ibid., p. 48.
33. Negrea, 1936, p. 45.
34. Cernea, 1970, p. 55.
35. LeVine, 1965, pp. 200-204.
36. Lewis, 1951, pp. 322-338.
37. Stephens, 1963, p. 329.
38. Cernea, 1970.
39. Zaretsky, 1973, p. 39.
40. Thompson, 1963, p. 306.
41. Zimmerman, 1947.
42. Le Play, 1935 (originally 1866), in Farber, 1966, p. 20.
43. Ibid., p. 14.
44. Parish and Schwartz, 1972.
45. Aries, 1962.
46. Ibid., p. 414.
47. Maspetiol, in Cernea, 1970.
48. Berkner, 1972, p. 418.
49. Cernea, 1970, p. 55.
50. Berkner, 1972, p. 401.
51. Handlin and Handlin, 1971, p. 8.
52. Stone, 1960.
53. Goode, 1963, p. 19.
54. Parish and Schwartz, 1972.
55. Lasch, 1975, p. 37.
56. Berger et al., 1973, p. 4.
57. Hagen, 1962, p. 56.
58. Goode, 1963, p. 6.
59. Wrigley, 1972.
60. Ibid., p. 229
61. Murdock, 1949, pp. 203-204.
62. After Blumberg and Winch, 1972.
63. Nimkoff and Middleton, 1960, p. 225.
64. Winch and Blumberg, 1968.
65. Wrigley, 1972.
66. Zaretsky, 1973, p. 43.
67. Goody and Watt, 1962; Parsons, 1965.
68. LeVine, 1970, p. 585.
69. Bruner, 1964.
70. Riesman, 1960.
71. Ibid., p. 113.
72. Cipolla, 1969.
73. Ibid., pp. 65-66.
74. Shorter, 1975.
75. Ibid., p. 3.
76. Ibid., p. 205.
77. P. Laslett, 1965.
78. Jeffrey, 1972.
79. Demos, 1970, p. 186.

Chapter Five
Families in Modern Society

☐ *The word alienation is part of the cant of the mid-twentieth century and it began as an attempt to describe the separation of the worker from his world of work. We need not accept all that this expression has come to convey in order to recognize that it does point to something vital to us all in relation to our past. Time was when the whole of life went forward in the family, in a circle of loved, familiar faces, known and fondled objects, all to human size. That time has gone forever. It makes us very different from our ancestors.*

Peter Laslett, *The World We Have Lost*

Around the turn of the century it was a sociological truism that the coming of the urban industrial society was causing the family to lose its functions and wither away. Not just the extended group but the nuclear family as well was included in predictions of decline.

The ideas of such scholars were paralleled in the arguments of feminists of the period, but with a different emphasis. Whereas the scholars regretted or had mixed feelings about the passing home and family, the feminists applauded it:

> The family, they thought, once the most important unit of production, had gradually surrendered its functions to institutions outside the home—manufacturing to the factory, control over property to the state, the education of children to the public schools. . . . The tasks formerly performed by the housewife and the family in general were now performed elsewhere, and the function of the housewife in consequence was reduced to the passive role of consumption. The feminists did not regret the passing of the family; on the contrary, as staunch evolutionists, they regarded it as highly desirable. . . . [1]

In 1903 Charlotte Perkins Gilman saw in the kindergarten and the day nursery the liberation of both women and children:

> There is no more brilliant hope on earth today than this new thought about the child . . . children as citizens with rights guaranteed by the state; instead of our previous attitude towards them of absolute personal ownership—the unchecked tyranny, or as unchecked indulgence, of the private home. [2]

During the period under discussion the issues raised by the feminists preoccupied the leading intellectuals as well as the pages of the women's magazines, just as today. Yet during the fifty-year eclipse of the feminist movement, the idea that the demise of the family was a mark of progress passed from popular consciousness, remaining alive only on the fringes of society in bohemian and socialist groups.

Assessing the Family in Modern Society

Until very recently, much social-science literature on the family in modern society was written as an attack on scholars who had predicted the death of the family as a result of urban industrialism. Unlike the feminists, the social scientists who believed the family would wither away were not happy about the prospect. Some of these writers, most notably Le Play and Zimmerman, argued that "civilization" itself was threatened by the breakup of traditional paternalistic authority. They felt that the conjugal family, which Le Play called "the unstable family" and Zimmerman called "atomistic," was only a way station on the road to the total collapse of family life and civilization. Once individualism replaced tradition and filial duty as the ruling principle of life, people would ultimately reject the burdens of family responsibility.

Another group of writers—notably Louis Wirth and Ralph Linton—agreed that urban-industrial society presaged the demise of the family, but they did not go along with the idea that the quality of civilization would also decline. Wirth acknowledged that city life was accompanied by a more impersonal and superficial level of human relations, but he also credited the city with the production of cosmopolitan tastes and sophisticated ideas.

All these writers recognized that "modernization" and urbanization introduced profound transformations in the culture and personality.

In traditional societies, although there are many differences among them, ways of behavior continue with little change from one generation to the next. Individual attitudes and behavior are shaped by norms and customs governing familial obligations. Persons of a particular age, sex, and family status are supposed to behave in prescribed ways toward others occupying particular sex, age, and kinship categories. The individual's position in the society is inherited rather than achieved, and he or she usually has little say in the choice of a marriage partner. In any event, marriages are not based on "love."[3]

Although, as we've noted earlier, there are debates about the concept of modernization and its applicability to non-Western societies, there seems little doubt that an industrialized economy—and all that it implies for education, the mass media, urbanization, and so on—tends to undermine the traditional pattern of customary kinship practices, patriarchal authority, and inherited status. In Western societies, the modern emphasis on the conjugal family and marriage for love has been accompanied by an ideology of individualism and personal freedom. In socialist countries such as the U.S.S.R. and China, however, the values of equality and the subordination of the individual to the state community have also undermined traditional family obligations.

Parsons' Assessments

Despite these changes, many sociologists have argued that the family remains as important as ever in modern society. For example, Parsons and his associates agreed that the traditional family, linked by economic and residential rights and obligations as well as kinship bonds, was undone by industrial society. But, in contrast to earlier writers, Parsons argued that an industrial society still requires a stable family system to socialize children and to maintain the psychological balance of the men who face the pressures of competition in their work life.

As evidence for the separation of the nuclear family from kinship groups, Parsons

People of various ages working together in China.

Assessing the Family in Modern Society

pointed to the rise in jobs not based on kinship and the decline in family-operated economic units such as farms, small retail shops, and the like. Further, he pointed out that households were increasingly limited to nuclear-family members. In 1960, for example, 82.7 percent of the total population of the United States lived in nuclear-family households (husband, wife, and children), while the proportion of household members who were other kinds of relatives declined to 5.5 percent.[4] Parsons also noted the strong preference for the single-family house as a family residence in America.

He found further support for the importance of the nuclear family in the high rates of marriage and remarriage after divorce, the drop in the average age of marriage, and the increase in the birth rate during the postwar era—the time of Parsons' major statements on the nuclear family. Thus, Parsons argues, rather than having lost its importance, the nuclear family under industrialism is more vital than ever, in both senses of the word. It has become specialized, as part of the general process of social change.

Parsons and his followers argued that the relative isolation of the nuclear family from the kinship group, and its loss of functions, made the family *more* rather than *less* important:

> . . . The family has become a *more specialized agency* than before, probably more specialized than in any previously known society. This represents a decline of *certain* features which have traditionally been associated with families, but whether it represents a ''decline of the family'' in a more general sense is another matter. . . . The family is more specialized than before, but not in any general sense less important, because the society is dependent *more* exclusively on it for the performance of *certain* of its vital functions.[5]

Parsons emphasizes the home as a place to escape from the pressures of work. It is the only place in urban-industrial society where a person can find love and trust—the only place, that is, where a person can find affection and acceptance for the self, apart from particular achievements and accomplishments. The family remains the only dependable primary group in modern society—that is, a group involving regular, face-to-face contact over a long period of time in a mood of intimacy and informality.

Parsons' Critics

Many criticisms can and have been made of Parsons' analysis, and some have been mentioned earlier in this book. He tends to disregard the diversity of family life and to concentrate on the "normal American family" as a middle-class urban couple with young children and reduced kin ties; the husband plays an "instrumental" role as the breadwinner, and the wife follows an "expressive" domestic role. Deviation from these patterns implies social disorganization, or personal psychopathology, rather than an alternative life style.

Parsons also confounds the meaning of the term "function"; for example, he asserts that the two functions of the nuclear family—the socialization of children and the psychological security of adults—are more important than ever, because now the nuclear family is the only place where such nurturing can be found. In this statement Parsons uses the term "function" to refer to both a need and the fulfillment of the need. He assumes that if a social need exists, it must be satisfied. This assumption flows from the general concept of Parsons and many other sociologists that societies are neatly organized and balanced social systems.

As noted in a previous chapter, however, not all sociologists hold to such a utopian model of social systems. Any society can give rise to contradictory functional requirements. Thus, although Parsons has offered a convincing explanation of why the family is desperately needed in modern society, he is overly optimistic about the ease with which the "psychological gold" of warmth and affection can be created, stored, and circulated in an urban-industrial society. (Parsons actually uses money as a metaphor for solidarity.) His argument overlooks the possibility that the same social changes generating the need for a stable and secure family life may also undermine society's capacity to fulfill the need.

Parsons' writing on the nuclear family gave rise to a wave of critical articles, but few of Parsons' critics dealt with the psychological aspects of modern family life. They focused their attack on the assumed isolation of the nuclear family. The critics opposed both Parsons and the earlier writers who had predicted the decline and fall of the extended family, and they asserted that kinship groups remained alive and well in urban and industrial settings. Thus, the argument went, people are not isolated from their kin groups: people visit their relatives, speak to them on the telephone, write letters, exchange Christmas cards, celebrate happy occasions, and help in emergencies. What's more, the argument goes, parents often help their married children, and children help support their aged parents.

The debate between Parsons and his critics has passed into the literature as a victory for the critics. For example, many reviews in textbooks agree with the verdict of Sussman, one the leading critics of Parsons:

> The isolated nuclear family is a myth. This has already been conclusively demonstrated. It does not merit any further attention of the field, and I for one refuse to waste any more time even discussing it.[6]

Instead of the isolated nuclear family as the typical family structure of modern societies, the critics offered such concepts as the "modified extended family" and the kin network.

Criticizing Parsons' Critics

An understanding of the debate between Parsons and his critics on the issue of the isolated nuclear family is basic to any analysis of the role of the family in contemporary society. If the critics are correct that the isolated nuclear family is a myth, it is obviously foolish to ascribe contemporary family problems to a nonexistent family structure. Still, despite widespread agreement that the critics won the debate with Parsons, their own arguments are riddled with conceptual and methodological flaws. A fairly mild critique of the nuclear-family critics was offered by B. N. Adams,[7] and a more devastating one has been published by Gibson.[8]

First, the critics create a straw man by making Parsons appear more extreme than he actually was. Parsons did not insist that the isolated nuclear family never saw any of its relatives. Indeed, as Parsons himself pointed out, his emphasis on the psychological importance of parent-child relations would suggest that people would not be likely to break off completely from their parents when they marry. It is worthwhile to look at Parsons' original statement about the isolation of the contemporary nuclear family:

> This "isolation" is manifested in the fact that the members of the nuclear family, consisting of the parents and their still dependent children, ordinarily occupy a separate dwelling not shared with members of the family of orientation (parents) of either spouse, and this household is in the typical case economically independent, subsisting in the first instance from the occupational earnings of the husband-father. It is of course not uncommon to find a surviving parent of one or the other spouse, or even a sibling or cousin of one of them, residing with the family, but this is both statistically secondary and it is clearly not felt to be the "normal" arrangement.

Of course, with the independence, particularly the marriage, of children, relations to the family of orientation are by no means broken. But a separate residence, very often in a different geographical community, and separate economic support, attenuate these relations . . . .

. . . A particularly significant aspect of the isolation of the nuclear family in our society is again the sharp discrimination . . . which it emphasizes between family members and nonmembers . . . .[9]

Obviously, then, Parsons was not talking about "isolation" in the sense of no social interaction, but rather about such structural issues as living in separate households—often in a different community from one's parents—about being economically independent, and about being emotionally as well as ideologically more focused on one's parents and blood relatives. One problem of Parsons' analysis, however, is that the isolated nuclear family is presented as a type, an either/or matter, rather than as a continuum along which different families can be arranged.

Yet the problem of many of his critics is similar: they also approached the issue in an either/or fashion. Asserting that Parsons had said there was no kin interaction at all among married couples, the critics point to family visiting and helping in times of need as evidence that the typical city dweller in modern society lives in close-knit kin networks. Gibson, however, points out that these critics often use "absurdly low levels" of interaction between members of different households to show that the nuclear family isn't isolated,[10] and they have overestimated their own statistics. Their assertions that kin networks play a major role in urban society show more enthusiasm than accuracy. For example, data showing that people turn *more* to banks than to relatives in times of financial need and *more* to clergymen and doctors in times of trouble, get *more* from friends and neighbors during illness, and so on, are interpreted as showing the strength of kinship ties in contemporary society!

Some writers, such as Litwak[11] and Sussman,[12] argue that the basic family system of the United States is "the modified extended family," consisting of coalitions of nuclear families; yet they never specify precisely what it takes for a group of families to become such a coalition. How much interaction or exchange of services is needed? What are the boundaries of such systems? Such questions are not answered by the proponents of the "modified extended family" notion. As Gibson states:

Unlike the classical extended structure, or the isolated nuclear family, for which clear identifying characteristics may be developed (i.e., household composition), the modified extended family is not clearly defined for either conceptual or research purposes. If the case is to be made of the primacy of kin relations over non-kin relations, much clearer definitions need to be provided. . . . It is hard to avoid the conclusion that the concept of the modified extended family is intended more as an ideological device to refute Parsons than as a meaningful research tool to describe reality.[13]

Whether or not the "modified extended family" exists as a reality, it is important only if it fosters a "radically different set of emotional arrangements" from those created by a more isolated nuclear family—for example, if it is associated with different child-rearing arrangements, such as multiple mothering, or with a diluted husband-wife relationship.[14] Yet the proponents of the concept do not make this claim. And, paradoxically, by applying the concept of "the modified extended family" to the society as a whole, they overlook those class and ethnic situations where extended-family

Peasant family life is embedded in the community.

structures do actually create a radically different set of emotional arrangements—such as the kin networks in poor black communities.

Even if the "modified extended family" does not alter relationships with the nuclear family, it would still be significant if it could be shown to have the same functions as kin and community groups in traditional society. But nobody argues that kinship plays the same role in modern society as it did in the past. Parsons and the earlier writers who saw a withering away of the family were not discussing family interaction such as visits so much as the role of kinship in the larger society. In comparison to other societies, relations between adult relatives in industrial society are peripheral to the functioning of the total society. That relations with all relatives, even close ones, are largely optional and voluntary places kin relations in industrial society on an entirely different plane from the obligatory roles found in traditional society.

Unlike kin relations in traditional societies, those in industrial society are not clearly prescribed. No strict rules dictate how often you should see your mother's brother or your father's sister's son, how you should act in his presence, or what precisely your mutual obligations are to each other. Rather, kinship in America and other industrial societies is much like friendship—people often interact with their relatives according to how they feel about them. Goode[15] calls such kin relations "ascriptive friendship."

Nor can we look to modern kin relations as the replacement for the intense community life that enmeshed families in previous eras. Although it is tempting, observes Edward Shorter, to regard the kin network, with its seemingly enhanced importance in the contemporary world, as a replacement for the web of community relations, the temptation should be avoided:

> As often as people nowadays see their kin, the intensity of such contact bears no resemblance to the intensity of sociability in traditional times. In terms of viewing oneself as part of a larger social unit, no number of visits with Mom and Dad will add up to the annual cycle of Carnival, Easter, St. John's Day, the harvest home, and so forth. . . . So, quantitatively, one would have to live with one's kin—and a wide circle of relatives at that—to get anything like the frequency of interaction achieved in village society.
>
> Qualitatively, kin contacts are no replacement for community contacts either. . . . Kinfolk today extend and complement the conjugal family's egotistical emotional structure. They don't rival it, or threaten to break it down. So despite the phoenix-like rise of the kin network from the ashes of village society, the nuclear family of the modern world remains in physical and spiritual isolation.[16]

Households as Intimate Environments

The key symbol of the "physical and spiritual isolation" of the modern nuclear family is the single-family home. In a previous chapter we noted the confusions about the universality of the nuclear family that resulted from failing to distinguish between kinship, living together, and domestic functions such as child care. Households do not always consist of family members, and family members do not always live together. Stephens,[17] for example, notes that one of the problems with the idea of the universal nuclear family is that, in many societies, husbands and wives do not live together, and it is also common for children to live with someone other than their own parents.

The advocates of the "modified extended family" fail to make crucial distinctions between degrees of interaction. They do not distinguish exchanging cards and telephone calls from face-to-face interaction, nor do they consider the significance of different amounts of interaction—daily, weekly, monthly. Above all they fail to take into account the differences between domestic functions and visiting. This is also the reason why it is important to know about who lives with whom—households are intimacy-producing environments.

Household structures are important in two senses. First, knowing about the typical household structure in a society tells us something about the kinds of relationships and experiences that a society encourages. For example, Bohannan[18] argues that the kind of houses people build, or would like to build, is an excellent indicator of the particular relationship emphasized in a kinship system. Mother-daughter, father-son, and husband-wife are the three relationships around which households most often are built. In the second sense, the household is the basic intimate environment in every society, and the process of living together, rather than the facts of kinship or marriage bonds, produces intimacy. Parsons observed that there is a

> central complex of privacy that seems to exist everywhere which consists of the sharing of "residence" in the sense of premises of daily living, perhaps above all sleeping, and . . . the privilege of eating in company with others. . . . Similarly, lines are drawn between clothing appropriate for public contexts and dress appropriate only to intimate occasions and company.[19]

An element of eroticism always exists in intimate environments, but the eroticism is neither the central feature nor the basis of intimacy. We tend to exaggerate the erotic aspects of intimacy because our own household structures are most often based on sexual relationships. When the household is built around the husband-wife bond, however, the eroticism of that relationship seems to intensify the intimacy already generated in any household through the mere fact of living together. Slater[20] has analyzed the tendencies to "dyadic" withdrawal when two people are deeply attached to each other; he includes mother-child relationships as also subject to dyadic withdrawal. Thus the nuclear-family household is more likely to withdraw from other relationships than any other kind of household structure. Gibson[21] reports data showing that nuclear-family households are more isolated from kin in comparison with other types of households—for example, those with single people and/or extended families.

It is a mistake to think that the intimacy of the household results only from deep emotional or sexual attachment. Much of the emotional atmosphere of households arises from the fact that they are what Goffman[22] has called a "backstage area." Goffman uses the terms "backstage" and "backstage behavior" to describe the way people act when they are relaxed, informal, and just being themselves rather than acting a role such as worker, teacher, host or hostess, and so on. Goffman gives the example of waiters who switch back and forth from scowling to smiling as they pass through the door from the kitchen to the dining room. Another example is the scene from a domestic comedy on television or in the movies in which a husband and wife smilingly say good-bye to the last guest, close the door, scowl at each other, and resume the argument they were having before the guests arrived.

Family secrets are not unique to families; all backstage regimes have them. Restaurant kitchens again serve as a prime example. The household also shares with other such backstage regions a kind of informality that permits a regression to "childish" ways. Goffman notes that backstage behavior has a certain uniformity whether it takes place in a worker's locker room, the backroom of a store, or in a home. "Polite" or public behavior requires certain styles of speech and posture indicating self-control and an appropriate distance from the other person. Backstage areas have their own code or "language" of behavior:

> . . . The backstage language consists of reciprocal first naming, cooperative decision making, profanity, open sexual remarks, elaborate griping, smoking, rough informal dress, "sloppy" sitting or standing posture, use of dialect or substandard speech, mumbling and shouting, playful aggressivity and "kidding," inconsiderateness for the other in minor . . . acts, minor physical self-involvements such as humming, whistling, chewing, nibbling, belching, and flatulence. The frontstage behavior can be taken as the absence . . . of this. In general, then, backstage conduct is one which allows minor acts which might easily be taken as symbolic of intimacy and disrespect

Households as Intimate Environments

for others. . . . It may be noted here that backstage behavior has what psychologists might call a "regressive" character.[23]

Goffman warns against concluding that backstage is full of the pleasant things in life such as warmth and generosity:

> Often, it seems that whatever enthusiasm and lively interest we have at our disposal we reserve for those before whom we are putting on a show and that the surest sign of backstage solidarity is to feel that it is safe to lapse into an asociable mood of sullen, silent irritability.[24]

Because family behavior is a backstage kind of interaction, it is of course extremely hard to observe. As Goffman notes, people in backstage regions know about their own unsavory secrets, but they are not in a position to know about those of other people. Thus families may think of themselves in terms of their backroom knowledge, but judge other families by their onstage performances. This may be why the discoveries of the new family studies[25] are at one and the same time so shocking and so familiar. By observing backstage family behavior, they have opened up for public discussion aspects of family life that could never be reached by means of questionnaires and formal interviews.

Rise of the Private Family

Although a distinction between public and private contexts may exist everywhere, the degree of family privacy in modern societies vastly exceeds that available elsewhere. Thus, as Parsons notes, although the places where people sleep and eat together seem always to be defined as intimate, private places, in most cultures and in our own historical past, households have been more open and accessible to outsiders. Furthermore, as we noted in the last chapter, the sense of a gulf between the home and the outside society seems to exist only in advanced industrial societies.

Indeed, there is reason to believe that the concept of the home as a sanctuary and retreat is a relatively recent cultural feature of the United States and, to a lesser degree, of England. In these countries we find not only the ideology but also the practice of family privacy. Sebastian de Grazia contrasts the "at-home-ness" of Americans with the more extensive out-of-the-house leisure life that exists in Europe. Citing a 1954 survey showing that at 6:00 P.M. of any workday three-quarters of the American male population from age 20 to 59 had arrived home from work, to stay for the rest of the evening, he writes:

> . . . The . . . separation of home and work . . . and the growth of cities into sprawling, black, transportation maps are two factors that help make the home a refuge against the impersonality outside. The trend seems to have begun in the reign of Victoria. Massive, comfortable chairs and sofas appeared in solidly appointed houses. By now the home as a sanctuary has legal and constitutional support in both England and the United States.[26]

Grazia notes that on the Continent, however, the concept of home as distinct from house is lacking. Particularly for men, the cafe and the bistro provide an out-of-the-house environment where they can "eat, drink, write letters or poetry, discuss women, and argue about politics and literature."[27]

The separation of the home from public life reflects not only a set of values, but also the technological self-sufficiency of the modern American home. The telephone, television, refrigerator, freezer, washer, dryer, air conditioner, backyard swimming pool—all increase the privacy and isolation of the household by reducing the need to go out for the necessities of life or for entertainment.

The less the household is a self-contained unit, the more family life goes on in the presence of nonfamily members. For example, in the Mexico City *vecindad* described by Oscar Lewis,[28] individual dwellings surround a central patio. People do most of their work in the patio and share a common toilet and washstand. This type of housing brings individuals from different and not necessarily blood-related households into intense daily interaction and enables people to maintain in an urban setting the extended-family pattern of the rural village. On the other hand, Lewis notes, such intense interaction also leads to problems of privacy and quarrels among neighboring children and parents.

To an American the unappealing aspects of the lack of family privacy in the *vecindad* do not need to be spelled out. But the drawbacks of too much family self-sufficiency and privacy are only beginning to be realized. Sociologist Barbara Laslett[29] argues that only in contemporary America has the ideology of the private nuclear family actually been put into practice, and hence only in America are its problematic aspects becoming apparent. The chief difference between the traditional family and its modern counterpart, according to this analysis, is the public-private dimension. The family of the past was a much more public institution:

> . . . When it is common practice for family life to occur elsewhere than within the confines of the [home], such as in parks or front stoops, when it is common for nondomestic activities—such as political and economic—to be pursued within the domestic context, when it is common for nonfamily members—such as servants, apprentices, and boarders—to constitute part of the household, then the family can be described as having a public character.[30]

By contrast, family privacy increases when most of family life goes on within the home, and when family activities are purely domestic rather than economic. Laslett sees the significance of the public-private distinction in the social-psychological effects of being observed

Life in an agricultural village is less isolated than in a city.

Households as Intimate Environments

while acting out family roles. Following Goffman's concept of backstage interaction, she argues that the increase in family privacy in recent years may result in less social control over what goes on in families, as well as less social support for family roles—hence the increases in family strains that have recently led to dissatisfaction with the nuclear family and the search for alternatives such as communes.

The Great Transformation

Of all of the changes in family life brought on by the emergence of the industrial society, the most dramatic and clear-cut was the separation of home and work. Despite its profound implications, however, this shift in the basic function of the family has rarely received the sustained analysis it deserves.

In preindustrial societies, the family is the basic economic and productive unit. Family life takes place in the midst of the daily cycle of labor, to which all members contribute except for the very young and the physically disabled. Thus, although the traditional-family system was patriarchal, the "head" of the family was as dependent on the contribution of wife and children to the family enterprise as they were on his.

In the modern industrial system, however, the "head" of the family leaves home to work elsewhere, and the rest of the family comes to depend on the father's wages for their support. Instead of sharing in the family's productive tasks, men exchange their wages for emotional support. The care of small children can no longer be carried out along with what society considers "real" work. Women, children, and older adults come to occupy a limbo outside the labor force. Given the demands of the factory or office—the time clocks, impersonal relationships, and monotonous work routines—people look to family life to ease the stresses of the outside world.

These changes, along with the other social and cultural changes that have accompanied the emergence of mass industrial society, have had a profound impact on the daily realities of family life and the experiences of family members. Yet rather than examine these changes, family scholars have been preoccupied with the debate over the isolation of the nuclear family and its relations with kin. Thus the questions raised by the decline-of-the-family school have never been dealt with in a detailed and serious way by students of the family. Le Play, Zimmerman, Wirth, and Linton had seen in urban-industrial society forces inimical to all family ties, both of marriage and of blood. Parsons turned the issue aside by declaring the nuclear family the basic unit. He separated its fate from that of the traditional family by arguing that while modern society was undermining extended-family ties, it rendered the nuclear family more necessary than ever. The nuclear-family critics confused the issue still further by arguing that the traditional family never died.

By assuming that the nuclear family was either the norm or nonexistent, both the Parsonians and the anti-Parsonians failed to come to grips with the structural problems of modern family life. They did not consider the possibility that modern social conditions unglue family ties and at the same time make them more needed. What happens to family life when the household stops being a workplace and father and older children leave for most of the day? What happens to women when they are freed from working on the family farm or trade and are left alone in isolated households with young children? What happens to the quality of family relationships when home becomes a refuge from the rest of society, and the family is the main place for people to enjoy intimate sociability?

Both Parsons and his critics share an optimistic view of family functioning in contemporary society. The structural-differentiation model assumes that changes are adaptive:

When a social organization becomes archaic under changing historical circumstances, . . . it differentiates . . . into two or more roles or organizations which function more *effectively* in the new historical circumstances.[31]

But why make the assumption that the changes are adaptive? Goode[32] suggests that the fit between industrialism and the conjugal family may be one-sided: the nuclear family may suit the needs of the industrial economy, but urban-industrial society may not serve the needs of the family. Further, the nuclear family may not be as ideally suited to a complex industrial society as is usually thought. Like the early generation of writers, Goode asks whether the ultimate thrust of advanced societies is to do away with the family altogether, making the individual the basic unit of society.

Goode and Parsons do recognize the strains placed on family members living in an advanced industrial society. But both Parsons and, to a lesser extent, Goode suffer from the sociologist's bias in favor of seeing societies as balanced and stable, or else changing in a controlled fashion—in a state of dynamic equilibrium. They also tend to see people as being integrated into their societies and social roles, and the family as the basis of this integration. In short, using the methods of sociological analysis, Parsons and Goode come close to seeing the nuclear family as caught in a tragic contradiction, but their functionalist framework prevents their going very far with it.

Very few social scientists have ever argued that the modern family itself contained built-in flaws. C. Wright Mills was one such critical voice. He used marriage as an example of how personal troubles could be viewed as social issues. Mills wrote that though a man and a woman could have personal troubles inside a marriage, when 250 out of every 1,000 marriages ended in divorce (the rates are now approaching 500 out of 1,000 in some places),

there had to be a "structural issue having to do with the institutions of marriage and the family and other institutions that bear upon them."[33] He suggested, as some of these structural strains, a "crisis of ambition" for men in a corporate economy, and the stultifying role prescribed for women within the family:

> Insofar as the family as an institution turns women into darling little slaves and men into their chief providers and unweaned dependents, the problem of a satisfactory marriage remains incapable of purely private solution.[34]

Another critical sociologist writing during the family-togetherness celebration of the fifties was Barrington Moore. At a time when it was axiomatic among social scientists that the family is a universally necessary institution in all societies, past, present, and future, Moore asked: ". . . to what extent may we regard the family as a repressive survival under the conditions of an advanced technology?"[35]

With a frank cynicism Moore struck out at the "barbaric nature" of the duty of family affection:

> One of the most obviously obsolete features of the family is the obligation to give affection to a particular set of persons on account of the accident of birth. This is a true relic of barbarism. . . . In earlier times it was expedient to organize the division of labor and affection in human society through real or imagined kinship bonds. As civilization became technically more advanced, there has been less and less of a tendency to allocate both labor and affection according to slots in a kinship system, and an increasing tendency to award them on the basis of actual qualities and capacities that the individual possesses.[36]

Parent-child relations were included in Moore's dim view of all kin bonds. He wrote that if people were to talk to each other about the "sufferings brought on by raising a family today, the birth rate would drop to zero."[37]

Moore argued that the home of today is less effective than it was in earlier times as a place to rear children. The family was once an economic unit in which all members worked together, but the separation of home and work, brought on by industrialization, removed the father from the household during the day. This meant that the children could have no direct experience of father's work, but even if they did, it was no longer an automatic model for their own careers. Also, the father would spend part of the day in a separate world of social interaction. More recently, mass media and peer groups have come to compete with parents in shaping children. The loss of work ties between family members, involvement in outside interests, and the intrusion of the media into the home all make it harder for family members to form genuine emotional ties with each other.

> The mass media have succeeded in battering down the social cell the family once constituted in the larger structure of society. . . . Newspapers, radios, and television have largely destroyed the flow of private communications within the family that were once the basis of socialization. Even meals are now much less of a family affair. . . .[38]

Like Mills, Moore saw through the popular myths that the woman's place in the contemporary family was one of privilege and dominance as well as instinctual fulfillment:

> Is she, perhaps, the happy person whose face smiles at us from every advertisement, and whose arts justify the sociologists' case? A more accurate assessment might be that the wife suffers most in the modern middle-class family, because the demands our culture puts upon her are impossible to meet.[39]

Moore took his argument to its logical conclusion: the family is already a part-time thing for most people; in the future it would become more so. The trend toward more effi-

cient technology and a greater division of labor would be extended to the home and its tasks. The child-rearing function would be carried on by specialized agencies, developing from today's play schools, boarding schools, and so on. Moore recognized that infants have a special problem: they need affection, fondling, and the "illusion of being the center of the universe." But, he reasoned, mechanized and bureaucratized child rearing could be made warm and supporting, often more so than a family ridden by problems and conflict.

This analysis of the future of the family sounds even more chilling to many people now than it did during the togetherness era. Our sense of values has changed. Moore criticizes the family of the fifties in terms of the values of the fifties: technology, efficiency, rationality. These are, of course, the very values against which there is so much protest. No social scientist predicted anything, however, like the student revolts, the rise of the counterculture, the rebirth of feminism, and so on. So Moore could hardly have foreseen that the direction of value change would be opposite to the one he predicted: rather than technology and bureaucratic efficiency taking over home tasks, the family-togetherness principle moved out beyond the family into the commune movement, encounter groups, political-protest groups, the reawakening of religion, and so forth.

Nevertheless, Moore had pointed to strains in the midcentury American family that would shortly reach crisis proportions: the fact that, despite the ideology of "togetherness," mother, father, and children lived in different worlds of experience, values, and information. Moore also recognized the paradoxical quality of the emotional ties between family members—the obligation to love when the day-to-day relationship may not generate any feelings of warmth. Yet Moore also reiterated the concern of Le Play, Zimmerman, and other traditionalists: would

Physical and social environments have profound effects on individuals and families.

not reduction of family burdens in the interests of individualism result in a world of "shallow and fleeting erotic intrigues"? He acknowledged that Hollywood might be the "ugly prototype" of such a world:

> The most that might be claimed by any future apologist for such institutions . . . is that they give greater scope to the development of the creative aspects of the personality than did the family. . . .[40]

At the conclusion of his article, Moore notes that he is merely pointing to changes that seem to be happening already:

> It would appear that the burden of proof is on those who maintain that the family is a social institution whose fate will differ in its essential form from that which has befallen all the others.[41]

Moore in effect presented the dark side of "structural differention." Parsons and his students saw the nuclear family stripped down to

its basic psychological functions as an effective supplier of security for family members as well as the producer of new recruits to industrial society. The nuclear family was now the only source of the pure gold of solidarity. Moore, on the other hand, argued that the stripping away of work, education, and other functions from the nuclear family had left the members with little or nothing on which to base their relationships. The specialized function of the nuclear family amounts to a heightened emotionality, a pure togetherness paradoxically harder to achieve as a goal in itself than as a by-product of working together on some task.

Actually, despite the fact that Mills and Moore are critics of "establishment" sociology while Parsons and Goode, the latter to a lesser extent, are the establishment, the analysis of the family made by the four writers does not differ very much. The differences lie in the implications drawn from the analysis. Where Parsons and Goode saw tensions and points of strain in an otherwise stable and functioning social system, Mills and Moore saw fatal flaws, contradictions that call into question the viability of modern-family arrangements and the social system that supports them.

Yet the built-in strains noted by Goode and Parsons are fundamental ones; they exist for the old and the young, for men and women, at work and at home. In Goode's analysis of the human costs of both industrialism and the conjugal family, the first and most obvious "cost" of the conjugal as opposed to the extended-family system is to the elders. Viewed as a power struggle, the rise of the conjugal system represents a victory of youth over age. Years of experience make one obsolescent rather than wise.[42]

Parsons sees the plight of older people not so much in terms of power but as a by-product of modern kinship, residential patterns, and occupational structures:

> In such fields as farming and the maintenance of small independent enterprises, there is frequently no such thing as abrupt "retirement," rather a gradual relinquishment of the main responsibilities . . . with advancing age. So far, however, as an individual's occupational status centers in a specific "job," he either holds the job or does not, and the tendency is to maintain the full level of functioning up to a given point and then abruptly to retire. In view of the very great significance of the occupational status and its psychological correlates, retirement leaves the older man in a peculiarly functionless situation, cut off from participation in the most important interests and activities of the society.[43]

Yet work in industrial society also has strains built in. But Goode, like Parsons, believes that the industrial system, based on competition and acheivement, creates great psychological tension. Security and satisfaction in work are almost impossible, no matter whether one is janitor of the building or president of the corporation:

> The modern technological system is psychologically burdensome on the individual because it demands an unremitting discipline. . . . Lower-level jobs give little pleasure to most people. However, in higher-level professional, managerial, and creative positions, the standards of performance are not only high but are often without clearly stated limits. The individual is under considerable pressure to perform better than he is able.[44]

This recognition of strains built into male roles does not diminish Goode's and Parsons' estimates of the strains in women's roles in modern society. The values embodied in the conjugal system—freedom, individualism, sexual equality—contradict the daily realities of the housewife in a modern society. Ironically, the woman is liberated from the extended family only to find that her domestic burdens are increased rather than lightened:

> The modern woman is given little relief from child care, which is typically handed over to one person, the wife, rather than to several women, some of them elders, who are part of the family unit in the more extended systems. . . . Even the substantial development of labor-saving devices and technology has not lightened labor in the modern United States home. . . . Most of these devices merely raise the standards for cleanliness and repairs, and allow the housewife to turn out more "domestic production" each day. Every study of the time allocation of mothers shows that housewives work extremely long hours.[45]

Parsons' analysis of the strains in women's roles focuses not so much on the contrast between family structures—extended versus conjugal—but rather on the effects of the modern occupational structure on the family. The principal source of strain in women's roles, he notes, derives from the fact that the wife is no longer a partner in a common economic enterprise.[46] When the home was also a workplace, economic roles were not differentiated from family roles. Women—and men—could combine child care and reproduction with economic activities. Industrialization, however, moves work, and the father along with, out of the home. Men acquire the status that once was attached to the family as a group. The husband's occupation, more than any other factor, determines the status of the family in terms of prestige as well as standard of living.

> The common enterprise is reduced to the life of the family itself and to the informal social activities in which husband and wife participate together.[47]

In a society with a strong emphasis on individual achievement, the woman is left with the unstable, "pseudo-" occupation of housewife[48] and no claim to status in her own right. The instability of the housewife role, especially in the middle class, Parsons notes, is indicated by the prevalence of women's varying strategies for escaping it—by hiring maids, by dissociating their personality from the role of domestic drudge and emphasizing glamor or cultural activities, and so forth. But because none of these is clearly defined, there tends to be a rather "unstable oscillation" between them, along with a considerable degree of neuroses in women.

The child does not escape built-in strains either, in Parsons' view. In the small modern conjugal family, the emotional intensity of family bonds is increased at the same time that a greater necessity to become emancipated from them is imposed. Thus adolescence is a particularly difficult time in advanced societies.

Summary

The turn-of-the century feminists and social theorists who predicted the end of family life as the inevitable result of urbanization and industrialization were both right and wrong. They were right in predicting the demise of the traditional preindustrial family pattern, in which the whole family was an economic unit. But they underestimated the continuing, and even increased, needs of people in industrial societies for the emotional supports that can be provided only by intimate relationships.

Similarly, the sociologists who argued that the family was more important than ever in modern society were both right and wrong. Whether they stressed the nuclear or the modified extended as the typical contemporary family form, they too easily assumed that family life could fulfill the new demands that were placed on it. They overlooked the possibility that the same social conditions that create the need for the emotional support of the family—the impersonality and competition of the work and public life—make it difficult for the family to fulfill its emotional tasks. Family ties have become more intense than they were in the past and, at the same time, more fragile and conflicted.

Families in contemporary society differ from preindustrial families in at least two major ways: they are more private than families in the past, and they are no longer held together by their dependence on each other's labor. In the past, the family was embedded in the community, and outsiders such as neighbors and kin could supervise relations between parents and children and husbands and wives. Now the family is a "backstage" area where family members can express themselves with more freedom, more emotionally and irrationally, than they can in public. While privacy permits the family to be more loving and intimate, it also permits the expression of more negative feelings.

When the family stopped being a productive unit, relationships between family members were transformed in other ways. Women, children, and old people were placed in an ambiguous position outside the world of productive work. The wife and children came to be dependent on the husband's wages, and his ability to fulfill his masculine role came to be defined by his success in the economic marketplace.

Source Notes

1. Lasch, 1965, p. 47.
2. Gilman, 1903, p. 335.
3. Goode, 1963.
4. Parsons, 1965, p. 32.
5. Parsons and Bales, 1955, pp. 3–9.
6. Sussman, in Rosow, 1965, p. 341.
7. Adams, 1968.
8. Gibson, 1972.
9. Parsons, 1955, pp. 3ff.
10. Gibson, 1972, p. 14.
11. Litwak, 1965.
12. Sussman, 1959, 1965.
13. Gibson, 1972, p. 17.
14. Demos, 1972, p. 562.
15. Goode, 1963.
16. Shorter, 1975, p. 244.
17. Stephens, 1963.
18. Bohannan, 1971, p. 56.
19. Parsons, 1971, p. 428.
20. Slater, 1963.
21. Gibson, 1972.
22. Goffman, 1959.
23. Ibid., p. 128.
24. Ibid., p. 132.
25. Boszormenyi-Nagy and Framo, 1965.
26. Grazia, 1962, p. 184.
27. Ibid.
28. Lewis, 1965, p. 501.
29. B. Laslett, 1973.
30. Ibid., p. 70.
31. Smelser, 1963, p. 2 (italics added).
32. Goode, 1963.
33. Mills, 1959, p. 10.
34. Ibid.
35. Moore, 1958, p. 409.
36. Ibid.
37. Ibid., p. 410.
38. Ibid., p. 411.
39. Ibid.
40. Ibid., p. 417.
41. Ibid.
42. Goode, 1963, p. 379.
43. Parsons, 1949, p. 231.
44. Goode, 1963, p. 14.
45. Ibid., p. 15.
46. Parsons, 1949, p. 223.
47. Ibid.
48. Ibid., p. 224.

□ . . . *it is after all this division into working class and business class that constitutes the outstanding cleavage in Middletown. The mere fact of being born upon one or the other side of the watershed roughly formed by these two groups is the most significant single cultural factor tending to influence what one does all day long throughout one's life: whom one marries; when one gets up in the morning; . . . and so on indefinitely throughout the daily comings and goings of a Middletown man, woman, or child.*

Robert S. Lynd and Helen Merrill Lynd, *Middletown*

Class and Caste in the American Family

In the last chapter, we took a bird's-eye view of the historical transformation of the family brought about by industrialization. That family breadwinners go out of the home to work for wages seems an obvious fact of life. Yet as a way of life for the majority of the population it is scarcely a century old. The impact of this change on families varies according to their places in the social order. American families share the same culture, but they confront marriage, child rearing, work, and relations with kin and others in very different ways according to their resources and their class, racial, and ethnic experience.

Blue-Collar and White-Collar Families:
The Rediscovery of Social Class

In the decades after World War II, America was widely celebrated as an affluent society unique in human history. Television, advertising, and the other mass media portrayed a way of life in which practically every family lived on a tree-lined suburban street with two cars in every garage. Social scientists viewed America as a "middle-class society in which some people were simply more middle class than others."[1] Poverty was an "afterthought," soon to be abolished as affluence and middle-class life styles reached out to include those "left behind." Manual workers were also a minority, soon to be replaced by a highly educated, technologically sophisticated labor force. In any event there were no longer any significant differences between blue-collar and white-collar workers; manual workers were affluent and many even made more than most clerks and teachers. After work, people with both kinds of collars returned home to the suburbs where they enjoyed backyard barbecues and TV, and worried about crabgrass.

The first challenge to the image of America as a uniformly affluent society came with the "discovery" of poverty in the 1960s. Suddenly the government, the media, and social scientists realized that significant numbers of Americans were suffering from economic deprivation and even malnutrition. The "war on poverty," the crisis of the inner cities, and the welfare problem became major public issues that still have not been resolved. Yet the discovery of poverty did not really discredit the image of widespread affluence; economic deprivation was widely viewed as a problem peculiar to racial minorities. Not only was poverty viewed as a problem of discrimination and racism, but the "cultural deprivation" and disorganized family lives of the poor, especially the black poor, were blamed for the failure of these groups to have made it into the great middle class.

In short, the "discovery" of poverty in the 1960s obscured the persistence of class and ethnic differences among white Americans. In the 1970s, however, we appear to be experiencing the "discovery" of another "underclass," which like the poor had actually been there all along. There is no agreed-upon way to refer to these millions of people who probably constitute a majority of the American population. Working class, blue collar, and lower-middle class are some of the terms used by professional observers, but the people referred to are more likely to label themselves as "average," "ordinary," or "plain" people.[2]

It is easier to describe them in terms of what they are not: not black, not brown, not on welfare, not hippies, not intellectuals, not rich or even "affluent." These are the people who were hailed and condemned as the "silent majority" of the 1960s, although they emerged to promi-

"Hardhat" demonstrations in support of the war in Vietnam.

nence on the national scene as "hardhats" attacking student protesters and as white backlashers protesting school and neighborhood integration. Conservatives hailed them as the vanguard of an emerging right-wing majority; most liberals denounced them as violence-prone bigots, while others argued that they had legitimate grievances and are no more racist than other groups in America. In any event, the rediscovery of social class poses an even more

Blue-Collar and White-Collar Families

profound challenge to the image of America as an affluent and egalitarian society than did the discovery of racism and poverty in the 1960s.

This rediscovery reveals that the image of white America as a middle-class society is oversimplified. It suggests a homogeneity of income and life styles that simply does not exist. It is refuted by the statistical evidence on the distribution of income and wealth as well as by studies of how people at different income levels actually live their daily lives, and how they perceive the world and their place in it. For example, the economist Paul Samuelson warns in his introductory economics textbook against the assumption that a majority of Americans share an affluent way of life:

> In the absence of statistical knowledge, it is understandable that one should form an impression of the American standard of living from the full-page magazine advertisements portraying a jolly American family in an air-conditioned mansion, with a Buick, a station wagon, a motor launch, and all the other good things that go to make up comfortable living. Actually, of course, this sort of life is still beyond the grasp of 90 percent of the American public.[3]

The realities of sharp differences in income and opportunity among white Americans remain obscured, however, by the persistence of the myth of affluence. The image of America continues to be one of an affluent white middle class and a minority of poor ghetto blacks. Despite rising unemployment, the myth of the affluent worker persists, as a recent article by Tom Wolfe illustrates:

> In America, truck drivers, mechanics, factory workers, policemen, firemen, and garbagemen make so much money—$15,000 to $20,000 (or more) per year is not uncommon—that the word *proletarian* can no longer be used in this country with a straight face. So one now says *lower middle class.* One can't even call work-ingmen *blue collar* any longer. They all have on collars like Joe Namath's or Johnny Bench's or Walt Frazier's. They all have on $35 Superstar Quiana sport shirts with elephant collars and 1940s Airbrush Wallpaper Flowers Bunchagrapes & Seashell designs all over them[4]

Perhaps the best way to illustrate what is wrong with applying the notion of affluence to those at the middle of the economic scale is to examine the "intermediate" or "adequate" budget constructed by the Bureau of Labor Statistics for an urban family of four. Such a family would have had, in 1974, an income of $14,003, close to the national median income of $14,747. This budget clearly has a "no frills" character— shabby, but respectable. It assumes, for example, that the family will buy a two-year-old car and keep it for four years, that the husband and wife will go to the movies together once every three months, and that the television set will last for ten years. The budget leaves nothing for savings and, although it sets aside some money for medical care, it does not provide for serious illness. Half of American families have incomes less than this median level.

The tenacity of the image of the "affluent society" and of blue-collar workers as overpaid fat cats derives in part from the lack of communication between different locations in the class hierarchy. For most college students, professors, and others of the professional and managerial middle class, working-class people are shadowy figures. If we live in a middle-class suburb and work in an office, we may rarely see blue-collar workers. Our contact may be limited to a glance at construction workers eating lunch on the sidewalk or a few words exchanged with a postman, doorman, or telephone installer.

> It is likely that more students have walked through the slums of Mexico with a copy of Oscar Lewis in their hands than have ever done so in the working-class neighborhoods of Ham-

mond, Indiana, or Flint, Michigan. In fact, there is no comparable book for middle-class people to read.[5]

More is known about families of the very poor or those with known problems such as delinquency or mental illness. Thus, as Lillian Rubin observes, when "hardhats" and "white backlashers" appeared on the national scene, the nation was caught off guard:

> . . . we knew almost nothing of the forty million American workers—just under half the total work force—who are employed in blue-collar jobs, most . . . of them steady workers living in stable families; most of them asking nothing and getting nothing from government programs that give welfare to the rich and the poor—
> . . . .
>
> Seeking to redress the oversight, the media gave us such caricatures as Archie Bunker on television and Joe on film. Social scientists went back into the field to see what they had missed.[6]

Social Scientists Look at Social Class: A Brief Review

With some exceptions, the study of social class over the past several decades tells us more about shifting ideological fashions in scholarship than it does about the experiences and living conditions of people in different social strata. Many social scientists have been preoccupied with making comparisons, usually pejorative in tone, between classes. Thirty years ago, the comparision favored "the lower class," which was portrayed as warm and indulgent towards its children, while "the middle class" was described as repressive. More recently, the comparisions have favored the middle class; however, the two classes are always seen in a "contrapuntal and judgmental relationship."[7]

Furthermore, the traditional social-science treatment of social class has emphasized emotional and motivational differences between the classes, rather than differences in life conditions and perceptions of reality. For example, working-class and poor people are often described as passive, lacking in the ability to delay gratification, and fatalistic—believing that luck rather than hard work leads to success. Rather than reflecting deeply rooted inadequacies of personality, however, these differences—to the extent that they exist at all—may reflect realistic assessments of the opportunity structure and the amount of control lower-income people actually have over their lives. Now, by contrast, there is beginning to be a body of work that deals appreciatively with life styles other than middle-class ones.[8]

Despite the large amount of work that has been done, social scientists do not agree on terminology or a set of concepts defining social classes in America. There is disagreement about whether occupation, income, education, life style, subjective perception, community reputation, or some combination of these should be used as the major indicators of social class.[9] Perhaps this lack of consensus is to be expected in a topic with such obvious ideological and political implications. Surprisingly, income differences have received relatively little attention in the social-class literature. As Rainwater notes,[10] it is odd in a mass-consumption society, in which money buys not only the necessities of life but also identity and status, that there has been so little attention paid to the "social psychology of materialism":

> One would think that a principal activity of sociology and psychology would be to chart the intimate connections between access to economic resources and possibilities for self-realization. . . . Instead, sociologists, for example, have tended to shy away from systematic examination of income as an independent variable in accounting for social behavior. Instead, sociologists have sought to stake their claim as

interpreters of human reality on variables that are somehow more "social." In the area of stratification this has meant a preeminent emphasis on occupation and education and ultimately on "values." It is amazing how many sociological studies do not even present data on income as an independent variable or when they do measure income much more sloppily than other social structural variables.[11]

Given the lack of consensus about how to define social class, it is not surprising that there is also disagreement about where to draw the dividing lines between classes. Many social scientists, as noted earlier, have contrasted "the middle class" with "the lower class." This practice not only applies an invidious label to a large part of the American population, but it also creates a good deal of conceptual confusion. Miller and Reissman observe:

. . . one of the greatest sources of difficulty in understanding nonupper and nonmiddle-class behavior is the social scientist's frequent use of the omnibus category of "lower class" to encompass the stable, and frequently mobile, fairly high-income skilled workers, the semi-skilled factory worker, the worker in various service trades, the unskilled worker, and the irregular worker.[12]

It is important to make a distinction, these authors argue, between the working class—the stable blue-collar worker—and an underclass of the irregularly employed and the unskilled, as well as between the working class and the lower-middle-class white-collar workers. Some observers would place certain white-collar workers in the working class, while some radical sociologists would count as working class anyone who works for a large business or other

The term "working class" has traditionally meant those who do physical or manual work. Some social scientists argue that people in lower-level white-collar jobs or service occupations should also be included in the working class. Others argue that stably employed manual workers should be labeled "lower-middle class."

Class and Caste in the American Family

organization even if he or she makes a high income and has a managerial title.[13] On the other hand, some observers argue that the term "working class" is inappropriate in America, where a majority of people identify themselves as middle class; in England and in Europe, many people publicly label themselves as members of the working class, thereby aligning themselves with a defined political position. These writers propose using the term "lower-middle class" rather than "working class" for that vast population of blue- and white-collar workers who live above poverty but below secure affluence.

Despite these theoretical debates, it seems clear that a realistic image of America would contain at least two distinct classes between rich and poor. The upper group, consisting mainly of professionals, managers, executives, and businessmen, fulfills the image of the affluent society. The lower group, consisting of blue-collar workers and white-collar workers at the lower levels of income and status, is vulnerable to economic anxiety in a way that the upper group is not.

Life on the Installment Plan: Making Ends Meet

The great increase in consumer goods available to lower-middle-class blue- and white-collar workers since the end of World War II has obscured basic differences between them and the upper-middle class. The gap between the two groups has often been considered merely a matter of differences in life style and quality of possessions—smaller houses and yards, less-stylish cars, bowling and motorboats rather than skiing and sailboats, beer rather than wine, spanking rather than Spock. The acquisition of consumer goods, however, is a misleading indicator of economic security. As Shostak observes, blue-collar prosperity is pre-

cariously supported, maintained largely by heavy installment debt and steadily declining purchasing power.[14] What is seldom realized by upper-middle-class observers is that payments for the house, the car, appliances, and so on take a large chunk out of the worker's paycheck, leaving almost nothing for savings or leisure. Savings and other liquid assets provide a family with a cushion against disaster and enable it to invest in the future, as in college education for the children. But in 1969, nearly half the population had less than $500 in savings, and less than a third had more than $2,000.[15]

A more fundamental difference between upper- and lower-middle-class families concerns the main earner's lifetime income patterns. Most upper-middle-class jobs are "careers": the manager or doctor or professor may start out at a low level of income and responsibility, but over the course of time, he (or more rarely, she) will experience a series of advances that bring greater economic rewards. By contrast, most working-class and many lower-middle-class jobs lead nowhere: they involve doing the same routine tasks in the factory or the office throughout one's entire working life, even assuming that one can count on continuous employment.

Thus the typical working-class career has a rather "tragic fate" built into it.[16] Although life generally gets better and better over time for the upper-middle-class family—at least financially—the working-class or white-collar family very early reaches a plateau as the breadwinner reaches the limits of his capacity to earn by promotion or advancement. The young male single worker may make enough to support himself in style—recall Tom Wolfe's affluent workers in their fancy sport shirts—but by the time he has reached his earning peak, family needs may have greatly exceeded his ability to provide for them. Even though his income may have increased, expenses continue to rise as the last children are born, older children enter their teens, and support may be needed for aging parents.

Thus working-class and lower-middle-class families often live on the edge of financial crisis. A single economic setback—a father's loss of a job, a cutback in overtime, an illness or injury requiring an operation or long-term care—can wipe out a family's savings. The realistic fear of unexpected economic danger imposes a heavy psychological burden in the form of nagging anxiety and a loss of sense of freedom. In Robert Coles' book *The Middle Americans*,[17] a man who works in the loan department of a bank provides insight into the difficulties of his own relatively comfortable and secure white-collar family, as well as into the more desperate situations of the people he interviews for loans:

> Like my father used to tell us, it's a mean rotten world if you don't have any money. And there I am in the bank, deciding if people will get money—but I myself don't have very much! We're always behind on bills; and we run a tight ship, my wife and I—no waste and no luxuries except what we can pay for. I hate borrowing money, maybe because I can see what happens to people who do. It's like quicksand; they fall into it, and they nearly die trying to get out. And the banks and finance companies are whispering in everyone's ear that they can have money . . . and the commercials on television are telling you every half minute to buy this and buy that or else you'll really be behind the times and left out.[18]

The economic insecurities experienced by nonaffluent families create a vast psychological gulf between them and the more advantaged. For example, upper-middle-class women, when asked what they value most in their husbands, are likely to mention such things as emotional intimacy, sharing, and communication; working-class women are likely to say, "He's a steady worker; he doesn't drink; he doesn't hit me.[19] It is not that middle-class women do not consider financial security and support impor-

tant, or that working-class women are unconcerned about the emotional aspects of marriage. Rather, each group of women states goals that seem to be more problematic; when economic security is uncertain, it comes to be defined as a dominant issue in marriage. When financial security can be taken for granted, the emotional quality of the relationship comes to be a primary concern. Among working-class women, however, the material aspects of life are always problematic to some extent:

> . . . even when men are earning a reasonably good living, it is *never* "taken for granted" when financial insecurity and marginality are woven into the fabric of life. These crucial differences in the definition of a good life, a good husband, a good marriage—and the reasons for them—often are obscured in studies of marriage and the family because students of the subject rarely even mention class, let alone analyze class differences.[20]

Child rearing, husband/wife relations, and everything else in the family are influenced by financial problems. When money runs short, each spouse may blame the other; the wife may criticize the husband for bringing home an inadequate income, while he can argue that the blame lies with her overspending and inadequacies as a household manager.[21] The quality of a family's leisure-time activities is especially likely to suffer when paychecks don't stretch far enough. Levison notes that much that seems "parochial and limited" about working-class life stems from these restrictions:

> Many workers, in the elation of the first days after their honeymoon, lock themselves into a lifetime of debt when they buy a house and furniture to add on the payments they are already making on their car. From then on, their freedom to travel, or to try a new job, or just engage in a range of activities outside work is taken from them by the structure of debt in which they are enmeshed.[22]

Hiring a baby-sitter and going out to a restaurant and a movie, taking a family vacation, or going off for a weekend by themselves are activities taken for granted by upper- middle-class couples. To working-class families, these things seem like major investments. Such little "luxuries," though, help to make life interesting, provide relief from daily routines, and

One of the privileges that middle-class people take for granted is the ability to indulge in leisure-time activities away from home without the children.

Blue-Collar and White-Collar Families

ease the inevitable tensions of family life. Particularly for housewives with small children, the lack of such activities can make them feel as if the house is a prison. Little wonder that many working-class women "attribute their major problems in life to their lack of sufficient money for the necessities of life as well as such 'luxuries' as an occasional baby-sitter or a visit to the hairdresser."[23]

In recent years, as economic pressures on families have worsened due to inflation and unemployment, working-class women have responded by getting jobs. Thus the recent great influx of women into the labor market has been due not only to middle-class women seeking liberation, or divorced women trying to support themselves and their children, or single career women, but also to working-class wives pushed by economic necessity. With only 46 percent of all jobs paying enough to sustain the average family at a "reasonable" level, the two-worker family is rapidly becoming the national norm.[24] Of all the changes in family life that have occurred in the twentieth century, this may be the most profound. It is producing pressures for changes in marital roles, the division of labor in the family, and child care. It is creating new perceptions of self in both men and women.

Although the problems of adjusting to the new pattern cuts across class lines, the change in female roles creates the most problems in working-class families. Middle-class men have

Both husband and wife were earners in nearly half of the husband-wife families in 1973. (Source: _U.S. Bureau of Labor Statistics._)

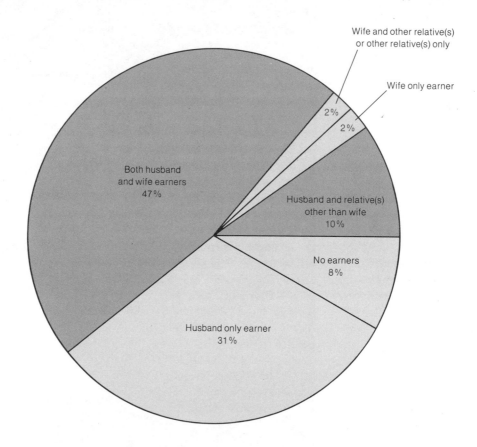

Wife and other relative(s) or other relative(s) only

Wife only earner

2%

2%

Both husband and wife earners
47%

Husband and relative(s) other than wife
10%

No earners
8%

Husband only earner
31%

Class and Caste in the American Family

traditionally been more willing to accept the ideology of sexual equality than working-class men, even if in daily life they have failed to act accordingly. For working-class men, sharing the breadwinner role with one's wife poses a serious challenge to self-esteem and masculinity:

> Despite the enormity of the burdens they carry, many men still feel they must go it alone if they are to fill their roles successfully. Often they cannot, as the soaring proportion of women who work attests. For the working-class man, that often means yet another challenge to his already uncertain self-esteem—this time in the only place where he has been able to make his authority felt—the family. For his wife, it means yet another burden in the marriage—the need to somehow shore up her husband's bruised ego while maintaining some contact not only with her own desires but with family needs as well.[25]

Love and Money

The impact of economic realities on the quality and structure of family life is not restricted to hard times. Though the impact of poverty and deprivation has received the most attention from family researchers, there is impressive evidence that variations in economic resources above the poverty line are also related to variations in family satisfaction and stability. However, the notion of a direct link between love and money flies in the face of some of our most cherished beliefs. The romantic-love complex in our popular culture tells us that true love is not supposed to depend on the economic resources of the loved one—special terms such as "gold diggers" or "fortune hunters" have been used to refer to those who seemed to place material gain above more emotional considerations in the search for a mate.

Similarly, sociological theory—the functionalism that has been predominant until lately—has postulated that the chief task of the family in industrial societies is to compensate for the harsh world outside the home by supplying a warm refuge where the person is treated as a whole and valuable person independent of his value in the market place. Much of the literature on marriage stresses personality factors—maturity, stability, or compatibility—as the chief ingredients in marital success. Clinicians often view marital conflicts over money as a reflection of presumably more basic personality problems. Those in the marriage-and-family field who specialize in giving advice on "how to do it" also present an image of marriage as an emotional and sexual relationship in which all problems can be solved through open communication.

Although communication and sexual issues are important, marriages are also based on economic realities. As Scanzoni points out, preparation for marriage should also include an understanding of how "the realities of an acquisitive society . . . impinge on marital interaction."[26] Although economic well-being does not guarantee marital happiness, economic insecurity is likely to have a profound impact on family relationships.

Our popular mythology, however, often seems to consider money somehow harmful to love. Thus there is an image of working-class families as warm and stable, while the well-to-do are supposed to have brittle, cold relationships that often end in divorce. The evidence, however, suggests the contrary: the distribution of rewards and resources in the economic world outside the family seems to be faithfully reflected within it. This is not to say that working-class and poor families cannot be loving and protective, or that affluent families do not have their own problems. But the trends are clear: studies of poor and working-class families do not reveal the warmth and stability extolled in the myth.[27]

Indeed, there is impressive cross-cultural and historical evidence of an inverse correlation between socioeconomic status and marital in-stability—that is, the higher a person's occupation, income, or education, the less is the likelihood of divorce.[28] (The inverse correlation seems not to hold for women—having a higher income seems to make for greater rather than

The work that people do affects their family lives. Men who enjoy respect and power in the business world may have less need than working-class men to dominate their wives and children.

Class and Caste in the American Family

less marital instability in women.[29] Evidently, deviation from the traditional pattern of male breadwinning increases marital tension and instability.) The popular belief that divorce is more common among the rich and fashionable probably arose during the era when divorce was expensive or difficult to obtain; during such times, legal divorce would be confined to the well-to-do, while less advantaged would have to remain in unhappy marriages or else resort to legally unrecorded separations and desertions. Another reason for the mistaken notion that wealth and status are associated with divorce is the publicity that attends the divorce of the rich or famous. Whenever there is a free market in divorce, however, the greater marital instability among the lower social strata reveals itself.

In short, economic resources come to be converted into emotional responses within the family. How this conversion takes place has been described in theoretical detail in survey studies by McKinley[30] and Kohn[31] for parent-child relationships, and Scanzoni[32] for marital relationships. And Lillian Rubin's recent study of working-class families[33] portrays the conversion process with the insight of a novelist. All of these studies confirm that the contemporary American male's occupational success or lack of it may set off a chain reaction of emotional responses within the family.

Beyond the question of income and making ends meet, which affect everyone in the family, there are the tensions and frustrations created by working conditions on the job, which also affect what happens at home. A husband whose every day at work is a bad day comes home grumpy, withdrawn, and uncommunicative— his family may even seem like the enemy at times.[34] Unable to assert himself at work, he may insist on his traditional male prerogatives at home, demanding service and deference from wife and children. Even within the same occupation, as McKinley finds, fathers whose jobs provide more autonomy, satisfaction, and power tend to be more supportive to their children, while those who suffer greater frustrations tend to be more severe.

Apart from working conditions that may be unpleasant in themselves, there is also what Sennett and Cobb[35] refer to as the "hidden injuries of class"—the bruises to self-esteem suffered by men at the lower ranges of the status hierarchy. In America, a man's personal worth both in his own eyes and those of others is tied to his success on the job market; his wife's "success" and self-esteem as well as her material well-being have traditionally been derived from her husband. It is little wonder, then, that his self-esteem and the respect he receives from the family are tied up with his occupational status. Ironically, the upper-middle-class father, who needs less ego-bolstering respect and submission from his wife and children, is more likely to find family members going along with him in everyday decision making. The frustrated lower-status father, more demanding of deference and obedience, is likely to find his wife and children less willing to accede to him; the less the father's occupational success, the less legitimate does the rest of the family regard his authority. Thus the stage is set for power struggles between husbands and wives and parents and children, resulting in strains, tensions, and ultimately the instability that is reflected in differential divorce rates.

Unemployment and the Family

The clearest illustration of the impact of economic realities may be found in what happens when the family breadwinner loses his job. Historically, one of the major distinctions between the upper-middle and the blue-collar class has been vulnerability to unemployment. The two classes differ not only in level of income and type of work done, but also in the likelihood of having no work and no income. Although the loss of income is the most visible effect of unemployment, it also places severe strains on the psychological functioning of families.

Although families may be drawn closer together as they struggle to get by, more often it appears that lengthy unemployment places strains on family relations, sometimes to the breaking point. Unemployment can be devastating to a man's self-esteem; men tend to blame themselves rather than the "system" for their lack of work, and their families may do likewise. Even during the Great Depression of the 1930s, when unemployment was massive and recognized as a national emergency, out-of-work men still felt guilty about their plight.[36] The symbolic importance of work is reinforced by the daily realities of household life for the unemployed man; his presence around the house all day with time on his hands creates problems for the whole family.

A dramatic illustration of the effects of unemployment on family life is provided by the city of Flint, Michigan, a major auto-manufacturing center. When unemployment hit 20 percent, alcoholism and child-abuse rates also soared. A social worker describes exactly how unemployment damages the fabric of family life:

The story has become so common in Flint, it would be a cliché if it wasn't so terribly sad. A man has been employed for maybe ten years. He had a decent income, a modest house, perhaps a camper, and lots of payments. He had debts, sure, but he also had hope. Then came the layoffs. Still, he didn't worry. He had unemployment compensation and union benefits and felt he would be called back before long.

But he didn't get called back and the special benefits ran out. He lived by the skin of his teeth even in good times, because there was always something to pay for. And it gets worse and his optimism fades. He's around the house almost all day and he has fixed everything in sight. Something goes out of the family because he's around. He sees the kids when they are dirty and noisy and misbehaving. And they don't pay him the same attention they used to when they greeted him at the door when he came home from work.

He had always had the disciplinary role around the house. He was the boss, the breadwinner. So his relationship with his wife changes. He bosses her around and demands she bring him a beer because he has to prove that he's still the man of the house. In a situation like that, everybody in the house gets bent out of shape.

I don't know how many cases I've had where the father admits that what his child did would normally not have been cause for reprimand. Or it would have been overlooked. But in the house of the unemployed, there is so much tension it's like striking a match in a room full of gas fumes. The child misbehaves, the father loses his temper, and smacks him harder than he intended.

There is no evidence of sadism or serious emotional illness in most of the child-beating cases we have been seeing. . . . The hospital or the doctor shows me a child covered with bruises and when I ask the parents what happened, the father breaks down and tells me he did it. He says over and over again that he's sorry, that he simply lost control, that if he could only find a job he would make it up to the child.

I may sound crazy, but most . . . child beaters are concerned and loving fathers, and in a way they are driven to child beating because they are.[37]

A growing body of statistical evidence also documents the effects of unemployment on the family. A major study by Harvey Brenner[38] found significant correlations between unemployment and seven measures of stress-related pathology: suicide, homicide, admission to mental hospitals, admission to prisons, mortality from heart and kidney disease, as well as mortality from all causes. The data were from the United States, England, and Sweden, and covered the period from World War II to 1973. The correlations between unemployment and all the pathological indices held steady across age, sex, and racial groups in different states and three different countries.

Of course, most families manage to cope with the hazards of unemployment and do not contribute to the statistics on suicide, child abuse, or mental-hospital admissions. But the correlations reveal the kinds of stress that, with less dramatic outcomes, affect the families of the unemployed. As one writer puts it:

> . . . For every case of child abuse to which unemployment might have contributed, there are many more where parents no longer have the psychological resources to respond warmly to their children; for every divorce, there are several more lifeless marriages; for every admission to a mental hospital, several more individuals whose abilities to function as worker, spouse, and parent have been broken down.[39]

Black Families: Myths and Realities

In January 1977, the television dramatization of Alex Haley's book *Roots* became a national event. Appearing for eight consecutive nights, it told the story of seven generations in an American black family, beginning with the capture of a young African man and his enslavement in America, and ending with the birth of his descendant, the author Haley. The dramatization of *Roots* made history for a number of reasons. It attracted and held an enormous audience for the whole eight days, at the end exceeding previous viewing records set by the Superbowl and *Gone with the Wind*. Further, these records were set by a program presenting black history from a black point of view; *Roots* destroyed the myth that the mass television audience would not sit still for dramas with serious social content, especially if presented from a black perspective.

Finally, and perhaps most significantly, *Roots* challenged the stereotype of black-family life that had prevailed for decades in both popular opinion and the social sciences. This stereotype held that blacks had no family life to speak of: slavery had "destroyed" the black family, and the descendants of the slaves had never been able to overcome this damaging legacy.

Until very recently, family scholars have tended to deal with black-family life in one of two ways: the first has been to ignore the subject altogether in discussing the American family; the second is to consider black families only as a social problem. Thus social scientists as well as the mass media have helped to perpetuate a set of myths and stereotypes about black families. In fact, the term "black family" has come almost to be a shorthand form for "problem family," calling to mind a set of "pathological" conditions such as broken homes, matriarchal families, fatherlessness, and illegitimacy.

Probably the best-known presentation of the problem theory of the black family is Daniel Moynihan's *The Negro Family: The Case for National Action*. Combining several themes in both scholarly and journalistic accounts, he described the black family as the center of a "tangle of pathology," perpetuating itself from generation to generation without the assistance of the white world:

> At the heart of the deterioration of the fabric of Negro society is the deterioration of the Negro family. It is the fundamental source of weakness in the Negro community at the present time. . . . Unless this damage is repaired, all the effort to end discrimination and poverty and injustice will come to little.[40]

Like many previous writers, Moynihan traced the present disorganization of the black family to the heritage of three centuries of slavery. White America broke the "will of the Negro people by destroying the Negro family."[41] Thus slavemasters had encouraged promiscuity to increase the slave population, had prevented slaves from marrying, and had broken up families on the auction block. The slave household was fatherless and matrifocal (mother-centered).

Emancipation created still more disorder and disorganization. E. Franklin Frazier, a black historian, one of the leading scholars on the black family several decades ago, and one of the sources cited by Moynihan, had written about how black-family life disintegrated still further after the Civil War:

> When the yoke of slavery was lifted, the drifting masses were left without any restraint upon their vagrant impulses and wild de-

A rural black family.

Class and Caste in the American Family

sires. . . . Promiscuous sexual relations and constant changing of spouses became the rule. . . . Marriage as a formal and legal relation was not part of the mores of the freedman.[42]

Migration to the north, according to the Moynihan report and the writings on which it is based, reinforced the social and familial disorganization among southern blacks. Black women were forced to become breadwinners and the men became emasculated dependents or tried to assert their manhood in the bedroom and the streets. Family discipline broke down, producing juvenile delinquency and other forms of crime.

Although the Moynihan report acknowledges that decades of "catastrophic unemployment" rates have undermined black-family structures, it does not conclude that ending unemployment will cure the "tangle of pathology." Rather, it argues that the black family is so damaged that its children, especially sons, are unable to profit from school and job opportunities. Until the "damage" to the black family is repaired, "all the effort to end discrimination and poverty and injustice will come to little."[43]

The Moynihan report was greeted with a storm of protest and criticism. Despite its plausibility, it was replete with inaccuracies and distortions. While expressing concern for the victims of racism and discrimination, it perpetuated racial stereotypes, substituting sociological and psychological explanations for crude racist ones. In fact, as William Ryan[44] has pointed out, the report constitutes the classic case of "blaming the victim": attributing the cause of social problems such as poverty and discrimination to defects within the victim.

At first glance, the line of reasoning advanced in the report seems reasonable, even self-evident. As noted earlier, Moynihan had drawn upon conventional scholarly wisdom. Slavery was harsh and inhuman, emancipation did cause painful dislocations, and blacks migrating north had always encountered catastrophic unemployment rates. How could any people survive three centuries of such massive oppression with intact psyches and family structures? The 1960 census data cited by Moynihan seemed to provide contemporary evidence of a crisis in the black family: 25 percent of black families were fatherless, 30 percent of black children lived with only one parent, and 25 percent of black births were illegitimate, exceeding white rates by a ratio of eight to one. In recent years, increases in these statistical indicators for middle-class white families have led many to proclaim a crisis in the American family. But do the figures for black families indicate a disorganized, crumbling family structure and the perpetuation of a pathological "culture of poverty" from one generation to the next?

One problem with the conclusions usually drawn from these crude figures, as numerous critics of the Moynihan report have pointed out, is the focus on the smaller proportion; it is like describing a three-quarters-full glass of water as one-quarter empty. Although black-white differences are real, the same census figures cited by Moynihan could be interpreted as showing that 75 percent of black families meet his own criteria for "stability," that 70 percent of black children live with both parents, and that more than 75 percent of black babies are born to legally married couples. The interpretation in the report illustrates Billingsley's point that black-family life is usually studied only insofar as it can be considered a social problem. He describes an incident illustrating this tendency:

> In a symposium on the Negro family . . . a few years ago, after a nationally known sociologist referred repeatedly to the "problem of Negro family," a Negro wife and mother arose and took him to task. "Why do you always consider us a problem?" The sociologist was undaunted.

He didn't know why she needed to be so defensive. Thus, despite the fact that the vast majority of Negro families are stable, conforming, and achieving, and cause no problems to anybody, the tendency to view them in negative terms persists.[45]

Further, attributing problems to *all* black families ignores the diversity of life styles and economic levels within the black community. It is as inappropriate to speak of "the black family" as it is to speak of "the white family." Although the black population does not contain a variety of ethnic groups—blacks themselves, as Billingsley suggests, can be considered one large ethnic group—it does contain the other social divisions that mark the white population. Black families may be upper class (about 10 percent), middle class (about 40 percent), or lower class (about 50 percent), with additional subgroupings within these categories.[46] They may be urban or rural or suburban, northern or southern or western; and they vary in child-rearing practices, values, and family roles.

Even within the lower class, distinct groupings exist. There are stable blue-collar families, comparable to the stable white working-class families described earlier. The working poor with marginal incomes, employed in unskilled and service occupations, constitute the largest sector of the lower class. The third segment of the lower class, which has attracted the most public and scholarly attention, includes the unemployed and people living on welfare. According to Billingsley, this group constitutes about a quarter of all lower-class black families. Even within this category, there are wide variations in family values and practices.[47]

Another serious shortcoming of the Moynihan report—and other studies making racial comparisons—is neglect of socioeconomic differences. Since almost half of black families can be considered poor, whereas only 10 to 15 percent of white families are, simple black-white comparisons will automatically produce distor-

tions. The black sample will contain large numbers of low-income families, while the white sample will contain large numbers of middle- and upper-income families. If, however, we compare black and white families at similar income levels, most of the differences diminish or disappear completely. As Hylan Lewis[48] and others have pointed out, when the effects of both income and race on family structure are examined, the income differences are more striking than the color differences. Poverty among whites is correlated with family instability and illegitimacy, while higher income and status among black families goes along with more stable and conventional family arrangement.

For black families, the problem of poverty is compounded by the problem of racial discrimination; the castelike barrier makes it difficult to compare black and white families at similar income levels. Poor black people are not simply poor white people with black skins; they face additional hardships due to discrimination. For example, suppose we establish categories in terms of a range of income, say under $3,000 or over $10,000. The incomes of the white families will cluster toward the top of the range, while those of the black families will cluster toward the bottom. Even when black and white families match on income, education, and occupation, they are not wholly comparable. The black group "must reflect its experience with the caste barrier as well as its distinctive history, both of which set the conditions for growing up black in America."[49]

Actually, Moynihan and his critics do not disagree about the correlations between poverty, family disorganization, and social pathology. Rather, the debate is about how these correlations should be interpreted. Moynihan insists that the family plays a central causal role in sustaining poverty and disorganization in the black community. Family deviance, he argues, is at the "center of the tangle of pathology," the crucial intervening variable between socioeconomic discrimination and community pathology. Here again, the Moynihan report relies on a traditional mode of theorizing in the social sciences—the tendency to see the family as the "primary" institution in society. Thus poor families do not suffer simply from a lack of money or opportunity; they also supposedly suffer from a number of personality defects and deviant values that keep them from getting ahead. This package of deviant attributes, the theory goes, constitutes a "culture of poverty" that is passed along from parents to children, thereby ensuring that the children of the poor remain poor. Thus in the Moynihan report, correlations between family types such as single-parent families and social pathology such as juvenile delinquency are used to support the conclusion that family structure is a "fundamental cause of weakness" in the black community.

As numerous critics of this line of reasoning have pointed out, the connection between poverty and community pathology such as crime and delinquency is direct, and the connection between socioeconomic discrimination and family instability is also direct. In short, poverty is a sufficient "cause " of whatever family and social disorganization occurs in the black community. It is unnecessary to assume family structural defects or a "culture of poverty" in the black family. Further, empirical research among blacks and other impoverished groups does not support the idea of a subculture of poverty passing on deviant values and life styles from one generation to the next. On many value aspirations for their children—a belief in the value of education and the desire for a stable family life and material well-being—a majority of the poor and of black people give allegiance to dominant American values.

In short, at the heart of the debate between Moynihan and others of the "culture of poverty" school on the one hand, and their critics on the other, is how to interpret observable differences between lower-income people and the advantaged. There is empirical evidence of inadequacy and incompetence among people living in slums and ghettos. Living in poverty is decidedly much worse for one's physical and mental health than living at an adequate economic level. Further, nobody doubts that economic stress can impair the ability of parents to provide for the physical and emotional well-being of their children. But the central issue is: are these "disabilities" passed on from parent to child as a cultural heritage in the process of child rearing? Or do they arise from the conditions of life in slums and ghettos?

There is a good deal of evidence that the differences and disabilities that set the poor apart from the middle classes can be attributed to the realities of living at the bottom of the economic hierarchy.[50] For example, Elliott Liebow,[51] in a participant observation study of lower-class, unemployed black men, found little evidence of a self-sustaining cultural system set off from the rest of society. The men he studied were painfully aware of their failure to meet the dominant American standards for success. Because they shared the standards of the larger society, they saw themselves as failures. As Liebow put it:

> . . . . the streetcorner man does not appear as the carrier of an independent cultural tradition. His behavior appears not so much a way of realizing the distinctive goals and values of his own subculture, or of conforming to its models, but rather, as a way of trying to achieve many of the goals of and values of the larger society, of failing to do this, and concealing his failure from others and from himself as best as he can.[52]

Liebow's analysis of the "delay of gratification" idea is particularly useful, since this presumed defect is one of the central components of the culture of poverty. To be unable to delay gratification means to be impulsive, to spend rather than save, to do whatever you feel like doing right now without regard for the future. Supposedly induced by lower-class or black child-rearing practices, it is said to account for the poor child's failure to succeed in school and the poor adult's inability to get ahead. One of the problems with this concept is that the middle classes, who are supposed to exemplify the virtues of delayed gratification, have been described in recent decades as increasingly hedonistic, impulsive, and devoted to spending rather than saving.

Despite the dubious existence of the delayed-gratification pattern in the middle class, Liebow argues that the current realities of life in lower-income populations are sufficient to cause what appears to be an inability to delay gratification. What appears as a "present-time orientation" to the outside observer, he argues, may actually take the future very much into account:

> . . . the young streetcorner man has a fairly good picture of [the future]. . . . It is a future in which everything is uncertain except the ultimate destruction of his hopes and the eventual realization of his fears. The most he can reasonably look forward to is that these things do not come too soon. Thus, when Richard squanders a week's pay in two days, it is not because, like an animal or a child, he is "present time" oriented, unaware of or unconcerned with his future. He does so precisely because he is aware of the future and the hopelessness of it all. . . . Thus, apparent present-time concerns with consumption and indulgences—material and emotional—reflect a future-time orientation. "I want mine right now" is ultimately a cry of despair, a direct response to the future as he sees it.[53]

Although some of Moynihan's critics dispute the extent of pathology in the black community and attribute whatever pathology does exist to economic stress and discrimination, other critics refuse to take a completely negative view even of lower-class family patterns.

Without denying the painful social and psychological costs that have been inflicted on black Americans, they nevertheless insist that lower-class black-family life is not necessarily "disorganized." They argue that many of its features are sources of strength that have helped the black community cope with its enormous burdens. For example, the supposedly "matriarchal" character of poor black families may have been an important contributor to black survival. As Robert Staples observes, rather than being a "matriarchal villain," the poor black woman:

> . . . has developed her personality out of the necessary role adjustments required to withstand the oppressive odds against her family's survival in an admittedly racist society.[54]

Since the Moynihan report appeared in 1965 the bias implicit in the concept of male dominance and female submission as the norm for marital "health" has become starkly apparent.

Other critics have pointed to the fact that adult women have traditionally played strong roles in the families of oppressed groups. For example, the Jewish family, the Irish family, and the working-class English family could be caricatured as matriarchal, yet these families have also been regarded as "strong" and "cohesive," not as part of "a tangle of pathology." Schneider and Smith[55] observe that there is nothing inherently disorganized or abnormal about "matrifocal" families. Mother-centeredness is not confined to any particular cultural tradition, but derives from the relationship of individuals and families to the economic system:

> Steady employment for males, with involvement in a range of welfare plans such as medical and unemployment insurance, savings and life insurance, and home-purchase schemes, provides a stabilizing effect upon marriage and reinforces middle-class normative stress upon the nuclear family. Unemployment and irregular

When southern agriculture became mechanized, black families moved north in search of work. They found massive unemployment and living conditions often as bad or worse than those they had left behind.

employment, coupled with high rates of female participation in the labor market, has the opposite effect. In neither case is this relationship to economics determinative in any simple way of familial structure at the behavioral level. For the lower class, it often results in the emergence of the perfectly normal configuration of domestic units based on a stable female core, to which males are related in a variety of supportive, dominant, or dependent ways.[56]

Black Families: Myths and Realities

Although such adaptations of people living under oppressive conditions may appear to the surrounding culture as excessive or pathological, once the social pressure that created it is removed, a new adjustment develops. As Laura Carper observes: "A people is not destroyed by its history. What destroys a people is physical annihilation or assimilation, not its family life."[57]

Carol Stack's[58] anthropological study, *All Our Kin*, provides vivid insights into some of the adaptive strategies of black families at the lowest income levels. Like the work of Elliot Liebow, it reveals that observations of how people actually live yield a very different picture of reality than census or survey data.

For example, what census records indicate as a fatherless or female-headed household does not necessarily mean that a woman is isolated and alone. Also, ethnographic studies like these reveal that if you look closely at so-called "disorganized" families and communities, you may find distinct forms of social organization. Stack describes how networks of kin and quasi-kin—good friends who can be relied on—meet daily needs:

> Black families living in the flats need a steady source of cooperative support to survive. They share with one another because of the urgency of their needs. Alliances between individuals are created around the clock as kin and friends exchange and give, and obligate one another. They trade food stamps, rent money, a TV, hats, dice, a car, a nickel here, a cigarette there, food, milk, grits, and children.
> . . . Without the help of kin, fluctuations in the meager flow of available goods could easily destroy a family's ability to survive.[59]

The adaptations to poverty described in Stack's book do not lock people into a "cycle of poverty" or prevent the poor from marrying. But her work does show that trying to become more middle class through marriage or employment involves a dubious risk. For a poor black woman to withdraw from the kin network means sacrificing the security gained through the system of exchange, and giving up her welfare payments as well, to depend on the precarious employment of an unskilled black man. It is a dubious proposition indeed. The kin group also has a vested interest in keeping its members loyal and avoiding marital commitments. Ironically, official welfare policies also discourage social mobility and formation of nuclear families, and encourage the maintenance of domestic networks. They do so by rewarding only fatherless families and preventing the poor from inheriting even small amounts of cash, or from acquiring investments typical for the middle class, such as home ownership.

The women Stack encountered in the course of her study provide vivid evidence of the futility of trying to live up to middle-class family standards under these conditions:

> Julia Ambrose estimated the man she married to be a good provider and a reliable risk. After her husband was laid off from his job, Julia was forced to apply for welfare benefits for her children. Ruby Banks returned to the flats without her husband within a year of marriage, embarrassed, disappointed, depressed. Her pride was injured. She acquired a bitter resentment toward men and toward the harsh conditions of poverty. After the separation, Ruby's husband moved into his older sister's home in a neighboring town. His spirit and optimism towards family life had also been severely weakened.[60]

Although the critics of the Moynihan report disputed his analysis of the "pathology" of contemporary black families, few of them disagreed with his description of slavery, or the view that slavery had "destroyed" the black family. In recent years, however, this traditional view of black families under slavery has been radically revised by new historical discoveries. Herbert Gutman's book, *The Black Family in Slavery and Freedom*,[61] is the most important

Class and Caste in the American Family

work in this line of research, but other scholars have also contributed to the new view. The book and television version of *Roots,* with its vivid emphasis on the strength of family bonds among slaves, dramatizes the findings of the new scholarship.

Gutman's work was originally inspired by the Moynihan report. Trying to evaluate what has been called the "slavery-specific hypothesis" presented in the report—the view that contemporary black-family "disorganization" is a legacy of slavery—Gutman looked at census data for a number of cities between 1880 and 1925. He discovered that two-parent households were the norm among blacks during this period, and that single-parent households were no more common than among comparable whites. There was no evidence among lower-class blacks of the "tangle of pathology."

Trying to explain how this stable family pattern could have arisen, Gutman used a variety of statistical and other evidence to explore the structure of the black family during the

Reconstruction and slavery. He discovered that the two-parent household prevailed among slaves and continued to do so after Emancipation. He found that slave unions tended to be remarkably long-lasting, forced separation through sale being the major reason for family breakups. The various letters and statements made by ex-slaves reveals the strength of the attachments of slave families and the deep and lasting grief caused by these separations.

Yet the nuclear family was not the only kind of family structure discovered by Gutman. He also discovered evidence of a strong extended-kinship structure. The existence of distinctive slave-marriage rules, such as taboos against blood-cousin marriage, and the fact that slave children were often named for blood kin such as aunts, uncles, and grandparents provide part of the evidence for the importance of slave kin groups. This kinship structure, and the sense of community and interdependence it fostered, may have been the chief means by which African cultural traditions were preserved, as

A middle-class black family.

Black Families: Myths and Realities

well as an important survival mechanism of black people under slavery.

The major conclusion of Gutman and the other historians who have contributed to the new black history is this: to the extent that contemporary black families are "matrifocal" or "disorganized," it is not a legacy of slavery but a result of the destructive conditions of northern urban life encountered by a massive number of migrants from the rural south. Gutman compares the twentieth-century migration of blacks to the Enclosure Movement in eighteenth-century England, when millions of farmers were driven from the land when landowners turned to sheep herding.

The modern "enclosure movement" was caused by the mechanization of southern agri-culture, particularly by the cotton-picking machine. As a result, the migration from American rural areas between 1940 and 1970 was equal to the century of European immigration between 1820 and 1920.[62] In 1940 half the black population lived on the land; by 1965 it was four-fifths urban. The Moynihan report acknowledged that black employment rates in northern cities have continued at disaster levels for thirty-five years. Yet the report preferred to blame "the black family" rather than the economic conditions that had uprooted millions from the land and failed to provide jobs in the cities. It is much easier, as one recent article put it, "to lament the sins of one's forefathers than to confront the injustices of more contemporary socioeconomic systems."[63]

Summary

The removal of work from home to factory transformed the family from a productive unit to a group of consumers dependent on the income of the family breadwinner. The impact of this change differs according to the family's location, the hierarchy of occupation, and income. Although the effects of the husband's occupational situation can be seen most clearly in working-class families living with economic uncertainty, or among black families coping with chronically disastrous employment levels, the dependency of the wife and children on the breadwinner's income affects all families.

Above all, the exchange of the husband's money for the wife's service creates the potential for each to feel exploited by the other. We live in a mass-consumption society in which money buys not only the necessities of life but also identity and status. People are encouraged to have limitless appetites for goods and services, making most people feel that their incomes are inadequate. Thus family members must compete with one another in the allocation of the family's limited resources. Further, when income seems insufficient, the family breadwinner, traditionally the husband, may feel his dependents are squandering his hard-earned money, while the wife and children may blame the husband for failing to be more successful.

In recent years, women have entered the labor market in massive numbers, in part to help fill the gap between the husband's income and the family's needs and wants. Once again, a shift in the economic functions of the family seems to be changing the nature of family relationships and producing a redefinition of family roles and obligations.

Race and ethnicity add another dimension of variation in family experience. The black-family experience in America is unique because of the heritage of slavery, discrimination, and massive unemployment persisting for generations. Many social scientists, however, have tended to blame black-family life for the continuing poverty of much of the black population — the classic case of blaming the victim. The view of the black family as a "tangle of pathology" not only ignores the role of economic and social discrimination in perpetuating the disadvantages of racial minority, but also overlooks the diversity of black families. Further, family scholars often fail to see that many features of poor, urban, black-family life are successful ways of coping and surviving in a difficult environment.

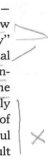

Source Notes

1. Bottomore, 1966, p. 105.
2. Coles, 1971.
3. Samuelson, 1967, p. 12.
4. Wolfe, 1976, p. 31.
5. Levison, 1974, p. 43.
6. Rubin, 1976, p. 5.
7. Miller and Reissman, 1964, p. 28.
8. Howell, 1973; Rubin, 1976; Sennet and Cobb, 1973; Shostak, 1969.
9. Otto, 1975.
10. Rainwater, 1974.
11. Ibid., pp. xi–xii.
12. Miller and Reissman, 1964, p. 26.
13. For example, see Anderson, 1975.
14. Shostak, 1969, p. 274.
15. Parker, 1972, p. 8.
16. Hamilton, 1972.
17. Coles, 1971.
18. Ibid., p. 91.
19. Rubin, 1976, p. 93.
20. Ibid., p. 94 (italics in original).
21. Ibid.
22. Levison, 1974, p. 106.
23. Shostak, 1969, p. 130.
24. Ginzberg, 1976.
25. Rubin, 1976, p. 184.
26. Scanzoni, 1970, p. 196.
27. Blood and Wolfe, 1960; Komarovsky, 1959; McKinley, 1963; Rubin, 1976; Scanzoni, 1972.
28. Goode, 1970.
29. Ross and Sawhill, 1975.
30. McKinley, 1963.
31. Kohn, 1968.
32. Scanzoni, 1972.
33. Rubin, 1976.
34. Ibid., p. 160.
35. Sennett and Cobb, 1973.
36. Elder, 1974.
37. Hilliker, quoted in Mondale, 1976.
38. Brenner, 1976.
39. Grubb, 1977, p. 29.
40. Moynihan, 1965, p. 5.
41. Ibid.
42. Frazier, 1949, p. 89.
43. Moynihan, 1965, p. 5.
44. Ryan, 1976.
45. Billingsley, 1968, pp. 198–199.
46. Ibid.
47. Lewis, 1968.
48. Ibid.
49. Billingsley, 1968, p. 201.
50. Ryan, 1976; Valentine, 1968.
51. Liebow, 1967.
52. Ibid., p. 222.
53. Ibid., pp. 64–68.
54. Staples, 1971, p. 132.
55. Schneider and Smith, 1973.
56. Ibid., p. 107.
57. Carper, 1967, p. 467
58. Stack, 1974.
59. Ibid., pp. 32–33.
60. Ibid., p. 126
61. Gutman, 1976.
62. Ibid., p. 466.
63. Furstenberg et al., 1975, p. 233.

Chapter Seven
Sexual Destiny and Sexual Knowledge

□ *The domestic career is no more natural to most women than the military career is natural to all men; although it may be necessary that every able-bodied woman be called upon to risk her life in child-bed just as it may be necessary that every man should be called upon to risk his life in the battlefield . . . . If we have come to think that the nursery and the kitchen are the natural sphere of a woman, we have done so exactly as English children come to think that a cage is the natural sphere of a parrot—because they have never seen one anywhere else.*

George Bernard Shaw, *The Womanly Woman*

People have been theorizing about sexuality for thousands of years, yet the scientific study and public discussion of sexual matters is barely seventy years old. Many of the questions that earlier generations have puzzled over remain unanswered, the experts in disagreement. The study of sexuality illustrates in an extreme way many of the problems that beset the social sciences in general and the family in particular.

The Study of Sexuality

In speculating why the social sciences have "lagged behind" the natural sciences like physics and chemistry, some writers have argued that the social sciences are too new; they are only now at the point that physics was when Galileo was dropping balls off the Leaning Tower of Pisa. Others who have thought about the matter come to the opposite conclusion: the social sciences have lagged because they are too old. People have always had theories about what social life is all about, and these folk psychologies and folk sociologies get in the way of, and even get mixed up with, the more scientific models.[1] Still others have argued a third position: that the social sciences can never attain the precision and predictability of the natural sciences for the simple reason that the subject matter is so different; the physicist, watching a ball roll down an inclined plane, does not have to worry about the ball's reactions to being observed—that it might be too embarrassed to roll at all or, just to be contrary, might decide to roll uphill.

Prudery and Patriarchalism

Besides sharing in the general difficulties that beset the study of human behavior, the study of sexuality has been hampered by cultural attitudes surrounding sexuality with anxiety, making it a taboo topic for private or public discussion, and by cultural biases defining women as the natural subordinates of men because of biological and intellectual inferiority.

Thus, in approaching the study of either the physical or the social relations between the sexes, it is important to understand how the prevailing assumptions of male dominance and female submissiveness may have influenced both popular and professional conceptions of sexuality and sex differences. The new feminism has made us aware how deeply entrenched sexist attitudes are in men and women, even in our language and habits of expression. It is difficult for students of sexual biology and behavior to escape the patriarchal image of the passive egg, waiting for purposeful, active sperm to impregnate it, or of female animals during their periods of sexual interest as being "receptive," when in fact their behavior shows them to be the initiator of the sex act.[2] Anthropologists have applied male-female stereotypes to the study of human evolution, emphasizing the importance of "man the hunter" and overlooking the contributions of "woman the food gatherer" in prehistoric times.[3]

As John Stuart Mill and later feminists have argued, the history of relations between the sexes is analogous to those between different races, classes, and castes. All such relationships have involved the domination of one group, defined by birth, by members of another group, also defined by birth. Thus patriarchy—the rule of men over women—must be placed alongside feudalism, despotism, slavery, aristocracy, and racism. When in practice, however, such power arrangements appear natural and inevitable, and alternatives to them unthinkable. When religion is given as the major justification for behavior, subordination of one group by another is explained in religious terms. More recently, domination is usually justified in terms of biological necessity, irrevocable instincts, and inherent inferiority.

Since the line between biology and culture has not yet been drawn precisely, there has been a tendency to emphasize the inevitability and significance of existing differences between the sexes. Albert Memmi's analysis of racism applies well to the issue of sex differences. He notes that the essence of racism is the way it emphasizes differences that may be either real or imaginary. Memmi writes:

> . . . Revealing a characteristic differentiating two individuals or two groups does not in itself constitute a racist attitude. After all, this is part of what any student of the human sciences does. The assertion that there is a difference takes on a special *significance* in the racist context: by emphasizing the difference, the racist aims to intensify or cause the *exclusion,* the *separation* by which the victim is placed outside the community or even outside humanity.[4]

Thus Memmi goes on, colonialists argue that the natives are too culturally inferior to be included in the community, anti-Semites argue that Jews are too strange and clannish to live and work near non-Jews, and so forth. Extending this analysis to women, alleged sex differences are used to justify keeping women in their place—preferably at home. Memmi continues:

Making use of the difference is an essential step in the racist process: *but it is not the difference which always entails racism, it is racism which makes use of the difference.*[5]

There are several other aspects to the racist mode of thought. The "difference" is generalized to encompass all of the victim's personality and all the members of his or her group. Every manifestation of the person's being is marked by membership in the group. In terms of sex difference, a woman is "all woman" in whatever she does, and all women are presumed to be alike.

Science and Sexuality

In general, social-science models of sexuality have remained remarkably similar to folk or popular models of sexuality. Sexuality is said to represent the instinctive "animal" side of human nature, separate from and opposed to the higher forms of human behavior that are learned and cultural.

The prevailing ideas about sex and sex differences are that sex is a powerful natural drive, necessary for reproduction, but one that must be socially controlled. Learning and culture enter into the process only as controls, not as influences on the patterning or development of sexuality.

Sexuality in the folk model includes more than the urgency of lust. It accounts for masculine and feminine behavior, the choice of sex partners, and the differences between the father's and mother's role in child rearing. Thus the natural model of sexuality implies that the person intuitively knows whether he or she is male or female. His or her behavior follows naturally the patterns laid down by the body's biological gender. And, in the same way, a person will naturally be sexually attracted to and fall in love with members of the opposite sex.

Sex is used to mark off humanity into two separate species. At birth children are divided into males and females, with the assumption that everything else about them is secondary to, or flows from, that basic distinction. If the child is a boy, he will be active, assertive, aggressive; he will go out into the world and seek his fortune. If the child is a girl, she will be gentle, passive, dependent, intuitive; her place will be at home. The notion that maleness or femaleness necessarily determines social role and behavior runs deep in many cultural traditions. Ancient Chinese sages divided the world into male and female qualities: yang is bright, hot, active, and positive; yin is dark, moist, cold, and passive. The essential feature of the folk beliefs about sex differences is duality, with gender being a matter of either/or rather than both/and or more/less. Social-science theorists similarly hold that the biological division of labor between the sexes, and a sharp differentiation between men and women, is necessary to the functioning of any society. The prevailing tendency takes the present relations between men and women for granted, and looks for biological "reasons" to explain these relations.

Sex Roles and Biology

Biological determinism often seems more compelling to both laymen and scholars than the notion that sexual destiny is also based on culture and learning. For the layman it is relatively easy to believe that innate biological forces transform boy babies into men and girl babies into women, since most men and women until very recently have lived up to the prescribed sex roles. Such exceptions as obviously "gay" homosexuals could also be accounted for on biological grounds.

Scholars, however, should find it harder to ascribe to biological determinism of adult sex roles, since evidence clearly reveals cultural variation. In American culture, for example, it is considered "feminine" to be artistic and emotional, but in other cultures men are supposed to be more emotionally expressive and artistic than women. Margaret Mead's[6] classic study of sex and temperament in three cultures is the best example of the variability of sex-role patterning. In one of the New Guinea tribes, the Arapesh, both men and women were found to be cooperative, unaggressive, and gentle. In contrast, the Mundugumor tribe prescribed what would be a masculine temperament in our culture for both sexes—ruthlessness, aggressiveness, and severity. Neither the Arapesh nor the Mundugumor emphasized a contrast between the sexes. In a third New Guinea tribe, however, the Tchambuli, there was such a contrast, but it was the reverse of sex-role temperament in our culture. Tchambuli women tended to be aggressive, domineering, and managerial, whereas the men tended to be dependent, artistic, and sensitive. In short, the study concludes that sex differences are arbitrary and do not reflect any underlying predisposition.

Further, the realities of everyday social life in modern societies do not support the notion that biological differences automatically assign certain activities to men and others to women. Evelyne Sullerot[7] has pointed to a time lag in sex-role differentiation in modern societies: social changes seem more rapid for men. For example, when cars were scarce and driving was prestigeful, few women drove. Driving seemed a "masculine" activity. Now driving a car is a commonplace necessity of everyday life in many places. But piloting airplanes still seems more a masculine activity than driving cars.

Parents encourage their children to be "masculine" or "feminine," and the training begins in infancy.

Nor does simply looking around at people support the notion that every male is bigger, stronger, and more aggressive as well as more logical than every female.

In trying to reconcile social reality with the notion of innate biological differences between the sexes, scholars have come up with a variety of compromise positions. They all share a belief

Sex Roles and Biology

in some degree of biological determinism, but they allow room for culture and learning to influence the patterning of sexual attitudes. These modified or partial determinism theories differ, however, in the way they conceive of the "natural" forces and the "cultural" forces working together.

Roger Brown,[8] for example, puts forth what could be called an "overlap" theory. He argues that although there is a natural biological tendency for males to be rougher and tougher and more active than most females, there is also considerable overlap between the sexes: some women are bigger and stronger and rougher and tougher than some men. Most cultures, moreover, subscribe to sex-role stereotypes that force people into predetermined molds regardless of their individual inclinations. Thus a tough, dominant woman is regarded as a deviant female in our culture, but among Tchambuli she would be considered a normal female. In Mundugumor society she would be regarded as merely a normal person, but in Arapesh society she would be regarded as a deviant human being, not merely a deviant from a sex role. In similar fashion the fate of a temperamentally gentle, sensitive male would vary from culture to culture. Brown concludes that the sex difference is an inadequate method of assigning people to roles.

The essential difficulty is this: temperaments and tastes and attitudes are usually prescribed on the basis of biological sex when they actually reveal an imperfect natural linkage with sex. Men aren't always big, tough, and logical; women aren't necessarily small, gentle, and flighty. If you want your furniture moved, you would be better off with a heavyweight woman than a bantamweight male. Or, to use one of Brown's examples, if you want to hire a door-to-door salesperson, you'd be wiser to hire a determined, aggressive woman than a shy, retiring male.

A similar difficulty often arises when roles are assigned on the basis of other inherited attributes:

> . . . not all brahmans have a religious "vocation"; not all elderly men are wise; not all sons of kings are equipped to lead a nation. . . .
>
> The answer must be to detach leadership, aggressiveness, aestheticism, wisdom, and the like from irrelevant ascribed attributes and incorporate them in pure achievement roles. . . .[9]

In a certain sense all theories about sex and sex roles agree that there is some interaction between biological determinants and social factors. But they disagree over the source of the patterning of sexuality. Are sex roles biologically determined, is biology tempered by social learning, or are the learned factors the means by which undirected biological capacities are shaped?

Freudian Biological Determinism

To Freud, "anatomy is destiny." He also believed in one prototype for humanity—the male. This "sexual monism," as one writer described it,[10] is not unique to Freud. Indeed, it is built into the English language. Thus "man" or "mankind" is used to describe the human race, and "he" is the generalized term for person. But Freud went further: he presented an elaborate psychological theory based on the idea that the female constitutes a defective or incomplete male. For Freud there were not really two sexes, but only one. Freud believed that the little girl thinks of herself as a little man until she discovers, to her horror, that she is castrated. This discovery represents the crucial point in her development, according to Freud and his followers. She can either accept her biological destiny, transform the wish for a penis into the wish for a child, and become a passive female as nature intended her to be, or she can persist in the misguided belief that she is really a man and can do things men can do.

In the perspective of the 1970s it seems remarkable that psychoanalytic writers of the forties and fifties—even women—could confidently interpret departures from wifely and maternal roles as abnormal. Helene Deutsch, a leading psychoanalytic authority on the psychology of women, believed that an "overgrowth" of a girl's intellect was a form of masculinization; it could only impoverish her own emotional life, wreck her marriage, and ruin her children. She believed that a healthy woman would renounce her own claims to accomplishment and originality, realizing herself instead through identification with her husband and sons:

> They are the loveliest and the most unaggressive of helpmates and they want to remain in that role; they do not insist on their rights, quite the contrary. They are easy to handle in every way—if only one loves them.[11]

The belief that the anatomical distinction between the sexes has the most fateful influence on a person's destiny persists among many writers in the psychoanalytic tradition. Anatomy is destiny, not only for Freud at the turn of the century but also for many psychologists, sociologists, and biologists down to the present time. Even Erik Erikson, who has changed Freud's libido theory in major ways, persists in the belief that anatomy is destiny; men are directed by their bodies to an interest in "outer space," whereas women will be forever focused on "inner space."[12]

Despite the biologism and bias against women in much psychoanalytic writing, it contains many insights into male and female psychology and the relations between the sexes. Recently there have been a number of attempts to disregard the obvious biases in order to extract these insights from Freudian ideas. Juliet Mitchell[13] and several other feminists—and nonfeminists—have been presenting social and cultural interpretations of the sex differences Freud describes. While accepting the Freudian account of sexual development—the Oedipus complex, castration anxiety, penis envy, and so on—they argue that these psychological reactions are not biologically determined but reflect the social and cultural realities into which children are born. Thus psychosexual development is viewed not as a simple unfolding of innate biological potentials but as a complex and often painful learning process. It is, as Althusser puts it, a "long forced march" toward "the Law that has been lying in wait for each infant since before his birth, and seizing him before his first cry, assigning him his place and role, and hence his fixed destination."[14]

A major social reality emphasized in these writings is the dominance of the mother in early infancy; every infant's "first love" and "first boss" is a woman.[15] By different routes, boys and girls must extricate themselves from this early relationship and find their proper places in a world divided into masculine and feminine roles and a hierarchical order in which adults rule over children, and men rule over women.

One of the outcomes of mother-dominated infancy is that both males and females grow up repudiating femininity and resenting female authority. Thus, on a deeply emotional level, most people—even some feminists—may find themselves uncomfortable at the prospect of women sharing equally with men in the ruling of the world. Dorothy Dinnerstein[16] argues that until men participate fully in the care of babies and young children, it will be difficult to overcome the present malaise between the sexes and achieve genuine equality. One need not agree fully with the diagnoses or prescriptions of the new approaches to Freudian writings to appreciate their usefulness; they help us understand our current sexual predicaments and some of the obstacles standing in the way of solving them.

The New Biological Determinism: Man as Ape

In recent years, in the writing of such men as Lorenz, Ardry, Morris, and Tiger, a new version of biological determinism has arisen. These writers have put forth a number of books arguing that human behavior can be understood as the result of powerful instinct or rigid patterns genetically programmed during the course of evolution. They offer a version of what is supposedly "natural" human nature by using primate societies as models of the earlier stages of human evolution. They argue that man evolved as a killer ape. He is genetically programmed, they assert, with implacable instincts to make war on his fellow man, to seize and defend territory, and to exclude and dominate females. Females, in this theory, are obviously programmed to attract males and to bear and nurture the young.

Although the books of Ardry, Morris, and the others have proved extremely popular, for the most part they are not taken seriously as contributions by other scholars. Because of the popularity of the man-is-an-ape school, a number of detailed rebuttals have appeared.[17] An article by Pilbeam states: "The fashionable view of man as naked ape is: . . . an insult to apes . . . simplistic . . . male-oriented . . . rubbish."[18] The basic flaw consists of exaggerating the similarities between man and other primates (as well as the similarities among the primates themselves) and ignoring the crucial differences between human beings and apes.

The naked-ape school of popular writing represents an exaggerated version of what was, until recently, accepted scholarly wisdom about the importance of man the hunter in human

evolution. Recent anthropological studies suggest that the economic role of women in hunting societies was more critical than had previously been assumed.[19] In fact, the gathering and sharing of plant food rather than hunting may have been the critical invention in human evolution. Instead of viewing women as passive creatures dependent on men for meat and protection, women emerge, in these theories, as central economic and social actors:

> Females gathered plant food and shared it with their young, and mother-centered units may have been the most enduring segments of the larger group. An important selective agent may have been the preference of females in mating with nonaggressive males whose presence in the mother-centered unit was least disruptive. In this model, hunting as an important economic activity, and the sexual division of labor, emerge late in hominid evolution.[20]

Other authors argue that hunting and gathering emerged together as the critical innovation in human evolution. Whatever the final version of human evolution turns out to be, it seems clear that the androcentric—that is, male-centered—model stressing male economic dominance overlooks important archeological and cross-cultural evidence.

The naked-ape school also represents in exaggerated form a kind of biological reductionism that has been stated somewhat more respectably by others. For example, Harlow, a psychologist, reports on some of his findings on the play behavior of infant macaque monkeys and generalizes his observations to humans:

> . . . Males threaten other males and females but females are innately blessed with better manners; in particular, little girl monkeys do not threaten little boy monkeys. . . . Play behavior in the playroom is typically initiated by males, seldom by females. However, let us not belittle the female, for they also serve who only stand and wait. Contact play is far more fre-

Two of woman's basic roles: sex object and food server.

quent among the males than the females and is almost invariably initiated by the males. Playpen data show that real rough-and-tumble play is strictly for the boys.

I am convinced that these data have almost total generality to man. Several months ago I was present at a school picnic attended by twenty-five second graders and their parents.

Sex Roles and Biology

While the parents sat and the girls stood around or skipped about hand in hand, thirteen boys tackled and wrestled, chased and retreated. No little girl chased any boy, but some little boys chased some little girls. . . .[21]

A curious paradox appears in Harlow's insistence on innate biological determinism. His most notable contribution to psychology is to have shown that certain kinds of behavior that had always been believed to be instinctive have large learned components. In the same article from which the preceding quotation is taken, Harlow reports on the sexual and maternal behavior of rhesus monkeys who have been raised in total isolation. These isolated monkeys did not know how to have sex relations when they grew up. When, after many attempts to teach them, some of the isolation-reared females became pregnant, they did not know how to "mother" the infants born to them, and even attacked them.

In any event, Harlow, the experimental psychologist working with monkeys, should be distinguished from Harlow, the maker of coy remarks comparing monkey and human behavior. The range of sex-role behavior among primates is actually much more diverse than is generally recognized. In some, for example, females are more aggressive than males; and in some, males participate in child care more than females.[22]

Regardless of whether monkey sex-role behavior is varied or rigid, its relevance to human beings is highly dubious. What does it mean to say that monkey behavior shows what human behavior "naturally" is? Does it mean that humans are biologically incapable of acting in any other way? If that were the case, "unnatural" sex or sex-role behavior would never occur, and there would be no need for writers to argue against women violating their natural sex roles. For example, a single instance of a little girl chasing a little boy would be enough to disprove Harlow's generalization that children's playground behavior is determined by innate biological differences.

Another way "natural" is used in talking about sex differences is to point to the way things ought to be, not the way they necessarily are.[23] Thus Harlow might argue that it is "unnatural" for little girls to chase little boys, and therefore they shouldn't. But in that case the burden would be on him to explain why it is "better" for human beings to act like certain species of monkeys. As another psychologist, Naomi Weisstein, puts it:

. . . There are no grounds to assume that anything primates do is necessary, natural, or desirable in humans, for the simple reason that humans are not nonhumans. For instance, it is found that male chimpanzees placed alone with infants will not "mother" them. Jumping from hard data to ideological speculation, researchers conclude from this information that *human* females are necessary for the safe growth of human infants. Following this logic, it would be as reasonable to conclude that it is quite useless to teach human infants to speak, since it has been tried with chimpanzees and it does not work.[24]

Sex Roles in Cross-Cultural Research

Cross-cultural research demonstrates that a division of labor by sex occurs in all currently known cultures. Women's work centers around preparing food and caring for children; men's work varies according to the economy of a particular culture, but it is more likely to involve being away from home—as in hunting, herding, traveling, and fighting—and is more often strenuous.[25]

The conclusion often drawn from such findings is that sex roles and the division of labor by sex are innate and biologically necessary.

The critical question is: What is "biological necessity"? Do the "biological necessities" similarly prevail in advanced industrial societies? The cultures in the cross-cultural surveys differ in three crucial ways from modern ones: they lack the technology of contraception and bottle feeding; they have high infant-mortality rates; and they highly value children's labor. Given these circumstances the lives of women in preindustrial societies are often dominated by an endless cycle of pregnancy, nursing for one to three years, then another pregnancy, and so on, until the end of fertility, which often coincides with the end of the woman's life itself. It makes sense then that while women are thus preoccupied, the tasks of hunting, herding, and so forth are carried out by the men.

Given the necessity for women to bear and nurse children, women's "nature" can be explained as part of the requirements of women's work. Their working role requires them to be giving, nurturant, responsible, unaggressive. Men's work may or may not require the opposite of such traits. In some cultures, as Margaret Mead pointed out, both sexes have "feminine" personalities, whereas in others both sexes are "masculine."

These differences in cultural emphasis, however, seem to depend to some extent at least on the type of work that is done in the economy. Where agriculture or herding represents the means of subsistence, both boys and girls are socialized to be compliant; but in hunting societies children are socialized to be independent and assertive.[26]

Hormonal Determinism

The primate analogy represents one form of the argument that sex behavior is biologically determined. Another version of the biological theory of sexual behavior is based on hormones. Females and males differ in the kinds and amounts of hormones their bodies produce. Hormones shape the bodies of men and women and cause the secondary sex characteristics to take their characteristic form—body and facial hair, voice depth, fat and muscle distribution. Hormones also enter the brain. Therefore, the theory goes, hormones explain everything there is to know about sex, the rise and fall of sexual desire, sex-role differences in interests and temperament, and choice of sex object.

Actually, however, as Ford and Beach[27] point out, the dominant fact with regard to human sexuality is the evolutionary trend away from hormonal control over sexual behavior and toward control by the higher centers of the brain—in other words, control by learning and by symbolic social meaning. Studies of the actual effects of hormones reveal that no simple relation exists between the amount of sex hormones in a person's blood and erotic arousal; that is, high arousal is possible at low levels of the hormones, and high levels need not necessarily lead to arousal. Furthermore, attempts to cure sexual problems such as impotence or frigidity with hormones generally have been unsuccessful.[28] In short, the research emphasizes the importance of social and psychological factors in erotic arousal. People are turned on by other people, situations, emotions, and imagination; hormones play a relatively minor role.

Sexuality: "Life Force" or Appetite?

The alternative to the "life force" or hormonal view of sexuality emphasizes the role of learning and the social context in the shaping and patterning of sexual experience and behavior. This concept of sexuality has been put forth by a number of social psychologists, sociologists, and anthropologists. Basically it conceives of sexuality, or any human biological motive for that matter, as a two-step process at least, involving a biological capacity that is shaped, directed, and amplified by social learning as well as individual cognitive processes. In other words, sex is in the head and in the social environment, as well as in the genitals.

Udry sums up the social-learning view of sexuality:

> The basic statement of the social-psychological explanation of human sexuality is this: sexual behavior is learned behavior. "Sex drive" is learned, sex interest is learned. If the requisite learning experiences occur, the individual becomes sexually interested and active; if they are absent, he does not. . . .[29]

Sexuality can begin in infancy. Hardy[30] has noted that there are two distinct constitutional bases around which sexual "appetites" can form: mild local stimulation of the genital area, and the more intense excitement-relaxation of orgasm. Although some children are capable of genital climax, cross-cultural evidence shows that sexual interest and behavior does not depend on the maturation of the sex glands or the ability to experience orgasms. Hardy notes that mild stimulation of the genital regions is pleasurable from infancy, and even in the preschool years may lead to orgasm. The cultural shaping of sexual appetites and sexual behavior, he argues, is built upon this constitutional basis. Thus some cultures encourage young children to masturbate and play at having intercourse. In such societies sexual behavior is continuous from childhood to adulthood.

Stephens[31] reports on a number of societies around the world where sexual stimulation is used as a pacifier for infants and as an aid in weaning older babies from the breast. In a number of cultures children play at intercourse all during childhood, and "real" intercourse may begin at the age of eight or ten. Some societies believe that children will not mature properly or be able to produce babies when they are adults unless they have regular sexual practice early in life.[32]

American parents typically discourage masturbation and any other form of sexual behavior in children, and try to keep them from observing sexual behavior. Most American

The world outside the home also encourages sex-typed activities.

Sexual Destiny and Sexual Knowledge

children, therefore, do not develop a sex interest until their teens, at which time it is expected of them. The male peer group encourages boys to have sexual interests in girls, but the girls' peer group, as well as parents, inclines girls toward a more social interest in boys.

Learning thus plays a role in the development of a general appetite for sex, as well as specific tastes. As with food, everyone needs to eat in order to stay alive, but beyond the minimal caloric requirements a great deal of individual variation is possible in what people like to eat, which is often what they have learned to like as children. As there are different cuisines in different cultures, with different tastes and styles of food preparation, there are varying symbols of sexual attractiveness and types of sexual behavior among cultures.

Even within one culture, such as ours, some people think about food often even when they are not hungry; other people express particular tastes in food and will refuse to eat certain dishes even when very hungry. Both obesity and an interest in gourmet cooking represent in different ways psychological approaches to food irrelevant to tissue needs.

Ultimately, however, the analogy between sex and food breaks down because there is little evidence that sex fulfills any tissue need. There is no sexual counterpart to starvation. As Beach puts it:

> No genuine tissue or biological needs are generated by sexual abstinence. It used to be believed that prolonged sexual inactivity in adulthood resulted in the progressive accumulation of secretions within the accessory sex glands, and that nerve impulses from these distended receptacles gave rise to sexual urges. Modern evidence negates this hypothesis. . . . What is commonly confused with a primary drive associated with sexual deprivation is in actuality sexual appetite, and this has little or no relation to biological or physiological needs.[33]

Physiological states alone are never enough to produce emotional arousal and behavior. As Silvan Tomkins has put it, the "oomph" of biological drives is an illusion. The "oomph" comes not from physiology but from the person's response to a physiological state. Tomkins offers the example of oxygen deprivation. What motive could be more urgent than that of a drowning or choking person for air? Yet, Tomkins notes, the tissue need for oxygen, by itself, does not create a psychological need for air. In fact, when oxygen deprivation is gradual, people become euphoric. Some pilots in World War II refused to wear their oxygen masks at high altitudes, and died with smiles on their lips. In the same way, argues Tomkins, sexual arousal is a state of conscious excitement, which amplifies the physiological arousal. No one, he writes, "has ever observed an excited penis. . . ."

> One is excited and breathes hard, not in the penis, but in the chest, the esophagus, the face, and the nose and nostrils. Both the sexual urge and the sexual pleasure of intercourse are ordinarily amplified by excitement as anoxia is amplified by panic. . . . To be fully sexually aroused and satisfied, one must be capable of excitement as well as tumescence.[34]

Tomkins notes that the concept of amplification helps explain how couples can report that they have orgasms and yet complain of the lack of sexual satisfaction:

> Sexual intercourse repeated with the same partner is vulnerable to such attenuation of satisfaction whenever the decline in novelty of the interpersonal relationship is such that excitement can no longer be sustained. Those who are generally bored with each other may also be unable to become sexually excited even when they are capable . . . of orgasm.[35]

Further, the experience of orgasm can even be perceived as a burden. Lillian Rubin[36] reports that among the working-class couples she studied, the sexual revolution has been a mixed blessing, especially for women. Once these women were expected to submit passively to sex. Now, however, new standards of sexual performance teach women—and their husbands—that if they don't have orgasms they are impairing their husbands' pleasure. Once an unexpected and pleasing occurrence, orgasms have become a requirement.

The women in Rubin's study not only worry about their ability to achieve orgasms at all, but they also worry about having them at the right time—at the moment of their hus-

bands' ejaculation. They also worry about the possibility of their husbands leaving them for women who can produce more and better climaxes. As Rubin points out, it seems clear that many women feel that their orgasms are for their husbands, not for themselves. Thus, although the new sexual freedom has brought increased satisfaction to many women, it has brought new anxieties and new demands to many others. Human sexuality remains, as always, a complicated psychological and social process, and not a simple physiological response.

New Views of Sexual Development

Challenges to the innate-determinism view of sexuality and sex-role development have also been emerging in recent years from research on the sexual development of normal children, as well as on people with sexual anomalies of various kinds. Probably the most striking illustration of the ambiguities of sex and gender is the phenomenon of transsexualism—the belief of a seemingly normal male or female that he or she is actually a person of the opposite sex. In recent years several such cases have made headlines; for example, a male tennis player who underwent a sex-change operation stirred up a controversy when she tried to enter a women's tennis tournament. In the San Francisco Bay area, a popular woman gym teacher who became a man was fired by the school board and sued to be reinstated, setting off a community controversy. Most sex-change operations are done confidentially, however. Although it is difficult to know how many people have changed their sex, it is estimated that, by 1975, approximately 1,500 such operations had been carried out in the United States.[37]

Why would anyone want to undergo the pain and humiliation of a sex-change operation? Although it's not possible to answer the ques-

tion in a final way, thanks to one gifted transsexual we do have some insight into what it is like to grow up believing that one was born into the wrong body. James Morris was a distinguished British newpaperman and writer of nonfiction books before he underwent a sex-change operation at the age of forty-six. He was the most prominent person to have had such an operation, and he seemed a highly unlikely candidate for one. He had climbed Mount Everest, had served four years in the army, and had married and become the father of five children. Yet since the age of three, he had felt that he really was a girl. After the operation, Jan Morris replaced James Morris and told the story of her life and transformation in an extraordinary book, *Conundrum*. It begins with the moment she "knew" she was a girl trapped in a boy's body:

I was three or perhaps four years old when I realized that I had been born into the wrong body, and should really be a girl. I remember the moment well, and it is the earliest memory of my life.

I was sitting beneath my mother's piano, and her music was falling around me like cataracts, enclosing me as in a cave. The round stumpy legs of the piano were like three black stalagmites, and the sound box was a high dark vault above my head. My mother was probably playing Sibelius; . . . .

What triggered so bizarre a thought I have long forgotten, but the conviction was unfaltering from the start.[38]

For more than forty years after that, Morris lived what was outwardly a man's life, all the while tormented by "the tragic and irrational ambition . . . to escape from maleness into womanhood."[39]

James Morris and other transsexuals illustrate the problematic nature of sexual identity. Maleness and femaleness do not spring automatically from anatomy or hormones; possessing a penis or a vagina does not necessarily make us a man or a woman. Jan Morris's female identity was clearly her own creation. The rest of us also construct sexual selves through experience and over time, but if the final outcome is in accord with our anatomical equipment, the temptation is to attribute our destiny to biology.

Some of the most dramatic evidence for the ambiguity of sexuality has emerged from studies of "sex errors of the body": people born with physical characteristics of both sexes. Studies of such people, generally referred to as hermaphrodites or intersexed individuals, have provided new insights into the development and patterning of sexuality. They have revealed that these processes are more complex than anyone had thought. These studies have also shown that popular discussions tend to use sexual terms in a confused and imprecise way, and some scholarly writing does so also. Thus Brown and Lynn[40] point out that the following terms are often used as synonyms:

male and masculine

female and feminine

homosexuality, sexual transvestism, inversion, and transsexualism

Actually, most contemporary sex researchers agree that it is important to distinguish between the biological aspects of sexuality and the psychological aspects. "Male" and "female" are the terms used to refer to biological aspects of sex, but "masculinity" and "femininity" are psychological and behavioral characteristics. We are so accustomed to thinking of all the aspects of sexuality as hanging together that it is difficult to get used to the idea that anatomy may be independent of the sense of gender identity ("I am a boy" or "I am a girl"). Table 7-1 presents the physiological and psychological aspects of sex differences.

Masculinity and femininity are not to be confused with gender identity. Thus a tomboy is a girl with boyish interests in, say, sports, tree climbing, and playing with soldiers, but there is no doubt about what gender she belongs to. A boy may have an interest in the things the culture places in the feminine world but he is still a boy. People may worry about their femininity and masculinity but, with rare exceptions such as Jan Morris, they have no doubts about their gender identity. Furthermore, there appears to be very little relationship between being worried about one's masculinity or femininity and the actual degree of discrepancy between one's behavior and the cultural standards. Thus a male who seems very "masculine" to other people may go through a crisis of doubt about his masculinity during adolescence, whereas an "effeminate" male may go through life without any such worries at all.[42]

Gender identity and masculinity-femininity are also to be distinguished from the third aspect of psychological sexuality, sex-object preference. Whether a person is sexually aroused by a member of his or her own or the opposite sex is independent of gender identity and masculinity-femininity. Homosexuals are not confused about their gender identity. Nor do

New Views of Sexual Development

TABLE 7-1   MALE/FEMALE CHARACTERISTICS

Characteristic	Male	Female	Explanation
Physiological:			
1 Chromosomal composition	XY	XX	At the moment of conception the unborn child's sex is determined by whether the father's sperm cell contains an X or a Y chromosome; if it is a Y chromosome, child will be a boy.
2 Gonads	Testicles	Ovaries	
3 Hormonal composition	Androgen, etc.	Estrogen, progesterone, etc.	These hormones operate before birth to differentiate male and female fetuses and again at adolescence to produce secondary sex characteristics— e.g., deep voices, beards, and body hair in men, breasts and menstruation in women.
4 Internal accessory organs	Seminal vesicles and prostate gland	Vagina, uterus, and fallopian tubes	
5 External genitalia	Penis and testicles	Vulva	
Psychological:			
1 Gender identity	I am a male	I am a female	The basic sense of one's social identity.
2 Masculinity-femininity	I am a masculine or effeminate male	I am a feminine or mannish woman	This refers to the person's conformity to the sex-role standards of the particular culture; it involves certain interests, attitudes, fantasies, ways of moving and speaking.[a]
3 Sex-object preference			Whether one is aroused by members of one's own sex or the opposite one.

[a]*Roger Brown caricatures American sex typing as follows: "In the United States a real boy climbs trees, disdains girls, dirties his knees, plays with soldiers, and takes blue for his favorite color. A real girl dresses dolls, jumps rope, plays hopscotch, and takes pink for her favorite color."*[41]

Sexual Destiny and Sexual Knowledge

homosexual men and women necessarily differ from their "straight" counterparts in masculinity and femininity. Some homosexual men view themselves as masculine and take the masculine role in sexual encounters. Others view themselves as feminine and take the feminine role, whereas still others see their masculinity as independent of homosexual roles.[43]

The argument that the psychological aspects of sexuality—gender identity, masculinity and femininity, or sex-object choice—are learned rather than innate comes in two versions. The first is a social-learning model of sex development.

The Social-Learning Model

According to this approach the child learns sex-typed behavior the same way he or she learns any other type of behavior, through a combination of reward, punishment, and observation of what other people are doing. Proponents of this view include psychologists, such as Mischel, Bandura, and Walters, and anthropologists, such as Margaret Mead in her early writings. In essence, proponents argue that it is unnecessary to invoke innate biological drives or tendencies to account for sexual behavior, particularly sex-role behavior, since learning can and does account for whatever behavioral differences are found between the sexes. Bandura, for example, describes sex-role learning as a process of indoctrination that begins at birth:

> Sex-role differentiation usually commences immediately after birth, when the baby is named and both the infant and the nursery are given the blue or pink treatment depending upon the sex of the child. Thereafter, indoctrination into masculinity and femininity is diligently promulgated by adorning children with distinctive clothes and hair styles, selecting sex-appropriate play materials and recreational ac-

tivities, promoting associations with same-sex playmates, and through nonpermissive parental reactions to deviant sex-role behavior.[44]

Besides direct indoctrination, the view of sexual development includes modeling as a way of learning: the boy will be rewarded for imitating his father and discouraged from using his mother as a model for his own behavior; the girl will be rewarded for the reverse. Eventually the child will find imitating the appropriate models rewarding in itself.

The Cognitive-Development Model

Unlike the social-learning model of sex-role development, which reflects a general approach held by a number of psychologists, sociologists, and anthropologists, the cognitive-development model of sexuality is mainly the work of one scholar, Lawrence Kohlberg.[45] Kohlberg's approach is largely an elaboration of the theories of Piaget, applied to the area of sexual development. Like the social-learning theorists, Kohlberg argues against the notion that sexuality is instinctually patterned. Nevertheless, he does not believe that sexuality and sex-role learning are based on learned conformity to cultural patterns. Rather, he argues, children's concepts of sexuality arise in the same way as all their other concepts about the world and the things in it. Sexual ideas and sex-role concepts result from children's *active structuring of their own experience,* rather than from something directly taught by other people.

The key cognitive event is the categorization of one's self as male or female. Once this recognition of self is acquired, between the ages of one-and-a-half to three, it organizes the way the child perceives and categorizes the rest of the world and his or her place in it. For example, other people are defined as belonging to one category or the other, male or female. The child places himself or herself in one of these categories, and begins the process of "cognitive rehearsal"—the lifelong accumulation of memories and fantasies in which he/she acts out the appropriate sex roles. A little boy will dream of being a fireman or a policeman or an astronaut when he grows up, and when he thinks of his future family life he will imagine himself as a daddy with a wife and children. A little girl will dream of having breasts and wearing grown-up clothes and lipstick and attracting men, and her fantasies of family life will feature her in the role of mother. The learning is gradual and changes with the child's stage of thinking—that is, young children may think that one's sexual identity is something that can change, like one's age.

Kohlberg also shows that genital anatomy plays a surprisingly small part in young children's thinking about sex differences. Clothing styles and social-role differences, such as the fact that males are policemen and firemen, are more impressive to childish minds. In short, learning to be male or female seems to be a process of understanding and interpreting the rules, both explicit and implicit, defining sex roles.

Kohlberg cites evidence showing that bright children tend to be ahead of their age mates of average intelligence in the maturity of their sexual attitudes. For example, between the ages of four and eight, all boys tend to show a number of changes in preference for masculine toys, and toward affiliation with male figures rather than female. Bright boys show these shifts earlier than average boys.

Kohlberg cites the work of Money and his associates as further evidence for the theory. These were studies of hermaphrodites, children born with genital abnormalities that make it hard to tell whether the child is a boy or a girl.[46] Certain tests now make it possible to tell whether the child is "really" male or female—that is, whether the chromosomes are male or female in pattern. But in previous years the doctor merely had to guess. Sometimes the doctor would find out later that he had assigned the child to the wrong sex. In such a case the child might be reassigned to the appropriate gender.

Body, Mind, and Gender

Money and his associates undertook a series of studies of children and adults with sexual abnormalities of one kind or another. The most striking discovery of this research was the finding that children with the same anatomical structures could be assigned to either sex and grow up to be a psychologically "normal" member of that sex. These researchers argued that the biological aspects of sexuality are independent of the psychological aspects—that is, the sex category to which one is assigned at birth and reared in, one's own sense of gender identity, and one's preference in sex objects. Thus, not only can intersexed or hermaphroditic children be raised successfully in either sex, but children erroneously assigned to the wrong category can grow up to be psychologically normal members of the sex to which they were assigned.

Money ultimately concluded that every child is "psychosexually neutral" at birth.* Because it is so extremely rare for a child to be assigned to the wrong sex, we assume that masculinity or femininity is a natural unfolding of innate biological inclinations. The psycho-

---

*In his more recent research, Money has moved away from the concept of complete psychosexual neutrality at birth. Although he acknowledges that prenatal hormone levels may influence behavior to some degree, he does not subscribe to the notion that sex-role differences are determined in a simple and direct way by biological forces. Money[47] argues that gender identity, despite hormonal influences, arises mainly from learning and social interaction.

sexual-neutrality concept argues that we *assign* children to one sex or the other on the basis of their anatomy and then believe that the psychological aspects of sexuality are caused by anatomy and physiology.

The child does not, however, remain psychosexually neutral for very long; once the child has established a gender identity (during the period of language mastery from one-and-a-half to three), it seems to be irreversible. Before that age a child can be reassigned to the other sex;

"I put my hair up once or twice a week. It's the only way I can get curls in it. When it's combed out, I'm willing to be seen in public."

after that age it becomes much more difficult. Money compares the process to "imprinting" in birds. In certain species of birds there is a critical period during which a young bird will follow any moving object it sees, and later will try to mate only with something that resembles the "imprinted" object. Usually the baby bird will see its mother and so become imprinted with appropriate responses. Experiments carried out by Lorenz and others, however, show that the baby birds can become imprinted on humans or vacuum cleaners or any moving object. Money suggests that sexual imprinting is something like that in humans. Kohlberg warns, however, that the notion of imprinting is only a metaphor in human sexuality. He argues that early sexual identities are difficult to reverse later because they are basic to other learning. They constitute the cognitive categories around which experience and memory have been organized, and any such categories learned early in life are hard to reverse.

Sex-Role Learning in Infancy

Regardless of whether one uses a social-learning or a cognitive model to explain the development of sex-role identity, the observational facts are that sex-role learning begins at birth. Lois Hoffman, in a review of the literature on early sex typing, writes:

> . . . One thing appears certain from this body of research on early mother-infant interaction, there are sex differences in both maternal and infant behavior in the first year of life. That sex-role learning is begun so early should not be surprising. Sex is a primary status—the first one announced at birth. The mother is very much aware of it. Her early behaviors towards the infant are not deliberate efforts to teach the child his proper sex role but she has internalized society's view and acts accordingly.

New Views of Sexual Development

She acts towards her son as though he were sturdy and active and she is more likely to show pleasure when his behavior fits this image. Her daughter is her doll—sweet and delicate and pink. . . . If the child exhibits behavior consistent with the female stereotype, such as dependency, she is not as likely to discourage it as she would with a son.[48]

As the infant grows the parent's behavior continues to be guided by traditional sex-role conceptions. Hoffman's review of the literature reveals that girls are protected more than boys and given less encouragement for independent, adventurous, exploratory behavior. As a result little girls do not develop skills in coping with the environment, but remain dependent on adults, particularly their mothers. As David McClelland[49] has put it, males tend to be interested in things, and females tend to be interested in people. Hoffman argues that these early childhood experiences help to explain how girls are turned away from the kinds of experiences that lead to achievement striving in later life, and develop an overemphasis on emotional relationships. In boys the emphasis is reversed. She suggests that a better balance of love and achievement would be desirable for both.

Sex in History

In this section we focus on the erotic aspects of sexuality, especially the question of how sexual experience is modified by the social and historical context.

In spite of the sexual revolution—the new morality and more open communication about sex—we have not escaped from the long shadow of Victorian morality, the so-called "civilized" morality that prevailed in Europe in the nineteenth century.

In recent years some scholars have been pointing out that Victorianism was not so monolithic as has usually been assumed. It was not so dominant on the Continent as in England, and even where it was most authoritative and repressive—in America—there were inconsistencies and ambivalence in people's attitudes toward sex.[50] Yet the evidence so far does not suggest that we should stop regarding "Victorian" as a synonym for "repressive." There does seem to have been a "more or less unified nineteenth-century style in sexual theory"[51] that has persisted, in some segments of the population, until very recently.

Above all, the Victorians believed that sexual experience was a threat to moral character and a drain on vital energies. If you were a woman, the leading medical authorities and their popularizers would have assured you that it was normal to have no sexual feelings at all—to have any would have marked you as a degenerate or a whore. It would have been wrong, however, for you to refuse your husband his "marital rights" since this would harm his health. Although men were acknowledged to have sexual desires, sex was dirty and dangerous for them also. Many doctors of the Victorian era warned against "excess" and its dire consequences to mental and physical health. One of the leading authorities warned married men that they should have intercourse no oftener than every seven to ten days, and that often only if they were very strong and healthy.[52]

The rise and fall of sexual morality is an uncharted part of history, only now beginning to receive the serious attention of scholars. Although Victorian morality was a more stringent form of the "civilized morality" that prevailed in Europe during the nineteenth century, American morality, as noted earlier, may have been more severe than that of England:

> American morality bore the stamp of Anglo-Saxon culture, evangelical Protestantism, and the absence of aristocratic or popular traditions of hedonism. The American code formally required mental chastity of both men and women, placed a special emphasis on female purity, and installed the mother as the guardian of morals. The sexual secretions, it was taught, must be conserved, lest character and intellect be weakened or destroyed.[53]

Obviously, these ideas have not disappeared.

The most notorious example of the tendency of Victorian doctors to mix morality with medicine is the concept of "masturbation insanity." A number of medical writers have described the rise and fall of this concept. Alex Comfort[54] shows how the promotion of sexual anxiety came to be practiced by the medical profession. Comfort argues that sex anxiety is an *iatrogenic* malady—a disorder produced as a result of medical intervention. He compares the history of masturbation insanity with the outburst of witch hunting that occurred in earlier periods of European and American history. Although masturbation had always been considered a sin by the Church, it was not regarded as a worse sin than any other form of disapproved sex; and medical authorities showed no particular concern with the subject. Some writers before the eighteenth century regarded masturbation as a useful form of sexual relief. The notion that masturbation not only is sinful but the leading cause of insanity, blindness, and epilepsy was put forth in the eighteenth century and reached its peak in the middle of the nineteenth. The preoccupation led to numerous devices for controlling masturbation, such as chastity belts and even surgical intervention.

Perhaps the most widespread and pernicious effect of the concern about the practice was its effect on child rearing. From the mid-nineteenth century to the first half of the twentieth, mothers were warned by child-rearing manuals to be ever watchful lest their children touch their genitals. Comfort quotes some advice given by Dr. Emma Drake in 1901:

> Mothers need to be Argus-eyed, to guard their babies from all the evils that beset them. . . . While very young . . . they can be taught that handling [the genitals] will hurt them and make them sick. Tell them that little children, when they do not know this, form the habit of handling themselves and as a result they become listless and sick, and many times idiotic and insane, or develop epileptic fits. . . .[55]

As late as 1928 an English child-rearing manual was still recommending "untiring zeal" on the part of the mother to prevent masturbation, and suggesting that it might be necessary to put the child to bed with the legs in splints.[56] Comfort writes that the outbreak of masturbation-insanity nonsense did not really end until the Kinsey reports of the late 1940s, showing that masturbation was practically universal for both sexes.

Ironically, the very prevalence of masturbation made it possible for the proponents of masturbation as the cause of insanity to give the appearance of proving their point: they found if they were to interrogate any mental patient, he or she would confess to being a masturbator.

Legacy of "Civilized" Morality

The current sexual climate in many ways appears to have been shaped by the previous era of repression. For one thing our very preoccupation with sexuality may be a backlash phenomenon, a sudden outpouring of all the questions that couldn't be asked, all the words that couldn't be said, all the sights that couldn't be seen. But the present sexual atmosphere is more than an outpouring of blocked impulses. The assumptions of "civilized" morality provide much of the framework for today's liberal morality, as well as for research into sex. For example, the view of sexuality as a powerful, natural force that civilized society holds in check was and is the prevailing model of sexuality for the Victorians, for Freud, as well as for *Playboy* magazine and the liberal morality it represents. The Victorians believed in taming sexuality and banishing it even from thoughts; Freud believed that people should control their sexuality consciously, and direct sexual "energy" into useful work. *Playboy* and other advocates of "liberal morality" believe it is healthy and natural to follow the dictates of nature, and act on one's sexual impulses. All agree with the "life force" model of sexuality.

Freud was an outspoken critic of the excesses of "civilized" morality, particularly the silence and secrecy that prevented even doctors and patients from discussing sexual problems. Yet he shared many of the assumptions of the most extreme representatives of sexual conservatism. The historian Nathan Hale has recently pointed out the parallels between Freud and Anthony Comstock, the guardian of American purity who campaigned for censorship and obscenity laws:

> Despite enormous differences . . . they agreed on certain fundamentals. They believed that civilization and progress depended directly on the control of sexuality and on the stable monogamous family. They believed in different ways that "mind" should govern the "sensual nature." Even Freud displayed some of the reticence Comstock would enforce by public censorship. It was only after great inner resistance that Freud brought himself to publish the sexual histories of his patients. These broad similarities between men so unlike testify to the strength of the common elements in European and American versions of "civilized" morality.[57]

Freud, too, in his earlier years, believed in a version of masturbational insanity. "Neurasthenia," a common psychiatric complaint of Victorian times—involving weakness, weariness, and lassitude—was attributed by Freud to masturbation. At the same time, however, Freud believed that the guilt and anxiety caused by the taboos on masturbation might cause more harm than the practice itself.

The Social Context of Sexuality

Not only the past theories about sexuality and sex differences influence present theories; in addition, the social context surrounding sexuality may influence sexual experience and behavior itself. Thus the common notion that the sexual drive is pretty much the same everywhere, only the openness of talking about it varies, is probably wrong. Whether or not one can talk about sex or think about it, who can talk to each other about it, and how one learns about sex—all of this may have an enormous influence on the experience itself.

Most discussions of sexuality focus on sexual behavior itself, or the content of people's information and beliefs, or their attitudes, rather than on the context in which sex is learned and acted out. A number of researchers have suggested that it is also useful to look not only at what people say and do but also at the context of the interaction. For example, Lennard and

Bernstein[58] suggest that when a patient goes to see a psychotherapist, the patient may be helped as much by the form of the interaction as anything the therapist may say. In this perspective, therapy is a process of going to a place one or several times a week where you speak your innermost thoughts in confidentiality with the complete interest and attention of another person, and with the assurance that you will not be criticized or scolded.

Lennard and Bernstein use television as another example of the contrast between content and context. They note, for example, that people tend to worry a great deal about the effect of the content of television programs on their children—whether watching violent programs will make children act aggressive. But few people worry about the effects of television as a medium or context—the fact that television turns experiences on and off arbitrarily, that reports of serious real-life events such as wars, disasters, and human tragedies are interrupted by cheery advertisements.

What is the medium or context in which information about sex, and sexuality itself, is exchanged? The most important of such features are secrecy; the aura of shame and anxiety; the transmission of information via childhood peer groups rather than by adults; the preoccupation with health, morality, and normality; the taboos about discussing sexuality; the fact that "any statement by an individual is presumed to be related to the sexual preferences and desires of that individual"[59]; and, as a corollary of the latter, the assumption that talking about sex is an act of seduction.

Until very recently sexual knowledge in America was in a state sociologists call "pluralistic ignorance"—everybody knew about his or her own sexual behavior, but nobody knew what anyone else was doing or feeling. Thus everyone had a "backstage" or undressed view of his or her own sexuality, and a frontstage, dressed-up view of other people's. The Freudian revolution had made sexual feelings more ac-

ceptable than previously, but this loosening up was accompanied by rather strict notions of normality. For many people the old concern with the sinfulness of sex was replaced by a concern with normality. For women the change from Victorian sexuality to Freudian was like jumping from the frying pan into the fire—or, more aptly, from the freezer into the refrigerator. The Freudian revolution discovered that women have sexual feelings after all, but it created the myth of two orgasms: the notion that the clitoris transfers its sensitivity to the vagina in "mature," nonneurotic women. Actually, as Kinsey and later Masters and Johnson have shown, all orgasms center on the clitoris, although the stimulation that leads to orgasm can come from any erogenous zone or from the imagination.

From the perspective of the 1970s it appears that the truly revolutionary event in the social context of sexuality was the publication of the Kinsey reports from 1948 to 1953. Kinsey's statistics not only broke through the curtain of pluralistic ignorance, but also made it permissible to discuss sexuality in conventional social situations. They revealed widespread deviance from conventional moral standards and upset previously held notions of rigid distinctions between normality and deviance in sexual matters. For example, Kinsey found considerable evidence of childhood sexual activity, homosexual experiences in the sex histories of "normal" heterosexual men, premarital and extramarital sexuality, as well as deviations from presumably "normal" patterns of intercourse in marriage.

The Effects of Secrecy

The secrecy previously surrounding sexuality has had profound effects. For one thing it sets the stage for guilt and anxiety. Masturbation is the classic instance of a practice that is practically universal, yet so taboo that countless millions of people have been tortured by the thought that "I must be the only one to have done this." One of the reasons the notion of masturbational insanity seemed plausible was that people were indeed "driven crazy" by guilt and worry over having ruined themselves physically and mentally.

Another effect of secrecy is to call attention to whatever the secret is about. Georg Simmel, one of the classic sociologists of the nineteenth century, described the secret as a sociological form. Any secret, he noted, creates a great atmosphere of tension. Does the other person know my secret? What would happen if I told?

> . . . The secret is surrounded by the possibility and temptation of betrayal; and the external danger of being discovered is interwoven with the internal danger, which is like the fascination of the abyss, of giving oneself away. The secret creates a barrier between men but, at the same time, it creates the tempting challenge to break through it, by gossip or confession—and this challenge accompanies its psychology like a constant overtone.[60]

Adding sexual guilt and anxiety to the general tensions of any kind of secrecy results in a very potent mix. The context of prudery and repression may well have had the effect of heightening the excitement and "oomph" of sexuality. Laing[61] has pointed out that repression has paradoxical effects. He notes that if you try very hard to have only clean thoughts, it is difficult to avoid thinking "dirty" ones. It is like being told "Do not think of a white monkey." To be constantly on guard against sexual thoughts is to live in a highly erotic atmosphere; the Victorians found piano legs guilty of indecent exposure. Further, as Laing also notes, warnings and injunctions against doing things also may incline people to do those very things. A classic instance is the little boy who was playing with a bean. His mother told him "Don't put that bean in your ear." The end of the story,

of course, is that the boy puts the bean in his ear. Why? Because the warning may have put an idea into his head that wasn't there in the first place, and also because telling someone not to do something suggests that they really are inclined to do it, if it weren't forbidden.

Freud and Secrecy

Breaking through the knots of secrecy that surrounded sex was one of the major achievements of the Freudian revolution. Part of the "miracle" cures of the early analysts—severe symptoms clearing up after only one session—may have been due to the fact that the early analysts were able to attack the social context surrounding sex.

The discoveries of Freud have transformed emotional life itself. There is a vast difference between a psychoanalytic patient in 1899 learning of his romantic attachment to his mother, and one in the 1970s. Mary McCarthy[62] once wrote about the banality of the insights she had gained from her psychoanalyst. She was disappointed to learn how unoriginal her neurosis was; she suffered from the same conflicts as everybody else.

For several decades now sophisticated parents have been watching their offspring for the first stirring of sexual attachment to mother, Oedipal hostility to father, and sibling rivalry for the little sister with the same parental interest as other milestones of development, such as the first tooth, the first word, the first step. In short, the Freudian revolution transformed what had been a private, unthinkable torment—what kind of monster must I be to have such thoughts and feelings—into a problem common to everyone. As the mama in the joke put it, "Oedipus, shmedipus, as long as he loves his mother."

Another aspect of the Freudian revolution was to legitimize thinking previously forbidden thoughts. Freud drew a sharp line between having a fantasy and acting it out. Victorian morality did not make this distinction. It was almost as much a sin to have unclean thoughts as to do unclean things. Much of the torment of Freud's patients as well as of their contemporaries must have come about through struggles with their own thoughts as well as reactions to them—the knots of Western conscience, as Laing has described them.

When Freud began his psychiatric career, it was unheard of for patients to discuss their sex lives with physicians. Patients tried hard to conceal any information about the subject, and doctors were as "prudish" and "lascivious" as any other "civilized" people of that time.[63]

Freud argued that every nervous illness could be traced to a sexual origin. As Freud freely admitted, this idea did not originate with him. But Freud's method of treatment, "the talking cure," was original, and it required that the doctor and the patient communicate with complete openness. In one of his early papers,[64] he pleaded that it should be possible to discuss sexual matters "without being stamped as a disturber of the peace or as a person whose aim is to arouse the lower instincts." He summarized the arguments against doctors' inquiring into their patients' sexuality:

> I hear it said that a physician has no right to intrude upon his patients' privacy in sexual matters, or to wound their modesty (especially that of his women patients) so grossly as such an interrogation would do. His clumsy hand would only ruin family happiness, and with youthful patients destroy innocence and undermine the authority of parents; with adults he would become the uncomfortable possessor of disquieting knowledge and his relations with his patients would suffer in consequence. It is therefore his ethical duty to hold himself aloof from the whole question of their sexual life.[65]

Sexuality in Early Modern Europe

Before the nineteenth century, European culture was not nearly so repressive as it was to become. Before the Protestant reformation of the sixteenth century, it was even less so. It is instructive to look at this pattern of sexuality because it contrasts both with the "civilized" morality of Victorian times and with our own. Anyone who has read Chaucer, or Boccaccio, or Rabelais is aware of the bawdiness of early modern literature. The evidence is that people's everyday behavior was more openly sexual than even today, in the sense that there were fewer taboos on sexual talk, and sexual horseplay was a usual part of adult interactions. Even more surprising than the ribaldries of adult life was the fact that adults felt no need to shield children from these goings-on. Aries writes:

> One of the unwritten laws of contemporary morality requires adults to avoid any reference, above all, any humorous reference, to sexual matters in the presence of children. This notion was entirely foreign to the society of old. The modern reader of the diary in which Henry IV's physician, Heroard, recorded the details of the young Louis XIII's life is astonished by the liberties which people took with children, by the coarseness of the jokes they made, and by the indecency of gestures made in public which shocked nobody and were regarded as perfectly natural. . . .
>
> There is no reason to believe that the moral climate was any different in other families, whether nobles or commoners; the practice of associating children with the sexual ribaldries of adults formed part of contemporary manners. . . .[66]

In the fifteenth and sixteenth centuries there began to be a new concern with protecting childhood innocence, but the new attitude was slow in separating children from adult sexuality.

"Broad talk," writes Aries, "was so natural that even later on, the strictest reformers would introduce into their sermons to children and students comparisons which would seem shocking today."[67] He also points out that sixteenth-century textbooks for schoolboys often included sex jokes and riddles as well as conversations about sexual matters in order to illustrate points of grammar and so forth. "The coarsest jokes, as well as topics of anything but educational value, are to be found in these dialogues."[68]

The campaign to desexualize childhood eventually succeeded in building the taboos we are familiar with today, taboos so firmly entrenched as to have been practically untouched by the sexual revolution. Even the educational discussion of sex in schools is extremely controversial today, in spite of, or perhaps because of, the fact that parents find it extremely hard to teach their children "the facts of life."

The campaign for childhood innocence did not succeed, of course, in eradicating children's sexual interests; it only succeeded in driving them underground. On their side of the sexual generation gap, children created their own cultural traditions of sexual lore and misinformation. Such works as the Opies' *Lore and Language of Schoolchildren*[64] and Martha Wolfenstein's study of children's jokes[70] document the pervasiveness of sexual interest in children, as part of a "subversive" (i.e., antiadult) culture passed on through generations.

The result of the taboos between adult-child sexual communication has resulted in a system of sex education in which the vast majority of people learn about sex from their peers. It is a system of negative teaching and nonteaching from parents and positive learning from peers. As the students of human communication point out, not communicating about sex is one form of communicating about it. This context of sexual learning has profound consequences for individual experience and for the relations between men and women.

Sexual Learning and Nonlearning in the Family

The sexual attitudes and feelings learned in early childhood have a way of persisting even in people who have reevaluated or rejected their parents' attitudes and values in politics, religion, and other matters. Thus changes in adult behavior and the liberalization of public attitudes may obscure the persistence of traditional patterns of parent-child communication—and noncommunication—about sexual matters. One rather dramatic bit of evidence on this point is the study of Leah Shaefer[71] of a group of middle-class women in their twenties and thirties when she interviewed them in the early 1960s. These women had all rebelled against the sexual Victorianism with which they had been brought up. Yet many or most of them seemed to be raising their daughters in the same way they had been raised. They were able to overcome the feeling of shame and guilt as far as their own sexual feelings were concerned, but found it difficult to think of their children as having sexual feelings. Particularly as far as their daughters were concerned, they were afraid that if they expressed approval of sexuality, this would lead to promiscuity.

John Gagnon[72] provides a cogent analysis of why early sexual learning tends to be so heavily negative and so persistent. First, he notes that American parents tend to respond to children's sexual behavior—handling the genitals, sex play, and so on—in one of two ways. One way is to tell the child not to do that—that the behavior is wrong or bad. This type of response from the parent will not surprise the child because he or she has heard many don'ts before—don't touch the stove or knife, don't step into the street. The other way is to avoid saying anthing to the child, but to try to distract the child by pointing to something more "enjoyable" to do, or by pointing out some other reason than the sexual one to stop the behavior—"it's too cold to have your pants down," or "kissing can spread germs." Both the negative injunction—"it's wrong"—and the distraction technique—nonlabeling or mislabeling—may have much the same effect. The child learns that there is something vaguely wrong with sexuality. Further, as a result of the parents' reluctance to label sexual parts and activities and acts of excretion, the child is left with an infantile vocabulary that will later be filled in by terms learned from other children.

Parent-child relations are influenced by the lack of a vocabulary for matter-of-fact discussions of sexuality: the four-letter words have been tainted by their long use as curse words. Adults are beginning to use them more easily, but they are not felt to be a proper medium of instruction for children. Medical terms are too forbidding and polysyllabic.

In any event, nonlabeling or mislabeling may result in profound consequences. First, early sexual negative learning is never corrected. Gagnon points out that the parents modify their early no's and don'ts about many things as the child grows older—thus the child later learns how to cross the street and how to use knives and manage stoves. But the primitive early learning about sexuality is rarely, if ever, corrected in the same way.

Further, the child's lack of a vocabulary to describe what he or she sees and feels, plus difficulties of communication with parents, permits fantasies to flourish for long periods of time without correction.

> The mysterious penis that must exist behind the female pubic hair, the feeling that females have been castrated, and other childhood fantasies are common because there has been no system of naming which will adequately control the child's nascent interest in his own or others' bodies. The second consequence of the lack of a controlling set of symbols is probably related to the tendency for children to identify their sexual organs with excretory functions. . . . This may also be related to some of the sexual differences between girls and boys; since boys may get dirty—therefore dirt is not so bad—and girls may not, the association may be more firmly entrenched among the latter.[73]

To point out the problems in early sexual education of children in this culture is not, however, the same as suggesting a solution. The sexual instruction or noninstruction of children in families is part of a complex cultural pattern that includes family structure as well as adult sexuality. The concept of childhood innocence is deeply rooted in our culture, even though we can trace its beginnings in relatively recent historical times. It may well have arisen as an intensified form of the incest taboo, made necessary by the intimate emotional climate of the nuclear family.

Sex and Sex-Role Socialization in Peer Groups

Because parents and other adults provide little in the way of sex education for children, the information gap is filled by the growing child's friends and acquaintances—his or her peer group. After a child becomes of school age, both sex education and sex-role learning are carried out in large part by sex-segregated groups of children of comparable ages. Evidence indicates that elementary-school children are no longer as rigidly separated into same-sex groups as they once were,[74] but for many generations the existence of separate male and female subcultures among schoolchildren has had profound effects on definitions of masculinity and femininity, as well as relations between the sexes.

As far as sexuality is concerned, the exchange of sex information by children is guilty and clandestine. It generally tends to reinforce the negative attitudes the child has acquired at home, as a result of the parents' direct teaching or silence. Actually, several studies show that

The Social Context of Sexuality

most American parents fail to provide any sex information at all to their children. Gagnon notes that "the myth of the good heart-to-heart talk between father and son seems to be just that."[75]

Although communication about sex is much more open in child and adolescent peer groups than in the family, much of what is said is not very informative. Male sociologists report that the sexual emphasis in the male subculture is both pornographic and achievement-oriented:

> The exchange of information between males in American culture is not sexually informative except in an indirect sense. The information comes as part of tales of sexual prowess or of humor in which emphasis is placed on heterosexual expertise or exploits. What evolves from this male-to-male interaction is an image of the sexual self rather than knowledge of sexuality.[76]

And Udry writes:

> Since status results from convincing other boys of one's heterosexual escapades, most early adolescent heterosexual activity is discussed in male groups. There is considerable fabrication and elaboration of experience, and boys learn to discount one another's tales of prowess. The emphasis in the descriptions is on anatomical and manipulative detail and erotic responses. . . . Sex emerges as something which boys "do to" girls. . . . Accounts of boys' early coital experience with girls show the boys to have been unconcerned with and largely unaware of the girls' own behavior. Among unattached adolescent boys, sex is sex, and it is divorced from emotional involvement, love, or romance.[77]

Udry notes that the male orientation to sex acquired in child and adolescent groups persists into adulthood, and does not disappear at marriage. He suggests it accounts for the man's greater interest in and participation in extra-marital affairs and pornography, and is the cause of much misunderstanding between husbands and wives.

In the girls' subculture the order of priorities is reversed. If boys like sex more than they like girls, little girls like boys much more than they like sex. Girls have more trouble arriving at an image of a sexual self. There is often a huge gap between the images of love and romance and thoughts of direct sexual activity. The girl has no role models for sexual behavior such as those provided by male pornography or even male-oriented literature. In adolescence the girl tends to be caught in a bind between the wish and need to be "popular" with boys and the fear of losing her "reputation" or being taken "advantage of" by "giving in" to male sexual demands. Parents often contribute to the bind by pressures on the girl to be popular and have lots of dates, but not to be "cheap" or to let boys go "too far." The anthropologist Jules Henry, in a perceptive analysis of teen-age culture in the fifties and sixties, saw the American girl as living on a "razor edge of sexual competition":

> Because boys are united in "flocks" by the requirements of their games, they are held together more tightly than girls, and hence the competition among girls for friends is more intense than among boys. . . . As courtship becomes more important to the girls, competition and gossip increase in intensity. What makes the courtship experience particularly intense for girls is that it is the only activity through which they can validate their femininity. Since boys can validate their masculinity in a greater variety of ways, the chase does not have the same self-validating importance for them. Behind the girls' courtship drive, of course, looms the parental—usually the maternal—image, tirelessly keeping tally of each date. . . .
>
> . . . It is not exaggeration to say that the teen-age American girl lives on a razor edge of sexual competition. Thus, beneath the gaiety of

any teen-age party throbs the anxiety of being left out next time, of losing a boy tomorrow that one has today or not getting the right one, of not getting the one you really want, of not getting the popular one, and so on.[78]

Since Jules Henry wrote, the teen-age world in America has been exposed to extraordinary changes in sex attitudes, culture, generation conflict, women's and gay liberation, as well as countermovements to all of these. The whole pattern of dating, going steady, and early marriage seems to have altered—to what extent we don't yet know. It appears, however, that teen-agers today are in the process of being liberated from the rigid rating and dating codes of the last two decades—and all the tensions they entailed—and are beginning to face the problems involved in making personal choices without the guidance of strict rules.

Sexual Changes Across Time and Space

A few scholars have tried to place the rise and fall of sexual moralities in broader historical and cross-cultural contexts. Taylor[79] has shown that European sex history has followed an uneven course, with periods of sexual freedom alternating with periods of greater strictness. Also, at any one time, there was great variation in sexual mores according to social class; the classes at either extreme of the social scale have traditionally been freer than the middle classes.

Taylor and other scholars have also noted that sexual mores seem to alternate with changes in family structure and the political order. Strict sex seems to go along with strict or authoritarian methods of child rearing in all areas—not just sex—and with nondemocratic political orders. William Stephens finds this general pattern across cultures as well. He writes, as we noted earlier, that primitive tribes tend to have relatively relaxed child-rearing methods, liberal sexual norms, and democratic political structures. At the middle range of social development, in patriarchal agrarian societies, there is a move toward strictness, while liberal patterns seem to reemerge in industrial democracies. Stephens writes:

> The development of the kingdom seems to bring with it certain basic changes in the family; among these are an elaboration of deference customs between family members and a tightening of sex restrictions. When the kingdom, the autocratic agrarian state, evolves into a democratic state, these family customs seem to gradually liberalize: family relationships become less deferential and more democratic, and sex restrictions loosen.[80]

The job of untangling the complex connections between sexual moralities and political, economic, and religious change remains to be done. In Europe sexual morality has been heavily influenced by religious factors. Christianity has always been a relatively ascetic religion, and the Protestant reformation marked a greater tendency toward strictness. The peak of repressive morality in Europe, however, occurred during the nineteenth century, at a time when political regimes were becoming less autocratic.

On Sexual Revolutions

The sexual revolution of the past decade or so represents the continuation of a trend that began around the turn of the century. The decisive break with Victorian morality was the Freudian revolution.

To those scholars who have studied the rise and fall of sexual moralities, the Freudian contribution was only part of a larger revolution in attitudes toward sexuality and toward the family. These social attitudes in turn seem to have been part of still wider changes in the society, especially in the economic and religious order. These changes accompanied the beginnings of the mass-consumption economy and the decline of the Protestant ethic with its distrust of idleness and pleasure. Thus Hale notes that the sexual revolution of the twentieth century coincided with the decline of:

> exactly those factors that caused the nineteenth-century addictions to "civilized" morality. The decline of religious controls over sexuality has been noted. By 1900 American observers had become aware of decisive changes in the economic system. The American sociologist Simon Pattern argued in 1908 that America was moving from an economy of deficit and saving to one of surplus and abundance. A new kind of character had to emerge, no longer dedicated to austerity and sacrifice but to leisure and rational enjoyment. Repression would give way to release. The new economy was giving a new place to women outside the home and family.[81]

It would be a mistake, however, to think of the sexual revolution as simply a liberation of previously repressed impulses. Like Victorian doctrines about the danger and ugliness of sex, modern ideas about sex as healthy and good are, above all, just that—a set of ideas with a complicated relationship to behavior and experience. There is no denying that, for many people, the sexual revolution has brought greater freedom, pleasure, and mutuality in sex. Yet at the same time, the new legitimation of sex and the new standards of sexual performance can create new tensions and anxieties.

For example, the working-class women described earlier illustrate how the new sexual freedom can be experienced as a kind of oppression; many of these women not only felt burdened by their husbands' demands for oral sex, but also felt alienated from their own orgasms.[82] Some of these women's problems can be blamed on lingering Victorianism, as well as distrust of their husbands' commitments to sexual "liberalism." But liberated attitudes do not necessarily lead to uninhibited joy. Lillian Rubin also interviewed upper-middle-class women in her study. These women and their husbands were much more relaxed and accepting in their attitudes toward sex. Yet they often felt guilty about their inability to overcome their inhibitions and live up to their beliefs. While the working-class women wished their husbands would be less demanding, their middle-class counterparts blamed themselves for what they saw as inadequacies in their own personal sexual adjustment.

Paradoxically, the new sexual freedom may have decreased people's enjoyment of sex by raising the standards of satisfaction. Morton Hunt, in a survey of contemporary sexual attitudes and behavior, puts it this way:

> . . . the progress our society has made toward fuller and freer sexuality has revolutionized our expectations and made so many of us intolerant of our dissatisfactions that we forget the improvement that has taken place in our lives; like all partially liberated people, we are more discontented now than we were before our lot began to improve.[83]

Rather than unleashing wild and insatiable instincts, the sexual revolution reveals that, for many people, a lack of sexual desire is a major problem; the number one complaint of people who go to sex clinics is an inability to get "turned on" as much as they would like.

Besides those people who worry about getting enough satisfaction, there are also those at the other end of the spectrum who are made uncomfortable by the new standards for fre-

In recent years, increasing numbers of women have become active in sports, even those traditionally reserved for men only.

and in the general community have observed an increase in complaints of impotence. A team of three psychiatrists have identified a syndrome they labeled "the new impotence" — the inability of the male to function in the new sexual climate with the increased assertiveness of women.[84]

There are still other contradictions and tensions in contemporary attitudes toward sex. As Paul Robinson points out, the sexual revolution has not yet solved "the most vexing problem of human sexual psychology: the paradoxical need for both companionship and variety in erotic life."[85] The modern revolt against Victorian prudishness has taken two inconsistent directions. One approach argues for a liberation of sex, but only in the context of a deep emotional bond between the partners. The other approach to sexual modernism emphasizes the sensuous, bodily aspects of sex and separates sex from love.

The first point of view, which has been called "romantic"[86] or "person-centered,"[87] is exemplified in the work of Freud, Havelock Ellis, and Van de Velde. The second point of view, "anti-romantic" or "body-centered," is best exemplified in the writings of Kinsey. He believed that the idea of restricting sex to persons who were truly in love was as absurd a notion as the idea that masturbation causes insanity. In the work of Masters and Johnson, both tendencies coexist in an "almost schizoid" fashion.[88] On the one hand, Masters and Johnson unromantically manipulate sex in the laboratory, treating it as a physiological response; on the other hand, they insist on the need for emotional closeness and communication in sexual relationships.

This kind of ambivalence applies to many people today. As Robinson observes, "As moderns, we remain permanently divided between a romantic past, whose repressions we would gladly rid ourselves of, and a deromanticized future, whose emotional emptiness we fear even while we anticipate its greater freedom."[89]

quency, variety, and intensity in sex. For example, we hear from college campuses about some students who are not only inconvenienced by the sexual activities of their peers, but also made to feel deviant because of their relative inactivity. It is not only women who are having negative reactions to the revolution. Contrary to the image of male sexuality as an insatiable animal force, psychiatrists on college campuses

Sexual Changes Across Time and Space

Scientific and Technological Changes

The present changes in sexual attitudes and behavior and in sex roles are not due to ideological changes alone. The first half of the twentieth century witnessed three advances with profound implications for sexuality, the family, and the roles of women – the demographic revolution, the contraceptive revolution, and the technological revolution.

The demographic revolution resulted from medical advances that reduced infant mortality and extended the lifespan. Before the nineteenth century, a married woman could expect to devote the greater portion of her adult years to reproduction. In the United States, for example, the average number of births per woman around 1800 was seven. Infant-mortality rates varied over time and place, but until the twentieth century many and at times most infants could be expected to die. Thus high fertility rates were "needed" to offset the high death rates.

The reduction of infant mortality, as well as the invention of contraception, made it possible to separate sexuality from reproduction. The invention, development, and widespread acceptance of contraception – and of abortion – will probably prove to be the decisive advance in women's liberation. At least some of what we take to be sexist thinking today reflects the realities of women's lives in the past. The idea that "all women are mothers" was not quite so much of a distortion during the centuries when women could exercise slight control over their own reproductive capacities. In those days women were not only mothers, they were mothers many times over.

Finally, the industrial revolution may finally, after a century and a half, enhance the freedom of women and encourage the development of their mental capacities and talents. Whether women can match men in brute strength has sometimes been an issue, but in a technologically advanced society it is irrelevant.

In short, the demographic revolution, the contraceptive revolution, and the technological revolution have radically altered the potential role, status, and the very destiny of women in society. The current ferment over sex, sex roles, and family life may accordingly be interpreted as a form of "cultural lag" – a method of bringing social practices into cohesion with already existing biological and technological realities.

Summary

In both popular thought and many social-scientific writings, thinking about sexuality and sex differences has been dominated by biological imagery. Sexuality has been defined as a life force pressing for release, and sex-role differences are assumed to reflect innate temperamental inclinations. Obviously, males and females differ in anatomy, physiology, and perhaps even in temperament to some degree. Neither sexuality nor sex differences, however, can be understood as being independent of background such as learning, culture, and the historical context.

Anatomy is destiny largely because children are assigned at birth to two different worlds of experience and self-definition on the basis of the genital difference. Further, the biological capacity of women to bear children is much more fateful in societies without contraception and with high rates of infant mortality.

As a human motive, sexuality fits the model of an appetite or craving rather than a "life force." In general, then, our sexual selves are not simple reflections of the animal side of human nature; in our sexual lives as elsewhere, we are shaped by our time, place, and situation.

Source Notes

1. Murphy, 1971.
2. Herschberger, 1948.
3. Martin and Voorhies, 1975.
4. Memmi, 1968, p. 187 (italics in original).
5. Ibid., (italics in original).
6. Mead, 1935.
7. Sullerot, 1971.
8. Brown, 1965, p. 171.
9. Ibid.
10. Shainess, 1971, p. 14.
11. Deutsch, 1944, p. 192.
12. Erikson, 1964.
13. Mitchell, 1974.
14. Althusser, 1971, p. 195.
15. Dinnerstein, 1976.
16. Ibid.
17. Alland, 1972; Pilbeam, 1972.
18. Pilbeam, 1972, p.
19. Martin and Voorhies, 1975; Stack et al., 1975.
20. Stack et al., 1975, p. 149.
21. Harlow, 1962, pp. 3-6.
22. Mitchell, 1969.
23. Pierce, 1971.
24. Weisstein, 1971, p. 218.
25. D'Andrade, 1966.
26. Barry, Child, and Bacon, 1959
27. Ford and Beach, 1951.
28. Hardy, 1964.
29. Udry, 1971, p. 98.
30. Hardy, 1964.
31. Stephens, 1963.
32. Ford and Beach, 1951.
33. Beach, 1956, p. 4.
34. Tomkins, 1965, pp. 118-119.
35. Ibid., p. 119.
36. Rubin, 1976.
37. Gagnon and Henderson, 1975, p. 4.
38. Morris, 1974, p. 1.
39. Ibid., p. 8.
40. Brown and Lynn, 1966.
41. Brown, 1965, p. 161.
42. Kohlberg, 1966, p. 91.
43. Hooker, 1965.
44. Bandura, 1969, p. 215.
45. Kohlberg, 1966.
46. Money, 1961; Money, Hampson, and Hampson, 1957.
47. Money, 1972.
48. Hoffman, 1972, p. 141.
49. McClelland, 1953.
50. Degler, 1975; Rosenberg, 1973.
51. Robinson, 1976, p. 2.
52. Comfort, 1967, p. 58.
53. Hale, 1971, p. 465.
54. Comfort, 1967.
55. Drake, 1901, p. 87.
56. Comfort, 1967, p. 111.
57. Hale, 1971, p. 25.
58. Lennard and Bernstein, 1969.
59. Gagnon, 1965, p. 215.
60. Simmel, 1950, p. 334.
61. Laing, 1969a.
62. McCarthy,
63. Hale, 1971, p. 10.
64. Freud, 1898.
65. Ibid., p. 221.
66. Aries, 1962, pp. 100-103.
67. Ibid., p. 109.
68. Ibid.
69. Opie and Opie, 1959.
70. Wolfenstein, 1954.
71. Shaefer, 1964.
72. Gagnon, 1965.
73. Ibid., p. 222.
74. Udry, 1971, p. 86.
75. Gagnon, 1965, p. 214.
76. Ibid.
77. Udry, 1971, pp. 77-78.
78. Henry, 1963, p. 181.
79. Taylor, 1954.
80. Stephens, 1963, p. 258.
81. Hale, 1971, p. 476.
82. Rubin, 1976.
83. Hunt, 1974, p.
84. Ginsberg et al., 1972.
85. Robinson, 1976, p. 3.
86. Ibid.
87. Reiss, 1967.
88. Robinson, 1976. p. 195.
89. Ibid.

Sexual Changes Across Time and Space

Chapter Eight

The Ultimate Human Connection:
The Love Relationship

The Ultimate Human Connection

□ . . . *Anyone who has seen the film* Casablanca *will not have forgotten its theme song and the memorable line from it which declares: "the fundamental things apply, as time goes by." . . . But do they? . . . For instance, when two lovers woo, do they still say, "I love you?" Or are they more likely to say, "I'm not really ready for an involvement at this stage in my life"?*

William Kilpatrick, *Identity and Intimacy*

Despite the great changes in attitudes toward sex, marriage, and family life in recent years, the vast majority of Americans eventually marry. Most people experience one or several "love" relationships in the course of their lives, and "love" remains the only legitimate reason for marriage. Even more than in the past, such relationships are based on the choices of the two individuals themselves. What is it that attracts people to one another in the first place? Why do some relationships end at the first encounter, while others develop into emotional attachments and permanent commitments? What keeps people together in enduring relationships? Why do some relationships decline and dissolve over time?

The rapid social changes of recent years seem to have made people even more concerned with love and intimacy than they were in previous decades. One sign of this increased interest is the flood of books offering advice on how to find and manage intimate relationships. Another is the current boom in social-science research on love.

Some people look to science to tell them how they can make a person fall in love with them, or to tell them what kind of person they should choose as a mate. Others fear that the scientific study of love will destroy and dehumanize it. Senator William Proxmire, for example, criticized a grant for research into love by stating: "200 million Americans want to leave some things a mystery and right at the top of those things we don't want to know is why a man falls in love with a woman and vice versa."[1]

Neither the hopes nor the fears are justified. Although social scientists have offered explanations of love and attraction, they have not, as yet, been able to predict in advance which individuals will fall in love with one another. And although we know a good deal about the processes that lead to problems in relationships, we still don't know which ones will succumb to the difficulties and which ones will survive in spite of them. Nevertheless, the study of love relationships may, as one researcher put it, "make a positive contribution to the quality of life"[2] at a time when rapid changes in attitudes and behavior concerning sex, love, and marriage have caused great confusion.

This Thing Called Love

Love is one of those words that everyone uses but no one can define. Writers on the subject agree on only one thing—that love is an elusive concept; otherwise they contradict one another about its nature and significance. As one writer put it almost a century ago: "Love is such a tissue of paradoxes, and exists in such an endless variety of forms and shades, that you may say anything about it that you please and it is likely to be correct."[3]

Disagreement exists not only among poets and novelists, but among scholars as well. To some people, love is a trivial notion concocted by Hollywood movies and popular songwriters, and therefore hardly worthy of serious discussion. To some biologists and ethologists, love is part of our evolutionary inheritance, comparable to the pair bonding found in certain mammals and birds.

Traditionally, many sociologists of the family have scoffed at love as kind of irrational frenzy, typical of teen-agers and the early stages of some adult sexual relationships, but having little to do with marriage. In this view, the American idea of love is "dysfunctional" because it encourages people to believe that "love and marriage go together like a horse and carriage" and thus sets them up to be disillusioned by the discovery that they don't. Others believe love is functional because it brings people together, saving the institution of marriage from disintegration in modern societies where marriages are no longer arranged by kin.

To some radical critics, love is a kind of "opiate of the people"—an ideology that leads people to seek happiness in personal relationships and to ignore the problems of the larger society. Some feminists have argued that love is a trap leading women to be exploited by men. But not all radicals disapprove of love; some feminists argue that when men and women are able to relate to each other as equal human beings and no longer use each other as objects, love will flourish. One Marxist writer has argued that love and fidelity, far from being abolished in a socialist culture, "only need to be freed from their narrow bourgeois existence."[4]

Psychologists who have examined love tend also to disagree. To some, love is a kind of selfishness, a preoccupation with one's own feelings rather than a genuine concern for the other person. In this view, lovers are more in love with love than with one another.[5] To others, love is a giving of the self, ennobling and enriching. Freud defined the healthy person as one who could love and work. Erikson made ability to love a major developmental stage in adulthood.

What are we to make of these inconsistent views? Perhaps, like the six blind men and the elephant, each writer on love has seized on a different aspect of love and declared it to be the essential nature of the beast. As Morton Hunt pointed out, something is wrong with the question, "What is this thing called love?" because it implies that love is a single entity. Yet the word is used to refer to many different things:

> There is making love and being in love, which are quite dissimilar ideas; there is love of God, of mankind, of art, and of pet cats; there is motherly love, brotherly love, the love of money, and the love of one's comfortable old shoes.[6]

Oddly enough, in spite of the difficulties of defining love, most people understand perfectly well what is meant by the terms "love relationship," "falling in love," or "being in love." A love relationship is usually symmetrical—that is, it occurs between equals, unlike, say, the love between parents and children. It involves a mixture of sex, love, and friendship, but a purely sexual relationship or a platonic friendship would not count as love. All close relationships may be similar in someways, but love relationships are more intense and involve much more fantasy and possessiveness than friendships. Love need not necessarily be confined to partners of opposite sexes.

Love in Cross-Cultural Perspective

One of the persistent puzzles about love concerns its relationship to Western culture. Is the capacity to fall in love built into human nature and hence found in all times and places? Or do Americans and Europeans experience a different set of emotions than people in other cultures?

The answer seems to be that both statements are partly true. Although there has been a great debate about the subject, no one who argues that love is universal denies that it occurs more widely and is more elaborated in Western society than elsewhere. In most of the world's cultures, marriages are arranged by kin, not by the bride and groom. Those who emphasize the uniqueness of love in the West admit, however, that love *can* bloom anywhere, even if it rarely does so. Thus the anthropologist

Ralph Linton, often quoted as a proponent of the notion that love is a trait peculiar to our culture, concedes: "All societies recognize that there are occasional violent emotional attachments between persons of the opposite sex."[7] On the other hand, he goes on to argue that our present American culture is practically the only one that makes them the basis of marriage. The rarity of such attachments in most cultures, he writes:

> suggests that they are psychological abnormalities to which our own culture has attached an extraordinary value, just as other cultures have attached extreme values to other abnormalities. The hero of the modern American movie is always a lover just as the hero of the old Arab epic is always epileptic.[8]

Arguing against Linton's position, William J. Goode[9] points out that the potential for falling in love is universal. Even in societies where romantic love plays no role in the decision to marry, individual love relationships may appear in literature and myth, and in real life as well. Thus the Bible contains several descriptions of love: the Song of Solomon, the love story of Jacob and Rachel. The classical literatures of India, Japan, and China also include tales of romantic passion and tragedy.

Goode goes on to note that since strong love attachments can occur in any society, those societies that do not allow free choice in marriage partners must control love. Typical strategies of love control range from child marriage, to constant chaperonage, to the isolating of young people from potential mates.

Nevertheless, Goode concedes that although the potential for falling in love is universal, the belief that falling in love is the only proper basis for marriage is peculiar to Western culture. In most traditional cultures, the emphasis is on congeniality rather than love between marital partners. Young people are brought up to believe that any reasonably well-adjusted man and woman will be able to live together contentedly.

Yet even in those cultures where the spouses have no say in the marriage, personal preference can enter the picture, if only to make the person miserable. Anthropologists have recorded numerous instances of people complaining bitterly about having been pushed into marriages with people they detested. On the other hand, many cultures with arranged marriages do offer escape routes for people with strong feelings about one another. Thus in many of these societies, a couple can disobey their elders and elope, hoping that the parents will eventually approve the marriage.

Love and Labeling

The question as to whether people in different cultures feel the same emotions is hard to answer because emotions are not simple reactions to events or people, but complex mixtures of feelings and ideas. Feelings acquire meaning only in relation to a specific social and historical context. In other words, emotional words such as "love" do not have a fixed meaning corresponding to a fixed set of human feelings.

Recent work in the psychology of emotion suggests that thought processes play a large role in emotional experience. We are not passion's slaves, in the sense that emotions are not events that "happen" to us. Rather, we construct emotional experience on the basis of culture, learning, and bodily responses. Currently, the most influential explanation of emotions has been advanced by Stanley Schacter, a social psychologist. Schacter[10] suggests that emotional experience consists of two parts: physiological arousal, as manifested in a pounding heart, breathlessness, weakness in the knees, and so on; and an interpretation or labeling of the experience. Various kinds of strong emotions—fear, anger, and love—are not clearly distinguished from one another physiologically. In a well-known experiment, Schacter injected research subjects with a drug that induced physiological arousal; the subjects experienced their arousal as either elation or anger, depending on the circumstances Schacter placed them in. Thus, Schacter argues, when people experience the symptoms of arousal, they look around for an explanation.

Other researchers have applied Schacter's two-part theory of emotion to love. One study[11] compared the reactions of men to a young woman encountered in the middle of either of two footbridges. The men on a high, rickety, swaying bridge were more likely to express sexual and romantic interests than were men on a more solid structure. Two thousand years ago, Ovid observed the same principle. In the *Art of Love,* he advised that a man could easily arouse passion in a woman by flirting with her at the arena where gladiators were disemboweling one another.

If Schacter's theory is correct, then social and cultural influences play a large role in determining how people will label their emotions. And, as Judith Katz[12] points out, culture helps to determine when people will become emotionally aroused in the first place because it shapes our desires and goals. Our culture encourages the experience of love in many ways. It teaches that practically everyone will fall in love, and it leads people to apply the label "love" to a wide range of feelings. An elaborate set of images presented in literature, movies, and other mass media provides images and ideas of what love is like.

Arlie Hochschild[13] has noted the various ways people process the inner stream of thoughts and feelings in terms of such cultural symbols. The first step is to attend to feelings. In a culture where the love ideology is lacking, a boy and a girl could be attracted to each other and yet pay little attention to such feelings.

Children in our culture, however, are primed for love from an early age. The little boy or girl who plays with a member of the opposite sex may be teased about his or her "boyfriend" or "girlfriend" and about being "in love." Even before children are old enough to read, they will hear fairy tales such as "Cinderella," "Snow White," "Sleeping Beauty," and many others:

> Hardly any child *believes* the tales, but they all have the same message. A handsome prince overcomes obstacles to marry the poor maid with whom he has fallen in love; they are married and live in bliss. Alternately, the handsome but poor peasant boy overcomes obstacles to marry the princess, with whom he has fallen in love; they are married and live in bliss. Always beauty, always obstacles, always love, always a class barrier . . . always married bliss. The unsaid last line of each story is, "Someday this may happen to you." Parents set the proper example for their children by relating to the child their own prince-and-beauty story. "Why did you marry Daddy?" "Because we fell in love."[14]

Once attended to, feelings are codified in accord with cultural understandings. Thus many people would label the following set of feelings as love: a sense of excitement at first meeting someone; daydreaming and preoccupation with the other person; yearning to be with him or her; jealousy of rivals; a feeling that this is the one and only love and that the feeling will last forever. On the other hand, a person experiencing a mild, nonphysical attraction with no sense of urgency and no jealousy would not be likely to label it as love.

Romantic love in Western culture seems to be a unique compound of many elements: not only a strong emotional attachment with sexual overtones, but also elements of tenderness and idealization of the beloved. What looks like love in another culture may have a different quality than Western love. Thus Margaret Mead observes, although Samoan love making has a superficial resemblance to our own, Samoan love songs and flowery love letters are merely conventionalized rituals that may have little to do with feelings or behavior.[15]

Other anthropologists have reported similar ritual declarations of love in other cultures. In Tepoztlan, Mexico, it is common for young men to begin courtships by sending flowery love letters that have been copied from an etiquette book.[16]

Finally, feelings, once codified and labeled, are managed. That is, we may do "feeling work" to help bring our feelings in line with "feeling rules."[17] For example, feeling rules tell us that we should feel sad at funerals and happy at weddings and christenings. If we don't feel the way we are supposed to, we may feel guilty and try to make ourselves feel the "proper" emotions. Thus we may try to suppress feelings of love if we feel that they are inappropriate, or stir them up when they seem to be lagging behind the situation. In students' reports of emotional experience, Hochschild[18] found many examples of feeling work. For example, several people reported trying to make themselves love another person to justify sleeping with him or her. Others reported trying to make themselves stop loving people.

In sum then, love is a constructed experience built with feelings, ideas, and cultural symbols. In addition to knowing about the inner, psychological processes involved in love, it is necessary to understand something of the historical roots of the idea of love in Western culture.

The Ideology of Love in Western Culture

Twentieth-century American attitudes toward love are a distillation of themes that have been evolving through many centuries of Western civilization. Although most of the ideology of romantic love was derived from courtly love—the formalized love relationships celebrated by the troubadours of the twelfth century—certain ideas about love reach back to the Greeks and Romans. Sappho listed symptoms of "lovesickness" that have lasted for twenty-five centuries: a faltering voice, blushing, heart palpitations, erratic eye movements, muscle tremors, faintness, and pallor.

But love in ancient times was very different from what it was to become later. Love was not part of courtship or marriage, but occurred between married men and prostitutes or between men and young boys. It is paradoxical, as Morton Hunt observes, "that modern love began with Greek love and owes so much to it, although the forms and ideals of Greek love are considered immoral and, to a large extent, illegal in modern society."[19]

Because of the inferior social position of women in Greek society, little importance was attached to heterosexual love. Since women were not educated, even the upper-class Greek man would have a wife who would have more in common with servants and slaves than her own husband. Many of the traditional antiwoman jokes about nagging wives originated in Greek times. The leading Greek philosophers praised love and friendship between men. And Sappho's original description of lovesickness depicted the love of one woman for another.

Among the Romans, love tended to be heterosexual rather than homosexual, but, as among the Greeks, it occurred outside marriage and applied only to adulterous affairs. As codified in Ovid's first-century *Art of Love,* love was an elegant game of deceit, not the basis of serious or long-lasting relationships. It is impossible, of course, to state how widespread extramarital affairs actually were among the Roman upper classes, but other writers of the period suggest that Ovid's textbook of flirting and adultery had educated his entire generation in the game of love. Like the modern-day advisor, Ovid argued that personal hygiene and good grooming were essential for lovers: the man was to wear spotless, well-fitting clothes, keep his hair and nails trimmed, and avoid body odor and bad breath. Women were advised to shave their legs and underarms, and to avoid getting tanned.

Deception played an important role in Ovid's love games: flattery was to be used, preferably in conjunction with expressions of tender concern. It was permissible to fake the symptoms of lovesickness to advance an affair. In one of his poems, Ovid describes how lovers at a party can secretly communicate through intense looks, subtle gestures, a special code, and the secret touching of feet under the table.

The American ideology of love owes more to the courtly love ideal of the Middle Ages than to the cool and sensual games described by Ovid. Courtly love is based on the idea that love between the sexes is a supreme value of life on earth. It included the following beliefs: that love is an overwhelming passion inspired by the beauty and character of the loved one; that it strikes suddenly and uncontrollably at the first sight of the beloved; that the lovers are fated for one another; that love leads to perfect bliss or utter misery; and that it uplifts and ennobles the lover. Courtly love included profoundly contradictory elements such as adulterous passion and Christian religious devotion, stereotyped flirtation games and serious moral purpose, betrayal and faithfulness, joy and suffering.

The great courtly love romances—for example, Tristan and Isolde, Lancelot and Guinevere—are tales of adultery. Some of the writers who propounded the doctrine of courtly love argued that it was impossible for love to occur in a marriage, while others insisted that it was still possible, although rare. Marriages were still being arranged according to the family's interests, on the basis of property and status consid-

erations; hence love was likely to be found outside of marriage.

One of the most significant contributions of courtly love was the social elevation of the woman to an object of devotion. The knight's worship of his lady, scholars generally agree, paralleled religious devotion to the Virgin Mary. The traditions of chivalry have survived in the codes of etiquette that still persist in diminished form. The customary signs of deference toward women—holding the door for a woman, lighting her cigarette, and so on—are not done in other cultures, such as India and Japan. Rather, women are expected to show deference to men.[20]

Women have rightly protested that being placed on a pedestal represents a stifling denial of their needs and capacities; further, the idealization of some women as ethereal beings puts others in the category of impure beings who can be treated disrespectfully. Nevertheless, the Western tradition of respect for women, however much it has interfered with the achievement of sex-role equality, has made the goal of equality seem closer to reality than in other cultures, where women have been, and still are, treated as not quite human, as property to be to be traded, exchanged, and used, as servants, childbearers, and sex objects. Courtly love invented the novel idea that love must be a mutual relationship, involving respect as well as passion.

Courtly love has remained part of the cultural tradition of the West since it began in the eleventh century. The theme of romantic love has dominated Western literature for 800 years, from the legend of *Tristan and Isolde,* to *Romeo and Juliet,* to *Love Story, The Graduate,* and even *Annie Hall.* Regardless of how this or that feature of the myth has been changed, passionate love between a man and a woman has preoccupied the Western mind and woven itself in the fabric of daily life. It sets us apart from the other cultures of the world and from the early stages of Western culture. C. S. Lewis observes that courtly love and the troubadours who celebrated it "effected a change which has left no corner of our ethics, our imagination, or our daily life untouched, and they erected impassible barriers between us as the classical past and the oriental present."[21]

From its origins as an adulterous love game played by the feudal aristocracy, the code of romantic love came to be grafted onto the institution of bourgeois marriage. Later still, with the coming of industrialization and urbanization, the ideology of love spread to the working class. And, in ways that we shall examine in more detail later, the ideal was transformed again by the sexual and cultural revolutions of the twentieth century.

The link between love and marriage came early in England, and has remained ever since. By contrast, continental European literature continued to maintain the courtly tradition that love occurred outside marriage. Writing of the French novel, for example, Denis de Rougemont observed, "to judge by its literature, adultery would seem to be one of the most characteristic occupations of Western man."[22]

This was not true in England, where the Puritan bourgeoisie sanctified marriage and the family and condemned the adultery and other sexual excesses of the aristocracy. The Puritans, contrary to their reputation, were not against sex; rather they argued that it should be contained in marriage. The Puritans redefined marriage as a partnership based on companionship, trust, fidelity, and premarital chastity. The joining of love and marriage was foreshadowed in such works as Chaucer's "Franklin's Tale" in The Canterbury Tales and Spenser's The Faerie Queene, but it received its supreme expression in Paradise Lost, one of the few works of world literature in praise of married love.

The ideology of romantic love, however, did not merge completely with marriage until the eighteenth century and the emergence of the middle class as a major factor in society. In The Rise of the Novel, Ian Watt[23] describes how the new social and economic order gave rise to a new literary form, the novel, which placed the search for love and social mobility at the center of the plot, with marriage providing the happy ending. Samuel Richardson's novel, Pamela, in which a servant girl comes to marry her master, is the first example of this genre. This basic plot has served as the prototype of the love stories that have dominated our popular culture.

Some people have suggested that the romantic-love myth functions like a religion in Western culture. It is not necessary to believe literally in a religion to be influenced by it; the lapsed Catholic or the unobservant Jew is still, in deep ways, a variant kind of Catholic or Jew. Ann Swidler[24] points out that the symbols of love in our culture, like religious symbols in more traditional societies, provide models that shape the experience and the course of individual lives:

> Although love in real life is not like love in the movies or in literature, the images of love in our culture provide a background, a language, a set of symbols within which people frame the meaning of their own lives. In loving and being loved, people give themselves for brief periods to a more intense level of experience, and achieve a new awareness of self and others.[25]

The Necessity of Love

The theme of love could not have persisted through so many centuries were it not linked to other basic themes in Western culture and, in turn, to social structure. At the core of the myth is the image of two individuals set apart from all others, obsessed with their own inner feelings and striving to communicate these thoughts and emotions to each other. In short, the love

Love is not only for the young and the beautiful.

myth includes the themes of individual self-awareness and the need for communion with a unique and freely chosen loved one. As Heer observes, courtly love began a long tradition of self-discovery that culminated in psychoanalysis.[26]

The individualism that lies at the heart of romantic love has deep roots in the religious, economic, and political life of the West. It is widely recognized that Western culture values individualism to a unique degree, and that two of its major historical sources are the rise of capitalism and the spread of Protestantism, particularly Puritanism. Christianity, as noted in an earlier chapter, has always encouraged attention to inner feelings as a form of religious duty to cleanse the mind from evil thoughts. Protestantism emphasized individualism and self-awareness by attributing supreme spiritual importance to the direct relation between an individual and God.

Capitalism is the other major source of individualism in the West. In feudal society, the individual's place was fixed from birth. The rising bourgeoisie overthrew these restrictions in the name of freedom. The new concept of individualism was based on the idea of each person as a free agent—independent of tradition, society, and even other people—with the right to rise or fall through one's own efforts. The right to choose a marriage partner oneself, rather than submit to a marriage arranged by parents, was an important step in the growth of individual freedom in Western Europe.[27]

The rise of industrialized mass society increased the practical possibilities of individualism still further. As Greenfield[28] has pointed out, there is no rational reason for anyone to marry in the contemporary United States: the division of labor between the sexes is not so extreme that people cannot survive without the services of a mate, and all needs, from food to clothing to sex, can be satisfied in the marketplace. Although, he goes on, it is not in the interests of individuals to marry, set up households, and have families, the social system

Love in Cross-Cultural Perspective

would cease to operate if they did not do so. Therefore the ideology of romantic love performs a vital function by driving people together to form families:

> What appears to be necessary for the maintenance of American culture in its present form, then, is a special mechanism that would induce these generally rational, ambitious, and calculating individuals—in the sense of trying to maximize their personal achievement—to do what in the logic of their culture is not in their own personal interest. Somehow they must be induced—we might almost say, in spite of themselves—to behave emotionally and irrationally and to desire and to occupy the positions of husband-father and wife-mother.[29]

This account, although it recognizes the importance of love in American society, overlooks the psychological processes that form a missing link between social structure and the individual's wish to enter into love relationships. The notion that the ideology of love is necessary to make people do what they would not otherwise want to do misses the point: the very technological advances that have made it possible to live as an unattached individual have created a cold, impersonal world that makes us crave intimate relationships. At the same time, these conditions make it hard to find and sustain them.

Paradoxically, individualism seems to foster not only a preoccupation with the self, but also an emphasis on close personal relationships. As Murray Davis[30] observes, a preoccupation with friendship and love emerged during every period of urbanization in Western culture: in ancient Greece, in the Roman empire, during the Renaissance, and, most recently and extensively, since the eighteenth century. Without the traditional bonds of kinship and community, the urban individual must construct a more consciously chosen social life to replace the world that was lost.

Love and Loneliness

According to John Bowlby,[31] all human beings have an innate terror of solitude inherited from our history as primates. Fears of darkness, of strangers, and of being alone, he argues, are natural responses to what were high-risk situations for primates and early humans, and still are even in the modern world. Throughout life, people need "attachment figures"—in each phase of our lives we tend to make strong bonds to one or more special and particular individuals; as long as these bonds remain intact, we feel secure in the world, and when they are broken by separation or death, we become anxious and distressed. Infants may experience separation distress when they are out of sight of the attachment figure; older children and adults can tolerate separation without distress when they know the attachment figure is available.

Other psychological theories have argued that attachment is a learned behavior—that the child comes to depend on the mother and later on other people because the mother or other caretaker fulfills the child's basic needs for food, warmth, and so on. Whatever theory is ultimately correct, the end result is the same: people tend to need people. Few of us would accept the offer of a life in which all material needs were met, but which had to be spent alone. Although individuals differ in the amount of social contact they need, and some can get by with very little, the experience of extended isolation, even under optimal circumstances, seems always to be stressful. The picture of isolation that emerges from many accounts and studies is

> one of a difficult experience that frequently produces fantasy and anxiety-like symptoms. There may be indications of nervousness, of depression, of a general going-to-pieces. . . . People seem to need contact with others to continue functioning in a healthy manner.[32]

In most times and places, attachment needs are fulfilled continuously throughout life because people remain rooted to the communities in which they were born. Relationships with parents do not undergo a major change at adolescence or marriage. The necessities of daily life make people dependent on one another, and there may be few or no occasions for being alone, much less lonely.

Many of the conditions of modern life conspire to make loneliness a potential problem for large numbers of people. First, as noted earlier, it is possible to supply all one's material needs without entering into close or committed relationships. Second, individuals in contemporary Western cultures are required to give up their original attachments to their parents. Willingly or not, the adolescent must withdraw emotionally from his or her parents and transfer attachment to peers: a best friend, a girlfriend or boyfriend, or a group of peers. Eventually, attachment feelings merge with sexual strivings, so a person of the opposite sex comes to fulfill both needs.

The conditions of modern life make social relations problematic, because the individual must construct his or her own set of intimate and friendly relationships: they are not supplied automatically by economic necessity or the kinship system. As Robert Weiss observes:

> The relinquishment of parents as attachment figures . . . provides the opportunity for there to be a total lack of attachment figures; . . . it becomes possible for there to be no figure in an individual's life whose accessibility would provide the comfort and security associated with attachment. The parents will not serve, and no replacement may have appeared. The adolescent can now experience all the symptoms of separation distress, but without an object. This is *loneliness.*[33]

How frequent is the experience of loneliness? Social theorists such as Eric Fromm and David Riesman have argued that loneliness is inescapable in modern society, and Robert Weiss, one of the few scholars who has taken a detailed interest in this disturbing subject, esti-

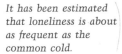

It has been estimated that loneliness is about as frequent as the common cold.

Love in Cross-Cultural Perspective

mates that it is about as frequent as the common cold. Surveys that have asked people if they often feel lonely have come out with estimates ranging from 10 to 80 percent.

It is not surprising that there is such variation in responses to the question; people in some situations—such as students away from home for the first time, widows, and people who have just moved—are more vulnerable to loneliness. And there are personality differences in susceptibility. Moreover, many people may be unwilling to admit to being lonely. Finally, people who have been driven into relationships out of loneliness would not show up in the typical survey.

Ironically, even when we find someone to love, we may find that love is not enough. Weiss's research suggests that there are two kinds of loneliness: *emotional* isolation, resulting from the lack of intimate ties with a spouse or lover; and *social* isolation, resulting from a lack of a network of relationships with peers, such as fellow workers, neighbors, relatives, or friends. Without such ties, people may feel lonely and depressed even though they are deeply in love with their spouses. Yet for many people, particularly those in the economically and geographically mobile middle classes, social networks may be harder to find and to sustain than intimate relationships. As Suzanne Gordon[34] observes, America is a "couple culture": love becomes the only thing of real importance, and people make or break other social bonds with friends, kin, and community in its interests.

Modern mass societies generate loneliness not only because they do not provide automatically for intimate or friendly relationships, but also because of the peculiar kinds of impersonal relationships they provide in abundance. Much of the person's daily life in modern society is spent in narrow roles such as worker, student, customer, client. People begin to experience themselves in a double way—as anonymous and replaceable players of such roles, and as unique and whole individuals with distinct thoughts and feelings. The discrepancy between the public roles we play and our "real" inner selves creates the need for a private world, a set of relationships where we can express those aspects of ourselves that must be denied at work and elsewhere.

Love in the Modern World

Until very recently, much of the literature in marriage and the family was fond of pointing to research data contradicting one or another tenet of the romantic-love ideology. Thus, to counter the romantic idea of the one and only love, writers would point to findings showing that people typically fall in love several times before they marry.

Nor does the research support the idea that love happens suddenly, one enchanted evening, when two strangers look at one another across a crowded room and their hearts stand still. There is much evidence that falling in love is usually a gradual process, coming after a period of acquaintanceship and repeated encounters.

Many people report growing to love someone whom they did not find overwhelmingly attractive in the first place, but with whom they develop deep rapport and enjoyable companionship. Burgess and Wallin[35] found that more than half the married men and women in their survey said they had no strong physical attraction until at least two months after they had met. Contrary to the idea that love is blind, that lovers idealize their beloveds so much that they cannot perceive any faults in them, Burgess and Wallin found that among the 2,000 engaged people they studied, two-thirds of the men and three-quarters of the women were able to mention defects in their loved ones.

The Ultimate Human Connection

Finally, to counter the notion that love overcomes all obstacles and transcends class barriers, sociologists point to well-established findings that the vast majority of marriages take place between men and women in the same class, race, religion, educational level, and even the same level of physical attractiveness.

Such debunkings of love could be found in much of the marriage-and-family literature of the 1930s, 40s', and 50s'. People married for practical reasons; whether anyone believed in the love myth or not, it had little effect on the choice of a marriage partner, and mates might just as well have been selected by parents or matchmakers. In recent years, many people have assumed that the sexual revolution must have killed off whatever remained of romantic love in America.

Such people had been persuaded by Freud's theory that the emotion of love is aim-inhibited sex; that is, they believed that a person experienced love as a result of the blocking of the sex drive. Courtly love seemed to fit this model perfectly, and the conventional norm against premarital sex seemed to ensure that couples would fall in love and marry to fulfill that love. Thus it seemed that the new sexual freedom, which permitted people to go to bed together shortly after meeting one another, would surely prevent the growth of love. And, with sex so easily available, most people, it seemed, would certainly prefer instant intimacy with an endless series of new partners to the dullness of monogamous marriage, or even to old-fashioned love affairs.

These reports on the death of love seem to be greatly exaggerated. It is true that marriages in America were rarely based on blind, heedless passion. And it is true that the sexual and cultural revolutions of recent years have revised the rules and meaning of love, sex, and marriage. But for most Americans in the twentieth century, love has been a strongly felt emotion, and intimate relationships continue to occupy a central place in people's lives.

Nor does the sexual revolution seem to have interfered with the capacity to form love relationships. There is little evidence to support the Freudian idea that love can flourish only if the lovers abstain from sex. In fact, recent research evidence suggests the opposite; among unmarried couples, sex can become the basis for the deepening of love relationships.[36] And Hunt argues that sexual liberation may have had the strongest impact within marriage itself; he found a great increase in the frequency and variety of sexual relations within marriage—a change that seems to be associated with a deepening of the emotional attachment between the spouses.[37]

In the Shadow of Love and Marriage: Being Single

Another recent change that many see as a sign that people are avoiding love relationships is the growth of the single life style. Recent statistics reveal a striking increase in the number of unattached individuals, and an increasing tendency for the unattached to live apart from families. According to the Census Bureau, the number of men living alone increased 60 percent between 1970 and 1977, and the number of women living by themselves rose 35 percent.[38] What are the implications of the growth of singleness for love and marriage? Does the new life style mean that large numbers of people are giving up the ideal of romantic love? Or are they merely giving up the idea of marriage? Or are they giving up neither?

There are several images of what it is like to be single in America today. One image is that of the "swinging single" as idealized by *Playboy* and *Cosmopolitan;* life is a continuous round of exciting sex partners, discotheque dancing, gourmet dining, ski weekends, and vacations to exotic places. Another image is suggested by television's Mary Tyler Moore: the single person as a self-contained, independent individual,

An idealized image of the unmarried—the "swinging singles."

finding satisfaction and contentment in work and a circle of good friends. Finally, there is an image derived from the old stereotype of the single person as a lonely, rejected loser at the game of love, the single life as a desperate search for love and escape from singleness.

There probably is some truth in all these images. People categorized as single include

The Ultimate Human Connection

those in very different social and psychological situations: young unmarrieds, the divorced, the widowed, the elderly, as well as the unmarried young person. It includes people committed to remaining single as well as those eager to marry at the first opportunity, and also people who, though officially single, are involved in love relationships of varying degrees of commitment. Since there has been very little research on singlehood—apart from studies of the widowed and the divorced—it is difficult to state with any certainty what the nature of the single experience is for different kinds of people. The rise of the singles life style, however, can be attributed to the increase in the age of first marriage, the increase in the divorce rate, and the tendency of the divorced to postpone remarriage longer than divorced people in the past. The growth of singles-only housing complexes and recreational facilities has made singles a visible part of the population.

Although there is an emerging ideology of singleness, relatively few single people seem to be committed to singleness as a permanent way of life. A 1974 survey of young Americans aged fourteen to twenty-five found that only 17 percent of women thought the single life was the most desirable life style, and only 5 percent expected to be single in five years. The corresponding figures for young men were 24 percent and 9 percent.[39]

Other evidence for a lack of commitment to singlehood may be found in the appeals offered by the various facilities and establishments catering to singles. Advertisements for such activities often suggest that singleness is a lonely state and that the advertised activity can lead to love or marriage.

Thus singleness in America appears to be an ambivalent and contradictory status. On the one hand, the single life offers extraordinary appeal in an individualistic society. Single people can spend their money as they like and do what they please when they please. They can live in

city or suburbs, often in housing complexes designed to provide them with recreational facilites and social activities. They can throw themselves into their work without having to worry about neglecting the family, or they can reduce their work commitments to a minimum without worrying about mortgage payments on the house or savings for the children's braces and college educations. Single people can enjoy the sexual freedom made possible by the pill and the new permissive morality. Or they can involve themselves in romantic attachments to be enjoyed as long as they last, without the commitment to permanence or marriage.

Yet the loneliness-making conditions of American society that previously drove people into early marriages have not vanished; rather than having found a way to avoid them, single people seem to be in a constant struggle against them. As Peter Stein observes in a study of singles: "The greatest need single people feel is for substitute networks of human relationships that provide the basic satisfactions of intimacy, sharing, and continuity."[40]

Yet it is often hard to find such substitute networks. Single people often look back nostalgically to high-school, college, or graduate-school days as a time of easy friendship, when an institution brought large numbers of young people together and provided a setting for relationships. But the cities to which singles flock usually don't encourage easy sociability. Most work settings seem to provide fewer candidates for friendship and love than did the college campus.

Single people often turn to other single people for friends. They tend to feel uncomfortable around married or living-together friends, and the feelings tend to be reciprocated. Yet single friendships are often undermined by the search for love and romance. It has been traditional for women to give priority to male relationships—that is, to drop a date with a female friend if a man invites one out. It is sometimes

High schools and colleges bring large numbers of eligible males and females together. Later in life, it becomes harder for people to find romantic partners.

difficult even for "liberated" women to overcome this habit.

In fact, looking at the various studies of the single life style, it often seems as if single people are caught between two standards of behavior—the stereotypes of previous decades and the new images of swinging singleness. Thus single people sometimes find themselves feeling as if they are missing something by not being part of a couple, that feeling lonely or not having a date

The Ultimate Human Connection

on Saturday night means one is a misfit and a failure.

This attitude is reinforced by the still-prevailing assumption that marriage is the only desirable and natural state. Unmarried people are continuously pushed toward marriage by parents, relations, coworkers, and married friends. One of the single women in Stein's study described the meaning of being single in this way:

> There is a whole part of me that sees as freedom the possibilities of meeting different people and having different kinds of relationships, which is the exciting part. And then, there is the part of me that looks at where I'm not doing what I'm supposed to be doing, where I'll ultimately end up lonely, where something is the matter with me because I'm not in love with somebody, whatever that means.[41]

On the other hand, single people may feel inadequate because they are not living up to the image of the swinging single. Writer Suzanne Gordon observes that there seems to be a new expectation that if you don't have somebody to love, then you should at least have somebody to have sex with. If you don't, then "something's really wrong with you." Yet after interviewing many single people, she concludes it's a myth that this is an age of easy sex. The myth suggests that you don't have to be married or in love or involved with one person to have sex:

> All you have to do is have the right attitude and step outside your door and there it is—sex. But according to hundreds of people I have interviewed, "easy sex" is painfully at odds with reality. As one young man in Berkeley succinctly put it, "Everyone I know is horny."[42]

It is not all that simple, Gordon learned, to find that one-night stand. According to her interviews, most people who begin an evening alone in a singles bar or encounter group end up going home without a companion for the night.

Since this report was a journalist's rather than a scientific study, we don't know much about the sample—maybe for one reason or another Gordon was able to interview only people who were having problems meeting and forming relationships with people.

Morton Hunt's survey[43] presents more systematic information about sex and the single person. Although he does not deal with the issue of how people perceive the availability of sex, he finds relatively few "swinging singles" and little evidence that a "recreational" as opposed to a "romantic" view of sex is becoming a widespread philosophy among singles. Although there has been a dramatic increase in premarital sex, and swinging singles do exist—more among older divorced people than young unmarrieds—there has not been a violent overthrow of the traditional link between love and sex. Hunt concludes:

> The new sexual freedom operates largely within the framework of our long-held cherished cultural values of intimacy and love. Even while it asserts its freedom from marriage, it is an apprenticeship for marriage, and is considered successful by its participants when it grows, deepens, and leads to ever-stronger commitment, and unsuccessful and a wasted effort when it does not.[44]

A thirty-two-year-old lawyer interviewed by Suzanne Gordon put it more vividly:

> For the most part, the eminently respectable sons-of-bitches walking around the financial district of San Francisco know how to get laid. The question is, "Is that what they want to accomplish?" and the answer is "no." But that's what they'll settle for. They want, however, more than that. They want to accomplish "it," of course, the ultimate, mind-blowing experience, make the ultimate human connection, the ultimate emotional experience. What it boils down to is falling in love.[45]

Contemporary Love:
Research Findings

Despite the sweeping changes in sexual morality and life styles in recent years, most people have not abandoned their belief in some form of love as an important value. In a recent national survey, when people were asked what was the primary reason for marrying today, a large majority—77 percent of the men and 83 percent of the women—mentioned love.[46] Obviously, this is the expected answer and gives us little information about what people meant by the terms.

We can get a somewhat better picture of what love means to contemporary young people from social-psychological studies of love and love relationships. Zick Rubin[47] has constructed a paper-and-pencil "love scale" to assess the kinds of feelings that constitute love relationships. Obviously, a paper-and-pencil scale cannot measure real feelings, but simply what people say their feelings are. But there is some behavioral evidence that supports the scale's validity. For example, couples with above-average scores on the love scale tended to spend a great deal of time gazing into each other's eyes, an activity that both folk wisdom and social scientists regard as one of the supreme expressions of intimate communication between two individuals.

Rubin's research revealed that couple relations seemed to have several components. His love scale is divided into two separate scales, a love scale and a like scale. The love scale contains three components: intimacy (I feel I can confide in _____ about virtually everything); attachment (It would be hard for me to get along without _____); and caring (If _____ were feeling bad, it would be my first duty to cheer him/her up). The liking scale dealt with admiration and respect for the other person on grounds of competence, good judgment, intelligence, the high regard of other people, and also the feeling of being similar to the self. The pattern of correlations within and between the items on each scale supported the idea that loving and liking are different phenomena. Although the love scale itself does not ask couples if they are "in love," when Rubin asked them this question, two-thirds of the men and women in his sample of 182 dating couples indicated that they were. Further, the correlation between the love scale and saying one was in love was reasonably high.

Rubin's data show that different kinds of love can propel people into more intense relationships and marriage. Although the people who scored high on the love scale thought themselves more likely to marry than those who scored high on the liking scale, when the actual progress of relationships was followed over time, liking was almost as good a predictor of marriage as love.

Along with the lovers for whom respect and admiration were sufficient grounds for marriage, Rubin found a large number of people who seemed to subscribe to the full-blown ideology of romantic love. These people obtained high scores on a romanticism scale by agreeing with such items as "To be truly in love is to love forever" and "A person should marry whomever he or she loves regardless of social position," and disagreeing with such statements as "Most of us could sincerely love any one of several people equally well" and "Economic security should be carefully considered before selecting a marriage partner."

Other researchers have developed more elaborate typologies of love. John Lee[48] has been less concerned with how much one person loves another than with the possibility that love has different meanings for different people. Using a long questionnaire dealing with many aspects of relationships, he found three different types of love, which he labeled with terms from classical literature.

The three types are *eros,* or romantic love, characterized by love at first sight, sensuality, close intimacy, and rapport with the partner; *storge,* or companionate love, but devoid of passion; and *ludus,* or playful love, in which the lover is hedonistic and free of commitment— love is a game and can be played with many partners, and dependency is to be avoided. Lee identified three subsidiary types of love: *mania*—obsessive and jealous; *agape,*—altruistic and self-sacrificing; and *pragma,*—practical and realistic.

The six types of love are ideal constructs— few people fit into just one type. People can be high or low on several scales. Some clinicians have found the scales useful in dealing with relationship problems. For example, two people may be having problems because they have different concepts of love. A "manic" lover involved with a "storgic" lover might feel un-loved, while the latter might think the former was "crazy."

The Romantic Male One surprising but per-sistent finding in love research is that, contrary to the stereotype of women as starry-eyed romantics, men turn out to be more romantic than women. Thus Rubin[49] found that men scored significantly higher than women on the romanticism scale. He also found that although men seemed to fall in love more quickly and easily than women, women seemed to fall out of love more quickly and easily, at least in premar-ital relationships. Also, women were more likely to be the ones to end relationships, to disengage themselves emotionally to do what Hochschild calls "feeling work."[50] Men tended to experience more grief and despair after a breakup than women.

In an earlier study, Kephart[51] had found a similar sex difference. He asked college men and women the following question: "If a man or woman had all the other qualities you desired, would you marry the person if you were not in love with him or her?" Although 65 percent of the men said no, only 24 percent of the women said they definitely would not marry such a person. Two-thirds of the women and one-third of the men were undecided. One woman re-marked, "It's rather hard to give a yes or no answer to this question. If a man had all the other qualities I desired and I was not in love with him—well, I think I could talk myself into falling in love."[52]

In short, while men can be romantic, women have a more practical, realistic ap-proach to love and take a more managerial attitude toward their own feelings. The differ-ence is understandable in terms of sex-role inequality, particularly the contrasting social and economic positions of sexes. Women are more economically dependent on marriage than men are. As sociologist Willard Waller once observed: "A man, when he marries, chooses a companion and perhaps a helpmate, but a woman chooses a companion and at the same time a standard of living."[53] Thus women stand to lose more than men by falling in love with the "wrong" person.

Also, as Hochschild[54] points out, there has been a "patriarchal etiquette" governing the courtship process; if a man is attracted to a woman, he has the right to initiate a relationship with her, to call her for a date, to pursue her, and to propose to her. Women have traditionally engaged in flirting and other strategies to get men to court them. But when a woman cannot directly pursue a relationship with a man who attracts her, and when she may be courted by men she might not have chosen in the first place but who have other desirable qualities, she is likely to try to manage and control her feelings. When women and men approach economic equality, these differences are likely to vanish.

Coming in out of the Cold:
The Development of Love Relationships

In the past, the development of a relationship not only was something to be worked out between the individuals, but it followed socially defined steps. Thus marriage used to be the endpoint of a series of distinct stages, each involving a greater degree of commitment— dating, keeping company, going steady, a private agreement to be married, a public announcement of the engagement, and finally marriage, presumably for life. A different level of sexual intimacy was permitted at each stage of the relationship.

In recent years, this whole system has collapsed. One by one, the various stages began to sound old-fashioned; "courtship" and "keeping company" were obsolete terms by the 1950s; in the '70s both "dating" and "engagement" were no longer appropriate to describe the development of relations between the sexes. The whole sequence of ever-increasing commitments have given way to a series of "involvements" that may or may not evolve into marriage.

Noting that marriage no longer implies monogamy and permanence, and that couple relationships outside marriage no longer exclude sex and a sense of commitment, Farber[55] has suggested that the American system of mate selection and marriage is best described as one based on the "permanent availability" of all adults as potential marriage partners, whether they are currently married or not. As McCall[56] has pointed out, there is a paradox in the new pattern of couple relationships. Marriage has become less exclusive and permanent, but in what used to be courtship there is an emphasis on deep personal intimacy or some kind of commitment. Yet neither type of involvement is expected to last if it turns out to be dissatisfying. Couple relationships are both more intensely personal and less stable and enduring. The notion of the "one and only love" has faded.

Although a love "involvement" no longer follows set, socially defined stages, it does follow a developmental course. It seems obvious that since in modern societies most lovers start out as strangers, their relationships must proceed through at least three different stages: first, the couple must have the opportunity to meet and be attracted to one another. Second, they must explore one another's interests and attitudes to see if they are compatible and whether they enjoy one another's company. Third, they develop a set of expectations and commitments about the relationship, or decide whether there is to be a relationship at all. Later, if the relationship is to be a long-term one, it will enter a more routinized and committed phase.

There have been several attempts to conceptualize this process. Murstein[57] has developed a theory of marital choice based on three stages: (1) a *stimulus stage* in which people are attracted to one another on the basis of physical appearance and other obvious traits; (2) a *value stage* in which the couple discovers whether they are compatible; and (3) a *role stage*, in which they consider how they will fit together as long-term partners.

Alternatively, Reiss[58] has proposed a "wheel theory" of relationship development. Different interpersonal processes form four spokes of a wheel: rapport, self-revelation, mutual dependency, and need fulfillment. The four spokes work together so that as the relationship moves in a positive direction, a sense of rapport will lead the couple to confide in one another, which will lead to mutual dependency and thus to the fulfillment of interpersonal needs. The wheel can also run backward; a loss of rapport will make people reluctant to confide in one another, and so on.

Although these explanations seem to be reasonably accurate descriptions of many, if not most, relationships, they seem to portray those based on liking and companionate love more than those based on passionate love. As Elaine Walster[59] argues, passionate love may be very different from liking someone, even liking him or her a great deal.

Liking is a very sensible emotion. As in the models described above, we tend to like people who are similar to us in interest and values, who offer us affection, and who reward our acts of self-revelation with approval and correspondingly intimate disclosures. We reject those who reject us. Although passionate love sometimes operates in this reasonable way, often it does not. As Walster observes:

> Individuals do *not* always feel passionate about the person who provides the most rewards with the greatest consistency. Passion sometimes develops under conditions that would be more likely to provoke aggression and hatred than love.[60]

For example, it would be reasonable to reject lovers who reject us or give us cause to be jealous, but experiences such as these often make people love even more passionately. Walster presents an array of anecdotal and experimental evidence suggesting that negative emotions such as fear, anger, and frustration can enhance passionate love.

In the first, or "stimulus," stage of a relationship, all that people know about each other is what they can see.

The Complexities of Love: Mixed Emotions

Although the connection between love and negative emotion is clearest in excited states such as anger, fear, and jealousy, there is reason to believe that an undercurrent of negative feelings accompanies love in all stages of its growth, from casual acquaintance to deep commitment. Theories suggesting that the development of a love relationship is based on the accumulation of "rewards" and "satisfactions" underestimate the complexities of human emotions. Freud theorized that all important human relationships are inherently ambivalent, and the insight that love and hate are closely related has been portrayed in literature throughout history.

Several other theorists have elaborated this view. Some writers have suggested that rather than a direct increase in positive feelings, the growth of love is marked by an oscillation between positive and negative feelings, or a series of crises and resolutions. Theodore Reik suggests that the prospect of love is actually frightening: "The person whom love approaches does not welcome it as a gift, but tries to chase it away as an intruder. . . . It is as if the ego were afraid of a danger, of a threatening loss."[61]

What is this mysterious fear? What have we got to lose in loving? The answer seems to be "several things." We dread loneliness, but we also fear being trapped in relationships where we are more committed than our feelings justify. We want love, but seeking it makes us run the risk of humiliation and rejection. Involvement with one person usually means giving up the opportunity to be involved with others. More fundamentally, perhaps, we fear the growing dependency that falling in love brings with it.

Several theorists have believed that an "anxiety of dependency"[62] is an inevitable component of love. As Berscheid and Fei observe, to become dependent on someone is to:

> give a portion of ourselves away as hostage. . . . As our dependency grows, we relinquish more and more control over our fate. . . . love involves a loss of freedom and independence. . . . As our happiness becomes more and more vested in another, our awareness—and dread—of the conditions and circumstances which may take the loved person away from us, and threaten our happiness, may grow also.[63]

Getting Together

For many people the first step in a relationship—meeting and attracting other people—is the most painful. At this stage a person's fantasies of love and his or her sense of self-worth confront the often brutal realities of the love market. "The individual is faced with a terrible thought: if he or she is not chosen, then he or she may not be worthy of being chosen."[64]

The relationship market does not fit the model of a just world in which rewards follow inner virtue. Although the "rating-and-dating" game may not be as snobbish and rigid as it was found to be in the studies of college social life in the thirties and forties, social hierarchies have not disappeared. Writing of the "dating-and-rating complex" that prevailed in the 1930s, Waller[65] noted that certain men and women were at the top of the social hierarchy. These "Class A" men and women tended to date each other. The men's prestige depended on belonging to the "right" fraternities, having a large supply of spending money, and being "smooth" in manners and appearance. Women students gained their Class A status by dating Class A men. The class system was recognized by students, creating problems of adjustment for those below the Class A category. Thus some Class B individuals could challenge the system by dating Class A women. Class D men developed a series of rationalizations putting down the women above them in the campus hierarchy, who usually rejected them. Class D women tried to rationalize going out with Class D men, but not very successfully, so that they often felt uneasy.

Although fraternities and "smooth" manners may no longer serve as criteria of prestige on today's campus, people still tend to rank one another in desirability. Recent social-psychological research suggests that physical attractiveness is still extremely important in forming impressions of other people. Further, there is

Getting together—the car remains an essential part of teenage dating.

little tendency for people to be attracted to partners whose desirability matches their own; everyone seems to prefer the most attractive date possible.

The collision between the matching principle—seeking out people like oneself—and the desirability principle produces what might be called the "Groucho Marx effect": Groucho once observed that he didn't want to belong to any club that would have him as a member. Those at the lower reaches of the rating-and-dating hierarchy are often faced with the choice between having no relationships or having one with a person less attractive than one would ideally like. Thus Burgess and associates[66] observed that dating often presented severe problems to those outside the minority of the very attractive. They quote a typical college student:

> One of the greatest troubles is that men here, as everywhere, I guess, are easily overwhelmed by physical beauty. Campus glamor queens have countless beaux flocking around them, whereas many companiable, sympathetic girls . . . go without dates and male companionship. . . . I will never understand why so many men (even, or maybe particularly, those who are the least attractive themselves) seem to think they may degrade themselves by dating or even dancing with a girl who does not measure up to their beauty standards.[67]

The singles bar provides the best and clearest example of the contemporary rating-and-dating complex. Most people seem to find going to these places an alienating experience. People are under pressure to give the most favorable impression of themselves as they can, and to assess very quickly the social desirability of possible partners. Surface characteristics count for a great deal—how pretty or handsome one is, how much money and status one has, what kind of car one drives, and what neighborhood one lives in.

Coming in out of the Cold

A man who had been a bartender at a singles bar told a reporter that the waiters think of the place as a "zoo":

> I used to stand around the bar and watch people, and the sense of values there is so incredible I used to just stand in awe, because I didn't believe people were actually like that. You'll hear a regular income rap, "Where did you go on your last vacation, what kind of car do you drive?" . . . Nobody actually cares who someone is, but what they have and where they come from.[68]

The chance of rejection is great for both men and women, and people are under pressure to make snap decisions in the first minutes of a conversation as to whether to end the encounter or indicate an interest in seeing the person again.

A demonstration of the importance of a good appearance was provided in a field study carried out in 1966 by Elaine Walster and her associates.[69] They recruited 752 college freshmen to attend a "computer dance." Although the students were led to believe that they had been matched by a computer on the basis of similar interests, actually couples had been paired randomly. The study was intended to test the matching principle—the hypothesis was that people would like, and prefer to see again, people who were close to themselves in social desirability. Each student was assessed in terms of intelligence, intellectual achievement, and personality, as well as appearance. During an intermission, the students were asked how they liked their dates. Although the researchers expected that intelligence and personality would have a lot to do with how well a person was liked, they discovered that for both men and women, the physical attractiveness of the other person was the most important determinant of how much students liked their dates.

This correlation between good looks and being liked contrasted strikingly with what college students say they are looking for on dates. Both men and women mention intelligence, friendliness, and sincerity as more important than appearance.[70] Yet in real-life situations, these traits seem not to be the ones people are looking for.

Although it might be argued that attractiveness would have played a lesser role if the students had had time to get to know one another better, or that physical attractiveness becomes less important as individuals get to be older than the eighteen-year-olds interviewed in the study, the evidence suggests otherwise. Numerous studies have shown that people of all ages and sexes are inclined to believe that physically attractive men, women, and even children possess more desirable personality traits as well. Although most people would deny it, they seem to act on the assumption that "what is beautiful is good."

A study of the dating habits of young and middle-aged adults in the San Francisco area revealed that the importance of physical attractiveness continues beyond the college years. In fact, sociologist Marsha Rosenbaum[71] found that middle-aged men's preoccupation with looks was "almost total." Although younger men rejected the standard media version of female attractiveness, they had their own versions of attractiveness. One young man said:

> Looks are playing less and less a role. I reject the *Playboy* image. It's a classical, exploitative bunch of garbage. I don't gravitate toward those kinds of girls. I like tall, lean girls.[72]

Eventually, however, most people find some way of reconciling their idealized images with reality. The vast majority of average people who do not look like models or movie stars, and even the majority of unattractive people, also meet, fall in love, and marry. There is strong evidence that people choose romantic partners who are comparable to themselves in

The telephone, along with the car and the movies, contributed to "dating" as an American cultural pattern.

looks and other desirable traits. Yet as Elaine Walster points out, people often do not submit to reality gladly; they may persist in trying to attract partners more "desirable" than themselves. "Thus, romantic choices seem to be a delicate compromise between one's desire to capture an ideal partner and one's realization that [one] must eventually settle for what [one] deserves."[73]

The Dilemmas of Commitment

Attractiveness may bring people together for a first encounter, but it cannot sustain a relationship in the absence of common interests and values. Once they have found each other, and have entered into a continuing relationship, a couple is likely to encounter a new set of difficulties. The classical love stories of Western culture typically end with death or the decision to marry. It's hard to imagine Romeo and Juliet growing old together. We lack an imagery that portrays enduring relationships in a romantic way.

The arbiters of courtly love believed that love was incompatible with marriage. In 1174, Marie, Countess of Champagne, wrote that "lovers give each other everything freely, under no compulsion of necessity, but married people are in duty bound to give in to each other's desires and deny themselves to each other in nothing."[74] Andreas Capellanus, who wrote the major treatise on love, observed that too many opportunities to see the beloved, and too much chance to talk to one another, would also decrease love.[75]

The traditional criticism of romantic love made by sociologists and marriage counselors also assumes the incompatibility of passion and marriage, of feeling and commitment. They argue that by generating impossible expectations, the myth of romantic love creates untold misery, dooming most marriages to disillusion and frustration and thus contributing to divorce. Although this view underestimates the normal human capacity to reconcile wishes with reality and to relinquish impossible dreams, it is true that there is a contradiction in the idea of a freely chosen commitment to a love relationship. Once the decision has been made, there is no more freedom of choice. Before the point of choice, feelings guide action; after the choice is made, feelings may lag behind the commitment to love.

Coming in out of the Cold

A tension between emotion and commitment is implicit in any ongoing couple relationship—most obvious in legal marriage but not eliminated in a "living-together" couple. As Haley observes:

> When a man and a woman decide their association should be solemnized by a marriage ceremony, they pose themselves a problem which will continue through the marriage: Now that they are married, are they staying together because they wish to or because they must?[76]

The living-together couple has the same problem without the religious and legal element. For example, are they staying together because they said they would or for convenience, or do they still want to be together as much as they did in the first place? But the free couple has the opposite problem as well, which also arises out of the tension between commitment and freedom. That is, is my partner going off without me or sleeping with that other person because he or she is exercising the right to freedom I happily granted, or because he or she is tired of me and really wants to leave me or live with that other person? If boredom and the feeling of compulsion are the occupational hazards of marriage, insecurity and jealousy are the corresponding hazards of the free couple.

A *New Yorker* short story[77] portrays the insecurity dilemma neatly. A young woman is living with a young man in San Francisco. He has moved into her apartment with some of his belongings. They have never made clear exactly what their commitment is to each other, except that they are both to be very cool and free. Usually he comes for supper, but he doesn't want to be held to account if he just doesn't show up. One day she returns home from work and finds a fur rug, his most prized possession, missing. Not knowing whether he has taken the rug to the cleaners or moved out of her life, she becomes upset with uncertainty and sense of loss. Finally, he calls and it turns out to her great relief that the rug has been "ripped off"—the title of the story—a possibility that hadn't occurred to her. The story ends with everything as it was before, except for the disturbing insight she got into the uncertainties of the relationship.

The commitment problem among living-together couples has been documented in a study comparing eighteen such couples with thirty-one "going-steady" couples in a college community.[78] Among the going-together couples, commitments to marriage were equal in both partners; among the living-together couples, however, the women were almost as committed to marriage as the more conventional going-together couples, but their male partners were not. Only three of the eighteen men voiced any marital commitment. On the other hand, couples in both groups were equally happy and emotionally involved in their relationships. Depending on one's assumption, these results can be interpreted as showing the immaturity and exploitiveness of the living-together men, the insecurity and unliberatedness of the living-together women, or a realistic assessment on the part of these women that marriage offers certain advantages in a sexist society.

The Green-Eyed Monster

Insecurity often takes the form of jealousy. Until very recently, social scientists gave little research attention to the subject of love, and still less to jealousy. In the past decade, however, as the study of love and attraction has become an important area of social psychology, there is beginning to be serious interest in love's frequent companion, jealousy.

Before the most recent sexual revolution, many people thought of jealousy as a normal part of love and marriage. Other people argued that jealousy was something rather easily controlled if recognized as bad, rather than as the expression of a just moral indignation. Albert Memmi observes that "great minds of left and right agree that jealousy is an outmoded emotion."[79] Yet for many people it just isn't as easy as that. It is difficult to imagine a firmer intellectual commitment to the total liberty of each partner than that of Simone de Beauvoir and Jean-Paul Sartre, two of the leading French intellectuals of the past three decades. Yet, according to Beauvoir's own writing, she suffered during his liaisons with others. For example:

> I often wondered if he did not care for M more than for me. . . . According to what he told me, M shared completely in his reactions, his emotions, his desires. . . . Was this perhaps the sign of a profound harmony between them—a harmony at the very well-spring of life, present in the rhythm of its ebb and flow— that Sartre did not sense with me, and which was more precious to him than our understanding?[80]

There are other instances of people without commitments to conventional morality who still suffer pangs of jealousy when their partners enter into liaisons with others. A fictional example is the revolutionary hero in Malraux's *Man's Fate*, who on the eve of the Shanghai uprising is devastated to learn from his wife of her fleeting affair with a colleague of hers. Jan Myrdal, the son of the famous Swedish sociologist and radical, writes in his autobiography of a fateful quarrel with the young woman he had been living with. He finds a letter in her coat pocket from a lover. He himself is also having an affair with someone else, but this does not prevent him from being overwhelmed by jealousy:

> I read the letter. I find it strange that such a letter—I myself have also written them—has such a totally different effect when you yourself are neither sender nor receiver but only the third party. It would be sane and reasonable to put it back again in its envelope and stick the envelope back in the pocket. Reasonable and calm . . . . But I don't do so. I know that I won't do it. Anyway, everything is unavoidable . . . I will stage a scene of jealousy. The consciousness of this disgusts me.
>
> . . . I stand for a couple of seconds in the hall before I enter the room. Beforehand I experience all that is going to happen. Once more I think: if I were really rational I would shut off all emotions, take a deep breath, and walk into the room and take a cup of coffee with her. But it is impossible. I am in a state of emotional tension. I observe my pulse, it is quickening, my mouth has become dry . . . I am *cocu*. Swindled, betrayed.[81]

The statements by Beauvoir and Myrdal correspond to some recent findings about sex differences in response to jealousy. A study by Gregory White[82] suggests that women are more likely to feel depressed if their partner has an affair with someone else, while men are more likely to feel angry and aggressive. These results seem due not to temperamental differences between the sexes, but rather to the imbalance of power between men and women. Generally, the partner with fewer alternatives outside the relationship is more likely to experience jealousy, even when no cause exists. Usually, but not always, the man holds the powerful position in a romantic relationship or a marriage because he is likely to have more economic resources and can more easily go out and find another partner. Thus the woman may respond to jealousy with feelings of loss and powerlessness, while the man may be responding to a sudden threat to his power position within the relationship.

A peculiarity about the psychology of jealousy and betrayal comes through clearly in the Myrdal passage cited. There is often a lack of parity in the perception of each member of a couple about the relations of each with another party. That is, consider any couple A and B (these could also be close friends of the same sex): A may feel that he or she can enter into a relationship with any third party X without taking anything away from the relationship with B; A may well even feel that he or she can love X without reducing the love for B. The relationship between A and X looks very different from B's point of view, however. No matter how uninvolved this relationship may be, it is likely to be magnified in B's perspective. And the same is true for a relationship between B and another person from A's viewpoint.

Carl Rogers presents a clinical case study showing these mechanisms in action. He describes how a sexually liberated couple returned to monogamy as a way of resolving conflicts over jealousy and openness. Both partners had love affairs with others, and each was willing to accept the other's outside relationships. But it turned out that this willingness was more intellectual than emotional.

> Eric experiences a full measure of primitive jealousy when he knows she is having sexual relationships with another man. And Denise, though ashamed of her feeling, is hurt when he is sexually involved with another woman, a hurt she feels even though she has been similarly involved with other men. . . .
>
> So they have come to a somewhat peculiar accommodation. If either feels such attraction to another person that he/she wants it to come to a climax in a sexual relationship, so be it. But they will keep these matters private from each other, simply because openness brings too much pain and hurt. But since they are accustomed to an astonishing degree of complete openness with each other, such deceit does not come easily and the result is to make them monogamous.[83]

Anthropologists have had more to say about sexual jealousy than the psychologists. William Stephens[84] observes that though there seems to be great variation in the jealousy potential of different societies and social arrangements, in no society is jealousy absent or incomprehensible. The peoples with the least amount of jealousy live in polyandrous societies —those very rare cultures in which women can have several husbands at the same time. Usually the cohusbands are brothers or other relatives. Yet even in these societies, some husbands experience jealousy and some do not.

One reason for the relative absence of extreme jealousy in polyandrous groups, according to Stephens, is the fact that husbands are given some say in whether the wife will take a cohusband, and, further, there is usually an economic benefit in bringing another man into the household. Although men's feelings in polyandrous societies are spared, women's feelings in polygynous societies are not. In most cases where men can take several wives, at least some of the wives suffer intensely from jealousy, and many polygynous families are strife-torn. Again, there is a great deal of individual variation.

Although the cross-cultural literature does not show monogamy to be a common human disposition, in only a few societies is adultery a permitted and expected form of behavior. Perhaps the most extreme example of institutionalized adultery occurs among the Lesu, a Pacific people. A woman's lover gives her presents— tsera—which are to be passed along to her husband. Yet even in this culture, jealousy is still a problem. Another anthropologist reports that among the Kaingang, "people are sexually promiscuous; yet they still wish—rather pathetically—for marital fidelity."[85]

The societies with the most extreme expression of jealousy are those Latin cultures where the ideals of machismo prevail. In Tepoztlan, Mexico, for example, husbands try to prove their virility by seducing other men's wives, but worry obsessively about other men seducing theirs. And in the United States there has been something called "the unwritten law"; if an irate spouse, especially a husband, were to shoot his wife's lover, a jury would be likely to let him off.

Explaining Jealousy

It would certainly be interesting to know what personality and situational factors give rise to greater and lesser degrees of jealousy. There are reports in the literature of couples who are able to maintain a close relationship with each other and tolerate affairs on the part of each other. Cuber and Harroff, for example, write that some very close couples were also adulterous:

> To some of them, sexual aggrandizement is a way of life. Frequently the infidelity is condoned by the partner and in some instances even provides an indirect (through empathy) kind of gratification. The act of infidelity in such cases is not construed as disloyalty or as a threat to continuity, but rather as a basic human right which the loved one ought to be permitted to have—and which the other perhaps wants also for himself.[86]

Another context in which jealousy appears to be controlled is in "swinging" groups, or mate-swappers. These couples are said to control their jealousy, however, by submitting their behavior to strict rules—for example, not engaging in certain sexual practices with others, not meeting sex partners outside the group setting, and so on. In effect, each spouse has veto power over the sexual behavior of the other.

Why should jealousy be such a deeply rooted—and hard to control—emotion? One obvious reason is that it is realistic to be jealous when a lover or spouse has an intimate relationship with someone else; people who try another partner are more likely to fall in love with the new person than those who do not get involved with third parties. But jealousy does not always seem to be based on realistic considerations. Jealousy can exist even when a person believes the partner's involvement does not involve a threat to the relationship. Nor are people jealous only of potential romantic competitors; one social-psychological experiment found that people were likely to be jealous when a same-sexed friend became interested in a third person.[87] And as writer Judith Viorst puts it, women can be jealous of their husband's families, business partners, psychiatrists, and bowling teams.[88]

Several psychological and sociological explanations of jealousy have been advanced. The psychological explanation would trace jealousy back to infancy and the nearly universal fact that infants are nurtured by, and form a primary attachment to, one person. An intimate attachment to someone later in life may bring back some of the earlier feelings—the sense of dependency and the wish to be the exclusive recipient of the loved one's love. Thus jealousy in adult life might be the equivalent of sibling rivalry in childhood. There is some recognition of this in the often-heard advice to parents about what to say when a new baby is brought home. The parent is warned not to tell the older child: "We love you so much we decided to have another baby." How would the parent feel if his or her spouse came home and said: "I love you so much I decided to have another one just like you"?

One sociological explanation of jealousy is based not on individual emotions but on the structural properties of the two-person group.

Georg Simmel[89] pointed out that the dyad differs from groups of all other sizes from three on up in a fundamental way. In groups larger than two a sense of groupness exists apart from the individual members. Even in a triad, for example, one person can leave and there is still the sense of a group carried on by the other two people. But in a dyad there is no group independent of the two people. If one person leaves or dies, that is the end of the relationship. Thus, argues Simmel, the peculiar properties of the dyad make it the most intimate of groups, and hence the most vulnerable to jealousy. The addition of a third party to a two-person group results in a very different social structure and changes the relationship between the original two. Where there was a relationship only between person A and person B, now there are three dyads: A and B, B and C, and A and C. This complication results in a certain instability:

> No matter how close a triad may be, there is always the occasion on which two of the three members regard the third as an intruder. . . . It may also be noted how extraordinarily difficult and rare it is for three people to attain a really uniform mood—when visiting a museum, for instance, or looking at a landscape—and how much more easily such a mood emerges between two.[90]

More recently, Sasha Weitman[91] has proposed a different sociological explanation of jealousy. According to this argument, sexual jealousy is just a specific instance of a general human tendency to feel excluded when witnessing other people engaged in acts of intimacy or friendship. Weitman argues that all acts of "social inclusion"—that is intimacy, love, and friendship, as well as membership in clubs or religious groups—are at the same time acts of exclusion as well. Thus, if a person invites friends A, B, and C for dinner, he or she is thereby excluding D and E. If a person confides in one friend, he or she is excluding others.

Weitman contends that witnesses to acts of social inclusion are likely to feel as if they had been subjected to aggression. Or as Judith Viorst puts it: "The everyday kind of jealousy has less to do with a fear of overt sexual betrayal than it does with a fear of intimacy that excludes us."[92]

Love and Conflict

Paradoxically, as we have seen earlier, intimate relationships are likely to experience more conflict than less-intimate ones. Around the turn of the century, the leading social theorists such as Simmel and Freud recognized the ambivalence inherent in close relationships. Families and other close-knit groups deal with each other in many areas of life, so there are more occasions for conflict to arise. Also, intimate relationships involve deeper layers of the personality—the more private and vulnerable parts of the self—so disagreements are likely to arouse more passion.

The self-disclosure that sets close relationships apart from more casual ones makes it possible for intimates to hurt one another more deeply than other people. One of the major reasons people need intimate relationships is to share their innermost thoughts. Yet the secrets revealed in moments of closeness can become weapons during an argument; a person who confides a childhood unhappiness might be told in the heat of a fight: "Your mother was right not to love you—you are unlovable"; or "Your father was right—you are incompetent."

Several studies have shown that people are likely to make the most intimate disclosures not to long-term intimates, but to strangers they don't expect to meet again—the "strangers on a train" phenomenon. There is also evidence of a curvilinear relationship between self-disclosure and satisfaction with relationships.[93] That is, up to a certain point, the more openness and self-revelation between two people, the more content they are with the relationship. After that point, however, increased openness may lead to discontent; people may find out more than they want to know about one another.

Lovers betray one another in several ways—not only by using knowledge of weakness and soft spots in arguments, or revealing them to others, but by reducing their opinion of the other person after learning of his or her failings. Thus lovers become emotional hostages of one another. The current popular idea that intimacy brings only benefits and no cost is a myth. People can be hurt emotionally and even physically when intimate relations turn sour.

Another reason intimate relations are so prone to conflict and violence is that the signals we use to communicate love and affections are very close to the ones that signal aggression and domination. Thus, although lovers stare at each other, so do enemies. Standing very close to a person, calling him or her "baby," remaining silent for long periods, or handling that person's possessions can signal either intimacy or hostility, depending on the emotional context of the situation. Since lovers are used to giving one version of these signals, it seems relatively easy for them to slip into the other mode.

In sum, then, many of the problems of love relationships are inherent in their very nature and hence are unsolvable. In fact, we may be on the verge of developing a new version of the romantic-love myth that recognizes the basic tensions between love and hostility, passion and permanence. As Ann Swidler observes:

> We hear of relationships in which "struggle" is the highest virtue, and in which loving means facing one after another crises in which two autonomous, changing individuals work to deepen communication, to understand each other, and to rediscover themselves.[94]

The new version of love may be seen in Bergman's *Scenes from a Marriage* and Woody Allen's *Annie Hall*. The great love stories of Western literature, from *Tristan and Isolde* to *Romeo and Juliet* to *Anna Karenina* to *Love Story*, are based on obstacles keeping the lovers apart. In the new love stories, the obstacles are internal; the new love "requires heroic struggles with the self and the lover. Love must stimulate and absorb perpetual changes."[95]

The new version of love recognizes that love does not always last forever. But among some couples, there seems to be a renewed emphasis on marriage as a permanent commitment. For example, Jane Ferrar[96] has described the new phenomenon of "spiritual marriage" in which the right to divorce is voluntarily renounced by couples commited to the struggle for spiritual advancement in Eastern religions. Thus, although the new values of self-realization and personal fulfillment are placing new strains on relationships, there seems also to be a growing recognition that relationships can never be perfect. As Murray Davis observes:

> It is my belief that the so-called crisis of intimate relations today is due to the increasing disparity between the rising expectation that all their problems can be solved and the intractable fact that many of them cannot be solved. Only by accepting the little tragedies of intimate relations as inherently necessary can the big tragedy of their breakup be avoided.[97]

Coming in out of the Cold

Summary

The essential themes of this chapter may be summarized in two statements:

1. Love relationships derive from our unique individuality and most private sense of self, and yet they are shaped by the time and place in which we live.

2. Close relationships are inherently problematic. In all stages of love and intimacy, there are psychological and social forces that pull the partners away from each other as well as forces that pull them together.

The ideology of romantic love has been part of Western culture for the past 800 years. It is deeply rooted in Western religious and economic traditions, and is strongly reinforced by the conditions of life in modern urban-industrial society. Although the potential for romantic love exists in all times and places, it is elaborated to a greater degree in Western culture than anywhere else. Also, some of the ideas in the romantic love tradition—deference to the woman, the mixture of sexual love and admiration, and the idea that love ennobles the lover—are uniquely Western.

In the course of history, the idea of love has been redefined. Although it started out as adulterous passion, romantic love was joined to marriage with the rise of Puritanism and capitalism. In recent years the connection between love and marriage has loosened once again; although love and sex are no longer necessarily linked to marriage, there is little evidence that large numbers of people are giving up the values of intimacy and love.

Source Notes

1. Proxmire, 1975, p. 73.
2. Rubin, 1977, p. 59.
3. Fincke, 1891, p. 244.
4. Reiche, 1971, p. 27.
5. Kilpatrick, 1975.
6. Hunt, 1959, p. 5.
7. Linton, 1936, p. 175.
8. Ibid.
9. Goode, 1959.
10. Schacter, 1964
11. Dutton and Aron, 1974.
12. Katz, 1977.
13. Hochschild, 1975.
14. Udry, 1971, pp. 162–163.
15. Mead, 1928.
16. Hochschild, 1975.
17. Ibid.
18. Ibid.
19. Hunt, 1959, p. 16.
20. Stephens, 1963.
21. Lewis, 1958, pp. 3–4.
22. de Rougemont, 1956, p. 3.
23. Watt, 1957.
24. Swidler, 1977.
25. Ibid., p. 12.
26. Heer, 1962.
27. Stone, 1964.
28. Greenfield, 1969.
29. Ibid., p. 360.
30. Davis, 1974.
31. Bowlby, 1969.
32. Middlebrook, 1974, p. 215.
33. Weiss, 1973, p. 92.
34. Gordon, 1974.
35. Burgess and Wallin, 1953.
36. Peplau, Rubin, and Hill, 1977.

37. Hunt, 1974.
38. *San Francisco Chronicle,* Sept. 26, 1977, p. 3.
39. Institute of Life Insurance, 1974.
40. Stein, 1977, p. 496.
41. Ibid., p. 528.
42. Gordon, 1974, p. 83.
43. Hunt, 1974.
44. Ibid., p. 154.
45. Gordon, 1974, p. 231.
46. Roper Organization, 1974.
47. Rubin, 1970.
48. Lee, 1975.
49. Rubin, 1973.
50. Hochschild, 1975.
51. Kephart, 1967.
52. Ibid., p. 473.
53. Waller, 1938.
54. Hochschild, 1975.
55. Farber, 1964.
56. McCall, 1966.
57. Murstein, 1971.
58. Reiss, 1960.
59. Walster, 1971.
60. Ibid., p. 87.
61. Reik, 1944, p. 185.
62. Klein and Riviere, 1953.
63. Berscheid and Fei, 1977, p. 104.
64. Sennett and Cobb, 1974, p. 62.
65. Waller, 1939.
66. Burgess, Wallin, and Schultz, 1953.
67. Ibid., pp. 63–64.
68. In Gordon, 1974, p. 226.
69. Walster et al., 1966.
70. Vreeland, 1972.
71. Rosenbaum, 1972.
72. Ibid., p. 6.
73. Walster, 1973, p. 6.
74. Quoted in Hunt, 1959, pp. 143–144.
75. Capellanus, 1957.
76. Haley, 1963.
77. Adams, 1971.
78. Lyness, Lipetz, and Davis, 1972.
79. Memmi, 1968, p. 148.
80. Beauvoir, 1968, p. 147.
81. Myrdal, 1968, p. 159.
82. White, 1977.
83. Rogers, 1972, pp. 195–196.
84. Stephens, 1963.
85. Henry, in Stephens, 1963, p. 253.
86. Cuber and Harroff, 1965, p. 63.
87. Branson, 1977.
88. Viorst, 1977.
89. Simmel, 1950.
90. Ibid., pp. 135–136.
91. Weitman, 1973.
92. Viorst, 1977, p. 21.
93. Cozby, 1973.
94. Swidler, 1977, p. 19.
95. Ibid.
96. Ferrar, 1977.
97. Davis, 1974, p. xiii.

Coming in out of the Cold

Chapter Nine
Marriage: Image and Institution

□ *Above all, it must not be thought that the couple relationship is a simple one: a man and woman bound by some obvious contract.*

Albert Memmi, *Dominated Man*

To many people the best evidence that the American family is falling apart is the seeming unpopularity of the institution of marriage. The divorce rate continues to rise, after reaching an all-time high point in the early 1970s, with the biggest increases occurring among couples with children.[1] Unmarried couples living together have become a commonplace and even accepted part of the social scene, especially among the upper-middle class. Recent census data reveal a rapid expansion of the number of people living alone; although many of these people will eventually marry, and many are older widows who are willing to marry but unlikely to find mates in their age group, a small but growing number of people are developing a commitment to singlehood.[2] Nor is marriage any longer the socially necessary prerequisite for homeownership or even parenthood. Despite the availability of abortion in recent years, many single women have chosen to continue their pregnancies and rear their children themselves.

Attitudes toward marriage have changed even more strikingly than behavior. In recent years marriage counselors have become concerned with saving the spouses rather than the marriages; feminists and social scientists have pointed out that for women, the legal, economic, and psychological costs of marriage often exceed the benefits. In Hollywood movies it has become almost a cliché to portray marriages as unhappy, particularly for middle-class or middle-aged partners.

Nevertheless, marriage is not about to disappear from the American scene. Despite the statistics on divorce and increasing singleness among young people, other indicators suggest that marriage may actually be as popular as it ever was. Of course, how one feels about the persistence of marriage depends on one's attitudes toward the institution. Some may celebrate the fact that marriage seems to be "here to stay"[3] while others may lament it.

Even the divorce rate itself can be interpreted as an indicator of the stability of marriage. It is true that the divorce rate is rising. Only 12 percent of the marriages of women born between 1900 and 1904 ended in divorce, but 30 to 40 percent of marriages of women born between 1940 and 1944 will do so.[4] Despite the tripling of the divorce rate, however, a majority of married couples are still remaining together. It is possible that in the future, most marriages will end in divorce, but that moment has not yet arrived.

Another way of putting divorce in perspective is by looking at the other great disrupter of marriage—death. Until very recently the rate of marital disruption in the twentieth century declined from what it had been in earlier times. In the Plymouth colony 40 percent of men and 26 percent of women over fifty had been married more than once, following widowhood.[5] Marital disruption due to the death of the spouse was about as common in 1910 as disruption due to divorce is today.[6] Of course, the death of a husband or wife is a very different psychological event than divorce. But the historical evidence does suggest that the loss of a marriage partner before advanced old age is not a new experience.

Other indicators of the persistence of marriage include the proportion of people who marry again after divorce or widowhood. A very high proportion of Americans marry at least once. As a feminist writer complained, "Just as God has been pronounced dead quite often, but has this sneaky way of resurrecting himself, so everyone debunks marriage, yet ends up married."[7] Over the past century, 90 to 95 percent of all American women married at least once. During the Depression, when the number of never-married women rose to a near record figure, only 9 percent of women remained unwed. At the height of the baby boom of the 1950s, all but 4 percent of those at the height of the childbearing years married.[8]

Marriage: Image and Institution

TABLE 9-1   *THE LIKELIHOOD OF DIVORCE*[a]

Sex and Year of Birth	Percent of Ever-Married Persons Whose First Marriage . . .		Percent of Persons Married Twice Whose Second Marriage . . .	
	Had Ended in Divorce by 1975	May Eventually End in Divorce[b]	Had Ended in Redivorce by 1975	May Eventually End in Redivorce[b]
Men:				
1945–1949	13	34	5	35
1940–1944	17	31	6	32
1935–1939	20	29	5	28
1930–1934	18	24	8	24
1925–1929	18	22	7	20
1920–1924	18	20	9	18
1915–1919	17	18	9	13
1910–1914	17	17	7	9
1905–1909	15	15	7	8
1900–1904	13	13	6	6
Women:				
1945–1949	17	38	8	44
1940–1944	20	34	12	40
1935–1939	21	31	10	31
1930–1934	21	26	11	26
1925–1929	21	24	14	23
1920–1924	18	20	8	15
1915–1919	16	17	11	16
1910–1914	16	16	10	12
1905–1909	15	15	9	9
1900–1904	13	13	5	5

[a]Percent of ever-married persons whose first marriage may eventually end in divorce and whose second marriage may eventually end in redivorce, by year of birth and sex, June 1975.
[b]If their future divorce experience is similar to that of persons in older age groups between 1969 and 1974.
Source: U.S. Bureau of the Census.

Thus our perspective on the state of marriage in America is distorted if we take the postwar era as the baseline for measuring change. Further, although singleness has been increasing in young people, it has actually decreased in people over thirty, at least for the period between 1960 and 1974. Thus, for people born before 1944, the proportion of those who marry at some point in their lives has continued to rise.[9]

Comparison with other cultures also helps to put American marital patterns in perspective. Americans have traditionally been a marrying society. Europeans, by contrast, have historically followed a different marriage pattern: they have married late, and a large proportion of the population have never married.[10] Marriage was a privilege reserved for those who had accumulated sufficient economic security under conditions of scarce land and jobs. It was a kind of gift bestowed on the individual by the community: "A place had to be vacant, land for the luckier ones, or a bakery, a joinery, a loom, or some other productive property."[11] In America, by contrast, for most of its history, land and jobs were abundant. Even today the European pattern exists to some extent. In many European countries the average age of marriage is about two years later than in America, and singleness persists for large numbers: in the 1960s, 28 percent of French women between the ages of twenty-five and thirty-four remained unmarried, as did 18 percent of British women of comparable ages and an amazing 45 percent of the Irish.[12]

The most frequently cited evidence for the argument that marriage remains an important part of American life is the rate of remarriage after divorce or widowhood. Until very recently, the remarriage rate has followed the divorce rate; when the divorce rate rose, so did remarriage, and when it fell, the remarriage rate also dropped. In 1972 the Bureau of the Census estimated that four out of every five divorced persons eventually remarry. At every age, peo-

ple who get divorced are more likely to marry again than those widowed or those who never married. Men are more likely to remarry than women, despite their tendency to malign marriage.

Since 1970, however, the remarriage rate has leveled off while the divorce rate has continued to rise. It is not clear as yet whether divorced people are simply waiting longer to remarry, or whether they are becoming disillusioned with marriage. As with a number of other statistical indicators, the slowdown in the rate of remarriage has demographers, social scientists, and policy makers anxiously waiting to find out whether people are simply postponing such commitments or opting out of them.

Although the statistics on marriage and remarriage do not support the idea that the institution of legal marriage is obsolete in America, neither should they be interpreted as showing that nothing has changed. But the changes have more to do with the quality of relationships—the kinds of values and expectations that people bring to marriage—than they do with absolute numbers or observable behavior. As Gagnon and Simon[13] point out, significant social change does not occur only when people's behavior changes. The moment of change may simply be the moment when new forms of behavior seem plausible. It is probably the shift of certain behaviors from the unthink-

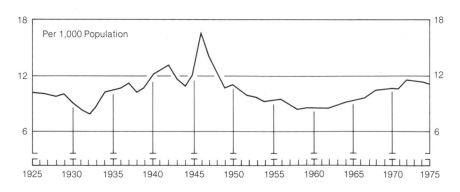

Marriage rate, 1925–1975. In 1975, the rate declined for the third year in a row. Because the proportion of marriageable people has increased, the specific marriage rate declined still more sharply. (Source: National Center for Health Statistics.)

Marriage: Image and Institution

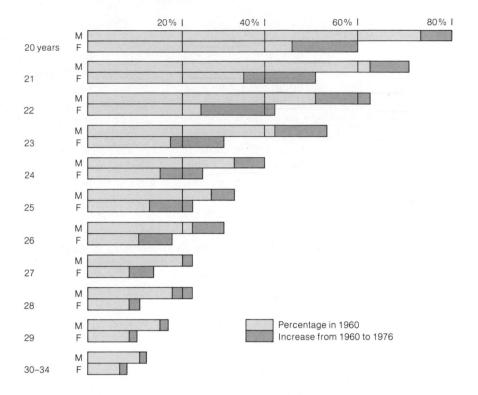

Percentages of young people who have never married, by age and sex. (Source: U.S. Bureau of the Census.)

able to the plausible that accounts for the widespread sense that the family is falling apart.

What is more significant than the absolute numbers of people engaging in such behaviors as remaining single, living together, having babies out of wedlock, getting divorced, and so on, is the fact that these things appear as options to many people, something they might think about doing even if they ultimately decided not to. Until recently social scientists often used demographic statistics to deny that anything

was changing in the area of marriage and the family. Today, however, it is hard to find anyone who will disagree with the statement made by two leading demographers from the Census Bureau: "There seems little doubt that a basic transformation of the institution of marriage is underway."[14]

If we are to understand how marriage is changing we need to explore what it has been—as image, institution, and personal relationship. This task occupies the rest of this chapter.

The Two Faces of Marriage

Marriage has always had a dual aspect that has puzzled students of marriage as well as ordinary folk; marriage is a relationship be-

tween two people, but it is more than a couple relationship—it is an institution. Marriage is an intensely private affair, but it is public as well.

"Marriage" seems to lead its own separate existence, quite apart from particular married couples. Indeed, many people today experience "marriage" as an alien presence, an unwelcome third party, intruding itself into what may be an otherwise delightful relationship.

Attacks on marriage as an institution are not a novelty brought on by the current wave of family and sexual unrest. Although some of these criticisms are new, hostility toward marriage has deep roots in Western culture. Usually, however, antimarriage attitudes have coexisted with respect for the institution and a sense of its inevitability. What is novel in the contemporary scene is that the positive side of the ambivalence has diminished, emphasizing the hostility.

This ambivalence toward marriage takes many forms, beginning perhaps with the statement of St. Paul that it is better to marry than to burn. Not marrying and not burning was better still, but was conceded to be beyond the capacities of most. Besides Christian ambivalence, the models of marriage put forth by the professionals in the field also have two faces. We shall look at the professional work on marriage later, but let us look first at what could be called the "classical ambivalence" of popular culture.

As Udry observes, there are two contradictory myths about marriage: one is cynical and the other romantic. Despite their inconsistency, many people hold to both.

> The first myth—"and they lived happily ever after"—portrays marriage as a continuous courtship. The second myth is the picture of the domestic grind: the husband sits behind the paper, the wife moves about in the morning disarray; the husband leaves for work, the wife spends the day among dishes, diapers, and dirty little children. Although, as with most myths, no one *really* believes either one of them, they continue to affect the behavior of most people.[15]

This popular ambivalence about marriage forms the basis of much of the humor on television and in the comics and cartoons, as exemplified in such fare as "Maggie and Jiggs," "I Love Lucy," "Dagwood and Blondie," mother-in-law jokes, and ball-and-chain jokes. George Orwell once took a long look at this kind of humor, in the particular form of obscene penny postcards. Orwell was writing of the English scene around the early 1940s, but the kind of humor he describes persists; it is, as he says, "something as traditional as Greek tragedy, a sort of subworld of smacked bottoms and scrawny mothers-in-law which is a part of Western European consciousness." He lists the conventions of the sex joke:

> . . . Marriage only benefits the woman. Every man is plotting seduction and every woman is plotting marriage. No woman ever remains unmarried voluntarily.
>
> . . . Sex appeal vanishes at about the age of 25. Well-preserved and good-looking people beyond their first youth are never represented. The amorous honeymooning couple reappear as the grim-visaged wife and shapeless, mustachioed, red-nosed husband, no intermediate stage being allowed for.
>
> . . . Next to sex, the henpecked husband is the favorite joke. Typical caption: "Did they get an X-ray of your wife's jaw at the hospital?"—"No, they got a moving picture instead."
>
> CONVENTIONS:
>
> (i) There is no such thing as a happy marriage.
> (ii) No man ever gets the better of a woman in an argument.[16]

Orwell explains this humor in much the same way as some sociologists have explained the persistence of prostitution and pornography, as a sort of safety valve, a harmless rebellion against virtue, which protects a stable family life by giving some expression to otherwise disrupting impulses. This humor, says Orwell, implies that:

> Marriage is something profoundly exciting and important, the biggest event in the average human being's life. . . . Jokes about nagging wives and tyrannous mothers-in-law . . . imply a stable society in which marriage is indissoluble and family loyalty taken for granted. . . . The working-class outlook . . . takes it almost as a matter of course that youth and adventure—almost indeed, individual life—end with marriage.[17]

Orwell overlooks something else about such jokes: practically all are based on the male viewpoint, expressing male resentment of women. There are no male counterparts to the stock figures of the wife in curlers wielding a rolling pin, the nagging mother-in-law, the crotchety old maid. Males appear only as victims of female domination—Dagwood Bumstead, Jiggs, Fred Flintstone, and others. There is no positive image of women other than the sweet young thing.

Such antifemale humor was encouraged during the Middle Ages when people who deviated from marital norms were publicly taunted. The historian Natalie Davis[18] has described communal festivals where all sorts of people were mocked, in something like the spirit of a school play making fun of the teachers. A prominent part of these festivities, or *charivari,* was the public humiliation of husbands who had allowed themselves to be henpecked or deceived, of widows and widowers who had remarried younger spouses, and newlyweds who had failed to produce a child in the first year of marriage. These customs were obviously an attempt to control family behavior, particularly women's. Davis notes, however, that they may have unintentionally encouraged the kind of rebellious behavior they mocked.

Sophisticated Ambivalence

Another brand of humorous ambivalence toward marriage occurs in the sophisticated tradition. This includes the French bedroom farce and the humor of such magazines as *Esquire* and *Playboy*. Here the main source of humor is adultery, and the complications arising from deception and discovery.

This brand of humor reflects the moral order of the Continental upper-middle class, where separation of love and marriage is assumed, love affairs are expected of both spouses, but especially the husband, and conjugal love, particularly of long standing, is perverse.

> I've been married 18 years,
> And still adore my wife.
> I have no hunger for other women,
> I am content to be faithful,
> I am resigned to decency.
> I actually think I have found love
>   and Life.
> What's the matter with me?
> —John Haynes Holmes[19]

The above poem, written in 1922, was quoted by a journalist who observed, "Even back in 1922, when those lines were written, people were asking themselves, albeit ironically, whether they were some kind of freaks because their marriages were happy."[20] Although this view of marriage has long been traditional in certain sectors of European society, only recently has it come to be publicly expressed in America. It now seems, however, to be the prevailing Hollywood image of marriage.

Cross-Cultural Ambivalence

It would be a mistake to conclude that marital conflict and ambivalence toward marriage are peculiar to Western European culture. William Stephens,[21] in his worldwide survey of family practices, has shown that divorce is as universal a custom as marriage. No known society forbids divorce—with the exception of Christian countries. Even here, however, escape can be found in the form of annulments and informal separations, as well as approved ways of not marrying at all, such as joining religious orders. In spite of the widespread belief that marital disharmony is unique to modern industrial society, no culture has found the formula for perfect marriage.

Marriage is not all "togetherness."

Sexual Politics and Power Struggle

Two separate sources of marital strain are often inextricably bound together in real life, but should be kept separate for purposes of analysis. The first results as the inevitable by-product of any prolonged intimate association between two people, regardless of their gender: difficulties may arise from basic temperamental incompatibilities and differences in tastes and opinions or from changes in these. There are also momentary disharmonies of mood—one partner may feel tired while the other feels lively. Further, there is always the issue of whose wishes will prevail at a given moment, and how to decide whose wishes will prevail. Such problems of rule making and communication will be discussed in a later section.

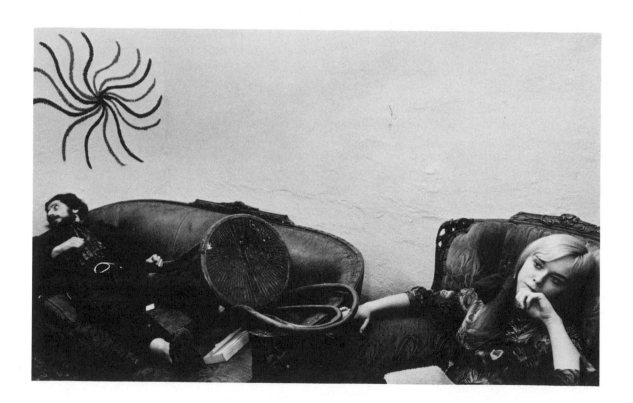

Marriage: Image and Institution

The other leading source of marital tension arises from the sexual politics implicit in a union between a man and a woman. Until sexual equality prevails, we will never know how much the sex difference in itself adds to the general strain of dyadic interaction. But until sex differences no longer imply differences in status and power, the stage will be set for the classic battle of the sexes: the struggle on the part of most men to keep women in their place, and the maneuvering of women to evade or exploit that place.

The social inequality of the sexes and the traditional stereotypes of masculinity and femininity have made it difficult for men and women to relate to each other as human beings. The social inequality of men and women creates psychological inequality; they have a hard time understanding each other, and tend to use each other as "objects" trying to win "in the game of exchanging sexuality for commitment and security."[22]

His Marriage Versus Hers

To the extent that sex roles are sharply marked off and the sexes differ in status and resources, marriage will continue to be a somewhat different institution for men and women; or, as Jessie Bernard puts it, every marital union contains two marriages, his and hers.[23]

Marital humor usually reflects prevailing cultural definitions of the husband's marriage. These define marriage as a trap set for men by women, and they encourage a myth of happy bachelorhood—if only women would let him alone, a man could lead a happy and free existence. This myth is part of the "masculine protest" aspect of male socialization: to be masculine in this culture is to be free of responsibility to females, particularly maternal females.

The cultural notion that men don't really need or want strong attachments to women may make them uncomfortable when they do wish such attachments. But the myth encourages them to a grudging resentment of wife and children. Simone de Beauvoir comments on how oppression by men paradoxically results in feelings of being oppressed:

> . . . In oppressing, one becomes oppressed. Men are enchained by reason of their very sovereignty; it is because they alone earn money that wives demand checks; it is because they alone engage in a business or profession that their wives require them to be successful. . . .
>
> . . . Man and wife together undergo the oppression of an institution they did not create. If it is asserted that *men* oppress *women*, the husband is indignant; he feels that he is the one who is oppressed—and he is; but the fact is that it is the masculine code, it is the society developed by the males and in their interest, that has established woman's situation in a form that is at present a source of torment for both sexes.[24]

Consider a man I shall call Eric S., a moderately successful business-man in his forties whom I interviewed as part of a longitudinal study of a normal population. As he thought over his life thus far, he said that though he liked his wife and loved his children, he probably wouldn't marry if he could live his life over. He liked freedom—the idea of always being able to come and go as he pleased, to take off for a fishing trip or a distant city whenever he felt like it, and not to be committed to eating his wife's cooking all his life. He also felt that, though his family was always struggling to get by on his salary, he would have been almost rich if he'd had it all to himself. On the other hand, his wife had wanted to take up a career when the children were all in school, but he had dis-

right?

couraged her from doing so. It was better for the children, he thought, if their mother were home all the time and not distracted by outside interests.

The attitudes and assumptions expressed by this man illustrate the obstacles that tradi-tional sex roles can place in the way of solving everyday problems. This man feels short of money, but he won't let his wife work; he can't stand her cooking, but it doesn't occur to him that he could help prepare the family meals himself.

Legal Images of Marriage: Institutionalized Sexism

We mentioned earlier that marriage always involves something more than just the relation-ship between people. The legal aspects of mar-riage are one of the important ways in which the institution goes beyond the interpersonal rela-tionship. For most people the legal side of marriage is experienced only at the time of marriage or divorce, or when inheritance of property becomes an issue. Yet there is more to marriage as a legal instituiton than a series of procedures one has to go through to get mar-ried or divorced.

Although few people realize it, when they marry they are legally committing themselves to a detailed set of duties, rights, and obliga-tions. Lenore Weitzman points out that no state gives the prospective bride and groom a chance to read the terms of their marriage contract, or asks them if they are willing to abide by its terms. The marriage contract is actually a more extreme form of legal obligation than other contracts: "·. . . its provisions are unwritten, its penalties are unspecified, and the terms of contract are typically unknown to the contract-ing parties."[25]

What are the obligations people are com-mitting themselves to? The specifics of the marriage contract vary in each state, of course. In New York for example, married couples are harnessed with several hundred sections of the Domestic Relations Law, the Family Court Act and Rules, and other related statutes and deci-sions that have the force of law.[26] Underlying all these specific kinds of regulations, there are, as Weitzman summarizes them, four essential provisions. These assume that (1) the husband is the head of the household; (2) the husband is responsible for support; (3) the wife is respon-sible for domestic services; and (4) the wife is responsible for child care.

The historical traditions of Western law, from Roman times on, have defined women as inferior beings who must be under the protec-tion of a man. The wedding custom of a father "giving" his daughter to the groom reflects this legal notion. Further, whatever women's status in general, they usually lose legal rights by marrying. In most countries there are two legal statuses for women: one for spinsters and one for married women.

The married woman's loss of legal rights can be traced to the feudal doctrine of cover-ture, the notion that the husband and wife are a unity.

Based in part upon biblical notions of the unity of flesh of husband and wife, the doctrine was described by Blackstone as follows: "By marriage, the husband and wife are one person in law; that is, the very being or legal existence of the woman is suspended during the marriage, or at least is incorporated and consolidated." . . . The doctrine . . . has worked out in reality to mean . . . the one is the husband.[27]

The clearest symbol of the married woman's loss of an independent identity is her assumption of her husband's name; she also assumes his residence and his social and economic status. Although some women are trying to retain their maiden names, there are many obstacles in their way: they may have trouble voting, obtaining a driver's license, or securing credit. The woman's assumption of her husband's residence also affects a number of rights and duties, such as where she must vote, register a car, pay taxes, and so on. Sometimes the residence rule can have serious consequences. For example, a woman who, as a state resident, receives free tuition at a state university may suddenly be charged out-of-state fees if she marries a fellow student whose legal residence is in another state.[28]

In the United States today, married women also lose some of their rights to control property, and they cannot enter into contracts on the same basis as men or single women. In some states the husband controls the wife's earnings and property, and can dispose of it without her consent. The wife, on the other hand, has no right to a share of her husband's earnings beyond that necessary to run the household.[29] She is not entitled to direct compensation for doing domestic work—her husband is merely obliged to "maintain" her. This distribution of obligations has been described by one observer as the economic relationship between an owner and his property, rather than between two free individuals.[30]

Discussions of family law can sound abstract and irrelevant for most people's lives, but family law is a part of an invisible web of forces maintaining family structures in the traditional forms. Family structures are backed in many ways that are not easily observable. As William Goode has pointed out, most people take family structures they live in for granted, and do not challenge them:

> They know in advance they would fail. In most families the structure is not overthrown, because it is viewed as inalterable or at best the only alternative. Thus, force plays a role even when no deviant act is actually committed. The rebellious child or wife knows that the father or husband is stronger, and can call upon outsiders who will support that force with more force.[31]

We do not see the application of force to maintain family patterns, but its threat creates and maintains an imbalance of power:

> For example, if in a patrilineal polygamous society an older woman were to announce that she is henceforth to be treated as the leader of her patriline, tried to sell its cattle, started to give orders, set dates for rituals, or chose a chief, very likely she would be beaten or treated as insane. Similarly, if a child in our society were to claim the headship of the family, give orders to his parents or siblings, try to write checks on his father's account, or trade in the automobile for a new one, the same result would occur.[32]

The legal restrictions and obligations enter in subtle ways into the social exchange between marriage partners. Even if both spouses try to have a more egalitarian arrangement than the law allows, they may run into legal difficulties. Thus a couple may agree that the wife should keep her maiden name, or maintain a residence in another state, or buy a house on her own, or open her own charge account, but legal traditions and business practices may prevent them from carrying out these wishes or may cost the wife or the couple certain privileges.[33] Or a couple may wish to challenge the legal precedent that a wife owes her husband household services and is not to be directly paid for them. The courts, however, may not grant a husband the right to pay for something he is entitled to free:

> In a Texas case, David promised his wife, Fannie, that he would give her $5000 if she would stay with him while he lived and continue taking care of the house and farm accounts, selling his butter, and doing all the other tasks which she had done since their marriage. After David's death, Fannie sued his estate for the money which had been promised her. The court held the contract was unenforceable since Fannie had agreed to do nothing which she was not already legally and morally bound to do as David's wife.[34]

It is obvious that the provisions of the marriage contract do not reflect current social realities. Marriages are becoming more "symmetrical"[35] if not egalitarian, with women contributing to the support of the family, and men becoming more responsible for household duties and child care. In addition, the legal system's rigidly prescribed roles allow no choice of family form or intensity of relationship. Thus, as Weitzman observes, a wide variety of individuals—homosexuals, communards, unwed couples—have been excluded from legal marriage. She concludes:

> . . . the legitimacy and relevancy of legal marriage would be greatly improved if the law permitted alternative family arrangements and judged them by the traditional legal standards developed in equity and contract law—instead of the outmoded family law.[36]

Recently there has been a growing trend for couples to write their own custom-designed marriage contracts, although alterations in the traditional contract face continued legal barriers. An individual premarital contract could be expected to deal with such issues as the following: the aims and expectations of the relationship, the management and control of wages, the allocation of responsibility for support and household duties, relations with others outside the marriage, and plans for children. Such contracts may clarify the intentions and expectations of each partner, hence they may be useful even if their provisions may be legally unenforceable.

The contract idea has also been applied to ongoing marriages. One such contract was described by Alix Shulman.[37] During the early days of the marriage, she writes, she and her husband both worked. They went out a lot and did the minimal household chores together, mostly on weekends. The arrival of two children drastically changed their roles. They moved to a larger apartment, and the amount of housework increased enormously. She had quit her job to stay home, and her husband had to work longer hours to support the family. When she revealed how dissatisfied she was, her husband agreed to participate in the child care and housework. They tried to recreate the equality that had prevailed during the first days of their marriage. But when the agreement was informal and verbal, she writes, they kept slipping back into their old division of labor. Ultimately, they resorted to a formal written agreement, including a detailed breakdown of the jobs that had to be done and the periods for which each spouse had to be responsible, so that each would end up with 50 percent of the responsibility. Perhaps the most striking aspect of this contract, aside from its businesslike breakdown of the minutia of domestic life—e.g., "Item: Nighttime—getting children to take baths, brush their teeth, go to bed, . . . reading with them, tucking them in, and having night talks . . . "—is the redefinition of the husband's career as a personal privilege rather than family duty:

We reject the notion that the work which brings in more money is more valuable. The ability to earn more money is already a privilege which must not be compounded by enabling the larger earner to buy out of his or her duties and put the burden on the one who earns less, or on someone hired from the outside.

We believe that each member of the family has an equal right to his/her own time, work, values, choices. As long as all duties are performed, each person may use his or her extra time any way he/she chooses. If he/she wants to use it making money, fine. If he/she wants to spend it with spouse, fine. If not, fine.[38]

Probably the idea of negotiated contracts between husbands and wives seems, to most readers, an intrusion of business practices into an intimate relationship. Yet it is not only women's liberationists who have argued for such explicit bargaining; some marriage counselors have advocated this approach to dealing with the nitty-gritty conflicts of daily life.

The Housewife Problem

The feminists quarrel with family law not only because the low status and impaired rights of women are unjust, but also because this injustice is reflected all too well in daily realities. Thus the assumptions of the law on the subject of domestic work are fairly descriptive of the realities of the division of labor in most marriages.

The concept of the housewife role is central to understanding the feminist complaint about marriage. Their argument has several facets. First, domestic work remains the last occupation to which a person is fated at birth. As Daryl and Sandra Bem[39] have pointed out, when a boy is born it is hard to predict what he will be doing in twenty-five years—his future is open. If the

newborn child is a girl, however, how she will be spending her time in twenty-five years can be predicted with almost complete statistical certainty. Looking at the two newborns, we can tell with even more certainty who will be washing socks and who will have them washed for him. It doesn't matter that the girl baby is nominally free to choose a career or not to marry. Until very recently socialization pressures have worked effectively to prevent all but a small minority of women from acting on the options presumably available. If they do try to enter the world of work, they will find not only lower pay and discrimination in a variety of forms, but they will never entirely escape the long shadow of domesticity.

Studies of working women indicate that the egalitarian family that supposedly prevails in America is largely a myth. Although husbands of working wives do more housework than husbands of nonemployed ones, they do not do as much as the wives. Thus Blood and Hamblin[40] estimated that nonworking wives in their sample did 85 percent of the housework and working wives did 75 percent. Another study of fifty-three couples in which both partners were professionals also revealed a marked inequality in the allocation of domestic tasks.[41] The research shows that married women can follow what Jessie Bernard[42] has called the "one-role option," either career as a single woman or the full-time housewife and mother role; or the "two-role option"—career woman plus mother and housewife. The "shared-role option"—both husband and wife working and sharing all domestic work—has rarely been tried, although many couples who are now marrying are attempting to follow this pattern.

Another feminist objection to the housewife role, apart from its castelike aspects, is that it is highly burdensome in terms of time and monotony and yet is devalued. Thus studies show that housewives spend an enormous amount of time at their occupation—99.5 hours a week accord-

The kitchen is no longer the exclusive territory of the wife.

ing to a Chase Manhattan Bank study—yet it is not counted as real work. The housewife is considered—by economists, the dictionary, and most people—as a person who does not work. In terms of prestige it is an occupation near the bottom of the scale.

Finally, the occupation of housewife does not even deliver the security it promises. The housewife has no guarantee that, after she has given her "best years" to marriage, she will not be traded in for a newer model. Many men would identify with the comedian who quipped that he wanted to trade in his forty-year-old wife for two twenties. Germaine Greer observes:

> The housewife is an unpaid worker in her husband's house in return for the security of being a permanent employee: hers is the *reductio ad absurdum* of the case of the employee who accepts a lower wage in return for permanence in his employment. But the lowest-paid employees can be and are laid off, and so are wives. They have no savings, no skills which they can bargain with elsewhere, and they must bear the stigma of having been sacked[43]

Furthermore, evidence suggests that the housewife role is debilitating to morale and well-being. Jessie Bernard has compiled a body of research findings showing that more married than single women are bothered by depression, worries and phobias of various kinds, severe neurotic symptoms, and physical pains and ailments.[44] A study of middle-aged women by Pauline Bart[45] revealed that the women who had made the deepest commitments to motherhood and domesticity were most likely to experience depression at the time of menopause. In a study comparing recent mental-illness rates among men and women, as indicated by community surveys, admissions to mental hospitals, and so on, Gove and Tudor[46] found women to have higher rates of "mental illness."

These higher rates of "mental illness" for women, however, are found mainly when married women are compared to married men. In studies of unmarried, widowed, and divorced people, the sex difference either does not appear or men may turn out to have higher rates. And among married women, full-time housewives seem to have more psychological problems than wives who work.[47] There is also evidence that higher rates of "mental illness" for women developed after World War II, and vary from community to community—small, traditional, culturally isolated communities showing lower rates for women than for men.

Gove and Tudor[48] give several reasons why the housewife's role in modern industrial societies may be stressful for many women. First, the full-time housewife is restricted to a single social role, while most men have two major roles—worker and father-husband. If one of a man's roles is unsatisfactory, he can look to the other for gratification. The housewife has no such alternative. Second, since much of the housewife's work is repetitive and undemanding, and does not call for a high degree of expertise, it is out of keeping with the educational attainments of many women. Third, the housewife's role is relatively unstructured. Her isolation and lack of structured job demands make it possible for her to brood over her troubles. By contrast, the person who has a job out in the world usually doesn't have the opportunity to be obsessed with his or her worries. Finally, the expectations confronting women are unclear and contradictory.

Models of Marriage: Paradise and Paradox

The omission thus far of detailed attention to the literature of marital satisfaction and adjustment is not, as the saying goes, an accident. Any social science dealing with the experience of daily life should consider popular or folk conceptions of the subject before proceeding to the ideas of "experts." In this field in particular there is cause to wonder whether the insights of the nonexperts are less valid than those of the marital-adjustment experts. Many studies on marriage have failed to recognize that, even under the most stable social conditions, marriage is a complex and ambivalent form of human interaction. Orwell recognized this when he described sex and marriage jokes as a kind of collective jeer, a protest against marriage on the part of people who take it very seriously.

In modern urban societies marriage becomes even more problematic as tolerance for divorce and adultery rises, individuals change, and the need for intimacy and personal realization increases. Marriage studies typically overlook the large social forces altering marital relations, marriage, and the people in them. They perpetuate a utopian romantic mystique of marriage.

Utopian Marriage:
The Adjustment Model

Probably the most famous single statement about family life is Tolstoy's opening sentence in *Anna Karenina:* "Happy families are all alike; unhappy families are unhappy each in its own way." It states a surprising yet obvious truth in a pithy way. And the prevailing images of family life in family sociology and marriage counseling coincide with it; there are normal families, all more or less alike in their normality, and there are sick and disturbed or unhappy families, each with its own particular tale to be told. We are going to suggest in this section, however, that Tolstoy's words tell us less about the realities of family life, in particular marriage, than they do about the kinds of imagery of marriage that people hold.

A dilemma lies at the heart of the attempt to study marital success scientifically: it is impossible to define a successful marriage in an objective way. To see the problem, perhaps the reader should take a moment to determine his or her own definition of a good, successful marriage. Then consider whether the definition contains a value judgment—that is, a notion of what a "good" marriage *should be*. People with different values will inevitably define success in marriage differently. In contrast, a group of doctors can agree, except in rare cases, on the health of a person, no matter what their personal values and opinions may be. As Ryder puts it:

> There is no descriptively defined entity that can reasonably be called a successful marriage because there is no general agreement as to what marriages should be. Yet study after study has contrasted "good" marriages with "bad" marriages as if there were such an entity. A successful marriage is clearly one of which we approve. The concept is a value judgment dressed up to look like a matter of objective descriptive fact.[49]

What are the value judgments that we "dress up" to look like facts in marriage? By and large these include contentment with middle-class values, conservative definitions of sex roles, and a stress on harmony and absence of conflict. If there is any conflict at all, it is confined to the "period of adjustment," that stage between the bliss of the honeymoon and the mellow years of pure conjugal love.

The concept of marital adjustment used in the major studies, and in particular the prediction-of-success type of study, has been severely criticized on several grounds. One complaint charges that the studies rely too heavily on self-reports—that is, the individuals themselves rate how happy their marriages are and how happy their childhoods were, so the correlations may reflect nothing more than the tendency of some people to describe themselves and their families in favorable terms. This point has been documented in a series of studies by Edmonds.[50] He put together a series of statements about marriage that would be too good to be true for anyone—for example, "If my mate has any faults, I am not aware of them"; "Every new thing I have learned about my mate has pleased me."[51] Agreeing with such statements is an indicator of what Edmonds calls marital "conventionalization." He finds that conventionalization is widespread and that marital-adjustment scales are heavily influenced by the tendency. Further, Edmonds' data show that, contrary to the prevailing views in the marriage literature, there is no connection between being conventional and conservative and having a happy marriage. He finds that when the distorting tendency of conventionalism is controlled statistically, people who hold traditional moral attitudes, who go to church regularly, and who abstain from premarital sex do not have a greater degree of marital adjustment than those who do not.

Edmonds' argument is with the measurement of adjustment in marriage rather than with the concept itself. Other critics have argued with the assumption that happiness is the criteria for a good relationship. George Simpson observes:

> On the happiness schedule of Burgess and Wallin any person who gets very high scores may not be happy but slap-happy. . . . Their general satisfaction schedule is no less unsatisfactory. . . . Here we find the question: Do you ever regret your marriage? Answers and scores are as follows: frequently, 0; occasionally, 1; rarely, 3; never, 5. But a mature answer is: of course, but the very regret is the ambivalent aspect of my joy in it. All human satisfaction is tinged with dissatisfaction; by taking up one option, we surrender others. The human psyche is not structured in such a way that answers

to such questions give any indication of fundamental personality traits or make possible understanding of an individual's capacity for being interrelated with another.[52]

Similar problems arise if happiness is defined as an absence of conflict and quarreling. One reason why a couple may not have any arguments is that they do not talk to each other very much in the first place. But as Simpson contends, quarrels and arguments are inevitable in marriage.

A Psychoanalytic Utopia: The Intimacy Model

Critics of the conventional adjustment notion argue that it is based on the wrong values, that it is superficial and does not deal with the quality of the couple's relationship and the kind of life they lead. Really "good" marriages, they say, focus on the qualities of openness, intimacy, trust, and personal growth. The classic statement on this ideal of marriage is provided by Erik Erikson.[53]

In this model of marriage the focus of marital success or failure rests squarely in the psyche of each spouse—more specifically, in the ego capacities. Marriage is seen as a critical developmental stage in the life of each individual, a sort of "maturity test" that a person must pass if he or she is to be a healthy, well-adjusted person. Erikson divides the lifespan into eight stages, each with its own point of conflict or encounter between the individual and the environment, and with its own distinctive outcome of personality "success" or "failure." Thus the first stage centers around how well the infant's need for "love" in the form of food and tender care is fulfilled, and the outcome is a basic sense of trust or mistrust. The most well-known of Erikson's stages, the adolescent period, focuses on the "identity crisis"—the problem of finding one's own identity.

The next stage of life after adolescence is called the stage of "intimacy versus isolation," and one passes it, in part, by having a successful marriage. Erikson describes this stage as follows:

> . . . The young adult, emerging from the search for an insistence on identity, is eager and willing to fuse his identity with that of another. He is ready for intimacy, that is, the capacity to commit himself to concrete affiliations and partnerships and to develop the ethical strength to abide by such commitments, even though they may call for significant sacrifices and compromises. . . .[54]

Only during this period can "true genitality" develop, adolescent sexuality being dominated by searching for one's own identity or for a competitive kind of sexual combat.

The idea that marriage makes a unit of two people is, of course, an ancient one. "A man shall leave father and mother and shall cleave to his wife and they twain shall be one flesh," says the Bible. Within social science the idea of marriage as mutual identification also goes back a long time, relatively speaking. In 1926, for example, Burgess[55] wrote of marriage as a unity of interacting personalities.

More recently a new version of the intimacy model of marriage has been suggested by people connected with the "human potential" movement, or humanistic psychology, or the encouter-group movement. For example, Herbert Otto writes:

> . . . Marriage can be envisioned as a framework for actualizing personal potential.
> . . . the New Marriage offers an ongoing adventure of self-discovery, personal growth, unfoldment, and fulfillment.[56]

Another version of "the new marriage" is described in the O'Neills' book *Open Marriage*.[57] Criticizing traditional marriage for the limitations it imposes on the individual, the O'Neills propose a model of marriage that stresses complete openness of communication, flexible roles, openness to outside contacts and interests, as well as "supportive caring" and the commitment of both partners to their own and others' psychological growth.

A major flaw shared by these models is their tendency to idealize marriage—to present utopian images of marriage rarely found in real life. The adjustment model, as we've noticed, leaves no place in marriage for conflict or disagreement between the spouses. Although the proponents of the intimacy model reject the idea that the marital relationship consists of only positive feelings, they do assume that conflicts are resolved through mature sacrifice and compromise. Each partner is conceived to be an individual with his/her own needs and wishes, and at the same time able to fulfill the other's needs within their own mutual genitality. Marital problems are attributed to the unresolved neurotic tendencies of each spouse. Goethals and associates point out the difficulties in equating genital maturation with the capacity for intimacy and note that most attempts to define love from the psycholanalytic point of view have been unsuccessful:

> The primary confusion seems to arise from the assumption in most psychoanalytic thinking that when one has reached a certain stage of genital development, an emotional state, love, is an automatic corollary. Even the most cursory reading of the anthropological literature or an examination of non-middle-class standards suggests that sexual gratification per se is by no means related to or a predictor of an emotional relationship. Many cultures and subcultures. . . . attach little if any emotional significance to adult sexual relationships. While tenderness and affection can be expressed toward children and while there can be extremely strong ties of family loyalty, the emotional overtones so characteristic of modern Western romantic attachment are entirely absent.[58]

In short, the psychoanalytic model of marriage overlooks macrosocial and cultural influences on personal relationships. Furthermore, both the intimacy and the adjustment models overlook the strains that life in contemporary society place on marriage. Rather than the average or expectable state of married life, a "good" marriage may be a rare achievement or lucky accident. Both models fail to deal with the social changes that have transformed the urban scene and increased the pressures on marriage. For example, the increasing acceptability of adultery and divorce may increase people's sensitivity to potential sources of dissatisfaction in their marriage. The emphasis on the nuclear family as the prime locus of intimacy may strain the marriage relationship by reducing the opportunity to satisfy needs for closeness and support within the larger community. As one writer observes:

> It is ironic that sophisticated psychoanalytic theorizing tends to perpetuate the romantic mystique that Americans have always attached to marriage; nowhere is one able to find the vaguest hint of the ennui, the struggle over the minute details of existence, the hostility, and the sense of confinement that *at times* characterize the very best of marriages.[59]

Finally, both models of marriage are unidimensional; they assume that all marriages can be lined up along a single dimension of adjustment, happiness, maturity, or else be clearly categorized as good or bad, healthy or pathological. A few studies, however, have attempted to explore the diversity that exists in marriage. Even during the 1950s there was much more diversity in marriage than social scientists recognized. As Elizabeth Bott has pointed out:

> It is often assumed that there is a large measure of agreement on familial norms in the society as a whole. . . . Such a view implies that given individuals will recognize that these

agreed-upon external standards exist, and that they will be able to make the norms explicit without difficulty.[60]

In her own research on marital roles in urban families, however, Bott found much more variation in the norms that is commonly assumed. Further, many of the people interviewed had a hard time generalizing about customary and proper behavior for husbands and wives. They were too much aware of variation among their acquaintances.

Marriage as Conflict: Exchange and Strategy Models

Although the prevailing models of marriage in the family literature have stressed adjustment, intimacy, and mutuality of interests between spouses, there has always tended to be a minority view stressing the competitive and conflictful aspects of marriage. Jessie Bernard has traced the history of this view of marriage:

> . . . The conception of the relation between the sexes as a bargaining situation is very old. Quite aside from the patent form of bride purchase or the dowry, the psychological give and take between men and women has long been viewed as essentially a duel of wits for advantage. . . .
>
> It was Waller who formulated most elaborately and insightfully the bargaining model of the relations between the sexes. His application was primarily to the premarital period, but the fundamental processes are the same, although the specific ''goods'' involved in the exchange may vary greatly—love, mink coats, sex relations, approval, ''freedom,'' etc.[61]

In recent years the old insight that the daily events of social life could be compared to economic transactions or the dealings between hostile countries has been greatly systematized.

Game theory, social-exchange theory, and strategic bargaining theory all represent attempts to offer precise analyses or models of various types of competitive—and cooperative—behavior.

Classical game theory, based on pure competition and the assumption that any loss incurred by one side is matched by pure gain on the other, is not regarded as an appropriate model for international relations, much less marriage, so it need not concern us here.

The kind of model that is applied to marriage, one called a "mixed-motive" or "cooperative" model, is based, among other things, on a situation in which both sides can win and both can lose. Here is a rather simple situation: John and Mary, a married couple, have had a fight. They have said some harsh things to each other. Each would like to make up, but each is afraid of being the first to act friendly and being rebuffed by the other person. A similar situation: a young man and woman, strangers to each other, are deciding whether to act friendly or to ignore the other. Each party's preferred outcome is to smile and to receive a smile in return, but since each fears a frown, neither smiles! (Those who know something about the literature on mixed-motive models will recognize the outline of the Prisoner's Dilemma game.)

All exchange approaches share a cost-benefit-analysis way of looking at personal relations, but they differ among themselves in assumptions and detail. Her are some observations on love, based on Peter Blau's version of exchange theory:

> The more an individual is in love with another, the more anxious he or she is likely to be to please the other. The individual who is less deeply involved in a love relationship, therefore, is in an advantageous position, since the other's greater concern with continuing the relationship makes him or her dependent and

gives the less involved individual power. Waller called this "the principle of least interest." This power can be used to exploit the other; the woman who exploits a man's affection for economic gain and the boy who sexually exploits a girl who is in love with him are obvious examples. . . .

To safeguard the value of her affection, a woman must be ungenerous in expressing it and make any evidence of her growing love a cherished prize that cannot easily be won. . . .

The aim of both sexes in courtship is to furnish sufficient rewards to seduce the other, but not enough to deflate their value, yet the line defined by these two conditions is often imperceptible.[62]

Social scientists have questioned whether game theory and similar models actually apply to the real-life situations, such as international relations, they are intended to describe. Their applicability to family life is even more questionable. Such models seem to rule out situations where simple self-interest is mixed with concern for the other person, or where the person changes his or her preferences in light of the other person's feelings. Nor do these models deal very well with ambivalence—where people are in conflict about what they want. Nor do they deal with the situation in which the exchange between the couple seems unbalanced to observers, who may say "What does she see in him?" or "He could do better than her." Consider the following instance, which arises out of the problem of defining the marital relationship as voluntary or compulsory:

. . . A young couple began having trouble a few years after marriage. . . . They separated, but continued to associate. When they entered therapy, the husband wanted to go back together again, but was uncertain about it. The wife, having taken up with another man, did not want to live with her husband, but wanted to associate with him and consider possible future

reconciliation. At one moment, the husband insisted on immediate divorce, at the next he asked for a reconciliation. Each time he spoke more firmly about his plans for divorce, the wife began to discuss the great potential of their marriage and how fond she was of him. When the husband began talking about going back together, the wife discussed how miserable their marriage had been. After several sessions of trying to clarify the situation, the issue was forced by a suggestion that if the couple continue treatment they do so in a trial period of living together. . . . The wife refused. The husband managed to arrange a divorce, although when he was no longer compulsively involved with her, the wife was finding him attractive again.[63]

A similar instance of ambivalence is that of a young mother who worked out an agreement with her graduate-student husband to divide child care equally between them; if he failed to live up to what seemed a full share of the burden, particularly if he forgot to be responsible for figuring out what needed to be done, she was angry. But the better he performed, the more useless and displaced she felt; after all, he had another identity in his work, but being a mother was what she was.

Marriage as Paradox: Communications Model

The objection to game-theory models is not their portrayal of marriage as a conflict-prone institution or one in which bargaining takes place, but rather the qualities they ascribe to marital conflict. In these models conflict consists of the coldly rational sparring of two opponents simply trying to maximize their own gains. Seemingly scientific descriptions of human behavior, in fact such models are probably quite limited hypotheses about behavior.

A model that seems to fit better the daily facts of marital and other family conflict is based on what has been called a "communicational" or "systems approach" to the family. It was originally developed by a group of psychiatrists and psychologists who studied the interaction in families with a schizophrenic member.[64] As we noted earlier, the insights developed by this research have been extended to normal family life.

The basic tenets of communication theory may be contained in a short set of statements. These statements are more like assumptions of theorems in mathematics than hypotheses that can be tested and possibly rejected. That is, within the perspective of the theory, they are self-evidently true.

The most basic principle is that it is impossible not to communicate—just as it is impossible not to behave. When two people meet, therefore, they have to decide how they are going to behave toward each other, and what kinds of messages they are going to exchange. They also must decide what sorts of things they will not say and do. This process is referred to as "defining the relationship."

Whenever one person speaks to another, the message either reinforces the ongoing definition or suggests a shift. For example, one of the issues they can't avoid dealing with is that of dominance versus equality: will they deal with each other as equals, or will they assume complementary positions in which one will show respect for the other? These decisions will determine how they will address one another—whether they will use each other's first names, call each other "mister," or whether one will use "mister" and the other the first name. The other basic dimension of social life is what Roger Brown[65] has called solidarity or affection. This will also determine the content of messages as well as such things as how far the two people will stand from each other when speaking and whether one may put an arm around the other.

Another basic concept of communications analysis is that human communication always takes place at several levels. People not only say something, but they qualify what they say by their tone of voice, facial expressions, and body movements, and by the context. For example, a person can say "yes" to a request in an almost infinite number of ways, expressing anything from eagerness to extreme reluctance. Incongruity often occurs among these levels. Teasing and sarcasm are familiar ways of qualifying statements; in each instance the main message is disqualified by the speaker: "Don't take this statement seriously."

Finally, communications theory sees in any statement a person makes to another an attempt to control or define that relationship. This does not mean that one tries necessarily to be the boss or to advance one's self-interest in an obvious way. Consider the example of a person who acts helpless; such behavior is an invitation for the other person to take care of the helpless one. But the helpless person may control the relationship since he or she has been able to exert influence over the behavior of the other person. The more extreme the helplessness of the dependent one, as for example a baby or a very sick person, the more the dependency may seem to be a form of domination.

One cannot avoid communicating, or qualifying one's communication, or controlling the definition of the relationship.

How does the communication perspective apply to marriage? Marriage in these terms is seen as a situation in which two people must define their relationship to each other. That is, they must work out rules for living together as well as rules for making the rules. The couple need not necessarily be aware of the rules they are following, but they cannot, accordingly, avoid having them:

. . . Whenever they complete a transaction, a rule is being established. Even if they should set out to behave entirely spontaneously, they would be establishing the rule that they are to behave in that way.[66]

For example, couples must make rules about what kind of work each will do, how much say each one will have in the other's work, whose responsibility the various household chores will be, whether or not each can criticize the other, whether when one person makes a mistake the other is to comfort or criticize him or her, what topics are open for discussion and what topics are too sensitive to bring up, what roles outsiders are to play in the marriage, whether in-laws are outsiders, and so on.

Conflicts arise over the rules themselves, over who sets the rules, and over incompatible rules. One almost inevitable source of conflict results from the fact that the two spouses come from two different families. Each family would have impressed its child with its own set of implicit and explicit rules for dealing with people, for managing household finances and routines, and even for the proper distance one should stand from another person while talking to him or her. Disagreements over the rules themselves can often be settled by compromise. The really emotional battles occur over who is to make the rules. These have to do with the control aspects of the marriage.

> For example, a wife could insist that her husband hang up his clothes so that she does not have to pick up after him like a servant. The husband might agree with his wife that she should not be his servant, and so agree to the definition of the relationship, but he still might not agree that *she* should be the one to give him orders on what to do about his clothes.[67]

The communications approach helps to explain why talking things out doesn't always lead to a resolution of the problem and why heated arguments can arise over trivial matters. The proponents of this view do not argue that improved communication leads to improved relationships, or that interpersonal conflicts result only from "failures of communication." Rather they point out that talking things over and expressing feelings openly may make things worse between a wife and husband, or a parent and child, as often as it clears the air.[68]

The communications perspective shows how anyone can become involved in irritating and disappointing hangups in the nitty-gritty struggles of daily life. It reveals how the interaction between two people has properties of its own, independent of their particular personalities. Consider, for example, the concept of paradoxical communication. A simple example of a paradoxical communication is the statement, "I command you to disobey me." The situation of the wife telling the husband to pick up his clothes also contains a paradox, but a more subtle one:

> The communication of bids for two incompatible types of relationships can occur whenever there is an incompatibility between (a) the rule defining a relationship, and (b) the type of relationship implicit in *who* is defining the relationship. For example, if a wife tells her husband to pick up his own clothes. However, *when she tells him to do this* she is defining the relationship as complementary—she orders and he is to follow the orders. The husband is then faced with two different definitions of the relationship so that whichever way he responds, he cannot satisfy both requests. If he picks up his clothes, accepting the symmetrical definition, he is following her directions and so accepting a complementary definition. He cannot accept one definition without the other unless he comments on the situation in a way that redefines it. More likely he will erupt in indignation while uncertain what he is indignant about and his wife will similarly be indignant because he erupts over this simple request.[69]

A similar kind of paradox occurs when one spouse tells another to be more independent, or expressive, or assertive. "I command you to be spontaneous," or "I command you to love me."

Sexual relationships are full of such paradoxical messages, providing further examples of the problems of communication. Not only are there taboos about talking about sex matters in the first place, but there are taboos against talking about the taboos. Laing has pointed out there are rules that one cannot talk about without breaking the rule that one should not talk about them:

> A family has a rule that little Johnny should not think filthy thoughts. Little Johnny is a good boy: he does not have to be told not to think filthy thoughts. They never have *taught* him *not* to think filthy thoughts. He never has.
>
> . . . Perhaps no one outside such a family rule system could knowingly embrace it—Rule A: Don't. Rule A-1: Rule A does not exist. Rule A-2: Rule A-1 does not exist[70]

Furthermore, even if a couple does talk to each other about sex, talking may often lead to conflicts that are difficult to resolve:

> For example, if a wife turns her back on her husband in bed, assuming that if he is interested in sexual relations he will turn her over, the husband might assume from her behavior that she is not interested in sexual relations and so he does not turn her over. Both spouses can then feel that the other is disinterested, and both can then feel righteously indignant. If this conflict is at the level of what kind of relationship to have, it can be resolved as a misunderstanding. Discussion and correction of the signals involved will lead to more amiable relations. However, if the couple is in a struggle over who is to define the type of relationship, discussion of the situation will not necessarily relieve the problem. After discussion, the wife may still feel that it is a law of life that only the man initiates sex relations, and she will not let him impose a different relationship upon her. The husband may continue to feel that he will not impose himself upon his wife until she has expressed some interest, and she is not going to tell him how to conduct himself. In this struggle, he might label her as frigid, and she might label him as unmanly.[71]

Similar problems can arise over specific practices; one partner might define a satisfactory sex relationship as one that includes oral sex, whereas the other partner might define oral sex as unnecessary or even disgusting.

There are still other paradoxes in sexual interaction. For example, sex is supposed to be the ultimate refuge from the rat race, but achievement pressures exist as much in the bedroom as elsewhere. On the one hand, sex is supposed to be a free surrender to basic impulses and instincts; on the other hand, what you do and when you do it are supposed to be in tune with the needs of the other person. Each partner is supposed to let the other know what he or she wants. If a person doesn't communicate this information, he/she may be frustrated, and this frustration may spoil the partner's pleasure directly or indirectly. But the other horn of the dilemma is this: if one person communicates his/her own needs too clearly or too insistently, then the partner is likely to resent being *told* what to do; he/she may feel like a masturbatory tool of the other person, rather than a free sexual being.

Sexual hangups between couples probably result as much from communicational knots as from purely sexual problems. One of the attractions of affairs may be escape from the old knots, and the exploration of a new set of rules and metarules for talking about sex.

It is interesting that the Masters and Johnson[72] therapy for couples having troubles in their sex lives is largely an attack on the couples' old communication or noncommunication patterns. This occurs at two levels. On the level of specifics, each partner is taught the preferences of the other by means of a hand-on-hand technique that eliminates the need for verbal communication. This technique and whole-therapy situation nearly disposes of the communications problem at the initial level. Now the therapists are telling the couple what to do and what not to do, thus extricating them from their impasse and presumably freeing them from their sex hangups by controlling their behavior and commanding that they be spontaneous.

Still another kind of communicational paradox occurs in the demand to be told what to do. Haley cites the example of a rebellious boy who says to his parents, "All right, tell me what to do from now on and I'll do it." If they tell him what to do, they are doing what the child tells them. The parents are likely to react to his statement of compliance with the same angry helplessness as they do to his demands. A similar situation is the following: a couple are trying to decide what movie to see or where to go on their vacation. After each one has suggested several alternatives and had them rejected by the other, one — say the husband — may say, "OK, *you* decide where we are going. Whatever you say, that's what we'll do." The recipient of such a message is likely to feel perplexed without knowing why. What has happened is that a symmetrical or equal relationship, deciding together what to do, has been changed to a complementary or unequal relationship in a paradoxical way. By demanding that the wife tell him what do do, the husband is in fact controlling her behavior, at the same time absolving himself of any blame if the movie or vacation spot turns out to be a dud.

In sum then, the communication analysis of conflict, with its emphasis on ambivalence, paradox, and shifting emotional preferences, seems to do more justice to the complexities of marriage than the rational, cost-benefit analysis of game and exchange theory, or the face-saving of strategic-bargaining theory. One question that remains to be answered is whether paradoxical communication occurs in all human interaction or only in Western culture, and particularly in contemporary family life.

Reality-Based Models

In recent years a number of studies of marriage have begun to explore some of the diversity in outwardly conventional marriages. Most previous marriage studies tended to assume that the most important feature of any marriage was a quality that could be referred to as adjustment, or satisfaction, or happiness. The notion was that all marriages could be lined up along a single dimension—with all the "good" marriages on one end of the scale and all the "bad" marriages on the other end.

The most well known of the descriptive studies is the one done by Cuber and Harroff.[73] These authors departed from the typical marriage study in several ways: they did not use the one-dimensional rationale of marital "adjustment"; they were more interested in collecting accounts of personal experience than in gathering statistics; they used no schedule of formal questions, but simply conversed with each person on the general subject of men and women for as many hours as the subjects felt like talking; and finally, they chose to study an elite group of subjects. Feeling that too many marriage studies had been done on families in crisis situations and too few on successful, "normal" upper-middle-class people, they chose their subjects from the top end of the income and occupation distribution: business executives, lawyers, government officials, and the like. They interviewed 437 such men and women, between the ages of thirty-five and fifty-five.

One of the most widely quoted findings of this study is its description of five types of enduring marriage. The authors discovered enormous variation within a group of stable marriages among people of similar class positions, thus destroying the myth that "happy families are all alike."

Conflict-Habituated Marriage Cuber and Harroff describe the "conflict-habituated marriage" as the type that is furthest removed from the notion of the happy/stable/conflict-free/adjusted couple as opposed to the unhappy/unstable/fighting/maladjusted couple. This type of marriage, though not the most prevalent, was the most dramatic one in the sample. In such marriages the couples simply fight with each other often. Being together usually suffices to trigger an argument, and the couple has a reputation for battling among the rest of the family. They do not, however, define the fighting as grounds for dissolving the marriages—to use communication terms, the husband and wife define it as acceptable to talk to each other that way. Cuber and Harroff speculate that such spouses feel a lot of hostility that must be expressed, and the marital battles therefore bind them together.

Devitalized Marriage In the second type, the "devitalized" marriage, the term applies to the couple relationship, not the individual wife or husband. Starting out their marriages romantically with love and closeness, these couples have drifted apart over the years but still get along with each other and want to stay married.

Passive-Congenial Marriage In the third type of marriage, called "passive-congenial," the couples differ from the devitalized couples in that they were never highly emotional about each other to begin with. Rather, they view being married as a convenient and comfortable way to live while directing one's true interests and creative energies elsewhere. Unlike the devitalized couples, these people do not regret the failure of their marriages to attain romantic

stereotypes. Such a marriage can free the individuals to become absorbed in their careers or other social commitments. In other words these couples define their lack of intense involvement in each other as the way marriage ought to be—at least for them.

Although such a utilitarian version of marriage does not go along with popular romantic attitudes toward marriage or with the psychoanalytic intimacy model, it coincides with the European approach to marriage mentioned earlier. Moreover, it is not just upper-class or upper-middle-class circles where this type of marriage is found. Elizabeth Bott,[74] in her study of English working-class and lower-middle-class families, found many marriages in which husband and wife led rather separate lives. Rather than having high-powered careers as did the Cuber and Harroff subjects, however, these people were involved in close-linked social networks of relatives, friends, and neighbors in relation to which the marriage tie was secondary.

Although all marriages must be understood in the context of their social and environmental surroundings, the dependency on outside forces is highlighted in the utilitarian type of marriage. If the strong involvement in career or community is missing, then such marriages can become drab cages of empty togetherness. Mirra Komarovsky,[75] in a sensitive study of blue-collar marriages, deals with a group of white, Protestant, native-born American workers and their wives in a town she calls "Glenton." These people do not hold romantic or psychological notions about marital companionship or intimacy, but—in contrast to Elizabeth Bott's Londoners and the Cuber and Harroff jet-setters—they also do not have many or strong outside associations and interests. Komarovsky argues that outside sources of stimulation, interest, and accomplishment may nourish a marriage while too much togetherness may overburden it, particularly for people who have not cultivated the skills of reflecting on and verbalizing their reactions to their experiences as daily life unfolds. She writes:

> Many couples in their late thirties, especially among the less educated, seem almost to have withdrawn from life. There they sit in front of the television set: "What's there to say? We both see it." "If you had two extra hours every day, how would you like to spend them?" asked the interviewer, and a man mused: "This would make the evening long and tiring if you're watching TV."[76]

The passive-congenial or utilitarian marriage, though failing to live up to the ideal of what marriage should be, nevertheless confirms a common belief that a person must choose between work involvement and family involvement, that a hard-driving professional or successful executive must inevitably have an atrophied family life, and conversely that a man or woman deeply involved with spouse and children must lose out in the work rat race. There are, of course, plenty of examples of this stereotype. Most of the people studied by Cuber and Haroff fell into this category. But other findings by them and by Komarovsky dispute the notion that the more a person invests in the family, the less time he or she has for work and outside friendships, and vice versa.

Komarovsky found that the people who were most involved in their work were the same ones who had more emotionally intense marriages. Similarly, the women who engaged in more leisure-time activities with their husbands also spent more time in club work and with women friends. The active, involved people had more education, which in this sample of blue-collar people meant having graduated from high school.

Vital Marriage   In the elite sample of Cuber and Harroff, there were also couples who belied the either/or stereotype about work involve-ment versus family involvement. The last two of their five types of marriage, the "vital" and the "total," conform more closely to the ideal image of what marriage is supposed to be. About one out of six of the marriages they studied fell into these two types. Again, the term "vital" refers to the relationship, not the personalities of the spouses. In the vital relationship the couple not only spends a lot of time together, but enjoys being together. The relationship itself is extremely important to each one, although the spouses do not lose their separate identities. Since the entire sample in this study was highly successful in work, there were of course no differences on that score between the vital couples and those with more utilitarian marriages.

Total Marriage   The last of the Cuber and Harroff types, the "total" marriage, differs from the vital marriages in that there are more aspects of life in which the couple participates together. For example, the wife often is involved in various ways in the husband's work.

An interesting feature of these types of relationship, which the authors call "intrinsic," is the sense of being deviant among their friends and neighbors. Many of them felt that they had to hide their true feeling about their spouses for fear of being laughed at or doubted. That they were correct in judging how most people would react to them is shown by the comments of the Cuber and Harroff subjects in the more utilitarian types of marriage when the intrinsic types of marriage were discussed: some people doubted that there really were any such marriages, and some thought the people must be "oddballs" or immature. Others who knew people in such marriages disapproved of them—they felt that the spouses were so involved with each other that they weren't as devoted to their children as parents should be, or that they expressed too much affection in front of the children. The intrinsic couples, on the other hand, felt they did enough for their children, and that many couples not that interested in each other often compensated by becoming overinvolved in their children's lives.

Other Typologies   Cuber and Harroff do not claim that their typology is the last word on marriages, or that their study is as high on methodological rigor as it is on human interest. They have presented suggestive findings and pointed out how some of the supposedly more "scientific" studies of marriage fall short as descriptions of real-life marriages. Inevitably, however, their own study leaves many questions unanswered. Would different researchers, looking at the same sample of subjects, divide the subjects the same way and arrive at the same five types of marriages? Would another researcher perhaps have emphasized the sexual aspects less and considered other dimensions more—such as attitudes toward parenthood? Or, granting that the five types of marriage do have validity for the sample in the Cuber and Harroff study, would the same five types appear in a sample of people less affluent and of a different ethnic background?

Other researchers, looking at other families, have come up with different schemes for analyzing family life. For example, a study of families by Hess and Handel[77] dealt with such matters as the images each family member has of the others, the ways each member establishes his/her separateness and connectedness, the way families deal with experience—how intensely they feel things, whether they evaluate their experiences and family themes. A family theme is a particular notion or motivation that determines how a particular family sees things, and all family members share it. For example, one family might be dominated by the theme of acquiring and displaying possessions, another by the theme of blaming and avoiding blame. One family might draw a tight boundary around itself in trying to maintain the home as a secure island in a threatening outside world; another family might see the world as its oyster, a place to explore and savor. Hess and Handel were dealing with whole families, but the same concepts could be applied to the study of married couples.

Still another way of looking at marriages is found in a study carried out by researchers at the National Institute of Mental Health. The original sample included 2,162 young, recently married couples in the Washington, D.C., area. The particular study we are concerned with here is only a small part of a large and still ongoing research project. To arrive at a typology of couples, one of the researchers, Ryder,[78] selected at random two hundred interview abstracts, read them, and grouped together the couples who seemed to belong together. The basis for the similarity of the couples grouped together and their differences from the other types was certain combinations of husband and wife characteristics.

The husbands seemed to differ from each other in terms of their effectiveness in fulfilling middle-class male roles. Ryder calls these variables "potency" and "impulse control"; the former term is a bit misleading because it refers not to sexual performance but to some combination of occupational success, intelligence, and personal dynamism.

The women seemed to differ from each other in terms of their dependency, their attitudes toward sex, and their investment in marriage—the extent to which the wife's interests and satisfactions are bound up in the marriage. (It seems odd that the women differed from each other on this, but not the men.)

Let us look at some of the twenty-one types of marriages that emerged from this analysis. One recurrent pattern is called "competent husband/incompetent wife":

. . . The husband is said to be highly intelligent, capable, planful, ambitious, but not very colorful, who is married to a woman seen by both of them as inferior: less organized, less attractive, unintelligent, etc. The wife wants and gets frequent reassurances that she is not worthless or unloved; but even with these reassurances the wife may feel that if she were more worthwhile her husband would be more attentive. . . .[79]

This pattern seems to have validity as a description of some marriages (I have encountered quite a few couples like this among the Institute of Human Development sample). It's surprising though that Ryder found this pattern among fairly young couples whom one might have expected to start out their marriages more nearly equal to each other in competence. The IHD sample is in their forties and fifties, and the competent-husband/incompetent-wife pattern seems to occur more often in that group of couples where the husband has been very successful in business and the wife has had no career or major interest outside the roles of wife and mother.

A variation of this pattern, called "stern husband," differs from the first in that the husband does not reassure his wife:

> . . . They are more ostentatiously "masculine," i.e., stern, hard, unfeeling, and may find it desirable to be deliberately unkind or unsympathetic to their wives' distress. The wife . . . cries more and is more depressed than in the preceding pattern. . . . Further, she may have some private sorrow about which she cannot speak to her husband, since he would take it to be a sign of weakness. . . .[80]

Another type of marriage in which the husband rates high on the "potency" dimension is called "husband negative about children." The husband is not really impulsive in the sense that he can't or doesn't control his impulses and feelings or isn't dependable, but he is not as tightly controlled—up tight, some would say—as the previous types:

> These husbands . . . tend to be exciting and active in physical ways. They may swim, boat, engage in contact sports, enjoy sports cars (and perhaps sell them). There is a fun emphasis, particularly on the part of the husband. He was not eager to acquire the restrictions of being married, and is less eager to be further restricted by having children. The wife may feel neglected, but wants to participate in her husband's active life.[81]

There turned out to be more types of marriages in which the husband rated low on the "potency" dimension than ones in which he was both occupationally ambitious or successful and had a strong personality: "[These] husbands may be hard-working and ambitious, but their most salient characteristic is that they are, in a word, dull. . . ."[82] One such type is called "second-choice husband." In this pattern the wife had lived an adventurous, sexually free life while single. Then, for some reason, perhaps pregnancy or an unhappy love affair,

> she lowers her sights to select a sturdy, responsible, dependable husband, who is probably thought physically unattractive. The wife is pretty, impulsive, competitive with other women, and not very sexually interested in her husband.[83]

Most of the types of marriages in which the husband rates low in "potency" differ from each other in terms of the wife's characteristics, her dependency, whether or not she enjoys sex, and how much her marriage is a consuming part of her life. One type of couple in which the wife has what Ryder calls a "nonmarriage orientation" is named "easy wife":

> A wife in this group likes the feeling of having men interested and attentive to her and is perfectly willing to go to bed with them. The husband may be considered unexciting or dull, but is valued as a secure home base. The other men involved are for that matter not thought to

be unusually wonderful. In the clearest case of this pattern the wife consciously intended to move from one affair to another from time to time, for as many years as she could manage it.[84]

We shall not describe all of the twenty-one types; there are several types in which, as Ryder saw it, the wife "pushes the husband around in various ways"; in another group of marriages the husband is violent, or footloose and irresponsible. In one rather large group, called "lonely spouses," both husband and wife have tended to have had lonely, frustrating lives, including job failures, mental hospitalization, suicide attempts, and so on. Very little interaction occurs between the spouses, but what does occur is positive.

At the very least this catalog of couples makes interesting reading, and seems to resemble couples that one encounters in real life. There are other types of marriages that did not seem to get into this catalog—marriages in which the couples are more nearly equal in competence and dependency, or the "intrinsic" or "total" kinds of relationships found by Cuber and Harroff. All of the twenty-one types of couples seem to be described in terms of some weakness or inadequacy, as if in trying to avoid the "happy marriage" concept Ryder leaned over backward and considered all marriages as bizarre in one way or another. Actually, Ryder found he couldn't classify about one-third of the couples because they seemed to be "unique."

The task of making sense, scientifically, out of marriage as a phenomenon is an elusive one. It is difficult to point to a piece of marriage research that has the theoretical elegance or predictive value of some of the best studies in individual psychology or the other branches of sociology. The foregoing typological studies are certainly inelegant and difficult to use for predicting anything, but at least they describe couples, rather than fitting marriages into an abstract, unidimensional scheme.

The Social Contexts of Marriage

Some writings that present the communicational or systems approach to marriage and the family portray the family as a closed world of interaction. Paradoxically, the same theorists who argue that a person's psychological problems cannot be understood apart from the context of his or her family sometimes treat the family group as if it exists in a social and cultural vacuum. Lennard and Bernstein[85] note that some family therapists fail to recognize the "family's vulnerability to prescriptions, demands, and values originating from outside its boundaries." Thus family interaction may reflect and be sensitive to the values of the children's peer group, the husband's coworkers, the wife's friends and neighbors, the images of family roles in the mass media, and a variety of conflicting norms in the community.

Family definitions and roles, as we noted earlier, are backed by legal and economic sanctions. There are limits beyond which family roles cannot be changed, no matter what the outcome of open communication, without major changes in the larger social structure:

For all their efforts at openness and communication, father and son are bound to each other . . . by the social requirements of their respective roles (being a son the father can be proud of) and the social institutions within which they have to exist. This last is vitally important. There are inevitable hegemonies built in the present family structure. For example, the child is quite simply financially dependent on the parent. The parent has legal control and responsibility. The father is compelled by a society that holds *him* responsible morally and psychiatrically for his son's troubles.[86]

A similar analysis may be made of husband-wife interaction. Marriages are surrounded by a complex network of social pressures and rewards and sanctions that pull the partners apart, push them together, and limit their options. Proposals for "open" or "liberated" marriage often overlook these realities. They suggest that couples can turn their marriages into unions of two free and independent beings merely by resolving to respect each other's individuality and by dividing economic and domestic responsibilities. Open marriage, like open communication, is an attractive-sounding goal that is difficult to achieve for most people. Apart from the fact that "openness" does not guarantee harmony but may increase conflict, advocates of open marriage overlook the harsh realities of the marketplace, both economic and sexual, in which couples find themselves:

. . . The average working man does not have an easy life; being king of his castle is at least some compensation for job tensions.

The average woman learns early that she had better catch a man if she wants to avoid a future of low-paying dead-end jobs and the social stigma of being unmarried. . . . Every housewife knows that there are lots of younger, prettier women around and that her residual secretarial skills from 20 years ago are worth zilch on the job market.

Is it surprising if she is possessive and jealous?

There is no way for a married couple to escape the pervasive effects of the sex-role system. For one thing, our entire economy is based on the premise that men should work and women should stay home.

A husband and wife may decide that they would really like to exchange roles—that she loves holding down a job, while he would rather take care of the children and garden. But if his job pays twice as much as any she could get, chances are they can't afford to switch.

. . . Most part-time jobs pay next to nothing and offer no fringe benefits, security, or opportunity for promotion. . . .

. . . Until there is genuine equality between the sexes, ''open marriage'' can be nothing but a cotton-candy slogan.[87]

Marriage over the Life Cycle

It is ironic that during the togetherness era of the 1950s and '60s, when the adjustment and intimacy models of marriage were idealizing it, empirical studies were revealing a dismal picture of what happens to marriage over time.

Despite the fact that they are based on self-reports, which are heavily influenced by conventionality, the leading studies use as their key terms disenchantment, disengagement, and corrosion. An important study is one Blood and Wolfe[88] made in the Detroit area. They conducted extensive interviews in the mid-1950s with 731 urban and suburban wives and with 178 farm wives. In contrast to many studies of marriage, the sample was not limited to middle-class people, but it did not include the husband's point of view. The authors summarize their findings on the course of marriage over time as follows:

> The first few years of marriage are a honeymoon period which continues the romance of courtship. With the birth of the first baby, satisfaction with the standard of living and companionship decline. In subsequent years, love and understanding lag. If children do not come, their absence is an alternative source of dissatisfaction.

> These trends do not involve all couples, but affect a very large proportion of the total. In the first two years of marriage, 52 percent of the wives are very satisfied with their marriages, and none notably dissatisfied. Twenty years later, only 6 percent are still very satisfied, while 21 percent are conspicuously dissatisfied. These figures suggest that a majority of wives become significantly less satisfied in later marriage than they were at the beginning.

> Some of this decline involves the calming of enthusiasm into satisfaction as a result of getting used to the partner, no matter how fine he may be. . . . However, much of the decline in satisfaction reflects observable decreases in the number of things husbands and wives do with and for each other. Hence, corrosion is not too harsh a term for what happens to be the average marriage over the course of time. . . .[89]

This study was cross-sectional—that is, at one point in time it looked at couples of different ages who had been married differing lengths of time. A number of other studies done in the same cross-sectional way found similar declines in marital satisfaction with length of marriage.

Studies, however, of the same couples over time—longitudinal studies—yielded essentially similar conclusions. In the best known of these longitudinal studies, researchers interviewed couples during their engagement period, again after three to five years of marriage, and a third time after they had been married eighteen to twenty years. They found a decline over time in the following areas: companionship, demon-

Do marriages "corrode" over the years? Recent research suggests that marital satisfaction declines when children are part of the family, and then, for many couples, rises again after the children leave home.

Marriage over the Life Cycle

stration of affection including both kissing and intercourse, common interests, common beliefs and values, belief in the permanence of the marriage, and marital adjustment. Feelings of loneliness increased. On the other hand, marital happiness, sex adjustments, and ratings of the spouse did not decline.

Using the term "disengagement" to describe these changes, one writer, Pineo,[90] sees them as the inevitable result of mate selection based on choice. Since the couple begins marriage at a high point of love and "fit" between their personalities, they have nowhere to go but down. According to this view, then, marital unhappiness is a normal operating feature of the institution. The description is rather far from the genital utopia that psychoanalysis offers as a model for marriage.

Some more recent studies have challenged this dismal view of what happens to marriages over time. In a cross-sectional study of 1,598 husbands and wives ranging in age from the twenties to the seventies, Rollins and Feldman[91] found that the later stages of marriage have as high a satisfaction level as the earlier ones. The curve of marital satisfaction over time followed a U shape: satisfaction was highest in newlyweds, declined with the coming of children, and turned up again when the children left home. Similar findings appeared in a national survey of life satisfaction.[92]

Some studies show that couples in later life actually experience a new high in marital happiness. One found that a majority of middle-aged couples saw the later stages of marriage as a time of new freedoms: freedom from being economically responsible for children; freedom from housework and other chores; and finally, freedom to be oneself for the first time since the children came along.[93]

In my own studies at the Institute of Human Development, there was no decline in marital satisfaction over time, nor did the older couples in the sample, who were in their fifties, differ significantly from the younger ones, who were in their early forties. (The satisfaction ratings were made by psychologists on the basis of lengthy interviews.) In comparing interviews that had been obtained from the same eighty-four people about twelve years apart, I was struck by the great variety of changes that had occurred in the marriages.

Although a little more than half the marriages stayed within the same range of satisfaction, almost half changed markedly in both directions. Situational changes seemed to have a great deal to do with changes in the marital relationship. The work situation of the husband and the child-rearing burdens of the wife seemed to have the greatest impact on marriage. Money started coming in after a period of struggle, or finances became tight; the frazzled, overwhelmed mother of a young child would become calmer as the children grew up; conversely, teen-age problems might emerge, causing friction between the parents; health problems came and went. In-law problems could lessen as the couple grew older, or aged parents could become a burden.

It was interesting that often what in the earlier interview looked like a deep-rooted personality incompatibility between the husband and wife had disappeared in the second interview, when circumstances had changed. For example, the overwhelmed mothers were likely to feel that their husbands were aloof and unsupportive. In the later interviews, when the children were older, the husband and wife had become closer. Here are some examples of couples whose marriages improved over time. During the first interview, they were in their early thirties; in the second they were in their early forties:

1958: John A. and his wife and child live in a cramped graduate-student apartment. He worries about how he will do in his finals, and whether he will find a good job after graduation. He wife works as a nurse and her salary supports the family, a fact that makes him very uncomfortable. He feels his wife is too reserved; she doesn't discuss problems. He also has a strained relationship with his father.

1971: John's family now lives in an expensive home. John has been very successful in his profession. Their teen-aged son is doing very well. His wife has become more outgoing and they are closer than they have ever been. His father has been dead for several years.

1958: Mary A. is overwhelmed with four small children under five. She finds her husband noncommunicative and unavailable when she needs him. She expected married life to be a lot more fun than it turned out to be.

1971: Mary feels she and her husband have matured quite a bit. He is now a very involved father. The marital relationship is close and understanding.

1958: Joan J. reports her husband seems to be undergoing some sort of crisis or breakdown. He is under extreme tension at work; he drinks heavily, stays out late, and refuses to discuss his feelings with her.

1971: Joan's husband is now president of his corporation. They have become much closer to one another.

The marriages that declined in satisfaction over the years did not follow any consistent pattern, although alcohol seemed to be involved in one way or another in most of them. For example:

1958: Ellen B. describes her husband as easygoing and very considerate. Their lives are centered around boating and fixing up their house. Her husband is on the verge of quitting his job to start his own printing business in partnership with another man.

1971: Ellen's next interview is dominated by her concern with her husband's drinking problem. She says it began several years ago when the partnership went sour. She recently gave him an ultimatum to quit, which he did, but he still goes on binges. Since he began to drink, he has lost all interest in sex.

In recent years there has been much talk of a "mid-life crisis." Unlike the slow corrosion of the marital relationship described earlier, the mid-life crisis is supposedly more sudden, and is centered in the individual rather than the marriage. It has been compared to adolescence, in that it involves a questioning of one's basic identity and a concern with sexuality. Only two of the eighty-four marriages seemed to be affected by anything like the mid-life crisis as it has been described. In one, a seemingly contented marriage of seventeen years broke down when the husband became convinced he was a homosexual; after some experimentation, he decided he wasn't, but the relationship with his wife was seriously impaired. Another man reported he was vaguely dissatisfied with his marriage, although he couldn't figure out why, and thought about finding "a cute young mistress."

Probably the most important point about marriage over the life cycle is the fact that it has changed dramatically in recent years. Because people live longer and have fewer children than in the past, today's couples will spend an unprecedentedly small number of years in their married lives taking active care of children.

According to Census Bureau estimates, we are entering a period in which marriages will follow a very different pattern than those of a century ago. For example, a statistically average woman born in the middle of the nineteenth century would marry at twenty-two and have

Marriage over the Life Cycle

her first child a year and a half later. Her last child would be born when she was thirty-six. She would be widowed at age fifty-six, and her last child would be married two years later. By the 1930s, however, two-thirds of the married life of a couple would be free of the burdens of young children, and one-third would be free of children in the home. In the future, the length of time couples are likely to spend alone together, without children, will increase still more. Child-free marriage on a mass scale is a new phenomenon in human history with as yet unknown implications for marital stability and satisfaction.

The Future of Marriage

To many people, marriage as we have known it is a dying institution. As one recent writer put it:

> All around me there is a marital turbulence. My editor has just remarried; an editor in the same firm has just separated from his wife; one of my doctors has left home and rented an apartment for himself and his mistress, leaving his wife with a flock of children to raise; one of my best friends is having an affair which his wife knows about; and another good friend is on the verge of divorce. My neighbor on the right is remarried, and the one on the left is also remarried.[94]

After viewing all this marital wreckage in her social landscape, she concludes that "old-fashioned, once in a lifetime, till death do us part marriage" is "going on the rocks these days."[95] Yet, as we have seen earlier, it is possible to look at the statistics on marriage, divorce, and remarriage and come away concluding, as Mary Jo Bane does, that "taken as a whole, the data on marriage and divorce suggest that the kind of marriage Americans have always known is still a pervasive and enduring institution."[96]

The imagery of death and decay as applied to marriage may be too extreme; the marital turbulence described above certainly exists in the professional and intellectual upper-middle class, but it couldn't apply across the whole population, since the majority of marriages are still stable.

Rather than "dying," marriage is in the process of being transformed. Marriages are becoming, all at once, more varied, more equal, more intense, and more fragile. First, we are experiencing a major restructuring of sex roles both inside and outside the family. The pressure for change derives from both feminist ideology and the economic reality that a majority of women are now in the labor force.

Although women are still a long way from achieving economic equality, and many families with working wives still accept traditional sex-role ideologies, a wife's working tends to shift the division of labor and the balance of authority in the family. Studies of working wives show that they have more influence in major family decisions than full-time housewives. Husbands of working wives are more likely to participate in the housework and child care, even if it is only "helping" the wife in "her" tasks, rather than redefining the roles within the marriage. Most observers believe the trend toward female labor-force participation will continue into the forseeable future.

There is evidence that although working seems to be good for women—in terms of both physical and mental health[97]—it can create conflict and dissatisfaction in marriage. These findings can also be attributed to other factors, such as the money problems that lead to lower-middle and working-class wives going to work in the first place. But since women's employment is a shift away from tradition, and entails changes in family routines, it is little wonder that it creates tension and conflict. Some observers feel that problems created by women working is a temporary phenomenon caused by the transition from one pattern to another. Eventually, they feel, when expectations conform with the realities of the two-worker marriage, the level of marital satisfaction is likely to rise.

On the other hand, some observers feel that the demands of two outside jobs, caring for home and children, and coordinating the leisure-time interests of all the family members will continue to be a source of strain. Young and Willmott, in *The Symmetrical Family*,[98] argue that we have moved from an era when there was "one demanding job for the wife and one for the husband" into a time when there are "two demanding jobs for the wife and one for the husband." In the future, they predict, the symmetry will be complete: there will be "two demanding jobs for the wife and two for the husband." Strains will be inescapable, and there will be more divorces, "because people will be seeking a more multifaceted adjustment to each other, with the two outside jobs clicking with the two inside ones; and because the task will be harder, there will be more failures."[99]

Another major transformation of marriage is the demand for personal fulfillment in marital relationships. In recent times the goal of personal "growth" and self-realization has come to be valued more than the obligation to fulfill social roles. As we noted earlier, most people have defined their "real selves" in terms of such roles—husband, wife, father, worker, student, and so on—whereas now, feelings and impulses are more likely to be defined as the "true self."[100]

Looking back, the togetherness era of the 1950s seems to have been a transitional period.

In the past marriages had been what was called "institutional." Marriage was a matter of duty and obligation to family and community; maintaining the stability of the family took precedence over the happiness of the individual. The "companionate" marriage came to be the ideal of the twentieth century. The goal of marriage was a close and satisfying relationship between husband and wife. The psychoanalytic view of marriage, which was widely influential even among people who never would think of going to an analyst, argued that in marriage, a person could—or should—have it both ways: both conformity to social roles and the fulfillment of one's deepest emotional needs. Personal growth was defined as taking place *within* the roles of husband, wife, mother, father, and worker. The wish to leave a relatively satisfactory marriage or job to "find oneself" would have been considered a neurotic symptom.

Today this supposed unity of social expectations and personal fulfillment has split apart, with the latter taking precedence over all other considerations. In contrast to the psycoanalytic ethos of the fifties, the new fulfillment ideology is found in the "new" psychologies—humanistic, gestalt, and so on.

In the future, as the trends toward sex-role symmetry and personal fulfillment follow the traditional path from the educated middle class to those lower down in the status hierarchy, we can expect a variety of sexual and marital life styles to coexist. Most adults will probably continue to live as couples, either in marriage or cohabitation. Traditional marriage is likely to continue to exist as a widespread option. Legal marriage will also continue to perform as a more committed form of relationship. Remarriages, already amounting to one out of four of all marriages today, are likely to continue and even increase along with the divorce rate. The "blended" families that result from second marriage will become a more common and accepted part of the social landscape. Noncouple life

The Future of Marriage

Number of unmarried couples living together, 1960–1977. (Source: U.S. Population Reference Bureau.)

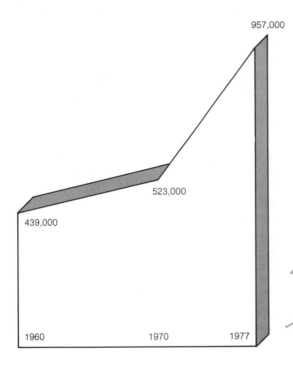

957,000

523,000

439,000

1960   1970   1977

styles, ranging from singleness, to communal households, to group marriage, are also likely to continue.

Despite the proliferation of changes and options, the idea of marital commitment is a symbol if not a reality that will continue to hold its appeal. It is interesting to note that even the authors of *Open Marriage* stress the emotional significance of a one-to-one relationship, which

> whether it is realized through monogamy or within other forms of marriage, fulfills man's profoundly human needs. . . . The relationship of two people to each other allows a closeness and psychological intimacy that no other kind of relationship offers.[101]

Similarly, Jessie Bernard, after a devastating feminist critique of traditional marriage, concludes that:

> The future of marriage is as assured as any social form can be. . . . For men and women will continue to want intimacy, they will continue to want to celebrate their mutuality, to experience the mystic unit which once led the church to consider marriage a sacrament. . . . There is hardly any probability such commitments will disappear or that all relationships between them will become merely casual and transient.[102]

There is support for this prediction in the findings of anthropologists. Robert Murphy points out expectations of permanence and faithfulness are almost universally held norms for marriage, even where the rates of divorce and infidelity are much higher than our own.[103] Ronald Cohen[104] reports on an African society, the Kanuri, where the divorce rate approaches the theoretical limit of 100 percent—almost every marriage ends in divorce. Yet even here, marriages are not entered into casually; furthermore, the Kanuri place a high value on marital stability and even perform a ritual at weddings to symbolize the desire of everyone that this particular marriage should be a lasting one.[105] Cohen's research refutes the assumption that such a high-divorce society must be a "quagmire of instability" for people who live in it. A high divorce rate can become a stable aspect of a stable society. Even so, there are tensions as well as adaptations. He concludes with some implications for our own society:

> If our own divorce rate is changing upward, we must prepare for widely ramifying effects in the society as a whole. I do not claim they would be the same as the ones described here, but I am certain they will be profound, and affect, in the end, the nature of the entire society and of the individuals who compose it.[106]

Marriage: Image and Institution

Summary

Some see marriage as an obsolete institution, doomed to pass into extinction in a few years. Yet despite the rise in divorce rates, marriage is not about to disappear. Most people marry, and most of those who do remain married for life. The majority of divorced people remarry. Yet marriage has become more fragile than it was in the past.

A couple marrying today can hardly do so with the sense of inevitability that was common only a few years ago. The lessened pressure to marry and remain married may revitalize marriage; people who feel reluctant to marry in their twenties or at all can follow their own feelings more easily than in the past, and there will be less and less justification for couples locked in "holy deadlock" to remain together.

Although marriage is a relationship between a man and woman, it involves more than the sum of these two personalities. It is a social institution, a legally defined status involving legal rights and obligations, and a social group—the dyad—with its own interactional properties. In addition, the partners have been socialized to be different and unequal in status.

A great deal of ambivalence about marriage occurs in our culture, but in no culture anywhere is marital harmony the general rule. In the marriage-and-family literature, four broad models of marriage may be discerned. Two of these stress the positive, harmonious side of marriage; the other two emphasize the conflictual aspects. The adjustment model sees happiness, harmony, and stability as the hallmarks of marital success. Psychoanalytic models reject the adjustment concept as superficial and emphasize the attainment of intimacy and personality growth. Both of these models tend to assume that conflict indicates marital difficulty or failure.

By contrast, the conflict models assume that all social interaction involves conflict. Game theory or exchange theory tends to see marriage as a battle of the sexes, a rational struggle of two parties to maximize their own positions. The systems or communications approach emphasizes ambivalence and the paradoxes of human communication as the source of conflict in marriage.

All four models tend to view marriage largely as an interpersonal relationship in a social vacuum. They tend to ignore the ways in which social, economic, and cultural factors influence marriages.

Source Notes

1. Glick, 1975.
2. Kobrin, 1976.
3. Bane, 1976.
4. Norton and Glick, 1976.
5. Farber, 1972, p. 4.
6. Bane, 1976.
7. Firestone, 1970, p. 251.
8. Glick, 1975.
9. Bane, 1976, p. 22.
10. Hajnal, 1965.
11. Bernard, 1973, p. 123.
12. Sanders, 1971.
13. Gagnon and Simon, 1970, pp. 10–12.
14. Norton and Glick, 1976, p. 17.
15. Udry, 1971, p. 270.
16. Orwell, 1946, p. 107.
17. Ibid., p. 109.
18. Davis, 1971.
19. In Klemesrud, 1971, p. 23.
20. Ibid.
21. Stephens, 1963.
22. Safilios-Rothschild, 1977, p. 3.
23. Bernard, 1972, p. 15.
24. Beauvoir, 1949, p. 454.
25. Weitzman, 1977, p. 288.
26. Sheresky and Mannes, 1972, p. 33.
27. Kanowitz, 1969, p. 35.
28. Weitzman, 1977.
29. Freeman, 1970, p. 8; Sullerot, 1971, pp. 207–211.
30. Crozier, 1935.
31. Goode, 1971, p. 625.
32. Ibid.
33. Kanowitz, 1969.
34. Pilpel and Zavin, 1964, p. 65.
35. Young and Willmott, 1973.
36. Weitzman, 1977, p. 311.
37. Shulman, 1970.
38. Ibid., p. 6.
39. Bem and Bem, 1970.
40. Blood and Hamblin, 1958.
41. Poloma and Garland, 1971.
42. Bernard, 1971.
43. Greer, 1971, p. 239.
44. Bernard, 1972.
45. Bart, 1970.
46. Gove and Tudor, 1973.
47. Shaver and Freedman, 1976.
48. Gove and Tudor, 1973.
49. Ryder, 1967, p. 807.
50. Edmonds, 1967, 1972.
51. Ibid., 1967, p. 286.
52. Simpson, 1960, p. 217.
53. Erikson, 1963.
54. Ibid., p. 263.
55. Burgess, 1926.
56. Otto, 1970.
57. O'Neill and O'Neill, 1972.
58. Goethals et al., 1976, p. 231.
59. Shaffer, 1970, p. 173.
60. Bott, 1957, p. 194.
61. Bernard, 1964, p. 705.
62. Blau, 1964, pp. 78–80.
63. Haley, 1963, p. 122.
64. Bateson et al., 1956; Haley, 1963; Ruesch and Bateson, 1968; Watzlawick, Beavin, and Jackson, 1967.
65. Brown, 1965, p. 57.
66. Haley, 1963, p. 123.
67. Ibid., p. 226.
68. Levenson, 1972.
69. Haley, 1963, pp. 127–128.
70. Laing, 1969, p. 113.
71. Haley, 1963, p. 130.
72. Masters and Johnson, 1970.
73. Cuber and Harroff, 1965.
74. Bott, 1957.
75. Komarovsky, 1962.
76. Ibid., p. 107.
77. Hess and Handel, 1959.
78. Ryder, 1970b.
79. Ibid., pp. 389–390.
80. Ibid., p. 392.
81. Ibid., p. 393.
82. Ibid., p. 394.
83. Ibid., p. 396.
84. Ibid., pp. 397–398.
85. Lennard and Bernstein, 1969, p. 210.
86. Levenson, 1972, pp. 128–129.
87. Willis, 1972, p. 16.
88. Blood and Wolfe, 1960.
89. Ibid., pp. 87–88.
90. Pineo, 1961.
91. Rollins and Feldman, 1970.
92. Campbell, 1975.
93. Deutscher, 1967, p. 516.

94. Westoff, 1977, p. 143.
95. Ibid.
96. Bane, 1976, p. 35.
97. Ibid.
98. Young and Willmott, 1973.
99. Ibid., p. 278.
100. Turner, 1976.
101. O'Neill and O'Neill, 1972, p. 24.
102. Bernard, 1972, p. 301.
103. Murphy, 1971, p. 215.
104. Cohen, 1971.
105. Ibid., p. 217.
106. Ibid.

Chapter Ten
The Parental Mystique

☐ *It may well be believed that if procreation had not been put under the dominion of a great passion, it would have been caused to cease by the burdens it entails. Abortion and infanticide are especially interesting because they show how early in the history of civilization the burden of children became so heavy that parents began to shirk it. . . .*

William Graham Sumner, *Folkways*

☐ *In some ways the romantic complex surrounding parenthood is even deeper and more unrealistic than that relating to marriage.*

E. E. LeMasters, *Parents in Modern America*

For most of human history, marriage has almost inevitably led to parenthood. Before reliable contraceptives were invented, children were the unavoidable by-product of sexual activity. They were usually welcomed, however, as contributors to the family's work and as insurance policies for their parents' old age. Although affection between parents and children was not unknown in other times and places, parental love did not receive the emphasis it does in our culture. In contemporary Western cultures, parents are expected to love their children—to be "crazy" about them, as one psychologist recently put it—and children are expected to return that love. Maladjustment in later life is attributed to lack of parental love.

Parent-child relations in traditional societies were in many ways comparable to those between husband and wife. As noted earlier, the premodern bride and groom would not be expected to be in love when they married, nor would their failure to be in love several years later be considered a sign that the marriage was a failure. Unhappy marriages were regarded as a curse, but most people did not expect more than relative contentment with their spouse's performance of the traditional roles and duties.[1]

In the same way, parents and children in traditional societies and in our own past were expected to fulfill their obligations to one another; cruel parents and disobedient children would be condemned, but love was not considered the central element in relations between parents and children. Before the seventeenth century, the European child-rearing literature rarely mentioned parental love as a significant factor in the child's development. God's love, not the parents', was regarded as the major influence on the child's future. "The child needed a good education and a faith in God; parents provided physical care, consistent discipline, and a model for proper behavior."[2]

Procreation and Parenthood: Nature and Necessity

Child rearing in traditional societies, like marriage, tended to be utilitarian or instrumental: from an early age, children could make material contributions to the family's welfare. If, however, the children's value to the parents was based on their being economic assets, what if a child came into the world as a liability rather than an asset? For thousands of years, people have been trying to break the link between sex and the production of infants.

Far from being a modern preoccupation, the search for some sure, safe way of preventing conception occurs in the oldest records and in the most primitive preliterate groups. The oldest written medical prescriptions for contraception are from ancient Egypt and date from 1850 B.C. They recommend the use of a paste made with crocodile dung to block the vagina.[3]

Unfortunately, such methods do not work very well in preventing conception, nor do the other ancient methods such as drinking potions, wearing magic amulets, jumping up and down after intercourse, or remaining passive during it. Since abortion until very recently has been a dangerous operation (the abortion laws were originally aimed at preventing the death of the pregnant woman), the leading method of birth control, historically and cross-culturally, has been infanticide.

Around the turn of the century, William Graham Sumner suggested that, if sexual relations were painful rather than pleasurable, human beings would probably have become extinct long ago. Sumner argued that the relation of parent to child is one of sacrifice; children add to the burdens of the parents in their own

The Parental Mystique

"struggle for existence." That there are compensations for the parents does not alter the fact that "the interests of parents and children are antagonistic."[4]

Now that we do have effective contraception, and raising children is a costly commitment with no economic return, why do people still have them? In the modern world children have an emotional and symbolic value to their parents that has no relation to practical economics. It is true that in 1972 the birth rate in America dipped to an all-time historic low, falling below the replacement level for the first time, and similar trends are found in the rest of the industrialized world. Public attitudes toward children and child rearing have surely moved away from the child-centeredness of the 1950s family-togetherness era. Yet very few people seem to want childless futures for themselves.

Recent studies demonstrate dramatic changes in attitudes toward family size as well as the continuing appeal of parenthood itself. Thus one study of 15,000 college women found a large majority disapproving of large families — defined as three or more children[5] Most did not think of having children as the major reason for getting married; they believed in birth control and thought it possible for women to combine motherhood with careers. In short, fewer rather than no children was the goal of these women.

A later study revealed a similar pattern of findings; 56 percent of male college students in the poll and 49 percent of female students said they wanted only two children. Roughly a third of each sex wanted three.[6] This is a dramatic change from the fifties and early sixties, when three children was the average family size. Public attitudes then favored families as large as the parents could afford, and people with small families were perceived as being "selfish."[7]

The vast majority of married couples want at least one child. According to both United States and Canadian census data, only about 5 percent of couples prefer to remain childless.[8] In recent years, however, there has been an increase in the percentage of younger married women who express a preference for no children. The younger the woman, and the higher her education, the more likely she is to reject motherhood.

Remaining childless, however, is not always the result of a clear-cut decision made early in a marriage. Couples who never become parents often do so by continuing to postpone having a child until a convenient time; the convenient time somehow never arises.[9] Currently, large numbers of women born during the post-World War II baby boom are entering their thirties and must decide whether their postponement of childbearing really is just a postponement or a final "no." If a majority of these women do decide to have children, there will be a dramatic rise in the birth rate, since they are part of such a large group.

The ability to decide whether or not to become a parent is, of course, a product of very modern times. But the availability of contraceptives is not the only explanation of the birth rate in any particular time or place. Given the impact of population growth in today's world, there is great interest in the motivations that lead people to have children. In a later section, we shall examine some of the recent findings concerning the individual reasons that account for why individuals want to have children. First, we will examine another view of the motivation for parenthood, one that has been much more common in both the psychological and popular literature: the view that it is natural for all people to want and to have children.

"Natural" Interpretation of Parenthood

Much thinking about parent-child relationships in the social sciences assumes a natural fit between the needs of the parents, particularly the mother, to nurture the child, and the need of society to support and encourage the parents. Thus psychoanalysts argue that every woman's deepest instinctual wish is to bear and nurture an infant; the child represents the substitute for the never-to-be-obtained penis, and being a mother represents the fulfillment of the girl's Oedipal wish to replace her own mother.

The more contemporary ego-psychology version of psychoanalysis defines parenthood in terms of the growth of skills and personality resources. For Erikson,[10] parenthood represents a stage of development in the course of the life cycle. Erikson asserts that the desire to care for very young children is built into the human nature of both men and women:

> Adult man is so constituted as to *need to be needed,* lest he suffer the mental deformation of self-absorption. . . . I have therefore postulated an instinctual and psychosocial stage of "generativity" beyond that of genitality.[11]

Erikson and other writers in the psychoanalytic tradition argue that within each society institutions arise that take into account the needs of the very young. Parents provide physical care and teach children what they need to know to deal with the environment and society, and society supports the parents in their efforts because it "needs" stable adults.[12] Sociological thinking about child rearing also tends to assume an intuitive fit between social patterns and the needs of children. The very term "socialization," or even "child rearing," implies that parental behavior toward children is usually dedicated to the child's education and welfare. Functional sociology interprets reproduction and child rearing in terms of society's need for "social replacement," the production of a new generation to replace the parents. This interpretation tends to assume that every child comes into the world with a fixed, positive value. It does not allow for the possibility that a new mouth to feed may, at a particular time, be dysfunctional for the parent or the community,

possibilities seen very clearly by Sumner and still earlier by Malthus and Darwin.

The belief that "biology" guides and directs parental behavior pervades both popular and "expert" thinking. The older notion of "blind" instinct has given way to the more sophisticated view that mother and child are genetically "programmed" to be attracted to each other. An animal infant provides the specific stimulus to release an appropriate response in the mother, which in turn will evoke a further response in the infant and so on in a chain of coordinated behavior. Thus the human child is said to be equipped with an innate tendency to attach itself to a mothering figure early in life. This tendency is said to be matched by a built-in responsiveness on the part of the mother.[13] Or the seeking, sucking infant is guided to the breast, relieving both the infant's hunger and the mother's fullness. As the introduction to an anthology put it, parenthood is part of:

> the process of evolutionary biology as it repeats itself in each human being and directs human behavior, under the aegis of the genetic code, toward procreation and parenthood. . . . Parenthood is a manifestation of "natural man" and, as such, is governed by the laws of biologic processes that are universal.[14]

Misuses of Biology Both the old and the newer versions of the idea that mothering is a "natural" biological process are seriously flawed. Like arguments about the biological determination of sexual behavior, they underestimate the role of culture and social context. Furthermore, the belief in innate nurturance is based on an oversimplified version of biology and evolution. First, the argument that maternal instincts in animals reveal the biological source of human mothering overestimates the similarities between humans and other species. Furthermore, it presents only one side of animal behavior. As Pohlman puts it:

If research from comparative psychology and anecdotal observation of animal life are cited to try to show innate tendencies toward parenthood, in fairness we should note that some animals, including mammals, will kill and eat their own offspring.[15]

Animal analogies can offer useful and interesting illustrations for understanding human behavior, but they certainly should not be used to define the human condition.

The innateness-of-parenthood argument also rests on a misunderstanding of evolutionary process. It assumes that evolution works on the principle of preserving every individual newborn animal or human. Rather, evolution works on the principle of species survival, and this may involve considerable waste of individual lives.

Margaret Mead,[16] for example, argues that breast-feeding seems to fit the model of a process designed to eliminate all but the strongest, "fittest" babies. She criticizes the etholo-gist's model of nursing, which pictures every mother as biologically able to nourish every infant she brings into the world, and nursing itself as a chain of mutually beneficial responses.

The War of the Breast   It is well known that women in contemporary society have a great deal of trouble breast-feeding their children. The very fact that there are organizations devoted to convincing women to breast-feed and to helping them do so indicates how far from automatic nursing is. Nursing difficulties usually are attributed to the hectic pace of modern life, to the fact that women are rejecting their children or are just unwilling to do their motherly duties, or to some combination of these. Yet the irony of blaming somebody for failing to do something instinctive usually passes unnoticed. As far as the child is concerned, the prevailing assumption is that the availability of bottles represents a loss for the child.

Although nursing is a "natural" function, it does not go on apart from culture and society.

Procreation and Parenthood: Nature and Necessity

In spite of the belief that breast-feeding has been a problem only in recent times, the historical records indicate otherwise. The nursing of children has been a matter of serious concern in Western civilization for the past two thousand years. William Kessen,[17] in a history of ideas about child development, writes about the "war of the breast." He notes that the most persistent theme in the history of the child is the reluctance of mothers to suckle their babies. "The running war between the mother, who does not want to nurse, and the philosopher-psychologists, who insist she must, stretched over 2,000 years."[18]

Margaret Mead's analysis of mother-child relations in early infancy is more consistent with the historical picture than the alternative image of nursing as a mutually beneficial instinctive relationship. She writes that lactation and early maternal care may be biologically a life-*selecting* process as much as a life-*saving* one. In other words, "nature" is not a benevolent, child-saving force. Rather, the biological factors seem to be arranged to ensure that only the strongest, most vigorous babies will survive, and only if they are born to women with the right physical qualifications to feed them. Far from being a simple process by which any mother can feed any baby born to her if only she wants to, lactation seems to require a specific set of physical and constitutional capacities on the part of both mother and child.

Many babies have individual quirks of temperament that make them hard to feed. Thus there are "rejecting" babies—babies who shortly after birth seem to fight the whole feeding process. There are also babies born with a seemingly innate disinterest in being fed, as well as babies with breathing difficulties and mouths too small to nurse.

Further complications arise from the shape of the mother's breast. One study found that the suckling response in human infants is elicited by the whole front of the mother's breast filling the entire oral cavity of the child. About one-quarter of mothers do not have breasts of the right shape or elasticity to fill the child's mouth.

Finally, the production of milk is based on a "letting down" reflex that is highly vulnerable to anxiety. When a child sucks well and thrives, a mother has little anxiety and much milk. But if there is some difficulty such as those just suggested, a vicious circle starts. The child fails to suck well or thrive, the mother is made anxious, her milk supply fails, the infant receives still less food, and soon, if there are no other ways to feed the child, it will die.

This, argues Mead, is the "natural" biological fate of an "unfit" infant under survival conditions. She sees a parallel in the maternal behavior of herd animals such as reindeer, sheep, and goats. Immediately after giving birth, such animals are highly attentive to their infants. The mother will nuzzle the infant, lick it, feed it, try to get it up on its feet. But she will do this only for a certain number of hours. If the baby does not stand up and walk well enough to follow the herd, the mother will no longer recognize it as hers. She will abandon it and go with the herd, because that is the only way she can survive. Mead suggests that the human situation is comparable. The very vulnerability of the mother's milk supply, the ease in which it can be turned off, may have been in evolutionary terms a selective device for ensuring that the mother's energy would not be wasted on trying to rear a child who did not have a vigorous grasp on life.

Thus it is not "nature" but culture that values human life and holds it as an ideal that every infant shall live, the weak as well as the strong, the premature as well as the full term. And it is not instinct but human inventiveness that found other ways to nurture infants than by the lactation of their biological mothers.

The Nurturance Gap   The invention of bottles to feed babies illustrates one of the paradoxes of the human condition. The same evolutionary pressures that created a brain able to conceive of inventing something to save infants' lives, and a pair of hands capable of actually making it, resulted in human infants' being born into a nurturance gap: the human infant comes into the world the most helpless of all the primates, and yet its care is less assured than that of any other.

The idea that evolution works by the principle of guaranteed nurturance is at odds with recent studies of human evolution. Mother Nature appears to be more of a trickster than a Lady Bountiful. The trick nature played on humans was to give them the most burdensome infants of all the primates, while removing the detailed genetic instructions that guide maternal behavior among other species. The extreme helplessness of the human newborn, its existential plight, results from the same evolutionary pressures that created human intelligence.

Most people know what newborns look like, but our imagery of babies comes mostly from photographs, paintings, and advertisements showing plump, smiling, rosy-cheeked little cherubs. Therefore some parents are disappointed and perhaps even shocked when they first see their scrawny, limp, unresponsive offspring. It takes about six months for the child to resemble the cherubic advertising image.

The human infant is, in primate terms, at least six months premature at birth, perhaps more. That is, if human infants were born at a comparable point to other primate newborns, they would be like six-month-olds. The burdensomeness of the human infant is a by-product of the evolutionary process. Chimpanzee or baboon babies are much more developed at birth. They can, in part, determine their own relationship to the mother, and after weaning they gather their own food.

At one stage in human development, babies were born in such an advanced state. The large human brain developed rather late. Our earliest immediate ancestors—the Australopithecines,

the so-called apemen of southern and eastern Africa—were tool-using bipeds with ape-sized brains. The Australopithecines lived two million years ago, but protohumans did not look like today's people for about a million years. The tool-using, cooperative way of life of these hominids led to the enlargement of the human brain. This is a relatively new version of human evolution; it used to be thought that human beings first acquired the physical form that distinguished them from the apes, then developed culture. It now appears, however, that tool use and cultural life shaped the human body and brain by favoring the survival of those with small teeth and big brains.

Tools, language, and cultural life set human beings apart as a species. Humans are "incomplete" apes or, as Geertz[19] puts it, they are born into "an information gap." The human nervous system evolved in interaction with culture. It cannot direct behavior or organize experience without the guidance of language and other significant symbols.

> Beavers build dams, birds build nests, bees locate food, baboons organize social groups, and mice mate on the basis of forms of learning that rest predominantly on instructions encoded in their genes and evoked by appropriate patterns of external stimuli: physical keys inserted into organic locks. But men build dams or shelters, locate food, organize their social groups, or find sexual partners under the guidance of instructions encoded in flow charts and blueprints, hunting lore, moral systems, and esthetic judgments: conceptual structure molding formless talents.[20]

While the brain and head were growing larger during the course of evolution, the human pelvis was (and is) more limited in the size it could grow. Thus the same selection pressures that led to larger brains led to earlier births. The psychological effects of this change in the direction of premature birth were momentous. As Washburn and DeVore describe it:

> The psychological consequences of the change from the monkey pattern to the human are profound. . . . When the baby baboon is born, it has its own reflexes and motor development that enable it to help determine its own relationship to the mother. . . . The helpless human infant is exposed to maternal whim, custom, or vagary in a way that is true of no other primate.[21]

The relationship between the monkey or ape infant and its mother is not completely determined by the infant's reflexes and its mother's drives and physiology. Learning and even custom play a role in primate maternal behavior patterns. For example, one study[22] has shown that female rhesus monkeys raised in isolation do not treat their infants in a "normal" way when they become mothers. They may ignore, reject, or even beat them. They evidently have to learn how to handle infants from living in a social group of other monkeys, although even when the isolation continues, the rhesus mother acts more "normally" when she has a second and third child.

But biological drives and reflexes play an even smaller role in human mothering:

> Although female monkeys appear to learn part of their maternal behavior patterns, and older juvenile females hold and carry infants before they have any of their own, the role of learning, culture, and custom in determining the care of the young is vastly greater in man than in any nonhuman primate.[23]

In short, the human infant is born into a nurturance gap. Once the large brain had been built, people no longer lived in a world of things, of simple stimuli, but a world of meanings, concepts, and significant symbols. Furthermore, the human consciousness can negate the world, can imagine the hypothetical. A human parent is uniquely capable of imagining the nonexistence of a child. This capacity can lead to a cherishing of the child as an irreplaceable treasure, to resentment, or to a search for a means of birth control. No ape ever tried to invent a contraceptive device. Even supposing an ape had the capacity to think of doing such a thing, it would have no need to. The nonhuman primates are tropical creatures. Each one finds its own food in the rich vegetation. Humans developed as a separate species in response to the food scarcities of the Ice Age. Therefore a human infant can never be considered a bundle of stimulus patterns that can call forth a predetermined response in the mother; each infant comes into the world carrying a very specific set of meanings for that particular mother, at that particular moment, in that particular set of circumstances, in that particular culture. This freedom may have tragic implications.

The analysis of the evolution of human mother-child relations offered by Washburn and DeVore makes it clear that nothing is guaranteed about the reception an infant will receive on being born. "The helpless human infant is exposed to maternal whim, custom, or vagary in a way that is true of no other primate."[24] Everything people do is mediated by language and culture. There is no such thing as "natural" childbirth and child rearing, in the sense of a process unmediated by learning and cultural rules.

For example, Margaret Mead[25] has filmed a childbirth in a "primitive" tribe, the Iatmul of New Guinea. In an article she gives a detailed description of this film, which is called "First Five Days in the Life of a New Guinea Baby." The film begins immediately after the birth, before the cord is cut, and shows the mother-child relationship during the next four days. On first glance it seems to show a perfect model of "natural childbirth." The mother is overtaken by labor pains while on an errand and gives birth alone. There are no complications. Although people quickly come to her aid, she attends to the baby and herself with very little help and walks back to the village. She breast-feeds the child easily.

This seemingly natural childbirth is actually highly stylized—that is, governed by arbitrary cultural rules. The umbilical cord has to be tied in a certain way, and the placenta has to be placed in a coconut shell and ritually disposed of. A wet nurse is on hand to give the baby its first feeding. The wet nurse, a neighbor and also a new mother, qualifies for the job because she observes the same food taboos the new mother must observe. The mother has to toss the baby up and sideways in the air after birth, give the child a patterned set of baths in clay and warm and cold water, and shape the baby's nose with fingers warmed on a leaf laid on a glowing log. Thus, even among the "simplest" people, technologically speaking, there is enormous cultural complexity in the practice of childbirth.

Infanticide As mentioned earlier, infanticide has been a leading means of population control in precontraceptive societies. Not only is the infant not guaranteed a warm welcome through natural mechanisms in the mother, but in many times and places a new infant would simply not be allowed to live. When we think of such practices at all, we think of them as barbaric customs existing only at primitive levels of culture, and as incompatible with "civilization." (There is a paradox here in the idea of the maternal instinct needing civilization in order to flourish.) Actually, however, infanticide has been much more widespread in Western civilization than is generally recognized.[26]

Further, one savage practice has flourished during most periods of European history, but has not been reported for other cultures: the maiming and crippling of children to use them as beggars. The fact that such practices now seem horrible beyond belief indicates that our feelings about maimed children, not to speak of adults, has changed drastically.

The historian William Langer[27] reviewed the history of infanticide as a means of population control in Europe and Britain. He notes that Plato, Aristotle, and other writers of the same period advocated infanticide as a means of regulating the size of the population as well as ridding society of deformed and diseased infants. During later times both the church and governments made infanticide a crime punishable by death. Yet, as late as the last century, infanticide was frequent as well as publicly noticeable. Langer concentrates on the period of 1750–1850 when the population of Europe nearly doubled. He argues that the two major brakes on population growth were celibacy and infanticide, and that without these controls the population of Europe would have outrun the food supply. He notes:

> In England as late as 1878 about 6 percent of all violent deaths could be classed as infanticides. . . . In the 18th century it was not an uncommon spectacle to see the corpses of infants lying in the streets or in the dunghills of London and other large cities. . . .
>
> . . . In 1862 one of the coroners for Middlesex county stated infanticide had become so commonplace "that the police seemed to think no more of finding a dead child than they did of finding a dead cat or a dead dog." The *Morning Star* (June 23, 1863) declared that infanticide "is possibly becoming a national institution"; the *Morning Post* (September 2, 1863) termed it "this commonest of crimes."[28]

Public attitudes toward infanticide were remarkably lenient, according to Langer. In contrast with the attitudes of most people today, and with religious and legal authorities then, public sympathy tended to be on the side of any woman who was charged with killing her child. Very few culprits were discovered anyhow, and very few of those ever reached the courts. One London coroner said he had never known a woman to be punished for killing her baby, "no matter how flagrant the circumstances." Usually the women involved in court cases were destitute workers or servants who had been abandoned by the men involved.

Before recent times it was difficult to draw a line between infanticide, child abandonment, and putting an infant in a foundling home. The mortality rates of the latter tended to be 80–90 percent. Foundling homes were started by reformers such as St. Vincent de Paul, Thomas Coram, and Napoleon, who were shocked at infanticide. Whenever one opened, however, it was swamped by more babies than it could handle. Conditions were so bad that foundling homes became, ironically, another form of the infanticide they were designed to prevent:

> When Coram's London Foundling Hospital was finally opened in 1741, it immediately became evident that he had underestimated the need. The pressure of applicants was so great that women fought at the hospital gates. Eventually, in 1756, Parliament undertook to provide the Foundling Hospital with funds on the understanding that all children who were offered would be accepted. . . .
>
> The policy of open admissions completely swamped the Foundling Hospital; in the first four years nearly 15,000 children were accepted. It was impossible to find enough wet nurses for such a number and thousands died in early infancy; only 4,400 of the foundlings lived to reach adolescence.[29]

Wherever foundling homes sprang up as a way of saving abandoned children, the same tragic irony was repeated. At the height of his power Napoleon decreed that foundling homes be set up in every region of France and if possible in every arrondissement (neighborhood). Again the facilities were overburdened and the expenses staggering to local govern-

ments. Napoleon tried to make it possible for a baby to be left without anyone seeing the person who was leaving it. The method was so successful that one-fourth to one-third of the foundlings were thought to be *legitimate* children whose parents either could not or would not care for them. The mortality rates led one writer to suggest that the homes put up signs saying "Children killed at government expense."[30]

Langer's article deals mainly with demographic issues: the factors that led to the population explosion in Europe between 1750 and 1850, and the checks on population growth. He does not deal with the many questions that might be asked about the psychological and social aspects of the situation. How did the factors to which Langer attributes the rise in population—the introduction of the potato and corn from the New World—actually get translated into the production of more children? How did the need for checks on population become translated into individual acts of infanticide? Why were mothers increasingly likely to abandon children until 1850, and why did the attitude toward children change thereafter?

Evidence emerging from the work of Langer and other historians shatters easy notions of an intuitive fit between the needs of children, the inclinations of parents to nurture them, and the functional need of every society to care for infants. Langer's work also illustrates how technological changes enter into the parent-child relationship. For example, better sanitation and the introduction of smallpox vaccination seem in part to have been responsible for the rise in population. Malthus had described smallpox as one of the major natural checks on population. Before the vaccination was invented, 96 percent of the population contracted the disease, which was fatal in one-seventh of the cases.[31] The chief victims of this "hideous illness" were children in the first year of life. The eradication of smallpox and the plague, another epidemic killer, must have tremendously reduced infant mortality. Contraception, however, was not widely known or practiced. Hence the result was a baby glut dealt with by the means just discussed.

Parenthood in Early Modern France

David Hunt's work [32] on parenthood in seventeenth-century France similarly raised questions about the intuitive wisdom and benevolence of parents. Hunt's work dealt not with abandoned children, but with well-born infants. One of his major sources was a journal of the infancy of the future King Louis XIII, the most precious infant in France. Although dealing mostly with the children of the nobility and upper classes, Hunt nevertheless described the situation he found as a "breakdown in parental care."

Hunt's aim in writing *Parents and Children in History* was to combine the insights of Erikson and Aries in trying to understand the psychology of family life in early modern times. As we noted earlier, Aries had described infancy in medieval times as a period of "benign indifference." Infants did not count for much emotionally in the lives of their parents, but they were treated kindly.

Hunt takes issue with Aries. He argues that parents of the Old Regime were neither as benign nor as indifferent to their infants as Aries says they were. Rather, parents appear to have been destructive and irrational toward their infants. Hunt argues that parents were deeply disturbed by infants' physical needs — their hunger and messes — as well as, later on, their assertive willfulness. Each one of Erikson's three earliest stages was typically met with a failure to satisfy the particular need involved; or, to put it even more strongly, the child was met with attack at each stage in its area of greatest vulnerability. Thus the oral stage was met by a reluctance to nurse on the part of mothers, the stage of autonomy was met with beatings to break the child's will, and infant sexuality was met with cruel and seductive teasing.

The Feeding Problem   If anything symbolizes the instinctive naturalness of motherhood, it is the image of a nursing mother and her infant. Hunt presents evidence showing that even in families where the child was accepted and highly valued, there was a large-scale failure to nourish infants. He argues that infant feeding represented a major crisis and contributed to the huge infant-mortality rates.

Hunt's book as well as other evidence shows that the unwillingness of large numbers of women to nurse their infants preceded by several centuries the technology of bottles and prepared baby foods. In the absence of this technology the prevailing substitute for those who could afford it was a wet nurse, supplemented by various prepared concoctions. Hunt cites evidence showing that infants were seen as not quite human. He emphasizes the emotional quality of this view: people tended to see children as "gluttonous little animals . . . sucking away the mother's blood."[33] This feeling stemmed from the belief of the medical experts of the time that mother's milk was actually whitened blood rather than a special secretion made to feed infants. Although the act of giving birth was regarded as a proud occasion, child rearing itself tended to be viewed as tedious and degrading. For any woman who could afford it, a wet nurse was the preferred way of feeding an infant.

Hunt is probably in error when he writes of wet-nursing and other practices in the seventeenth century as a "breakdown in parental care," implying a sudden decline from a level of better care. Rather, as we noted earlier in this chapter, a conflict between the needs of infants and the willingness of mothers to nurse them has been going on, at least in Western culture, for the past two thousand years.[34]

Unfortunately, we don't know the prevalence of the various forms of infant feeding in specific times and places, and the ups and downs of trends in the use of wet nurses. Kessen does present some evidence, however, as to distribution of various feeding practices at one particular time and place: Paris in the year 1780. Of 21,000 children born each year, 700 were nursed by their own mothers, 700 were wet-nursed at home, 2,000–3,000 well-to-do were sent to the suburbs to be wet-nursed, and 17,000 or so went to the country. These baby farms were notorious for their high mortality rate. Sending an infant to one meant a two- or three-day journey without food. If a child managed to survive the trip, he or she would remain at the farm for two to three years.

Kessen uses the "war of the breast" as a model for the history of child development in general; the same themes and issues keep reappearing in each new generation. The problem of baby feeding exemplifies both the redundancy of the basic argument and the way new concepts are grafted onto old issues. Thus Plutarch argued against wet nurses because their affection was spurious: "they love for hire."

Rousseau argued that if only mothers would nurse their own children, there would be a general reform of morals. In our times the prevailing arguments have been based on the child's physical and, in the teachings of the psychoanalysts, psychological welfare. In the literature of the past, when wet nurses rather than bottles were the "unnatural" means of feeding, the "natural mother" seemed to be treated less harshly than the wet nurse, whose character, morals, and intelligence were regularly assailed. As Hunt notes, these women are the hated scapegoats of the literature on child rearing.[35] The children who concern the philosopher-psychologists are more often the upper-class children who will imbibe the inferior qualities of the lower-class nurse along with her milk. An occasional voice was raised on the part of the wet nurse's own children; thus Montaigne wrote:

> . . . We tear . . . their own infants from their mothers' arms and make these mothers take charge of ours. We cause them to abandon their children to some wretched nurse, to whom we do not wish to commit our own, or to some goat. . . .[36]

The voice of the wet nurse herself is not entirely missing from the record. It occurs in the form of a lullaby sung by American slave nurses to their white charges:

> Husha bye don't you cry
> Go to sleep, little baby
> When you wake, you'll have cake
> And all the pretty little horses . . .
>
> Over yonder in the meadow
> There's a poor little lambie
> Bees and butterflies
> Buzzin' round its eyes
> Hear the poor little thing cry mama

The "lambie" in the last stanza refers to the child of the nurse.

Parenthood and Power

If a generalization can be made about parenthood on the basis of the foregoing historical evidence, it is that no easy generalizations can be made. John Stuart Mill, writing about the Victorian family, argues that one should not judge a social institution by its best examples nor by its worst. One must look at each institution as a system, considering not only the virtues of its best practitioners but also the abuses it allows and encourages. Thus absolute monarchy produced some enlightened kings and queens—truly benevolent despots. The problem with despotism, as Mill puts it, was not that most despots were bloodthirsty ogres, looking down with glee at the suffering of their subjects; rather, the problem was that nothing was built into the system to prevent the ogres from coming to power and carrying out their whims.

Mill finds the key to the problem of the family in the distribution and control of power. He argued that the Victorian family concentrated enormous power in the hands of the husband-father, made women and children powerless economically and legally, and yet did nothing to prevent the worst sort of brute from finding some poor woman to marry and doing with her whatever he liked.

Today the most flagrant abuses of the Victorian family have been reformed. Women are no longer legally defined as having a child-like status in relation to their husbands. The official version of child rearing no longer makes a virtue of beating children in the interests of breaking their will and shaping their character. Even parents who believe in strictness and obedience tend to think of spankings more as a last resort than as a good thing in themselves.

Yet the structural problems resulting from the power imbalances in the family remain. These are more subtle but no less real for women, although women are not typically in as much physical danger as in Victorian times. Children, however, in the isolated nuclear-family household, face physical risk. This does not mean that all or most parents are ogres, but that our system is not structured to prevent child abuse, and may even encourage it. Babies and young children really are weak and dependent—that is, powerless—emotionally, physically, and intellectually. Notions such as permissiveness and the child-centered society obscure the basic inequality with which parent and

A crying child is a powerful stimulus.

child confront each other at the outset of the child's life. The basic imbalance is corrected in other societies by the presence of other people in or near the household.

Child Abuse

Researchers point to the difficulty of drawing a line between "normal" discipline and child abuse because the parent is legally empowered to use corporal punishment to enforce rules, no matter how arbitrary they may appear to the child or to others. If a parent should kill a child in the course of administering a "deserved" beating, some states would consider the event an excusable homicide.

It is also difficult to state how abusing parents differ from normal parents. There is a strong tendency to interpret child abuse as the result of some gross psychological abnormality—what sort of parental monsters would abuse their children? Yet the literature on battered children reveals no clear line of demarcation between battering parents and "normal" ones. Nothing sets them off in terms of social class, occupation, I.Q., urban-rural residence, or psychopathology. Research has found nothing more striking than a pattern of child rearing merely exaggerating the usual one.[37]

Most instances of physical abuse occur when the parent or caretaker gets carried away in anger and goes too far. Some battering parents expect strict obedience from very young children; they possess a marked sense of righteousness, and feel they are encouraging their children to behave and be respectful. Or they may be under severe economic or other strains. For example, B. F. Steele and C. B. Pollock observe that there seems to be an "unbroken spectrum" of parental disciplinary behavior, ranging from mild pats on the bottom, through severe spankings, through bone-breaking beatings:

> To be aware of this, one has only to look and listen to the parent/child interactions at the playground and the supermarket, or even to recall how one raised one's own children or how one was raised oneself. The amount of yelling, scolding, slapping, punching, hitting, and yanking acted out by parents on very small children is almost shocking. Hence, we have felt that in dealing with the abused child we are not observing an isolated, unique phenomenon,

but only the extreme form of what we would call a pattern or style of child rearing quite prevalent in our culture.[38]

It is impossible to determine accurately the number of instances of child abuse. About 10,000 cases of serious injury to children inflicted by parents or their caretakers are recorded annually by child-abuse registries. The rate is nine cases per 100,000 children per year. Researchers in the field assume this to be merely the tip of an iceberg; it is impossible to estimate the number of injuries passed off as accidents or never even reported. An English study of parents whose children were hospitalized for treatment of burns found many instances of what appeared to be willful negligence on the part of parents; for example, the parent was angry at the child and somehow just didn't move fast enough to prevent the child from tipping a pot of boiling soup onto himself.

Accidents constitute the leading cause of death in young children, almost three times more frequent than the next leading cause. Assuming that many of these accidents actually represent cases of child abuse, or willful negligence shading into carelessness, some researchers have suggested that parental abuse and neglect may be the most frequent cause of death to children in the United States today.[39]

On the other hand, David Gil, another child-abuse researcher, argues that physical abuse of children may not be the major killer and maimer that others have claimed. Gil argues that individual acts of violence against children within the family may be overshadowed by collective societal abuse through poverty and discrimination:

> America has sometimes been described as child-centered; however, any unbiased observer of child life in this nation will find that many millions of children are living and growing

up under circumstances of severe social and economic deprivation which tend to inhibit the fullest possible development of their innate capacities. . . . Many of these children lack adequate nutrition, medical and dental care, and educational vocational opportunities. Any serious student of child life in American society would have to conclude that, however high the prevalence of physical abuse of individual children within their families and homes may be, the abuse inflicted upon children collectively by society as a whole is far larger in scope and far more serious in its consequences.[40]

Although child abuse may not overshadow the child problems caused by poverty and inequality, Gil agrees with other researchers that the propensity toward child abuse is extremely widespread in the population. In a national survey carried out by Gil, about 60 percent of all the adults interviewed thought that "almost anybody could at some time injure a child in his care."[41] He suggests these results show that the infliction of physical injury on children is viewed as an "almost normal occurrence" in the course of caring for a child. His results are all the more striking in that the survey defined as physical abuse only those incidents resulting in actual injuries. Gil notes that if the definition had included attacks that did not result in injury, an even higher proportion of people would have agreed that almost anyone could at times abuse a child in his or her care.

Thus child abuse must be seen as *potential* behavior in many families, but actually may be relatively rare. The research on actual incidents of child abuse suggests that other factors have to be added to this general propensity in order for an attack on a child to occur. One of these extra factors appears to be the experience of the parents themselves as children. Many of the abusing parents who come to the attention of social agencies and researchers appear to have been—or felt—unloved or unlistened to as children. They expect their own children to supply the love they missed when they were children. Such a parent may take a baby's crying, or the failure of an eighteen-month-old to obey commands instantly, as a sign that the child really doesn't love him or her.

Child-abusing parents tend to find themselves entangled in a complicated web of emotions. They tend to see their children as both their own unloving parents and their bad, needy, childhood selves. When parents hit children, they sometimes seem to be reenacting a scene from their own childhood. Often parents report feeling as if hitting the child is like hitting themselves.[42]

Such psychological mechanisms do not operate in a vacuum. Situational pressures and the social context also contribute to the chain of events leading to physical child abuse. Money worries, unemployment, and illness are some of the other factors that can tip the delicate balance of parental inclinations toward the child one way or the other. Despite our initial horror and indignation when we first learn of child abuse, many of the actual incidents reveal familiar feelings and understandable—if not forgivable—responses to a difficult situation.

The following case of child abuse, for instance, came to my attention. A school counselor in a California suburb told me there were many instances where she and the teachers in the school suspected child abuse. Most often the children would not "tell" on their parents, but one instance was confirmed. An eleven-year-old boy came to school with a broken arm. He said he had fallen out of a tree. The counselor was working with the boy on learning problems, and eventually he took her into his confidence. He said his father had broken his arm, but made him swear not to tell anybody.

The circumstances were as follows: the boy's mother had died shortly before, leaving the husband with four children, of which this boy was the oldest. The father, who was a skilled worker in an aerospace industry, had been struggling to manage the housework and child care as well as keep up his job. One after another, a series of housekeepers had been hired, but they all quit. The incident of the broken arm occurred when the most recent housekeeper walked off. The father had done the wash and asked the boy to hang it on the line. Through carelessness or accident, the whole wash landed in the dirt in the back yard. That was the last straw for the father, and he hit the boy in the arm with a baseball bat.

Reactions to incidents of child abuse are complicated: on the one hand we are horrified and cannot understand how a parent could harm a child; on the other hand, as Gil's statistics indicate, most people feel that almost anyone could abuse a child at one time or another. The following letter from a mother to a child psychologist illustrates both the accepting attitude toward child abuse and the ease with which a conscientious middle-class mother can find herself cast in the role of child abuser:

One Saturday morning, I was rushing to gather the children's clothes, bottles, and diapers, preparing to leave for the weekend.

I was making some hot milk for the girls. While the baby was crying in the high chair and throwing his breakfast on the floor, the milk boiled over. June, my 5-year-old, was giving me her tenth excuse why she didn't want to put on her shoes, even though she was sick and the floor was cold. I blew up: "Do I have to start screaming before you'll listen to me?" (Thinking to myself at that moment—this isn't me—this is my mother yelling.)

June stood there holding her ground. I picked her up in a sweep of anger, dragged her to her room, and heaved her onto the floor yelling, "and don't come out until your shoes are on!" She landed on her stomach and chin and I immediately saw that she was hurt. I ran in, picked her up, and laid her on her bed.

Under her chin was a gash so deep I couldn't see the end of it. I don't remember what I said to comfort her. All I remember is how I felt: I had taken a child who was whole and broken her.

I ran out into the front hall and rang my neighbor's doorbell. He is a doctor. When no one answered immediately, I rang another bell. Two neighbors came to the door at the same time. I told them what had happened and they came in to help. The doctor wasn't home but his wife knew what to do. She stopped the bleeding, and told me to get hold of myself. She phoned my pediatrician and told him that June had had an accident and described the wound. The doctor asked for me. I told him the truth. He laughed and said, "It happens in the best homes."

He told me to take her to the emergency room at the hospital and assured me that she would be all right. Both my neighbors told me to forget it, "It was an accident, it happens all the time." The doctor's wife said she had hurt her sons a few times by throwing them against the wall and the other neighbor, a minister's wife, told me that once she had thrown a shoe at her youngest daughter and cut her forehead open.

"Forget it. It was an accident," they all advised. It took six stitches to sew my daughter up. She was wrapped in a sheet like a mummy, and taped down to the table. She kept crying: she was afraid that I would be angry with her because her tights would be dirty from the tape.

I never understood how a parent could hurt a child. I learned that it was very easy, and that it's accepted by friends and neighbors as an accident, as something to forget.

When June got home from the hospital, I held her in my arms and told her that I never meant to hurt her, that I loved her and that we were going to have a new rule in our home: People are not for hurting.[43]

The Parental Mystique

Parenthood in Cross-Cultural Perspective

As the preceding incidents illustrate, there is something peculiar about American child rearing that has been remarked upon by a number of anthropologists. This peculiarity apparently stems from the isolation and privacy of the nuclear family, which leads to intensive parent-child interaction. Thus the isolated family may tend to produce child abuse along with overprotection and other forms of psychological engulfment.

The issue has been stated most bluntly by Jules Henry:

> In our culture babies are a private enterprise—everybody is in the baby business as soon as he gets married. He produces his own babies; they are his; only he has a say-so in their management. . . . Pinched off alone in one's house, shielded from critical eyes, one can be as irrational as one pleases with one's children as long as severe damage does not attract the attention of the police.[44]

Henry contrasts this private-enterprise version of parenthood with the social regulation of parent-child relations in other cultures. In primitive cultures or large households many eyes watch what a mother does; she cannot do what she pleases with the child. Of course, this means a mother may have to carry out what she or a medical authority from another culture might consider harmful traditional practices, but the child is shielded from the mother's whims or gross incompetence. Often, as Henry points out, the child is thought of as belonging to the clan or whole family as much as to the parents.

The point is further documented by William Stephens[45] in his cross-cultural survey of family life. Stephens writes how, in a number of ways, American child-rearing practices are "strikingly deviant" from those of other cultures; it seems, says Stephens, that practically the whole world does things one way, while we do it another way. One of the areas of great deviance concerns this matter of the isolated nuclear-family household. In every other society but one, the Copper Eskimo, Stephens finds the nuclear family living with or near the husband's or wife's kin. Regardless of the degree to which the nuclear family is thought of as a separate unit, ecologically it is part of a larger household or complex of households.

The chief feature setting American parenthood apart from its traditional counterparts is not so much the loosening of kinship bonds as the absence of what the anthropologist John Whiting calls the "microcommunity."[46] A microcommunity is a group of about twenty or thirty mothers and their children—with or without fathers or their relatives—who live close to one another. All the mothers know the names of all the children. It is the microcommunity, Whiting argues, not the extended family, that serves as the basic support group for parenting in preindustrial societies.

Although something resembling the microcommunity may exist to this day in some small towns and urban ethnic neighborhoods, the mobility of American life, both social and geographical, and the strong value placed on family privacy have encouraged the separation of the family unit from the surrounding community.

In the microcommunity the child is surrounded by parental surrogates. The influence of the nuclear-family ideology has led to this situation being described at times as a deprivation for the child, as if the child can receive only a fixed amount of love—all of it from the mother or the same amount divided in several ways. Actually, however, the presence of stand-ins and helpers for the mother may increase the amount of warmth and attention the mother can give to the child. For example, one six-culture study[47] found that the more mother substitutes available, the warmer and more stable the mother was in interacting with the child. Lambert writes of this as perhaps the most important finding of the study: "It suggests that the mental health, or at least the style of emotional life, of both the mother and her child is enhanced by the availability of acceptable surrogates."[48] Whiting[49] reports that the attention and comforting a child receives is roughly proportional to the number of adults living in the household. For example, the more adults there are in a house, the more time an infant is likely to spend in someone's arms, and the sooner he or she will be attended to after starting to cry.

Once the point has been made, it seems rather obvious that the all-your-eggs-in-one-basket system of the isolated family imposes strains on both mother and child. As Stephens[50] puts it, mother's feelings become very important because she is the only mother you have. If she gets angry with you, there's no place else to go; nor is there anyplace for her to go to rest or to get out of an angry mood. This sets the stage for emotional outbursts, which at the extreme may result in child abuse, but more frequently result in scoldings and complaints, perhaps spankings, sometimes accidents. It's not a matter of villains, or bad parents, but rather an ecological one: great demands being placed on limited parental resources of time, energy, and money.

The lack of social regulation of parenthood by the clan or community has many disadvantages for parents even as it increases their power over a child. Again we encounter one of the many paradoxes of freedom: in the tribal family or traditional kin group, children not only do not belong to parents in the same way as they do to isolated modern parents, but also the parents deal with their children according to a script written by the larger culture. The culture's traditional beliefs and superstitions strengthen the parents' position in dealing with children and, again paradoxically, can make the parents more relaxed, warm, and affectionate.

In the old system the parent resembles an administrator in a large bureaucracy, carrying out policies made by higher authorities. Children may disobey or fail to carry out assigned tasks, but they are unlikely to argue with very many of the rules themselves. Even if they do, however, the parents can argue back that it's beyond their power to change the rules. What the parents lose in personal power they more than make up for in institutional backing for their position. By contrast, the American parent is often uncertain about rules because no community tradition exists, and advice from experts may be contradictory and difficult to apply. Whether or not the parent is unsure, the child recognizes the parent as the source of the rules—the parent is the legislator as well as the executive and the judiciary. Thus the stage is set for submission or resentment or rebellion.

No matter what the outcome, it is a two-party conflict, a win-or-lose game between parent and child. Books of advice to parents often suggest that parents state rules impersonally, not in the form of orders. Thus they are advised not to say to their children "Go to bed" but "It's bedtime"; not to say "Pick those toys up off the floor" but "There are some toys on the floor that need to be put away." Parents can even say "I know you want to stay up, but it's bedtime," indicating even further separation of themselves from the rules and a closeness to the child. This technique often does work since it prevents confrontations between parents and children. But it hardly duplicates the situation of the parent in a traditional society. The child usually comprehends that the buck really does stop at the parent, and that there is only a remote authority, if any at all, supervising both the parent's and the child's acts.

The most extreme form of social support for parental authority is the supernatural. Consider the following incident, reported by a Hopi Indian man about his childhood:

> I later saw some giantlike Katchinas (masked dancers who impersonate supernatural beings) stalking into the village with long black bills, and big sawlike teeth. One carried a rope to lasso disobedient children. He stopped at a certain house and called for a boy. "You have been naughty," he scolded. "You fight with other children. You kill chickens. You pay no attention to the old people. We have come to get you and eat you." The boy cried and promised to behave better. The giants became angrier and threatened to tie him up and take him away. But the boy's parents begged for his life and offered fresh meat in his place. The giant reached out his hand as if to grab the boy but took the meat instead. Placing it in his basket, he warned the boy that he would get one more chance to change his conduct.[51]

Notice the role of the parents in the anecdote—from the child's point of view they are benevolent protectors saving him from a terrible fate. In the American family system, the frightening giant and kind protector are one person.

Modern Motivations for Parenthood

In looking at parenthood as an institution, we have not yet focused on the parents themselves. What is the meaning of parenthood in the lives of parents? Given the burdensomeness of children and the difficulties of being a parent in the modern world, why do people choose to have children?

One reason is that it is still the expected thing for a married couple to do. Although "pronatalist" pressures have lessened in recent years, they have by no means disappeared. Organizations such as NON (National Organization for Non-Parents) complain that American society still assumes that all married people should have children, and that serious biases exist against those who do not.[52]

A study of more than fifty voluntarily childless couples by sociologist Jean Veevers reveals some of the social pressures toward parenthood.[53] All of the wives interviewed reported being stigmatized by their decision not to have children. There is, they feel, a widespread stereotype of the childless woman that includes such negative traits as selfishness, abnormality, immorality, and irresponsibility. In addition, the stereotype assumes that the childless woman feels unhappy, unfulfilled, and unfeminine. Many of the women had experienced direct pressures from family and friends: they had been subjected to arguments in favor of having children, as well as more subtle pressures such as being asked to explain their failure to become parents and being asked when—not if—they were going to have children. However, the social sanction associated with childlessness seemed to be the only serious problem encountered by these women. They reported feeling content with their decision. (It should be emphasized that these women had chosen not to have children. The psychological situation of the involuntary childless would, of course, be very different.)

Despite the negative view of childlessness, however, Veevers points out that these women were quite well defended against such sanctions. They drew support from their husbands, and they found various ways of "discrediting the discreditors."

Children give parents the opportunity to cuddle and romp.

In addition to the biases against childlessness, pronatalist pressures encourage people in a variety of ways to become parents. Although the United States does not make cash grants to parents, some people feel that our tax laws encourage parenthood through the $750 deduction allowed to parents for each dependent child.[54] A more pervasive inducement to have children is the idealization of parenthood in both popular culture and the social sciences.

Although in recent years there has been a growing tendency to look at parenthood in less idyllic terms than once was common, from the late 1940s to the 1960s parenthood was defined as happy self-fulfillment. Psychoanalysis contributed to this prevailing mystique of parenthood. The older version of Freudian theory saw parenthood as the realization of infantile wishes. In the newer ego psychology, parenthood became a stage of normal personality development. For a woman especially, the coming of children represented the crowning achievement of her life, the justification of her own existence. For men, the father role has traditionally been seen as proof of manhood. Along with the notion of parenthood as inherently rewarding and fulfilling have gone some subsidiary ideas, such as the notion that children bring a couple close together and thus can repair a bad marriage or improve a good one.

LeMasters has listed seventeen "folk beliefs" about parenthood that have been popular in American culture—a folk belief being an idea that is widely shared yet not supported by evidence. Some examples of these include:

Rearing children is fun.

Children are sweet and cute.

Children will turn out well if they have "good" parents.

Children appreciate all the advantages their parents give them.

The Parental Mystique

Two parents are always better than one.

Love is enough to sustain good parental performance.

All married couples should have children.

Childless married couples are frustrated and unhappy.

Children improve a marriage.

Child rearing is easier today because of modern medicine, modern appliances, child psychology, etc.[55]

But social pressures are not the whole explanation of why people want to have children. The experience of parenthood provides many emotional and symbolic rewards, despite the costs. Life in a modernized society—urban, industrial, bureaucratic, impersonal—as we've observed before, exerts paradoxical pressures on the family and on intimate relations generally. They are both more difficult to sustain and more deeply needed. It is not only love that we crave, but power and influence. As Jerome Kagan observes:

> As modern environments make a sense of potency and individual effectiveness more difficult to attain, freedom from all affective involvements becomes more and more intolerable. Involvement with a family is the only viable mechanism available to satisfy that hunger.[56]

Thus it is not as surprising as it may seem at first glance that there is an inverse relationship between social class and fertility—as in the saying that the "rich get richer and the poor get children." The explanation is not simply that poor and working-class people don't know about contraceptives or are careless about using them, though there are still large numbers of unplanned and unwanted children born to them. Rather, as several studies have shown, lower-status couples may want more children than their middle-class counterparts because

children provide satisfactions that cannot be had any other way. For women who lack the opportunity for satisfying work outside the home, the bearing and rearing of children can provide emotional rewards as well as a recognized social role.[57] For the working-class man, fatherhood can provide a source of pride and the opportunity to exercise a degree of power not possible at work or anywhere else but in the family. As Blau and Duncan observe:

> Whereas successful achievers have their status as adult men supported by their superior occupational roles and authority, the unsuccessful find a substitute in the authority they exercise in their role as fathers over a number of children.[58]

It is not only for working-class people that parenthood promises compensatory rewards—that is, gratification to compensate for lacks and deprivations in other areas of life. Many people have children because they want to feel important and needed, or because life seems empty and pointless and children promise excitement. Perhaps the most basic deprivation that leads people to have children is death; having children has always symbolized a kind of immortality. Through children one takes one's place in the chain of generations, linking ancestors with generations yet unborn. Children have assured the continuation of the family name and lineage, as well as the perpetuation of the family farm or business. In recent years, however, people have come to care less about what historian Edward Shorter calls "the posterity business."

There have been a number of studies dealing with motivations for parenthood, many of which have been summarized by Pohlman.[59] One of the most common reasons people give for becoming parents is that they "like" or "love" children. Sometimes this statement seems to be given as an easy answer when a person is asked why he or she wants to have children. But as Pohlman points out, some of the commonsense reasons for liking children are important: "Children provide action and stimulation and change, some of the factors that attract one to raise pets or watch a television program."[60] Adults can relax with children and relive some of their own childish ways by joking, teasing, and roughhousing. They can also hug, cuddle, and kiss their children, thus fulfilling a basic human need for touch that is otherwise hard to express in adult life. In many families, particularly working-class ones with rigid sex roles, the affection provided by children may make up for a lack of closeness between husband and wife.

The Costs of Parenthood

Although parenthood often brings the satisfactions that people hope for before they have children, there are costs as well. In recent years there has begun to be a trend away from the notions of parenthood-as-fulfillment and of child rearing as part of the grand design of the social system. There is a growing awareness that even wanted and dearly loved children seem to bring heavy costs to parents. One of the landmarks of this trend was a 1957 article by E. E. LeMasters entitled "Parenthood as Crisis." LeMasters argued that the romantic complex surrounding parenthood goes even deeper than the one surrounding marriage, and he especially challenged the notion that the coming of children improves marital relationships. He and other writers have documented some of the ways in which the coming of children disrupts marriage.

One study reported that following childbirth the amount of time the wife and husband converse with each other is cut in half.[61] The sexual relationship is disrupted and may even be discontinued for as long as four months—eight weeks before birth and eight weeks after birth while tissues heal. Some women remain indifferent toward sex even after their physical recovery from childbirth. The presence of the child looms large, and parental sex may be interrupted by the baby's cries. The exhaustion of the new mother hovers constantly in the background, and at times is overwhelming.

Another of the themes of this literature on the costs of parenthood is the feeling on the part of many parents, particularly fathers, that they are competing with the child for the attention and love of the spouse. In many homes the coming of the first child changes the household from husband-centered to child-centered.[62] Some of the earlier literature on parenthood as crisis saw the crisis as a "normal" one. Just as in the conventional literature on marriage there is the notion of the "period of adjustment," after which the couple settles down to a mature marriage, so the crisis-of-parenthood literature emphasized the transitory nature of the problems brought on by the coming of children.

Alice Rossi[63] takes issue with the "normal" crisis idea. She argues that the crisis need not always have a positive outcome: people need not always "mature" in response to the strains of parenthood, but may suffer deterioration. This is particularly so for women, she notes, since the cultural pressure to bear children is so great that many women may have children in the absence of a genuine desire for them or the ability to perform well at the task.

A novel feature of this analysis is Rossi's comparison of parental roles with those of marriage and work. She argues that the parent role is much more difficult in American society than the other two roles. Marriage and work often involve a long period of preparation, with gradual transition to the role. The transition to parenthood, on the other hand, occurs abruptly and totally, as if a person shifted from being a graduate student to a full professor with little intervening apprenticeship experience of slowly increasing responsibility. The new mother starts out immediately on twenty-four-hour-a-day duty with full responsibilities. Further, in contrast with other commitments, parenthood is irrevocable. Rossi notes that we can have ex-spouses and ex-jobs but not ex-children.

Rossi argues that failures in mothering should be blamed not on individual women but on the isolated nuclear-family structure and the failure of society to provide institutionalized substitutes for the extended kin to assist in the care of infants and young children. Pohlman likewise concludes that since so many women have dreary reactions to their first ten or twelve years of motherhood, a society-wide problem seems to be present, and he calls for a society-wide solution.

> It seems illogical that each one of many thousands of mothers should conclude she has some peculiar individual problem, and should go through a period of soul-searching and hostility and repression and guilt in her relations to her children.[64]

Not only the transition to parenthood but also the continuing financial and psychological costs of raising a child have received attention from a number of writers. One estimate arrives at a cost of $40,000 to raise a child from birth to age eighteen. If the income the mother would have made had she been working is counted, the price reaches $100,000. As to the psychological impact, John and Suzanne Clausen report the following findings:

> Especially during the early years, children connote broken sleep, noise, confusion, and when there are several, congestion. Mothers of young children put in an inordinately long work week and tend to be confined to the home much of the time. The early years of mother-

hood are frequently remembered as the period when one constantly yearned for a full night's sleep and for a day free of demands. In our longitudinal data at the Institute of Human Development, mothers with three or more children fairly closely spaced, looking back at the early years of motherhood, from the perspective of the late 40's, are likely to recall those early years as years of extreme exhaustion and discouragement.[65]

Pohlman notes that many parents find interacting with children, especially over long periods of time, a strain:

> Parents want the child to do one thing; the child wants to do another. The battle between wills can prove wearying. Demanding strict and unwavering obedience may be the simplest procedure, but even this is a strain on parents. And many parents doubt whether this is the right approach. . . . They may alternate between permissiveness and irritated punitiveness. If they punish physically, they may feel guilty for this; if they fail to do so, they may feel guilty for the omission.[66]

But the strains of parenthood are not the inevitable battle of wills and the temperamental incompatibilities of adults and children. In part, they are the responsibility of social arrangements that make parents solely responsible for children and fail to provide even minimal assistance for parents as they go about their daily rounds of work and chores.

Moreover, despite the myth of the child-centered society, we are remarkably adult-oriented, with few places where children can be integrated into adult activities. One mother has described the result as follows:

> I have three children, 8, 2½, and 1. They are beautiful children, and most times I delight in them. But there are times when I see them as encumbrances, the objects of my frustration and anger. They are welded to me not only at birth, but by a society that sees them as totally

The Costs of Parenthood

Parents are also adults with their own concerns. They are not always "parenting" when with their children.

even for an hour—the scheduling and logistical arrangements that must be made would spin the most grizzled heads in the Pentagon.

Though free universal community-controlled child care is one goal, child-care service of another sort is equally important. Part-time child care. Hourly child care. Child care provided on sites our dreary but necessary chores lead us to. Dragging the children along to places where adults don't even want to go doubles the frustration . . . and more often than not, turns the children into recipients of our frustrations.[67]

The inconveniences this middle-class mother experiences are magnified to greater torment for the poor, who must spend hours waiting with their children in welfare offices, hospital clinics, and the courts.

The everyday trivial strains of parenthood have been increased by changes in American life having nothing to do with children or families. The decline of the urban neighborhood, with its local stores and lively sidewalk life, the suburban automotive way of life, the general feeling that public places are unsafe—all this has resulted in a dehumanization of life in general that makes it harder than ever to integrate children into everyday adult life.

Parents as Pygmalions: Prescriptions for Perfection

my problem, my burden alone. Wherever I move, they move with me: to the drugstore, to the newsstand, the fish market. Where once I moved on two legs, now I move on eight.

As parents, my husband and I are the sole providers, protectors, entertainers, and watchdogs for our young. We have no "extended family" to help care for them, no communal group to share the tasks. . . . When there are errands to be run or places we want to go—

As we have noted, modern parenthood can be a burden because parents lack the support of kin and community in the daily tasks of rearing children, and also because children have come to be consumers of the family's resources rather than productive contributors to it. But there is another reason why modern parenthood has become burdensome. The modern parent is responsible not only for the child's physical well-being, but also for the child's psychological adjustment. Since the beginning of the twentieth century, the leading psychological theorists and their popularizers have argued that parents play an omnipotent role in their children's psychological development. Only if parents do the right things at the right time will children turn out to be happy, successful adults. Conversely, any flaws in a person's adjustment, even in adulthood, can be traced to a lack of parental love or some other parental failing.

In historical and anthropological perspective, this preoccupation with the psychological consequences of parental behavior is unusual, if not unique. Earlier generations of parents were concerned with the bodily health and moral virtue of their children. In times of high infant mortality and strong religious beliefs, God, Fate, and the Devil reduced the perceived influence of the parents over the child's life. As two anthropologists put it:

> For the whole of human history up to the turn of the present century, simple physical survival has been the dominant issue in child rearing: a question not of "How shall I rear my child?" but "*Will* I rear him?" . . . child psychology is a luxury which only a small section of the world's parents can afford to consider. . . .[68]

A concern with child psychology may indeed be a costly luxury for modern Western parents, but it does not make child rearing any easier. Just as improvements in household appliances have failed to reduce the housewife's working hours, but merely have raised standards of housekeeping, so have child psychology and improved pediatrics raised the standards for child rearing.

Child-development experts—psychologists, psychiatrists, and doctors—have been "worshipped as the high-priests of child rearing,"[69] yet the advice of the experts is often inconsistent and usually difficult to apply to specific situations. One expert may write, for example, that hugging and kissing is good for babies and children, whereas another writes that physical affection is seductive and disturbing. Some experts favor permissiveness; others argue that children need firm rules and authoritative direction. In a classic article, Martha Wolfenstein[70] reviewed the changes in advice given in various editions of the pamphlet *Infant Care,* published by the United States government on consultation with the experts in the field. In ten editions issued over forty years, there have been remarkable alterations in concepts of the child's psychological and physical needs, and the kind of parental behavior recommended:

> In the earlier period, the mother's character was one of strong moral devotion. There were frequent references to her "self-control," "wisdom," "strength," "persistence". . . . In the 1929–1938 period, parenthood became predominantly a matter of know-how. The parents had to use the right technique to impose routines and keep the child from dominating them.
>
> In the most recent period, parenthood becomes a major source of enjoyment for both parents. . . . The parents are promised that having children will keep them together, keep them young, and give them fun and happiness. . . . Enjoyment, fun, and play now permeate all activities with the child. "Babies—and usually their mothers—enjoy breast feeding," nursing brings "joy and happiness" to the mother. At bath time, the baby "delights" his parents, and so on.[71]

A review of child-rearing research by Bronfenbrenner[72] revealed that middle-class parents seemed to reflect in their actual child-rearing practices the swings in expert opinion. During the first half of the twentieth century, middle-class parents tended to be more strict with their children than working- and lower-class parents, but by the fifties they had crossed over and become more permissive. During the earlier period, for example, middle-class parents tended to wean and toilet train their infants earlier and to keep them on stricter schedules than did working-class parents; in more recent years, however, middle-class parents have swung over to later weaning and toilet training and to more flexible schedules. Bronfenbrenner, attributing these changes to the great sensitivity of middle-class parents to expert opinion, writes:

> Taken as a whole, the correspondence between Wolfenstein's data and our own suggests a general hypothesis extending beyond the confines of social class as such: *child-rearing practices are likely to change most quickly in those segments of society which have closest access to and are most receptive to the agencies or agents of change (e.g., public media, clinics, physicians, and counsellors).*[73]

Ironically, attention to the experts among middle-class people seems to raise anxiety rather than reduce it. Research on middle-class mothers, such as that conducted by Sears and his associates, suggests that the more awareness a mother has of the child-rearing literature, the more uncertain she feels that she is doing the right thing:

> ". . . I spend most of my time thinking I am a perfectly lousy mother and I suppose all mothers feel that way. The thing of motherhood brings out my own inefficiencies, my own deficiencies, so terribly, that . . . the outstanding thought in my mind is that I should try to be a better mother each new day."[74]

Problems such as bed wetting or stuttering tend to be interpreted by middle-class parents as a negative reflection of their parenting. But in former days, particularly in the working classes, parents more often blamed such problems on the child's character or on physical difficulties. Furthermore, working-class parents show relatively more concern for the child's outward behavior than his or her inner states.[75] A concern for the inner life of the child may make things harder for both parent and child.

The notion that parenthood is fun may lead paradoxically to greater strains for parents:

> The characterization of parenthood in terms of fun and enjoyment . . . may express a new imperative: You ought to enjoy your child. When a mother is told that most mothers enjoy nursing, she may wonder what is wrong with her in case she does not. Her self-evaluation can no longer be based entirely on whether she is doing the right and necessary things but becomes involved with nuances of feeling which are not under voluntary control.[76]

The Future of Parenthood

We have focused so heavily on the dark side of parent-child relations in this chapter because the prevailing views of the subject have been so romantic and unrealistic. It is possible, however, to end on an optimistic note.

As we have emphasized throughout this chapter, the care children will receive when they come into the world is not guaranteed by genes, instincts, or societal necessity. The first requirement for adequate child care is this: children should be wanted by whomever is responsible for them, although loving and wanting children do not guarantee competence in a parent. Anything that reduces the likelihood of unwanted births can only increase the chances that children who are born will be treated

Fathers often relate to their children in a playful way, with mothers assigned the more responsible caretaking roles.

humanely. The ability to exercise control and choice about parenthood must mark a milestone in what Erich Fromm has called the "revolution of the child."

Many other ongoing social changes now—the abortion movement, women's liberation, the concern with overpopulation and the environment, the increasing acceptability of singleness, childlessness, and homosexuality—can only mean that fewer children will be born as a result of carelessness or social pressure. When parenthood is romanticized, when it is asumed that all women are endowed with maternal instincts and innate competence in caring for infants and young children, any alternative means of child care can only be seen as a deprivation for the child. The prevailing myths of parenthood obscure the possibility that child-care facilities may rescue children from physical and emotional mistreatment and may even improve the relationship between the parents and children. After reviewing the literature on the experiences of women during the first ten or twelve years of parenthood, Pohlman suggests that neighborhood child-care and education centers are a vital necessity for the well-being of both mothers and children. He writes:

> We believe that most mothers need to be away from their children for a few hours each day, whether they are employed outside their homes or not. Such a "recess" probably permits a mother to relate to her children with greater zest and effectiveness when she is with them. Many mothers cannot bring themselves to leave their children, because of justifiable concern with the quality of substitute care they will receive. Also many mothers lack even the small initiative needed to arrange to be away from children, under existing circumstances. All of this seems to imply the need for a systematic program of child care and education, a program of excellent quality.[77]

The prejudice against child-care facilities outside the home has become a self-fulfilling prophecy. The relatively few day-care facilities that do exist are woefully inadequate in terms of both quantity and quality. They are conceived to be places where only a mother in extreme circumstances would consider sending a child. And they are conceived to be total substitutes for family child care—five days a week, eight hours a day, all year long.

Such forms of child care are needed, but there is another kind for which the need is even greater—part-time, drop-in child care for parents to use as they go about their business. Pohlman also mentions the need for visiting nurses or other parent surrogates to help out when parents or children are sick. Such services would relieve the kinds of strains that led the widowed father to break his son's arm in the incident reported earlier in this chapter.

Further, trends within the family itself promise to relieve some of the strains of parent-hood, which until now have fallen most heavily on women. In young middle-class families, that segment of the population most sensitive to changes in the intellectual climate, parenthood is coming to be defined more and more as a joint enterprise of both the husband and the wife. The trend seems to be motivated not only by women who are insisting that the men share some of the load, but also by many young professional men who no longer accept as their fate the compulsive male careerism that dominated the 1950s.

Finally, parent-child relations are being affected by far-reaching changes in definitions of both adulthood and childhood. We will consider these changes in the following chapters.

Summary

The prevailing conceptions of parenthood in the social sciences and popular thought have emphasized the naturalness of parenthood and the societal need for children. Early mother-child relations in particular are assumed to be governed by innate processes of mutual attraction, independent of social contexts.

Actually, however, the evolutionary evidence suggests that human infants, in contrast to our primate relatives, are born into a nurturance gap. The same factors that led to the evolution of the human brain resulted in the greater helplessness of human infants and a greater dependency on learning and culture for carrying out maternal activities.

Parent-child relations cannot be understood apart from specific social, cultural, and historical settings. The feeding and care of young children can be a heavy burden or an easily assumed one, depending on the food supply, cultural attitudes toward infants, and the particular circumstances of individual parents. The fact that infanticide has been widely practiced in Western society and else-where is evidence that benevolence toward children is not built into human nature and is not a societal imperative.

To understand parenthood in our own society, we must realize how modern kinship and work patterns may make parenthood more difficult than in traditional societies. In most cultures and in our own historical past, parenthood is carried out in the midst of the community and along with economic responsibilities. It is a less self-conscious process because traditional ways can be followed, and the child's future status is already known. Our own society, however, imposes great demands on parents while providing minimal institutional support to replace the kin and community assistance of former times.

Source Notes

1. Goode, 1977, p. 382.
2. Kagan, 1977, p. 42.
3. Himes, 1963.
4. Sumner, 1960.
5. Westoff and Potvin, 1967.
6. Blake, 1974.
7. Rainwater, 1965.
8. Current Population Reports, 1972, 1974.
9. Veevers, 1972, 1973.
10. Erikson, 1963.
11. Ibid., p. 130.
12. Levy, 1965.
13. Bowlby, 1969.
14. Anthony and Benedek, 1970, p. xvii.
15. Pohlman, 1969, p. 52.
16. Mead, 1957.
17. Kessen, 1965.
18. Ibid., p. 1.
19. Geertz, 1965.
20. Ibid., p. 112.
21. Washburn and DeVore, 1961, p. 39.
22. Harlow et al., 1963.
23. Washburn and DeVore, 1961, p. 42.
24. Ibid., p. 39.
25. Mead, 1957.
26. Shorter, 1973; Trexler, 1973.
27. Langer, 1972.
28. Ibid., pp. 96-97.
29. Ibid., p. 96.
30. Ibid., p. 98.
31. Ibid.
32. Hunt, 1970.
33. Ibid., p. 121.
34. Kessen, 1965.
35. Hunt, 1970, p. 101.
36. In ibid., p. 104.
37. Gil, 1971.
38. Steele and Pollock, 1968, p. 104.
39. Fontana, 1964, p. ix.
40. Gil, 1970, pp. 15-16.
41. Ibid., p. 56.
42. Steele, 1970.
43. Ginott, 1972.
44. Henry, 1963, pp. 331-332.
45. Stephens, 1963.
46. Whiting, 1977.
47. Lambert, 1971; Minturn and Lambert, 1964; Whiting, 1961.
48. Lambert, 1971, p. 55.
49. Whiting, 1961.
50. Stephens, 1963.
51. Ibid., p. 341.
52. Peck and Senderowitz, 1974.
53. Veevers, 1973.
54. Peck and Senderowitz, 1974.
55. LeMasters, 1970, pp. 18-29.
56. Kagan, 1977, p. 54.
57. Rainwater, 1960.
58. Blau and Duncan, 1967, p. 428.
59. Pohlman, 1969.
60. Ibid., p. 60
61. Feldman, 1962.
62. Waller and Hill, 1951.
63. Rossi, 1968.
64. Pohlman, 1969, p. 153.
65. Clausen and Clausen, 1971, p. 7.
66. Pohlman, 1969, p. 105.
67. Francke, 1972, pp. 27-28.
68. Newson and Newson, 1974, p. 55.
69. Pohlman, 1969, p. 102.
70. Wolfenstein, 1955.
71. Ibid., p. 173.
72. Bronfenbrenner, 1958.
73. Ibid., p. 411 (italics in original).
74. Sears et al., 1957, p. 43.
75. Kohn, 1963.
76. Wolfenstein, 1955, pp. 174-175.
77. Pohlman, 1969, p. 153.

The Future of Parenthood

Chapter Eleven
The Construction of Childhood

□ *Nature wants children to be children before they are men. If we deliberately pervert this order, we shall get premature fruits which are neither ripe nor well flavored. . . . Childhood has ways of seeing, thinking, and feeling, peculiar to itself; nothing can be more foolish than trying to substitute our ways for them.*

Jean-Jacques Rousseau, *Emile*

□ *There seems little doubt that, in our . . . culture, a contributing factor to the characteristic features of "child mentality" that we have discovered is the positive efforts we make to keep our children childish.*

A. Irving Hallowell, *Culture and Experience*

The Construction of Childhood

Americans have long been considered the most child-centered people in the world. Foreign observers throughout our history, as well as anthropologists who have observed other cultures, have commented on the American preoccupation with child rearing. No other group of parents seems to have been so anxious about children or so uncertain about how to deal with them. And no other society has so persistently experienced a sense of crisis over the future of children and the family. For the past century, public concern over children has resulted in wave after wave of reform movements and social policies.

Despite our reputation for child-centeredness, however, the 1970 White House Conference on Children, whose task was to assess the status and needs of children in America, warned of "national neglect of children."[1] One conference participant argued that the alarm was not made urgent enough:

> . . . The evidence indicates that American society, whether viewed in comparison to other nations or to itself over time, is accordingly progressively less attentive to its children. The trend is already apparent when the child is born. America, the richest and most powerful country in the world, stands thirteenth among the nations in combatting infant mortality.[2]

The participants not only had in mind children from disadvantaged families when they wrote of the neglect of children. Children from all classes, the conference report notes, suffer from being isolated from adult society. Within the home there is evidence of a decline in parent-child interaction over the past twenty-five years.[3] Further, the parent-child interaction that does occur is not all beneficial to children: one out of four fractures diagnosed in children under three results from physical abuse by parents; two children die every day from parental abuse.[4]

The coexistence of concern and neglect, or worse, in the treatment of children is not unique to our time and place. Perhaps the greatest gap between popular imagery and reality concerning children occurred in the Victorian era when, as Peter Coveney[5] points out, the *myth* of innocent childhood prevailed along with the *practice* of savagery toward children. Coveney refers not only to the exploitation of children in mines and factories, but also the the severe child-rearing practices approved by Victorian families.

In addition to the gap between ideal and reality in the treatment of children, our attempts to understand the child's place in society are complicated by contrasting images of the child which not only have succeeded each other but have coexisted side by side. Ideas about children taken for granted in one era come to be regarded as false by the next. In medieval times, for example, children were seen as miniature adults. They wore adult clothing, and when painters gave them adult proportions, no one seems to have noticed that the representations were inaccurate. To later ages such paintings appear quaint and funny.

The image of the child as an incomplete adult was replaced by the demonic child of Calvinism and the Jesuits, a child whose corrupt nature and evil will called for severe discipline, of which whipping was a ritual part, in order to fit the child to be a moral citizen. "Spare the rod and spoil the child" was once a literal prescription for child rearing.

The corrupt child in turn became—for the romantic school of writers, such as Blake, Wordsworth, and Rousseau—a noble savage, whose "doors of perception" and capacities for experiences were not yet deadened by an industrial society. The serious social criticism implied by the image of the romantic child wilted away to become the Victorian cult of the innocent child; childhood became a never-never land of fun and games.

The Construction of Childhood

Actually, the image of childhood innocence never entirely replaced the demonic child of the Puritans; particularly in England and America, attitudes toward childhood have been marked by "a curious conflict between childhood as innocence and the grim portrait of an evil being who must be scourged to his salvation."[6] At the end of the nineteenth century, Freud revived the image of the demonic child and made it the focus of a new psychology. Freud's theories of infantile sexuality attacked the image of childhood innocence and ushered in the first of the "developmental images" of the child which have dominated the twentieth century. Since that time the leading images of the child have been supplied by scientific professionals—psychologists, psychiatrists, pediatricians—rather than by religionists and poets. Thus the child is defined by a place on a staircase of development—the child of ages and stages.

In view of the profound changes that have occurred in our culture's theories of childhood, we can hardly rest assured that we have at last discovered childhood as it really is.

What Is a Child?

The enormous variation in the ideas different cultures and historical eras have had about children, their needs, capacities, and the dynamics of growth suggest that the answer is not as obvious as it seems. In this chapter we are going to explore such issues as the following: Is the nature of childhood universal, or do childhood experiences and the characteristics of children vary? To what extent has childhood as we know it been shaped by our family life and other social practices regarding children? Does a society's recognition of the various stages of childhood and youth indicate sensitivity to children's needs? Or does age grading represent a means of segregating children from adult society and exerting greater social control over them? Is the history of childhood one of uninterrupted progress?

In trying to define a child, we face many of the same problems we faced earlier in trying to arrive at a definition of the term "family." The very word "child" carries with it a number of assumptions that get in our way. For example, the term exists in opposition to another term—"adult"—like light and dark, male and female. Thus our language suggests an opposition, a discontinuity between children and adults, which fits with actual social practice in our society. We tend to assume that children have a separate and distinct nature that distinguishes them from adults: adults work and are responsible, children play and are irresponsible; adults are controlled and rational, children are emotional and irrational; adults think abstractly, children think concretely; adults are sexual, children are asexual; and so on.

Above all, we tend to view children through the lenses of the developmental model or paradigm: the assumptions that the child develops naturally by passing through a number of stages, that these stages follow one another in a constant order, that each order is appropriate for a particular age, and that the child has a built-in timetable of development. The essential principles of the developmental paradigm, first elaborated in 1762 by the philosopher Rousseau in *Emile,* continue to guide the field of child study.

In premodern societies, in our own historical past, and in groups outside the middle class, a different concept of childhood has prevailed: children are seen as miniature adults—small or inadequate versions of their parents, often totally subject to traditional or parental authority.

By contrast, the "modern" industrial, middle-class view tends to treat the child as a distinctive social category: children have their own special psychology and their own special needs, patterned processes of growth often elaborated into ideas about developmental states that may postpone advent to "full" adulthood well into a person's twenties, and still later.[7] Most professional and popular writings on childhood seem to take for granted that there is a closer fit between the child's special nature and his or her place in modern societies than in the premodern model where children are treated as little adults.

The prevailing assumption is that when the discontinuities between adults and children are not recognized, the child's nature is being violated. For example, we find the fact that young children work in some cultures both anomalous and distasteful. Even a sophisticated anthropo-logist can express surprise at the failure of Indian mothers, for example, to appreciate children's work:

> . . . Even those children who did work regularly were not accorded recognition. For instance, Narayan's mother, when asked about her son's chores, reported that he did not do very much work. It would seem that walking an average of 12 miles a day, and carrying a load for 6 to 9 of those miles, might be considered a rather arduous undertaking for a slightly built 7-year-old boy, but his mother was not impressed.[8]

Other failures to mark off childhood from adulthood also strike us as incongruous—as when children wear adult clothing—or horrifying—as when, as in many cultures, children are not shielded from sexual knowledge. In general,

Women's work begins early in life.

The Construction of Childhood

the failure of preindustrial societies to recognize childhood is taken to be an indicator of the backwardness of primitive peoples. Indeed, anthropologists of the late nineteenth and early twentieth centuries often equated the mentality of adult "savages" with that of the child in Western culture. Hence the failure to separate adulthood from childhood could be interpreted as a sign of arrested development: if children and adults acted in similar ways, it must be because the adults never progressed beyond the earliest stages of mental development.

Although anthropologists have rejected the notion that the norms of child development in Western cultures are the measuring rod against which other cultures are to be judged, the equation of preliterate adult with Western child persists as strongly as ever in psychology. Further, psychological concepts of childhood not only are *ethnocentric*—biased in favor of Western culture—but also they may be *chrono-centric*—biased in favor of a particular historical period. As Kenneth Keniston has put it:

> Every epoch tends to freeze its own unique experience into an ahistorical version of life in general. Modern developmental psychology witness this universal trend.[9]

The Ideology of Childhood and the Developmental Paradigm

The concepts of childhood that prevail in our culture, particularly among the most educated parts of the public, are those of developmental psychology. Psychologists and psychiatrists are generally conceded to be the experts in the field; most research in human development is carried out by psychologists.

The models of the child in psychology reflect prevailing cultural attitudes and practices concerning children as well as the intellectual traditions of psychology as a field. Childhood became an object of scientific inquiry in the psychology laboratory beginning in the second half of the nineteenth century, although there had been increasing concern on the part of parents, literary figures, and social reformers for about two centuries before. Darwin's theories stimulated the rise of scientific interest in the child. It is almost impossible to overestimate the dramatic impact of evolutionary theory on our notions of children as well as on psychology in general. "Development" became the guiding metaphor for theorizing about chil-dren. As Kessen puts it, there was a "riot of parallel-drawing" between the mind of the child and what were presumed to be earlier historical stages of the human species:

> The irreducible contribution of Darwin to the study of children was . . . in his assignment of scientific value to childhood. Species develop, societies develop, man develops. From the publication of *The Origin of Species* to the end of the nineteenth century, there was a riot of parallel-drawing between animal and child, between primitive man and child, between early human history and child. The developing child was seen as a natural museum of human phylogeny and history; by careful observation of the infant and child, one could see the descent of man.[10]

Although psychology has outgrown its historical origins, evolutionary doctrines continue, in many subtle ways, to influence the study of the child. Contemporary developmental psychology, like psychology in general, is divided into two radically different ways of looking at human nature—the mechanistic approach and the organismic approach. Both reflect, in different ways, the biological frame of reference inherited from Darwinism.

The Mechanistic Approach

The mechanistic approach consists of behavior or learning theories, as exemplified by the work of Skinner, Hull, Dollard and Miller, Bandura, and many others.[11] The intellectual ancestors of these theories were the empiricist or associationist philosophers who assumed that the child's mind was a blank slate (tabula rasa). Where the earlier versions of this position attempted to analyze the contents of the mind into basic elements, current proponents have dispensed with the concept of mind. The child is shaped not by original nature, but by the environmental contingencies to which he or she has been exposed, just like any other organism from animal to adult human. The Darwinian influence on mechanistic theories is evident in the influence of animal psychology on the study of the child.

At first glance, one might think that mechanistic theories see little difference between adults and children since the same "laws of learning" apply to both. In fact, however, adult and child differ as much in mechanistic developmental theories as in any other kind. Though not qualitatively different from adults, children—along with animals—are assumed to be much simpler organisms:

> The animal and the child are imperfect adults for the associationist and imperfect in a critically important way. They can be assumed to have fewer, or more simple, units of behavior than the full man, and their apparent simplicity may permit finding the beginning of the thread that is woven into the inexplicably complicated pattern of adult human behavior. . . .[12]

The Organismic Approach

Mechanistic theories use the term "development" in a general and descriptive sense. Organismic theories use the term in a more restricted way. They define development as a qualitative change of the whole organism from one state or form to another. The organismic approach may be further subdivided into psychoanalytic theories and what Langer[13] has called "organic lamp" theories. The psychoanalytic theories include, besides the work of Freud, principally that of Erikson. By organic-lamp theorists, Langer refers to the work of Piaget and Heinz Werner. Like psychoanalytic theories, organic-lamp theorists assume that innate, biologically rooted functions are the organizing forces that govern development, although they operate in interaction with the environment.

Although each theory selects a different aspect of the child as the key to understanding the process of development, they all agree on several things. First, development is self-propelled and teleological—that is, the "push" to change comes from within the organism, and the endpoint of development is implicit at the beginning. Second, the adult is categorically, or qualitatively, different from the child. The different stages of childhood are also qualitatively different from each other. The endpoint of development is placed in the twenties. The legal designation of eighteen or twenty-one as the age of adult status thus accords well with developmental theories. Finally, developmental theories are organized around specific concepts of adult competence. For Freud the endpoint of development is the genital, heterosexual adult, who is parent to children and has a place in the occupational world. For Piaget the endpoint of development is the stage of formal operational thinking—the ability to think hypothetically and abstractly.

Thus, by definition, these theories set up a polar opposition between child and adult nature. If the adult end of the scale is defined as logical and rational, then the child is by definition autistic, irrational, emotional, and lacking in perceptual and cognitive structures. These qualities are conceived of as being appropriate for children.

Developmental theories claim to be universal. In Freudian theory, development is caused by changes in the body's erotic emphasis. The theory allows for different outcomes depending on how the child's development crises are met, but the psychosexual basics of orality, anality, genitality, and the Oedipal crises are held to be universal. Piaget's progressions are based on maturation of the brain and nervous system along with the child's encounters with the physical and social environment found in all cultures. As Langer puts it, "The environment . . . in organic lamp theory is merely the *occasion* for or *scene* of, and not the cause or *agent* of, development."[14]

Although both organic-lamp and psychoanalytic theories fit the developmental framework or paradigm in both of the above senses, they differ in important ways. In some ways the Piagetian image of the child is the polar opposite of the Freudian image. If the Freudian child is a demonic little beast, seething with lust and aggression, Piaget's is a scientist bubbling with curiosity. The baby dropping toys out of the crib is revealed to be a little Galileo, observing the behavior of falling bodies. Not only does the Piagetian child exhibit a thirst for knowledge as strong as the sexual urges of the Freudian child — even stronger, because less satiable — but also the child has an active and independent intellect.

In Freud's imagery of the child as well as that of most socialization research, the child is more or less a passive recipient of the demands and teachings of the culture; the only alternative

Children can make playthings out of the most unpromising objects. In becoming adults, most people lose their creativity.

to acceptance is resistance. The choice of weaning and toilet training as the central events in the socialization of the child are significant: these are precisely the areas that allow no room for innovation on the part of the child. All children are eventually weaned and toilet trained; in these struggles the culture always wins, and the child always conforms.

The Piagetian child, however, does not merely internalize the standards of adults as he or she grows up. Piaget's model of development

The Ideology of Childhood

credits the child with more autonomy and creativity than any other. The child participates in his or her own development, and is not the passive victim of either an internal process unfolding on its own or social pressures.

Yet the Piagetian child is not so unlike the Freudian one as may appear at first glance. The child is curious like a scientist, but the capacity to process information is as yet unsophisticated. Thought processes are egocentric, animistic, and easily tricked by appearances: show the child two equal balls of clay, roll one into a sausage, and he or she will tell you there is now less clay in it because it is thinner. The child has a very long way to go before being ready to participate in adult life.

Limitations of the Developmental Paradigm

The problem with all of these images of the child is not so much that they are wrong but that they are limited in a variety of ways, despite the many valid insights they provide. We shall argue here that developmental psychology has overemphasized the view of development as an individual process unfolding from within and has neglected the influence of social and cultural contexts on children and concepts of childhood, and that it has emphasized grand theories and laboratory tests rather than empirical studies of children in their ordinary environments.

One surprising limitation is that most developmental research has little to say about children and their daily lives. As a review of the literature on early child care put it:

> The study of human development is nowhere more highly developed than in the United States, where hundreds of investigators monthly fill the pages of the numerous journals and books devoted to scientific inquiry concerning children's development. . . . But

most of this research has little to do with the process of development as it occurs in daily life.[15]

Thus American developmental psychology, as Bronfenbrenner and others have observed,[16] has tended to emphasize laboratory studies in which the child performs an unfamiliar task in a strange situation with a strange adult. It has tended to neglect the study of social settings in which children live and the persons who are central to them emotionally.

As a result of the emphasis on laboratory studies, developmental psychology tends to deal with bits and pieces of the child. The rationale for this approach is that eventually all the bits and pieces can be added together to give a comprehensive picture. It is rare, however, for anyone to try to construct the comprehensive picture. More often, there is a tendency for the bits and pieces to be taken for the real things they represent. Von Bertalanffy[17] calls this the fallacy of the "nothing-but." In the field of child development, the "nothing-but" fallacy takes the form of assuming that a child is "nothing-but" the developmental stage or test performance typical of that age. Even if the attempt were made to put the pieces together, it is doubtful that they could compose a valid and comprehensive picture of the child. A review of developmental research summed up the problem in this way:

> Social scientists, it is sometimes said, are forced to look at small bits and pieces and construct from them a model of reality. In doing this they are often forced into a kind of shorthand. The problem is that this shorthand tends to become a substitute for reality, in interpreting results, in reporting them, and in making recommendations based on them.[18]

The grand developmental theories of Freud, Piaget, and Werner, though much richer in their descriptions of children and their behavior than laboratory studies, also fail to portray children in terms of their day-to-day lives. For example, parents who have studied Freud before having children are often surprised to find that the very young infant does not seem to spend all the time being "oral" and that toilet training doesn't occupy most of the toddler's days. Robert White has written of the discrepancies between theoretical notions of children at different ages and their actual daily behavior. Even in infants, such discrepancies are striking:

> Somehow, the image has gotten into our minds that the infant's time is divided between eating and sleep. . . . this is not true even for newborn infants, who show distinct forerunners of what will later become playful exploratory activity.
>
> Gesell notes that at four weeks there is apt to be a waking time in the late afternoon during which visual experience begins to be accumulated. At 16 weeks this period may last for half an hour, and then increase steadily up to one year. Gesell's typical "behavior day" shows an hour of play before breakfast, two hours before lunch, an hour's carriage ride and another hour of social play in the afternoon, and perhaps still another hour after being put to bed. At the age of 12 months, the child is already putting in a six-hour day of play, not to mention the overtime that occurs during meals and the bath.[19]

Piaget's model of the child is as incomplete as Freud's even though it focuses on the very things that the Freudian theories slight—the young child's eagerness to learn, to explore, and to make sense of environment. Piaget's work on the first two years of life is rich in detailed descriptions of actual behavior, but the incidents are selected to illustrate the stages of intellectual growth rather than to give a rounded picture of the child in the framework of daily activities.

After the first two years, Piaget's writings serve as an even less useful guide to the activities and interests of children than his description of infant activities. He becomes less interested in the child's thinking, especially the limits of the child's conceptual capabilities.

Baldwin points to a gap between the ordinary, everyday functioning of preschool children and their performance on Piagetian tests of their thinking. It is surprising, he notes, that sensitive observers of children had never discovered Piaget's findings before he published his research:

> Nursery school teachers with years of experience find it impossible to believe that the child thinks the number of objects changes as one spreads them out or clusters them together. For some reason, in an experimental situation where he must deal with the problem in terms of language and engage in conceptual thinking about it, the child reveals weaknesses and defects that are seldom, if ever, manifested in his overt behavior.[20]

A similar point is made by the sociologist Norman Denzin. He finds that the actual behavior of children is more complex, both intellectually and socially, than developmental theories would lead one to assume. He summarizes his findings as follows:

> Children's work involves such serious matters as developing languages for communication; presenting and defending their social selves in difficult situations; defining and processing deviance; and constructing rules of entry and exit into emergent social groups. Children see these as serious concerns, and often make a clear distinction between their play and their work. This fact is best grasped by entering those situations where children are naturally thrown together and forced to take account of one another.[21]

The Ideology of Childhood

The argument is not that the concept of development is wrong and ought to be abandoned; rather, the concept should be used sparingly and critically. Susan Isaacs, a psychologist who studied cognitive development in preschool children, sums up her findings by noting that the overall impression one gets from her records is that the cognitive behavior of little children, even in the very early years, is not very different from that of adults:

> . . . Allowing for the immense difference in knowledge and experience, they go about their business of understanding the world, and what happens to them in it, very much as we do ourselves. . . . If we stress maturation in mental growth too strongly, and treat it too readily as literal, organic fact (of the same order as the facts of embryology), we are likely both to overemphasize the difference between children and ourselves, and to underestimate the part played by experience in their development. . . .[22]

The Recapitulation Hypothesis

Part of the reason for psychology's relative neglect of children in daily life is the emphasis on laboratory methods and the attempt to emulate the experimental sciences. Another reason is the impact of evolutionary theory on developmental psychology. As we noted earlier, modern child study was stimulated by the evolutionary theories of Darwin. The use of biological models of development as lenses for viewing children can be traced to these origins.

One of the most influential concepts to emerge from the new interest in evolution was the recapitulation hypothesis, the notion that the development of the individual repeats the history of the species ("ontogeny recapitulates phylogeny"). The starting point for the recapitulation hypothesis was the development of embryos. Thus it was noted that the human embryo starts out as a single-celled organism, becomes a multicelled organism, then resembles a fish, and so on. Extending this idea, the mental development of the growing child was assumed to repeat the mental development of the human race, reaching its highest point in the adult rational mind of Western man.

G. Stanley Hall's work is the prime example of how Darwin's biological concepts were translated into psychological ones. Hall is widely recognized as the father of child study in America.[23] He divided child development into stages corresponding to prehistoric eras in the development of the human race. Thus infancy, the first four years of life, corresponded to the animal stage of the human species when it was still using four legs. Childhood—ages four to eight—was supposedly a recapitulation of an earlier cultural era of hunting and fishing, and the period of eight to twelve, which Hall called "youth," was a reenactment of the "humdrum life of savagery" before the higher human traits emerged. (Hall's conceptions of childhood seem to have influenced the founding of the Boy Scouts. Scouting was thought to provide a means of satisfying the various prehistoric instincts such as hunting, fishing, and gathering.) Adolescence, in Hall's scheme, represented a turbulent, transitional stage in the history of the race after which the highest levels of civilization were attained:

> The child comes from and harks back to a remoter past; the adolescent is neo-atavistic, and in him the later acquisitions of the race slowly become prepotent. Development is less gradual and more saltatory, suggestive of some ancient period of storm and stress when old moorings were broken and a higher level attained.[24]

Hall's ideas sound rather farfetched to modern ears; indeed, his highly literal version of the recapitulation theory, based on the inheritance of acquired characteristics, is no longer acceptable scientifically. Yet in some basic ways, Hall's views of human development are retained in much current psychological theorizing. The following are some of the assumptions of recapitulation theory that correspond to those of contemporary views of development: (1) psychological development consists of a succession of genetically determined stages that are relatively independent of environmental factors; (2) each stage in the sequence is necessary for the emergence of the next; (3) there are direct parallels between child development and cultural development; at the apex of each developmental sequence stands the Western adult. Thus both the development of the individual and the development of the species follow a unilinear progression from lower, simpler, and more primitive functioning to higher, more complex, more advanced functioning. "Primitive" people now living are the psychological equivalents of both prehistoric man and contemporary Western children.

Almost every major developmental theory today has been shaped by the assumptions of recapitulation doctrine, although this is rarely acknowledged explicitly. McCullers, however, has pointed to important parallels between Hall's ideas and those of five eminent developmental psychologists: Freud, Jung, Werner, Vygotsky, and Piaget. Although most of these men rejected aspects of Hall's thinking and did not consider themselves his intellectual followers, Hall was the senior psychologist of this group of men and had many opportunities to influence them both directly and indirectly. As a group, McCullers observes, these men had a surprising number of things in common: (l) all were evolutionists with some grounding in biology; (2) all found some parallel between racial-cultural development and the development of the individual; (3) all conceived of development as progressing from a primitive to more complex organization through a series of stages or levels, determined by a continuous interplay between what is biologically given and environmental stimulation.[25]

If this analysis of the intellectual origins of developmental theory is correct, then much is explained about current ways of thinking about children as well as human development in general. The metaphor of development, based on embryology, leads one to think of psychological development as an internal process unfolding according to its own laws. It encourages a heavy emphasis on biological maturation in developmental theory, to the neglect of social, cultural, and historical influences. In short, child psychology assumes, as Riegel puts it, that the child grows up in a "sociocultural vacuum."[26]

Individual Growth and Social Context

No developmental psychologist disregards entirely the influence of the environment or claims that development is purely a matter of biological maturation. Both Freudians and Piagetians, for example, stress the interaction between internal change and environment. But to emphasize a point made earlier, the environment in these theories is the mere scene of development; it does not cause development to happen or determine its nature or direction. Like the effects of soil and climate on plants, the effects of environment in the prevailing developmental theories are important but limited; growth can be stunted or stimulated, but the nature of the organism remains the same.

Recently, some psychologists have begun to go beyond this limited view of how individual development interacts with the social and cultural context. Rather than looking at development as a process whose outcome is somehow inherent in the child from the beginning, they are arguing that the growth of the individual is inextricably bound with sociocultural conditions and changes.

> . . . The paradigm traditionally applied in child psychology pretends that individuals grow up in a sociocultural vacuum. Growth of the individual, as depicted by all the tables and curves in articles and textbooks, is likely to be a mere artifact generated by systematic disregard of historical changes in education, communication, welfare, etc.[27]

Failing to recognize the interdependence of individual psychology and the social matrix may invalidate many research results. Thus findings may be valid for one historical era but not for another. Although anthropologists have for some time argued that many psychological concepts may be *ethnocentric* or biased in favor of Western culture, it is only recently that there has begun to be an awareness of what Keniston calls *chronocentrism* — that is, the possibility that findings may be valid for one historical era but not for another. Also, some psychologists have come to realize that individual change has often been confounded with social and cultural change. For example, it was once regarded as well-established fact that a person's I.Q. inevitably declines with aging. This has turned out to be untrue, however; the seeming decline with age was an artifact of the cross-sectional method of comparing people of different ages to each other. There has been a tendency in the twentieth century for succeeding generations or cohorts to score better on I.Q. tests. Thus, at any one point in time, older adults will score lower than younger adults, but not necessarily lower than themselves at earlier ages.

More far-reaching psychological change may be found in the psychiatric literature. Since the beginnings of psychoanalysis around the turn of the century, psycho-therapists have been observing changes in the character structures and symptomatology of the patients who appear for treatment. The pre-World War I patients differed from those of the twenties and thirties; the post-World War II patients differed from those of the sixties and seventies.[28] The most dramatic instance is the disappearance of hysteria as a medical problem.[29] For 2,000 years, since the beginnings of recorded medicine in ancient Egypt, medical writers and practitioners were preoccupied with the "disease." Paradoxically, the understanding of hysteria that emerged in the twentieth century may have led to its disappearance.

Writing of developmental psychology in particular, Keniston describes the problem of chronocentrism:

> . . . Despite recent advances in our understanding of human development, our psychological concepts have generally suffered from an historical parochialism that takes the patterns, timetables, and sequences of development prevalent among middle-class children in contemporary Western societies as the norm of human development.[30]

The Discovery of Adolescence

Nowhere is chronocentrism clearer than in the development of the concept of adolescence. The emergence of this concept illustrates how a set of social and cultural changes that shaped children's lives came to be interpreted as a natural process. The history of adolescence illustrates the relativity of stages of the life cycle, the looseness of the relationship between biological maturation and psychological development, and the interdependence of individual experience and the social and cultural context.

The dramatic physiological changes of puberty are often thought to be the cause of

A bar mitzvah—a traditional Jewish rite of passage. The thirteen-year-old boy still says "Today I am a man," but in contemporary society, he merely becomes a teen-ager.

adolescent psychological characteristics, such as storm and stress emotionality. It is important to distinguish, however, between the physiological changes marking sexual maturation and the changes in behavior and social status that may or may not accompany them. *Puberty* is a universal occurrence, but *adolescence* can be viewed as a social invention of advanced technological societies. For example, Muuss observes that the anthropological evidence concerning the relationship between pubescence and adolescence is complicated:

Individual Growth and Social Context

In some instances, the transition from childhood to adulthood is smooth and without social recognition; in other instances puberty rites bring about a transition not from childhood to adolescence but from childhood to adulthood.[31]

In earlier eras of our own society, puberty was not considered the decisively important transition it was later to become. The historian Joseph Kett argues:

> The onset of male puberty failed to coincide with any fundamentally new life experience; boys at puberty simply were not conspicuous in the way they later became. . . . the twentieth century has argued that no matter where the boy is, what he is doing, or what he has been through, with the onset of puberty he becomes an adolescent. In the 1830's, in contrast, popular definitions of youth took their cue more from social status than from physiology. If a sixteen-year-old boy were in district school, he was called a child, and for the most part treated like one. If in college, he was usually described as a youth. Strictly speaking, the same boy could be a child for part of the year, and a youth for the remainder.[32]

Historical evidence from our own culture permits us to observe adolescence in the process of being "invented." Rousseau is generally credited with introducing the concept into Western culture. Describing adolescence as a second birth, he was the first to list the emotional traits that have come to be the hallmark of adolescence: the frequent outbursts of temper, moodiness, and so on. "A perpetual stirring of the mind makes the child almost ungovernable. He becomes deaf to the voice he used to obey; he is a lion in fever; he distrusts his keeper and refuses to be controlled."[33]

Rousseau wrote in the eighteenth century, but the idea of adolescence did not become part of everyday social reality until the dawn of the twentieth century. G. Stanley Hall is generally credited with popularizing the concept. His monumental two-volume work on adolescence not only made the term a household word, but also stimulated a vast amount of scientific investigation.

Rousseau and Hall, of course, did not invent adolescence. Rather, their work reflected social and cultural changes that were transforming human experience. The years between puberty and the achievement of adulthood were coming to have a significance they did not possess in previous eras.

The emergence of adolescence is related to the decline of the working family as the unit of economic production. In stable agricultural societies, where occupations are passed from father to son, one generation quietly merges into the next. The decline of this tradition opened a gap between the experience of parents and children, and transformed the teen years into a time of occupational choice. The prolongation of education and the removal of childhood from the labor market by means of compulsory education and the child-labor laws also contributed to adolescent experience. The age-graded school created a separate world of children and youth. Without such peer groups, the emergence of the "teen-ager" and youth cultures could not have taken place.

Thus economic, familial, and cultural changes transformed the experience of growing up; adolescence became an important stage of the individual's biography. The opening of a gap between being physically and socially an adult led to the psychological characteristics that have come to be known as the adolescent experience: the urge to be independent from the family, the discovery of the unique and private world of the self, the search for an identity, and the questioning of adult values and assumptions, which may take the form of idealism or cynicism—or both at the same time.

There is still debate among psychologists about the precise nature of adolescence—whether it is strictly a social phenomenon or whether it is based on some neurological, if not hormonal, substrate and thus in some sense culturally universal and "natural." Yet even those who argue for universality recognize the role of environmental stimulation and that the adolescent experience is not inevitable.[34] Indeed, some researchers argue that even in contemporary America, much of the population does not experience adolescence, but goes directly from childhood into adulthood without passing through the stage of emotional turbulence, questioning, search for self, and so on.[35]

On the other hand, some observers have noted that the adolescent experience is taking longer and longer to come to a close, and that the transition to adulthood is becoming harder to discern. Keniston has argued that the same factors that give rise to adolescence are now at work in later decades of life: (1) the extension of education through college and graduate school for masses of the population; (2) rapid social changes making it hard to achieve a settled identity, occupationally or otherwise. As a result of these changes, Keniston argues that a new stage of life, which he calls "youth," has emerged between adolescence and adulthood.[36]

The Discovery of Childhood

If adolescence may be viewed as a socially constructed stage of life, is it possible that childhood—the years between infancy and adolescence—can also have undergone the same process of social construction? In fact, recent historical work on the history of childhood parallels the findings on adolescence. Philippe Aries, the historian who first enunciated this thesis, writes:

In medieval society, the idea of childhood did not exist: this is not to suggest that children were neglected, forsaken, or despised. The idea of childhood is not to be confused with affection for children; it corresponds to awareness of the peculiar nature of childhood, that particular nature which distinguishes the child from the adult, even the young adult. In medieval society, this awareness was lacking. That is why, as soon as the child could live without the constant solicitude of his mother, his nanny, his cradle-rocker, he belonged to adult society. The infant who was too fragile as yet to take part in the lives of adults "did not count."[37]

Aries' work sketches the movement of the infant from a limbo outside society to a central place in the family. But the movement of the middle-aged child was from a place in the adult community to a segregated existence outside the world of adults. Aries argues that the recognition of childhood was brought about by the emergence of specific social institutions, namely the modern school and the bourgeois family, which created distinct roles for children. Children came to be perceived as not yet ready for life; they needed a "sort of quarantine" before joining adults.

. . . The solicitude of family, Church, moralists, and administrators deprived the child of the freedom he had hitherto enjoyed among adults. . . . But this severity was the expression of a very different feeling from the old indifference: an obsessive love which was to dominate society from the eighteenth century on.[38]

Though Aries' assertions may seem startling, his thesis that premodern Europe lacked a clearly distinguished concept of childhood was not entirely unprecedented. Anthropologists have often made the same point for non-Western cultures. They have often voiced objection to the assertions of psychologists concerning universal developmental stages and the incompetence of children.[39]

Margaret Mead's study of adolescence in Samoa was one of the earliest critiques of the notion of adolescence as an inevitable period of emotional crisis.[40] Another supposedly "universal" stage of development that anthropologists have failed to find in other cultures is that of latency—the period from about six to adolescence which Freud has described as free of sexual drives and interests. In many cultures genital sexual behavior is continuous from infancy through adulthood.[41]

In fact, as Ruth Benedict[42] has written, our culture is distinctive because of the sharp discontinuities between the behavior demanded of children and that demanded of adults: children play and are nonresponsible, adults work and take responsibility; children are supposed to be obedient, adults dominant; children are supposed to be sexless, adults are supposed to be sexually active and competent. In few other cultures, Benedict points out, do children have to learn one set of behaviors as children and then unlearn or reverse these patterns when they grow up.

Meyer Fortes makes a similar point. In many traditional African societies, he writes:

the social sphere of adult and child is unitary and undivided. . . . Nothing in the universe of adult behavior is hidden from children or barred to them. They are actively and responsibly part of the social structure, the economic system, the ritual ideological system.[43]

The major contrasts between premodern societies and our own society focus on middle-aged children, those seven to twelve years old. In a worldwide and historical perspective, our culture is decidedly unusual in that children of this age are not involved in productive work. Stephens points out, for example, that in nearly all societies, children go to work by the age of ten, after a period of apprenticeship:

Typically, work begins somewhere between the ages of three and six, the load of duties is gradually increased, and sometimes between the ages of nine and fifteen the child becomes—occupationally speaking—a fully functioning adult.[44]

Aries' description of premodern European practice is similar:

Generally speaking, transmission from one generation to the next was insured by the everyday participation of children in adult life. . . . Everyday life constantly brought together children and adults in trade and craft. . . . The same was true of the army. . . . In short, wherever people worked, and also wherever they amused themselves, even in taverns of ill repute, children were mingled with adults. In this way, they learnt the art of living from everyday contact.[45]

How do we resolve the contradiction between the "small adult" conception of childhood and the early entrance of preindustrial children into adult life, and psychological theories proposing that children are not ready for participation in adult life until they have completed a series of developmental tasks lasting into their twenties? The issue has rarely been raised explicitly, but it is possible to discern three general approaches to an answer.

The first approach might be called *psychological universalism*. Some psychologists assume that development universally runs its course whether or not children wear adult clothes and take part in adult life.

The second interpretation might be called an *arrested-development approach*. It assumes that the sequence of development is the same everywhere, but the different stages may be reached later or not at all under some circum-

Down on the farm, there has always been work for children.

stances. As we noted earlier, most developmental theories look on the "primitive" adult as psychologically comparable to the Western child. Thus a child in such a society would not have as far to go as the child in an advanced society in order to be fully developed.

The basic flaw in the arrested-development model lies in its choice of the endpoint of development or, more precisely, its failure to observe that a choice is being made at all.[46] The researcher who wishes to study development must choose some conception of adult competence as an endpoint toward which the child will develop. Developmental theories take the modern Western educated adult as the norm of development. Observations of the child are then organized around this concept of competence. As one critic argues, such an approach is:

a grandiose, ethnocentric conception that regards the post-Renaissance ways of thinking of Western man, and more particularly the mathematical-physical scientific modes of apprehending and interpreting reality, as the self-evident norm for cognitive development. It elevates one possibility of human nature into the grand design, the secret intent, of biologically given human nature.[47]

An alternative point of view might be called *cognitive pluralism*. Rather than regard the course of development in middle-class Western children as the unfolding of a "basic human potential," which is everywhere the same, or as the internalization of the only valid forms of knowledge, development can be viewed as the emergence of particular sets of adaptive *skills* that are geared to particular social and environmental circumstances.

If nonliterate peoples are not intellectually retarded, we cannot conclude that their failure to recognize childhood as a separate state of life leads to developmental arrest. But it would be wrong to equate premodern Europe with contemporary underdeveloped societies. Economically, politically, and culturally, medieval society was more developed than contemporary preliterate cultures. Furthermore, the bulk of the historical data pertains to the upper social classes of the times—people most advanced in such matters as literacy. Thus the pattern described by Aries and other historians represents an important test case for developmental psychology: the concept of childhood as we know it may not have existed, but the adult forms of competence were similar to our own. The evidence points to the conclusion that, under such conditions, children become competent at earlier ages.

Children in preindustrial Europe not only performed such craft occupations as farming, baking, and shoemaking, they also could be apprentices to lawyers, merchants, pharmacists, administrators, and, of course, the Church. the strongest evidence against equating the absence of childhood with developmental arrest is the evidence of precocity in premodern Europe. Young children not only could enter apprenticeship, but also could enter college at the age of nine or ten and complete their studies at thirteen. Aries notes that up until a certain time, "whether this [precocity] was the result of talent, as in the case of Descartes, or of forcing . . . precocity implied a superiority which opened the way to a great career."[48] Only later did the idea appear that there was something not quite right about doing adult things or older child things before one was "ready."

Developmental Stages Revisited:
The Great Transformation
at Five to Seven

At this point the reader may be wondering whether there is anything left at all of the concept of development. In this section we shall argue that the concept is useful, if used carefully, and will advance the hypothesis that there are two major psychological stages of development—infancy and postinfancy—during which time the child comes into possession of essentially adultlike mental capacities. Developmental theorists may have wrongly designed their staircases of growth by making the upper steps as steep as the bottom ones. The historical studies raise the question of whether it is useful and valid to consider the changes from childhood to adolescence, and from adolescence to adulthood, as fully comparable to the change from infancy to childhood.

The historians, as noted earlier, report a transition in the child's social status between the ages of five and seven. This same age is often the point of assuming adult work responsibilities in primitive societies; it is also the age of first communion in the Catholic Church, and used to be the age of legal responsibility for crime in the common law. Within psychology also, evidence shows that this age represents a major transition, although the assumption usually is that this is the age when the child becomes ready for school, rather than, as in other periods and cultures, ready for participation in adult life.

Thus Baldwin, in his survey of the major theories of child development, concludes that despite their differences, there is a consensus among the theories that there are two main types of psychological functioning. The first is primitive, direct, impulsive, and noncognitive, or primary process; the second is more controlled, thoughtful, and logical, or secondary process. One is essentially childlike, the other adultlike.[49] Baldwin does not specify the age at which the transition from one type of functioning to the other occurs, but there is remarkable consensus on this point also.

At about the time Baldwin was writing, Sheldon White, a psychologist, published a paper on the significance of the five to seven period.[50] White was intrigued that different types of learning experiments revealed a marked change in children's performance between five and seven, so he looked for more evidence of such shifts. He lists twenty-one behavior changes from age five to seven gleaned from his survey of the research literature. Perhaps the most striking single item in this list is the finding that the adult I.Q. can be predicted with a high degree of accuracy at this age. Other changes include the following: children are becoming more abstract and symbolic, less concrete; they are re-

Children playing the violin. Even very young children are more competent than the prevailing images of childhood suggest.

Individual Growth and Social Context

sponding to stimuli less in terms of physical properties and more in terms of the way they are categorized in terms of language; they are learning to string together images of the past and of the future, and so can plan behavior in advance; they are learning to locate themselves in space, and gaining knowledge of left and right and memory of where things are in relation to each other. In practical terms this means that children can get from one place to another and back again without getting lost.

At a more general level, theoretical treatments of child development also describe the five-to-seven period as a major turning point. For Piaget this age represents a transitional period between major epochs of thought. For the Russian developmental theorists Vygotsky and Luria,[51] this is the decisive turning point in behavior. Soviet researchers after Pavlov emphasize language (the second signal system) as the basis for higher human thought. They explain the changes at five to seven as resulting from the internalization of speech; speech becomes the vehicle of thought and the regulator of behavior. For Freud the age of five to seven is a time when infantile sexual impulses are repressed, and parental prohibitions are internalized to form the superego. Finally, for learning theory this is a time when children's responses to stimuli come to be guided by their own mediating responses rather than the stimulus itself.

White concludes:

> Perhaps the 5–7 period is a time when some maturational development, combining perhaps with influences in the . . . environment, inhibits a broad spectrum of first-level function in favor of a new, higher level of function.[52]

In White's model of learning processes we have a picture of human development that is fully compatible with the premodern life style as portrayed by the historians. Both suggest that there is essentially one step up from the childhood to the adult level and that the transition takes place at around five to seven. The conception of two major stages of thought does not imply that there are no important changes before or after this major watershed. Particularly during infancy, important developmental changes occur—for example, the toddler's learning how to talk. But the model does suggest that changes occurring after the age of five to seven are not as momentous and, further, the basis of development changes. Before five to seven, maturation plays a major role in developmental change; after five to seven, learning and culture become major forces influencing psychological development. Since psychologists, as we noted earlier, typically do not study the effects of the enduring environments in which children live, they have overlooked the possibility that schooling may have a profound effect on psychological development. Actually, the fact that virtually all normal children in America and Europe go to school between the ages of five and seven poses a major theoretical challenge to contemporary psychological theory.[53]

School and Society as Developmental Contexts

The institution of schooling in Western societies has had profound effects on conceptions of childhood, as well as on children themselves. It is school, along with the family, that defines the child's place in contemporary Western culture. For us school is the "natural habitat" of childhood, the schoolchild is the child. The concept of childhood, the emergence of the private, emotionally intense family, and the idea of the school as part of the "normal" socialization of the child were different aspects of the historical process of modernization.

The assumptions about childhood and education that we regard almost as part of human nature grew up gradually over the past four hundred years. We assume, for example, that stages of education should correspond to the age of the student. Thus we take it for granted that all the children in a class should be the same age, or close to it. Only in college and graduate school is the connection between level of subject matter and age of the student loosened somewhat. But even here there is an appropriate age for a particular level of work, and a person much younger or older than the standard will be noticeable and perhaps feel out of place.

By contrast, in medieval times and for a while after, school was not associated with age. A person attended school whenever he was ready and it was convenient, regardless of age. A seven-year-old could join a class where most other students were fifteen and over. Or a young man could work at a trade during his childhood and begin school at adolescence, without spoiling his chances for a higher-level career.

Futhermore, within the early school the child enjoyed the same status as outside—a free adult in a world of other adults. In fact, schoolchildren were frequently armed, and schools established regulations for student firearms and swords.

> Old men, young men, adolescents, and children could all be found sitting in the same classroom, learning the same lessons. They turned up for classes, but no one cared about the rest of their lives. Sometimes, as we learn from Thomas Platter's story of his school days in the early sixteenth century, groups of students ranging in age from the early twenties to a mere ten would wander in search of learning from France to Germany and back again. They lived like hippies and wandered like gypsies, begging, stealing, fighting; yet they were always hungry for books. Platter was nineteen

before he could read fluently, but within three years he mastered Latin, Greek, and Hebrew. And in the end he became rector of Basel's most famous school.[54]

Only gradually did the following ideas emerge: that the different ages ought to be separated, that there is an appropriate age at which students ought to do a certain grade level of work, that the subject matter should be divided into grade levels, that students need to be protected from the vicissitudes of adult life and subjected to a special discipline to develop their characters. Authoritarian regimes, corporal punishment, and constant surveillance replaced student autonomy. Aries argues that these changes in education were developed by moralists who should be sharply distinguished from humanists concerned with spreading intellectual ideas and culture.

The new moral ideology stressed by Aries is but one possible explanation for the growth of schooling. Another is that an emerging capitalist society began to need increasing numbers of skilled and trained men for commerce, law, and diplomacy:

> The turning point that gave rise to most of the traits peculiar to our culture is essentially to be found between the eleventh and the twelfth centuries when towns grew in number as well as in size and established their predominance over the countryside. . . .
> As an urban life based in the main on trade and manufacture developed, the division of labor grew and social structures became progressively more complex. The needs for literacy and literate persons became . . . obvious. Growth of an urban society and growth of schools and literacy were closely related phenomena. The areas that experienced higher rates of economic expansion and more revolutionary social change were also the areas in which schools and teachers were relatively more numerous.[55]

Individual Growth and Social Context

Imperialism and conquest also increased the demand for skilled manpower:

> The great empires—the French, the British, the Spanish, and the Dutch—required men with the habit of authority. The proconsuls of empire had to be stamped with the image of gentlemen, aware of obligations as well as privileges. Discipline, best enforced by regular schooling, proved the most efficacious mold.[56]

Nor was it only the gentlemanly arts of diplomacy and law that required education. In the sixteenth century one had to be literate to be a gunner, to navigate a ship on the open sea, to be a printer, or to be a maker of maps, clocks, and precision instruments.[57] Although schooling and literacy spread in response to social need, they soon began to acquire an independent value. To be illiterate came to be a mark of social shame.

Although schools, as we noted earlier, began by mixing people of all ages, they gradually developed into private worlds of children, distinct from adult life. There began to be a culture of childhood, developed in part by adult regulations of children's dress, reading, and deportment, and in part by the children themselves. Kept out of the adult world, children began to develop their own "lore and language."[58] Among the European upper classes of the nineteenth century, children were separated from adults even within the home. Children lived in their own section of the house, with nurses, governesses, and tutors, visiting their parents only for short periods: ". . . the difference between the life of a sixteenth- and a late nineteenth-century child is so vast as to be almost incomprehensible. Three centuries had created a private world for children."[59]

Besides their social effects in creating a separate world of childhood, schools may have profound consequences for the thought processes of the individual. A good deal of evidence shows that many of the psychological changes once thought to represent the unfolding of the innate capacities of the human mind may actually be the result of literacy and the experience of going to school. For example, schooling has dramatic effects on cognitive development in nonindustrial cultures. Tribal children or adults with a few years of schooling think and carry out intellectual tasks more like American schoolchildren than like their own unschooled brothers and sisters.[60]

All societies educate their children, but those without formal schools do so in the course of everyday adult activities, in which, as we've noted earlier, the children take part according to their abilities. In this type of learning—or "informal education,"[61] as the anthropologists call it—children learn by looking and doing rather than by verbal instruction. In school they learn abstract concepts without any immediate functional use. Even the attempts to make school education more real or interesting for children still proceed at high levels of conceptualization and abstraction. Thus the school environment and the demands it makes on the child push cognitive development in a particular direction:

> . . . many modes of thinking—categorizing, inferring, abstracting, grouping and ordering arrays of information—that we asociate with a certain age of child and use as an index of the intelligence or cognitive level of the child may in fact be heavily dependent on Western-type schooling.
>
> . . . It seems likely that without the specific contribution of the Western-type school, . . . the whole direction of the children's cognitive development would be different.[62]

In our own and other advanced industrial societies, school does not introduce new ways of thought that are discontinuous with daily life outside school. Rather, it extends and elaborates ways of thinking that pervade the society at large, particularly in the middle classes. Sociologists agree that modernization is not merely an economic or technological change, but involves profound social and psychological changes also. It changes all aspects of life: physical environment, the types of communities people live in, the way they view the world, the way they organize their daily lives, the emotional quality of family relationships, and on down to the most private aspects of individual psychological experience. Thus children growing up in modern societies face radically different sets of demands from those of children growing up in more traditional societies. These demands, rather than the inherent psychological differences between children and adults, may account for the gulf that seems to separate children and adults in modern societies.

Childhood and Social Reform

Although the history of childhood may not fit the model of uninterrupted progress, changing attitudes toward children were often motivated by genuine concern for children's welfare. The brutal exploitation of children in the mines and mills of nineteenth-century England served as a horrible example to discredit the idea of children working. In 1842 a Commission on the Employment of Young Persons and Children included among its findings a report that children sometimes as young as five were employed as beasts of burden in the mines, harnessed to heavy carts which they had to pull through tunnels that were long, low, dark, and wet:

> The child is obliged to pass on all fours, and the chain passes under what, in that posture, might be called the hind legs; and thus they have to pass through avenues not so good as a common sewer. . . . By the testimony of the people themselves, it appears that the labor is exceedingly severe; that the girdle blisters their sides and causes great pain. ''Sir,'' says an old miner, ''I can only say what the mothers say; it is barbarity, absolute barbarity.'' Robert North says, ''I went into the pit at 7 years of age. When I drew by the girdle and chain, the skin was broken and the blood ran down. . . . If we said anything, they would beat us. . . .''[63]

The reaction against this exploitation made it difficult to see anything but deprivation in the image of a child doing real work. Women, of course, were exploited in the factories along with children. Again the reaction against this led reformers, even a Karl Marx, to protest against women working outside their homes.

In short, the industrial revolution transformed cultural attitudes toward children and work because it changed the nature of work. Before the rise of factories and other large-scale institutions, as we have noted earlier, there was no separation of workplace and residence. Work went on at home, as part of family life. Indeed, in the early years of industrialization in England, whole families went to work together in factories. During this time, some evidence suggests, factory work was experienced by the workers as less oppressive than it was later.[64]

Another reformist trend that helped shape our current ideas about childhood was aimed at changing schools. One of the reasons that teaching very little children how to read and write fell into disrepute was the harshness of the early schools. Fowler writes:

> . . . At all levels of the infant (ages 2–7) and grammar school systems, serious deficiencies prevailed which persisted well into the last half of the nineteenth century. . . . Curricula were narrowly restricted to religious dogma and [the three R's]. . . . Authoritarian discipline, enforced by harsh physical punishment, was the rule. Teaching methods were rigid and tedious, being based on rote learning through incessant drills on isolated elements. The lecture system was used freely, making little concession to age differences. Enormous classes were charac-

teristic. Infant schools typically confined immobile for hours from 50 to 200 and sometimes as many as 1,000 undernourished children, crowded into galleries. They were watched over by the petty, severe, and ignorant eyes of monitors only slightly older than the children. Over such a mass only one or two adult teachers presided, who were poorly trained, if at all.[65]

The kindergarten and nursery-school movement arose as a protest against harsh schools. Such reformers as Pestalozzi and Froebel argued that young children would learn best through their own activities, that they needed sensory-motor experiences rather than rote drills, and sensitive understanding rather than harsh discipline. Although some of the leaders of the nursery-school movement invented ways of combining teaching with play—e.g., in the form of educational toys—the major thrust of the movement was to define early childhood as a time for play and social and emotional development. Thus the school-reform movement tried to liberate children from harsh, repressive, and really antieducational schools, but it also contributed to the definition of the child as a weak,

incompetent, and fundamentally unserious creature. Such institutions as the nursery school and kindergarten widened the gap that separated children from adults.

Thus our present images of the child originated from a complex of trends and conditions. The image of the child as weak and dependent both mentally and physically was constructed by the rise of the bourgeois family, by moralists trying to save the child's soul from original sin, by schoolmasters rationalizing their institutions, and by reformers trying to save the child's body from industrial slavery and the mind from the shackles of rote learning and authoritarian discipline.

All these influences contributed to the image of the child that took shape in developmental psychology. But the theories and images of the child put forth by the professional specialists amplified and specified the differences between adults and children, and between children of different ages. Further, they replaced religious dogma, educational theories, and sentimental notions as the authoritative source of information concerning the child's nature and competence.

The Costs of Childhood

Those who have examined childhood in history and across cultures agree that the roles of children and adults in contemporary Western societies are out of balance. Just as casting the sexes into the roles of strong, breadwinning male and weak, dependent female imposes costs on both men and women, so does a sharp split between child and adult roles take its toll. Economist David Stern observes that adult work roles seldom allow for the imaginative, growing, and feeling parts of human beings. Dependent children, by contrast, are often

given opportunities to play, experiment, and make mistakes, but "they lack power, social standing, and responsibility."[66]

The roles of child and adult, as we have seen in this chapter, have not always been far apart. Aries' description of medieval culture as "lacking a concept of childhood" may be misleading. The period seemed equally lacking in a concept of adulthood; it was a society lacking age consciousness as an important definer of role, behavior, and status. Today one's age is almost as much a part of one's identity as one's name—for example, people are identified by names and ages in newspaper stories. People in earlier times were not unaware of age differences, but age consciousness and age grading were simply not that important.

In this minimally age-graded society, no activities were set aside for children or adults only. Sexual talk and play was not defined as something from which the child had to be protected. Children gambled, drank wine and beer, and carried swords and guns; adults collected dolls, played blind man's bluff, and rolled hoops. Fairy tales provided amusement for all ages, as did frequent communal festivals such as May Day, Twelfth Night, the European counterpart of Halloween, and others. In all these festivities, children and adolescents participated fully, although sometimes the two age groups had special roles. Further, the polarity of work and play was as lacking as age distinctions. In traditional society, work took up less time during the day and did not have the existential value it has in modern society. On the other hand, observes Aries, "games and amusements extended far beyond the furtive moments we allow them: they formed one of the principal means employed by a society to draw its collective bonds closer."[67]

Dependency and Self-Validation

We have heard much in recent years of the costs of children to parents, not only in money, but in freedom and opportunity as well. Very little has been said about the costs to children themselves—and to the adults they will later become—of their prolonged dependency. Although the participation of children in economic life has been the practice in all times and places up until the twentieth century, we persist in regarding the role of the playful, self-indulgent child as the only natural one. One could just as easily argue that industrial society's creation of

In many third-world countries, older sisters share in the care of younger children.

an extreme discontinuity between child and adult roles is "unnatural."

Arguments about naturalness are seldom conclusive; more significantly, there may be profound psychological consequences arising from the modern child's having to spend the first two or even three decades of life in a state of uselessness. As women have been discovering, economic dependency can easily lead to emotional dependency and to doubts about one's worth as a person. Women experience these doubts even though they know they are doing vitally important work in the home.

Children, excluded from the workplace, are in a more extreme psychological position. Children's "chores," such as taking out the garbage, are regarded by no one, least of all children, as productive work. The persistent restlessness of young people at school indicates that school also is not regarded by them as serious, socially useful work.[68] Perhaps most schoolchildren, particularly older ones, realize that one of the major functions of the school is simply to warehouse a portion of the population that is not needed anywhere, but which cannot simply be let loose on the streets. And many of the most dedicated students view their school years as a bureaucratic hurdle they must pass on the way to adult careers, rather than as a time of meaningful work or learning.

By Love Obsessed

Four decades ago, Ruth Benedict[69] pointed out how the discontinuities between child and adult roles create problems for the individual as he or she progresses from one role to the other; adolescent turmoil can be understood as a result of having to perform in ways that were forbidden to children. It is little wonder, she observed, that many people find it hard to "put off childish things" and so remain "fixated" at immature levels of behavior. Thus the removal of children from productive work roles and, more generally, the dichotomy between child and adult roles may be responsible for much psychological maladjustment.

Apart from the problem of having to bridge the gap between the child's role and the adult's, the prolonged economic uselessness of modern children may deprive them of a major source of self-validation, and make them more dependent on the parental affection and the opinions of other people. Children working on the family farm or as apprentices in a trade could, as Jerome Kagan[70] points out, see evidence of their virtue in the results of their work.

The daily life of the peasant's son or daughter, as we saw in Chapter 4, was hardly idyllic. Yet such activities as plowing fields, tending to animals, cutting wood, spinning and weaving cloth, and making soap, candles, butter, and cheese provided clear physical evidence of contributions to the family's welfare.

By contrast, the middle-class child has historically lacked that advantage, while enjoying many others. Unable to point to any physical product of their labor, middle-class children have had to base their sense of worth on their psychological qualities. "As a result," Kagan observes, the middle-class child "may have been more uncertain of his value, more dependent on parental communication assuring him of his worthiness, and more preoccupied with parental attitudes towards him."[71]

Kagan's speculations are in line with what we know about the origins of self-esteem. Traditionally, social psychologists have emphasized the affection and approval of other people as the source of our attitudes toward ourselves—the well-known "looking-glass self." But researchers recently have become aware that love may not be enough to guarantee self-esteem.

The other major source of self-esteem derives from our own activities—from the feeling of having an effect on the physical or social environment. Seeing the products of our labor, solving a problem, influencing someone, having some control over the events in our lives—these experiences produce a sense of competence and mastery. One psychoanalyst has succinctly expressed the difference between the two sources of self-esteem. Both are important, he notes, but the experience of mastery is steadier and more dependable; the opinion of others is always more uncertain:

> Unhappy and insecure is the man who, lacking an inner resource for self-esteem, must depend for this almost wholly upon external sources. It is the condition seen by the psychotherapist almost universally among his patients.[72]

It is also the condition that prevails almost universally among contemporary children and youth.

Thus the great emphasis on the power of parental love in contemporary culture may have arisen as a substitute for the self-validation children used to achieve through productive work. Kagan observes that non-Western cul-tures, and Western society before the seventeenth century, did not recognize parental attitudes as a source of physical or mental illness. By contrast, twentieth-century society believes that a lack of parental love can have disastrous consequences later on. These beliefs can act as self-fulfilling prophecies: parents believe they will harm their children if they fail to love them enough. Children and adolescents learn of scientific and popular theories relating lack of parental love to unhappiness and psychological illness; and adults interpret their emotional problems as delayed reactions to a lack of love during childhood, rather than, say, fate, witchcraft, or evil spirits.

> Our books, magazines, and television dramas all announce the healing and prophylactic power of parental love and the toxicity that follows closely in its absence.
>
> Americans seek out psychiatrists, new love objects, or peers whom they hope will love them and dissolve their anguish. This faith in love is not unlike the faith in the curative power of the potion or the incantations of the shaman.[73]

The Future of Childhood

In view of the profound changes in the social place of children and in theories of childhood that occurred in our culture, it would seem unreasonable to assume that our present conceptions of childhood will remain in force indefinitely. New stages of life have been added to the life cycle. The child's future at birth has changed from one of almost certain death to one of almost unlimited possibility. In the eyes of parents, the growth and development of the child has shifted from being the object of mild concern or indifference to the major emotional focus of the family. If the nature of childhood and of human development have changed in the past, they are capable of changing again. Although it is difficult to predict the next directions of social change, a new view of childhood may be visible on the horizon. And new stages of development may emerge from these changes.

The Child's Changing Place

There is evidence that contemporary social changes are altering the child's place, both inside the family and in society at large. In a variety of ways the norms of conventional age grading appear to be losing their previous decisive influence. Although the adult world is still sharply marked off from the world of the child, there is a certain blurring around the edges. "Adolescence" is spreading at both ends—younger children are absorbing teen-age culture and attitudes, and many people in their twenties are refusing to progress to "adulthood." Some of the indicators of separate status used by Aries, such as dress and amusements, no longer distinguish children and adults as sharply as they once did. Current clothing styles not only are unisex, they are increasingly uniage. Where fairy tales once were shared by all age groups, now television is.

The future of schooling as the child's place and hence definitions of childhood itself are being changed by the current crisis surrounding education. As we noted earlier, schools helped to invent childhood by creating places and roles for children. Educational change now in prospect seems to be in the process of unmaking such places. James Coleman argues that we live in an "information rich" society, in which children at young ages begin to have large amounts of vicarious experience through radio, television, and other media.[74] The present educational system was designed for societies that were "information poor." Children obtained most of what they knew from direct experience, supplemented by reading. The schools were the community's gateway to information.

Television has altered the ratio between direct and vicarious experience for everyone, but especially for children. Long before they enter a schoolroom, young children have acquired an enormous amount of knowledge about the world. In past ages a child entering school would have the adventure of discovering many simple but exciting facts. Coleman cites the example of a man born in 1870 who wrote in his autobiography of his amazement at hearing in school of a train that could go sixty miles an hour.[75] Thus children may have outgrown the schools.

On the other hand, more and more adults want and need to continue their learning over the lifespan. Some have suggested that the schools should be opened to people of all ages, and that children should be integrated into work activities. The distinction between economic and educational institutions would become blurred. Schools might become communities in which children would carry out responsible service activities, but also include time for learning. The White House Conference on Children suggested something like a revival of the apprentice system: workplaces would be modified to include the young in productive work; they would divide their time between learning and actual work.[76] The life cycle would no longer consist of an early period of full-time school and then full-time work later, but a combination of the two activities over many years.

In short, traditional notions that work is "bad" for children and separation from the adult world is good are being reexamined. The exploitation of children in the mines and mills of the last century may have blinded us to the fact that responsible and productive action may reward children and aid in their development. A series of studies by Mary Engel and her associates[77] produced findings that challenged the prevailing assumptions about child work. These researchers found that child work—defined as working part-time for strangers for pay—is much more prevalent among fourth- to eighth-grade boys than is generally believed. (The study did not include girls.) Nor did they find that only boys from the poorest homes worked: child work was most prevalent in the lower-middle and middle-class groups. As for the psychological effects of working, these researchers found that having a part-time job not only was not harmful, but also could actually aid in the development of competence and personality. On the other hand, as we observed earlier, the prolonged uselessness of children today may be demoralizing and even debilitating.

The Construction of Childhood

Although nobody advocates reversing history and returning to the era of childhood exploitation, there is a growing recognition that the roles of self-denying adult and irresponsible child are frustrating for both parties. The challenge for theorists and policy makers is to devise new kinds of settings that could function in an industrial society to integrate children and adults, and at the same time develop the full range of children's abilities.

Summary

The concept of childhood as a separate stage of life, having its own psychology and requiring separate institutions, is an invention of modern times. In premodern societies, including Western society several centuries ago, children did not live in a separate world from adults. In the premodern pattern, children after the age of infancy participated in the economic life of society. The modern concept of childhood seems to be a product of the process of modernization: a complex occupational structure calls for an educated population.

Schools during the medieval era were for anyone who wanted to learn Latin. There was no sequence of courses and no notion that a person could be too young or too old to study a subject. School was a part of the adult world; schoolboys made their own rules and came and went as they pleased. Precocity, particularly among preadolescent children, was common in school as well as in the professions, arts, and trades.

During this period there was little emphasis on love as the essential ingredient in parent-child relationships. Parent-child relationships were weakened by the practice of apprenticeship, with children often residing and working in other homes by the age of seven.

Over several centuries, definitions of childhood, school, and family changed. Childhood came to include adolescence, being defined as the preparatory stage of life for the not fully socialized. Accordingly, schools became instruments of discipline and character training. The home became a place to nurture children and prepare them for later life. Precocity came to be seen as unwholesome. Adults abandoned the toys, games, and stories they shared with children and became more serious. The work ethic replaced the old sociability, and the nuclear family's importance rose.

In recent years, scholars in a number of fields have pointed out that the sharp contrasts between child and adult roles in our culture impose costs as well as benefits on both sides. Children who must spend at least the first two decades as economically unproductive dependents may grow up doubting their own self-worth. Current social trends as well as changes in educational and work policies may, in the not too distant future, reduce the discontinuity between age groups.

Source Notes

1. White House Conference on Children, 1970, p. 252.
2. Bronfenbrenner, in ibid.
3. Bronfenbrenner, 1970.
4. Kempe, 1973.
5. Coveney, 1967.
6. Kessen, 1965, p. 33.
7. Berger et al., 1972, p. 11.
8. B. Whiting, 1963, pp. 356–357.
9. Keniston, 1971a, p. 332.
10. Kessen, 1965, p. 33.
11. See Baldwin, 1967; J. Langer, 1969b.
12. Kessen, 1965, p. 129.
13. Langer, 1969b, pp. 1–11.
14. Ibid., p. 157.
15. Robinson et al., 1973, p. 1.
16. Bronfenbrenner, 1974.
17. Von Bertalanffy, 1960.
18. Herzog and Sudia, 1973, p. 207.
19. White, 1960, pp. 110–111.
20. Baldwin, 1967, p. 584.
21. Denzin, 1971, p. 14.
22. Isaacs, 1966, p. 57.
23. See Grinder, 1969; McCullers, 1969.
24. Hall, 1904, p. xiii.
25. McCullers, 1969, p. 1113.
26. Riegel, 1973, p. 3.
27. Ibid.
28. Hale, 1971; Levenson, 1972.
29. Veith, 1965.
30. Keniston, 1971, p. 329.
31. Muuss, 1962, p. 6.
32. Kett, 1971, pp. 283, 294–295.
33. Rousseau, quoted in Kessen, 1965, p. 93.
34. Kessen, 1965, p. 93.
35. Douvan and Adelson, 1966.
36. Keniston, 1971.
37. Aries, 1962, p. 128.
38. Ibid, p. 413.
39. Benedict, 1938; Goodman, 1970.
40. Mead, 1938.
41. Hardy, 1964; Stephens, 1963.
42. Benedict, 1938.
43. Fortes, 1970, pp. 14, 18–19.
44. Stephens, 1963, p. 386.
45. Aries, 1962, p. 222.
46. Kessen, 1966.
47. Schmidt, 1973, pp. 145–146.
48. Aries, 1962, p. 222.
49. Baldwin, 1967, pp. 591–592.
50. White, 1965.
51. Luria, 1961; Vygotsky, 1962.
52. White, 1965, p. 213.
53. Cole, Gay, and Glick, 1971.
54. Plumb, 1972, p. 84.
55. Cipolla, 1969, pp. 41–45.
56. Plumb, 1972, p. 84.
57. Cipolla, 1969, p. 49.
58. Opie and Opie, 1959.
59. Plumb, 1972, p. 84.
60. Greenfield, in Bruner et al., 1966, pp. 225–256.
61. Scribner and Cole, 1973, p. 553.
62. Schmidt, 1973, pp. 145–146.
63. Cooper, 1842, p. 49.
64. Smelser, 1968.
65. Fowler, 1962, p. 129.
66. Stern, 1975, p. 117.
67. Aries, 1962, p. 73.
68. President's Panel on Youth, 1973.
69. Benedict, 1938.
70. Kagan, 1977.
71. Ibid., p. 43.
72. Silverberg, 1952, p. 26.
73. Kagan, 1977, p. 44.
74. Coleman, 1972, p. 72.
75. Ibid.
76. White House Conference on Children, 1970.
77. Engel, Marsden, and Woodaman, 1967, 1968.

Chapter Twelve
Socialization: Generational Politics

☐ *Conformity to norms is sometimes said to be the end result of a positive or successful socialization. This is much too narrow a conception. The norms of a language are the rules of pronunciation, spelling, semantics, and grammar. Some who have learned these rules very well—children, poets, the Beatles—elect on occasion to violate them. Others who know them well undertake to reform them: to make spelling consistent, or to strip certain works of ambiguity. Similarly, the moral theory an individual forms by working over his moral experience can lead him to reject some part of the conventional morality. He is likely to argue . . . the change he favors will make the total morality more consistent or . . . will more truly realize the basic values of the culture. . . . Saints and revolutionaries and reactionaries all take some such position. It does not seem correct to consider such persons . . . failures of socialization.*

R. W. Brown, *Social Psychology*

In the ideal societies of the utopian writers, the only recurrent threat to changeless peace arises out of human mortality. People die and new people are born. The social structure is conceived as a set of roles that must be filled, like the positions on a baseball or football team. The whole society must be duplicated anew in every generation. Utopian writers from Plato on, therefore, have been preoccupied with the regulation of reproduction, the training of the young, and the assignment of young people to their adult places in society. In the literary utopias these processes are arranged so as to affirm the status quo. The rise of the new generation is conceived to be part of the grand design of the social system.

Ralf Dahrendorf has pointed to striking similarities between sociological theorists and utopian writers. Like the utopians, the functional sociologists conceive of society as a social system in a state of equilibrium; and they also have been preoccupied with the problem of generational replacement. They conceive of socialization in the same terms as the utopians, as a regular, patterned process that maintains the status quo:

> The system is the same, however often we look at it. Children are born and socialized, and allocated until they die; new children are born, and the same happens all over again. What a peaceful, what an idyllic world the system is. . . .[1]

Although marches and demonstrations are no longer routine on the nation's campuses, the rebelliousness of youth in the 1960s still challenges such theories of socialization. If conformity to norms is conceived to be the end result of socialization, there is no way to explain such nonconformity as student protest except as a failure of socialization. A "generation gap" is precisely what should not happen according to theories defining socialization as a direct transmission of the cultural heritage from one generation to another. The youth protests of the last decade have been upsetting to prevailing social-

Antiwar protesters of the 1960s. The sign shows that people can learn the rules of their culture very well and still be nonconformists.

Socialization: Generational Politics

science assumptions. They were, as Keniston[2] observes, like experiments that fail and therefore refute the hypotheses they set out to test. From the point of view of scientific theory, such experiments are often more useful than those that confirm our expectations. When scientific prediction fails, it is necessary to reexamine the assumptions on which they were based. The emergence of youthful dissent in the past decade raises fundamental questions about human nature and society and about the transmission of culture and social structure from one generation to the next.

Were the student protesters of the 1960s psychological misfits? These campus protesters are the most studied rebels in history—not only psychologists but also commissions of distinguished citizens investigated the various student protests and the participants. There is remark-able agreement in findings of a variety of different researchers as to the characteristics of the student protesters. Activists typically have come from the ranks of the better and more serious students.[3]

It could not be said that the majority of activist students were rejecting the values of their parents and the nation. Rather, as the Cox report and other investigations concluded, they took very seriously the ideals taught in schools and churches; their protests were directed at what they saw as society's deviation from its professed ideals, particularly racial injustice and the war in Vietnam. Thus the traditional explanation for deviance—that there will always be a certain number of misfits who, through faulty child rearing or some inherent defect, will fail to absorb the values of their society—did not apply.

Generational Conflict and Continuity

There was, and is, a good deal of confusion about the meaning of the "generation gap," among the experts as well as the public. For most people the notion of a generation gap refers to parent-child conflict. Thus a spate of theories defined student protesters as being in rebellion against their own parents and taking it out on school authorities and society in general.

Some writers argued that the generation gap was a myth because lots of parents got along fairly well with their children. Then it turned out that student protesters often agreed with their parents on values although they had experienced conflicts about *actions* at the same time. It was the hippies, it seemed, not political activists, who were more extreme in rejecting the *actions* and *values* of their parents.[4] Other writers argued that young people could not be neatly separated into political activists or hippies. Margaret Mead entered the debate by declaring that the generation gap doesn't have anything to do with parents and children at all: "The generation gap is between all the people born and brought up after World War II and the people who were born before it. It's not at all about children and getting on with parents."[5]

In contrast to Margaret Mead's view of the generation gap as something that "happened only once," other observers noted that rebellion has long been recognized as an inevitable part of growing up—a "stage," like the temper tantrums of the two-year-old. Piaget, for example, has noted that the newly maturing intellectual powers of adolescents make them aware of the general moral rules of the society and enable them to be shocked by the failure of adults to live up to them. Adolescents are idealistic because their limited experience has not yet taught them how hard it is to put ideals into practice.[6] As they "mature" further, they will settle down, give up youthful ideals, and become members of adult society. S. M. Lipset has pointed out that almost every country has a version of the saying: "He who is not a radical at twenty does not have a heart; he who is still one at forty does not have a head."[7]

A Multiplicity of Gaps

The profusion of contradictory explanations of "the generation gap" suggests that social-science experts were overtaken by events and caught with their theories in disarray. Many social scientists are aware that the prevailing models of socialization don't fit with the complex realities of generational relations in contemporary society, but have not been able to abandon them. Norma Haan has attributed the predicament of developmental psychologists and sociologists in dealing with the generation gap to the persistent notion that the mind of a young person is simply a blank slate:

> Parental power and social countervention are still the foci of much research, as if empty-headed children are automatically stamped with effects or simply duplicate their elders. This supposition continues to determine the research design, and in the realm of common sense, leads the older generation to expect that there *should* be a generational replacement, but to their subsequent chronic dismay, there isn't.[8]

On the other hand, the theories of rebellion as an inevitable stage tell us nothing about the rise and fall of youthful protest in particular historical periods; they do not tell us why the college generations of the fifties were the silent generation, why campuses erupted all over the United States and in many parts of the world during the late sixties, and why they became quiet in the early seventies. Nor do they explain why large numbers of the not-so-young have not settled down on reaching thirty or even

forty. Margaret Mead is correct in pointing to the social changes going on in society as a whole as a source of the generation gap, but she seems to underestimate the complications these changes introduce into parent-child relations. The realities that impinge on families may result from conditions having nothing to do with families, but they affect families in profound ways. If the balanced, homogeneous social system is not a tenable model of society, the idea of socialization as smooth replacement is no longer tenable either. "Socialization" then becomes problematic: what is the child being socialized to fit into?

> . . . If every society contains within it important internal conflicts, then growing children are exposed not to a stable, self-consistent set of social expectations and cultural values, but to social and cultural contradictions. . . . Furthermore, in times of rapid historical change, the societal conflicts to which one generation is exposed will differ from those of the previous generation; partly for this reason, individuals of different historical generations will typically differ from each other in basic personality.[9]

In short, if we give up the notion that socialization involves the smooth replacement of one generation by the next, we are driven to the conclusion that some sort of generation gap is inevitable. Yet we must also explain why it appears more acute at some periods rather than others. In fact, there seem to be several kinds of generational cleavage, not just one.

Generational Conflict

To most people the term "generation gap" implies conflict between parents and children. Actually, there can be generational conflict without a generation gap, and a generation gap without conflict. Maybe it is because the assumption of generational continuity is so ingrained that little attention has been paid to the variety of ways generational cleavage can come about.

Let us look at generational conflict first. In its purest form generational conflict does not involve a challenge to the social order; it is simply a power struggle between parents and children. The son, for example, may want to take over the father's position, as in a peasant family where the son remains a "boy" until he has taken over the family farm. In general, it seems that tension and hostility follow patterns of inheritance. Thus LeVine notes that in societies with patrilineal inheritance and descent there are antagonisms between father and son; in matrilineal societies, where the son inherits from his mother's brother, tensions occur between uncle and nephew.[10] Some societies overtly recognize intergenerational antagonism. Among the Tallensi of northern Ghana, for example, sons eventually do take the places of fathers in the life of the community, and are suspected of wanting to hasten the day when this will happen:

> . . . Tallensi themselves make no bones about the matter. ''Your oldest son is your rival,'' . . . the men say bluntly. . . . This candor in fathers is not matched by their sons, who never admit the rivalry. . . .
>
> Tallensi explain the rivalry between father and son by means of the mystical concept of the Yin or personal destiny. There is, they say, an inborn antagonism between the Yin of a father and the Yin of his oldest son. . . . The son's Yin wants to destroy the father's Yin; but the father's Yin wants the father to live and be well and remain master of the house. . . . Therefore it will try to destroy the son's Yin, and if it is the stronger Yin it will cause misfortune and perhaps death to the son.[11]

Freudian writers have emphasized the sexual aspects of conflicts between parents and children, particularly fathers and sons. Although sexual feelings enter into such struggles, an overemphasis on the Oedipal feeling—the sexual rivalry with the parent of the same sex—has obscured the situational realities of power as a source of generational conflict. Thus we have the Freudian explanation of revolutionary activism as a disguised attack on father.

In 1940 Kingsley Davis[12] published a still relevant article in which he outlines the sociological reasons why conflict between parents and children is inevitable, and why for most societies in history there has been relatively little awareness of the generation gap. Davis argues that the ingredients for generation conflict exist in any society. In traditional societies, however, these inescapable conflicts between parents and children are counteracted in various ways. Part of the potential for conflict arises out of biological and psychological differences between organisms of differing ages, part from the power relations of child and parents. Davis also sees social complexity and social change as sources of parent-child conflict, but these are best considered separately from the more universal power and organismic differences.

Davis notes that parental power is sociologically one of the most extreme forms of authority. Unlike the authority of boss over worker, for example, parental power is unlimited, personal, and inescapable. In traditional societies, however, the power conflicts inherent in parent-child relations are mitigated in several ways. The authority of the parent is supported by the rest of the kinship group and the community in general. There are no competing authorities, such as schools, the mass media, or peer groups. Another reason for the relative lack of challenge to the older generation in traditional societies is the sense of the unbroken continuity of life—the sureness of all concerned that the lives of the children will duplicate the lives of the parents and grandparents.

Another source of parent-child conflict lies in the contrast between ideals and reality. Parents tend to offer their children idealized versions of the culture during the course of socialization. In daily interaction as well as in more formal teaching situations, the child learns such ideals as: be sincere, don't lie, don't steal, treat other people as you want to be treated yourself, be kind and generous, love your relatives. Since no society ever observed has lived up to its ideal norms, sooner or later the child discovers that the adults don't practice what they've been preaching.

This credibility gap can become a source of conflict between seemingly hypocritical elders and their children. In traditional, slowly changing societies there is what Keniston has called the "institutionalization of hypocrisy."[13] Violations of the rules are built into the rules. Children are taught that for certain situations and people, the rules don't apply. Or they are told that what appears to be an inconsistency isn't really that after all. Thus the ideal of honesty may be ignored in business dealings, the ideal of kindness may not be extended to foreigners or war-time enemies. In times of rapid social change, however, the institutionalization of hypocrisy may break down. New rules and ideas come into being, and there is a lag in the development of rules to justify hypocrisy. For example, modern parents trying to follow the latest expert advice on child rearing may have no rationalization to fall back on when they fail to live up to the new principles. Instead of being able to explain confidently why they departed from the rule, the parents may feel guilty and anxious. In such a situation, the children are likely to "see the emperor's nakedness with unusual clarity."[14]

Experience Gaps

Social change increases the likelihood that the potentials for conflict inherent in parent-child relations will emerge in consciousness and behavior. But social change need not lead to conflict; it does, however, add an experience gap

to the other, more universal gaps. Margaret Mead has described the sense of timelessness that traditional cultures depend on for continuity:

> It depends upon the adults being able to see parents who reared them, as they rear their children, in the way they themselves were reared. . . . The answers to the questions: *Who am I? What is the nature of my life as a member of my culture? How do I speak and move, eat and sleep, make love, make a living, become a parent, meet my death?* are experienced as predetermined.[15]

Social change breaks up this smooth continuity of generations, no matter how it comes about— whether by immigration, revolution, catastrophe, conquest, new technology, or anything that invalidates the experience of the older generation as a model for the young. The parent can no longer use his or her own youth or present reality as a model for the child. The classic example of discontinuity occurs in the immigrant family. The children can easily grow into natives, but the parents forever bear traces of the old country—in their speech, manners, and standards of propriety.

It is remarkable how long the social sciences have viewed growing up as a process of psychological and physical changes in individuals, set against a background of social stability. There is a superficial awareness that we live in a changing world; we are used to a steady stream of innovations in fashion, popular music, intellectual trends, and so forth. But we lack an appreciation of how profoundly social change affects us, and how greatly it differentiates American society from more static ones.

> The assumption is . . . that the normal course of a human life would be cast under conditions where all the ancestors had lived for several generations in the same place; where social changes are registered in the living

Like father, like son —but children can also choose not to model themselves on their parents.

habits of two generations was slow enough to be easily assimilable by adults, and where young people would in turn grow up to marry others of almost exactly the same background.[16]

Margaret Mead and other observers have suggested that today's parents and children are in something of the same position as immigrants. People born before World War II, she writes, are immigrants in time. It is more difficult to adapt to new circumstances when you have to unlearn previous knowledge and attitudes. For example, the parents of today's college students grew up believing that technology and economic growth could produce limitless abundance and solve all problems. They were taught that new products must inevitably be better than older or less-processed ones. Disposable products were the wave of the future; when people thought about the year 2000 during the forties and fifties, they thought in terms of plastic or paper clothing and furniture, and electrically controlled weather. Energy seemed to be an unlimited resource that could be called upon to do an ever-increasing variety of jobs. For many people who grew up with these attitudes, the new concerns over environmental pollution, ecology, the problems of waste, and the idea that unlimited growth and meddling with nature can lead to catastrophe are hard to grasp emotionally, even when they can be accepted intellectually.

The Persistence of Generational Continuity

Why has the idea of generational continuity been so persistent in the social sciences? Daily reality, as well as literary tradition, suggests that conflict and discontinuity between the generations are far more common than most theories suggest. Part of the answer probably arises from the fact that much socialization research has been guided, as Danziger[17] points out, by social-policy needs of the moment rather than by purely scientific considerations. Thus socialization researchers have focused on the mentally ill, criminals, juvenile delinquents, and the poor.

During World War II and the Cold War, researchers looked into the child-rearing practices of America's adversaries—the Germans, the Japanese, and then the Russians—to find the origins of their belligerent attitudes toward us. Thus war, revolution, and all kinds of deviance seemed to arise from faulty socialization of one kind or another. The field of socialization came to be dominated by a "social engineering" approach that looked for reliable techniques of child rearing, therapy, and correction that would produce well-adjusted individuals who would fit smoothly in society's roles. In short, socialization came to connote something that the powerful do to the powerless in the interests of social order.

The Psychology of Socialization

Psychological theories of socialization have absorbed, sometimes inadvertently, sociological and anthropological emphases on the continuity of generations and the social-control features of socialization. Psychological theories are also based on assumptions of social stability. The child presumably grows up to mirror the parents, doing so through two models of socialization—"social molding" and "impulse taming."

The first model emphasizes the plasticity of human nature and stresses the seeming inevitability that infants in any culture, starting out very much like each other, will end up as little replicas of adults of their cultures—talking like them, doing things like them, thinking like them. Stimulus-response or conditioning psychology is one version of a social-molding theory. The rules and prohibitions of the culture become the rewards and punishments the parents use to shape the child's behavior.

The other view emphasizes the control of impulse. The child is not so much a bit of clay, waiting to be shaped, as a willful, aggressive, dirty little animal who must be tamed. Freudian theory provides the most emphatic expression of a basic conflict between biological drives and the demands of organized social life. The key to successful socialization in the Freudian conception is the child's identification with the parent of the same sex as the resolution of the Oedipus complex. Thus the child acquires the roles, values, and morality of the culture as these are embodied in the parent.

In both of these conceptions, socialization is defined as the inculcation of conformity. Although they differ in their estimates of the forces opposing socialization, in both approaches the terms are set by the society and by the family acting as society's agent. One presents an image of human nature easily adapted to any social order, and whose strongest motive is conformity; the other portrays children in the image of the cruel but clever savages of Golding's *Lord of the Flies*. There is no room in either model for legitimate autonomy, dissent, or conflict, no way to conceive of the forces opposed to socialization in any positive way.

Both the social-molding model and the impulse-taming model have to define any behavior that deviates from the norms as representing some defect in childhood experience.

Rethinking Socialization

In sum, then, socialization theorists have been faced with the dilemma of choosing between an oversocialized view of human nature on the one hand, or an antisocial view on the other. This impasse is revealed in a striking way in Dennis Wrong's[18] widely quoted critique of sociological conceptions of socialization. Wrong attacks the (then) prevailing ideas about the nature of society and human motivation. The overintegrated view of society, he writes, is the counterpart of an oversocialized view of human nature. Thus, if one defines society as stable, consensual, and harmonious, one must go on to assume a psychology in which the need to conform is the most important human motive. Wrong argues that socialization theorists have overlooked the "forces in man that are resistant to socialization."

In trying to identify these forces, Wrong can only point to the Freudian id, powerful drives that resist the restraints that civilization places on them. At the time he was writing, there was no other image of human nature that seemed strong enough to compete with the oversocialized models. Further, the turbulence of the 1960s had not yet broken the silence of the previous decade. The years of dissent and protest were to make many observers dissatisfied, as Wrong had been, with the oversocialized, overintegrated view of society and human nature. But the idea of bodily instincts as the major force opposing social equilibrium also seemed inappropriate as an explanation of social turbulence. Although some writers tried to explain ghetto revolts and student protest in such terms, others felt that psychology simply

had nothing to contribute to an understanding of historical realities. But there was, in fact, a new psychological perspective emerging from research and theory, one that was not committed, as the older psychologies had been, to assumptions of social stability and generational continuity.

During the 1960s and into the 1970s, the field of psychology as a whole, and child development in particular, has quietly been passing through a conceptual revolution that has received little attention outside the discipline. There has been a return to basic psychological questions that have been ignored for half a century—the nature of human thought, language, perception, memory, and imagination. From the 1920s to the 1960s, American psychology had been dominated by ideas derived from behaviorism and psychoanalysis. Freud taught that unconscious sexual and aggressive impulses were the source of human behavior, and that conscious, rational thought was the least powerful and important part of the mind. Watson, Skinner, and other behaviorists argued that people are almost infinitely malleable by the environmental forces of reward and punishment; mental processes were only an illusion.

These psychological models are still alive and well; and both provide valid, if partial, insights into human nature. By the early 1960s, however, the claims of behaviorism and psychoanalysis were shaken by findings in a number of related areas of research—children's play, animal curiosity and exploration, and most important of all, the study of human language. These new findings made it necessary to redefine human beings as active seekers, processers, and users of information, rather than as the passive victims of inner drives or environmental forces.

Another major reason for the new interest in thought and language was the emergence of the computer. Psychologists have always liked to compare the mind to a machine. Before the computer, however, such mechanical models had been very simple ones; the behaviorists had likened the mind to a telephone switchboard hooking up stimuli and responses. Freud had based his model of the mind on nineteenth-century physics. The computer, by mimicking such mental activities as taking in information, storing information in memory, solving problems, manipulating symbols, recognizing patterns, and so forth, provided evidence that such mental acts were real and could be studied. The computer provided metaphors of the mind rich and varied enough "to encompass our wildest psychological speculations."[19]

The insights of the new cognitive psychology suggest a new view of socialization. Instead of defining socialization as the growth of conformity, or as a struggle between the forces of "instinct" and the forces of "civilization," the new vision emphasizes the autonomy and activity of the child in his or her own socialization. Further, the new vision sees both conformity and nonconformity as arising out of the same psychological processes. The nature of human thought and language suggests there may be inherent limits to the prediction and control of behavior.

The Experiencing Child

The traditional views of socialization have tended to assume that what the child experiences can be directly inferred from parental behavior or environmental events. Recently there has been a growing realization that socialization cannot be described without taking into account the point of view of the central character in the drama—the child. The parents' power is limited by the ability of children to interpret their experiences in their own ways.

The most basic generation gap, then, is the gap between the selfhood of the growing child and the attempts of other people to control and define him or her. Yet the prevailing theories of socialization have tended to ignore a conscious "I." They have, as Erik Erikson puts it, deleted "the core of human self-awareness."[20]

Many psychologists, under the influence of Freud's teachings, believed that the decisive events in a person's life occurred in the first few years of life and centered around nursing, weaning, and toilet training. A huge number of studies were carried out to show that different patterns of infant care, such as breast or bottle feeding, gradual or abrupt weaning, or strict versus relaxed toilet training led to differences in adult personality. The results of these studies have been disappointing. It is by now generally conceded that specific practices, in and of themselves, have no demonstrable effects on adult personality.[21]

H. R. Schaffer observes that these studies were based on the assumption that a particular practice must have the same effects on different children:

> The nature of the experiencing child, that is, is left out of consideration. . . . It is probably this factor more than any other which accounted for the failure of the above line of investigations and which has now convinced developmental psychologists of the need to pay attention to the experiencing infant. . . ."[22]

It is significant that Schaffer, an experimental child psychologist, is writing of the first year of life. Even working with infants at this very young age, Schaffer finds he cannot make meaningful statements about the child's behavior without taking into account the child's thoughts, feelings, and representations of reality. Even newborns show selective attention. They like to look at certain patterns more than others. Furthermore, the child is now coming to

Psychologists used to think that what happened during toilet training determined personality for life.

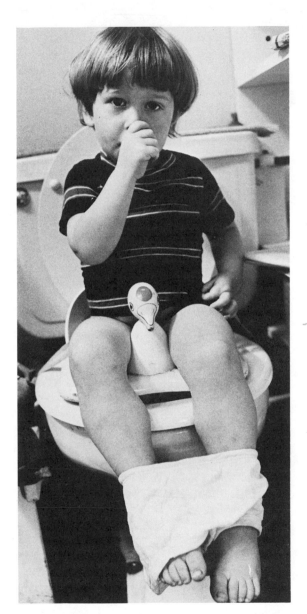

be seen as a socializer of the parents. With the cry and the smile, the infant commands two powerful means of controlling the caretakers. Harriet Rheingold[23] has described how the infant makes "fathers and mothers" out of "men and women." Even very young infants have the power to reward and punish the parents and to let them know the things that please and displease them. Through fretting sounds of impatience and facial expressions, the infant lets the caretakers know what to continue doing and what to stop.

The Tasks of Childhood Defining socialization as weaning, toilet training, and the control of aggression and sexuality stresses just those aspects of growing up in which the child is "wrong," the adult is "right," and conformity is the only outcome. Such an emphasis on what the child must suppress in the course of growing up overlooks the staggering amount of learning the child has to do, starting from birth. Piaget's studies[24] of the first two years of life show that the everyday world we live in—the world of things and people, time and space, and cause and effect—is not built into the child's perception but has to be constructed. The child cannot tell the difference between the self and the world beyond the skin. The child cannot distinguish the mother from other people or tell the difference between people and inanimate objects. Piaget has documented the many milestones of learning the child has to pass to acquire such a fundamental concept as that of "object permanence": the realization that an object or a person still exists even when one is not looking at it. Yet, by the end of the first year, the child has accomplished all this:

> The child (as Konrad Lorenz once put it) has now joined the human race. He has learned to distinguish familiar people from strangers, he has developed a repertoire of signaling abilities

The Psychology of Socialization

which he can use discriminatively in relation to particular situations and individuals, and he is about to acquire such social skills as language and imitation.[25]

Most of this early learning occurs without direct teaching. During the first year and a half, the child learns about causation, objects, space, and time through an active exchange with the environment. Thus Piaget's theories, as well as observational studies of young children, simply do not support the notion that basic knowledge is acquired only socially, from parents or other people.

Language Learning to speak is the child's next large task, one with very great consequences. What sets human beings off from animals is their capacity to translate experience into symbols. Language does two things: it makes society and culture possible, and it increases awareness of self. Thus, paradoxically, language both *socializes* and *individualizes*.

Recent discoveries in linguistics have made clear that children, in learning to speak their native language, face an enormously complex task. It used to be thought that children learned to speak through a process of trial and error, imitation of and correction by the parents. Bit by bit, according to the same principles that animals learned to perform tricks, the theory went, the child built knowledge of language. The stimulus-response explanation of language learning is not supported by observations of young children. It fails completely to account for the fundamental fact about language: its creativity, the fact that the speaker of a language can understand and produce sentences never heard before. A child learns not words and particular sentences, but a system of rules. Out of the welter of speech sounds, the child constructs the basic principles of grammar.

The new awareness of the complexities of early socialization have, as noted earlier, transformed the image of the young child from that of a seething cauldron of lust, or a passive lump of clay, to that of a tireless explorer. The single most characteristic thing about human beings is the will to learn, writes Bruner.[26] Similarly, White[27] presents evidence for a competence motive, an intrinsic need to deal with the environment. The new views of the child echo the spirit expressed sometime earlier by the Soviet children's poet, Kornei Chukovsky, who described every two-year-old child as a "linguistic genius":

> It is frightening to think what an enormous number of grammatical forms are poured over the poor head of the young child. And he, as if it were nothing at all, adjusts to all this chaos, constantly sorting out into rubrics the disorderly elements of the words he hears, without noticing, as he does this, his gigantic effort. If an adult had to master so many grammatical rules within so short a time, his head would surely burst. . . .[28]

Jerome Bruner has pointed out that when children acquire language, they learn not only to represent the world but to transform it. Transformation of reality is built into the grammar of every language.

> . . . The transformational rules of grammar provide a . . . means of reworking the "realities" one has encountered. Not only, if you will, did the dog bite the man, but the man was bitten by the dog, and perhaps the man was not bitten by the dog, or was the man not bitten by the dog? The range of reworking that is made possible even by the three transformations of the passive, the negative, and the query is very striking indeed.[29]

Bruner does not exhaust the possibilities: after all, there is still "the man bites the dog" as another alternative. Indeed, very young children like to play with language in order to "violate the established order of things," as Chukovsky puts it, as in nursery rhymes, nonsense verse, and so forth. Thus the oversocialized view of human nature overlooks more than bodily impulse as a source of nonconformity. It ignores the possibility of using the cultural rules and tools in nonconforming ways.

The Limits of Behavior Control

The new cognitive psychology has important implications for the possibility of predicting and controlling behavior, as well as for socialization. Many people believe, either hopefully or fearfully, that psychologists possess powerful techniques of behavioral control that could change the world if only they were fully unleashed. B. F. Skinner is a well-known proponent of this point of view, which is shared by many other behavior modifiers.

Other people feel that such psychological techniques pose a threat to human freedom. Both the hopes and the fears may be undeserved. As one cognitive psychologist sums up the argument: "The facts of human cognition imply that the psychological manipulation of behavior is bound to fail; it cannot lead to systematically predictable outcomes under ordinary cultural conditions.[30] This is not to deny that much human behavior is predictable. Society could hardly exist if everyone's behavior was random. Nor do the facts of human cognition imply that people's behavior cannot be manipulated in tightly controlled laboratory experiments, or in coercive and closed environments such as prisons, mental hospitals, prisoner-of-war camps, and the like. There is little evidence, however, that the control techniques used in these settings, such as behavior modification or brainwashing, have predictable or lasting outcomes once the individuals are released.

The question is not whether people can be coerced into behaving in particular ways; people with guns and not much knowledge of psychology can be very successful at manipu-

lating others. Theorists of socialization have always recognized that it's not enough to induce the proper *behavior* in children, but to win their hearts and minds; they are supposed to believe in or, to use the jargon term, to *internalize* the values and attitudes of their society.

The traditional views of socialization, however, have tended to overestimate the amount of internalization that actually takes place in society. They have done so in two ways: by underestimating the role of coercion in inducing compliant behavior, and by assuming that conforming, nonrebellious behavior has to imply an inward acceptance of the values and rules of the society.

On the first point, William Goode[31] has noted that most social theories have tended to underestimate the role of force and violence in maintaining social arrangements. They have assumed that because force is not visible, it is not there. But Goode points out that the threat of force keeps people in line and creates "a relatively stable, unchallenged set of understandings, behaviors, and imbalances of influence or dominance."[32] Thus many would-be rebellious wives or children do not actually commit deviant acts because they know that the father or husband is stronger, has more economic resources, and can call on outsiders who will support his force with additional force. The community will back up traditional family patterns, particularly dominance of adults over children.

But behavioral compliance does not necessarily lead to internal change. Psychologist Gerald Davison,[33] in a discussion of the limits of behavior modification, points to a "Kol Nidre" effect. During the Spanish Inquisition of the fourteenth century, all Jews had to convert to Catholicism or else be executed or banished. Most Jews complied, and many became well known as devout Catholics. Despite their seeming change, however, most did not really convert. Each year, on the eve of the Jewish day of atonement, small groups of "Catholics" met secretly to sing a prayer called "Kol Nidre" and to inform God that, despite their outward behavior the rest of the year, they had not given up their original faith.

Davison argues that much behavioral modification that goes on in institutions is probably the Kol Nidre effect, rather than change of hearts and minds. He also points out some facts well known to behavior modifiers themselves, but not to the general public. Most people tend to think of behavior modification as a powerful technique that can be applied against a person's will—as, for example, subjecting homosexuals to electric shocks or other "aversive conditioning" in conjunction with homosexual images. In fact, nearly everything that behavior modifiers do requires the active cooperation of the subject. Conversely, the subject can sabotage the procedures. For example, the homosexual who gets electric shocks when shown homosexual images can imagine heterosexual scenes while undergoing the unpleasant stimulation,[34] and thus reverse the effects intended by the conditioner.

In short, human cognitive processes, such as deciding what to pay attention to and thinking of images and ideas, impose limits on the manipulation of behavior, including that of children.

Indeterminacy and Unanticipated Consequences in Socialization

Thus, despite its dependency, the infant comes into the world with a certain degree of distance and autonomy from other people and the environment. For if the child selectively interprets situations and events, we cannot confidently predict behavior from knowledge of the situation alone. The search for direct and simple cause-and-effect relationships between what the parent does and what the child does is bound to fail.

Parents who turn to "the experts" for advice on how to rear their children are often surprised to learn that the expert may not have very specific advice to offer. If he or she does offer a specific technique, chances are another expert will disagree with the first one. "Children need firmness," says one. "Children need understanding above all," says another. "The worst thing a parent can do is vacillate and be inconsistent," says another.

Jane Loevinger[35] suggests that one of the reasons for such disagreement is that none of the theories work. She provides an amusing and insightful account of how "the experiencing child" introduces indeterminacy into the child-rearing process. There is no guarantee, she writes, that when a parent tries to get a disciplinary message across to the child, the child will interpret that message in the way the parent intends. She offers the following illustrative situation: a mother has come upon her five-year-old son hitting his two-year-old sister. She wants to teach him that this is wrong. How will she do it?

Some mothers believe in strong discipline. They feel that unless children feel pain for wrong behavior, they will tend to repeat it the next time the impulse arises. Such a mother may spank an offending child. Another mother may feel that a child has to be made to understand why it is wrong to hit a little sister, so she will explain the error of the child's ways. This mother would be following an insight theory of learning, in contrast to the first mother who is following a reinforcement or punishment-and-reward theory. A third kind of mother might believe that the strongest influence on the child is the example or model provided by the parent's own behavior. Such a mother would hesitate to use physical punishment for fear the child would learn that it is all right for a bigger person to be mean to a smaller one.

Thus the inescapable parental dilemma: there is no way for any of the mothers to make sure the child will learn what she tries to teach. This, Loevinger claims, is the fallacy common to all parental-teaching theories. The mother can decide to spank or not, but she cannot control how the child will interpret her action. Thus the child whose mother spanks for reinforcement may learn according to identification theory that it is all right for a big person to hit a little person if you really feel strongly about something and if nobody bigger is around to get you for it.

The children of the insight- and identification-teaching mothers may learn, according to the reinforcement theory their mothers disavow, that nothing much will happen if you do beat up your little sister. The parent teaches by one theory; there is no guarantee the child will not learn by another.

Thus researchers as well as parents have been frustrated in the search for clear or simple cause-and-effect relationships between the things parents do or don't do and the way children turn out. There are no cookbook recipes for producing a particular kind of child. Although it was widely believed a few years ago that the crucial determining events of a person's life were those that occurred early in infancy, in the ways that the parents handled the infant's oral, anal, and genital impulses, there is little evidence that specific practices such as breast or bottle feeding or early or late weaning or toilet training have any profound influence on later development. The same may be said about different disciplinary practices, such as strictness or permissiveness. Whatever specific techniques the parent may use are influenced by the emotional context—most importantly, whether the parent is relatively warm and loving, or cold and hostile, or ambivalent.

The research literature even documents the idea that certain parental actions may produce quite opposite effects. Wesley Becker,[36] in a review article on the effect of parental discipline, cites studies showing that in boys strict discipline on the part of parents may result either in sons who are extremely nonaggressive or extremely aggressive. Becker also points out that all the different approaches to discipline entail certain costs or risks, even if they do result in the very kind of behavior the parent is aiming at. Strictness may foster well-controlled, obedient behavior, but it may also result in children being fearful, dependent, and submissive; further, it may dull their intellectual striving and inhibit their ability to deal with aggression in themselves and others. On the other hand, permissiveness may result in children who are outgoing, sociable, assertive, and intellectually striving, but it may also lead to less persistence and more aggressiveness.

Pearlin[37] has discovered another paradoxical outcome of parental pressure in a different set of circumstances. He found that working-class parents who want their children to reach a level of occupation much higher than their own often urge their children to work hard to succeed in school. The children, however, are likely to respond to these pressures not by working hard but by cheating.

Another instance of socialization pressures leading to paradoxical effects is found in Jessie Pitts's[38] description of French family life. The upper-middle-class French child is not supposed to make friends with other children. The extended family is a "total society," and no one is supposed to have any relationships outside it. The child is supposed to find friendship among cousins or among children of adult "friends of the family," who have a family-like status. Nevertheless, the child eventually goes to school and participates with peer groups. This is where the paradox comes in. Because the family does not recognize sociability among unrelated children, whenever peer groups do arise they possess a delinquent, antiadult quality.

By contrast, most American parents, who want their children to be popular and to participate in group activities such as sports, often encourage and manage their children's social lives. Parents may even take over and run peer-group activities, such as Little League baseball. But among comparably situated French families, the peer group has no legitimate or constructive meaning. Hence all its activities are directly or indirectly tinged by a subversive, antiadult atmosphere.

Finally, Ronald Laing has described a common family scenario in which the parent, trying to produce one kind of behavior in the child, actually succeeds in encouraging the opposite. How many times have we heard parents say something like the following to a child?

> "I'm always trying to get him to make more friends, but he is so self-conscious. Isn't that right, dear?"

> "He's so naughty. He never does what I tell him. Do you?"

> "I keep telling him to be more careful, but he's so careless, aren't you?"[39]

Usually the parent is exasperated and confused about why the child persists in being self-conscious, naughty, and careless in the face of such pleadings. Laing argues that such statements as those quoted contain a double message. The child is being told "Do X (the good thing), but you really are the kind of person who does Y (the bad thing)." Being told what you *are,* argues Laing, is a much more powerful message than an order merely to do something. In this way the parents, without realizing it, may be teaching the child to persist in the very behavior they are trying to change.

Conflict and Growth

One reason for the persistence of the idea of the family as a harmonious, balanced social system is a line of thought that goes something like this: (*a*) the society needs stable adults to survive; (*b*) stable adults are produced by warm, harmonious, stable families; (*c*) society is surviving; so (*d*) families *must* be warm, stable, and harmonious. The concept of the family as a difficult environment, which has emerged from the study of family interaction, has been hard to accept because of these assumptions.

Recently some writers have suggested that we need to rethink the role or conflict in human development. In looking at an individual or a family, the prevailing assumption of most psychologists has been that conflict was neurotic and undesirable. Now, however, it appears that conflict is not necessarily something of which the less one has the better. Rather, the optimal dose is somewhere in between—not too much, but not too little either. Piaget and other students of cognitive development have argued that intellectual and moral growth occurs as a result of conflict. The child must feel some "perturbation," some sense that something is wrong with the way he or she is thinking.

Intellectual growth occurs not through a smooth process of adding on pieces of knowledge bit by bit, but rather by a constant series of small crises in the way the child looks at the world. The child has a certain idea or interpretation or expectation—the moon follows me, people can see my dreams and thoughts, shadows are a substance, if you pour water into a tall, skinny glass there will be more of it, and so on. If these beliefs were never challenged by experience or other people, the child's reasoning processes would remain at this "primitive" level. If we think of what kind of environment is most likely to stimulate intellectual skill, it would be one providing some surprise, contradiction, and challenge rather than a merely bland and pleasant one.

There is reason to believe that the same is true of the child's emotional development. The pleasant, conflict-free family atmosphere idealized in the sentimental model of the family may not prove the optimal environment for child

*Play is an important
source of learning.*

The Psychology of Socialization

development, even in those rare instances where it occurs. Thus the findings of the new anthropology of the family are not, in the end, as shocking as they seem to be at first glance.

Such notions as the politics of experience, family myths, family rules, paradoxical communication, struggles over definitions of the situation, family secrets that everybody knows but doesn't dare talk about—all these concepts and others as well were found to be characteristics of family life in general, and not unique to schizophrenic families. The very usefulness of the new ways of describing family interaction led to disillusion with the concept of schizophrenic families. This disillusion could lead in two directions: it could let schizophrenic families off the hook, or put all families on it.

For some writers the failure to find some unique quality specific to schizophrenic families meant that mental problems had to arise from some other cause than family experience—most likely some kind of organic defect.[40] For R. D. Laing the lack of uniqueness meant that all families are guilty of psychological double-dealing and emotional blackmail. In his later works Laing comes to look on the schizophrenic as a hero, one who refuses to be cowed by the duplicities in family and society that most of us conform to.

There is a compromise position between these two views. The first one ignores the evidence of problematic aspects of ordinary family interaction. Laing's position seems to ignore differences of degree between families as well as the autonomy of children and their ability to deal with the "perturbations" of family life in the same way as they deal with the rest of the environment. Laing's concepts may suffer from the same psychiatric fallacy we noted earlier—generalizing from clinical cases to the population at large. The schizophrenics treated by Laing may indeed have experienced double binds and other forms of psychological mayhem, but Laing obviously did not observe those people who grew up under similar conditions and managed to survive without coming to the attention of psychiatry. In the next section we look at the surprising findings of studies that did make such observations.

The Uses of Adversity

The image of a troubled adult scarred for life by an early trauma, such as the loss of a parent, lack of love, or family tensions, has passed from the clinical literature to become a cliché of our popular media. Yet the assumption of childhood vulnerability, the belief that only a stable and supportive family life with gentle parents attuned to the child's inner needs can assure a child's personality development, is not supported by the literature. The idea that childhood stress must inevitably result in psychological damage rests on a methodological flaw inherent in the clinical literature—that of starting with adult problems and tracing them backward in time.

Thus many studies trying to document the effects of early pathological and traumatic conditions have failed to demonstrate more than a weak link between such conditions and later development. It is true that whenever the backgrounds of delinquents, mental patients, or psychiatric rejectees from military service are investigated, a large number are found to come from broken or troubled homes, overpassive, domineering, or rejecting mothers, or inadequate or violent fathers. The argument is typically made that these circumstances cause the maladjustment of the offspring. The difficulty, however, is that if "normal" or "superior" people are samples—college students, business executives, professionals, military officers, creative artists, and scientists—these same pathological conditions occur in the same or greater proportions.

Although such findings have been appearing in the literature at least since the publication in 1949 of Stouffer's massive studies on the American soldier,[41] they have never attracted very much public and professional attention. One of the most thorough studies of the effects of childhood stress on later development was the midtown Manhattan study[42] by Srole and others. Some of the most striking findings concerned the effects of broken homes on mental health. Among psychiatric patients included in the study, 20 percent had reported a history of a home broken in early childhood by death, divorce, or separation. But 35 percent of the nonpatient, control population also came from broken homes. This is not to say that having a broken home has no effects at all. The severity of effects seemed to depend on the age of the child, whether the parent lost was the mother or the father, and the social class of the family.

The recent work of Norman Garmezy[43] of the University of Minnesota on the subject of "invulnerables" has received considerable coverage in the press. Garmezy began his work by studying adult schizophrenics and later turned to developmental studies comparing children judged to be at high and low risk to develop schizophrenia and other disorders at a later age. When these children were studied over time, only 10 or 12 percent of the high-risk group became schizophrenic, while 85 to 90 percent did not. He became increasingly fascinated by these seeming "invulnerables"—children who thrived in spite of genetic disadvantages and environmental deprivations. Through interviews with teachers and principals, he has identified many such children; for example, a ten-year-old facing extreme poverty, with a dying exconvict father, an abusive, illiterate mother, and two mentally retarded siblings, is described as charming, popular with peers and teacher, a good student, and a natural leader.

The striking differences between retrospective studies—starting with adult misfits and looking backward to childhood conditions—and longitudinal studies—starting with children and following them through time—was shown earlier in a study at the University of California's Institute of Human Development. Jean Macfarlane[44] and her associates studied, through test and interview over a period of thirty years, a group of 166 infants born in 1929. The purpose was to observe physical, mental, and emotional growth in average people.

Over the years this study has generated several significant research findings, but the most surprising of all was the difficulty of predicting what thirty-year-old adults would be like even after the most sophisticated data had been gathered on them as children. Macfarlane, the director of the project, writes that the researchers experienced shock after shock as they saw the people they had last seen at age eighteen. It turned out that the predictions they had made about the subjects were wrong in about two-thirds of the cases! How could a group of competent psychologists have been so mistaken?

Above all, the researchers had tended to overestimate the damaging effects of early troubles of various kinds. Most personality theory had been derived from observations of troubled people in therapy. The pathology of adult neurotics and psychotics was traced back to disturbances early in childhood—poor parent-child relations, chronic school difficulties, and so forth. Consequently, theories of personality based on clinical observation tended to define adult psychological problems as socialization failures. But psychiatrists see only disturbed people; they do not encounter "normal" individuals who may experience childhood difficulties but who do not grow into troubled adults. The Berkeley method, however, called for studying such people.

The experience of the Berkeley subjects showed the error of assuming that childhood stress must inevitably lead to adult maladjustment, or that similar childhood conditions must affect all children the same way. The adult data showed that early difficulties could be overcome or compensated for. "In fact," as Macfarlane pointed out:

> many of the most outstandingly mature adults in our entire group, many who are well integrated, highly competent, and/or creative, who are clear about their values, who are understanding and accepting of self and others, are recruited from those who were confronted with very difficult situations and whose characteristic responses during childhood and adolescence seemed to us to compound their problems. . . .[45]

The theoretical predictions of the researchers were also jarred from the other direction by the adult status of the children who had seemed especially blessed with ability, talent, popularity, or easy and confidence-inducing family lives. Those who had enjoyed admiration, success, and approval as children failed to live up to the expectations that the researchers, along with everybody else, held for them. As adults they seemed strained and dissatisfied, wondering what went wrong and longing for the good old days. This pattern was particularly strong for boys who had been athletic leaders and girls who had been extremely beautiful and popular in high school.

Summing up the implications of the Berkeley study, Macfarlane noted:

> . . . we had not appreciated the utility of many painful, strain-producing, and stressful experiences . . . nor had we been aware that early success might delay or forestall continuing growth, richness, and competence. . . . We need to look at and to try to conceptualize the configurations of what kinds of stress, in what graded doses, with what compensating supports, and what developmental periods, and in what kinds of organisms, forestall maturity and strength or facilitate them.[46]

Recently, a more precise explanation of the kind of evidence described above has been presented by Martin Seligman[47] in his theory of "learned helplessness." Summarizing a vast array of data including animal experiments, clinical studies, psychiatric case literature, and reports from prisoner-of-war camps, Seligman proposes that the key to whether one copes with difficulty or gives up in despair is the feeling of helplessness—the expectation that our efforts have little or no important effect. The feeling of helplessness can come about through actual experiences of uncontrollable events, simply believing that we have no control over what will happen. The expectation of having some control, not the objective conditions of controllability, is the crucial determinant of helplessness.

The expectation of helplessness can result from being told by someone authoritative that you are helpless, or it can come about through actually experiencing uncontrollable events. Thus, in experiments studying the stressful effects of loud noise, subjects who were told they could turn the noise off if it became too disturbing suffered from less stress than those who were told the noise was uncontrollable. And, in other experiments, children who were given unsolvable arithmetic problems were later unable to solve easy ones.

A key point in the theory is that good events that happen outside our control can produce a sense of helplessness as much as bad ones can. Thus the theory helps explain both of the puzzling findings from the Macfarlane study—not only the positive outcomes of many of the people who had troubled early lives, but the finding that many of those who had had "everything" as children failed to realize their potential later on. The theory of learned helplessness suggests that the experience of controllable stress may be better for a child's ego development than good things that happen without any effort on the child's part.

The statements of Macfarlane's subjects seem to confirm this hypothesis. A central theme running through the accounts of those who successfully coped with difficulty seems to be the perception that their own actions could have some effect on what was going on in their lives. Looking back at their early lives at the age of thirty, these individuals convinced the researchers that what had looked like disturbed behaviors were actually ways of coping with difficult situations.

Even at their most troubled periods, they do not reveal themselves as passive victims of circumstance or of uncontrollable symptoms or impulses. Rather they seem to have been trying to deal with difficult situations, to exercise some degree of choice no matter how extreme the situation, to construct a self of their own choosing, even if that meant engaging in behavior that looked bizarre and meaningless to others. For example, a woman who had been seen as a "full-blown schizophrenic" during adolescence, but who turned into a competent adult, said:

> "The only stabilizing aspect of my life during that period was the undeviating and all-enveloping homicidal fantasies against my mother. I believe they prevented my complete disintegration until I could escape my home and achieve other methods of handling my strains."[48]

A man who had been in constant trouble in school, and who was finally expelled at age fifteen, said:

> "Granted that my defiance of authority precluded a college education. I desperately needed approval, even if it came from kids as maladjusted as I was. Yet I can see positive results too. To maintain my rebel status called for a commitment that demanded my disciplining *all* of my intelligence and stamina which, I believe, has contributed to my adult strength and to my self-confidence in tackling later tough problems. . . ."[49]

Another subject who defied expectations was a girl who also spent most of her adolescent energies defying authorities. She too was expelled from school at age fifteen. At age thirty she was described as an understanding, compassionate mother. She had taken specialized training and was working with physically handicapped people.

The ability to cope does not mean that the child does not suffer; in that sense, the term "invulnerables" is misleading because it suggests an imperviousness to pain. One woman who successfully overcame a childhood marked by the death of her beloved but alcoholic and abusive father, and rejection by her mother and stepfather, put it this way: "We suffer but we don't let it destroy us." This woman became active in her school and community and sought support from peers, teachers, and other adults. Recent studies of children of divorce show that successful coping seems to imply the ability to function on two levels, to experience one's misery and yet to go on with living.[50]

Another problem with the term "invulnerables" is that it implies that the ability to cope is a trait, something internal to the child. In the case histories of successful and unsuccessful copers, one often finds external supports that integrated the impact of the traumatic event. Thus, in many of Macfarlane's cases, something in the child's environment provided alternative sources of love and gratification—one parent compensating for the inadequacy of the other, a loving sibling or grandparent, an understanding teacher, a hobby or strong interest, a pet, recreational facilities.

Indeed the local community may play an important role in modulating the effects of the home environments on the child. Once at a seminar discussing the life histories of Macfarlane's longitudinal subjects, Erik Erikson, who had worked on the study, was asked how so many of these people overcame the effects of truly awful homes. Without hesitation, he an-swered that it was the active street life in those days, enabling the child to get out of the house and play with other children when relations with parents got to be too difficult.

Social Class and Family Environment

If we take seriously the notion that family interaction is difficult, it may be that the various modes of child rearing may differ not so much in degree of strain as in what kind of problem they pose for the child growing up in them. Despite the size of the literature on child rearing and the diversity of the populations studied and mea-sures used, two broad patterns of child rearing appear again and again. These two patterns stand as polar contrasts to each other (see Table 12-1). One is organized around obedi-ence, the other around the personality of the child. The first pattern is typically called tradi-tional, repressive, or authoritarian socialization; the second is called modern, democratic, or child-centered. The chief characteristics of each style are contrasted in the table. Needless to say, these represent ideal types rather than patterns one can observe in every family. At the present time most researchers agree that the traditional style of socialization tends to be found in the working class, whereas the demo-cratic style typifies the middle classes—or at least those segments of it most influenced by the literature on child-rearing advice. In the past, however, the pattern seems to have been re-versed, with the middle classes more "repres-sive" in child rearing.[51]

Most writers see the repressive style as creating a less benign environment for the child and as impairing the child's intellectual and emotional development. It appears, however, that both these environments are best seen as problematic for the child, each in its own way. For example, a number of writers have sug-gested that predicaments such as the double bind may not reflect personality traits of parents so much as the built-in structure of the middle-class nuclear family. To understand how the middle-class nuclear family has such strains built into it, it is necessary to contrast this family form with two different ones: the traditional extended family of preindustrial society and working- or lower-class family patterns in in-dustrial societies. The characteristic of the modern middle-class family that sets it off from both of these others is the emphasis on individ-ualism and autonomy on the part of the child. Paradoxically, individualism represents both the chief glory and the chief source of difficulty in modern middle-class socialization. To the extent that the nuclear family and middle-class values represent the norm to which these other groups will move, the attendant problems will be found in these groups also.

The contrast between socialization in tradi-tional kin groups and in the modern nuclear family has been summarized by Hsu as follows:

> There is . . . [in the nuclear-family sys-tem] . . . an inherent tendency to conflict be-tween the generations not known in other types of kinship systems. On the one hand, parents view their children as their exclusive posses-

TABLE 12-1   TWO PATTERNS OF SOCIALIZATION

"Traditional" or Status-Centered	"Modern" or Person-Centered
1 Each member's place in family is a function of age and sex status.	Emphasis is on selfhood and individuality of each member.
2 Father is defined as boss and more important as agent of discipline; he receives "respect" and deference from mother and children.	Father more affectionate, less authoritative; mother becomes more important as agent of discipline.
3 Emphasis on overt acts—*what* child does rather than *why*.	Emphasis on motives and feelings—*why* child does what he or she does.
4 Valued qualities in child are obedience, cleanliness.	Valued qualities in child are happiness, achievement, consideration, curiosity, self-control.
5 Emphasis on "direct" discipline: physical punishment, scolding, threats.	Discipline based on reasoning, isolation, guilt, threat of loss of love.
6 Social consensus and solidarity in communication; emphasis on "we."	Communication used to express individual experience and perspectives; emphasis on "I."
7 Emphasis on communication from parent to child.	Emphasis on two-way communication between parent and child; parent open to persuasion.
8 Parent feels little need to justify demands to child; commands are to be followed "because I say so."	Parent gives reasons for demands—e.g., not "Shut up" but "Please keep quiet or go into the other room; I'm trying to talk on the telephone."
9 Emphasis on conforming to rules, respecting authority, maintaining conventional social order.	Emphasis on reasons for rules; particular rules can be criticized in the name of "higher" rational or ethical principles.
10 Child may attain a strong sense of social identity at the cost of individuality, poor academic performance.	Child may attain strong sense of selfhood, but may have identity problems, guilt, alienation.

sion, since they are given unbridled authority to order the youngsters' lives. On the other hand, privacy and self-reliance keep parents and children apart even before the latter reach majority in ownership of property, correspondence, relationship with friends, romance, and in the choice of life partners. Therefore, parents often find it hard to let their children go their own way as the youngsters advance in age, while children often find it necessary to reject their parents as the most important sign of maturity and independence. As a result, the parent-child tie is not only terminated legally upon the youngster's reaching majority, it may be socially and psychologically broken long before.[52]

In short, Hsu points to a contradiction between the values of independence and self-reliance for children, and two other aspects of the nuclear-family system: the actual power of parents and the emotional significance of children in their parents' lives. Thus modern nuclear parents are both more powerful and more affectionate than traditional parents, although their ideology underplays the parental authority as an ideal.

Social Class and Family Environment

Behavioral Versus Attitudinal Conformity

In traditional societies children depend less on parents alone, and individuality and independence are less valued; children are supposed to conform behaviorally. In middle-class Western society, especially American society, parents don't generally want their children to conform for the sake of conformity. They want them to internalize the rules the parents are trying to teach, to believe in them as the right thing to do. Whereas working-class parents tend to value neatness, cleanliness, and obedience in a child, the middle classes tend to value happiness, considerateness for other people's feelings, curiosity, and self-control. They want not only behavioral conformity but attitudinal conformity.[53] The prototypical working-class parent, as he or she emerges from research findings, is happy when the child obeys and does not mind spanking the child for disobedience. The middle-class parent may actually spank the child sometimes, but disapproves of spanking for two reasons: first, he or she believes in the child-centered, psychologically oriented child-rearing teaching of the experts.[54] Second, having to spank the child is in itself proof that the parent has failed to get the child to internalize the parent's values—to want to do the "right thing" because it is right. Kohn argues that the emphasis on different values in different social classes reflects both the circumstances of life in each social class and the qualities necessary for the advancement of the child. For the working-class child, cleanliness, neatness, and obedience may actually be necessary to attain respectability and success. The middle-class family, however, can take these values more for granted. Further, lower-class occupations stress working with the hands; middle-class occupations involve working with symbols and people. Kohn has described the "message" of middle-class socialization as follows:

The child is to act appropriately, not because his parents tell him to, but because he wants to. Not conformity to authority, but inner control; not because you're told to, but because you take the other person into consideration—these are the middle-class ideals.[55]

Thus modern middle-class socialization is both more permissive and more demanding than traditional, restrictive socialization. As Bronfenbrenner puts it:

Though more tolerant of expressed impulses and desires, the middle-class parent . . . has higher expectations from the child. The middle-class youngster is expected to learn to take care of himself earlier, to accept more responsibility about the home, and—above all—to progress further in school.[56]

The prevailing emphasis in the literature has been that the middle-class pattern of child rearing is better—and that, in fact, the lower-class pattern is a social problem because it is associated with poor school performance. On the other hand, a number of observers have pointed out the problematic qualities of middle-class socialization. For example, Arnold Green[57] has contrasted the neurotic tendencies of the middle-class male child with the freedom from guilt of his lower-class peers. The very repressiveness of lower-class parents, Green argues, makes it easier to reject them and assert one's own autonomy.

In a similar vein Rose Coser has pointed out that the "schizophrenogenic" mother who exposes her child to the double bind of love and hostility is none other than the ordinary middle-class mother caught between contradictory demands placed on her by society. The schizophrenogenic mother is described in the writings of many clinicians as having the following characteristics. She dominates her children and is strongly ambivalent. She is both punitive and overprotective. She shrinks from the children when they try to get close to her, but if they withdraw from her, she tries to bring them closer or else punishes them for implying that she is not a loving mother. The classic example is Bateson's[58] tale of the mother who comes to visit her schizophrenic son in a mental hospital. He hugs her and she shrinks from his embrace. He withdraws. "Don't you love your mother?" she asks. He blushes. "You mustn't be ashamed of your feelings, dear," she says. He stays with her only a few minutes; after she leaves he assaults an aide.

Coser argues that double binding results from the mother domination and mother-child ambivalence that are built into the middle-class family. Mom is such a dominant force in middle-class children's lives for several reasons. She is the source not only of affection, but of both attitudinal and overt conformity—that is, she is concerned with both their inner dispositions and the details of their everyday behavior. Since it is the mother's task to supervise all the children's activities, her position of control tends to outweigh the control that a busy and absent father can have over his children.

> . . . Being interested in the children's attitudes as well as their behavior, her supervision makes it possible to weigh all their acts not only in terms of the immediate situations, but also in terms of their symbolic meaning in regard to attitudes and future development. The scolding phrase, "It's not that I mind you not doing the dishes—I do them myself faster anyway—it's your attitude that I object to" expresses criticism both of the youngster's inability to do the task . . . as well as of his underlying disposition. Such control is aimed at both levels of the personality at the same time.[59]

Adding to the magnification of the mother's impact on the children is a child-rearing ideology in which the raising of perfect children offers the chief justification for the mother's life.

Thus everything the children do not only validates or invalidates their own inner worth, but that of the mother.

The child is also exposed to contradictions arising out of the mother's various roles. Being a wife, mother, and housekeeper involves opposing demands and pressures. The traditional, obedience-demanding mother has little difficulty in resolving conflicts between household cleanliness and childhood messes, but the modern middle-class mother, faced with finger paint on the walls or a clock broken in the pursuit of intellectual curiosity, may experience personal conflict over whether to scold or praise the child for creativity. Besides the conflict concerning the immediate versus the long-range view of the child's behavior, the mother may also be in conflict between her own interests and what she conceives to be those of the child. The child wants to spend Saturday morning watching those awful cartoons. Should she, in the interests of the child's future development, forbid this? Should she permit it in the name of the child's autonomy to choose his or her own activities? Or should she let the child watch the awful stuff to gain two or three hours of peace and quiet for herself and her husband?

The role of the father in the modern middle-class family contains paradoxes of its own. On the one hand the cultural script calls for the father to be a warm family man, even a pal to his children. The literature comparing the American father with fathers in other cultures shows how much the distribution of authority and affection within the family contrasts with the stereotypical Victorian family. The father is no longer used as the ultimate threat to enforce obedience: "Wait till your father comes home." This means that the middle-class mother can no longer pretend to be the sheltering buffer between the child and the father's wrath and power. Thus the figure of "Mom" takes on witchlike proportions in the child's eyes, while "Dad" seems to embody the gentler virtues.

On the other hand, the middle-class father role competes with occupational demands. The highly career-oriented father may be available to his children hardly at all, partly from necessity and partly because he finds that life in the family is mundane when compared with life outside the home, where the responsibility and the power he can command are exciting.[60]

In recent years a new set of values has complicated the lives of middle-class fathers. The new morality of self-realization and self-fulfillment demands a commitment to self that may conflict with work and family commitments. Further, the sexual revolution, particularly in its *Playboy* aspects, has added aspects of the single-man's role to that of husband and father.

Still another contradictory aspect of the paternal role concerns achievement. Both parents teach achievement values, but father is supposed to embody them. However, most men in this culture are ambivalent, to say the least, about their work. Work in industrial societies is more often than not burdensome and unfulfilling for all classes.[61] In general, the system makes failures of most men. They fail if they occupy a low-status job, and in high-status jobs they judge themselves against impossibly high standards of creativity and success. The middle-class father communicates standards that define him as a failure, or else he communicates dissatisfaction with the cultural standards. Thus the middle-class child receives confusing messages about achievement.[62] In the working class, by contrast, the child acquires either a fatalistic attitude—success is all a matter of luck—or else the world of achievement can be held out as a promised land that the child may reach, but the parents may never enter. That world is not discredited through familiarity.

Middle-class socialization may be paradoxical at an even deeper level. For example, the demand that a child internalize a rule creates a double-bind situation. The point has been made by Sluzki and Eliseo.[63] They gave the following example: a university student in therapy reported that his parents had always stressed the importance of having clean teeth. When he was a child they had emphasized that brushing his teeth regularly, on his own initiative, would be clear proof of his being grown up—that is, independent. Sluzki and Eliseo argue that this example represents in effect a pathological double bind or paradoxical communication: "Do just what we say, but do so on your own initiative." The parental demand to brush one's teeth on one's own initiative is a model of the paradoxical nature of all socialization based on internalization rather than obedience.

"If you do not obey, we shall be angry with you, but if you obey only because we are telling you, we shall also be angry, because you should be independent" (that is to *want* to do whatever one *should* do of one's own will). This injunction creates an untenable situation, because it demands that an external source be confused with an internal one. But, on the other hand, it is also the almost ubiquitous model for the internalization of social rules. Its universal occurrence in no way alleviates its paradoxical nature. . . .[64]

In short, middle-class families embody in an acute way the strains in the larger culture. The reason they convey contradictory messages to the child in the course of socialization is that the society itself contains contradictions. Thus, as we noted earlier, the middle-class parent is torn between responding to the child's behavior in the here and now and thinking of its meaning for future development. In the society at large a similar conflict occurs between present and future orientations:

In the schools, the media, and the churches, such contradictory values as self-denial and self-expression, discipline and

The peer group also socializes.

indulgence . . . are being preached, drama-tized, and fostered all at once. On the one hand, television and magazines advocate hedonism, consumption and living it up, while schools and churches continue, uneasily, to embody the Protestant ethic. The economy demands dis-cipline and self-control in order to *make* a living and spending and self-indulgence as a *way* of living.[65]

These contradictions in contemporary val-ues are vividly shown in a recent survey of 2,000 American families with children under twelve. Ironically, the youthful protesters of the 1960s have given rise, a decade later, to a new kind of American parent. According to Daniel Yankelovich,[66] who conducted the poll, the new breed of parents is self-oriented, not ready to sacrifice for their children, questioning of all authority, including their own, and scornful of traditional values such as marriage as an insti-tution, religion, patriotism, and material suc-cess. They have a "laissez faire attitude that says both they and their children should do as they like."[67]

One surprising finding of this poll is the large proportion of parents—43 percent—who fit the new pattern. Another is the finding that the new kind of parents hesitate at imparting their new values directly to their children. They join the more traditional parents in stressing values such as "duty before pleasure," "hard work pays off," "my country right or wrong," "people in authority know best," and "sex without marriage is wrong." As Yankelovich observes, "The upshot of all this at the moment is confusion for both the children and the adults."[68]

Social Class and Family Environment

Summary

Social scientists have tended to look on socialization as a process by which new generations replace their elders; the social system itself remains the same, like a long-run play performed by a succession of different actors. Some social theorists have regarded socialization as a process of shaping and molding; others have emphasized "internalization" as the key: the child takes into his or her own personality the norms and values of the culture. In spite of their differences, however, the prevailing theories have tended to define the end result of socialization as conformity to social norms.

This view of socialization has been undermined by several developments. First there is the rise of a youthful opposition in the United States and the other industrially advanced countries. The wide-scale dissent of upper-middle-class youth could not be accounted for simply as failures of socialization. Rather, the dissent seemed to arise from taking all too seriously the ideas that had been taught in schools, churches, and homes. Thus it became clear that rebellion and dissenting behavior as well as conformity could be the outcome of otherwise successful socialization.

The turbulence of the 1960s undermined theories of social stability and consensus as the normal state of social life; many scholars became persuaded that change and conflict were the rule rather than special circumstances in need of explanation. If society were not stable and consensual, however, then growing children would be exposed to social and cultural conflicts and inconsistencies. The idea that stable societies are maintained by stable families passing the cultural heritage from one generation to the next becomes increasingly untenable.

The demise of theories of socialization based on stability and consensus brought to the fore a number of concepts that had been anticipated earlier but were analyzed and developed more fully in the 1960s. These include: the idea that generation gaps are inevitable in any culture; that the child is an active and autonomous agent in his or her own socialization; that the child is an experiencing self that interprets events in his or her own way; that conflict may be useful for emotional and intellectual development.

Recent psychological research and theorizing suggest that there may be inherent limits to the manipulation and control of human behavior, even in young children. Rather than being the passive objects of inner impulses or environmental conditions, people are active seekers and processors of information.

Ultimately, patterns of socialization reflect the technology, organization, and dynamics of society. The process should not be regarded as a constant, and new societies may produce socialization patterns for children and adults that are as yet unimagined.

Source Notes

1. Dahrendorf, 1958, p. 21.
2. Keniston, 1971b.
3. Cox, 1968, p. 41.
4. Keniston, 1971b.
5. Mead, 1971, p. 50.
6. Piaget, 1967, pp. 64-68.
7. Lipset, 1967, p. 58.
8. Haan, 1971, p. 260.
9. Keniston, 1971b, p. 390.
10. LeVine, 1965, p. 195.
11. Fortes, 1949, pp. 225-227.
12. K. Davis, 1940.
13. Keniston, 1971b, p. 297.
14. Ibid.
15. Mead, 1970, pp. 5-6 (italics in original).
16. Mead, 1947, p. 633.
17. Danziger, 1971.
18. Wrong, 1961.
19. Kessen, 1966, p. 57.
20. Erikson, 1968, p. 218.
21. Caldwell, 1964; Schaffer, 1971.
22. Schaffer, 1971, p. 16.
23. Rheingold, 1969.
24. Piaget, 1952, 1954.
25. Schaffer, 1971, p. 13.
26. Bruner, 1966.
27. White, 1959.
28. Chukovsky, 1966, pp. 9-10.
29. Bruner, 1964, p. 4.
30. Neisser, 1976, p. 177.
31. Goode, 1971.
32. Ibid., p. 625.
33. Davison, 1973.
34. Bandura, 1969.
35. Loevinger, 1959.
36. Becker, 1964.
37. Pearlin, 1971.
38. Pitts, 1968.
39. Laing, 1969, p. 81.
40. Frank, 1965.
41. Stouffer, 1949.
42. Srole et al., 1962.
43. Garmezy, 1976.
44. Macfarlane, 1964.
45. Ibid., p. 121.
46. Ibid., p. 123.
47. Seligman, 1975.
48. Macfarlane, 1964, p. 121.
49. Ibid.
50. Wallerstein and Kelley, 1976.
51. Bronfenbrenner, 1958.
52. Hsu, 1961, p. 418.
53. Kohn, 1959.
54. Bronfenbrenner, 1958.
55. Kohn, 1959, p. 351.
56. Bronfenbrenner, 1958, p. 424.
57. Green, 1946.
58. Bateson et al., 1956.
59. Coser, 1964, p. 378.
60. Flacks, 1971, p. 29.
61. Goode, 1963, p. 380.
62. Flacks, 1971.
63. Sluzki and Eliseo, 1971.
64. Ibid., pp. 398-399.
65. Flacks, 1971, p. 33.
66. Yankelovich, 1977.
67. Ibid., p. 1.
68. Ibid.

Chapter Thirteen
The Future of the Family: Prospects and Policies

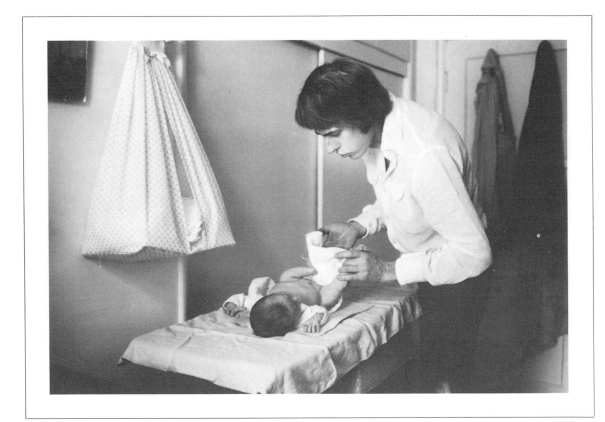

☐ . . . *perhaps some day we will cease to relate to families just as we no longer relate ourselves to clans, and instead be bound up with some new, as yet unnamed principle of human association. If and when this happens, we may also see a world of unisex, multisex, or nonsex.*

Suzanne Keller, "Does the Family Have a Future?"

☐ *Long after the last reader of this volume has moldered into dust, the vast majority of human beings will continue to be born into a family unit with two spouses, male and female, with or without another child already there. They will live most of their lives entwined closely in family relations and will experience much of their anguish and happiness because of what takes place there.*

William J. Goode, *Principles of Sociology*

For many people today, the main question about the future of the family is: will it have one? For a much smaller number, the question is: should it have one? The current debates about the family, sex roles, and sexuality involve not only definitions of social reality, but also deeply felt notions about how people ought and ought not to live. Social science can never be a purely objective pursuit—least of all when it deals with such touchy matters as sex and family. Complicating things further, the very concept of the family itself, as we observed earlier, is a slippery one. Discussions can become even more elusive and confusing when the concept of the family is joined to other vague terms, such as the "survival" of the family, or its "strengthening" or "weakening."

Scholars disagree about whether the family is or is not breaking down, and they disagree about whether the decline of the family is good or bad. Most fundamentally, they disagree on what the nature of the family really is.

Both conservatives and radicals interpret recent trends in the family as symptoms of decline and decay. The conservative looks at the increases in divorce, women's entrance into the labor force, sexuality outside marriage, youthful rebelliousness, and the increasing openness about homosexuality and sees moral breakdown and decadence. The radical, however, sees not a breaking down but a breaking free, an overthrow of artificial, repressive restraints. Both agree that basic impulses are being unleashed, but they differ drastically as to the nature of impulse. To the conservative, impulses are dangerous, uncontrollable, and rather ugly; to the radical, they are beautiful and innocent.

To the conservative, children are cruel, ignorant, but clever savages who must be tamed by moral and rational adults. The radical, by contrast, sees the moral tables turned the other way. The child has a clarity of perception and moral sensitivity that has been corrupted in adults: socialization is an "almost complete holocaust of the child's experience on the altar of conformity."[1]

The "breakdown" perspective includes many popular writers who are fond of alluding to the fall of Rome. It also includes the older generation of family scholars such as Zimmerman who predicted decades ago that the decline of the traditional patriarchal family and the rise of the "atomistic" conjugal family would lead to the general erosion of moral and responsible behavior.[2] In 1972, Zimmerman offered his interpretation of the turmoil of the 1960s.[3] He saw the emergence of the "no-family" and an anarchic society where irrationality, mob rule, and public fornication are the order of the day.

The most extreme as well as the most widely known advocate of the radical perspective is David Cooper. In *Death of the Family*,[4] Cooper asserts along with Zimmerman and others that the contemporary family is in a state of extreme decline. Unlike them, he applauds rather than denounces its passing. For Cooper, the family as well as schools and other social institutions are enemies of the individual. He sees the family as an "ideological conditioning device" to regiment its members and prepare them for psychological exploitation.

But not everyone who deplores the decline of the family is a conservative. For example, Urie Bronfenbrenner,[5] a leading child psychologist, also takes a dim view of the present state of the family. Bronfenbrenner is not concerned with sexual morality, but with a breakdown in socialization. He contrasts child-rearing patterns in America and Russia and concludes that, though Soviet child rearing produces responsible citizens, American child rearing consists of "the unmaking of the American child." Bronfenbrenner writes that there has been a decline in the interaction of parents and children over a twenty-five year period in the United States. The vacuum left by the parents is filled by peers and television, resulting in antisocial, alienated attitudes and behavior. In milder forms this alienation expresses itself as cheating, lying, playing hooky, and teasing; in stronger form it emerges as drug abuse, delinquency, and violence.

Although in recent years the idea that the family is in crisis has come to be taken for granted as a fact, many scholars have argued that the reports of the death of the family are greatly exaggerated. The litany of statistics cited by the doomsayers—the rising divorce rate, the number of single-parent homes, the increasing numbers of employed mothers—seems convincing enough at first glance, until we remember the number of times in previous eras that obituaries were written for the family. Recall, for example, Theodore Roosevelt's warning about race suicide. As Goode points out, for generations people have been observing the breakdown of the family, yet it shows no signs of disappearing.[6] Every major social change in American life generated worry about the future of the family.

For every recent trend that seems to show the family is declining, historians can point to evidence showing that things were no better, and even worse, in the past. Today's divorce rate, for example, seems to provide the most striking statistical indicator of family conflict and instability. Yet during some periods in American history, the statistics of marriage and family life were more dismal than they are today. Until fairly recently, death broke up more families than divorce currently does. Besides those marriages broken by death, many marriages in the past ended in desertions, which were not legally recorded. Thus the statistics on legal divorce are not an accurate guide to the extent of marital disruption in the past.

There is also statistical evidence suggesting that the erosion of the family's child-care role is more myth than fact. Mary Jo Bane,[7] taking issue with those who believe that the decline of the extended family, the increasing number of working mothers, and the isolation and mobility of American life has undermined family life, writes:

> . . . [t]he extended family is not in fact declining; it never existed. Family disruption has not increased but has only changed its character. The proportion of children living with at least one parent has gone up, not down. The increased proportion of children living in single-parent families results mostly from mothers keeping their children instead of farming them out. Mothers have changed the location and character of their work, but there is no evidence that this harms children. Nor is there any evidence that contemporary families have fewer neighbors and friends to call on than in the past.[8]

Thus the sense of crisis concerning the family may be an illusion generated by other social changes; or it may arise from our unrealistic images of family life. We idealize the family as a provider of

unconditional solidarity, homey affection, and a satisfying place for a moderate amount of sexuality. Continually obliged to admit that the image does not correspond to reality, we find that we can give it more substance by projecting it back into the past.[9]

The Future of the Family: Prospects and Policies

The Future of the Family

Events of the past fifteen years should worry anyone who would dare to predict social futures. Those who foresaw a continuation of the public turbulence of the sixties turned out to have been as mistaken as those who thought of the tranquility of the fifties as the permanent and natural state of an advanced technological society. Nevertheless, in the near future, it seems reasonable to expect present trends to continue.

The major reason is that these trends—in life styles, behavior, and attitudes—are not simply fads based on personal whims. Rather, they are reflections of and reactions against American society and its institutions—its economy, its occupational structure, its values. Thus, instead of viewing recent challenges to traditional family life such as the women's movement, the sexual revolution, the aware-ness and encounter-group movement, the homosexual-rights movement, and so on as coming from the lunatic-fringe groups disconnected from the rest of the society, we can see them as vanguard groups heralding changes in the mainstream of society. As Gartner and Reissman observe:

> The basic motion of the sixties has not been lost. Some of the values are vulgarized, commercialized, and watered down. But others have been institutionalized, accepted in consciousness and everyday life. They have deeply affected human relations and some have contagiously spread to new areas, including the workplace.[10]

Two cautions are in order. First, the trends are not intended to describe everyone. They describe emerging tendencies, rather than sta-

Unisex, bisex, multisex, or nonsex—challenges to traditional family life or a vanguard heralding changes in the mainstream of society?

The Future of the Family: Prospects and Policies

tistical majorities. Second, in the long run, things may look very different. Although social scientists, like weathermen, tend to predict more of whatever is happening today, historians often take a more cyclical view. Thus, though it is hard to see, for example, how an era of sexual restraint could follow upon a period of relatively free sexuality, the historians can point to many instances when precisely this change occurred. If, as we have repeatedly seen in this book, the family is a product of its time and place, when and if social conditions change drastically, the family will change also.

The following, then, are some of the major changes in marriage and family arrangements in recent years that seem to be here to stay, at least for the immediate future.

Increasing Symmetry in Sex Roles

Women are likely to spend a substantial portion of their lives doing paid work outside the home. This is a long-term trend that began decades before the women's movement of the 1960s. It is likely to continue for a variety of reasons. First of all, the evidence is that women like to work. Second, women are living longer and are having fewer children closer together than in the past. These changes in the life cycle mean that women will have more time to spend working even if they stay home until their children are married—an increasingly rare choice. If they stay home only until their children reach school age, they can work 80 percent of their adult years.[11] Finally, women are likely to work because of strong economic pressures. As we noted in an earlier chapter, most men's jobs do not pay enough to support a family at a standard of living most Americans would consider good. As more families come to have two earners, those with nonworking wives will be at a competitive disadvantage. As Ross and

Sawhill observe: "It is difficult enough to keep up with the Joneses under normal circumstances, but when both of them are working, it becomes virtually impossible."[12]

Sexual equality is likely to be pursued if not achieved in the next decade. The backlash to the women's movement—such as the opposition to the Equal Rights Amendment and to abortion, and the "total woman" movement—is not the most important obstacle. Women's continuing economic handicaps and the persisting difficulties of combining family life and a career pose more significant difficulties.

Women do not yet receive equal pay for equal work, and they do not enjoy equal employment opportunities. Most women continue to do traditional "women's work"—teaching, clerical work, sales, and so on—although increasing numbers are beginning to pursue male careers such as law and medicine. Apart from the problems of job discrimination and segregation, most jobs are designed for men who can work long hours without attending to child care and other family needs.

As long as women continue to bear major responsibilities for child care and housework, they will have a hard time achieving economic equality. Many of the early feminists resolved this dilemma by remaining single, but later generations were unwilling to trade marriage, maternity, and domesticity for careers. Although the options to remain single, or childless even if married, are readily available, relatively few people will choose them as lifetime patterns. Thus the dilemma will remain.

There are two ways out of it: one way is shifting part of the burden of child care to public facilities; the other is shifting part of it to men. The issue of publicly provided child care is a complicated and controversial one; there is no room here to discuss the pros and cons about the extent of the need for child care, its purposes and effects, and various proposals to organize and fund it.

The number of married
women in the labor force
has more than doubled
since 1950. (Source: U.S.
Bureau of Labor Sta-
tistics.)

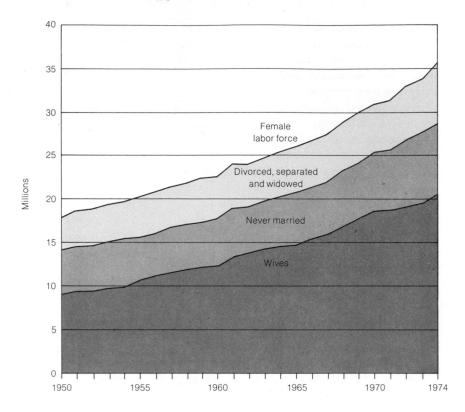

In any event, since even free, universal day care would not replace the family, there would still remain the question of who would be responsible for the child care that goes on in the home—changing diapers, doing laundry, feeding, amusing, helping, disciplining, and so on. In addition, there is the issue of all the rest of the housework. At present, men's roles inside the home do not seem to have changed as much as women's roles outside it. But there is some evidence that wives' employment changes the division of labor in the home. In two-worker families, husbands are more likely to share in the child care than in the routine responsibilities for housework.

In the future, the division of labor and responsibility in the home may become more even, as the value of sexual equality comes to be more widely shared and as women exert more pressure for male participation. Finally, males may find genuine satisfactions in greater participation in the home. As noted earlier, young people are placing less emphasis than the older generation on occupational achievement, and more on personal life, including the family, as a source of meaning.

One clear indication of men's increased willingness to shoulder the responsibilities of parenthood is the great increase in the number of divorcing men who ask for, and often get, custody of their children. As of 1974, close to 900,000[13] American children, more than half of them of preschool age, lived with their fathers. Most fathers who seek custody, according to one article on the subject, maintain they do not seek it out of vindictiveness or to win concessions from their wives. Rather:

> They stress coming to terms with their own untapped nurturing instincts—and what they view as the best interests of their children. As they accept the fact that today's women are fighting for equality, the men demand nothing less than equality in their fight for custody.[14]

Continuing Fragility in Marriage

No one expects the divorce rate to go down in the near future. Several trends seem to be making marriages harder to sustain. First, the prevalence of divorce itself reduces the pressure on couples to remain in unsatisfactory marriages. Second, the new roles for women not only make women less dependent on marriage, but women's new demands and expectations, plus the changes in family living that come about when a woman works, also may contrib-

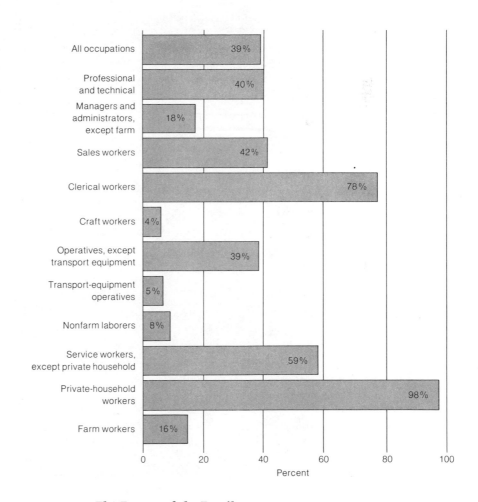

Women as a proportion of all workers by occupation, 1974. The majority of clerical and service jobs are held by women; they make up about 40 percent of professional, technical, sales, and operative workers. (Source: U.S. Bureau of Labor Statistics.)

Occupation	Percent
All occupations	39%
Professional and technical	40%
Managers and administrators, except farm	18%
Sales workers	42%
Clerical workers	78%
Craft workers	4%
Operatives, except transport equipment	39%
Transport-equipment operatives	5%
Nonfarm laborers	8%
Service workers, except private household	59%
Private-household workers	98%
Farm workers	16%

The Future of the Family

Although women still are responsible for most of the housework, men are doing more than they used to.

The Future of the Family: Prospects and Policies

ute to marital tensions and conflicts. Eventually, after the period of transition, as the new patterns become institutionalized and husbands and wives enter marriage with similar expectations, tensions arising out of women's new roles may subside. On the other hand, two-worker marriages may always be more complicated than the more traditional kind. And when men's and women's roles are more symmetrical, spouses can be less dependent on one another.

Another source of marital instability stems from the new set of demands placed on marriage by the ideal of finding personal growth and self-fulfillment in intimate relations. The "radical new romanticism" asserts that there are unlimited possibilities of choice in close relationships, and that life is a series of self-discoveries in which we proceed from one relationship to another as we grow and change.[15] Although the new romanticism seems to rule out the idea of permanent commitments in the first place, many people try to combine marriage with the new goals of personal growth and self-realization. One major example of this kind of new ideal for marriage is "open marriage," in which the spouses try to combine an intense personal relationship based on openness and mutual trust, as well as individual freedom and independence for each partner, including the freedom to enter into intense relationships with other people.

Ironically, by creating new expectations, this new romanticism in marriage creates new sources of discontent as well. In the past and in traditional families even today, married people seemed to require very little from each other except a bit of compatibility. Marriages were held together by practical necessity, moral commitment, and community opinion. Even today, in working-class areas and ethnic enclaves of large cities, husbands and wives often lead rather separate lives; the wife may be intensely involved with her kin, the husband with his work, friends, and relatives. When marriage becomes more intense and intimate, it also becomes more difficult. In traditional societies, as Philip Slater observes:

> . . . spouses are not asked to be lovers, friends, and mutual therapists. But it is increasingly true of our society that the marital bond is the closest, deepest, most important, and putatively most enduring relationship of one's life. Therefore it is increasingly likely to fall short of the demands on it and to be dissolved. . . .[16]

More Fluid Individual Life Cycles

People live much longer than they used to, and fertility patterns have changed so that women spend a smaller portion of their time bearing and raising children. This creates new problems as well as new opportunities. Husbands and wives have many more years alone together; on the average, couples born in the 1930s will live two-thirds of their married lives without the responsibilities of young children at all in the home.[17] It is little wonder then that the personal relationship between the spouses has taken on so much importance in recent years.

Not only has the marital life cycle changed, but also the individual life cycle. The idea of development, once applicable only to growing children, is applied to adults, as new stages of adult life are "discovered." The link between a person's age and his or her family and work roles has been dramatically loosened in recent years. Instead of following an age-graded ladder of roles, people make changes in their commitments all through the life cycle. Schooling lasts longer, and is no longer confined to early youth. People leave school and continue their education at some later point. Older people move to new careers or drop out for a while to explore new possibilities of self-realization.

All of this change and possibility of change creates new scources of stress. People experi-

Married couples can expect to spend many more years alone together, after the children are grown, than earlier generations.

Diversity of Life Styles

For the first time in history, it is becoming legitimate to choose from a number of family and life-style options: singleness, living together, single parenthood, communal living, custom-designed marriage contracts, and dual-career marriage, as well as traditional marriage.

The trend toward living together—what used to be called "living in sin"—has emerged as the most persistent and widespread legacy of the sexual revolution of the 1960s. Between 1970 and 1977, according to the Census Bureau, the number of unmarried men and women living together in a single household has doubled, from 640,000 to 1.3 million.[18] Undoubtedly, these figures underestimate the actual number of cohabiting couples, but the very fact that the Census Bureau is counting them shows that this way of life has become an important part of the social scene.

The change occurred with remarkable speed. In 1968, a Barnard College sophomore became front-page news when she was almost expelled from college for living with a man. Today, few colleges place restrictions on student living arrangements. And the people who live together are not only college students, but also adults of all ages, including senior citizens for whom marriage often means the loss of social-security benefits. Although surveys reveal that a majority of Americans disapprove of living together, in some circles a couple who announced they were getting married without having lived together would be greeted with raised eyebrows.

The other major change in family life style has come about because of the increase in divorce. New kinds of family ties are emerging as a result of divorce and remarriage. The formerly married, particularly those who have children, continue to maintain relationships as part of what Daniel Bell once described as "the ex-kinship" system, and various kinds of

ence a heightened awareness of time's passing and a sense that all commitments are fluid and open to redefinition and renegotiation. The awareness that options remain open creates sensitivity to the inner self and to its wishes and potentials. This fluidity of self and its commitments contributes to the instability of marriage and other family ties.

"blended" families and step-relatives are being produced in vast numbers by the high rate of remarriage.

In the second chapter of this book, I noted that anthropologists have had trouble coming up with a definition of the family that would fit all societies. In recent years the same problem has come to plague those who would define the family in our own society. One think-tank group concerned with the current state of the family defined a family as "any two or more biologically related or legally related people."[19] The limitations of this definition—it seems to exclude a living-together couple from being a family, and it doesn't say whether biologically related people have to live together to be a family—only illustrate the complexities of family life today.

Some people have suggested that we stop talking about *the* family and talk about families instead. One psychiatric social worker complained about a meeting of family therapists she attended:

> I sat there during the whole time listening to talks about THE family, studies of THE family, arguments about THE family, until I couldn't stand it any longer. I got up and said, "What on earth do you mean . . . THE family? There is no such thing. There are two-parent families, one-parent families, no-parent families, three- or four-parent families, families without children"—there was a burst of applause when I finished."[20]

Yet even substituting "families" for *the* family may be too restrictive to capture the variety of intimate relationships that exists today. Perhaps "personal life" would be a better term; in the fifties, social scientists saw the

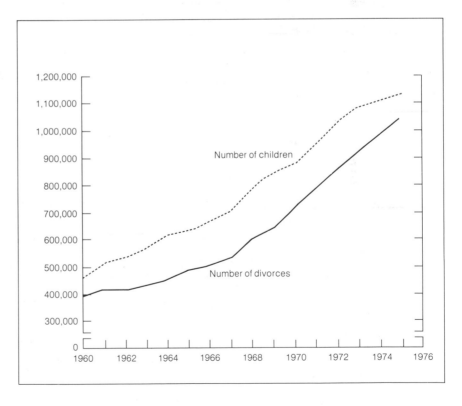

Divorce and children, United States, 1960–1976. The year 1975 was the fourth in a row in which more than one million children under eighteen had been affected by divorce. The total number of persons involved in divorce—husbands, wives, and children—was 3,195,000, more than double the number involved in 1965. (Source: National Center for Health Statistics.)

Number of children

Number of divorces

1,200,000
1,100,000
1,000,000
900,000
800,000
700,000
600,000
500,000
400,000
300,000
0

1960 1962 1964 1966 1968 1970 1972 1974 1976

The Future of the Family

family as the place where people could express the aspects of themselves that couldn't be expressed in the world of work. Yet people today are expressing themselves in other kinds of relationships—in friendships of varying degrees of intensity, in living-together arrangements with varying degrees of commitment, and in leisure-time pursuits that may or may not include other people.

Deepening Commitments to Intimate Relationships

The concern with personal growth, awareness, and self-fulfillment is often viewed only as a threat to the family. According to its critics, the "new narcissism" leads to mindless self-indulgence and living for the moment. It encourages people to avoid commitments to love and friendship, and to treat all relationships as casual encounters, to be enjoyed while they last, and then replaced by later models.

As in all caricatures, there is some truth in this one. But by exaggerating the dark side of the new concern with personal development, it completely overlooks the positive aspects. It sees the possibility for viciousness and psychopathology in the new values, just as the advocates of self-realization exaggerate their morality and mental-health potential. Every personality style or ethical stance has its vices and weakness, but also its virtues.

Thus the new ideology of self-fulfillment can lead to a greater fragility in relationships, but it also encourages a deeper emotional involvement between people. The new awareness of self goes along with an increased sensitivity to others and a greater capacity for sharing and caring.

Surprisingly, recent changes in sexual behavior provide a good illustration of the two-sidedness of the new ideology. When we think about the liberalization of sexual behavior and attitudes in recent years, we are likely to think of such unconventional behavior as casual sex with all kinds of sex partners, "swinging," bisexuality, and so on. There have been striking increases in sexual relations among the unmarried and the formerly married. Yet sexual liberation may have had its greatest impact for most people within marriage itself. Thus, in his survey of sexual behavior in the 1970s, Morton Hunt[21] finds that "a dramatic and historic change" has taken place in the practice of marital sex in America.

Hunt's data reveal a great increase in marital eroticism in recent years: married people of all ages are having sex relations more often, they are spending more time in both foreplay and intercourse, and they are engaging in formerly taboo activities, such as oral sex. Further, women appear to be equal, rather than reluctant, participants in this increased eroticism. Thus many more women report having regular orgasms than they did in the past, and only a tiny fraction complain that their husbands are too demanding sexually, in contrast to the large majority who previously made that complaint.

It would be a mistake, however, to think that the sexual revolution has brought nothing but uninhibited joy. Although for many people it has permitted the enjoyment of long-denied pleasures, for others it has brought new burdens and anxieties. Lillian Rubin,[22] for example, has written of the difficulties experienced by blue-collar couples as they try to explore the new sexual options. For wives caught between the new standards for sexual performance and previous training to be "good"—that is, asexual—orgasms and experimental sex can be just another chore in a life full of chores. Middle-class women, on the other hand, may worry about being neurotic if they fail to live up to their own "liberated" standards.

But in spite of these complications, both men and women are becoming more concerned with their partner's gratification as well as their own. Lillian Rubin argues that if working-class men ever were the boorish, insensitive studs they have been portrayed to be in both literature and social science, they no longer are. In line with Hunt's findings, she notes that men at all educational levels have become more sensitive to women's sexual needs, with the most increase among high-school educated men.

The new sexuality also implies greater attention to the sexual and psychological needs of adults. It reflects the new definition of adulthood as a time of growth and change. As Ann Swidler observes, in American culture, sex used to belong to the young, and was played down, if not renounced, in adulthood. But "the new clinical approach to sexual fulfillment, which seems lacking in romance, may be seen as an attempt to keep sexuality gratifying for people who are not in the first blush of romantic involvement."[23]

Some writers have worried that the sexual revolution and the increase in divorce will lead people to avoid permanent commitments and to treat all relationships as casual encounters. There is little evidence for this view. Despite the increased eroticism within marriage—and the marked increases in premarital sex—the new permissiveness does not seem to have blurred the difference between marital and extramarital sex.

There is disagreement about the extent of extramarital sex in contemporary America. One writer suggests that only about 30 percent of marriages live up to the ideal of monogamy;[24] another, citing survey data, suggests the figure ought to be about 50 percent.[25] Although Hunt's survey did find that extramarital intercourse is three times as frequent among wives aged eighteen to twenty-four as it had been in Kinsey's time, the percentage of women engag-

ing in it is only 24 percent, still below the incidence for males in that age bracket. Furthermore, Hunt found little evidence of an increase in extramarital sex for men.[26] Thus, in spite of all the talk about open marriage, affairs, and "swinging," there has not been a sharp break with the ideal of monogamy. What has changed is the double standard—the pursuit of extramarital sex is no longer confined to husbands.

The majority of married people interviewed by Hunt expressed the feeling that extramarital sex could be damaging to the marriage and would be emotionally devastating to the spouse. Yet they were also more aware of their own extramarital desires and the various possibilities of permissive or nonexclusive marriage than people in previous generations. As a result of all the talk, Hunt observes, many people tend to overestimate the amount of the extramarital sex actually going on, and come to wonder if their own reluctance to engage in it is a sign of some neurotic hangup.

Other researchers have come to different conclusions about the possibilities for reconciling marital commitments with extramarital relations. A number of studies suggest that in many instances, such relationships can actually bolster the marriage. Cuber and Harroff[27] found that many mature couples with good marriages could have outside relationships as a matter of principle. In general, couples following such nontraditional life styles do not seem to lose sight of the difference between the primary, committed relationship with spouse and outside relationships.

Despite their differences as to the incidence and emotional implications of extramarital sex, the above writers agree that the marital relationship remains central to contemporary Americans, even to those engaging in sexually variant life styles. In sum then, the sexual liberation of recent years does not appear to have led people to abandon marital commitments in favor of casual sex and a search for kicks.

A variety of other evidence supports the contention that commitments to family relationships are not being abandoned wholesale. For example, especially in middle-class families, divorce does not mean the end of parental involvement in the lives of their children. As we noted earlier, men are increasingly asking for and getting custody of their children after divorce, which means that they are also rejecting the life of unencumbered singleness that men were traditionally supposed to prefer. There is also an increase in joint custody—husband and wife sharing the care of children. In contrast, in the not-too-distant past, mothers who lost their husbands through death or divorce were likely to send their children to live with relatives or in orphanages.[28]

Another area in which increased choice seems to have led to increased commitment is childbearing. Despite the availability of contraceptives and legal abortion, many young women are choosing to give birth to, and keep, their "illegitimate" babies. They are less inclined than women in the past to give up a child they have borne to adoptive parents—an inclination that is often a mixed blessing, or worse, for the child if the mother herself is very young.

Other evidence for increased commitment may be found in the mass movement of women to change the way hospitals and the medical profession handle childbirth and the care of the newborn and the mother. Many women are pressing for birth practices that are more child-centered; they want fewer anesthetics and "nonviolent" handling of the child. In addition, many women also want encouragement for breast-feeding and increased contact between

A home birth. Many people are now defining birth as a normal family event rather than an illness to be treated in a hospital. Some hospitals are trying to create homelike settings for birth so mothers and babies can have the best of both worlds.

The Future of the Family: Prospects and Policies

mother and child during the postpartum period. Further, a study of women in alternative or nontraditional families—communes, unmarried couples, unwed mothers—revealed that these women wanted to be at home with their children more than women in conventional families.[29] As one unmarried mother put it, "I didn't have my baby to leave her with a baby sitter."

Out of Eden: The Rise and Fall of the Communal Ideal

Although there have been striking changes in both behavior and attitudes concerning women's and men's roles, sexuality, and child rearing, there has been no massive shift toward the more experimental forms of the family. During the 1960s, new models of the family were proposed to resolve the limitations of conventional family life. Along with their novelty these views have also lost much of their claim to be the instant solution to the problems that beset the family. To the extent that these alternatives have been tried, it is fair to state that none of them has proved as workable in practice as their originators had hoped.

It was the commune more than any other alternative family form that was looked to as the hope and model of the future. Although communes have declined in numbers and in the attention of the media, there are communes in practically every major city in the world, and religious communes have shown striking persistence. But, as sociologist Ben Zablocki[30] observes, we are at the tail end the communitarian social movements of the 1960s. It is impossible to know how many individuals were involved in the movement, but Zablocki estimates that there were at least 10,000 separate communal experiments between 1965 and 1975. "What was unique about this resurgence," he observes, "besides its size, was that it centered around a search for alternatives to the family, rather than around economic or utopian issues."[31]

The communes of the sixties and seventies attempted to create a protective environment against the harsher and more materialistic pressures of contemporary social and economic life. In large part communes can be understood as a protest against modern industrial society, in particular against the tense and constraining role assigned to the isolated nuclear family. The contemporary communal movement sought to combine the presumably warm and supportive group life of the extended family with a greater degree of personal freedom than is afforded by conventional middle-class family life.

Although the researchers who have studied communes observed the great diversity of living styles, they found remarkable unity in the beliefs of communards—excepting those who believe in systematic religions. Zablocki, for example, notes three motivations leading people to enter communal life: (1) to enjoy more freedom, (2) to recreate the extended family on the basis of fellowship rather than kinship, and (3) to escape from the city.[32]

Yet the vision of a harmonious, warm, loving, supporting community did not emerge very easily or very often from attempts at group living. In part, the difficulties of building communes could be attributed to problems inherited from the larger society—the inability of people reared in a materialistic, individualistic environment to adapt to a life of sharing and deep commitment to a group. In part, some of the difficulties of communes occurred because some communal values contradicted other values—freedom versus commitment, privacy versus sharing, spontaneity versus the need to get work done. Tensions arising from such conflicts often led communes to shift from anarchism to extreme authoritarianism. For example, one commune that still survives turned away from the freedoms on which it had been founded. In the past, they promoted free love and rejected absolute authority; now they accept their leader as unquestionable and unchallengeable—and they insist on marriage and bar adultery.[33]

A basic problem with the communal idea may lie in its resemblance—which several authors have observed—to the sentimentalized model of the nuclear family that it apparently rejects. Bennett Berger and associates,[34] for example, have pointed out the similarities between the ideology of the rural commune and the middle-class flight to the suburbs of the postwar years; both seek to withdraw from the problems of urban life and define happiness in terms of a perfected family life based on togetherness. Kirk Jeffrey[35] has pointed out how dominant American ideas about home and family in the nineteenth century and today resemble the ideas of utopian planners. In fact, the modern American idealization of the home can be traced to the same nineteenth-century sources as the communes of that era. The home was seen, in fact, as a kind of utopian community; writings on the family were pervaded by the utopian themes of retreat from urban society, conscious design, and perfectionism:

> . . . Whether they [nineteenth-century writers on the family] regarded home as an utter and permanent retreat from life in a shocking and incomprehensible social order, or as a nursery and school for preparing regenerate individuals who would . . . remake American society, they agreed that domestic life ought to be perfect and could be made so. Through careful design of the home as a physical entity, and equally painstaking attention to the human relationships which would develop within it, the family could actually become a heaven on earth.[36]

The utopian idealization of the home contained two flaws. First of all, the goal of creating a perfectly blissful, harmonious, smoothly functioning home was an impossible one. Indeed, such goals undoubtedly created greater frustration and guilt about the inevitable imperfections of family life than people would otherwise have experienced. Besides leading to unrealistic expectations, the turning away from the problems of the larger society may have made those problems worse. Writing of the nineteenth century, Jeffrey observes:

> In terms of the relationship between family and community, the middle-class yearning for a small corner of peace in the form of a happy family may actually have furthered the social trends which Americans deplored and which caused them to turn inward in the first place: the misgovernment of the city, the frantic race for status through conspicuous consumption, the degradation of politics in the Jacksonian era.[37]

One of the most useful outcomes of the recent social ferment is the undermining of the perfectionist expectations about the home and family that have persisted in America through the twentieth century. Although the sentimental gush of the nineteenth-century writers gave way to the "scientific" concern with psychological needs and mental health, a similar romanticization of family life persisted.

But it may be as unrealistic to look at the family as the cause of our troubles as to look up to it as our salvation. Nor is the restoration of the extended family the solution either. If utopianism is one pitfall to avoid in trying to deal with the problem of the family, familism—the tendency to see in family forms themselves either the cause or solution to family problems—is another. The sentimentalization of the family is often as extreme as that of the nuclear family. Every family system has its own set of strains, its costs as well as its benefits.

The Future of the Family: Prospects and Policies

The Dialectics of Intimacy

There is good reason to believe that some problems of the family may never be solved. Even after the problems of poverty, inequality, racism, and sexism have been solved, the family will still be problematic. As we have emphasized in a previous chapter, there are some cogent reasons for believing that social life in general is never in a steady state of conflict-free equilibrium. There is always change, conflict, disagreement over means and ends, and gaps between ideal norm and the activities of everyday life. Rather than being the exception to the general state of social life, the family is best seen as a model of conflict, change, and ambivalence. Indeed, as Freud and Simmel have argued, the more intimate social relations are, the more likely they are to give rise to conflict. Yet the norms that people bring to family life cannot be left out of the picture either. The struggles between the sexes and the generations cannot be understood as power struggles pure and simple. Even the most extreme instances of physical violence between family members usually arise from a complex mixture of hate and love rather than cold, uncaring hostility. Indeed, as Freud has taught us, love and hate are closely linked—we do not love or hate, but love and hate.

David Schneider has noted that when kinship is stripped of its economic and political functions, it remains as a symbol of a particular quality of human relationship. Kinship ties

Despite all the recent changes, family life still serves as a sanctuary from the impersonality of urban-industrial society.

The Dialectics of Intimacy

symbolize love or, in sociological jargon, "enduring diffuse solidarity":

> They symbolize those kinds of interpersonal relations which human beings as biological beings must have if they are to be born and grow up. They symbolize . . . a special kind of trust which is not contingent and which does not depend on reciprocity.[38]

It is significant that no revolutionary movement, however opposed to conventional forms of the family, has dispensed with the symbolism of kinship as an ideal form of human relatedness. Revolutionaries may wish to abolish the family, but only in the name of brotherhood or sisterhood.

In a very real sense the family has stood for the best in human feeling between people. Marx, for example, took the natural relation between man and woman as the ideal model of human relatedness. Brotherhood, sisterhood, motherly love, fatherly concern—we still use family terms when we want to describe good relationships between people, even though these terms have often been abused. A most striking example of this paradox is found in David Cooper's often brilliant and more often outrageous book, *The Death of the Family*.[39] Cooper proclaims "the end of the age of relatives" and declares that a family is a trap, an ideological conditioning device of an exploitive society, and a destroyer of all autonomous initiative and spontaneity. Yet he dedicates the book to his brother and sister-in-law and their children, who, during a mental and physical crisis that occurred while he was writing the book, treated him with "immense kindliness and concern . . . just as a true family should."

The need for intimacy and commitment seems to persist after the traditional ideologies of the family have lost their validity. Each model of the family has its own set of virtues, but also a set of liabilities. Thus it is currently popular to romanticize the traditional extended family—

the communes, in fact, base themselves on this model of the family—but when this form of the family prevails, it is experienced by many of those in it—especially by women and young people—as highly oppressive. In looking at extended-family systems in other societies, Western observers tend to be highly impressed by their benefits and to overlook their strains. The extended family is seen as providing care for the aged, the sick, and the unemployed. It seems to provide security for all its members, ensuring that no one will have to face life's troubles alone. Yet, as anthropologist Robert LeVine notes, a growing body of anthropological evidence indicates that extended families confer not only benefits on family members, but considerable fear and hostility as well:

> We hear of the frequency of suicide among the desperate young married women of traditional China seeking to escape their tyranical mothers-in-law. From North India it is reported that young wives develop hysterical seizures when marital obligations force their return to residence with their husbands' families. Assassins are hired to help settle internal family quarrels in Egyptian villages. Fraternal tensions within domestic groups are extremely widespread from China to West Africa. . . . Accusations of witchcraft and sorcery—a common medium for the expression of hostility—tend to be concentrated among kinsmen in East African societies. Parricide is a marked phenomenon in at least one Uganda tribe. . . . The burden of such disparate fragments of data is that the very structures which entail kinship obligations beyond the nuclear family engender antagonisms which may ultimately be registered in homicide, suicide, litigation, and other forms of interpersonal conflict.[40]

In general, then, it appears that the tensions that arise in family systems are not separate and distinct from their benefits. The intimate environments of the extended family provide security because of each member's lifelong obligation to the other members, but these very commitments often give rise to intense conflicts that cannot be expressed in an open and direct way. If conflict does occur it often takes an explosive and disruptive form, such as witch-craft accusations.

In short, the search for some ideal form of the family may be futile. Every principle of family organization, whatever its benefits, entails certain costs. The anthropologist Paul Bohannan[41] has stated the point in terms of household structure. Every family system, he notes, must solve the problem of how to organize households. There are a variety of problematic side effects. Bohannan examines three types of household structure: where the father-son relationship provides the cornerstone, as in the Tiv; the mother-daughter-based household that prevailed among the Iroquois Indians in the eighteenth and early nineteenth centuries; and finally the American nuclear-family household, grounded on the husband-wife relationship.

We have already noted structural problems of the nuclear-family household: it places a great burden on the marital relationship and it is vulnerable to disruption through divorce and death. By contrast, among the Tiv both parenting and spousing are highly diffuse activities, leading to a seemingly idyllic stability, continuity, and calm.

But the security and continuity provided by the extended-family household also entail certain costs not immediately evident in an idealized version of extended-family life. In Tiv and Iroquois societies, parent-child conflicts are not expressed directly; instead they emerge in the form of preoccupations with witchcraft.

Modest Proposals

Rather than trying to reform the family itself, the best strategy for improving family life would be to reduce the stresses and strains that flow from the larger society to the family. Despite the rhetoric idealizing the home and family in America, the fact is that American society does not place a high priority on providing a supportive environment for families and children. As one report to the 1970 White House Conference on Children put it, "A hard look at our institutions and way of life reveals that our national priorities lie elsewhere."[42] For example, the United States is the only industrialized country without a family health-care program that includes prenatal, maternal, and child-care services. This lack may partially explain why our infant mortality is higher than that of many other countries. Other social indicators suggesting that all is not well with American families are: the large number of families and children living in poverty, the unavailability of child-care options, and the high prevalence of child abuse.

There is little mystery about what needs to be done to improve the lot of American families and their children. It is significant that at its 1977 convention meeting on the state of the family, the American Orthopsychiatric Association did not call for more mental health clinics or more research money, but instead made three basically economic proposals:

1. Establishment of an income transfer or maintenance program for all families, guaranteeing a basic level of economic support and stability.

2. Development of a national system of high-quality maternal and child health-care ser-

Adequate health care is one of the great unmet needs of American children and families.

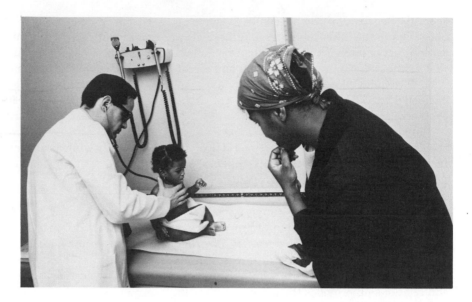

vices, including prenatal and obstetrical care, well-baby clinics, and adequate follow-up and treatment resources.

3. Special programs to assure vital family and child supports, such as maternity leave, sick leave for parents who must attend to seriously ill children, quality day care, visiting housekeeper services, constructive after-school programs, job programs for youth, etc.[43]

These proposals are not new. Every decade for the past sixty years, the White House conferences on children and youth have been issuing almost identical recommendations. Indeed, the economic answer to much family stress, poor health, and other problems would be even simpler and less controversial than guaranteed-income proposals—that is, a full-employment policy, with a job for every American man, woman, and young person who wants one. The problem seems to be that though full employment, guaranteed incomes, national health insurance, and a variety of child-care options are in the interests of families, they are not in the direct interests of those who make the final policy decisions.

Besides the basic needs of families for adequate incomes and health care, there are other kinds of policies that can help families cope with the difficulties of living in a time of great social change and reduced traditional supports for family functioning.

Reconciling Work and Family Life

The separation of work and home in modern times, as we have seen earlier in this book, has had profound implications for family life. It demanded new arrangements for child care and made women an expendable part of the labor force. The change created a new role for women—the full-time housewife-mother—and a new ideology justifying women's absence in the workplace and her presence in the home.

The world outside the home also based itself on this division of labor. Most jobs were designed for men who could work long hours without attending to family needs because they had wives at home to back them up. The suburb removed the home far from the workplace, adding commuting time to the workday. Schools could arrange their hours and vacation schedules on the assumption that there would always be somebody home to receive the child.

Although these arrangements created structured strains on family life, they did not become acute until recently, with the growth of the two-worker family and the single-parent household. We now appear to be in a transitional period during which the need for restructuring work is coming to be recognized, and various solutions are tried. Part-time work and maternity and paternity leaves have been suggested. One innovation that may have a promising future is flexible working hours, or flex-time.

Some companies are experimenting with the idea of allowing employees to arrange when they will begin and end their workdays. The idea has been more widely used in Europe, with apparently positive results. Flex-time possibilities would be especially useful for single-parent families, dual-career families, and those who would like to care for the sick or elderly at home.

Community-Based Family-Support Services

In recent years there has been a proliferation of people-helping services that have been less professional, less hierarchical, and less expensive than traditional ones—free clinics, hot lines, encounter groups, cooperatives, and switchboards. For example, parental-stress hot lines and groups such as Parents Anonymous help deal with the problems of child abuse in ways that seem to be more helpful and less stigmatizing and disruptive to families than traditional ways of dealing with the problem. However, large numbers of people in need of services do not get them.

Restoration of the Local Community

As Bronfenbrenner observes, much of what happens to children and families is determined by the ecology of the neighborhood in which the family lives.[44] The design of housing developments and urban environments has emphasized privacy and the separation of people by age and income. There is evidence that the isolation of the family has negative effects on families and children. The emotional closeness of a family is not enough to make up for the lack of a social network of outsiders. There needs to be research into how communities can be designed to encourage a sense of community and yet preserve the family's privacy from outside intrusion. Many older urban neighborhoods had this kind of social environment.

Family- and Community-Impact Statements

There has been growing recognition in recent years that the home is not an isolated retreat, immune from outside influence. Rather, the daily lives of families are affected by government policies and laws, the mass media, the design of housing and communities, availability of transportation, as well as the corporations and other large-scale organizations that determine where their employees work and live.

When Vice-President Mondale was a senator, he headed a subcommittee on children and youth which revealed that government programs have had a major impact on families. Because of insensitivities to the ways policies affect families, many decisions have had negative effects on families: the income-tax system, for example, penalizes married working couples and, through the deduction system, provides more money to rich families for each dependent than to poor ones. The social-security system penalizes older couples, who lose their pensions if they marry. The welfare system in many states encourages families to break up because a mother and children can't be eligible for benefits if there is a man in the home. Basic economic policies have a profound impact on families. Levels of unemployment and inflation that are acceptable to economists can have devastating effects on the health and psychological well-being of families.

One of the conclusions of the hearings was the suggestion that "family-impact statements" be attached to selected public policies. Based on an analogy with environmental-impact statements, these would encourage decision makers at various levels of government to consider what pending policies might mean to families and children. Although the proponents of the idea approach the idea cautiously, and do not propose attaching family-impact statements to every piece of legislation, they feel it is important for decision makers to be conscious of how their policies affect children and families.

Extending the idea, Rosabeth Kantor has recently suggested that large-scale organizations also might file "family-responsibility statements." In a review of the relationship between work and family life, she concludes that "the nature of the work world plays a dominant role in the possibilities for families and for personal satisfaction in and out of work life"; thus "the organizations in which most Americans work might begin to take some responsibility for their effects on families and personal relations."[45] Such organizations would provide family-responsibility statements dealing with the major policies that affect the personal lives of the employees, such as the scheduling of work, promotion practices, employee transfers and promotions, along with consideration of how such policies might affect employees and their families, and how the organization intends to deal with major stress.

Finally, Ralph Keyes[46] has suggested that there ought to be community-impact statements. He suggests the government could evaluate programs according to their effects on the community, whether they bring people together or drive them apart. Thus urban-renewal projects would be evaluated in terms of their effects on existing neighborhoods.

The advocates of family-impact statements have proposed the idea cautiously. No one has advocated that every law or policy would have such a statement. And it is much more difficult to measure family well-being than it is to measure air or water pollution. Further, there is the problem of defining what a family is—a policy might be good for some kinds of families and individuals and bad for others. Nevertheless, though the feasibility of such family- and community-impact statements needs to be explored further, the human impact of government and business policies has been ignored for too long.

Last Words

All fixed, fast-frozen relations, with their train of venerable prejudices and opinions, are swept away, all new-formed ones become antiquated before they can ossify. All that is solid melts into air, all that is holy is profaned, and man is at last compelled to face, with his sober senses, his real conditions of life and his relations with his kind.

In these words Marx described the destruction, by the modernizing forces of capitalism, of the myths that had sustained traditional society. It is a description that few students of "modernization" would dispute.

What a chilling prospect—to face the real conditions of life and our relations with others with sober senses! The other side of liberation from the constraints of religion, family, hereditary status, and small community has been described as alienation. As Peter Berger points out, the alienation or "homelessness" of modern social life is most clearly seen in the fate of religion in the shift from traditional to modern society.[47] For most of human history, religion has provided an "overarching canopy" of symbols that explained the meaning of life, death, suffering, and one's place in the universe. Religious beliefs in traditional societies are experienced as certain and real because they are taken for granted by everyone. In modern societies religion is pluralized and certainty is lost. The individual encounters others who do not share his or her beliefs. Religion is no longer socially given, but becomes a matter of individual choice or preference. Yet, although religion in modern society suffers from a "crisis of plausibility," the experiences that called for the comforts of religion are still with us—sickness, death, loss, and pain.

Much of the same sort of analysis can be applied to the family today. For most of human history, intimacy and community were the by-products of kinship systems and economic necessity. Families were economic units, and they monopolized, albeit imperfectly, the supply of sexuality. The freedom to choose one's spouse was the first step in the liberation of personal life from these restraints. In our own day we are witnessing a further pluralization: one chooses not merely a spouse, but whether to marry, or have children, at all. Individual men and women are no longer dependent on the family for economic support or for the fulfillment of sexual needs. Women, having won control of their own biology through the pill and other forms of contraception, are no longer bound by the double standard and no longer dependent on men for their economic survival. Only children and the ill remain unable to fend for themselves. But the ability to live as isolated individuals does not mean that most people will *want* to live that way. Like death and sickness, the need for intimacy and enduring commitment has outlasted the social institutions that provided for them in the past.

Source Notes

1. Laing, 1971, p. 101.
2. Zimmerman, 1947.
3. Zimmerman, 1972.
4. Cooper, 1970.
5. Bronfenbrenner, 1970.
6. Goode, 1976.
7. Bane, 1976.
8. Ibid., p. 70.
9. Lautman, 1976, p. 252.
10. Gartner and Reissman, 1974, p. 94.
11. Bane, 1976.
12. Ross and Sawhill, 1975.
13. Molinoff, 1977.
14. Ibid., p. 13.
15. Goode, 1977, p. 394.
16. Slater, 1968, 90.
17. Bane, 1976.
18. *Newsweek,* 1977, p. 46.
19. *McCall's,* 1977, p. 63.
20. Westoff, 1977, p. 3.
21. Hunt, 1974.
22. Rubin, 1976.
23. Swidler, 1977, p. 33.
24. Schultz, 1977, p. 20.
25. Ramey, 1977, p. 43.
26. Hunt, 1974.
27. Cuber and Harroff, 1965.
28. Bane, 1976.
29. Warren, 1977.
30. Zablocki, 1977.
31. Ibid., p. 9.
32. Ibid.
33. Wenner, 1977.
34. B. Berger et al., 1972.
35. Jeffrey, 1972.
36. Ibid., p. 22.
37. Ibid., p. 37.
38. Schneider, 1968, p. 116.
39. Cooper, 1970.
40. LeVine, 1965, p. 189.
41. Bohannan, 1971, p. 59.
42. White House Conference on Children, 1970, p. 241.
43. Reported in *American Psychological Association Monitor,* 1977, p. 6.
44. Bronfenbrenner, 1970.
45. Kantor, 1977, p. 96.
46. Keyes, 1973.
47. P. Berger, 1974.

The Future of the Family: Prospects and Policies

Bibliography

ACKERMAN, N. (1958). *The psychodynamics of family life: Diagnosis and treatment of family relationships.* New York: Basic Books.

ADAMS, A. (1971). Ripped off. *New Yorker, 47:*14.

ADAMS, B. N. (1968). *Kinship in an urban setting.* Chicago: Markham.

ALLAND, A., JR. (1967). *Evolution and human behavior.* Garden City, N.Y.: Natural History Press.

——— (1972). *The human imperative.* New York: Columbia Univ. Press.

ALLPORT, G. W. (1968). The historical background of modern social psychology. In G. Lindzey and E. Aronson (eds.), *The handbook of social psychology,* 2nd. ed., pp. 1–80. Reading, Mass.: Addison-Wesley.

ALTHUSSER, L. (1969). Freud and Lacan. *New Left Review, 55,* 48–65.

American Psychological Association Monitor (1977). *8:*6, 6.

ANDERSON, C. H. (1975). *The political economy of social class.* New York: Prentice-Hall.

ANTHONY, E. J., AND T. BENEDEK (1970). *Parenthood: Its psychology and psychopathology.* Boston: Little, Brown.

ARENSBERG, C. M., AND S. T. KIMBALL (1968). *Family and community in Ireland.* 2nd ed. Cambridge, Mass.: Harvard Univ. Press.

ARIES, P. (1962). *Centuries of childhood: A social history of family life.* Robert Baldick (trans.). New York: Knopf.

BACK, K. W. (1972). *Beyond words: The story of sensitivity training and the encounter movement.* New York: Russell Sage.

BAKAN, D. (1971a). *Slaughter of the innocents: A study of the battered child phenomenon.* San Francisco: Jossey-Bass.

——— (1971b). Adolescence in America: From idea to social fact. *Daedalus,* Fall, 979–995.

BALDWIN, A. (1967). *Theories of child development.* New York: Wiley.

BALL, D. W. (1972). The "family" as a sociological problem: Conceptualization of the taken-for-granted as prologue to social problems analysis. *Social Problems, 19:*3, 295–307.

BANDURA, A. (1969). Social-learning theory and identificatory processes. In D. A. Goslin (ed.), *Handbook of socialization theory and research,* pp. 213–262. Chicago: Rand McNally.

BANE, M. J. (1976). *Here to stay.* New York: Basic Books.

BARRY, H., I. L. CHILD, AND M. K. BACON (1959). Relations of child training to subsistence economy. *American Anthropology, 61,* 51–63.

BART, P. (1970). Mother Portnoy's complaint. *Transaction, 8,* 69–74.

BARTELL, G. D. (1971). *Group sex.* New York: Wyden.

BATESON, G., D. D. JACKSON, J. HALEY, AND J. WEAKLAND (1956). Towards a theory of schizophrenia. *Behavioral Science, 1,* 251.

BEACH, F. A. (1956). Characteristics of masculine "sex drive." In M. R. Jones (ed.), *Nebraska symposium on motivation, 1956,* pp. 1–32. Lincoln: Univ. of Nebraska Press.

BEAUVOIR, S. DE (1949). *The second sex.* (Paris: Gallimard.) New York: Knopf, 1953.

——— (1968). Cited in A. Memmi, *Dominated man.* New York: Orion.

BECKER, W. C. (1964). Consequences of different kinds of parental discipline. In M. L. Hoffman and L. W. Hoffman (eds.), *Review of child development research,* vol. 1, pp. 169–208. New York: Russell Sage.

BEM, S. L., AND D. J. BEM (1970). Training the woman to know her place: The power of a non-conscious ideology. In D. J. Bem, *Beliefs, attitudes, and human affairs.* Monterey, Ca.: Brooks/Cole.

BENDER, D. R. (1967). A refinement of the concept of household: Families, co-residence, and domestic functions. *American Anthropologist, 69:*5, 493–504.

BENEDICT, R. (1938). Continuities and discontinuities in cultural conditioning. *Psychiatry, 1:*2, 161–167.

BERGER, B., B. M. HACKETT, AND R. M. MILLAR (1972). Child-rearing practices in the communal family. Unpublished progress report to National Institute of Mental Health.

BERGER, P., B. BERGER, AND H. KELLNER (1973). *The homeless mind.* New York: Random House.

BERKNER, L. K. (1972). The stem family and the developmental cycle of the peasant household: An eighteenth-century Austrian example. *American Historical Review, 77,* 398–418.

BERNARD, J. (1964). The adjustments of married mates. In H. T. Christensen (ed.), *The handbook of marriage and the family,* pp. 675–739. Chicago: Rand McNally.

——— (1971). *Women and the public interest.* Chicago: Aldine.

——— (1972). Paper presented at symposium on sex role

learning in children and adolescence. American Association for the Advancement of Science Meetings, Washington, D.C., December 1972. Reported in *Science, 177,* 1128.

———— (1973). *The future of marriage.* New York: Bantam.

BERSCHEID, E., AND J. FEI (1977). Romantic love and sexual jealousy. In G. Clanton and L. G. Smith (eds.), *Jealousy.* New York: Prentice-Hall.

BILLINGSLEY, A. (1968). *Black families in white America.* Englewood Cliffs, N.J.: Prentice-Hall.

BIRDWHISTELL, R. L. (1968). The American family: Some perspectives. *Psychiatry, 29,* 203–212.

BLAU, P. M. (1964). *Exchange and power in social life.* New York: Wiley.

BLOOD, R. O., JR., AND R. L. HAMBLIN (1958). The effect of the wife's employment on the family power structure. *Social Forces, 36,* 347–352.

————, AND D. M. WOLFE (1960). *Husbands and wives: The dynamics of married living.* New York: Free Press.

BLUMBERG, R. L. AND R. F. WINCH (1972). Societal complexity and familial complexity: Evidence for the curvilinear hypothesis. *American Journal of Sociology, 77:*5, 898–920.

BOHANNAN, P. (1963). *Social anthropology.* New York: Holt, Rinehart and Winston.

———— (1971). Dyad dominance and household maintenance. In F. L. K. Hsu (ed.), *Kinship and culture,* pp. 42–65. Chicago: Aldine.

BOOCOCK, S. S. (1975). Children and society. Paper prepared for presentation at the American Association for the Advancement of Science Annual Meeting, January 1975. Reprinted in A. Skolnick (ed.), *Rethinking childhood.* Boston: Little, Brown, 1976.

BOONE, P. (1958). *'Twixt twelve and twenty.* Englewood Cliffs, N.J.: Prentice-Hall.

BOSZORMENYI-NAGY, I., AND J. L. FRAMO (eds.) (1965). *Intensive family therapy.* New York: Harper & Row.

BOTT, E. (1957). *Family and social network.* London: Tavistock.

BOTTOMORE, T. B. (1966). *Classes in modern society.* New York: Pantheon.

BOWLBY, J. (1969). *Attachment and loss.* New York: Basic Books.

BOYERS, R., AND R. ORILL (eds.) (1969). *R. D. Laing and anti-psychiatry.* New York: Harper & Row.

BRENNER, H. (1976). *Estimating the social costs of national economic policy: Implications for mental and physical health and criminal aggression.* Joint Economic Committee, 92nd Congress, October 26, 1976.

BRODERICK, C. B. (1971). Beyond the five conceptual frameworks: A decade of development in family theory. *Journal of Marriage and the Family, 33:*1, 139–159.

BRONFENBRENNER, U. (1958). Socialization and social class through time and space. In E. E. Maccoby, T. M. Newcomb, and E. L. Hartley (eds.), *Readings in social psychology,* 3rd ed., pp. 400–425. New York: Holt, Rinehart and Winston.

———— (1970). *Two worlds of childhood: U.S. and U.S.S.R.* New York: Russell Sage.

———— (1974a). Developmental research, public policy, and the ecology of childhood. *Child Development, 45:*1.

———— (1974b). The origins of alienation. *Scientific American, 231,* 53–61.

BROWN, D. G. (1958). Sex role developments in a changing culture. *Psychological Bulletin, 55,* 232–242.

————, AND D. B. LYNN (1966). Human sexual development: An outline of components and concepts. *Journal of Marriage and the Family, 28,* 155–162.

BROWN, R. W. (1965). *Social psychology.* New York: Free Press.

BRUNER, J. S. (1964). The course of cognitive growth. *American Psychologist, 19,* 1–15.

————, ET AL. (1966). *Studies in cognitive growth.* New York: Wiley.

BRYSON, J. (1977). Situational determinants of the expression of jealousy. Paper presented at the American Psychological Association, San Francisco.

BRZEZINSKI, Z. K. (1970). *Between two ages: America's role in the technetronic era.* New York: Viking.

BURGESS, E. W. (1926). The family as a unity of interacting personalities. *The Family, 7,* 3–9.

————, AND P. WALLIN (1953). *Engagement and marriage.* Philadelphia: Lippincott.

————, ————, AND G. D. SCHULTZ (1953). *Courtship, engagement, and marriage.* Philadelphia: Lippincott.

BURTON, R. V., AND J. W. M. WHITING (1961). The absent father and cross-sex identity. *Merrill-Palmer Quarterly, 7,* 85–95.

BUTTERWORTH, E., AND D. WEIR (1972). *Social problems of modern Britain.* London: Fontana/Collins.

CALDWELL, B. M. (1964). The effects of infant care. In M. L. Hoffman and L. W. Hoffman (eds.), *Review of child development research,* vol. 1, pp. 9–87. New York: Russell Sage.

CAMPBELL, A. (1975). The American way of mating: Marriage, si; children, maybe. *Psychology Today,* May 1975.

————, P. E. CONVERSE, AND W. L. RODGERS (1976). *The quality of American life.* New York: Russell Sage.

CAPELLANUS, A. (1968). The art of courtly love. Excerpted in W. M. Stephens (ed.), *Reflections on marriage,* pp. 39–46. New York: Crowell.

CARPER, L. (1967). In L. Rainwater and W. L. Yancey (eds.), *The Moynihan report and the politics of controversy,* p. 466. Cambridge, Mass.: M.I.T. Press.

CERNEA, M. (1970). *Changing society and family change: The impact of the cooperative farm on the peasant family.* Stanford, Ca.: Center for Advanced Study in the Behavioral Sciences.

CHAMBLISS, W. J. (1973). *Sociological readings in the conflict perspective.* Menlo Park, Ca.: Addison-Wesley.

CHAPPLE, E. D. (1970). *Culture and biological man: Explorations in behavioral anthropology.* New York: Holt, Rinehart and Winston.

CHASE, R. (1958). *The democratic vista.* Garden City, N.Y.: Doubleday.

CHESLER, P. (1971). Patient and patriarch: Women in the psychotherapeutic relationships. In V. Gornick and B. K. Moran (eds.), *Woman in sexist society,* pp. 362-392. New York: Basic Books.

CHOMSKY, N. (1968). *Language and mind.* New York: Harcourt Brace Jovanovich.

CHUKOVSKY, K. (1966). *From two to five.* Miriam Morton (trans. and ed.). Berkeley: Univ. of California Press.

CIPOLLA, C. M. (1969). *Literacy and development in the West.* Baltimore: Penguin.

CLAUSEN, J. A., AND S. CLAUSEN (1971). The effects of family size on parents and children. Unpublished ms., Institute of Human Development. Univ. of California, Berkeley. Published in James Fawcett (ed.), *Psychological perspectives on population.* New York: Basic Books, 1973.

COHEN, R. (1971). Brittle marriage as a stable system: The Kanuri case. In P. Bohannan, (ed.), *Divorce and after,* pp. 205-239. Garden City, N.Y.: Doubleday (Anchor).

COLE, M., J. GAY, AND J. GLICK (1971). *The cultural context of learning and thinking.* New York: Basic Books.

COLEMAN, J. S. (1972). The children have outgrown the schools. *Psychology Today, 5:9,* 72-75, 82.

COLES, R. (1971). *The middle Americans.* Boston: Little, Brown.

COMFORT, A. (1967). *The anxiety makers.* New York: Dell (Delta).

CONGER, J. J. (1971). A world they never knew: The family and social change. *Daedalus,* Fall, 1105-1138.

COOPER, A. A. (1842). A speech before the House of Commons, U.K., June 7, 1842. Reprinted in *Speeches of the Earl of Shaftesbury, K.G.,* pp. 31-58. London: Chapman & Hall, 1968.

COOPER, D. G. (1970). *The death of the family.* New York: Vintage.

COSER, L. A. (1956). *The functions of social conflict.* New York: Free Press.

COSER, R. L. (1964). Authority and structural ambivalence in the middle-class family. In R. L. Coser (ed.), *The family: Its structure and functions,* pp. 370-383. New York: St. Martin's.

COUGHLAN, R. (1956). Changing roles in modern marriage. *Life,* December 24, 1956, pp. 109-111.

COVENEY, P. (1967). *The image of childhood.* Baltimore: Penguin

COX COMMISSION (1968). *Crisis at Columbia.* New York: Vintage.

COZBEY, P. (1973). Self-disclosure: A literature review. *Psychological Bulletin, 79,* 73-91.

CROZIER, B. (1935). Constitutionality of discrimination based on sex. *Boston University Law Review,* 1935, 723, 727-728. Cited in L. Kanowitz, *Women and the law.* Albuquerque: Univ. of New Mexico Press, 1969.

CUBER, J. F. (1970). Alternate models from the perspective of sociology. In H. A. Otto (ed.), *The family in search of a future,* pp. 11-23. New York: Appleton-Century-Crofts.

————, AND P. HARROFF (1965). *Sex and the significant Americans.* Baltimore: Penguin.

DAHRENDORF, R. (1958). Out of Utopia: Toward a reorientation of sociological analysis. *American Journal of Sociology, 64:2,* 115-127.

D'ANDRADE, R. (1966). Sex differences and cultural institutions. In E. E. Maccoby (ed.), *The development of sex differences.* Stanford, Ca.: Stanford Univ. Press.

DANZIGER, K. (1971). *Socialization.* Baltimore: Penguin.

DAVIS, F. (1971). Why all of us may be hippies someday. In E. Z. Friedenberg (ed.), *The anti-American generation,* pp. 61-80. Chicago: Aldine (Transaction).

DAVIS, K. (1940). The sociology of parent-youth conflict. *American Sociological Review, 5,* 523-535.

DAVIS, M. (1973). *Intimate relations.* New York: Free Press.

DAVIS, N. (1971). The reasons for misrule: Youth groups and charivari in sixteenth-century France. *Past and Present, 50,* 41-75.

DAVISON, G. C. (1973). Counter-control in behavior modification. In L. A. Hamerlynck, L. C. Handy, and E. J. Marsh (eds.), *Behavior change: Methodology, concepts, and practice.* Champaign, Ill.: Research Press.

DEGLER, C. N. (1974). What ought to be and what was: Women's sexuality in the nineteenth century. *American Historical Review, 79:5,* 1467-1490.

DEMOS, J. (1970). *A little commonwealth.* New York: Oxford Univ. Press.

———— (1972). Demography and psychology in the historical study of family life: A personal report. In P. Laslett and R. Wall (eds.), *Household and family in past time,* pp. 561-569. London: Cambridge Univ. Press.

Bibliography

DEUTSCH, H. (1944). *The psychology of women: A psycho-analytic interpretation.* New York: Grune & Stratton.

DEUTSCHER, I. (1967). The quality of postparental life. In B. L. Neugarten (ed.), *Middle age and aging,* pp. 263–268. Chicago: Univ. of Chicago Press.

DIAMOND, M. (1965). A critical evaluation of the ontogeny of human sexual behavior. *Quarterly Review of Biology, 40,* 147–173.

DICKSTEIN, M. (1977). *Gates of Eden.* New York: Basic Books.

DINNERSTEIN, D. (1976). *The mermaid and the minotaur.* New York: Harper & Row.

DOUVAN, E., AND J. ADELSON (1966). *The adolescent experience.* New York: Wiley.

DOWNS, A. (1977). The impact of housing policies on family life in the United States since World War II. *Daedalus, 106,* 163–180.

DRAKE, E. (1901). *What a young wife ought to know.* Cited in A. Comfort, *The anxiety makers.* New York: Dell (Delta), 1967.

DUTTON, D. G., AND A. P. ARON (1974). Some evidence for heightened sexual attraction under conditions of high anxiety. *Journal of Personality and Social Psychology, 30,* 510–517.

EDMONDS, V. H. (1967). Marriage conventionalization: Definition and measurement. *Journal of Marriage and the Family, 29,* 681–688.

———, G. WITHERS, AND B. DI BATISTA (1972). Adjustment, conservatism, and marital conventionalization. *Journal of Marriage and the Family, 34:*1, 96–104.

ELDER, G. H. (1974). *Children of the Great Depression.* Chicago: Univ. of Chicago Press.

ELLENBERGER, H. (1970). *The discovery of the unconscious.* New York: Basic Books.

EMMERICH, W. (1959). Parental identification in young children. *Genetic Psychological Monographs, 60,* 257–308.

ENGEL, M., G. MARSDEN, AND S. WOODAMAN (1967). Children who work and the concept of work style. *Psychiatry, 30,* 392–404.

———, ———, AND ——— (1968). Orientation to work in children. *American Journal of Orthopsychiatry, 38,* 137–143.

———, ———, AND S. W. POLLOCK (1971). Child work and social class. *Psychiatry, 34:*2, 140–155.

ERICKSON, E. H. (1963). *Childhood and society,* 2nd ed. New York: Norton

——— (1964). Inner and outer space: Reflections on womanhood. *Daedalus,* Spring.

——— (1968). *Identity: Youth and crisis.* New York: Norton.

ESHELMAN, J. R. (1971). *Perspectives in marriage and the family: Test and readings,* 3rd ed. Boston: Allyn & Bacon.

FALLERS, L. A. (1965). The range of variation in actual family size: A critique of Marion J. Levy's argument. In A. J. Coale et al., *Aspects of the analysis of family structure,* p. 77. Princeton, N.J.: Princeton Univ. Press.

FARBER, B. (1964). *Family organization and interaction.* San Francisco: Chandler.

——— (1966). *Kinship and family organization.* New York: Wiley.

FARNHAM, M., AND F. LUNDBERG (1947). *Modern woman: The lost sex.* New York: Harper.

FELDMAN, H. (1962). Unpublished research. Cited in E. H. Pohlman, *Psychology of birth planning.* Cambridge, Mass.: Schenkman, 1969.

FERRAR, J. W. (1977). Some casual thoughts on spiritual love and marriage. Unpublished manuscript. See also J. W. Ferrar, Marriages in urban communal households: Comparing the spiritual and the secular. In P. J. Stein, J. Richman, and N. Hannon (eds.), *The family: Functions, conflicts, and symbols,* pp. 409–419. Reading, Mass.: Addison-Wesley.

FILENE, P. (1975). *Him, her, self: Sex roles in modern America.* New York: Mentor.

FINCKE, H. T. (1891). *Romantic love and personal beauty: Their development, causal relations, historic and national peculiarities.* London: Macmillan.

FIRESTONE, S. (1970). *The dialectic of sex: The case for feminist revolution.* New York: Morrow.

FLACKS, R. (1971). *Youth and social change.* Chicago: Markham.

FLAVELL, J. H. (1963). *The developmental psychology of Jean Piaget.* Princeton, N.J.: Van Nostrand.

FONTANA, V. J. (1964). *The maltreated child.* Springfield, Ill.: Thomas.

FORD, C. S., AND F. A. BEACH (1951). Human sexual behavior in perspective. In C. S. Ford and F. A. Beach, *Patterns of sexual behavior.* New York: Harper.

FORTES, M. (1949). *The web of kinship among the Tallensi.* London: Oxford Univ. Press.

——— (1970). Social and psychological aspects of education in Taleland. In J. Middleton (ed.), *From child to adult,* pp. 14–74. Garden City, N.Y.: Doubleday (Natural History Press).

———, R. W. STEEL, AND P. ADY (1947). Ashanti survey, 1945–46: An experiment in social research. *Geographical Journal, 110,* 149–179.

FOWLER, W. (1962). Cognitive learning in infancy and early childhood. *Psychological Bulletin, 59:*2, 116–152.

FRAIBERG, S. (1959). *The magic years.* New York: Scribner.

FRAMO, J. L. (1965). Systematic research on family dynamics. In I. Boszormenyi-Nagy and J. L. Framo (eds.), *Intensive family therapy,* pp. 407–462. New York: Harper & Row.

——— (1972). *Family interaction: A dialogue between family researchers and family therapists.* New York: Springer.

FRANCKE, L. (1972). Tot lots: Integrating children into everyday life. *Ms., 1:*1, 27ff.

FRANK, G. H. (1965). The role of the family in the development of psychopathology. *Psychological Bulletin, 64,* 191–205.

FRAZIER, E. F. (1948). *The Negro family in the United States,* abridged ed. New York: Dryden.

FREEMAN, J. (1970). The building of the guilded cage. Unpublished ms., University of Chicago, Reprinted in *Green Hearings,* U.S. House of Representatives, Sect. 10. Washington, D.C.: U.S. Government Printing Office, 1970.

FREMONT-SMITH, F. (1970). Comment cited by I. C. Kaufman, Biologic considerations of parenthood. In E. J. Anthony and T. Benedek, *Parenthood: Its psychology and psychopathology.* Boston: Little, Brown, 1970.

FREUD, S. (1898). *The future of an illusion.* Garden City, N.Y.: Doubleday (Anchor), n.d.

——— (1909). *Analyse der Phobie eines S-jährigen Knaben.* Vienna: Deuticke.

FRIEDENBERG, E. Z. (1971). *The anti-American generation.* Chicago: Aldine (Transaction).

FROMM, E. (1970). *The crisis of psychoanalysis.* New York: Holt, Rinehart and Winston.

FURSTENBERG, F. F., JR., T. HERSHBERG, AND J. MODELL (1975). Family structure and ethnicity: The black family. *Journal of Interdisciplinary History. 6:*2, 211–233.

GAGNON, J. H. (1965). Sexuality and sexual learning in the child. *Psychiatry, 28,* 212–228.

———, AND W. SIMON (1970). *The sexual scene.* Chicago: Aldine (Transaction).

———, AND B. HENDERSON (1975). *Human sexuality: An age of ambiguity.* MagaBack, Social Issues Series, no. 1. Boston: Little, Brown (Educational Associates).

GAMBINO, R. (1975). *Blood of my blood.* Garden City, N.Y.: Doubleday (Anchor).

GARMEZY, N. (1976). Vulnerable and invulnerable children: Theory, research, and intervention. Document MS 1337. Journal Supplement Abstract Service. American Psychological Association, Washington, D.C.

GARTNER, A., AND F. RIESSMAN (1974). *The service society and the consumer vanguard.* New York: Harper & Row.

GEERTZ, C. (1965). The impact of the concept of culture on the concept of man. In J. R. Platt (ed.), *New views of the nature of man,* pp. 93–118. Chicago: Univ. of Chicago Press.

GELLES, R. J. (1972). *The violent home.* Beverly Hills, Ca.: Sage.

——— (1976). Demythologizing child abuse. *The Family Coordinator, 25:*2, 135–141.

GESELL, A. AND F. L. ILG (1943). *Infant and child in the culture of today.* New York: Harper.

GIBSON, G. (1972). Kin family network: Overheralded structure in past conceptualizations of family functioning. *Journal of Marriage and the Family, 34:*1, 13–23.

GIL, D. G. (1968). Incidence of child abuse and demographic characteristics of persons involved. In R. E. Helfer and C. H. Kempe (eds.), *The battered child.* Chicago: Univ. of Chicago Press.

——— (1970). *Violence against children.* Cambridge, Mass.: Harvard Univ. Press.

——— (1971). Violence against children. *Journal of Marriage and the Family, 33:*4, 637–648.

GILMAN, C. P. (1903). *The home: Its work and influence.* New York: McClure Phillips.

GINOTT, H. (1972). Being a parent. King Features Syndicate, 1972. Reprinted in *San Francisco Sunday Examiner and Chronicle,* Feb. 11, 1973.

GINZBERG, E. (1976). Quoted in "Women at work," *Newsweek,* December 6, 1976, p. 69.

GLICK, P. (1975). A demographer looks at American families. *Journal of Marriage and the Family, 37,* 15–26.

GOFFMAN, E. (1959). *The presentation of self in everyday life.* Garden City, N.Y.: Doubleday.

GOODE, W. J. (1956). *Women in divorce.* New York: Free Press.

——— (1959). The theoretical importance of love. *American Sociological Review, 24,* 38–47.

——— (1963). *World revolution and family patterns.* New York: Free Press.

——— (1964). *The family.* Englewood Cliffs, N.J.: Prentice-Hall.

——— (1971). Force and violence in the family. *Journal of Marriage and the Family, 33:*4, 624–636.

——— (1976). Family disorganization. In R. K. Merton, and R. Nisbet (eds.), *Contemporary social problems,* pp. 511–554. New York: Harcourt Brace Jovanovich.

——— (1977). *Principles of sociology.* New York: McGraw-Hill.

GOODMAN, M. E. (1970). *The culture of childhood: Child's-eye views of society and culture.* New York: Teachers College Press.

GOODY, J., AND I. WATT (1962). The consequences of literacy. *Comparative Studies in Society and History,*

5, 304–326, 332–345.

GORDON, S. (1974). *Lonely in America.* New York: Simon & Schuster.

GOTTLIEB, E. (1974). *Youth and the meaning of work.* Washington, D.C.: U.S. Department of Labor (U.S. Government Printing Office).

GOUGH, K. E. (1959). The Nayars and the definition of marriage. *Journal of the Royal Anthropological Institute of Great Britain and Ireland, 89:*1. Reprinted as "Is the family universal?—The Nayar case," in N. W. Bell and E. F. Vogel (eds.), *A modern introduction to the family,* pp. 76–93. New York: Free Press.

——— (1971). The origin of the family. *Journal of Marriage and the Family, 33:*4, 760–771.

GOULDNER, A. W. (1970). *The coming crisis of Western sociology.* New York: Basic Books.

GOVE, W. R., AND J. F. TUDOR (1973). Adult sex roles and mental illness. *American Journal of Sociology, 78:*4, 812–835.

GRAZIA, S. DE (1962). *Of time, work, and leisure.* New York: Twentieth Century Fund.

GREEN, A. W. (1946). The middle-class male child and neurosis. *American Sociological Review, 11,* 31–41.

GREENFIELD, S. J. (1969). Love and marriage in modern America: A functional analysis. *Sociological Quarterly, 6,* 361–377.

GREER, G. (1971). *The female eunuch.* New York: McGraw-Hill.

GREER, S. (1962). *The emerging city: Myth and reality.* New York: Free Press.

GREVEN, P. (1970). *Four generations: Population, land and family in colonial Andover, Massachusetts.* Ithaca, N.Y.: Cornell Univ. Press.

GRINDER, R. E. (1969). The concept of adolescence in the genetic psychology of G. Stanley Hall. *Child Development, 40,* 355–370.

GRUBB, N. (1977). The relation of home and work. Working paper for Childhood and Government Project, Univ. of California Law School, Berkeley.

GURIN, G., S. VEROFF, AND S. FELD (1960). *Americans view their mental health.* New York: Basic Books.

GUTMAN, H. G. (1976). *The black family in slavery and freedom, 1750–1925.* New York: Pantheon.

HAAN, N. (1971). Moral redefinition in families as the critical aspect of the generational gap. *Youth and Society, 2:*3, 259–283.

——— (1972). Personality development from adolescence to adulthood in the Oakland Growth and Guidance Series. *Seminars in Psychiatry. 4:*4.

———, AND N. LIVSON (1972). Sex differences in the eyes of expert personality assessors: Blind spots. Unpublished ms., Institute of Human Development, Univ.

of California, Berkeley.

HAJNAL, J. (1965). European marriage patterns in perspective. In D. V. Glass, and D. E. Eversley (eds.), *Population in history,* pp. 101–143. Chicago: Aldine.

HALE, N. (1971). *Freud and the Americans.* New York: Oxford Univ. Press.

HALEY, J. (1963). *Strategies of psychotherapy.* New York: Grune & Stratton.

HALL, G. (1904). *Adolescence: Its psychology and its relations to physiology, anthropology, sociology, sex, crime, religion, and education.* New York: Appleton.

HALLOWELL, A. I. (1955). *Culture and experience.* Philadelphia: Univ. of Pennsylvania Press.

HAMILTON, R. F. (1972). *Class and politics in the United States.* New York: Wiley.

Handbook on women workers (1976). U.S. Department of Labor, Bulletin no. 297, chap. 1, sect. 8.

HANDLIN, O., AND M. F. HANDLIN (1971). *Facing life: Youth and the family in American history.* Boston: Little, Brown.

HARDY, K. R. (1964). An appetitional theory of sexual motivation. *Psychological Review, 71,* 19–26.

HAREVEN, T. (1971). The history of the family as an interdisciplinary field. *Journal of Interdisciplinary History, 2:*2, 399–414.

HARLOW, H. F. (1962). The heterosexual affectional system in monkeys. *American Psychologist, 17, 1–9.*

———, M. K. HARLOW, AND E. W. HANSEN (1963). The maternal affectional system in infant monkeys. In H. J. Rheingold (ed.), *Maternal behavior in mammals.* New York: Wiley.

HARRINGTON, C., AND J. W. M. WHITING (1972). Socialization process and personality. In F. L. K. Hsu (ed.), *Psychological anthropology,* pp. 469–507. Cambridge, Mass.: Schenkman.

HARRINGTON, M. (1966). *The accidental century.* New York: Macmillan.

HARRIS, M. (1964). *The nature of cultural things.* New York: Random House.

——— (1968). *The rise of anthropological theory: A history of theories of culture.* New York: Crowell.

HAUSER, P. M. (1970). Comments in *The Millbank Memorial Fund Quarterly, 48:*2, part 2.

HAWKES, J. (1963). *Prehistory.* In *History of mankind: Cultural and scientific development,* vol. 1, part 1. New York: New American Library (Mentor).

HEER, F. (1962). *The medieval world.* New York: Praeger.

HENRY, J. (1963). *Culture against man.* New York: Random House.

——— (1971). *Pathways to madness.* New York: Random House.

HERSCHBERGER, R. (1948). *Adam's rib.* New York: Pellegrini

Bibliography

& Cudahy.

HERZOG, E., AND C. E. SUDIA (1973). Children in fatherless families. In B. M. Caldwell and H. N. Ricciuti (eds.), *Child development research,* vol. 3, pp. 141–221. Chicago: Univ. of Chicago Press.

HESS, R. D., AND G. HANDEL (1959). *Family worlds.* Chicago: Univ. of Chicago Press.

HICKS, M. W., AND M. PLATT (1970). Marital happiness and stability. *Journal of Marriage and the Family, 32,* 553–574.

HILL, R., AND D. A. HANSEN (1960). The identification of conceptual frameworks utilized in family study. *Marriage and Family Living, 22,* 299–311.

HILLIKER, G. (1976). Quoted in W. F. Mondale, Government policy, stress, and the family. *Journal of Home Economics, 68:*5, 14.

HIMES, N. E. (1963). *Medical history of contraception.* New York: Gamut.

HINDUS, M. (1971). Historical trends in American premarital pregnancy. Paper presented at American Historical Association, New York, December 1971.

HOCHSCHILD, A. R. (1973). A review of sex role research. *American Journal of Sociology, 78:*4, 1011–1029.

——— (1975). Attending to, codifying, and managing feelings: Sex differences in love. Paper presented at American Sociological Association, San Francisco, 1975.

HODGSON, F. *America in our time.* Garden City, N.Y.: Doubleday.

HOFFMAN, L. W. (1972). Early childhood experiences and women's achievement motives. *Journal of Social Issues, 28:*2, 129–155.

HOOKER, E. (1965). Gender identity in male homosexuals. In J. Money (ed.), *Sex research.* New York: Holt, Rinehart and Winston.

HORNEY, K. (1932). The dread of women. *International Journal of Psychoanalysis, 13,* 359.

HOWE, L. K. (1977). *The pink collar ghetto.* New York: Putnam.

HSU, F. L. K. (ed.) (1961). *Psychological anthropology.* Homewood, Ill.: Dorsey.

HUNT, D. (1970). *Parents and children in history: The psychology of family life in early modern France.* New York: Basic Books.

HUNT, M. (1969). *The affair.* New York: World.

——— (1974). *Sexual behavior in the 1970's.* Chicago: Playboy Press.

ICHHEISER, G. (1970). *Appearances and realities: Misunderstandings in human relations.* San Francisco: Jossey-Bass.

ILLICH, I. (1971). *Deschooling society.* New York: Harper & Row.

INKELES, A. (1968). Society, social structure, and child socialization. In J. Clausen (ed.), *Socialization and society,* pp. 75–129. Boston: Little, Brown.

INSTITUTE OF LIFE INSURANCE (1974). *Youth.* New York: Institute of Life Insurance.

ISAACS, S. (1966). *Intellectual growth in young children.* New York: Schocken.

JANEWAY, E. (1971). *Man's world, woman's place.* New York: Morrow.

JEFFREY, K. (1972). The family as utopian retreat from the city: The nineteenth-century contribution. In S. TeSelle (ed.), *The family, communes, and utopian societies,* pp. 21–41. New York: Harper & Row.

KAGAN, J. (1977). The child in the family. *Daedalus,* Spring, pp. 33–56.

KANOWITZ, L. (1969). *Women and the law: The unfinished revolution.* Albuquerque: Univ. of New Mexico Press.

KANTER, R. M. (1968). Commitment and social organization: A study of commitment mechanisms in utopian communities. *American Sociological Review, 33,* 499–518.

——— (1972). *Commitment and community: Communes and utopias in sociological perspective.* Cambridge, Mass.: Harvard Univ. Press.

——— (1977). *Work and family in the United States: A critical review and agenda for research and policy.* New York: Russell Sage.

KATZ, J. M. (1977). Discrepancy, arousal, and labeling: Towards a psychosocial theory of emotion. Manuscript in process. York University, Toronto.

KEMPE, H. (1973). Quotes from personal interview. *Woman's Day,* March 1973, p. 62.

KENISTON, K. (1971a). Psychosocial development and historical change. *Journal of Interdisciplinary History, 2:*2, 329–345.

——— (1971b). *Youth and dissent: The rise of a new opposition.* New York: Harcourt Brace Jovanovich (Harvest).

——— (1974). *Do Americans really like children?* New York: Carnegie Council on Children.

KENNEDY, D. M. (1970). *Birth control in America: The career of Margaret Sanger.* New Haven, Conn.: Yale Univ. Press.

KEPHART, W. M. (1967). Some correlates of romantic love. *Journal of Marriage and the Family, 29,* 470–479.

KERR, M. (1958). *The people of Ship Street.* London: Routledge.

KESSEN, W. (1962). "Stage" and "structure" in the study of children. In W. Kessen and C. Kuhlman (eds.), *Thought in the young child,* pp. 65–82. *Monogr. of the Society for Research in Child Development,* no. 83.

Bibliography

———— (1965). *The child.* New York: Wiley.

KETT, J. (1971). Adolescence and youth in nineteenth-century America. *Journal of Interdisciplinary History, 2,* 283, 294–295.

KEYES, R. (1973). *We, the lonely people.* New York: Harper & Row.

KILPATRICK, W. *Identity and intimacy.* New York: Dell (Delta).

KLEIN, M., AND J. RIVIERE (1953). *Love, hate and reparation.* London: Hogarth.

KLEMESRUD, J. (1971). Happy duos aren't so rare. *San Francisco Chronicle,* June 8, 1971. (Copyright 1971, N.Y. Times News Service.)

KOBRIN, F. K. (1976). The primary individual and the family: Changes in living arrangements in the United States since 1940. *Journal of Marriage and the Family, 38,* 233–240, 480–494.

KOHLBERG, L. (1966). A cognitive-developmental analysis of children's sex-role concepts and attitudes. In E. E. Maccoby (ed.), *The development of sex differences,* p. 91. Stanford, Ca.: Stanford Univ. Press.

KOHN, M. L. (1959). Social class and parental values. *American Journal of Sociology, 64,* 337–351.

———— (1963). Social class and parent-child relationships. *American Journal of Sociology, 68,* 471–480.

KOMAROVSKY, M. (1967). *Blue-collar marriage.* New York: Vintage.

KUHN, T. (1962). *The structure of scientific revolutions.* Chicago: Univ. of Chicago Press.

LAING, R. D. (1969). *Self and others.* Baltimore: Penguin.

———— (1971). *The politics of the family.* New York: Random House.

————, H. PHILLIPSON, AND A. R. LEE (1966). *Interpersonal perception: A theory and a method of research.* New York: Harper & Row.

LAMBERT, W. W. (1971). Cross-cultural backgrounds to personality development and the socialization of aggression: Findings from the six-culture study. In W. W. Lambert and R. Weisbrod (eds.), *Comparative perspectives on social psychology,* p. 433. Boston: Little, Brown.

LANDIS, P. H. (1955). *Making the most of your marriage.* Englewood Cliffs, N.J.: Prentice-Hall.

LANGER, J. (1969a). Disequilibrium as a source of development. In T. Mussen, J. Langer, and M. Covington (eds.), *Trends and issues in developmental psychology,* pp. 22–37. New York: Holt, Rinehart and Winston.

———— (1969b). *Theories of development.* New York: Holt, Rinehart and Winston.

LANGER, W. L. (1972). Checks on population growth: 1750–1850. *Scientific American, 226,* 93–100.

LANTZ, H. R., AND E. C. SNYDER (1969). *Marriage,* 2nd ed. New York: Wiley.

LASCH, C. (1965). *The new radicalism in America.* New York: Vintage.

———— (1975). The family and history. *New York Review,* November 13, 1975, pp. 33–38.

———— (1976). The narcissist society. *New York Review,* September 30, 1976, pp. 5–8, 10–13.

LASLETT, B. (1973). The family as a public and private institution: A historical perspective. Unpublished ms., Univ. of Southern California, Los Angeles, September 1972. Published in shortened version in *Journal of Marriage and the Family,* August 1973, *35,* 480–494.

LASLETT, P. (1965). *The world we have lost: England before the industrial age.* New York: Scribner.

———— (1977). Characteristics of the Western family considered over time. *Journal of Family History, 2:2,* 89–115.

LAUTMAN, F. (1976). Differences or changes in family organization. In R. Forster and O. Ranum (trans. and eds.), *Family and Society,* pp. 251–261. Baltimore: Johns Hopkins Univ. Press.

LEE, J. (1975). Styles of loving. *Psychology today,* August 1975, pp. 20–27.

LEE, R., AND I. DE VORE (1968). *Man the hunter.* Chicago: Aldine.

LE MASTERS, E. E. (1957). Parenthood as crisis. *Marriage and Family Living, 19,* 352–355.

———— (1970). *Parents in modern America: A sociological analysis.* Homewood, Ill.: Dorsey.

LENNARD, H. L., AND A. BERNSTEIN (1969). *Patterns in human interaction.* San Francisco: Jossey-Bass.

LENSKI, G. (1966). *Power and privilege: A theory of social stratification.* New York: McGraw-Hill.

LE PLAY, F. (1866). *La réforme sociale.* In C. C. Zimmerman and M. E. Frampton, *Family and society,* Princeton, N.J.: Van Nostrand, 1935.

LEVENSON, E. A. (1972). *The fallacy of understanding: An inquiry into the changing structure of psychoanalysis.* New York: Basic Books.

LE VINE, R. A. (1965). Intergenerational tensions and extended family structures in Africa. In E. Shanas and G. F. Streib (eds.), *Social structure and the family: Generational relations,* pp. 188–204. Englewood Cliffs, N.J.: Prentice-Hall.

———— (1970). Cross-cultural study in child psychology. In P. H. Mussen (ed.), *Carmichael's manual of child psychology,* 3rd ed., pp. 559–612. New York: Wiley.

LEVISON, A. (1974). *The working-class majority.* Baltimore: Penguin.

LEVY, M. J., JR. (1955). Some questions about Parsons'

treatment of the incest problem. *British Journal of Sociology, 6,* 277–285.

——— (1965). Aspects of the analysis of family structure. In A. J. Coale, L. A. Fallers, M. J. Levy, Jr., D. Schneider, and S. S. Tomkins, *Aspects of the analysis of family structure.* Princeton, N.J.: Princeton Univ. Press.

LEWIS, C. S. (1958). *The allegory of love: A study in medieval tradition.* New York: Oxford Univ. Press.

LEWIS, H. (1968). Child rearing among low-income families. In L. Ferman, J. Kornbluth, and A. Haber (eds.), *Poverty in America,* rev. ed. Ann Arbor: Univ. of Michigan Press.

LEWIS, O. (1951). *Life in a Mexican village: Tepoztlan restudied.* Urbana: Univ. of Illinois Press.

——— (1965). The folk-urban ideal types. In P. M. Hauser and L. F. Schnore (eds.), *The study of urbanization,* pp. 491–503. New York: Wiley.

LIDZ, T. (1963). *The family and human adaptation.* New York: International Universities Press.

LIFTON, R. J. (1965). Woman as knower. In R. J. Lifton (ed.), *The woman in America.* Boston: Houghton Mifflin.

——— (1969). Protean man. *Yale Alumni Review,* January, 14–21.

LINDZEY, G., AND E. ARONSON (1968). *The handbook of social psychology,* 2nd ed. Reading, Mass.: Addison-Wesley.

LINTON, R. (1936). *The study of man.* New York: Appleton-Century-Crofts.

——— (1959). The natural history of the family. In R. N. Anshen (ed.), *The family: Its function and destiny,* rev ed., pp. 30–52. New York: Harper & Row.

LIPSET, S. M. (1960). Student activism. *Current Affairs Bulletin, 42.*

——— (1967). *Student politics.* New York: Basic Books.

———, AND R. B. DOBSON (1972). The intellectual as critic and rebel: With special reference to the United States and the Soviet Union. In Intellectuals and change. *Daedalus,* Summer, 137–198.

LITWAK, E. (1965). Extended kin relations in an industrial democratic society. In E. Shanas and G. F. Streib (eds.), *Social structure and the family: Generational relations.* Englewood Cliffs, N.J.: Prentice-Hall.

LOEVINGER, J. (1959). Patterns of child rearing as theories of learning. *Journal of Abnormal and Social Psychology, 59,* 148–150.

LOMAX, A., AND N. BERKOWITZ (1972). The evolutionary taxonomy of culture. *Science, 177,* 228–240.

LURIA, A. (1961). *The role of speech in the regulation of normal and abnormal behavior.* New York: Pergamon.

LYND, R. S., AND H. M. LYND (1959). *Middletown.* New York: Harcourt Brace Jovanovich (Harvest).

LYNESS, J. L., M. E. LIPETZ, AND K. E. DAVIS (1972). Living together: An alternative to marriage. *Journal of Marriage and the Family, 34:*2, 305–311.

MC CALL, M. M. (1966). Courtship as social exchange: Some historical comparisons. In B. Farber (ed.), *Kinship and family organization,* pp. 190–200. New York: Wiley.

McCalls Magazine (1977). How the government affects family life. May 1977, p. 63.

———(April 1954). Quoted in B. Friedan, *The feminine mystique.* New York: Dell, 1963.

MC CLELLAND, D. C., J. W. ATKINSON, R. A. CLARK, AND E. L. LOWELL (1953). *The achievement motive.* New York: Appleton-Century-Crofts.

MC CULLERS, J. C. (1969). G. Stanley Hall's conception of mental development and some indications of its influence on developmental psychology. *American Psychologist, 24,* 1109.

MACFARLANE, J. W. (1963). From infancy to adulthood. *Childhood Education, 39,* 336–342.

——— (1964). Perspectives on personality consistency and change from the guidance study. *Vita Humana, 7,* 115–126.

MCKINLEY, D. G. (1964). *Social class and family life.* Glencoe, Ill.: Free Press.

MALINOWSKI, B. (1964). The principle of legitimacy: Parenthood, the basis of social structure. in R. L. Coser (ed.), *The family: Its structure and functions,* pp. 3–19. New York: St. Martin's.

MANDER, J. (1969). In defense of the 50's. *Commentary,* September.

MARKS, F. R. (1975). Detours on the road to maturity: A view of the legal conception of growing up and letting go. *Law and Contemporary Problems, 39:*3, 78–92.

MARTIN, M. K., AND B. VOORHIES (1975). *Female of the species.* New York: Columbia Univ. Press.

MASPETIOL, R. (1970). Sociologie de la famille rura de type traditionnel en France, in *Sociologie comparée de la famille contemporaine.* Cited in M. Cernea, *Changing society and family change: The impact of the cooperative farm on the peasant family.* Stanford, Ca.: Center for Advanced Study in the Behavioral Sciences.

MASTERS, W. H., AND V. JOHNSON (1970). *Human sexual inadequacy.* Boston: Little, Brown.

MEAD, M. (1928). *Coming of age in Samoa.* New York: Morrow.

——— (1935). *Sex and temperament in three primitive societies.* New York: Morrow.

——— (1947). The implications of culture change for personality development. *American Journal of Ortho-psychiatry, 17,* 633ff.

——— (1949). *Male and female.* New York: Morrow.

——— (1957). Changing patterns of parent-child relations in an urban culture. *International Journal of Psycho-analysis, 38,* 369–378.

——— (1966). Marriage in two steps. *Redbook,* July.

——— (1970). *Culture and commitment.* Garden City, N.Y.: Doubleday (Natural History Press).

——— (1971). Future family. *Transaction,* September, 50–59.

MEMMI, A. (1968). *Dominated man.* New York: Orion.

MIDDLEBROOK, P. (1974). *Social psychology and modern life.* New York: Knopf.

MILLER, D. T., AND M. NOWACK (1977). *The fifties: The way we really were.* Garden City, N.Y.: Doubleday.

MILLER, H. (1965). *Income of the American people.* New York: Wiley.

MILLER, M. (1954). In *Esquire.* Quoted in D. T. Miller and M. Nowack, *The fifties: The way we really were.* Garden City, N.Y.: Doubleday.

MILLER, S. M., AND F. R. REISSMAN (1964). The working class subculture: A new view. In A. B. Shostak and W. Bomberg (eds.), *Blue collar world: Studies of the American worker.* Englewood Cliffs, N.J.: Prentice-Hall.

MILLS, C. W. (1959). *The sociological imagination.* New York: Oxford Univ. Press.

MINTURN, L., AND W. W. LAMBERT (1964). *Mothers of six cultures: Antecedents of child rearing.* New York: Wiley.

MITCHELL, G. D. (1969). Paternalistic behavior in primates. *Psychological Bulletin, 71,* 399–417.

MITCHELL, J. (1974). *Psychoanalysis and feminism.* New York: Random House (Vintage).

MODELL, J. (1972). Strangers in the family: Boarding and lodging in industrial America. Paper read at National Conference on the Family, Social Structure and Social Change, April 27–29, 1972, Clark University, Worcester, Mass.

MOLINOFF, D. D. (1977). Life with father. *The New York Times Sunday Magazine,* May 22, 1977.

MOLLER, H. (1971). Childhood before the enlightenment. *Psychotherapy and Social Science Review, 5:*9, 16–18.

MONEY, J. (1961). Sex hormones and other variables in human eroticism. In W. C. Young (ed.), *Sex and internal secretions.* Baltimore: Williams & Wilkins.

——— (1972). Paper presented at symposium on sex role learning in childhood and adolescence. American Association for the Advancement of Science Meetings, December 1972, Washington, D.C.

———, J. HAMPSON, AND J. HAMPSON (1957). Imprinting and the establishment of gender role. *Archives of Neurological Psychiatry, 77,* 333–336.

MOORE, B. M., JR. (1958). Thoughts on the future of the family. In *Political power and social theory.* Cambridge, Mass.: Harvard Univ. Press.

MORGAN, E. S. (1944). *The Puritan family.* Boston: Public Library.

MORGAN, L. H. (1870). *Systems of consanguinity and affinity of the human family.* Washington: Smithsonian Institution.

——— (1877). *Ancient society.* New York: Holt. Modern edition by E. Leacock (ed.), *Ancient society.* New York: World (Meridian), 1963.

MORRIS, J. (1974). *Conundrum.* New York: Harcourt Brace Jovanovich.

MURDOCK, G. P. (1971). *Social structure.* New York: Macmillan.

MURPHY, R. F. (1971). *The dialectics of social life: Alarms and excursions in anthropological theory.* New York: Basic Books.

MURSTEIN, B. I. (1971). A theory of marital choice and its applicability to marriage adjustment. In B. I. Murstein (ed.), *Theories of attraction and love,* pp. 100–151. New York: Springer.

MUUSS, R. E. (1962). *Theories of adolescence.* New York: Random House.

MYRDAL, J. (1968). *Confessions of a disloyal European.* New York: Pantheon.

NEGREA, A. G. (1936). *The sociological theory of the peasant household.* Bucharest: 1936, p.·45. Cited in M. Cernea, *Changing society and family change: The impact of the cooperative farm on the peasant family,* p. 114. Stanford, Ca.: Center for Advanced Study in the Behavioral Sciences, 1970.

NEISSER, U. (1976). *Cognition and reality: Principles and implications of cognitive psychology.* San Francisco: Freeman

NEWSON, J., AND E. NEWSON (1974). Cultural aspects of child-rearing in the English-speaking world. In M. P. M. Richards (ed.), *The integration of the child into a social world.* London: Cambridge Univ. Press.

NIMKOFF, M. F., AND R. MIDDLETON (1960). Types of family and types of economy. *American Journal of Sociology, 66,* 215–225.

NISBET, R. A. (1961). The study of social problems. In R. K. Merton and R. A. Nisbet (eds.), *Contemporary social problems.* New York: Harcourt, Brace & World.

NORTON, A. J., AND P. C. GLICK (1976). Marital instability: Past, present and future. *Journal of Social Issues, 32,* 5–20.

O'NEILL, N., AND G. O'NEILL (1972). *Open marriage.* New York: Evans.

Bibliography

O'NEILL, W. L. (ed.) (1969). *The woman movement*. Chicago: Quadrangle.

OPIE, I., AND P. OPIE (1959). *The lore and language of school children*. London: Oxford Univ. Press.

ORWELL, G. (1946). The art of Donald McGill. In *A collection of essays,* p. 107. New York: Harcourt, Brace, 1953.

OTTO, H. A. (1970). *The family in search of a future*. New York: Appleton-Century- Crofts.

OTTO, L. (1975). Class and status in family research. *Journal of Marriage and the Family, 37,* 315-332.

PARISH, W. L., AND M. SCHWARTZ (1972). Household complexity in nineteenth-century France. *American Sociological Review, 37,* 154-173.

PARKER, R. (1972). *The myth of the middle class*. New York: Harper & Row (Colophon).

PARSONS, T. (1949). *Essays in sociological theory: Pure and applied*. Glencoe, Ill.: Free Press.

——— (1951). *The social system*. Glencoe, Ill.: Free Press.

——— (1955). The American family: Its relations to personality and the social structure. In T. Parsons and R. F. Bales, *Family socialization and interaction process,* pp. 3-21. Glencoe, Ill.: Free Press.

——— (1965). The normal American family. In S. M. Farber, P. Mustacchi, and R. H. L. Wilson (eds.), *Man and civilization: The family's search for survival,* pp. 31-50. New York: McGraw-Hill.

——— (1971). Kinship and the associational aspect of social structure. In F. L. K. Hsu (ed.), *Kinship and culture,* pp. 409-438. Chicago: Aldine.

———, AND R. F. BALES (1955). *Family socialization and interaction process*. Glencoe, Ill.: Free Press.

PAYNE, G. H. (1916). *The child in human progress*. New York: Putnam.

PEARLIN, L. I. (1971). *Class-context and family relations: A cross-national study*. Boston: Little, Brown.

PEPLAU, L. A., Z. RUBIN, AND C. T. HILL (1977). Sexual intimacy in dating relationships. *Journal of Social Issues, 7,* in press.

PIAGET, J. (1952). *The origin of intelligence in children*. New York: International Universities Press.

——— (1954). *The construction of reality in the child*. New York: Basic Books.

——— (1967). *Six psychological studies*. New York: Random House.

———, AND B. INHELDER (1969). *The psychology of the child*. New York: Basic Books.

PIERCE, C. (1971). Natural law, language and women. In V. Gornick and B. K. Moran (eds.), *Woman in sexist society: Studies in power and powerlessness,* pp. 242-258. New York: Basic Books.

PILBEAM, D. (1972). Evolutionary anthropology. Review of *The brain in hominid evolution* by P. V. Tobias. *Science, 175,* 1011.

PILPEL, H. F., AND T. ZAVIN (1964). *Your marriage and the law*. New York: Macmillan (Collier).

PINEO, P. C. (1961). Disenchantment in the later years of marriage. *Marriage and Family Living, 23,* 3-11.

PITTS, J. (1968). The family and peer groups. In N. W. Bell and E. F. Vogel, *A modern introduction to the family*. New York: Free Press.

PLUMB, J. H. (1972). The great change in children. *Intellectual Digest, 2,* 82-84. (Originally in *Horizon,* Winter 1971.)

POHLMAN, E. H. (1969). *Psychology of birth planning*. Cambridge, Mass: Schenkman.

POLOMA, M. M., AND T. N. GARLAND (1971). The married professional woman: A study in the tolerance of domestication. *Journal of Marriage and the Family, 33:3,* 531-540.

POPE, H., AND D. KNUDSEN (1965). Premarital sex norms: The family and social change. *Journal of Marriage and the Family,* August, 314-323.

PROXMIRE, W. (1975). Quoted in National science foundation funded projects controversy: Senator William Proxmire vs. social scientists. *Wisconsin Sociologist, 12,* 72-86.

RABKIN, R. (1970). *Inner and outer space: Introduction to a theory of social psychiatry*. New York: Norton.

RAMEY, J. W. (1977). Alternative life-styles. *Society, 14:5,* 43-47.

REICHE, R. (1971). *Sexuality and class struggle*. New York: Praeger.

REIK, R. (1944). *A psychologist looks at love*. New York: Lancer.

REISS, I. L. (1960). *Premarital sexual standards in America*. Glencoe, Ill.: Free Press.

——— (1970). How and why America's sex standards are changing. In J. H. Gagnon and W. Simon (eds.), *The sexual scene,* pp. 43-57. Chicago: Aldine (Transaction).

RHEINGOLD, H. L. (1969). The social and socializing infant. In D. A. Goslin (ed.), *Handbook of socialization theory and research,* pp. 779-790. Chicago: Rand McNally.

RICOEUR, P. (1973). Psychiatry and moral values. In S. Arieti et al. (eds.), *American handbook of psychiatry,* 2nd ed. New York: Basic Books.

RIEGEL, K. (1973). An epitaph for a paradigm. *Human Development, 16,* 1-3.

RIESMAN, D. (1960). The oral and written traditions. In E. Carpenter and M. McLuhan (eds.), *Explorations in communication,* pp. 109-124. Boston: Beacon.

——— (1964). Two generations. *Daedalus,* Spr., 711-735.

Bibliography

ROBINSON, H., N. ROBINSON, M. WOLINS, U. BRONFENBREN-NER, AND J. RICHMOND (1973). Early child development and care. *International Monographs on Early Child Care,* vol. 4, no. 3.

ROBINSON, J. P., AND P. E. CONVERSE (1972). Social change reflected in the use of time. In A. Campbell and P. E. Converse (eds.), *The human meaning of social change,* pp. 17-86. New York: Russell Sage.

ROBINSON, P. (1976). *The modernization of sex.* New York: Harper & Row.

RODMAN, H. (1965). The textbook world of family sociology. *Social Problems, 12,* 450.

ROGERS, C. (1972). *Becoming partners: Marriage and its alternatives.* New York: Delacorte.

ROLLINS, B. C., AND H. FELDMAN (1970). Marital satisfaction over the family life cycle. *Journal of Marriage and the Family, 32,* 20-28.

ROPER ORGANIZATION (1974). *The Virginia Slims American women's opinion poll.* New York: Roper.

ROSENBAUM, M. (1972). Patterns of seduction: The young and the middle-aged. San Francisco State University. Abridged version published in J. P. Wiseman (ed.), *The social psychology of sex.* New York: Harper & Row, 1976.

ROSENBERG, C. (1973). Sexuality, class, and role in nineteenth-century America. *American Quarterly, 25,* 131-153.

ROSOW, I. (1965). Intergenerational relationships: Problems and proposals. In E. Shanas and G. F. Streib (eds.), *Social structure and the family: Generational relations,* pp. 341-378. Englewood Cliffs, N.J.: Prentice-Hall.

ROSS, H. L., AND I. V. SAWHILL (1975). *Time of transition: The growth of families headed by women.* Washington, D.C.: Urban Institute.

ROSSI, A. S. (1968). Transition to parenthood. *Journal of Marriage and the Family, 30,* 26-39.

ROTHMAN, D. J. (1971). Documents in search of a historian: Towards a history of childhood and growth in America. *Journal of Interdisciplinary History, 2:2,* 368-377.

ROUGEMONT, D. DE (1956). *Love in the Western world.* New York: Pantheon.

ROUSSEAU, J. J. (1762). *Emile, or on education.* London: Dent, 1911. (Original French edition in 1762.)

RUBIN, L. B. (1976). *Worlds of pain.* New York: Basic Books.

RUBIN, Z. (1970). Measurement of romantic love. *Journal of Personality and Social Psychology, 16,* 265-273.

—— (1973). *Liking and loving: An invitation to social psychology.* New York: Holt, Rinehart and Winston.

—— (1977). The love research. *Human Behavior,* February, 56-59.

RUESCH, J., AND G. BATESON (1968). *Communication: The social matrix of psychiatry,* 2nd ed. New York: Norton.

RYAN, W. (1976). *Blaming the victim.* New York: Random House (Vintage).

RYDER, R. G. (1966). The factualizing game: A sickness of psychological research. *Psychological Reports, 19,* 563-570.

—— (1967). Compatibility in marriage. *Psychological Reports, 20,* 807-813.

—— (1970a). Dimensions of early marriage. *Family Process, 9,* 51-68.

—— (1970b). A topography of early marriage. *Family Process, 9,* 385-402.

RYLE, A. (1967). *Neurosis in the ordinary family: A psychiatric survey.* London: Tavistock.

SAFILIOS-ROTHSCHILD, C. (1970). The study of family power structure: A review of 1960-1969. *Journal of Marriage and the Family, 32,* 539-552.

—— (1972). *Toward a sociology of women.* Lexington, Mass.: Xerox College Publishing.

—— (1977). *Love, sex, and sex roles.* Englewood Cliffs, N.J.: Prentice-Hall.

SAHLINS, M. (1968). In R. Lee and I. DeVore, *Man the hunter.* Chicago: Aldine.

SANDERS, M. (1963). The case of the vanishing spinster. In W. Goode (ed.), *The contemporary American family.* Chicago: Quadrangle.

San Francisco Chronicle (1977). Big increase in men who live alone. September 26, 1977, p. 3.

SARTRE, J. P. (1963). *Search for a method.* New York: Knopf.

SCANZONI, J. H. (1970). *Opportunity and the family.* New York: Free Press.

SCHACTER, S. (1964). The interaction of cognitive and physiological determinants of emotional state. In L. Berkowitz (ed.), *Advances in experimental social psychology,* vol. 1, pp. 49-80. New York: Academic Press.

SCHAFFER, H. R. (1971). *The growth of sociability.* Baltimore: Penguin.

SCHMALENBACH, H. (1961). The sociological categories of communion. In T. Parsons et al. (eds.), *Theories of society,* vol. 1. New York: Free Press.

SCHMIDT, W. (1973). *Child development: The human, cultural, and educational context.* New York: Harper & Row.

SCHNEIDER, D. M. (1965). Kinship and biology. In A. J. Coale, L. A. Fallers, M. J. Levy, Jr., D. M. Schneider, and S. S. Tomkins, *Aspects of the analysis of family structure.* Princeton, N.J.: Princeton Univ. Press.

—— (1968). *American kinship: A cultural account.* Englewood Cliffs, N.J.: Prentice-Hall.

———, AND R. T. SMITH (1973). *Class differences and sex roles in American kinship and family structure.* Englewood Cliffs, N.J.: Prentice-Hall.

SCHULTZ, D. A. (1977). Sex and society in the seventies. *Society, 14:5,* 20–24.

SCHWARTZ, T., et al. (1977). Living together. *Newsweek,* August, pp. 46–50.

SCRIBNER, S., AND M. COLE (1973). Cognitive consequences of formal and informal education. *Science, 182,* 553–559.

SEARS, R. R., E. E. MACCOBY, AND H. LEVIN (1957). *Patterns of child rearing.* Evanston, Ill.: Row, Peterson.

SELIGMAN, M. P. (1975). *Helplessness: On depression, development, and death.* San Francisco: Freeman.

SENNETT, R. (1970a). *Families against the city: Middle class homes of industrial Chicago, 1872–1890.* Cambridge, Mass.: Harvard Univ. Press.

——— (1970b). *The uses of disorder: Personal identity and city life.* New York: Knopf.

———, AND J. COBB (1974). *The hidden injuries of class.* New York: Random House.

SHAEFER, L. C. (1964). Sexual experiences and reactions of a group of thirty women as told to a female psychotherapist. An unpublished Ph.D. thesis, Teachers College, Columbia Univ., 1964. Cited in E. M. Brecher, *The sex researchers.* Boston: Little, Brown, 1969.

SHAFFER, J. B. P. (1970). Review of recent books on marriage. *Harvard education review, 40,* 165–174.

SHAINESS, N. (1971). "New" views of female sexuality. A book review of *Female sexuality: New psychoanalytic views* by J. Chasseguet-Smirgel et al. *Psychiatry and Social Science Review, 5:4,* 13–19.

SHEEHY, G. (1976). *Passages.* New York: Dutton.

SHERESKY, N., AND M. MANNES (1972). A radical guide to wedlock. *Saturday Review,* July 29, p. 32.

SHORTER, E. (1971). Illegitimacy, sexual revolution and social change in modern Europe. *Journal of Interdisciplinary History, 2:2,* 237–272.

——— (1973). Infanticide in the past. A review of *Slaughter of the innocents* by David Bakan. *History of Childhood Quarterly, 1:1,* 178–180.

——— (1975). *The making of the modern family.* New York: Basic Books.

SHOSKAK, A. B. (1969). *Blue-collar life.* New York: Random House.

SHULMAN, A. (1970). A marriage agreement. *Out from Under, 1:2,* 5–8.

SILVERBERG, W. V. (1952). *Childhood experience and personal destiny.* New York: Springer.

SIMMEL, G. (1950). In K. Wolff (ed.), *The sociology of Georg Simmel.* New York: Free Press.

SIMPSON, G. (1960). *People in families.* New York: Crowell.

SJOBERG, G. (1965). Cities in developing and in industrial societies: A cross-cultural analysis. In P. M. Hauser and L. F. Schnore (eds.), *The study of urbanization,* pp. 213–263. New York: Wiley.

SKOLNICK, J. H. (1969). *The politics of protest.* New York: Simon & Schuster.

———, AND E. CURRIE (1973). *Crisis in American institutions,* 2nd ed. Boston: Little, Brown.

SLATER, P. E. (1963). On social regression. *American Sociological Review, 28,* 339–364.

——— (1968). Some social consequences of temporary systems. In W. G. Bennis and P. E. Slater, *The temporary society,* pp. 77–96. New York: Harper & Row.

——— (1970). *The pursuit of loneliness.* Boston: Beacon.

———, AND D. I. SLATER (1965). Maternal ambivalence and narcissism: A cross-cultural study. *Merrill-Palmer Quarterly, 2,* 241–259.

SLUZKI, C. E., AND V. ELISEO (1971). The double bind as a universal pathogenic situation. *Family Process, 10:4,* 397–410.

SMELSER, N. J. (1963). *Social change.* Englewood Cliffs, N.J.: Prentice-Hall.

——— (1968). *Essays in sociological explanation.* Englewood Cliffs, N.J.: Prentice-Hall.

SMITH, R. T. (1956). *The Negro family in British Guiana: Family structure and social status in the village.* London: Routledge.

SORENSON, R. C. (1973). *Adolescent sexuality in contemporary America.* New York: World.

SPECK, R. V., et al. (1972). *The new families: Youth, communes and the politics of drugs.* New York: Basic Books.

SPENCER, H. (1946). *Essays on education.* New York: Dutton.

SPIEGEL, J. (1971). *Transactions: The interplay between individual, family, and society.* New York: Science House.

SPIRO, M. E. (1954). Is the family universal? *American Anthropologist, 56,* 840–846.

——— (1956). *Kibbutz: Venture in utopia.* Cambridge, Mass.: Harvard Univ. Press.

SROLE, L., J. S. LANGNER, S. T. MICHAEL, M. K. OPLER, AND T. A. C. RENNIE (1962). *Mental health in the metropolis: The midtown Manhattan study.* New York: McGraw-Hill.

STACK, C. B. (1974). *All our kin.* New York: Harper & Row.

———, et al. (1975). Anthropology (review essay). *Signs, 1:1,* 147–159.

STAPLES, R. (1971). Towards a sociology of the black family: A theoretical and methodological assessment. *Journal of Marriage and the Family,* February, pp. 119–135.

STARK, R., AND J. McEVOY, III. (1970). Middle class violence. *Psychology Today,* November, pp. 52–65.

STEELE, B. F. (1970). Parental abuse of infants and small children. In E. J. Anthony and T. Benedek, *Parenthood: Its psychology and psychopathology,* pp. 449–477. Boston: Little, Brown.

———, AND C. B. POLLOCK (1968). A psychiatric study of parents who abuse infants and small children. In R. E. Helfer and C. H. Kempe (eds.), *The battered child.* Chicago: Univ. of Chicago Press.

STEIN, P. J. (1977). Singlehood: An alternative to marriage. In A. S. Skolnick and J. H. Skolnick (eds.), *Family in transition,* 2nd ed. Boston: Little, Brown.

STEINMETZ, S. K., AND M. A. STRAUS (1974). *Violence in the family.* New York: Dodd, Mead.

STEPHENS, W. N. (1963). *The family in cross-cultural perspective.* New York: Holt, Rinehart and Winston.

STERN, D., S. SMITH, AND F. DOOLITTLE (1975). How children used to work. *Law and Contemporary Problems,* no. 3, p. 93.

STIERLIN, H. (1976). The dynamics of owning and disowning: Psychoanalytic and family perspectives. *Family Process, 15:3,* 277–288.

STONE, L. (1960). Marriage among the English nobility. *Comparative Studies in Society and History, 3,* 182–206.

——— (1964). Marriage among the English nobility. In R. L. Coser, *The family: Its structure and functions.* New York: St. Martin's.

STOUFFER, S. A., S. A. STAR, AND R. M. WILLIAMS (1949). *The American soldier: Studies in social psychology in World War II.* Princeton, N.J.: Princeton Univ. Press.

SULLEROT, E. (1971). *Woman, society and change.* New York: McGraw-Hill.

SULLIVAN, H. S. (1953). *The interpersonal theory of psychiatry.* New York: Norton.

SUMNER, W. G. (1960). *Folkways.* New York: New American Library (Mentor).

SUNLEY, R. (1955). Early nineteenth-century American literature on child rearing. In M. Mead and M. Wolfenstein (eds.), *Childhood in contemporary cultures,* pp. 150–167. Chicago: Univ. of Chicago Press.

SUSSMAN, M. B. (1959). The isolated nuclear family: Fact or fiction. *Social Problems, 6,* 333–339.

——— (1965). Relationships of adult children with their parents. In E. Shanas and G. F. Streib (eds.), *Social structure and the family: Generational relations.* Englewood Cliffs, N.J.: Prentice-Hall.

SWIDLER, A. (1977). Love and adulthood in American culture. Unpublished paper prepared for conference on love and work. May 6–7, Palo Alto, Ca.

SZALAI, A. (1972). *The use of time: Daily activities of urban and suburban populations in twelve counties.* The Hague: Mouton.

SZASZ, T. S. (1961). *The myth of mental illness.* New York: Harper & Row.

TAVRIS, C. (1976). The Cory complex. *Psychology Today,* August, p. 32.

———, AND T. JAYARATNE (1973). What 120,000 young women can tell you about sex, motherhood, menstruation, housework—and men. *Redbook, 140:3,* 65–69, 127–129.

TAYLOR, G. R. (1954). *Sex in history.* New York: Ballantine.

TEELE, J. E., AND W. M. SCHMIDT (1970). Illegitimacy and race: National and local trends. *Millbank Memorial Fund Quarterly, 48:2,* 127–144.

THOMPSON, E. P. (1963). *The making of the English working class.* New York: Random House (Vintage).

THOMSEN, M. (1965). The culture shock of quiet death. *San Francisco Chronicle,* April 25, 1965, p. 26.

TOFFLER, A. (1970). *Future shock.* New York: Random House.

TOMKINS, S. S. (1965). The biopsychosociality of the family. In A. J. Coale, L. A. Fallers, M. J. Levy, Jr., D. M. Schneider, and S. S. Tomkins, *Aspects of the analysis of family structure.* Princeton, N.J.: Princeton Univ. Press.

TREXLER, R. C. (1973). Infanticide in Florence: New sources and first results. *History of Childhood Quarterly, 1:1,* 98–116.

TROLL, L. E. (1969). Issues in the study of the family. A review of *The psychosocial interior of the family,* G. Handel (ed.). *Merrill-Palmer Quarterly, 15:2,* 221–226.

TURNBULL, C. (1961). *The forest people.* New York: Simon & Schuster.

TURNER, R. H. (1976). The real self: From institution to impulse. *American Journal of Sociology, 81:5,* 939–1016.

UDRY, J. R. (1971). *The social context of marriage,* 2nd ed. Philadelphia: Lippincott.

VEITH, I. (1965). *Hysteria: The history of a disease.* Chicago: Univ. of Chicago Press.

VIORST, J. (1977). Confessions of a jealous wife. In G. Clauton and L. G. Smith (eds.), *Jealousy.* Englewood Cliffs, N.J.: Prentice-Hall.

VON BERTALANFFY, L. (1960). General system theory and the behavioral sciences. In J. Tanner and B. Inhilder (eds.), *Discussions on child development,* vol. 4, p. 155. New York: International Universities Press.

Bibliography

VREELAND, R. (1972). Is it true what they say about Harvard boys? *Psychology Today,* January, pp. 65–68.

WALLER, W. (1938). *The family: A dynamic interpretation.* New York: Dryden.

———, AND R. HILL (1951). *The family: A dynamic interpretation,* rev. ed. New York: Holt.

WALLERSTEIN, I. (1974). *The modern world system.* New York: Academic Press.

WALSTER, E. (1961). Passionate love. In B. D. Murstein (ed.), *Theories of attraction and love,* pp. 85–99. New York: Springer.

——— (1973). Equity theory and interpersonal relations. Paper presented at American Sociological Association, New York.

———, V. ARONSON, D. ABRAHAMS, AND L. ROTTMAN (1966). The importance of physical attractiveness in dating behavior. *Journal of Personality and Social Psychology, 4,* 508–516.

WARREN, J. (1977). Alternative families: So what's new. *American Psychological Association Monitor, 8:*6, 9.

WASHBURN, S. L., AND I. DE VORE (1961). In S. L. Washburn (ed.), *Social life of early man.* Chicago: Aldine.

WATT, P. (1957). *The rise of the novel.* Berkeley: Univ. of California Press.

WATZLAWICK, P., J. H. BEAVIN, AND D. D. JACKSON (1967). *Pragmatics of human communication: A study of interactional patterns, pathologies and paradoxes.* New York: Norton.

WEISS, R. S. (1973). *Loneliness: The experience of emotional and social isolation.* Cambridge, Mass.: M.I.T. Press.

WEISSTEIN, N. (1971). Psychology constructs the female. In V. Gornick and B. K. Moran (eds.), *Woman in sexist society: Studies in power and powerlessness,* pp. 207–224. New York: Basic Books.

WEITMAN, S. R. (1973). Intimacies: Notes toward a theory of social inclusion and exclusion. In A. Birenbaum and E. Segarin (eds.), *People in places: The sociology of the familiar.* New York: Praeger.

WEITZMAN, L. J. (1977). To love, honor, and obey: Traditional legal marriage and alternative family forms. In A. S. Skolnick and J. H. Skolnick (eds.), *Family in transition,* pp. 288–313. Boston: Little, Brown.

WENNER, K. (1977). How they keep them down on the farm. *New York Times Magazine,* May 8, pp. 74, 80–83.

WESTOFF, L. A. (1977). *The second time around.* New York: Viking Press.

WHITE, G. (1977). Inequality of emotional involvement and jealousy in romantic couples. Paper presented at American Psychological Association, San Francisco.

WHITE, R. W. (1959). Motivation reconsidered: The concept of competence. *Psychological Review, 66,* 297–333.

——— (1960). Competence and the psychosexual stages of development. In M. R. Jones (ed.), *Nebraska Symposium on Motivation,* pp. 97–141. Lincoln: Univ. of Nebraska Press.

WHITE, S. (1965). Evidence for a hierarchical arrangement of learning processes. In L. P. Lipsitt and C. C. Spiker (eds.), *Advances in child development and behavior,* pp. 184–220. New York: Academic Press.

WHITE HOUSE CONFERENCE ON CHILDREN (1970). *Profiles of children.* Washington, D.C.: U.S. Government Printing Office.

WHITING, B. B. (1963). *Six cultures: Studies of child rearing.* New York: Wiley.

WHITING, J. W. M. (1961). Socialization process and personality. In F. L. K. Hsu (ed.), *Psychological anthropology.* Homewood, Ill.: Dorsey.

——— (1977). Cross-cultural perspectives on parenthood. Paper presented at Groves Conference on Marriage and the Family, May.

———, R. KLUCKHOHN, AND A. ANTHONY (1958). The function of male initiation ceremonies at puberty. In E. E. Maccoby, T. M. Newcomb, and E. L. Hartley (eds.), *Readings in social psychology,* 3rd ed. New York: Holt.

WILLIS, E. (1972). Open marriage: A fantasy. *San Francisco Chronicle,* November 8.

WINCH, R. F. (1968). Some observations on extended familism in the United States. In R. F. Winch and L. W. Goodman (eds.), *Selected studies in marriage and the family,* 3rd ed. New York: Holt, Rinehart and Winston.

———, AND R. L. BLUMBERG (1968). Societal complexity and familial organization. In R. F. Winch and L. W. Goodman (eds.), *Selected studies in marriage and the family,* 3rd ed. New York: Holt, Rinehart and Winston.

WOLF, M. (1972). *Women and the family in rural Taiwan.* Stanford, Ca.: Stanford Univ. Press.

WOLFE, T. (1976). The me decade. *New West Magazine,* August 30, p. 31.

WOLFENSTEIN, M. (1954). *Children's humor: A psychological analysis.* Glencoe, Ill.: Free Press.

——— (1955). Fun morality: An analysis of recent American child-training literature. In M. Mead and M. Wolfenstein (eds.), *Childhood in contemporary cultures,* pp. 169–178. Chicago: Univ. of Chicago Press.

WRIGLEY, E. A. (1972). The process of modernization and the industrial revolution in England. *Journal of Interdisciplinary History, 3:*2, 255–260.

WRONG, D. (1961) The oversocialized conception of man in modern sociology. *American Sociology Review, 26,* 183–193.

WUTHNOW, R. (1976). *The consciousness reformation.* Berkeley: Univ. of California Press.

YANKELOVICH, D. (1977). Quoted in: A new kind of parent. *San Francisco Chronicle,* April 21, p. 1.

YOUNG, M., AND P. WILLMOTT (1973). *The symmetrical family.* New York: Random House (Pantheon).

ZABLOCKI, B. (1971). *The joyful community: An account of the Bruderhof, a communal movement now in its third generation.* Baltimore: Penguin.

—— (1972). Lecture presented at symposium on middle-class communes. Univ. of California, Berkeley, February 12.

—— (1977). Quoted in: Communes in retrospect—A search for family ties. *American Psychological Association Monitor, 8:*6, 9.

ZARETSKY, E. (1976). *Capitalism, the family and personal life.* New York: Harper & Row (Colophon).

ZELDITCH, M., JR. (1964). Cross-cultural analyses of family structure. In H. T. Christensen (ed.), *Handbook of marriage and the family,* pp. 462–500. Chicago: Rand McNally.

ZIMMERMAN, C. C. (1947). *The family and civilization.* New York: Harper.

—— (1970). Quoted in: The American family: Future uncertain. *Time,* December 28, pp. 34–39.

—— (1972). The 1971 Burgess Award Address: The future of the family in America. *Journal of Marriage and the Family, 34:*2, 323ff.

Bibliography

Name Index

Subject Index

Sex education (cont.)
in peer group, 191–193
Sexism, effect of, on marriage,
241–247
humor as, 238–239, 241
study of sexuality affected by,
166–167
see also Sex roles, female, male
Sex jokes, 238–239, 241, 247
Sex-object preference, 179–181
Sex roles, female, in agrarian
societies, 174–175
in courtship, 192–193, 217;
see also Couple
relationships; Love
future trends in, 369, 373
historical, an overview, 31–34
in hunting-and-gathering
societies, 97, 172, 174–175
in industrial society, 131, 132,
134–135
mother as, 7, 9–11, 32, 34,
73–74, 171, 175, 196,
358–359, 369; see also
Matriarchal family;
Parenthood
in patriarchal family, 101
postwar, 7, 9–11, 13, 21–22
sex education and, 192–193
technological changes
affect, 196
wife as, 13, 21–22, 32, 34, 101,
131–132, 134–135,
241–242, 245–247, 369,
373; see also Marriage;
Wife, legal status of
see also Feminist movement;
Working women
general, biological determinism
and, 168–170
Freudian, 170–172
hormonal, 175
man-as-ape, 172–174
social-learning and, 175–178
cognitive-development model
and, 181–183
cultural variation in, 168, 170,
175–177, 193
gender identity and, 179–180,
182–183
learning of, in infancy,
181–184

Sex roles (cont.)
limitations imposed by, see
Sexism
masculinity-femininity and,
179–180
sex-object preference and,
179–181
social-learning model and,
175–178, 181
transsexualism and, 178–179
male, in courtship, 192, 217;
see also Couple
relationships; Love
father as, 11, 13, 101, 151–152,
359–360, 370–371; see also
Parenthood; Patriarchal
family
future trends in, 370–371
husband as, 7, 12–13, 101,
131, 148–149, 151–152,
241–242, 370; see also
Marriage
in industrial society, 131,
134, 135
in patriarchal family, 101; see
also Patriarchal family
postwar, 7, 9, 11–13, 21
sex education and, 192
working-class, 148–149,
151–152
Sexuality, adolescent, 177,
192–193, 249
in children, 176–177, 185,
187, 190
feminist perspectives on,
171–172
folk models of, 167–168
in hunting-and-gathering
societies, 97–98
sexual revolution and, see
Sexual revolution
social context of, historical,
184–186, 189–190, 193
importance of, 186–187
Kinsey reports and, 187
secrecy as, 187–189
sex education and, 190–193
study of, cultural attitudes
affect, 166–168
Victorian attitudes toward,
184–186
Sexual politics, see Sexism

Sexual relationships,
communications problems
in, 255–256
Sexual revolution, effects of,
177–178, 194–195, 211,
215, 376–378
origins of, 185–186, 193–194, 196
Singleness, 9, 211–215, 237; see
also Divorce
Singles bars, 221–222
Slavery, black family under,
154–155, 161–162
Social change, effect of, on
developmental
psychology, 313–326; see
also Developmental
psychology, social-change
effects
family change and, see Agrarian
societies, family in;
Evolutionary theories of
family; Family, changing,
and social change;
Family, study of, as
study of society; Modern
family
generation gap and, 340–341
population control via, 299
sexual revolution and,
193–194, 196
Social class, blue-collar, see
Working class
defined, 143–145
lower-middle, see Working class
marital instability and, 149–151
rediscovery of, 140–142
socialization and, 356–361
unemployment and, 151–153
upper-middle, defined, 145
see also Black family;
Working-class family
Social engineering, 342
Socialization, behavior modification
and, 347–348
cause-and-effect, uncertain, in,
348–350
conflict a factor in, 350–356
defined, 336, 342, 344
experiencing child a factor in,
344–347 passim
generational continuity and,
340–342